GOD'S PLENTY

27 May 2012

For Paul Gareau
With very best wishes,
Bill.

God's Plenty

Religious Diversity in Kingston

WILLIAM CLOSSON JAMES

McGill-Queen's University Press
Montreal & Kingston • London • Ithaca

ISBN 978-0-7735-3889-4 (cloth)
ISBN 978-0-7735-3925-9 (paper)

Legal deposit third quarter 2011
Bibliothèque nationale du Québec

Printed in Canada on acid-free paper that is 100% ancient forest free (100% post-consumer recycled), processed chlorine free

This book has been published with the help of a grant from the Canadian Federation for the Humanities and Social Sciences, through the Aid to Scholarly Publications Programme, using funds provided by the Social Sciences and Humanities Research Council of Canada.

McGill-Queen's University Press acknowledges the support of the Canada Council for the Arts for our publishing program. We also acknowledge the financial support of the Government of Canada through the Canada Book Fund for our publishing activities.

Frontispiece: View of Kingston from Fort Henry Hill.

Library and Archives Canada Cataloguing in Publication

James, William Closson, 1943–
God's plenty: religious diversity in Kingston / William James.

Includes bibliographical references and index.
ISBN 978-0-7735-3889-4 (bound). – ISBN 978-0-7735-3925-9 (pbk.)

1. Kingston (Ont.) – Religion – 21st century. 2. Religious pluralism – Ontario – Kingston – History – 21st century. I. Title.

BL2530.C3J35 2011 200.9713'7209051 C2011-902294-X

This book was typeset by Interscript in 10/13 Sabon.

Once more for Carolyn,
the love of my life

Contents

List of Illustrations ix
Preface xi
Introduction xv

1 Situations of the Sacred in Kingston: From Downtown to the Suburbs 3

2 Mainline Christian Denominations: Roman Catholic, United, Anglican, Presbyterian, Baptist 36

3 Protestant Evangelicals: Pentecostal, Christian and Missionary Alliance, Free Methodist 80

4 Proselytizing Groups: Salvation Army, Mormons, Jehovah's Witnesses, Brethren 118

5 Ethnic Christianity: Protestant, Eastern Christian, Roman Catholic 147

6 Liberal Religion: Quakers, Reform Jews, Unitarians 180

7 Diversity of Religions: Islam, Bahá'í, Hindu, Sai Baba, Sikh 213

8 Women's Roles in Religions: Mainline Denominations and Alternative Spiritualities 248

9 Religion in Institutions: Universities, Hospitals, and Prisons 282

10 Religion in the City: Public Religion and the Religious Imagination 317

Conclusion 356
Appendices
A Interview Questions 377
B Religious Site Profile Template 380
C List of Interviews Conducted 382

D Interviews Broadcast in the *Profiles: People of Faith* Series 385
E Letter of Information and Consent Form 387
F 2001 Census, Kingston Religion 390

Bibliography 393
Index 419

List of Illustrations

MAPS

Kingston, Ontario, in relation to other urban centres xxx
Kingston's city boundaries xxx
Downtown Kingston xxxi

PHOTOGRAPHS

View of Kingston from Fort Henry Hill frontispiece
St George's Anglican Cathedral 12
St Mary's Roman Catholic Cathedral 14
Beth Israel Synagogue 21
St Joseph's Roman Catholic Church 22
Chalmers United Church 45
St Andrew's Presbyterian Church 66
First Baptist Church 68
Kingston Gospel Temple 87
Third Day Worship Centre 95
Salvation Army Citadel 123
Church of Jesus Christ of Latter-day Saints 127
Jehovah's Witness Kingdom Hall 131
Kingston Chinese Alliance Church 156
Greek Orthodox Church 163
Sydenham Street United Church 184
Kingston Unitarian Fellowship 199
Islamic Centre of Kingston 217
Prayers at the Islamic Centre 228
Heathfield, Sisters of Providence Motherhouse 253

Kuluta Buddhist Centre 266
Funeral of Capt. Matthew Dawe, Royal Military College, 14 July 2007 300
North Gate, Kingston Penitentiary 308
Salvation Army at Confederation Park 313
Manger scene at Confederation Park 326
Interfaith vigil, Kingston City Hall, Good Friday 2004 364
Bronwen Wallace's poem "Mexican Sunsets" 371

Preface

Shortly after the turn of the millennium – a momentous phrase for a monumental phase – several things turned me toward this project on religious diversity in Kingston. The Department of Religious Studies at Queen's University had just begun a new master's program in religion and modernity for which I was the coordinator. For the first time during my three decades in the department, we would have graduate students available as research assistants. My teaching of a fourth-year course, The Contemporary Religious Situation in Canada – also to be opened up to master's students – had for a number of years been augmenting my knowledge of the local religious scene, as annually I directed students in the task of doing fieldwork projects on Kingston's religious sites. My book dealing mostly with Canadian literature and its religious dimensions had recently been published, the culmination of many years of teaching and research in that area, and I was ready to turn toward something different. I had also just concluded a year as acting director in international programs and was leaving administrative duties to go back to classroom teaching and research. Many things, then, conspired to make a study of religious diversity in Kingston a timely and engaging enterprise for me.

The assistance of many individuals helped to enable the success of this project. Above all else, the research assistants who were hired, both senior undergraduates and master's students, were industrious and creative beyond my expectations. They threw themselves into this work, providing suggestions, helping to shape interview questions, investigating little-known byways of the religious character of Kingston, organizing my files, and then devising finding aids for me to recover what was in them. Over one hundred interviews with representatives of local religious groups, each interview about an hour in length, were tape-recorded and then transcribed (see the interview questions, appendix A, and the list of interviews conducted, appendix C). Students provided executive summaries for each interview so that the contents could be readily accessed, and then compiled an index of themes to enable comparison among the interviews. Some research assistants prepared reports, or presented papers at conferences, that dealt with the work they had been doing. Much of this book, therefore, draws on their reports, the taped and transcribed interviews, the indexes and summaries, and the completed templates of site visits made by students in the course Religious Studies 451 (see the template in appendix B).

The Census of 2001 provided invaluable data enabling the comparison of local findings with larger, national trends in religion on the Canadian scene. The availability of Statistics Canada material and information on the web has greatly facilitated this project. Although books and articles on religious groups and on religion in Canada have proliferated lately – and, as well, religion has been much better covered by news media than it was a few decades ago – religious groups themselves, both nationally and locally, have made themselves accessible on the Internet. Churches, denominations, and other faith communities small and large have organized and presented themselves online, advertising their times of worship and special events, sharing newsletters, annual reports, and financial statements, and even podcasts of sermons. While the availability of so much material is a boon to the researcher, it also presents challenges. Something that is available one month disappears the next, making referencing a headache. A researcher's life used to be easier when the source was fixed in print and kept in a library – but after all, religions themselves are fluid rather than fixed. Except for a few instances that are noted, the references to websites listed in the bibliography remained current by the end of 2010.

As already indicated, my greatest thanks are due to the research assistants for this project. They are, in alphabetical order: Hannah Dick, Jo Ann England, Laurie Gashinski, Joe Green, Lee Wing Hin (Vivian Lee), Nicole Mailman, Ryann Miller, Lisa Pim, Dolores Turner, and Amanda Walker. Other students – Jodi Baine, Gillian Cornie, Amy Fisher, Taryn Ling, and Megan Unterschultz – provided additional assistance. In almost every instance where an interview is cited in these pages, that interview was conducted and transcribed by one of these student researchers. Their work fleshed out and brought to life the skeleton of this project. Some of them collaborated more actively with me in the interpretation of the data: Hannah Dick presented a conference paper on religious clubs at Queen's University (see chap. 9; Dick 2007), and prepared a report on spiritual mapping (see chap. 10); Laurie Gashinski presented a paper on the project to the Canadian Society for the Study of Religion (Gashinski 2006). Laurie also co-authored with me an article published as "The Challenges of Religious Pluralism in Kingston, Ontario," which appeared in the *Canadian Journal of Urban*

Research in 2006. A revised version is used with permission of the publisher in chapter 10, in the section "Performing the Act of Religion in Public."

A second major obligation of gratitude is owed to the clergy and representatives of religious groups in Kingston who so graciously agreed to participate in this project. They answered our questions, told us about their hopes and goals, detailed what was distinctive about their way of being religious, and shared their histories with all of the attending triumphs and struggles. That willingness to be open and candid, in many cases to interviewers who could not be expected to understand with full sympathy their group or its vision, was impressive. Some local members of the clergy and laypeople generously agreed to read and comment on parts of the manuscript. While the responsibility for sifting through and interpreting what they all have provided to us is entirely my own, I hope those who appear in these pages will recognize themselves in the resulting tapestry of Kingston's religious diversity. A similar kind of willing acceptance and collaboration was exhibited by the twenty-four guests who agreed to be interviewed by me on the local cable television channel for the series *Profiles: People of Faith*, which aired on TVCogeco from September 2004 to April 2005 (see appendix D). Every one of these guests, many of them strangers to me before the interviews, consented to sit down before television cameras – with no opportunity for subsequent editing or retractions – and to share with me the details of their respective spiritual journeys. To encounter such honesty and openness of spirit was a humbling experience, leaving me convinced, whatever their theologies and convictions and religious paths, of the basic human goodness shared among people of faith. My thanks to Scott Meyers and Michael Pontbriand of TVCogeco in Kingston, who came to me with the idea of the series.

A third indebtedness is to colleagues in religious studies in Canada and elsewhere. Some were embarked on similar projects; others invited me to discuss my work at conferences; and, still others shared their research with me, gave suggestions, and provided in their own writing and published material much of the basis on which this project could be built. My friends and colleagues in the Department of Religious Studies at Queen's University were unfailingly helpful in their guidance and support. They volunteered suggestions about contacts and interview subjects in the community, helped enhance my understanding of local religious organizations, and, when requested, they read parts of this manuscript. A sabbatical leave in 2007–08 provided a large piece of the time necessary for the writing of this book. For that kind of support and so much else I remain grateful.

The maps for this book were drawn by Marc Letourneau, a Queen's University Ph.D. in geography who shares my interests in the city of Kingston and in sacred space. The photographs were taken by the author, almost all of them during 2010. Jonathan Sugarman of Sugarman Design provided some final image editing in the preparation of some of the photos. My thanks to both Marc and Jonathan for their contributions to the published look of *God's Plenty*.

Finally, I want to express my appreciation for the excellent editorial help I have received through the stages leading to the appearance of this book from the staff of McGill-Queen's University Press, especially Kyla Madden, Joan McGilvray, and Maureen Garvie. The two anonymous readers for the press were careful and thorough in their assessments, offering suggestions and advice from which I benefited greatly.

Permission to quote from Bronwen Wallace's poem, "Mexican Sunsets," from her collection *Common Magic* (Ottawa: Oberon Press), was kindly granted by the publisher and by the poet's son, Jeremy Baxter.

The research project Religious Diversity in Kingston was supported by a standard research grant from the Social Sciences and Humanities Research Council of Canada (SSHRC) from 2003 to 2006.

Introduction

Let us situate the geographical context for this book. To stand almost anywhere on Kingston's waterfront – on top of Fort Henry Hill is a good vantage point – is to stand at a place of the merging and parting of waters. To the south lies Wolfe Island, now studded with scores of giant wind turbines, their blades rotating in the same winds that make Kingston the world's freshwater sailing capital. The Great Cataraqui River empties into Kingston Harbour at the terminus of the Rideau Canal, which joins together various lakes and rivers over the distance of two hundred kilometres from Ottawa. Lake Ontario, last and smallest of the Great Lakes, begins its outflow at Kingston, where the St Lawrence River gathers up the waters of the Great Lakes and embarks on its twelve-hundred kilometre passage to the east down to the sea. On a calm summer day, calibrating my sailboat's knotmeter – it measures speed by water rotating a small paddlewheel – a downstream current is already perceptible off Kingston's waterfront. Sometimes, when the wind blows from the east, it is a "river flowing both ways," as Morag Gunn observed in Margaret Laurence's novel, *The Diviners*, bringing past and future together: "And yet it never lost its ancient power for her, and it never ceased to be new" (1974, 285). The subtitle of the first part of Laurence's novel, "River of Now and Then," suggests the simultaneity of past and present for Morag as narrator, who carries three generations within herself. Kingston is a place where waters meet and part, and where past and present converge too.

Seen from the air, Kingston lies amidst a blue and green constellation of big and small islands – Wolfe, Amherst, and Howe, Simcoe, Garden, and Cedar. Cedar Island, part of the National Parks system and located opposite Fort Henry, just where the St Lawrence begins, sometimes gets identified as the first of the Thousand Islands because of the granite composition it shares with the rest of the famous archipelago. For a traveller by road or rail,

Kingston is a kind of halfway point on the five or six hour journey between Toronto and Montreal. The trip from Kingston to Ottawa or to Syracuse, New York – for the great river unites as well as divides Canadians and their American neighbours – is similarly a matter of only a few hours. Kingston occupies a strategic location, a place of arrivals and departures for waters and people.

In the geography of places renowned for spiritual energy, Kingston is reckoned by some as especially charged with the sacred. The Kingston and Area Dowsers, for example, one of seventeen such groups in Canada, has about a dozen members who practise the old art of divining for hidden water with a rod. They, like some other Canadian Dowser chapters – and perhaps, too, like Laurence's character, the scavenger Christie Logan – engage in various alternative spiritual practices ranging from healing therapies and energy work to Feng Shui, essential oils, and protective jewellery, and including intuition and hypnosis, all aimed at achieving wholeness and balance. When researcher Laurie Gashinski interviewed Barbara Caldwell, then a contact for the Kingston Dowsers, she described her farm on the Napanee River as situated "in a geological fault you might say that is millions of years old," with an artesian well and other "water sources that have not been studied because they are just too complex." On her property is a woods "like a cathedral," where other members of the Kingston Dowsers have reported seeing fairies. Another local dowser by the name of Lloyd, so Caldwell related, has a hundred acres near Gananoque, with a spot at the back where "the earth erupts," which has "been a burial site for native peoples for centuries." Lloyd has the gift of being able to summon up the names of people who have done anonymous or unwitnessed deeds; he identified a pair of teenage vandals that way (interview, 9 June 2005). The two farms are situated respectively to the west and to the east of Kingston, each about a half-hour's drive.

This kind of attention to unseen processes and energies detectable by special powers is reminiscent of the ancient religions based in nature, and identifies the Kingston area as particularly charged with power. A place where the important water routes of the Great Lakes, the Rideau Canal, and the St Lawrence converge, begin, and end, and where the limestone plain of eastern Ontario touches the Frontenac arch of the Canadian Shield, readily lends itself to being interpreted as a locale of the sacred. The native peoples who lived in the area before European contact saw the Thousand Islands as such a place when they called it Manitonna, the "Garden of the Great Spirit." Some of the Kingston Dowsers too have native ancestry and join other members in the effort to reawaken their ancient memories, harking back to the Druids with whom they identify themselves, and explore their deep connection to the currents of nature. The Dowsers, like so many other informal groups, have developed these spiritualities of nature independently of the major religious traditions.

For many other religions, revelation does not come through nature, nor is the sacred even to be found within nature. Instead, the divine is revealed on the stage of history, and for Christians, in Jesus Christ. Adam Hood Burwell, minister of the Catholic Apostolic Church in Kingston from 1836 until his death in 1849, has been acclaimed as "probably the best lyric poet Canada produced in the early nineteenth century" (MacDonald n.d.). In his poem "Summer Evening Contemplations," published in 1849, Burwell expresses the orthodox Christian view that nature does not provide an avenue to God. Instead, as he puts it in this extract from his poem, revelation comes through Jesus Christ alone:

> Gold, silver, precious stones, the earth itself,
> With all its furniture of mountains, hills,
> Valleys, and streams, deserts, and fruitful plains;
> The northern cold; the moulding of the snow;
> The generation of the hail and storms;
> The changing winds, the restless roaring sea,
> That casts up mire and dirt; – these man should read,
> And "look through nature – *up to Nature's God?*"
> Not so! – He hath ordained another way.
> The mystic ladder Isaac's son beheld
> Of intercourse between the seen and unseen,
> Prefigured naught of Nature. God in manhood,
> Th' Eternal Word made flesh! He is the Way
> Up to the God of all.

The three great western monotheistic traditions of Christianity, Judaism, and Islam understand God as acting within the historical process, intervening and shaping its course. Their religions are highly organized, their sacred texts rigorously interpreted, their doctrines and teachings carefully expounded, and their clergy subject to prescribed training and ordination. All three monotheisms observe holy days and annual occasions of observance. Their predominance tends to fix the definition of what counts as "religion," thereby excluding some other ways of being religious, including the religions of native peoples (see chap. 9). While not all organized religions locate the divine in the linear processes of history progressing toward an ending – Buddhism and Hinduism see life as cyclical and recurring – the western religions tend to follow this pattern. In Kingston the major buildings devoted to religion – many Christian churches, an Islamic Centre, and a Jewish synagogue – are within the traditions of western monotheism. Much of this exploration of religious diversity in Kingston focuses on contemporary local congregations within these traditions, examining their histories, their origins, and their similarities and differences.

Some people, including many sociologists of religion, assumed a scant generation ago that religion would die away, or at least become unnecessary, as Canada became more secular. Instead, a boom in personal spirituality and a pluralism forged out of growing diversity have emerged as the most noticeable features of a transformed religious situation. The nature and extent of religious diversity in multicultural Canada has firmly impressed itself on many observers. As one scholar comments, "Among immigrants specifically, almost 52 percent of those admitted to Canada between 1991 and 2001 stated that they belonged to a non-Christian tradition" (Milot 2009, 108). While this transformed religious scene has mostly been examined in Canada's large urban centres, it is happening in smaller cities too – such as Kingston – where it has not been much studied to this point.

Only nine cities in Canada have a population of more than a half-million people. The twenty next largest cities range from 500,000 down to 100,000 people. In 2006 Kingston ranked twenty-fifth among the thirty most populous cities in Canada. When Kingston with its metropolitan population of 152,358 in 2006 is compared with Canada at large, we find that it mirrors the national distribution of population by age, but with fewer immigrants, a larger proportion of highly educated people, and more employment in health and social services and in education. In the popular view, Kingston epitomizes Upper Canada's Anglo-Celtic customs and values. It is characterized as "an institutional town" that has changed little over the past three hundred years. How do these factors show up in religion in Kingston? What does religion look like in the city's university, military, hospitals, and prisons, and how do these institutions affect religion in the city generally? Has increased ethnic and religious diversity of the past generation altered the traditions of religious sites and groups within this mostly unilingual city?

Using interviews that followed the questions outlined on the Religious Diversity in Kingston website (see appendix A), from 2003 to 2006 this research project examined most, though not all, of the religious groups, sites, and activities in the city. The interviews began in October 2003, with many of them being conducted over the next twelve months. When the process was already underway, the decision was taken to transcribe each taped interview to make it easier to consult, either in hard-copy format or electronically. The additional work of transcription, requiring of the research assistants an extra four to six hours for each interview, slowed down the schedule of meetings with faith representatives, with the result that the interviews continued over the next three years and more, with the last one being conducted in April 2008. That prolonged schedule meant that our interviewees were often reacting to different events in the world or in the city – the tsunami of 2004, the native residential schools settlement, proposed legislation on same-sex marriage, public statements from their faith group, or local news stories of religious significance. In a very few cases, after repeated requests to some groups did not lead to a meeting, the decision was made to omit that organization or representative. Even less frequently, a group declined to be interviewed. Sometimes we decided that to consult with yet another congregation representative of the same denomination was unlikely to add much to the picture that was emerging of local religious sites. Over the period of our research, the personnel changed at some of the sites, or the group relocated or closed. Necessarily, then, the interviews do not always reflect subsequent developments. In short, whether due to exigencies or to choices made because of limited time and resources, we cannot claim to have conducted interviews with every single religious group in Kingston. As the pages of this book reflect and document, religions and people change over time, often within a space of a few years.

In addition, the project studied what was going on at various sites representative of minority religions. Many of these groups, often newer or smaller, using temporary space or meeting infrequently, were studied too. Local trends have been compared with provincial and national ones. The project looked too at the degree to which religion has departed from the public sphere for the inner self. Is religious life and practice in Kingston marked by an increased personal spirituality? If so, how have religious traditions adapted to this more individualistic turn? Perhaps a multi-layered spirituality in which people "mix and match" several different ways of being religious has replaced an exclusive loyalty to one tradition. Alternatively, perhaps substitute forms of religion only supplement, without replacing, that ongoing religious commitment. Not only that, but many of the religions that are relative newcomers to Canada are seeking their place in the public sphere. *God's Plenty* examines mergers and separations within historic religious traditions, and the creation of alternate traditions – all focused within the context of a medium-sized city in central Canada during the first decade of the twenty-first century.

In the effort to maintain continuity with their pasts, some religions vigorously oppose themselves to the world around them and to other religions; they continue to affirm their traditions in resistance to the pressures of modernity. Other religions strive to adapt their traditions, seeking to update them, in the face of these pressures for change. Such resistance and transformation of religions, mostly studied in Canada's large urban centres, is occurring in smaller cities too, where it has not been much examined. Since this municipal mapping of the religious in Kingston was initiated, parallel studies have begun in several other small to mid-sized cities among Canada's thirty largest urban centres. Many such places are ripe for a similar examination, especially in cities where a university is situated – for example, in Victoria, St John's, Windsor, Saskatoon, Regina, Kitchener-Waterloo, Sherbrooke, Trois-Rivières, Moncton, Sudbury, and Thunder Bay. Further, this Kingston project adds concreteness and specificity to investigations of more general and nationwide trends pertaining to religion in Canada. Although Canadians almost never speak this way – perhaps it is too "American" or inappropriate for a country characterized by its regions – this might be said to be a study of religion in "middle Canada," though in this book's conclusion I borrow Hugh MacLennan's more regional term, "Laurentia."

Three areas of exploration are the focus of this book. The first objective is to chart the groups and record the activities present at the established religious sites in Kingston. The visible monuments of downtown ecclesiastical architecture, many originating from the nineteenth century, represent "mainline" Christian denominations: Roman Catholic, Anglican, United, Presbyterian, Lutheran, and Baptist (see chaps. 1 and 2). About twenty-seven centres of worship representative of mainline Christianity – that is, denominations whose membership is greater than 2 per cent of Canada's population – are situated in the "old" city of Kingston, between the Great Cataraqui River and Little Cataraqui River. Several dozen more buildings house "non-mainline" groups extending from the old city to include its newer suburbs: for example, Brethren, Pentecostal, Salvation Army, Christian Reformed, Unitarian, Free Methodist, Seventh-day Adventist, Missionary Alliance, Christian Science, and Jehovah's Witnesses (see chaps. 3 and 4). Some Christians assemble to worship on the basis of shared ethnicity: the Chinese Alliance, Greek Orthodox, Ukrainian Catholic, Coptic Christian, or South Indian churches; additionally, there are Korean, francophone Roman Catholic, and Dutch congregations (see chap. 5). For a century Kingston has had an Orthodox synagogue, while a Reform congregation with its own part-time rabbi has become established in the last generation (see chaps. 1 and 6). More recent still is the Islamic Centre in the suburban area north of Highway 401 and the relocated Kuluta Buddhist Centre downtown (see chap. 7).

The second objective of this project is to map some of the other, less visible religions present in Kingston. Many of these groups use temporary space or meet infrequently, such as Sai Baba, Spiritualists, Bahá'ís, Hindus, Sikhs, and Wiccans or other New Religious Movements (NRMs). As well, people assemble for meditation, tai chi, yoga, or in groups for personal growth or consciousness-raising in response to ads placed in a public library, a New Age bookshop, or a health food store. Students on the campus of Queen's University gather for meetings of Navigators, Inter-Varsity Christian Fellowship, the Newman, Geneva, or Hillel houses, or for special lectures sponsored by Transcendental Meditation, the Raelians, Krishna Consciousness, or Soka Gakkai International. In addition, religious activities, including services provided by institutional chaplains, take place at other organizations in the city such as schools, hospitals, and prisons, Queen's University, the Royal Military College, or the Spirituality Centre run by the Sisters of Providence (see chap. 9, also chap. 8). All these deserve a place in the account of the religious panorama to be found in Kingston.

A third objective here is to examine the extent to which religion has left the public sphere and become lodged in the private self. Recent trends indicate that religious life and practice are marked by an increased personal spirituality. If so, how have religious traditions adapted to this less social or communitarian and more personalistic and individualistic turn? Here it would be useful to correlate local trends with national ones. A number of scenarios are possible. Perhaps an eclectic, multi-layered spirituality, in which people "mix and match" several different modes of religiousness, alters a previously exclusive commitment or loyalty to a single tradition. Or, perhaps substitute secular correlates of religion may supplement, without replacing, that ongoing and traditional religious commitment (see chap. 8). Among the issues to be explored are the shifts that have taken place over the past decade or so as more such options increase and attendance at long-established worship sites decreases. How have the changing roles of women in society, or an aging population, or the generation of baby boomers affected religious groups? Another development in our research was to seek new spaces in which public forms of religions can be manifest in the city. How has Kingston accommodated this new public face of religion so that religions not part of a Canada once overwhelmingly Christian (see chap. 10) find their place in the public square?

The Pluralism Project emanating from Harvard University and supervised by Diana L. Eck stands as the immediate inspiration and model for this research. That project's first explicit goal is comparable to the impetus for this one: "To document and better understand the changing contours of American religious demography." Over the past decade and more, though limiting itself to the American scene, and focusing mostly on the religions of immigrants, this massive project has produced extensive materials, on CD-ROM, in print, and on the web, covering many of the towns and cities of the United States. The tools and templates developed from Harvard provide a valuable pattern for similar work in Canada, though, remarkably, no one else had yet applied those methods when the Religious Diversity in Kingston project began. Further, our project aimed to cover the entire religious landscape of the city, including – as the Pluralism Project mostly does not – the faith communities of Jews and Christians. Of course, the differing Canadian context demands a somewhat altered mandate. As compared with the United States, to name only a few factors, Canada has fewer evangelicals, more Roman Catholics, different patterns of immigration, and no "civil religion" – which is to say that unlike in the United States, the nation itself does not assume a sacred character in Canada.

Related studies on religions in Canada are both more general and more specific than this one. Books by Reginald Bibby (1987, 2002) and Peter Emberley (2002) and others edited by Paul Bramadat and David Seljak (2005, 2008) and Lori Beaman (2006, 2008) are but a few examples of surveys of national religious trends. The same kind of comprehensive examination has been conducted in relation to specific religions in Canada; see, for example, the essays on Hindus, Muslims, and Sikhs nationally, written respectively by Harold G. Coward, Sheila McDonough, and Joseph T. O'Connell (in Coward, Hinnells, and Williams 2002) or on Jews in Canada by Gerald Tulchinsky (1992, 1998, 2008). More specifically, other studies have documented Asian Buddhist communities in Toronto (McLellan 1999), immigrant religions in Ottawa, and comparative studies of Christian or Jewish congregations elsewhere. Canadian scholars I consulted about this project at its beginnings in 2002, all of them engaged in their own research on some aspect of religion in Canada, assured me they knew of no Canadian application of the approach and methods of the Pluralism Project.

Locally, Queen's University scholars such as sociologists Marion Meyer (1983) and David Lyon (1995) have published books on, respectively, Jews in Kingston and St James' Anglican Church. Other studies of particular congregations – some informal, some scholarly – abound in Kingston. Among the scholarly books are a volume of essays on St George's Cathedral (Swainson 1991) and a detailed examination of St Andrew's Presbyterian Church (Osborne 2004). Both historian Donald Swainson and geographer Brian S. Osborne in their wide-ranging co-authored book *Kingston: Building on the Past* (1988) stress the function of Kingston as a religious "sub-capital" in one aspect of its role as "an institutional town." They claim that Kingston's distinctive personality lies in three hundred years of continuity, making it one of the least changed of Ontario cities. Those observations are worth testing on the religious front: How does religion manifest itself in the city's institutions – university, military, hospitals, and prisons? Further, how has the increased ethnic and religious diversity of the past fifty years affected the continuity of religious sites and groups within Kingston?

A significant context for the research reflected here is my teaching of the required honours seminar Religious Studies 451, The Contemporary Religious Situation in Canada, for majors in religious studies at Queen's University. For more than twenty years I conducted this year-long course for a group of between six and twenty students. My early realization was that these fourth-year students, who had spent as much as half their time at Queen's in Religious Studies courses, might have read a great deal about religions and theories of religion but had not always seen much religion being practised. Therefore, a required aspect of the course became four fieldwork visits to observe groups engaged in cultic exercises, ranging from "Mainline Christian," and "Christian, but Not Mainline," through "Religious but Not Christian," to "Secular Correlates of Religion." Sometimes, in directing students about how to write up the results of their fieldwork research, I suggested that they imagine two hypothetical readers, one who knew nothing about the site being described, the other a lifelong member. Similarly, this book aims at setting forth the beliefs and practices within any faith community to readers having at best an external knowledge of the group, while being recognizable to congregants well acquainted with its inner workings.

Students have responded with enthusiasm to this fieldwork component. One of them commented that "having the opportunity to observe firsthand the practices and rituals of several faith groups in Kingston was an invaluable experience as a religious studies student ... Attending synagogue and listening to the chanting of the kaddish, observing the breaking of bread at the Union Street Gospel Chapel, and admiring the beautiful neo-Classical architecture of St George's Cathedral drew my studies out of the textbook and into my senses, becoming tangible sights, smells, and sounds." Much of the field research became incorporated into term essays. Some students wrote extended papers for the course on the local religious scene and presented them at a departmental colloquium. Because these site visits at first followed relatively informal guidelines, no systematic body of research information was initially built up. Once the formal research for Religious Diversity in Kingston was underway, students in Rels-451, joined each year by a few master's students enrolled in the parallel Rels-851, began to file profiles on each group they visited, using the model provided by the Pluralism Project (see appendix B). The other products from the class have been their largely narrative and descriptive critical essays, some submitted as term papers, some presented at academic conferences, and some subsequently incorporated into this book (see James and Gashiniski 2006; Dick 2007). These years of observations and studies from my students have contributed to my own impressions of the changes and trends in local religion.

The many-sided methods of short-term ethnography were used in the further gathering and analysis of the data. In effect, the ethnographic researcher wants to know how a particular religious site operates and what it means to be a member of the group being investigated. In the study of a local religious group, the researcher seeks to discover how the people associated there categorize their activities and what they call one another, how they construct and discover meaning in life-events that are significant to them, and what processes of individual and collective self-definition characterize their situations. This study is a kind of "backyard anthropology," an examination of the local and familiar as if it were foreign and other.

No single investigative technique – nor any one kind of resulting data – was employed or derived here. Written documents from parallel researches, the observers' own notes of their observations, and any record of things said in discussion, informal conversation, interviews, and even overheard remarks have become part of the picture – though admittedly, not all of that material can be quoted and attributed. Photographs, audiotapes, and transcriptions of scores of interviews provide an archivable spoken and visual record, and an eventual contribution to local religious history. This material is now held in the Queen's University Archives for future researchers. The twenty-four half-hour interviews I conducted with various individuals about their personal religious histories for the local cable channel (see appendix D) became an important resource, also held in the Queen's University Archives, and now deposited in DVD format in Stauffer Library. The series, *Profiles: People of Faith*, was a dialogue with men and women about their own spiritual autobiographies. In these television interviews these "people of faith" were not acting as spokespersons for a particular faith tradition, unlike the formal interviews that were the centre of the Religious Diversity in Kingston project. Instead, they related their own religious histories and convictions.

To acquire and assemble a coherent narrative of a religious group or centre depends more on having an open mind and continued qualitative observation than on quantitative methods. Ethnographers have endorsed such a seemingly grab-bag approach in positive terms as a "magpie" attitude, in which knowledge is gained simply by "hanging around" and "picking things up" (see Massey 1998). On the one hand, assembling an account as experienced by participants is a "phenomenological" enterprise that describes rather than explains, and is as concerned about ritualistic and symbolic expression as much as ideas and doctrines. Asking what it means to be a member of a particular religious group suggests representing the world as it appears to an insider. Yet, while the researcher may have an open mind and endeavour to suspend judgment, he or she still possesses prior knowledge and assumptions. There is no *tabula rasa;* nor is "cognitive atheism" or total objectivity required or desirable. The final story remains etic rather than emic – that is, it comes from an external observer rather than a participant who shares the group's beliefs. The description and analysis found here is structured by someone who is and remains an outsider to the group, who has decided what questions are to be asked, who has made a selection from what has been seen and heard, and who has interpreted the results. Such a procedure is of course largely congruent with methods used throughout the field of religious studies. Since human subjects were the focus of this research, this project required the approval and direction of the General Research Ethics Board at Queen's University. The requisite letters of information and consent forms were used with all of the interview subjects (see appendix E).

The terms of the book's subtitle, *Religious Diversity in Kingston*, need some definition. What is "religion"? What is "diversity"? And, even, what is "Kingston"? Defining the scope and nature of such an exploration is essential to determining its dimensions and limits. How far do we go? What do we look at along the way? Further elaboration of the parameters of this book is provided to a greater extent in the course of the chapters that follow. In a preliminary way, let us consider what is to be expected of this examination.

For now it is enough to say that the subject is religion of almost all kinds and varieties available in the city of Kingston, Ontario, early in the twenty-first century. Some groups, therefore, that were once here but have since disappeared are not dealt with at all. Christian Science – or officially, the First Church of Christ, Scientist – faded from the Kingston scene more than a decade ago. Other groups, less well known because they were one-of-a-kind house churches or briefly visible alternative religions, were present here for a time but have disappeared with almost no trace. The obvious beginning place for anyone wanting to canvass a city's religious resources – as strange as it might initially seem – is the Yellow Pages of the phone book, under the entry "Churches." Even if it's a mosque or synagogue you're looking for, that's the place to start. The actual heading that begins the listing reads: "Churches & Other Places of Worship." It also has sub-listings for "Muslim" and "Buddhist," including the Kingston Islamic Centre and the Kuluta Buddhist Centre. As Will Herberg pointed out fifty years ago (1960), by the middle of the last century Judaism in the United States was conforming to a pattern of religious denominationalism already characteristic of the existing institutional system of Protestantism in America. When Leslie K. Kawamura was writing about the history of Japanese Buddhists in southern Alberta, he referred to the priests as "ministers," and to their buildings as "Buddhist churches" (Kawamura 1977). There are other accounts of

Buddhists taking over disused Christian churches in Canada and using existing notice boards in front to display the time of worship and of their "Sunday School." Given that kind of adaptation to the prevailing religious landscape, it is perhaps not surprising that religious groups that are not Christian are listed in the phone book under "Churches."

The category of "religion" for the purposes of this study was made deliberately broad and was by no means restricted to the "Churches & Other Places of Worship" listed in the telephone book. After all, those places had to have a fixed address and phone number and the wish to be publicly identified in this way. Other possibilities included clubs and organizations that appeared to be at least quasi-religious and advertised in local newspapers or on campuses, or else made themselves known by word of mouth or were mentioned on the web, in health food stores, on various notice boards, or at the public library. The line was drawn, however, so as to exclude groups or events whose religious significance would be largely "implicit," defined by Edward Bailey in a preliminary way as involving "commitment," "integrating foci," and "intensive concerns with extensive effects"; he analyzes the British pub as an instance of implicit religion (1997, 8–9). Our focus, by way of contrast, was primarily on instances of explicit religion, as exploring possible examples of implicit religion would simply have expanded the project beyond any reasonable limits.

The question of what "diversity" might mean is discussed in chapter 7. Briefly, religious diversity would seem to refer to an assortment of religions, suggesting the variety of different religious traditions that exist side by side in a pluralistic and multicultural society. To that end, the pages that follow give special attention to faith traditions other than Christianity and Judaism. For example, Islam, Buddhism, Hinduism, Sikhism – all of which have come comparatively recently to Kingston and contribute greatly to the enrichment of the tapestry of religions in the city – get particular examination in chapter 7. Minority and alternative traditions – including what is sometimes called "New Age religion" or personal spiritualities that flourish apart from, or alongside, longstanding or monolithic institutions and traditions – are also studied (see chap. 8). Meditation groups, religions that follow a contemporary leader or guru, forms of dance or exercise, and movements that aim at consciousness-raising add to the religious or quasi-religious options available in any contemporary Canadian city (partially dealt with in chap. 8). Because in multicultural Canada religious diversity is frequently elided with ethnic diversity, we conducted extensive research of ethnically based Christian congregations within Kingston (see chap. 5), though even a diversified Christianity might still be understood to be a single religion. We also studied the way in which Kingston's institutions (see chap. 9) provided more religious options – especially on the campus of Queen's University – than would have existed otherwise.

A consideration of "diversity" led to examining the variety existing within specific religious traditions as well – what has been provisionally termed "intrinsic" as opposed to "extrinsic" religious diversity. Today a wide spectrum of belief and practice can be found within a single faith tradition such as Christianity; see, for example, how the Roman Catholic, United, Anglican, and Baptist churches exhibit this range in chapter 2. That kind of intrinsic diversity can also be found within a single denomination and even with a single congregation. In Judaism too the extremes of theological liberalism and conservatism are evident (see chaps. 1 and 6). To that end, Reform Judaism and Unitarianism comprising instances of liberal religion at one end of the spectrum (chap. 6) are contrasted with evangelical Christianity and Orthodox Judaism at the other (see chaps. 1, 3, and 4). Perhaps it ought to come as no surprise, but we found that the particular religiosities of some women led to an expansion of the religious options on the contemporary scene as well (see chap. 8), as they explored ways of developing alternative traditions, liberalizing their own, or combining a traditional way of being religious with another, minority practice. Again, not surprisingly, in almost every faith the question of the place of gays and lesbians, same-sex relationships and marriages, and other issues characterized by sexuality and gender became indicative of either the preservation of values seen as significant to maintenance of the tradition or, alternatively, of the degree to which the religion can adapt to modernity, changing according to alterations in society. In short, then, for this book "diversity" came to characterize the variety and range of religious options presenting themselves and encompassing a wide assortment of beliefs, theologies, liturgies, and practices.

And, as for the third term in our project's title, what is "Kingston?" Here the answer was simple, almost mechanically so. Kingston was taken to consist of the area lying within the boundaries of the municipality – an artificial distinction, perhaps, especially because outlying suburbs, and smaller places just beyond the reach of those boundaries, were excluded. Not only such villages and hamlets as Odessa, Napanee, Yarker, Gananoque, Harrowsmith, and Joyceville were left out, but even Wolfe, Amherst, and Howe islands, partly visible from Kingston's waterfront, and part of the political constituency of Kingston and the Islands, were similarly put aside. To include these nearby places would have enlarged our study beyond the readily achievable. To restrict ourselves to the municipality of Kingston allowed for a focus on the religious nature of this urban centre – see the characterizations and conclusions offered in chapter 10, "Religion in the City," which itself rounds out some of the preliminary observations of chapter 1, "Situations of the Sacred in Kingston."

God's Plenty, then, is a unique study of the entire religious landscape of one medium-sized Canadian city early in this new century. Partly in homage to this "Limestone City," several books about religion in Kingston use the metaphor of rock in their titles: there is Louis J. Flynn's history of St Mary's Cathedral entitled *Built on a Rock* (ca. 1976), with its companion, *Springing from the Rock* (McKinnon 2002), about the Catholic archdiocese of Kingston; there is also Brian Osborne's history of St Andrew's Presbyterian Church, *The Rock and the Sword* (2004). The religion being examined in this present book, though, is less stony and fixed than these metaphors, or the prevalence of limestone as the preferred ecclesiastical building material, might lead one to think. Like the rivers and lakes of the watercourses that surround Kingston, religion is fluid and in motion, though these waters may run or rest in ancient channels and beds. The continuing story of religion in Kingston includes groups that have merged and ones that have separated, new groups that have sprung into existence and ones that have disappeared. The nature, quality, and direction of faith groups change over time; the surfaces may be calm or ruffled or tumultuous – and at times frozen; and any efforts to fix, contain, or stop that fluidity is bound to misrepresent or distort its nature. A snapshot is not a movie, and a map is not reality. The cartography of religions bears testimony to something, however framed and focused it might be, that, for a period at least, was there.

In Norman Maclean's memoir, *A River Runs through It*, a tribute to his brother and to their shared love of dry-fly fishing in Montana, Maclean reflects on the antiquity of water. As their father, a Presbyterian minister, sits by the river reading St John's Gospel in Greek, he explains, "In the part I was reading its says the Word was in the beginning, and that's right. I used to think water was first, but if you listen carefully you will hear that the words are underneath the water" (95). Maclean, once my professor at the University of Chicago, tries to sort out the relative priority of water and words – and of rocks too. He thinks that a river "has so many things to say that it is hard to know what it says to each of us" (102), perhaps alluding to what his father knew as *logos*, the central divine Word or creative principle, but which gets interpreted in manifold ways by human words. He concludes that "eventually, all things merge into one, and a river runs through it" (104). It is that perennial and enduring religious impulse within humanity – but even more, the many ways in which that impulse gets expressed and symbolized as people create and shape their religions – that *God's Plenty* bears witness to.

The book's title needs some explanation. It was the English poet, critic, and dramatist John Dryden (1631–1700) who remarked, speaking of *The Canterbury Tales* of Geoffrey Chaucer (ca. 1340–1400), "'Tis sufficient to say, according to the Proverb, that here is God's Plenty." Dryden was praising the panoramic grasp of Chaucer's poetic imagination, the range and variety of his characters, his ability to take in so much of the length and breadth of the world of his day. In characterizing the richness of this comprehensive reach, Dryden spoke of Chaucer's imagination as incorporating the divine plentitude, "according to the proverb." The phrase, therefore, "God's plenty" was already proverbial in Dryden's time. Casting about for my title, I though it fit perfectly the diversity of religions in Kingston and the people who practise them, except for one possible problem: is it too exclusively monotheistic? After all, I am critical at several places in this book of those who regard "God" in the singular as the sole and proper subject of religion, thereby installing western monotheism as normative.

I intend the phrase "God's plenty" in a similarly metaphoric way, as an inclusive means of referring to the fullness and variety of "everything under heaven." At the end of his book *Lest Innocent Blood Be Shed*, about saving Jewish children in a French village during World War II, the Jewish philosopher Philip Hallie says: "Our awareness of the preciousness of human life makes our lives joyously precious to ourselves." Then he adds: "For me, that awareness is my awareness of God," by which he might be taken as meaning, using Paul Tillich's words, that his "ultimate concern" is the recognition of how valuable human life is. Tillich, after all, said that whatever concerns a person ultimately is God for that person. Hallie goes on to quote the central confession of the Jewish faith, the Shema Israel: "Hear, oh Israel, the Lord our God, the Lord is One." Yet he wants to pry that formulation loose from the particularities of the Jewish religion and make it accessible to everyone when he explains: "For me, the word *Israel* refers to all of us anarchic-hearted human beings, and the word *God* means the object of our undivided attention to the lucid mystery of being alive for others and for ourselves" (1994, 293). In Hallie's humanistic application and extension of the Shema, all human beings are included within "Israel," and "God" refers to their ultimate concern, whatever that might be. So it is with "God's plenty." The phrase as applied to the religious diversity of Kingston encompasses theists, polytheists, and nontheists; it includes those who consciously subscribe to a religious faith, those who are but casual followers, and those – "religious nones," the census calls them – who belong to no religion. For all of these, once more, "'Tis sufficient to say, according to the Proverb, that here is God's Plenty."

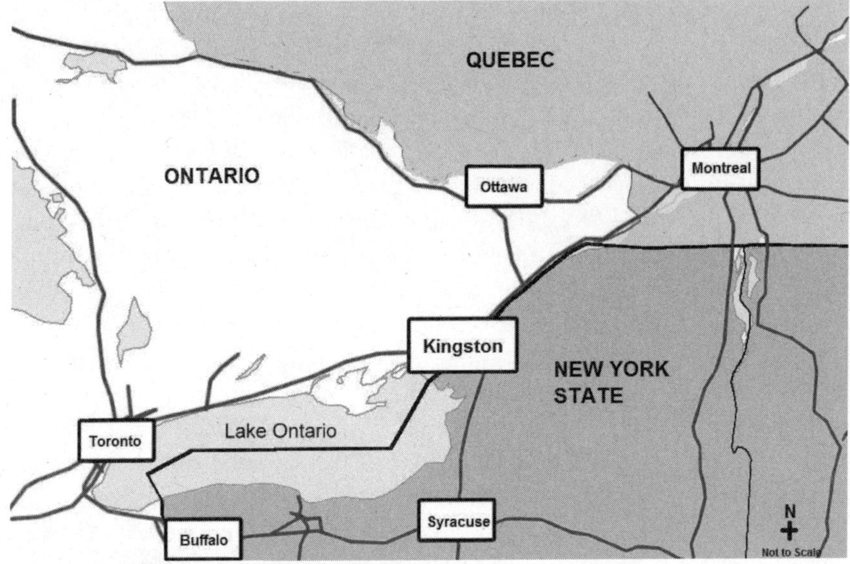

Kingston, Ontario, in relation to other urban centres

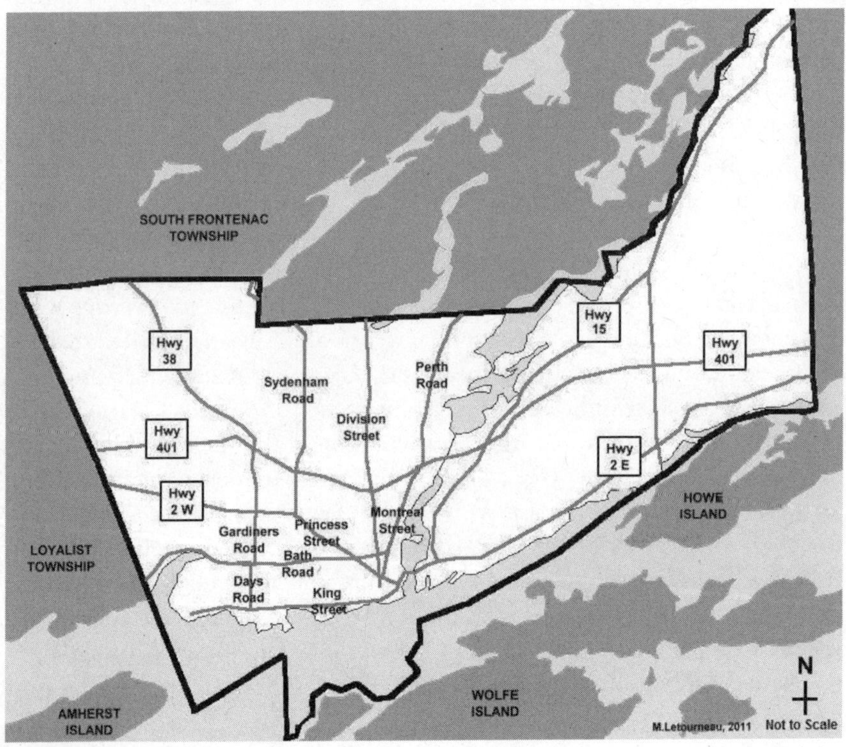

Kingston's city boundaries

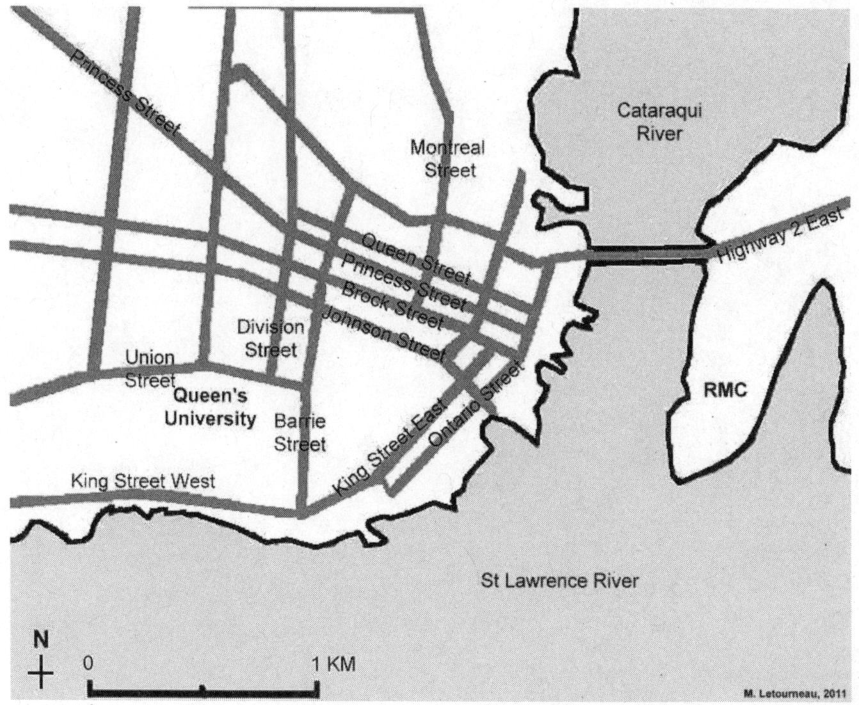

Downtown Kingston

GOD'S PLENTY

'Tis sufficient to say, according to the Proverb, that here is God's Plenty.

John Dryden (1631–1700)

1 Situations of the Sacred in Kingston: From Downtown to the Suburbs

KINGSTON AND RELIGION IN THE LITERARY IMAGINATION

Every city possesses certain obvious characteristics that we associate with an urban environment – a stated population, a specific geographical location, a particular economic composition, and a social history. Yet cities have religious characteristics too. In the religious mind the status of the city has ranged all the way from being the abode of demonic and sinister forces to being regarded as a holy place where one encounters the divine (see chap. 10). What, then, is the religious character of Kingston, Ontario, this mid-sized Canadian city situated about halfway between Toronto and Montreal at the strategic point where the Great Lakes empty into the St Lawrence River? Because we are dealing with the role of the imagination, one possible answer lies in considering the ways that writers of fiction have portrayed Kingston religion in their works. Kingston has been the hometown of an unexpectedly large number of first-rate writers. Others not resident here have also created images of Kingston in their novels, short stories, plays, and verse. This "literary Kingston" both represents and contributes to its religious character.

Robertson Davies, who before moving to Kingston spent his life in rural and small-town Ontario, distinguished Kingston from other places he had lived. With his customary overstatements and rhetorical flourishes, Davies declared in a 1973 CBC Radio interview that Kingston "isn't a small town" but a "city of gothic romance" and furthermore has "something that is very rare in Canada." He stated that "Kingston is twice a city" simply by virtue of having two cathedrals (qtd in Ross 2008, 30), alluding to the fact that in England the status of city was accorded only to a settlement having a cathedral. The same point is made in Davies' fictional depiction of Kingston as "Salterton" in his novel *Tempest-Tost*:

> Though not a large place it is truly describable as a city. That word is now used of any large settlement, and Salterton is big enough to qualify; but a city used to be the seat of a bishop, and Salterton was a city in that sense long before it became one in the latter. It is, indeed, the seat of two bishoprics, one Anglican and one Roman Catholic. As one approaches it from the water the two cathedrals, which are in appearance so strongly characteristic of the faiths they embody, seem to admonish the city. The Catholic cathedral points a vehement and ornate Gothic finger toward Heaven; the Anglican cathedral has a dome which, with offhand Anglican suavity, does the same thing. St Michael's cries, "Look aloft and pray!"; St Nicholas' says, "If I may trouble you, it might be as well to lift your eyes in this direction." The manner is different; the import is the same. (1951, 9–10)

Later in this chapter we explore in more detail some of the architectural differences between these two nineteenth-century cathedrals. Davies found Kingston a "fascinating city" partly because of its churches and partly because it was the abode of "many strange people" (CBC Radio interview qtd in Ross 2008, 30). His depiction of his one-time home, despite his assertion of its uniqueness in Canada, stands in tandem with his well-known endorsement of Douglas LePan's poetic depiction of the Canadian character as "wild Hamlet with the countenance of Horatio." That is, Canadians present to the world a Horatian façade of bland – even uninteresting – ordinariness beneath which seethes a cauldron of darkly gothic imaginations and double-mindedness. In the same vein he writes in *Tempest-Tost*, "the real character of Salterton is beneath the surface" (1951, 9).

Such unreliable and ambiguous qualities comprise exactly the "fascinating" material that Davies incorporated into much of his fiction. Dunstan Ramsay of Davies' *Fifth Business* found the Bible, like *The Arabian Nights*, to be psychologically rather than literally true. For Dunstan the world shows little of its face at the surface, for reality lies in the magic and myths lurking beneath. While Davies' characterization is exaggerated and romanticized, nonetheless any excavation beneath the surface appearances of Kingston potentially discloses layers of intriguing substrata. Perhaps that possibility of a gothic allure, of strangeness, and of secret complications that Davies so astutely remarked on – and portrayed in his Salterton trilogy of novels set in Kingston of the 1950s – lurks within the religious aspects of Kingston's life with their own richness and texture.

Other writers too have incorporated religion in Kingston into their fiction. David Helwig in *The Bishop* (1986) fictionalizes the dying of an Anglican bishop. Helwig's novelistic depiction of the bishop's funeral was inspired by the 1983 service at St George's Cathedral for Professor George Whalley. As well, the model for the protagonist seems to be Henry Hill, the Anglican bishop of the Diocese of Ontario from 1975 to 1981. Though Bishop Hill engaged in dialogue with Christians of the Eastern Orthodox tradition, Helwig's bishop – also named Henry – dies with an Inuit shaman by his side. In his memoir, Helwig comments on his writing of *The Bishop*, at the same time suggesting how religious participation may vary in form: "I had been singing in an Anglican church every week for several years, and while I didn't have it in me to believe in their religion, I was willing to take the imaginative leap and inhabit a man who was a committed and serious believer" (2006, 242). Another novel, *Our Lady of the Lost and Found* (2001) by Diane Schoemperlen, is set against the lore and historical background of the Marian apparitions though the centuries. Schoemperlen makes an imaginative leap similar to Helwig's when she has the Virgin Mary appear on the doorstep of a Kingston writer, "wearing a navy blue trench coat and white running shoes" (30). Schoemperlen – by no means a conventionally Catholic or even Christian writer – has her Mary resting in town for a few days, befriending the writer whose house she has chosen. These novels by Helwig and Schoemperlen plumb the depths of spiritual mysteries and the nature of belief amidst the prosaic features of an ordinary Kingston setting.

Margaret Atwood, probably Canada's most esteemed novelist, provides a nineteenth-century instance of clairvoyance and hypnosis among otherwise conventionally regular churchgoing Kingstonians in *Alias Grace* (1996). Grace Marks, sentenced to life imprisonment for a double murder, is subjected to these techniques by a group of reforming Christians to help her recover her memory of the deeds she is accused of committing. As Atwood explains in her afterword, Spiritualism "was at its height in the late 1850s, being especially strong in upstate New York and in the Kingston-Belleville area." She continues, "Spiritualism was the one quasi-religious activity of the times in which women were allowed a position of power – albeit a dubious one, as they themselves were assumed to be mere conduits of the spirit will" (1996, 466). Atwood also incorporates into her novel such other practices of the day as mesmerism and the "neuro-hypnotism" of James Braid, both precursors of new methods of treating mental illness. *Alias Grace*, then, stands with other contemporary fictions representing religion in Kingston as at once staid and institutional, while generating an opposite, underground current of unconventional and experimental spiritualities, a double-sided religiousness that continues to be observable today. The title suggests that Grace Marks has an alias, another name; perhaps what is known as "grace" in the religious sense has other names too.

Religion in Kingston has been fictionalized in more conventional terms as well – or, better, the conventional life of faith has been portrayed in fictional terms. Alison Gresik's collection of short stories, *Brick and Mortar* (2000), depicts the life of the minister and congregants in a small Presbyterian church. Gresik's fiction grows out of her own Christian devotion, as she examines the lives of people in a faith community and how they are touched in ordinary ways by divine presence. The book is dedicated in part to "the members of Kingston Christian Fellowship." In another short story, "The Mikveh Man," Sharon Drache deals with some of the challenges of being an Orthodox Jew in a small city identified as "Queenstown." For instance, the problems of obtaining a supply of kosher meat: "Willingly, the Levys endured the inconveniences of small town Jewish life. Every Monday, Bertha [wife of the rabbi] made her long distance call to Feinstein's, the kosher butcher in Ottawa. When Jake Feinstein brought the order on Thursdays, Bertha piled the meat as neatly as she could into her already crowded freezer" (1984, 8). Most of Drache's story illustrates the debate in the community around the construction of a *mikveh*, or ritual bath, for purification purposes.

While the literary examples could be extended further – including an incidental mention of the connection between Kingston Penitentiary and the Church of the Good Thief in the Village of Portsmouth in *The Convict Lover* (Simonds 1996) – those provided here demonstrate how religion provides a fertile resource for fiction writers, and how the portrayal of religion in Kingston has been so ably enriched by those authors.

A DOWNTOWN PRESENCE

The observable reality of Kingston's religion is presented, usually less imaginatively and more diagrammatically, by the cartographer. After all, as a character in Anne Michaels's novel *The Winter Vault* explains, "Every trade … has its own map of the city: the rat and cockroach exterminators, the raccoon catchers, the hydro and sewer and road repair workers" (2009, 249), as well as mothers and knitters and lovers of coffee and chocolate. A Rand McNally map of downtown Kingston shows about a dozen clustered crosses locating the major church buildings. The two cathedrals mentioned by Robertson Davies, St Mary's and St George's, are included among these churches, most of them built of limestone and originating in the nineteenth century; Kingston, nicknamed "the Limestone City," is renowned for possessing North America's largest stock of nineteenth-century limestone buildings outside of Quebec City. The monuments of ecclesiastical architecture are mostly situated within a block or two of Princess Street, Kingston's major street and the old Montreal-Toronto route by which Highway 2 finds its way through the city. Kingston's limestone churches garner the attention of visitors and tourists, and are the objects of local pride. Such distinguished architects as William Coverdale, John Power and his son Joseph, and Joseph Connolly designed these structures and established the stamp of Kingston's ecclesial architectural character in the 1800s. Scott K. Anderson includes a map with his published "walking tour" of historic churches and begins with these words: "Kingston is blessed with fine old churches rich in historical and architectural beauty. An hour or two spent walking downtown is an excellent way to get to know some of these unique local landmarks" (1988).

In its broadest contours the story presented in this chapter – the account of how these churches got there, why they are still there, and where other religious sites have been located more recently – could be duplicated in its major outlines in dozens of other cities across Canada. Put simply, it is a typical narrative of mammoth downtown religious edifices left behind in the push to the suburbs, about scarcity of parking space for congregants who live too far away to walk to church, and about sanctuaries constructed without heed to the economies of heating and maintenance for the liturgies of a bygone age when most people went to church on any given Sunday. This consideration of Kingston's version of this pattern atypically includes Judaism alongside Christianity – an aspect often neglected in other accounts – to amplify and provide some variation to the standard narrative. The history and sociology of religion in Canada has frequently focused on the Christian church, as if religious history began and ended with Christianity, the majority religion (see, for example, Choquette 2004 and Hewitt 1993). Even to begin this account of Kingston's religious diversity without telling the earlier story of the religions of indigenous peoples who lived here before Europeans would be another egregious omission if a full chronological history were intended here. Though Kingston is not a large city, other religious traditions than Christianity have been present for a long time. While at the beginning of the twentieth century Jews comprised only 0.2 per cent of Ontario's population, John Webster Grant describes them as "modest harbingers of the religious pluralism of a later era" (1988, 225). To include at the outset, therefore, Kingston's Jewish congregations alongside Christian ones anticipates the more fully developed religious diversity of Kingston dealt with in greater detail in later sections of this book.

According to Queen's professors Brian Osborne and Donald Swainson in *Kingston: Building on the Past*, Kingston became defined in the last half of the nineteenth century as "an institutional town" (1988, chap. 12). Following historian Arthur Lower, they suggest that Kingston found its unique role as a "sub-capital," serving the needs of various institutions, municipal and beyond, in educational, health, judicial, and other realms. By the 1850s Kingston was a sub-capital for a trio of important religions: Anglican, Presbyterian, and Roman Catholic. Methodists were present too, to the extent of about 10 per cent of Kingston's population, Osborne and Swainson point out, and Congregationalists and Baptists lived in Kingston as well, though in smaller numbers. It was the Christian churches of these groups– despite some later denominational changes and closures – that initially marked out the sacred in Kingston's downtown.

On 3 March 1908 the *Daily British Whig* carried an account of the results of a "religious census" conducted in Kingston: "The total tally, 20,072, was broken down by ward, by age – under 18 years and over 18 years – by religion – Anglicans, Baptists, Congregationalists, Holiness Movement, Methodists, Free Methodists, Presbyterians, Roman Catholics, Salvation Army, Catholic Apostolic [a nineteenth-century movement sometimes termed Irvingism], Hebrews [i.e., Jews] and no preference – and by residence – in household, domestics and lodgers." The information collected by the canvassers was turned over to the pastors of churches, though the results were regarded as incomplete because "mariners and students" were away from Kingston at the time of the census (reprinted in the *Whig-Standard*, 3 March 1999). This kind of detail from a century ago is interesting for the picture provided of the range of religious options available in Kingston, a diversity that has become much greater since.

Census data indicate that between 1871 and 1911 Anglicans, Presbyterians, and Roman Catholics comprised about 70 per cent of Canada's population. If to these groups one adds Methodists and Baptists, Roger O'Toole points out, "it is notable that more than 90 per cent of Canadians consistently claimed to belong to one or other of *five* major denominations" during this period of forty years when Canada's population rose from 3.7 to 7.2 million (2000, 43). The last part of the nineteenth century was a period of remarkable religious consensus in Ontario, when, according to John Webster Grant, newer religious movements were unable "to gain the adhesion of a significant proportion of the provincial population" (1988, 224). Almost everyone resident in Ontario, says Grant, expressed a religious preference in 1871, when "the only dissenters from orthodox Christianity were a few Universalists and Unitarians, the Longhouse people, and 518 Jews" (225). To leap forward by a century is still to see the lingering effects of this consensus. O'Toole states that in the 1990s two-thirds of Canadians still professed to belong to one of the "Big Three," that is, the Roman Catholic, Anglican, or United churches, the United Church having resulted from a 1925 union of Methodists, Congregationalists, and two-thirds of the Presbyterians. By the outset of the twenty-first century, however, data from the 2001 Census tell a different story, indicating that those claiming affiliation with the Big Three had declined to less than 60 per cent of Canada's total population. Amidst a Canadian population of 29.6 million in 2001, Roman Catholics comprised 12.4 million, while United and Anglican affiliates were 2.4 and 2.0 millions respectively (O'Toole 2000, 45; 2006, 9–10).

Peter Beyer of the University of Ottawa has proposed that a model for religion in Canada lies somewhere between the denominational type that applies to the United States and the established church model found in the United Kingdom and elsewhere in Europe (2006, 71–91; 2000, 189–210). In the United States, where evangelical or born-again Christians are a significant portion of the population, and where 40 per cent of Americans regularly practise their religion, Christian denominations proliferate in what has been termed "competitiveness under conditions of religious deregulation" (O'Toole 2000, 204). In England, where the Church of England is established as a national church, what is called the "church form" predominates. Even as the regular practice of religion has declined to about 10 per cent of the British people, a "residual state church" remains (Martin 2000, 23). In contrast to the "arena of religious free-competition" in the United States, O'Toole suggests that the Canadian situation is a "protracted religious oligopoly" in which a surprising 80 per cent of Christians – just "Christians" this time, not the entire Canadian population as in the preceding paragraph – still profess allegiance to one or another of the Big Three churches (O'Toole 2000, 45). Though the Greek term *oligopoly* means "few sellers," in today's religious marketplace the sellers are numerous; but towering above the rest on the Canadian scene are the Big Three.

Brian Osborne in his history of St Andrew's Presbyterian Church in Kingston details the early struggles of Presbyterianism for its place amidst the "Anglican hegemony" (2004, 15). With the Constitutional Act of 1791. Anglicanism for a time had claimed the status of the established religion of Upper Canada: "The Church of England was the official state religion; Anglican clergy were to be the dominant voices in local education; Anglican clergy were to be appointed by the Lieutenant-Governor and to be paid out of provincial funds; the Anglican 'Society for the Promoting Christian Knowledge' ... got special grants; and, finally, government also provided extra support to the Anglican clergy in the form of glebe lands, military chaplaincies, and contributions to building funds" (15). The first half of the nineteenth century was fraught with debates about religious rights and the struggle for recognition by Catholics and Presbyterians alongside the Anglicans. The sectarian tensions among those and other groups are another part of the story, dealt with, to some extent, elsewhere in these pages (see, for example, chap. 10). Even an account of how the major Christian denominations with their shared nineteenth-century heritage continued as a quasi-establishment after 1925 too quickly relegates other less numerous groups on the sidelines, Jews among them.

Describing the origins of the Canadian Jewish community, Gerald Tulchinsky relates that by the middle of the nineteenth century various itinerant Jewish peddlers and merchants were travelling through the towns and villages of Ontario and elsewhere: "Men on the move they were ... moving their stock by wagon or buggy, or occasionally even hot-footing it out of town" (1992, 78). Though such itinerants remained largely marginal to the mainstream of Canadian commercial enterprise in the Victorian period, in Kingston Jewish entrepreneurs undertook some substantial and occasionally permanent business ventures. The Nordheimer brothers opened a music store in the 1840s, though within a few years they moved to Toronto where their reputation was built. Several decades later Simon Oberndorfer set up a cigar factory and stayed on to become one of the founders of Kingston's Jewish community (77–9; see also Beth Israel website). Despite such early endeavours, by 1861 there were only five Jews in Kingston.

With the establishment of a Jewish congregation in Kingston in 1902, various ethnicities and languages "came together," as Tulchinsky puts it, "uneasily, but of necessity, to assemble and pray in awkward union" (161). This kind of necessity, forging a more or less unified assembly out of existing differences among smaller groups, continues up to the present as a major theme in the ongoing account of Kingston's faith communities (see chap. 7). In larger centres such as Toronto or Montreal or Vancouver, sectarian differences brought to Canada from their countries of origin could be preserved among factional immigrant groups. Where numbers were small, and especially in less cosmopolitan villages and towns, such different groups lacked the critical mass necessary for their separate continuation. Tulchinsky locates this feature precisely: "With their mixture of national origins, cultural backgrounds, economic levels, and political affiliations, small-town communities emerged as special places where their tiny numbers forced Jews into a unity, sometimes discordant, and an unnatural cohesion" (161).

Predominantly Orthodox Jewish families from Central and Eastern Europe began to move into Kingston in the late nineteenth and early twentieth centuries. Many were merchants who lived above their shops or else close to the centre of the city's commerce. Marion Meyer (1983) maps their places of residence, mostly within walking distance of the hub of the city where, after meeting in one or more temporary locations, a permanent synagogue was finally located. Meyer mentions the existence of two – perhaps three – small fragmented congregations that came together and by 1910 had established the first Beth Israel Synagogue, located on Queen Street where a parking lot now stands across from St Paul's Anglican Church. To erect the substantial building shown in archival photographs must have been a struggle: another fifteen years would pass before the Jewish community in Kingston would increase to the point where it numbered two hundred people. Remarkably, when the resources of the Jewish community proved to be insufficient, 20 per cent of the cost of the synagogue came from contributions from Christians, a striking instance of early twentieth-century ecumenicity and generosity (28–9). The published history of Beth Israel congregation reproduces a list of contributors to the Queen Street synagogue, with several Christian donors and businesses among them (Koven and Rosen 1986). Whatever prompted this ecumenical assistance, it stands in contrast to the squabbles often present among Christian groups themselves through the mid-nineteenth century when they competed against and even impeded each other's building endeavours. Perhaps the new synagogue was not considered a competitor: brick rather than stone; with rounded windows rather than pointed Gothic arches and vaguely Moorish curved tops at the two corners of the facade, it boasted no spire standing above its surroundings. In all, the Queen Street synagogue might have looked to the ecclesial eye of the day more like a school building than a church.

The Jewish experience in Kingston can be used as a basis for generalization in the construction of this more inclusive proposed template. A congregation first establishes its presence in downtown Kingston in rented quarters preliminary to building a sanctuary dedicated to its own purposes. Especially in the nineteenth century the construction of a monumental edifice dedicated to religious purposes was the way for a group to declare its significance, to achieve recognition and acceptance, and generally to announce its arrival on the local religious scene. St George's Anglican Cathedral in its current form began to be built on King Street in 1825, a replacement for the nearby wooden church dating from 1792. Architecturally influenced by St Paul's, London, with its four massive columns on the façade and a great dome, St George's has been acclaimed as one of the finest churches in Canada of a pre-Gothic style. The opening paragraph of the church's website, after stating that its primary function is worship, goes on to emphasize the importance of the civic, state, and military associations of St George's, harking back to the "Anglican hegemony" of two centuries past: "For many years Royal Military College cadets and other military groups have marched into St George's for worship on special occasions" (St George's).

In the nineteenth century, cadets at the Royal Military College were required to attend services at St George's. Between 1878 and 1882 the tradition of Copper Sunday – or "Penny Sabbath" – was begun when cadets began noisily to throw coins on the collection plate (Preston 1991, 21–2). This practice has continued up to the present – in a quieter form – on the last

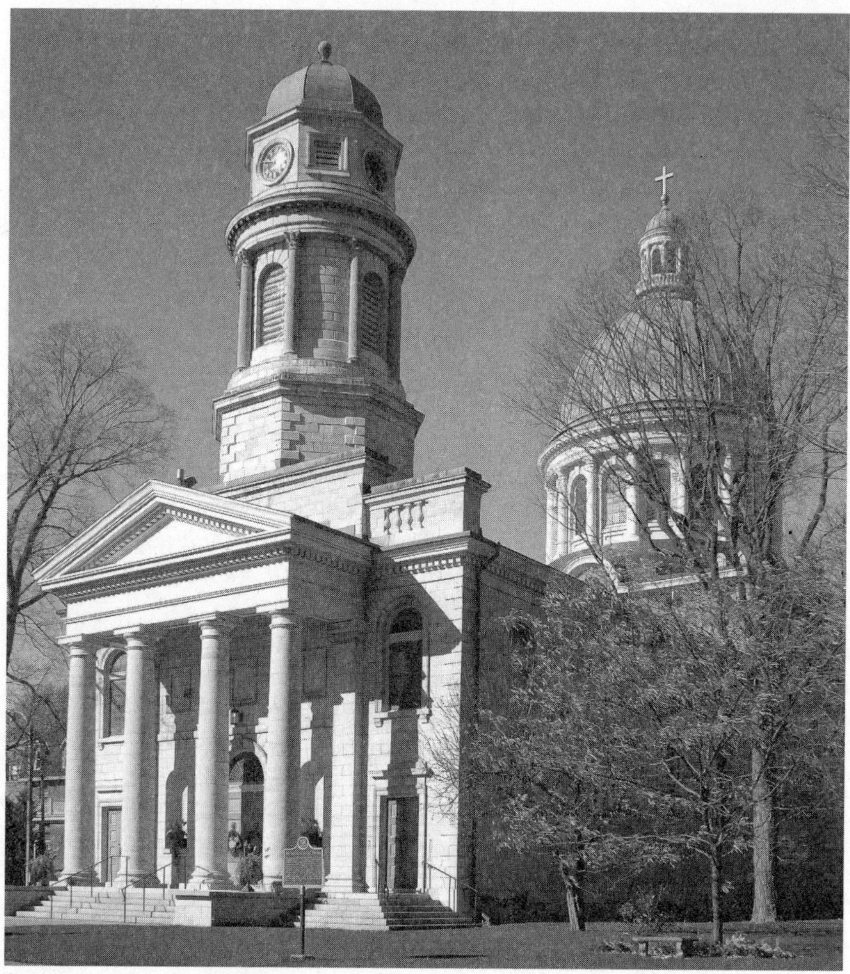

St George's Anglican Cathedral

Sunday before graduation each year. Now the pennies are gathered in black socks especially issued for the purpose. To the list of "approved" churches for cadets' attendance have since been added St Andrew's Presbyterian Church, Sydenham Street United Church, St Mary's Roman Catholic Cathedral, and the francophone Catholic St François d'Assise. Some more evangelical RMC cadets have been observed finding their way to such self-selected alternatives as the NeXt Church on Colborne Street.

After 1840, as part of the Romantic movement, Gothic architecture was widely promoted in church design, especially by Augustus Pugin, a British architect who saw medieval Gothic as the acme of human attainment in buildings. This revival had enormous influence in differentiating the symbolic presence of churches in the Victorian urban landscape, setting the sacred apart from the merely commercial and secular. So pervasive was its acceptance that Gothic architecture came to be known as "Christian" architecture, a style clearly not "pagan." William Westfall writes that the Gothic "became the most dominant and enduring symbol of the Protestant culture of Ontario" (1989, 127), to the extent that it "assumed the attributes of the sacred itself" (158). This revival of a medieval ideal affirmed the values of a spiritual realm in the midst of a Victorian culture thought to be increasingly materialistic. In Kingston the former Congregational Church on Wellington Street and the former Methodist – now United – Church on Sydenham Street remain as splendid fulfilments of this Gothic ideal. Yet the cathedrals of the two bishops – the classically domed shape of St George's Anglican Cathedral and the soaring Gothic spire of St Mary's Roman Catholic Cathedral – due to the size of these two buildings and their ecclesiastical significance, still contend for ecclesiastical architectural supremacy on Kingston's skyline.

Construction of St Mary's Cathedral began in 1842. In 1848, the year St Mary's was consecrated, a writer in the *Kingston Herald* predicted that it would be "an ornament to the city when finished": "It is built of cut stone, Gothic style, reaching from Johnson to Brock Streets, 210 feet long and 88 feet wide supported by massive pillars, surmounted with spiral cut stone, towering heavenwards; its roof covered with tin, being elevated very high and occupying the highest ground in the city, presents a magnificent appearance" (qtd in Flynn 1973). Bishop James Vincent Cleary summoned architect Joseph Connolly to design St Mary's new tower; built from the ground up and completed in 1892, its height reached 242 feet. By way of contrast, "down the road the Anglican Cathedral of St George would appear to the Puginian Catholic eye as a pagan temple," Malcolm Thurlby comments. Conveying what each successive stage of ecclesiastical architecture meant in Kingston's religious landscape, Thurlby adds: "If superiority of scale and correctness of style were not enough, the Irish Bishop of Kingston and his Irish architect dealt the ultimate blow to the Anglicans of the city by modeling their tower on 'Bell Harry,' the crossing tower of Canterbury Cathedral, the mother church of England" (1986, 103). The Anglican response on rebuilding their cathedral in the 1890s was to add transepts and a dome designed by Joseph Power and reminiscent of St Paul's, London. The dome of St Paul's, designed by Christopher Wren, had been inspired by St Peter's Basilica in Rome. Kingston's Anglicans and Catholics were thus emulating and borrowing from the great churches of the competing tradition.

Thurlby maintains that St George's use of a classical architectural model this late in the nineteenth century was unique in Ontario, considering how

St Mary's Roman Catholic Cathedral

widespread and influential the Gothic revival was. Before 1840 the use of classic-vernacular and neoclassical forms had predominated in both civic buildings and in churches. The portico and columns comprising the main features of the façade make St George's a perfect match with the City Hall and the Frontenac County Court House (Thurlby and Westfall 1986, 98). Architectural historian Jennifer McKendry notes how the details of the Roman Doric design allude to St George, who rescued a princess from a dragon; St George's Cathedral thus represents Christianity's triumph over paganism. Continuing this classical order at St George's despite the Gothic revival, Thurlby points out, indicates its conformity with the existing British and Anglican order of Kingston's non-ecclesiastical monuments. St George's, in other words, felt no need to differentiate itself architecturally from the secular fabric of the city of Kingston. As McKendry puts it, even its location – close by the market, courthouse, and city hall – was significant: "The 'official' nature of St George's was reinforced by its proximity to these public buildings" (1995, 59).

THE MOVE TO THE SUBURBS

The last half of the nineteenth century was a great era of church building, when mammoth architecturally imposing edifices were erected, primarily in Kingston's downtown core. In Ontario and Quebec during these years the number of church buildings soared by about 250 per cent while the population increased by 100 per cent (Beyer 2006, 77). By the beginning of the twentieth century, Canada's churches had enough seating for the population of the entire country, considering that most churches probably had two services on a Sunday. Despite this increased capacity the size of a typical congregation would appear to shrink in relation to the size of the sanctuary. The number of empty pews increased as new and rebuilt churches overestimated their future needs. As an example, when one of Ontario's largest Methodist churches in London was destroyed by fire in 1895, its replacement "seated nearly 1,400 worshippers, though the congregation was then half that size" (Metropolitan United Church). When churches were built outside of Kingston's downtown, they were generally to a smaller scale and not always in compliance with the Gothic demands. The "primitive medievalism" of St James' Anglican on Union Street, the solidly foursquare brick of the formerly Congregational Bethel Church, and the Romanesque Revivalism of the Roman Catholic Church of the Good Thief in Portsmouth Village departed from the Gothic norm. Even two of the downtown Presbyterian churches, Chalmers and St Andrew's, did not fulfil Gothic standards.

A century later, especially the 1950s and '60s, saw another great period of church expansion, this time corresponding to the growing population in Kingston's suburbs. Downtown worship sites began to be supplemented with or abandoned for newer buildings. Marion Meyer again tells the parallel story of Kingston's Jewish population. The number of Jews in Kingston, only 128 in 1901, increased to about 300 by 1951, climbing most rapidly in the three decades after 1921. By 1961 the number had reached 390 (1983, 36). Queen's University began to attract Jewish academics who were not Orthodox, thereby decreasing the percentage of Kingston's Jews who were members of the synagogue. The map Meyer provides shows how the locations of the residences of Beth Israel's members changed from the 1920s to the 1960s. In the 1920s fifty-nine Jewish families lived on sixteen streets, mostly in the area extending two or three blocks north of Princess Street and between Division Street on the west and Montreal Street to the east – all within an easy ten or fifteen minutes' walk to the synagogue on Queen Street. By the 1960s the 106 families attending Beth Israel, now located on Centre Street, lived on thirty-seven streets scattered throughout the city but almost all of them west of Barrie Street (54). Increased distances and changing religious practices meant that few congregants still walked to and from the synagogue on Centre Street to worship on the Sabbath.

Throughout the 1950s and early '60s the population of the immediate area in and around Kingston was growing at a rate greater than that of the province of Ontario as a whole. Whereas in 1941 most of the city's population lived downtown , within a few decades a shift had taken place to areas outside this central core, both within the existing boundaries of the city and to the adjoining townships to the east and west. In 1941, 80 per cent of the people in Kingston and these nearby townships lived within the city boundaries; by 1986 only half did. In less than half a century the population of Kingston and the surrounding area had trebled from about 36,000 to 108,000 (Osborne and Swainson 1988, 308). As in many other comparable places, factors such as reliance on the automobile for commuting, the provision of new residential housing – especially at first in the nearby "inner suburbs" – and the development of more commercial and shopping areas away from downtown created this shift. Then, too, annexation in the early 1950s extended municipal boundaries to the north and west, effectively enlarging the city's area and population. Partly due to the barrier to the east posed by the Great Cataraqui River with its single lift-bridge crossing, most of the new residential growth in Kingston occurred to the west, in the area known as Kingston Township prior to amalgamation in 1998.

In addition to this urban and suburban population growth and people moving away from the centre of the city, Christian churches were continuing to see steady ongoing increases in their numbers during the 1950s and '60s, providing an additional incentive to the construction of new sanctuaries. Yet, paradoxically, at the same time the percentage of Christians in Canada actually going to a church on a weekly basis was declining. Immediately after World War II, in 1946, 67 per cent of Canadian Christians, both Protestants and Roman Catholics, attended worship services weekly. Ten years later, the percentage was dropping but still relatively high at 61 per cent. After ten more years, by 1966, weekly church attendance had dropped to 55 per cent, a decline that would continue. Attendance among Roman Catholics had fallen slightly during this period, but still remained strong at over 80 per cent, while the percentage of Protestants in church on a given Sunday had plummeted from 60 per cent to 32 per cent (Bibby 1987, 17).

This phenomenon, which Bibby characterizes as a case of "numbers up, proportions down," explains why churches engaged in such a building boom during this period: most churches saw their membership increasing even as the percentage of those attending weekly was dropping. It would be some years yet before mainline churches began to notice that fewer people were in the pews week by week. In the meantime, some congregations moved from downtown to the edges of the expanding city, and denominations that were new to the city established new churches.

The Beth Israel congregation moved in 1961 from its downtown location at 148 Queen Street in this context of church growth when the national rate of synagogue attendance was also declining. Bibby assumes synagogue attendance for Canadians would be similar to that for Americans, declining from between 27 per cent and 15 per cent from the mid-1950s on, to 13 per cent in 1971 (1987, 22). Kingston's new synagogue was erected in an area of historic and professional homes at 116 Centre Street, a few blocks west of the Queen's University campus. When the Beth Israel Congregation was considering various properties in November of 1953, their first choice was a parcel of vacant land with two hundred feet fronting on Union Street at the southeast corner of Ellerbeck Street. The owner of that property, however, the Roman Catholic Diocese of Kingston, reportedly "declined to sell any portion of the land for synagogue building purposes" (Koven and Rosen 1986, 40). Was this Roman Catholic refusal to sell the property to Jews as anti-Semitic as it seems on the surface? Seven years earlier, in 1946, the Sisters of St Vincent de Paul had established St Mary's of the Lake Hospital on the southern part of the piece of property that bordered on King Street. Perhaps the Roman Catholics were already anticipating future needs, because that part of their hospital property was subsequently not sold to anyone else, and today forms an area of grass adjoining the facility's large parking lot.

At a meeting in May 1954 the congregation moved to accept its second choice, a nearby property on Centre Street backing on the land that is part of St Mary's of the Lake. In its short two blocks extending from Union Street south to the waterfront at King Street, Centre Street is favoured as the location of five remaining houses of historic significance dating from the 1830s to the 1850s. On the slope just above the lake sits Bellevue House, once the home of Sir John A. Macdonald – he referred to it as "Teacaddy Castle" – and now a National Historic Site. More or less across the street from Bellevue is the massive Elmhurst, at 26 Centre Street, while a little further up the hill is a one-and-a-half storey brick cottage at 68 Centre. Beth Israel itself is located between the classically elegant Barberry Cottage, another historically significant stone house, and Otterburn House, a heritage building owned by the congregation and situated at the corner of Union Street. This area, once known as the "Western Liberties," about a mile from downtown, was in the early nineteenth century the setting of country villas with extensive grounds.

Aside from being closer to the homes of most of the congregation's members, this new, more upscale location also identified the synagogue more closely with the university and the nearby Kingston General Hospital. After the 1930s, when Queen's had only thirty Jewish students, most of them from out of town, and only one Jewish professor (Meyer 1983, 42), the numbers of Jewish students and professors and doctors coming to Kingston was increasing dramatically. The Beth Israel website describes the changing makeup of the congregation of approximately 130 families: "Until 1960, the vast majority of the congregants were merchants or businessmen from Central and Eastern Europe. During the 1960s, however, the expansion of Canadian universities attracted numerous Jewish academics to Queen's University at Kingston. Within a short fifteen years, Beth Israel's composition changed to a bimodal membership: the old-timers/merchants and the newcomers/academics-professionals ... Today, Beth Israel remains an umbrella synagogue which accommodates members whose actual orientations range from Agnostic to Orthodox" (Beth Israel).

Reflecting this "umbrella" character, a survey from the mid-1970s reported that less than 5 per cent of Beth Israel members were Orthodox, while 61 per cent were Conservative, and 28 per cent Reform (Meyer 1983, 62). The new building with its contemporary facilities was more hospitable to this spectrum of observance and practice than the old Queen Street Orthodox *shul* would have been. While explaining the layout and conveniences available at the Centre Street building in 2003, the rabbi elaborated on patterns of attendance: "On a regular Shabbat we get thirty, forty, and on High Holidays we get three hundred" (interview, 3 November 2003). These figures, by the way, give local confirmation of the general estimates of about 10–15 per cent of affiliated Jews at worship each week. The large social hall, normally separated from the sanctuary by an accordion partition, can be opened up to accommodate an overflow.

The trend suggested by Beth Israel's relocation from downtown is repeated many times over among Christian churches. Among the mainline denominations, new church buildings were being erected at a great rate. Until St John the Apostle was built on Patrick Street in 1941, St Mary's was the only Roman Catholic Church in the city proper – remembering that the Church of the Good Thief, built in 1894 on King Street, would at that time have been in the Village of Portsmouth. In 1961 Holy Family Roman Catholic Church was created on Weller Avenue in Kingston's north end. In 1964 St Joseph's Roman Catholic Church was built on Palace Road, at the very western edge of the city prior to annexation in 1952. The decade of the 1960s also saw the creation of Our Lady of Lourdes Parish on Day's Road, located in Kingston Township further to the west. St François d'Assise, a francophone parish, was also established in 1961, closer to downtown and just north of Princess Street. Our Lady of Fatima, a Portuguese parish, was created in 1980, and by the mid-1980s St Paul the Apostle, to become Kingston's largest Catholic congregation with more than 3,000 family units, was built in a newer residential area in the western suburbs of Kingston. Remarkably, six of Kingston's nine Roman Catholic churches were built in the 1960s and later.

Several United churches also appeared in the 1950s and '60s. St Margaret's United Church, renamed Crossroads United Church in 2010 after an amalgamation with Queen Street United Church, was constructed on Sir John A. Macdonald Boulevard. St Margaret's was about as far west as St Joseph's and, like it, near to the then-new Kingston Shopping Centre, Kingston's first indoor mall. In a 2005 interview the minister, the Rev. David Iverson, outlined St Margaret's origins: "It began in 1954 at McArthur School. They built in 1957 – the church burnt down eighteen months later; the only thing that was left standing was the front door – and then rebuilt in 1961. And that's the present building we're in now. St Margaret's United Church was probably the first wave of expansion from the old city of Kingston, and so people who moved out into this area – and this was all fields, of course, in the 1950s" (interview, 10 November 2005). In Calvin Park, a subdivision created on former penitentiary farmlands, the Cooke's and Portsmouth congregations joined in 1967 to form the new Cooke's-Portsmouth United Church. Further to the west in Reddendale, St Andrew's by-the-Lake was built, and at Collins Bay, Edith Rankin Memorial United Church. Both of these churches had originally been created in the 1950s to serve farming communities that soon were to become suburbs. In the northern part of the city, St Matthew's United and Kingscourt United churches emerged in the 1950s. In all, half of the current fourteen United churches within the present city limits of Kingston were in existence before the 1950s, and until Queen Street United closed in 2010, five of them, all downtown, remained in their nineteenth-century buildings. Among the seven United Church congregations that have come into being since the early 1950s, only one, Faith United in the former Pittsburgh Township to the east of the city, was created after 1970. Faith United, which originated in 1989, does not have its own building; instead, the congregation has used rented space, in a nearby school or the Anglican church.

Seven of the eleven Anglican churches in the city of Kingston date from the nineteenth century, reflecting their greater prominence and antiquity as well as the quasi-establishment character of Anglicanism within Ontario.

Since the 1950s three new parishes have been established: one, the Church of the Redeemer, in the northern part of the city, and two in the west end, St Peter's at the extreme western municipal boundary and St Thomas' in Henderson Place just west of Day's Road. In addition, Christ Church Cataraqui has built a new Parish Centre on Sydenham Road just north of the church itself, adjacent to Cataraqui Cemetery, the resting place of such notables as Sir John A. Macdonald and poet Charles Sangster. The three newer Anglican churches are easily distinguished from their nineteenth-century antecedents in that brick rather than limestone has generally been used as the building material. The exception is St Luke's, an older brick church in the area of the city formerly known as Williamsville.

With this summary of church development among the "Big Three" since the 1950s, we have accounted for almost two-thirds – to be precise, 63.5 per cent – of Kingston's population. According to the 2001 Census, 33.0 per cent of Kingstonians are Roman Catholic; 17.2 per cent United Church; and 13.3 per cent Anglican. As compared with the corresponding provincial percentages of 34.3, 11.8, and 8.7 per cent, respectively (*Whig-Standard*, 14 May 2003), a suggestion of the greater Protestant character of Kingston emerges, especially when one adds in those selecting the undifferentiated "Protestant" category available in the 2001 Census. The result yields 48,000 Protestants (43 per cent) as compared with 37,000 Catholics (33 per cent) from a population of 111,000 Kingstonians. If one takes the top four religions listed in the 2001 Census for Kingston – Catholic, Protestant, Christian Orthodox, and Christian "not included elsewhere" – those categories include almost 80 per cent of the city's population. In Ontario as a whole, Catholics and Protestants are almost equal at about 34 per cent. Considering that Kingston consists of 78 per cent Protestants and Catholics, and that an additional 18 per cent are those who profess "no religious affiliation," the numbers of those counting themselves as Muslim, Jewish, Buddhist, Hindu, Sikh, "Eastern religions," or "Other Religions" is by comparison quite small, totalling 2,860 persons or 2 per cent of the total Kingston population of 142,770 in the metropolitan area census (see appendix F, "2001 Census, Kingston Religion"). Consider, by way of contrast with Kingston, the provincial and national picture: in 2001 the five largest groups after Christians – Muslims, Jews, Buddhists, Hindus, and Sikhs – comprised 6.0 per cent of Canada's population, and 8.7 per cent of Ontario's population. (Muslims, Hindus, and Sikhs in Kingston are dealt with in chapter 7.)

To return to the 1961 building for Beth Israel congregation on Centre Street, it is a typical example of the architectural innovations that the westward expansion among Kingston churches entailed. First, the new religious edifice fits in with, and is adapted to, its more residential surroundings. The

Beth Israel Synagogue

new structure is unlikely to be characterized by an imposing façade or monumental edifice or soaring spire; it is decidedly contemporary in appearance, usually wider than it is tall, and built of brick. At Beth Israel the brick is of varying shades of beige and yellow with a stylized seven-branch menorah as the predominant exterior decoration. Large expanses of glass reveal the interior to passersby and light the entrance foyer. The facilities too are adapted for uses other than worship services. The main floor of Beth Israel includes the sanctuary, a social hall, kitchen, rooms for storage, a secretarial office, the rabbi's office, and bathrooms. On the lower level there are classrooms. At the side of the building is the parking lot that, as the rabbi explained, "is closed on Shabbat and holidays because we don't drive, technically, so we don't allow parking in our parking lot" (interview, 3 November 2003). During the week the lot is used on such occasions as when parents drop off and collect their children studying at the Hebrew school.

Many of the new sanctuaries built in the 1950s and '60s were especially well adapted to the automobile. At St Margaret's United Church, situated on one of the main north-south arteries in Kingston, the minister in outlining the usefulness of the facilities, both for the congregation and the wider community, began with the parking available: "Well, one of the most notable things about St Margaret's, and why it is used a lot by the community, is that it is very accessible. There is a great parking lot, which most of the churches don't have, and there is no step. We have one level so it is easily accessible for people

St Joseph's Roman Catholic Church

who are in wheelchairs and who require assistance going in and out. From that perspective, it is a very useful building and is used quite extensively by the community in many ways" (David Iverson, interview, 15 July 2004).

Other church buildings established in the 1960s were similarly accommodating to parishioners travelling by car. St Joseph's Catholic Church, a few hundred metres to the south of St Margaret's, sits on a four-acre parcel of land, facing its extensive parking lot – described by the official history of the diocese as "huge" – that fills most of the block between Palace Road and Macdonald Boulevard. Vehicles can drive right up to the steps at the church's entrance with its folded-roof portico. Other churches built during the 1960s and after, such as Kingston West Free Methodist Church or the Pilgrim Holiness Church, have a roof extending over a circular drive at the entrance so that passengers can be discharged or picked up without exposure to the elements. The history of the first 150 years of Catholicism in Kingston refers to St Joseph's as "the first fully contemporary church in the Kingston Archdiocese" because "its main Altar was designed for Mass facing the congregation" (Flynn ca. 1976, 348). As a result of the reforms of Vatican II, new sanctuaries were being designed so that the altar was moved away from the rear wall; now the celebrant stood behind the altar rather than before it with his back to the congregation. Similarly, Protestant churches in the nineteenth century, particularly those at the Reformed end of the spectrum that held the Word as central to Christian worship, had modified the classic Gothic design by de-emphasizing the altar – that is, the communion table – and by arranging seating in a semi-circular amphitheatre shape that made lectern and pulpit central.

In general, however, liturgical needs did not play any large role in the determining the layout of contemporary churches. Many still echoed the nineteenth-century Methodist rectangular "preaching box," with a central aisle and rows of pews facing the front. Cooke's-Portsmouth United Church on Norman Rogers Drive, just west of St Joseph's, is typical of the architectural style of the 1960s. While both Cooke's-Portsmouth and St Joseph's have an imposing windowed façade above the front doors, neither is surmounted with a steeple. Cooke's-Portsmouth is almost entirely cedar-shingle roof, like a large A-frame cottage. The interior with exposed beams and roof planking soars to a lofty peak, carrying the eye upwards. The sheer volume of the space enclosed by the massive roof makes one realize that in the days when it was built, energy costs were not a major concern.

Holy Family Roman Catholic Church, in the north end of Kingston, was opened in 1962. Holy Family exhibits features similar to those of Cooke's-Portsmouth, particularly in its roofline and use of natural wood through the interior space of the sanctuary. L.J. Flynn describes the structure: "Modernistic in design, the new church has a laminated arch construction, with the arches completely exposed inside the building. Finished in a light-stained fir, these arches give a pillared effect to the interior side walls which, like the ceiling are of thick cedar planking… On the outside, the gable roof extends to within eight feet of the ground on either side of the building" (ca. 1976, 355). If liturgical requirements were not the sole or primary determinant in church projects during the 1960s, adaptation of the design to the immediate suburban surroundings and the provision of a flexible space that could be used by various groups became more important considerations.

As the minister of St Andrew's by-the-Lake United Church recounts the history of its founding, it was not even clear at the outset what denomination the new church would be. In the early 1950s, people – mostly Protestants in the community of Reddendale to the west of what was then Kingston – were worshipping in a school. They wanted to establish a church in the neighbourhood: "You know, we were kind of a community church; we were Baptists, we were Pentecostalists, we were Presbyterians, and we were Anglicans, I guess too. We weren't sure what we were going to be – maybe a community church or something. So then the United Church came along with $5,000, and we decided we'd be United" (Jean Barkley, interview,

26 February 2004). The same non-denominational emphasis continues fifty years after the church's founding, as the current website for the congregation reflects: "People of many traditions (and no tradition at all) find a home with our congregation. Our current family includes people who trace their church roots to: Baptist, Pentecostal, Roman Catholic, Lutheran, Anglican, Christian Reform and Unitarian. Membership within the United Church is offered but it is not stressed" (St Andrew's by-the-Lake).

THE 1960S AND AFTER

If denominationalism was already being muted in some congregations in the 1950s and after in favour of a community-based church, that could be taken as an outcome of the movements toward church union that had prevailed during the late nineteenth and early twentieth centuries. In part an outgrowth of the Social Gospel movement of the early twentieth century, belonging to a church and participating in weekly services of worship was the way most Canadian Christians contributed to the social project of building Canadian society. Peter Beyer has outlined how the religious market was not as "deregulated" in Canada as it was in the United States, nor was there an established form of religion here as in Britain and throughout much of Europe (2006, 72). As liberalization occurred within the Big Three churches, Beyer suggests, this process of "secularization from within" caused "their 'product line' to lose much of its supernatural character and thus its identifiable religiousness" (85). So long as those churches were playing a role in Canadian society, their success more or less continued. As the state took over an increasing share of efforts toward the betterment of people's lives within society, the part played by churches diminished. This trend helps explain the large decline in the membership within the United Church, which among all the Christian denominations especially supported and reflected the changing social character of Canada. In fact, the United Church aspired to position itself as a kind of national church, or at least as a distinctively and uniquely Canadian phenomenon. When Queen Elizabeth made a royal visit to Canada in 1959, she and Prince Philip attended worship at Sydenham Street United Church while in Kingston, partly as a result of overtures from the United Church of Canada. In an earlier day, attendance at an Anglican church would have been customary. A half century later Kingstonians still recall how the people of St George's were miffed by this "slight," and how around the time of the royal visit the Anglican bishop reportedly left town for a few weeks.

Through the 1960s the United Church continued to pass motions at its General Council meetings against alcohol, gambling, and Sunday sports, with the still-lingering expectation that its position on these issues would have some effect on the policies of the governments of the day. At the same time, however, some of its people began to wonder what remained that was distinctively religious about the United Church and the other mainline Protestant denominations in Canada. People joked that the United Church was "the NDP at prayer," an adaptation of the British quip referring to the Church of England as the Tory party at prayer. The implication was that the emphasis on social justice policies and a tendency to favour the political left was a central focus of the United Church mission. Some critics of the United Church might have felt that this characterization was a slur on the New Democratic Party whose positions were sometimes less radical than those of the church. Others might have wondered if it was not overstating the level of devotion within the United Church to imagine that prayer could be what differentiated that denomination from any political party!

Throughout the decade the decline of the supernatural began to be more widely felt as a changing experience of everyday life. Except among the conservative denominations, other churches too began to shift their attention away from the supernatural to secular, or this-worldly, emphases. Whatever else today might be taken to be the identifying markers of the 1960s, it witnessed enormous changes within the realm of religion. In 1966 a famous *Time* magazine cover posed the question "Is God Dead?" thereby raising issues about the relevance of the transcendent to the contemporary world. Some of this "Death-of-God" theology, in the lineage of the proclamation by Nietzsche's madman, was ongoing musing about the consequences of nihilism; some of it was reflection about the apparent irrelevance of religion in a world "come of age" in which people had outgrown their need for God; some of it was primarily rhetorical and for the sake of shock value. But there was nonetheless a strain within this radical mode of theological thought that was avowedly atheistic. Thomas J.J. Altizer, Paul Van Buren, Gabriel Vahanian, and William Hamilton were indicating that the supernatural deity of western monotheism could no longer be sustained as an object of belief. So largely felt were these challenges that Leslie Dewart, a professor at the University of Toronto, defended Christian theism from a Roman Catholic standpoint against contemporary attacks in his book *The Future of Belief: Theism in a World Come of Age* (1966).

In England J.A.T. Robinson published a bestseller entitled *Honest to God*. Bishop Robinson, following Paul Tillich, wanted God to be understood as "the Ground of Being" – or "the Beyond in the Midst of" – in preference to the projection of God as a kind of supernatural large-scale person located "out there," beyond the earth. Furthermore, Robinson, in line with the thinking of Rudolf Bultmann, made the case for a demythologization of the

New Testament. Understanding the message of Jesus did not require acceptance of an ancient worldview or a literal belief in miracles. Robinson called for greater candour among Church of England clergy in disclosing in their sermons and among parishioners the findings of a century of biblical scholarship rather than encouraging the assumption that a literal belief in the New Testament was a prime requisite of Christian faith. In the United States, Harvard theologian Harvey Cox tried in *The Secular City* (1965) to position the divine in the midst of everyday life as lived by most urban dwellers, rather than situating it in some domain beyond the earth.

Drawing on his own experience as a layman, and with special reference to the Anglican and United churches, the Canadian broadcaster and author-journalist Pierre Berton in *The Comfortable Pew* (1965) declared that the Christian Church needed updating in the direction of greater contemporary relevance. He castigated the church for its inability to communicate in intelligible language, for the failure of its leaders to address such issues of the day as nuclear weapons, racism, ethics in business, prison reform, capital punishment, a national health plan, birth control, and homosexuality (1965, 112), and for its assumptions that the future would be no more than an extension of the past. Pointing out that many Roman Catholics were no longer paying attention to admonitions of their priests against artificial means of birth control, Berton also wondered – perhaps with a bit of mock naïveté – whether the day would come among Christians, and especially Protestants, when "under certain circumstances and certain conditions, sexual relations between unmarried adults may not be considered altogether wicked" (63). In all, he was arguing for "a new kind of Church" appropriate to a changing society, a church that would be aware that the mindset of this new era would not be religious, but secular (139). With this, Berton came to the very heart of one of the issues of modernity. In a large and significant book, McGill philosopher Charles Taylor characterized what it means for a society to be secular, understanding secularism as entailing a shift from a context when "it was virtually impossible not to believe in God, to one in which faith, even for the staunchest believer, is one human possibility among others" (2007, 3). This shift to a largely secular society had become evident in many quarters by the mid-1960s.

The crisis of faith that was spreading throughout the membership of the Christian Church in the 1960s was partly the result of delayed adaptation to cultural changes, some of which were, after all, only being dimly apprehended in the larger world beyond the churches. Immediately following World War II and throughout the 1950s, the postwar baby boom and emphasis on the family and its values, the newly found prosperity and availability of consumer goods, and the general optimism in society all conspired to a kind of domestic complacency that disguised some of the larger issues that had been so present during the Depression and the war. Hugh MacLennan in *The Watch That Ends the Night* (1958), a classic of Canadian fiction, portrayed through his "everyman" narrator George Stewart the loss of community and collective social values, and the resulting individualism and isolation of these years. Stewart struggles with the meaning of human existence after the loss of faith in a providential God attending to the details of individual life or organizing the larger designs of history.

Following in the vein of other literary works by authors such as Sartre and Camus, existentialism enhanced this sense of the solitary decision-making individual, deprived of the consolations of a divine plan or an afterlife, as constitutive of what it is to be a human being. Whether or not these larger questions got any sustained reflection in the daily lives of ordinary Canadians, there surely was at least the sense that the existing norms of the church, or the conventions of society, no longer quite applied as they once had done. By the 1960s the reforms of Vatican II were being witnessed by Catholics as they saw unprecedented changes in the liturgy. Priests began to become laicized and nuns to leave their orders – or at least to change their habits for ordinary dress. Protestant clergy began to forsake the previously ubiquitous clerical collar and Geneva gown. Theological students, as well as university undergraduates, were debating the nature of religious language or claims about the existence of God. Ethical decisions based on consideration of context became popularized in such books as Joseph Fletcher's *Situation Ethics* of 1966 that suggested there might be exceptions to the universally binding moral principles of a deontological ethics.

While many churches still held two or even three services of worship on a Sunday, already some Christians, especially Protestant ones, were feeling that attendance at worship might not after all be an absolute requirement for being a Christian. Once again, Pierre Berton suggested that the church should consider the possibility of a "world in which many who call themselves Christians will not necessarily 'go to church' at all" (1965, 140). At the onset of what was to become a precipitous decline in participation at weekly services, here was an almost prophetic suggestion of what was to come within a generation. Berton and others foresaw the possibility that new forms of religious faith might emerge that could not be gauged by the older criteria.

Within Judaism, the situation of the 1960s might have appeared to the eye of the casual observer not very much different from Christianity. Weekly attendance at worship, already lower than what prevailed among Christians, had begun to decrease further. Yet an essential difference between these two western monotheistic traditions was that Jews did not regard credal affirmation or belief as the primary condition or means of definition of what it means to be a Jew. Even attendance at weekly worship was not a religious necessity for Jews. Elie Wiesel, giving advice in the later 1960s to a seventeen-year-old Jew troubled about his faith, downplayed the fact that this young man claimed not to believe in God: "I leave you the task of working out your own relationship with God. What matters to me is the relationship between the individual and the community" (1972, 217). For Wiesel the crucial thing for anyone born a Jew "is first to accept my destiny as a Jew, and then to choose it" (214). "To be a Jew," he states, "is to work for the survival of a people" (217).

At the same time, however, Wiesel was convinced that theology of the death of the God did not originate with any Jew who had survived the Holocaust, and especially a Jew who had been in the concentration camps (1974). That was his response at a conference to Rabbi Richard Rubenstein, whose work had been coupled with that of the Christian death-of-God theologians, especially Altizer and Hamilton. Like them, Rubenstein was declaring the impossibility of traditional theism. In *After Auschwitz* he asserted that the God of the Covenant was no longer credible in the aftermath of the Holocaust, an event that was impossible to understand as an expression of God's purposes in history: "How can Jews believe in an omnipotent, beneficent God after Auschwitz?" (1966, 153). Unlike Dietrich Bonhoeffer, the proponent of "religionless Christianity" who said that the difficulty was "how to speak of God in age of no religion," Rubenstein claimed that for Jews "our problem is how to speak of religion in an age of no God" (153). Rubenstein's view – and here he comes close to Wiesel's position – was that within Judaism the imperative remained to "share the decisive times and crises of life through the traditions of our inherited community" (153).

Other aspects of the changes occurring within Christianity after World War II find their parallels in Judaism. Gerald Tulchinsky sketches out some of these similar developments within Canada in the 1960s and '70s, including a larger degree of participation and integration among Jews in a multicultural Canada, in particular in the arts, politics, and higher education (1998, 288–321). Secular Judaism, "a broadly defined Jewish culture that does not exclude religion" (320), was visible among leftist, progressive, liberal or "non-Jewish Jews," although transformed from its earlier embodiments. Even if they no longer spoke Yiddish or participated in religious or ritual activities within Judaism, these secular Jews might, for instance, be active supporters of Israel. Like many who might be described as "post-Christians," they were participating in public debates on many of the issues of the day, either as an expression of the values of their inherited religious faith or else out of their roles as active citizens within a liberal democracy.

The exact source of the motivation might differ from one individual to the next, making generalizations difficult.

In *The Jews of Kingston* Marion Meyer focuses on the period preceding and following the creation of the Iyr HaMelech, Kingston's Reform Congregation, in 1976. By the mid-1970s, 95 per cent of the members of Beth Israel were other than Orthodox (1983, 62). Most of these – Conservative, Reform, agnostic, or atheist – seemed to have felt it desirable to accommodate their practice to the Orthodox minority in order to maintain the "umbrella" nature of the congregation. In the 1960s, while the Jewish population was increasing with an influx of academics, doctors, and other professionals, divisions were occurring within Beth Israel between the older members of the community and newcomers. Not everyone found that continuing as Orthodox, the affiliation of only a small proportion of the congregation's membership, was the best way to include those who found many of the traditional practices and beliefs alien to their own experience or else in need of adaptation and updating. Like many of their liberal Christian contemporaries, Reform Jews tend to hold that traditions need to be reinterpreted in the light of contemporary needs or individual conscience (see Meyer 1983, 101; chap. 6 below). In addition, many of the non-affiliated recent arrivals did not even hold being Jewish as the primary component of their identities.

The creation of the Reform congregation, Iyr HaMelech, in 1976 provided an option for those who had non-Jewish marriage partners or who were "religious skeptics." Some members shared the view that they wanted to see their children gain "some consciousness of just what it means to be Jewish," even if that meant they were to become "skeptical Jews," rather than being something else (Meyer 1983, 104). By the end of the 1970s the membership of the Reform congregation consisted of about thirty individuals, approximately a third of whom were married to non-Jewish partners. At the same time, about eighty Jewish individuals within Kingston preferred not to be affiliated with either Beth Israel or Iyr HaMelech. Meyer sums up the representative distinguishing marks of these three groups: "Beth Israel ... displayed the widest span of all. It reached from a sprinkling of Orthodox Jews all the way to atheism. Representative of Beth Israel was the Jew who chose Orthodoxy not because of religious convictions but as a higher model, 'the Orthodox tolerant Jew.' The Iyr-HaMelech member could best be characterized as a 'religious skeptic, but skeptically Jewish.' As for the non-affiliated Jew, 'intellectual-critical, emotional-compassionate' is possibly the best description" (118).

The situation of Jews in Kingston reflects a larger pattern prevailing over these years, according to Gerald Tulchinsky: "While on the whole traditional Judaism remained dominant in Canada, there was a significant increase in the number of Reform congregations" (1998, 317–18). Newcomers, especially academics, in places such as Kingston and Kitchener-Waterloo wanted a more liberal option than the existing congregations provided. From their small beginnings in borrowed or shared space, the new Reform congregations flourished and grew. While in Kingston Iyr HaMelech has increased over a thirty-year period to about seventy families, employing a rabbi on a part-time basis, it continues to use space on the university campus or at the local public library. Meanwhile, Beth Israel, which saw only three families leave at the time Iyr HaMelech was formed, also flourishes. Apart from their theological and liturgical differences, Beth Israel tends to be favoured by Kingston's Jewish business people, whereas Iyr HaMelech is the home of academics. Still, they cooperate well in many areas, especially where their common Jewish life is the focus, or when prospective members need to be directed to the appropriate congregation. Furthermore, following the pattern of Christian faith groups of the era, members of the newer congregation tended to be younger and therefore likely to have more children in the future.

In general it appears that religious groups – even small ones – in Kingston which are diverse and depend upon a spectrum of participants for their continuing existence are not much affected by internal divisions, nor even by a portion of their number splitting off and establishing a new community on their own. Among Christian churches, some congregations "planted" new churches in other areas to which they sent some of their members to help get the new church going. If older congregations withered and died, the process seems to be more often gradual than the result of a cataclysmic split resulting in the departure of people from the group.

While this chapter's focus has been principally on the initial downtown presence and subsequent spread to the suburbs of the "Big Three" – the Anglican, Roman Catholic, and United churches – together with a parallel account of Judaism in Kingston, there is of course much more to the story. As Margaret Atwood has noted (1996), Spiritualism had a strong presence in Kingston in the nineteenth century. As well, the religious census of 1908 reported in the *British Whig* (see above) pointed to the presence of other groups in Kingston not mentioned here: the Holiness Movement, Free Methodists, and the Salvation Army. Chapter 4, "Proselytizing Groups in Kingston," portrays how the Salvation Army, together with the Mormons and the Brethren, were active in this area more than one hundred years ago. Quakers, too, dealt with in chapter 6, also had a nineteenth-century presence in the Kingston area. Moreover, Protestant evangelical groups, including their nineteenth-century forerunners – for example, Free Methodists, the Holiness Movement, the Christian and Missionary Alliance, and Pentecostals – are the subject of chapter 3. Baptists, who have a lengthy history in

Kingston, are considered in chapter 7. The Presbyterians who continued after the Church Union of 1925, particularly the major downtown congregation at St Andrew's Presbyterian Church, are prominent too later on, in chapter 2 (see also chap. 10). Most of the denominations just named here have had, from the late nineteenth or early twentieth centuries, a building in Kingston's downtown or close to it. Many of those other churches followed the Big Three in their move, or expansion, to the suburbs during the 1960s.

Another feature, temporarily put aside in this chapter but part of the religious diversity of Kingston, is the presence of ethnic churches, especially from the 1950s on. These include the Lutheran Church (chap. 5), the Christian Reformed Church (chap. 3), and the Ukrainian Catholic Church (chap. 5), together with many others. St Mark's Evangelical Lutheran Church and First Christian Reformed Church, located respectively near Queen's University and in the Kingscourt area on Kingston's near north side, were built in the 1950s and continue in those locations today. The religion that takes place in institutions, most of them centrally situated – educational and penal institutions, the various hospitals and schools – is the subject of a separate chapter (chap. 9). In effect, then, the account given here has been somewhat attenuated for the sake of preserving a relatively uncluttered account of the history of Kingston's downtown churches and the subsequent growth to the suburbs. If this were a book about religious diversity in nineteenth-century Kingston instead of in the early twenty-first century, there is much more that would be worthy of inclusion in addition to the various groups dealt with in this initial chapter.

DOWNTOWN KINGSTON TODAY

What of existing religious sites still located centrally, that is to say within a kilometre of City Hall, in downtown Kingston today? Churches representing the major Christian denominations remain: Presbyterian, Anglican, Roman Catholic, United Church, and Baptist. In addition, there is the evangelical Bethel Church located near the corner of Johnson and Barrie Streets. Built in 1874, and formerly Congregational, Bethel became independent at the time of Church Union in 1925, when almost all of the other Congregational churches in Canada became part of the United Church. In 1949 Bethel became affiliated with the Associated Gospel Churches of Canada, and today has a huge ministry to evangelical students at Queen's University. The former Free Methodist Church at 89 Colborne Street became in the 1990s a "church plant" called the NeXt Church, aimed, as its name suggests, toward a "GenX" population. The church's website presents the NeXt Church as a thoroughly contemporary place, well adapted to electronic media (Next

Church). Podcasts of sermons are available online, and photos and blogs underscore the informal atmosphere. Many of the usual evangelical preoccupations with doctrinal and credal issues, as well as its association with the Free Methodist parent body, are muted.

At least one nineteenth-century sanctuary remained unused for religious purposes during most of the twentieth century: the former First Congregational Church on Wellington Street, designed by John Power in 1864, became a Masonic Temple with Church Union in 1925 and was recently leased as theatre space. For a few years it also housed a "café church" for alternative worship on Sunday mornings. Similarly, the plain stone building at 285 Queen Street, dating from 1837, was originally the site of the Catholic Apostolic Church, an apocalyptic renewal movement originating in Britain and based on a restored apostleship. After the twelve new "apostles" all died, the church declined, and the building was used as a Pentecostal church from the early twentieth century. When the Pentecostals relocated in 1959, it became the Scottish Rite Temple, a branch of Freemasonry. By 2008 the still-intact building – touted as "Kingston's oldest surviving church structure" – was renovated to live a new life as a banquet hall, the Renaissance Event & Wedding Venue (Jessup Food & Heritage).

The Salvation Army has several sites within the city of Kingston. The Citadel and Harbour Light residential treatment facility on Princess Street continues. The Army also maintains a storefront "Freedom Ministries" just further north on Division Street. The Thrift Store has moved away from downtown to a strip mall on the Bath Road, and a new worship space, though much delayed, opened in 2010 on Taylor-Kidd Boulevard in an expanding suburban area.

The Greek Orthodox Church stands on Johnson Street just west of the former First Congregational Church at the corner of Wellington and St George's Anglican Cathedral at the corner of King. All three buildings are visible in a row as one looks toward the foot of Johnson Street from the vicinity of the public library. Further out from the downtown core, but still within a few blocks of Princess, are two evangelical house churches, Calvary Bible Church on Nelson just north of Concession, and Faith Alive on Alfred Street at Princess. Other faith communities have also established places of worship near the downtown. After many years of meeting in space on the university campus, the Kingston Unitarian Fellowship in the 1990s hired a full-time minister and subsequently purchased a building for their use on Concession Street on the near north side. And though probably not so easily reckoned among Kingston's worshipping faith groups, the quasi-religious Taoist Tai Chi Society of Canada has its premises on Montreal Street. The website of the International Taoist Tai Chi Society explains that while tai chi may be engaged in merely as a form of exercise, its practitioners also use it as "a vehicle to tame the heart and help us recover our original nature ... In the Taoist tradition such a training path is referred to as 'cultivating both inner nature and life' (*xing ming shuang xiu*). A healthy body is considered to be one where the internal organs are interacting in a balanced and harmonious manner" (Taoist Tai Chi).

In 2005 the Kuluta Buddhist Centre moved from a limestone house in Calvin Park rented from the city, located just west of Macdonald Boulevard, to a tastefully restored building on Wellington Street in the heart of downtown. Part of the Kadampa Buddhist tradition, the centre incorporates a shop selling books and gifts, as well as a meditation room. This move arose from a wish to attract younger clientele from the university and downtown, to diversify the core of middle-aged women who comprised most of the attendees in Calvin Park. In a similar vein, just around the corner of Brock Street, in a block with upscale restaurants and a men's wear store, is the Sacred Source Bookstore. Most easily described as a New Age bookstore, Sacred Source is also the venue for proprietor Kellye Crockett to provide Tarot card readings, schedule her classes in sacred dance, and make available resources for the Pagan community in the store's upstairs space. Another religious bookstore, the Church Bookroom of the Anglican Diocese of Ontario, has long operated a block away on Johnson Street. Beginning in the summer of 2007, and continuing for three years, Kingston followers of Sri Chinmoy operated the Lotus-Heart-Blossoms vegetarian restaurant on Sydenham Street, between Princess and Queen streets. It paralleled other vegetarian restaurants inspired by the Indian guru Sri Chinmoy (d. 2007) located in the United States in New York, San Francisco, and Seattle – and in Canada, in Toronto, Ottawa, and Halifax.

In general, we have seen in the last generation or so no new religious sites being constructed from the ground up in or near the centre of Kingston's downtown. The mostly storefront sites that have emerged there could be interpreted as an attempt to re-centralize alternative groups that might be considered marginal to the familiar and well-established religious mainstream. Today, as with previously emerging faith groups in the nineteenth century, a downtown location visibly positions them in the city centre, enabling them to draw on the more venturous young and single folk – especially university students – living in or near the downtown core. Among the staid or trendy retail stores and restaurants surrounding them, the attractively renovated premises are a credit to Kingston's vibrant downtown. They are, like religious groups newly come to Kingston more than a hundred years earlier, seeking acceptance by presenting themselves as architecturally good neighbours in a city proud of its buildings.

With only a few exceptions, the expansion or new building of religious sites has taken place largely in Kingston's suburban west end beyond the Little Cataraqui River, sometimes called Cataraqui Creek. The United Church of Canada and other mainline Christian denominations over-expanded in the 1960s and left behind their older nineteenth-century downtown limestone church buildings for dwindling and aging congregations to repair, maintain, heat, and insure. Already too ambitiously large even when they were originally constructed, these buildings continue to pose difficulties for the people who worship there. Often historic purpose-built structures, they are not easily adapted to other uses, and are situated in areas far from the homes of their parishioners. Parking is scarce, yet congregational loyalty is often fiercely strong. Chalmers United Church had a 1960s building across from the church on Barrie Street, MacGillivray-Brown Hall, built principally to provide space for a gymnasium, meeting rooms, and a Sunday School. A generation later Chalmers was prepared to sell their church building and move to the church hall. Ironically, Bethel, the former Congregational Church that stayed out of Church Union, was one of the parties interested in purchasing this formerly Presbyterian Church. Chalmers wanted to build a multi-purpose centre on the site of their church hall to serve the community, but with a change of provincial governments, and disappearance of possible funding, the project fell through. Instead, Chalmers kept their original sanctuary and sold the MacGillivray-Brown Hall to Queen's University (Wayne Hilliker, interview, 3 October 2003).

Sometimes the possibility of uniting with one or more other congregations was raised, as, for instance, in the case of the three United Churches located within a few blocks of one another whose congregations customarily joined forces together for tri-church summer services. Though the attendees at Chalmers, Sydenham Street, and the former Queen Street United churches on almost any given Sunday could have been housed within a single one of their three spaces, the opposition was frequently vocal to proposals of uniting them, and the topic was finally dropped. In 2008 the congregation of Queen Street United put their building up for sale and joined the congregation of the west-end St Margaret's for worship, en route to exploring their eventual union. After all, most members of the church at the corner of Queen and Clergy Streets lived closer to the area where St Margaret's is situated than to either of the other neighbouring downtown United churches. In 2009 the Queen Street building and the four houses on the property were sold to a developer with an eye toward providing rental or possible future condominium accommodation. Queen Street's amalgamation with St Margaret's was finally brought to fruition in January 2010 when St Margaret's was renamed Crossroads United Church. The task of shutting down was easier at the postwar Kingscourt United Church on Kingston's near north side, which decided to close its doors at the end of 2007. Established in 1953, Kingscourt United had no long generations of families who had worshipped there, no significant endowments, and no historic building. In 2008 its space was leased, and later purchased, by a Free Methodist church plant, the Butternut Creek congregation, which for a decade or more had been using rented quarters in other locations.

This sketch outlining the history of the buildings associated with Kingston's major Christian and Jewish congregations might well seem to deal only with externals. As important as architectural matters are as a mark of the significance of a congregation, especially in the context of the nineteenth century, brick and stone alone, even given Kingstonians' strong pride in historic limestone buildings in the city, tell us little about the nature and character of these congregations as they continue today. Insofar as our focus is on the diverse entirety of Kingston's religious landscape in the early twenty-first century, much more remains to be said about other religious sites outside the Christian mainstream, and outside Kingston's downtown. Where they situate themselves, and whether or not they decide to build, rent, or share a building, remain important issues. While much of the character of religious groups can be determined by how their places of worship are constructed and how that space is organized, religious groups are, after all, about people, and what they do and how they see the world.

2 Mainline Christian Denominations: Roman Catholic, United, Anglican, Presbyterian, Baptist

DEFINING "MAINLINE"

Churches representing mainline Christianity in Canada are sometimes identified as the denominations represented by the acronym PLURA – that is, Presbyterian, Lutheran, United, Roman Catholic, and Anglican. PLURA was an anti-poverty coalition of Canada's mainline Christian churches, resulting from the ecumenical movement toward social justice that began in the 1960s (Hutchinson n.d.; Choquette 2004, 373). In the nineteenth century, Roger O'Toole points out, 90 percent of Canadians belonged to five major denominations of Christianity, almost the same as the PLURA churches, except that Baptists rather than Lutherans were on the list. The nineteenth-century "Big Five" were Anglicans, Roman Catholics, Presbyterians, Methodists – the last now usually considered to be part of the United Church – and Baptists (2000, 43). Near the beginning of his *Fifth Business*, which among its other riches portrays southwestern Ontario village life early in the twentieth century, sometime Kingstonian Robertson Davies has his narrator characterize the five churches of his fictional Deptford: "The Anglican, poor but believed to have some mysterious social supremacy; the Presbyterian, solvent and thought – chiefly by itself – to be intellectual; the Methodist, insolvent and fervent; the Baptist, insolvent and saved; the Roman Catholic, mysterious to most of us but clearly solvent, as it was, so we thought, quite needlessly repainted" (1970, 10–11). In Kingston, early in the twenty-first century, where Baptists continue to outnumber Lutherans, the contemporary descendants of the Deptford churches remain the Big Five.

In chapter 1, following O'Toole and others, these Big Five denominations were reduced to the "Big Three" – the Roman Catholic Church, the Anglican Church, and the United Church. In the 2001 Census Metropolitan Area of Kingston in 2001, in a total population of about 143,000, Roman Catholics number 44,000 people, members and adherents of the United Church 28,000, and Anglicans 19,000, all figures rounded to the nearest 1,000. That is, 64 per cent of Kingstonians consider themselves to be affiliated with one of these Big Three churches: 31 per cent are Roman Catholics; 20 per cent are United Church; 13 per cent are Anglicans. The other two PLURA churches add an additional 3 per cent of Kingstonians to this total of 64 per cent: 2 per cent of Kingstonians are Presbyterians (2,890), while 0.9 per cent are Lutherans (1,285). Baptists, numbering 2,050 or 1.4 per cent, are the only other large group of Protestant Christians to be found in Kingston. Because Lutherans in Kingston are relatively few and the sole Lutheran congregation is considered among the "ethnic" Christian churches in chapter 5, here we focus on the other Christian mainline denominations, namely – and ranked according to the number of adherents – the Roman Catholic Church, the United Church of Canada, the Anglican Church of Canada, the Presbyterian Church in Canada, and the Baptists. However, as three of the four Baptist churches in Kingston are logically included among the consideration of evangelical churches (see chap. 3), we pay attention here to the only one of these four congregations, First Baptist, the sole Baptist church in Kingston tending toward the mainstream of Protestant Christianity and the only Baptist congregation belonging to the more moderate Baptist Convention of Ontario and Quebec.

Probably other characteristics are more important than the numerical dominance represented by the so-called mainline Christian churches. As already indicated, their respective histories are linked with the history of Canada. They have frequently been in the forefront of establishing hospitals, colleges, and universities. Mainline churches have actively worked in the areas of social justice, politics, and environment. These churches are usually contrasted in their theology with evangelical Protestant churches, described in detail in chapter 3. Whereas evangelicals tend to hold conservative views on the nature of scripture, the person and work of Jesus Christ, and conversion and salvation, mainline churches are generally more liberal and less specific in their formulations of doctrinal matters. This is not to say, however, that uniformity of views marks these mainline churches. Rather, a split is often visible between mainline Christians who support what they claim to be their church's historic and biblical views against those who favour tendencies toward modern secular humanism.

ROMAN CATHOLICS

In Kingston as in Canada as a whole, the Roman Catholic Church is the largest religious body: about 31 per cent of Kingstonians are Roman Catholic.

Among about ten churches within the current boundaries of the city, only two existed in the nineteenth century, St Mary's Cathedral and the Church of the Good Thief in Portsmouth. The growth of Catholicism and the expansion of churches occurred more recently than among the other two of the Big Three, the United and Anglican churches. Father Joseph Lynch of St Joseph's on Palace Road explained that the Diocese of Kingston, about 175 years old, "was the first English-speaking diocese in Canada, so it was split off from the diocese of Quebec, which was the first diocese in Canada" (interview, 14 July 2005). Without the sectarian divisions that characterized Protestantism, Roman Catholics "were considered parishioners by reason of geography." That is, you were a member of a parish if you lived near a particular church. Today, by way of contrast, someone who lived near St Mary's but elected to go to St Joseph's would be a considered a parishioner of St Joseph's by virtue of regular attendance.

As we shall see, some Anglican churches in Kingston are able to characterize themselves by features of theology or liturgy, even within the overarching commonalities of Anglicanism that unite them. When Father Joseph Lynch was asked how St Joseph's differed from other Roman Catholic churches in the Kingston Diocese, his answer was, "I don't think it would be different at all." He continued, "I think the Roman Catholic Church has a structure that's pretty common. Obviously there would be some variations, but I don't think you would find much difference anywhere." With few variations in structure, polity, and governance, the obvious differences from one parish to another would be in such areas as "the ethnic mix, the income mix, the age mix."

Asked how Kingston looked from the perspective of Roman Catholicism, and whether the city is supportive of his faith, Father Lynch said that during his forty years in Kingston he had never detected "any issue in the community that has caused difficulty for the Catholic Church. The church has tried to be supportive of the community, and I think the community is supportive of the church." He referred to the response to the deadly Asian tsunami that occurred on Boxing Day 2004, about six months prior to our interview with him. Archbishop Anthony Meagher wanted "to gather people to pray" at St Mary's Cathedral, and within a few days arrangements were made with other Christian denominations, Muslims, and Jews that filled the church: "It was the general consensus that it was probably the first time the Cathedral had had an interfaith – not ecumenical – but an interfaith service of that kind and magnitude." Lynch was wanting to stress that this particular service involved people of different religions, not simply of different Christian denominations as the word "ecumenical" might imply. A few months later, Archbishop Meagher would gather a similar interfaith group at St Mary's

Cathedral again for a celebration of the life of Pope John Paul II, and again the cathedral was filled to its capacity of about one thousand people.

Anthony Meagher came to Kingston in 2002 as the diocese's eighth archbishop in its long history. He had just finished the onerous duties of being president of the World Youth Day 2002, when Pope John Paul II and many thousands of young people were welcomed to Toronto in an event that captured headlines for days. In the period of less than five years from his coming to Kingston to his death on 14 January 2007, Tony Meagher won the respect and admiration of Kingstonians of all faiths. His personal warmth, candour, energy, and humour charmed and impressed everyone who met him, and yet he was dying of cancer almost from the time of his arrival. He learned, two months after becoming archbishop, that he had a large tumour on his kidney that he apparently had been carrying around for three years. When I interviewed him on Cogeco television for *Profiles: People of Faith*, Meagher spoke of having been concerned about whether to make his disease public. "And the advice I got was this: 'There are a lot of people in this diocese who are suffering, who are sick, and if God has chosen somehow to give them a sick bishop, then maybe God wants you to relate to these people in a special way. So, be honest with people, let them know, and who knows, out of this you may be able to relate to people who are sick or suffering in a way that is special, and trust the providence of God in that'" (2 March 2005). Father Tim Shea, a close personal friend, spoke of how the illness changed Meagher: "The more he thought about it, he thought he'd serve as a bishop but serve in sickness. He wasn't going to roll over and die. He's chosen to live with cancer. He just wants to enjoy the people in Kingston for a little while" (*Whig-Standard*, 18 March 2006).

In 2002 Meagher was told that he had between eighteen months and three years to live. He commented that the more generous estimate of three years "would be stretching it because there isn't a cure for this. They don't have a cure for the kidney cancer cells which are now going all through you." By 2005 he had "at least five other tumours in bones and cracked ribs and cracked shoulder blade." In spite of these developments, he was also able to relate during our interview in March 2005 how "in some amazing way it's just stopped spreading in the last seven months and my energy is starting to come back." He expressed his appreciation for the support he had received and for the prayers that had been offered on his behalf – at a Toronto synagogue where a rabbi with whom he had been associated presided, at Anglican churches in Kingston at the request of Bishop George Bruce, by members of the local ministerial association who "prayed for me and anointed me with oil," and, of course, by Roman Catholics in the city and elsewhere. In an Advent message published in the local newspaper,

Meagher wrote, "My personal joy has been to know that I am being prayed for by name at a Jewish synagogue, Anglican and Protestant churches here in Kingston, my own Roman Catholic parishes, and God knows where else in this wonderful world" (21 December 2002). He told me, "We're all pretty frightened when we're sick and I was no different. And that support is so important when you're sick" (2 March 2005).

While the archbishop said that he hoped he had "always had the sense that he would accept what comes," he felt that the arrest in the spread of the cancer "borders on the amazing." It was probably deliberate that he did not use the word "miraculous." Despite the suffering he had endured, and with low prospects for recovery, he retained the twinkle in his eye and his sense of humour: "Mind you, I've talked with God a bit about it, and in fact I actually said to him there, 'You know, you could get a real bad rap if you don't listen to all these people praying for me. They may wonder whether you are capable or not.'" Early in our interview he spoke of growing up in a large family in Oshawa after his mother's death. He said that though faith was important in the family, it was the opposite of ostentatious, and that there was humour and practical joking in the household too. There was a sense that God was looking after things – that God would see you through.

After graduating from university in 1962, Tony Meagher went to St Augustine's Seminary in Toronto, but he continued to worry, "Who am I to be a priest? Am I cut out to be a priest? Because I didn't fit the mould." In the seminary he was not considered to possess the requisite qualities of earnestness and gravity – in addition to his uncertainties about his vocation. Although he agreed with the advice to take time away from the seminary, he implied that the assessment of his personality might have been incomplete, and based on a misreading of his apparent jocularity: "The more serious I am, the less serious I act." That observation could probably be applied too to the jokes he made in the context of his cancer.

His ministry to sick people in the diocese included giving a talk to staff at Hotel Dieu Hospital about the spiritual needs of cancer patients, and being available to other cancer patients who wanted to talk with him about their illness. My own path was to cross his again at the Regional Cancer Centre at the Kingston General Hospital when I became a fellow cancer patient there, something I could not have foreseen when I interviewed him in March 2005. Within a year I was diagnosed with malignant melanoma, a form of skin cancer. The cancer cells had already spread to my lymph nodes, necessitating more surgery and then daily interferon treatments throughout March 2006, with regular checkups following. It was on one of those visits when Tony Meagher, his illness now having progressed even further, mischievously confided that despite his disease he had made a recent trip to

Rome to witness a friend from South America being made a cardinal. In concert with Tim Shea's remark about Meagher enjoying the people of Kingston, he conveyed the feeling that you were one of those that he enjoyed being with, whether Catholic or not, and even at the Cancer Centre.

Meagher found ways, in the midst of his illness, of expressing gratitude. For instance, in a letter to the *Whig-Standard* published 12 January 2006, he affirmed that "one of the many Kingston blessings we can count is the Kingston Regional Cancer Centre and all the people associated with it." He recommended that "someone feeling a bit down after the holidays or jaded with the world" might be helped by spending "an observant hour some weekday morning or afternoon sitting in the waiting room of our cancer clinic here in Kingston, at 25 King Street West, across King Street from the beautiful lakefront park." He mentioned how a stranger had helped him with his coat there one day, and then commented: "Kindness, respect, thoughtfulness and love are a daily presence at the clinic, and they are a tribute to the secretaries, doctors, nurses, technicians, volunteers and patients who work and visit there" (*Whig-Standard*, 12 January 2006). As sick as he was at this time, about a year before his death, Meagher was expressing gratitude on behalf of those who benefited from the Cancer Centre's care, but who unlike him were too preoccupied or worried or frightened to be able to bear their witness to such human goodness amidst adversity.

During his tenure as archbishop Meagher had to address publicly two rather difficult issues confronting the Roman Catholic Church. One of them was, as one might expect, the legislation being considered in Parliament about same-sex marriage. The other was the unauthorized ordination of several Roman Catholic women within the Diocese of Kingston. On 25 July 2005 nine Roman Catholic women, mostly from the United States, were ordained as priests and deacons on board a Gananoque Boat Lines ship in international waters in the St Lawrence River. The three-hour ceremony was similar to one held on the Danube River between Germany and Austria in 2002 when the Danube Seven, as they were known, were ordained. They were subsequently excommunicated by Cardinal Joseph Ratzinger, who was later to become Pope Benedict. Archbishop Meagher issued a statement on the day following the ceremony on the St Lawrence in which he reiterated the position of the Vatican that ordination to the priesthood is a divine decree: "The Church has no authority whatsoever to confer priestly ordination on women and that this judgment is to be definitively held by all the Church's faithful." Furthermore, he continued, "A priestly ordination can be conferred only by a validly ordained bishop upon a candidate who is eligible to be ordained according to Church law. The proposed 'ordinations' cannot be called such, as they fail on both counts" (*Whig-Standard*, 26 July 2005).

Meagher also addressed the geographical ambiguity of the claim that the ordinations took place in international waters, pointing out that the boat departed from and returned to Gananoque, within the Diocese of Kingston. After speaking of opportunities for women to exercise roles of leadership within the church, he concluded with an expression of goodwill that served a bit to ameliorate the judgment he was bound to deliver: "Finally, it is very important to acknowledge the good faith and integrity of those who sincerely believe in the merit of this issue. While I cannot accept their position, I appreciate their sincerity."

Similarly, a few years earlier, at about the time that the matter of same-sex marriages was much in the news, the Vatican had called upon politicians of Roman Catholic background to uphold the principles of their faith when making legislative decisions. A proclamation on the website of the Congregation for the Doctrine of the Faith stated on 3 June 2003, "When legislation in favour of the recognition of homosexual unions is proposed for the first time in a legislative assembly, the Catholic law-maker has a moral duty to express his opposition clearly and publicly and to vote against it. To vote in favour of a law so harmful to the common good is gravely immoral." Meagher issued a statement to be read in churches on 2–3 August 2003 that, as one would expect, stated the Vatican position. In an interview with the *Kingston Whig-Standard* he commented, "Roman Catholic politicians are obligated to vote against any legislation that would give same-sex unions the same legal rights as heterosexual marriages" (5 August 2003). Yet he also stated, in a 2005 pastoral letter, that his own position derived from a love of Canada and a concern for its good, rather than because of what scripture says or because of a papal decree. Here and in later statements he cautioned against the negative effects on the family if same-sex unions were equated with marriage, in effect disagreeing with any attempt to "homogenize" all loving relationships. Again, in his statement to the Kingston parishes, published on the website of the Ontario Conference of Catholic Bishops, he also struck a positive note: "It is extremely important that we not resort to name-calling and blind criticism if others do not see things exactly as we do." Taking a position that might have been surprising to some Catholics, he went on to say, "There is evidence of same-sex unions that are stable, loving, and nurturing in many ways for each partner." He anticipated objections to this position by adding this affirmation: "If one interprets what I have said as being open to commending same-sex partners for stability, faithfulness, kindness, and perseverance when one or other is sick or incapacitated, such an understanding is perfectly correct." Notwithstanding these positive statements, he returned to the traditional Roman Catholic position with the reminder to all couples that sexual relations outside of marriage are sinful.

Archbishop Meagher's expanded statements on the women's ordination ceremony and same-sex marriage are perhaps unexpected because, despite the strict and unswerving Roman Catholic position on both issues, he found the opportunity to go beyond mere disapproval and censure to offer reasoned arguments in support of his position. He also used the opportunity to offer a positive comment, about the sincerity, good faith, and integrity of women seeking ordination, and about stability, love, and fidelity within same-sex unions. Rather than singling out same-sex relationships for particular criticism, he found little need to go beyond comments that the Roman Catholic Church might make of sexual relationships outside of marriage for heterosexual couples. He took the high road on the same-sex marriage issue, in contrast to Bishop Fred Henry of Calgary who publicly called Prime Minister Paul Martin a bad Catholic for introducing same-sex legislation. Bishop Henry's pastoral letter of 17 January 2005 stated, in terms that launched a complaint to Alberta's Human Rights Commission, "Since homosexuality, adultery, prostitution and pornography undermine the foundations of the family, the basis of society, then the State must use its coercive power to proscribe or curtail them in the interests of the common good." Far from identifying any positive or mutually supportive aspect within same-sex relationships, he wrote, "The committed union of two people of the same sex is not the same human reality as the committed union of one man and one woman."

In our interviews and studies of Roman Catholic churches in Kingston, evidence was repeatedly offered of healthy and thriving parishes, of programs that were flourishing, and of parishioners who were dedicated to the work of their churches and to the well-being of the city. With the exception of the Roman Catholic chaplain at Queen's University (see chap. 9), little was heard from any quarter to suggest that Kingston's Catholics felt besieged or in any way put upon within a secular or otherwise hostile environment. Asked about the effect of the presence of new religious traditions in the city, especially of ones other than Christianity, Father Charles H. Gazeley of Holy Family Roman Catholic Church offered this view: "If it has any impact, I would say it has a positive impact. That would be my opinion. It reminds me of when the Lord sent out the Apostles and they came back and said these other guys are curing the sick and so on, should we stop them? He said no. If they're not against us, they're with us. If there are other religions springing up and practising faithfully what their beliefs are, I think that can only strengthen all of us. Unless there's a church that is attacking other churches. If a non-Christian church is attacking a Christian church or a Christian church is attacking a non-Christian church … but I don't think that's happening. I'm not aware of it. Not now. Years ago I experienced some of that, but that's a long time ago" (interview, 26 November 2003).

THE UNITED CHURCH

Canada's largest Protestant denomination, the United Church of Canada stands as a uniquely Canadian body, formed in 1925 from a Union of Congregationalists, Methodists, and about two-thirds of Presbyterians. Another denomination, the Evangelical United Brethren, came into the United Church in 1968. One of the results of Church Union was that several large downtown churches in Kingston, formerly Presbyterian or Methodist, became United. Chalmers and Cooke's were originally Presbyterian; Sydenham Street and Queen Street were previously Methodist. Of these four congregations, two have since amalgamated with other United Church congregations, Cooke's in 1964, and Queen Street in 2010. In the era of developing suburbs and church building and expansion in the 1950s and '60s (chap. 1), Kingston saw its United churches doubling in number to fourteen. Today some of them are underused and one more, Kingscourt United, has closed its doors.

The United Church has at times had a quasi-establishment character in the minds of some, though never entirely fulfilling the vision of its founders of becoming Canada's national church. Efforts to influence national politics and to shape the making of legislation along the lines of its own social agenda have never been very successful. To be sure, its reputation has been of a church in the forefront of advocacy for social change, consideration of the lot of the poor, and solidarity with the outcasts and marginalized. The United Church has opposed unjust social structures, globally and domestically, that favour those in power and exclude those without. Yet it is a denomination – perhaps even more than the Roman Catholic and the Anglican churches which also share such tendencies – whose members and congregations range from conservative to liberal, both sociologically and theologically. There are United Church congregations, mostly in large cities, whose members are so broad-minded in their theological and social views as to be indistinguishable from Unitarians. Their position on same-sex marriage or with respect to traditional Christian doctrine is progressive (see Vosper 2008). In many respects, some United Church congregations could readily be included alongside other examples of "Liberal Religion" (see chap. 6). At the same time, however, many other United churches remain conservative in outlook and theology, continuing the old-fashioned values that have prevailed in their communities for decades and going back to Presbyterian or Methodist roots. Their members uphold traditional views of marriage and the family, especially in regard to matters of sexual conduct, with positions on biblical authority and personal salvation more in keeping with evangelical Protestants. The interim minister at Queen Street United Church in 2004, Stephen McAlister, confirmed this: "There is a part within our

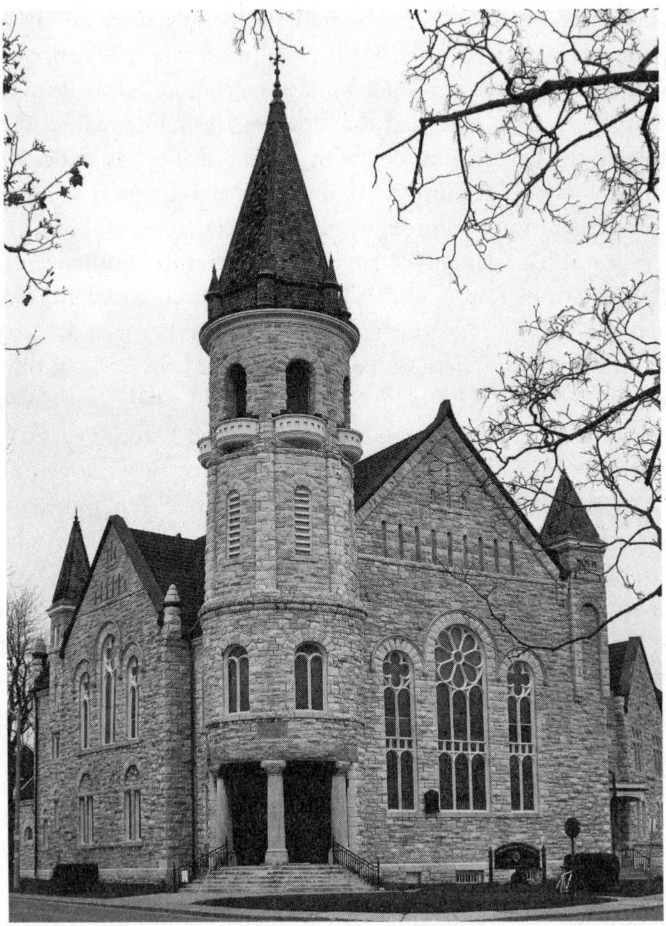

Chalmers United Church

church who have absolutely made it their mission to adhere to the twenty articles of faith [comprising the Basis of Union] that were written in the formation of the United Church in 1925 and their solid platform is they believe in family values. Family values, which means they have zero to do with anything that has the word homosexual in it" (interview, 5 February 2004).

Brian Yealland, part-time minister at Zion United Church, housed in a seniors' residence on the near north side of Kingston, spoke of his experience of declaring his support of gays and lesbians in a sermon: "Now that's probably the sermon that I have preached that was most controversial within Zion. Because although folks are very tolerant, quite open-minded and liberal-minded on all kinds of issues, that one does catch all kinds of people as a tough issue. So I would say maybe half the people were solidly with me and the other half were solidly against me" (interview, 6 February 2004). At about the same time, Mark Flemming, serving at Edith Rankin United Church in the west end, said that that congregation, like many others, dealt with change in the United Church "with a great deal of resistance." He commented that the people at Edith Rankin were "still reliving 'The Issue'" – that is, of sexual orientation and ordination – "but they're not talking about it as much as they did ten years ago." He predicted that in another ten to fifteen years "it's going to be non-news." When he tried to discuss with the congregation their position on marrying gays and lesbians they asked, "Do we have to talk about this?" (interview, 27 February 2004). Jean Barkley, the minister at St Andrew's by-the-Lake United Church in Reddendale in the west end of Kingston, summed up the character of the United Church of Canada this way: "People are in this denomination for lots of reasons. But certainly folks who want to be in a mainline Christian tradition but lean a little to the left, are going to be – there's nowhere else to be." She laughed. "As far as I'm concerned, there's nowhere else to be. The next step for me would be Unitarian and I think theologically there would be some difficulties there … In a sense the United Church's history and theological development [parallel] the Canadian story in a mainline kind of way" (interview, 26 February 2004).

The United Church's Statement of Faith from 1940 spoke of Jesus Christ in evangelical terms as "taking, at measureless cost, man's sin upon Himself," and of the cross as revealing "God's abhorrence of sin." Of the Bible the same statement says: "We believe that, while God uttered His Word to man in many portions progressively, the whole is sufficient to declare His mind and will for our salvation. To Israel He made Himself known as a holy and righteous God and a Savior; the fullness of truth and grace came by Jesus Christ" (United Church a). A new faith statement published in 2006 is presented as "A Song of Faith" that begins and ends by speaking of God as "Holy Mystery." There is nothing of personal salvation here, and sin is understood primarily in terms of a broken world and social injustice rather than individual misdeeds or an unredeemed nature that separate the individual from God. The Bible is now regarded as "a faithful witness to the One and Triune God, the Holy Mystery that is Wholly Love" (United Church b). As an appendix to the "Song of Faith" document explains, naming God in this way "throws into question any human claims to absolute truth." The United Church website, again in one of the appendices about the 2006 Statement of Faith, maintains that the distinctiveness of the United Church resides in "its approach to the interpretation of scripture, its affection for the concept of inclusivity, and its passion for social justice."

In its breadth and in the use of democratic procedures at all levels of decision-making, the United Church of Canada has the reputation of being a church that listens to its people, keeps up with social trends, and lacks the top-down structures of authority that mark the Roman Catholic Church. Ron Graham, in *God's Dominion*, his insightful if journalistic exploration of religion in Canada of a few decades ago, has written that "the United Church is the most Canadian of churches, and like Canada, its strengths may be the same as its weaknesses: diversity, tolerance, compromise, humility, practicality, and niceness." He continues: "Truth gets written by committee, mystery gets lost in the negotiation, decency gets translated into dullness, and the spirit gets hamstrung by the bureaucracy" (1990, 222). This characterization, in a chapter about the United Church's decision of the late 1980s that sexual orientation is not a barrier for ordained ministry, mostly deals with the church's process of decision-making. While presenting itself as a thoroughly democratic church, it appears in its organization and decision-making to be excessively bureaucratic. Gretta Vosper, a United Church minister who founded the Canadian Centre for Progressive Christianity, recalls that at the 2005 meeting of the Toronto Conference of the United Church, someone pointed out that "the conference had done nothing at their annual meeting that would have been the result of a Christian set of principles or values at all." Far from taking any stands on issues of social justice, government actions, or ethical issues, says Vosper, "this particular meeting had focused almost exclusively on administrative matters" (2008, 98).

The diversity of the United Church became obvious in the aftermath of its position on sexual orientation and ordained ministry in the late 1980s, an issue that for many raised questions about the authority of the Bible within the United Church. On the one hand (see chap. 6), a congregation such as Kingston's Sydenham Street United Church decided in the late 1990s to becoming an "affirming congregation." As the Affirm United website states, "Each United Church organization that is an Affirming Ministry declares itself to be fully inclusive of people of all sexual orientations and gender identities – and they back up their words with action." Yet in two other United Church congregations at Harrowsmith and Verona, within thirty minutes drive north of Kingston, petitions were signed "by a large majority" that rejected the recommendations of the 1988 report, *Toward a Christian Understanding of Sexual Orientation, Lifestyles and Ministry*. John Young, minister of these congregations at that time, writes that "the sense of alienation from decision-making felt by many people in the church raises questions both about our structures and about the processes our denomination uses to make decisions" (Young 1990, 143). Frequently grassroots members in rural pastoral charges feel that they are shut out of their church's legislative processes and committees.

The United Church has been known as a church that sticks its neck out, that sometimes takes risks – and makes mistakes – and that frequently has been in the advance guard on social issues. Sometimes subsequent history shows its positions to have been unfortunate or misguided. In the booklet *Unlock the Doors*, published by the United Church's Board of Evangelism and Social Service in the early 1960s, one chapter, "The Nasty Old Man," describes a scenario in which a pedophile is avoided by the other members of his church. The author, A. Phillips Silcox, decries this shunning but at the same time minimizes the sex offender's actions: "Indecent his conduct may have been, but of very little harm to the girls" because he only "fondled them gently" after offering them candy. His conduct, Silcox reiterates, did "very little real harm to the girls," one of whom "hadn't even bothered to tell her mother about it" (Silcox n.d., 36). He feels that the children would have forgotten the incident except for "the fuss and bother which mother and police made about it" (37). Drawing upon the legal and psychological wisdom of the day, this United Church report observes that "there have been times when the person accused of a sex offense has been more sinned against than sinning, when inflamed imagination has prevailed over sober observation" (39). Fifty years later attitudes have changed dramatically. The damage to victims of childhood sexual abuse has become widely recognized in cases such as this. Churches and popular media, as well as experts, now recognize the severity and longevity of the effects.

Of course, then and now the United Church may be said to be simply "following culture," hitching its wagon to whatever trends prevail at the time, observing the proclamations of the wisdom of the day. This kind of criticism has been made of the United Church by Reginald Bibby (1987), Ron Graham (1990), and Peter C. Emberley (2002). Bibby, having referred to gender-neutral references to God and to the ordination of gays and lesbians, cautions that religion may become "nothing more than culture in sanctimonious clothing." He sums up: "When religion becomes so wedded to culture, it finds that its authority is further eroded" (254). Graham says that the United Church's way of doing things does "not strike me as much of a rock upon which to build a church" (223). When United Church moderator Bill Phipps ignited controversy in 1997 with comments that Jesus Christ was not God – not divine – Emberley referred to Phipps's Christology as Arian, recommending that "his United Church detractors might want to consider shifting their devotion to the Church of England or Roman Catholicism" (107).

Other specific aspects of the United Church of Canada in its Kingston embodiments are to be found elsewhere in this book. The burdens of owning and maintaining an historic and underused building with a dwindling congregation in the downtown are dealt with in the initial section of chapter 6 using a United Church example ("To Rent or to Own"). The role of women in ordained ministry is considered, in part using the instance of United Church minister Nadene Grieve-Deslippe, in chapter 8. With the consideration of positions on same-sex marriage among liberal religious groups – Quakers, Reform Jews, and Unitarians – again in chapter 6, the United Church is offered alongside as a parallel example. In effect, the number and diversity of United Church congregations in Kingston, and the prominence of the denomination locally and nationally, provide many bases for comparison and reference within this study.

ANGLICANS

The eleven Anglican churches in the city are identical in polity and governance, similar in liturgy, and not greatly different in theological outlook. Distinctions within the Anglican Church have historically been made, especially in England, on the basis of low or high church, or evangelical or Anglo-Catholic. Sometimes within the Church of England the "high church" identification stressed an affinity with Roman Catholicism, emphasizing the preservation of the church's distance from Reformation Protestantism. In matters of ecclesiology, its episcopal ordination, and in liturgy, its sacramentalism, were regarded as crucial. The Church of England's status as an established church and the preservation of differences between clergy and laity were other continuing emphases. In Canada – though, as we have seen, some Anglican churches continue to cherish their historic roles in civic affairs – many of these issues are muted. Nonetheless, the high or low church distinction is employed in a general way as a convenient means of characterization, or when disputes arise – for example, about issues such as the ordination of women or same-sex relationships. Then traditionalists sometimes maintain a position closer to that of the Roman Catholic Church, even arguing that to alter the historical Anglican stance would be to hinder possible reunion with Rome. Of course, these distinctions are at best inexact, as we shall see. When Anglican clergy in Kingston identified themselves or their congregation as somewhere in between the high and low church positions, occupying a middle ground, they might have invoked the term "broad church," though none of them actually used that phrase.

In 2004 we interviewed Bill Clarke, then incumbent at St Luke's Anglican Church, a red brick building situated a block north of Princess Street, not far from the centre of downtown Kingston. He said that the local Anglican clergy, in discussions among themselves, acknowledge that "there are probably too many churches, Anglican Churches, in the city of Kingston to serve the numbers that we have." Clarke contrasted the difficulties of being a downtown Anglican church like St Luke's, Church of the Redeemer, the Good Shepherd, St Paul's, St John's, or St George's Cathedral, with those congregations that were "doing well" in the west part of the city, St Peter's and Christ Church in particular. "Downtown," Clarke said, "it's a struggle." He also referred to the lack of differentiation in Kingston's Anglican churches: "We offer virtually the same services. There is very little difference. We're all pretty much middle-of-the-road churches. There's no one that's really hard-core low evangelical church; there's really no one who's high church. We're all sort of in the middle, serving virtually the same thing every Sunday. Surprisingly, that works for Tim Hortons. They have fourteen stores in this city – same coffee, same donuts, packed every day. We have twelve Anglican Churches – same community, same services, virtually the same theologically – and it's not working, which is kind of funny, scary. A lot of it is, to a degree, sort of about busyness. It takes a lot of time and energy to just do the parish, never mind extra" (interview, 17 March 2004).

At about the same time, Wayne Varley, then priest at St Mark's Anglican Church, a traditional 1840s Gothic structure located to the east in Barriefield, was asked to characterize St Mark's on the spectrum ranging between "high" and "low" Anglican. Varley thought that that was a difficult task but said, "I would see us, for want of a better term, as a mainstream Anglican Church congregation. We are very sacramental, by at which at the very least, every Sunday is a celebration of the Eucharist." At St Mark's there is also "the reading, teaching, and understanding of scripture, both within Sunday service and in terms of neighbourhood Bible study, Sunday school programs, and the like." Given that, and the congregation's use of the hymnbook *Common Praise* and the Book of Alternative Services as the "two centrepieces of our liturgy," Varley concluded, "I would say therefore that we are mainstream and, in terms of the so-called high or Anglo-Catholic, or low or evangelical, we are a wonderful blend of the two." At that time, when Grace United Church was using space at St Mark's for their Sunday morning service at 9, Varley wondered whether St Mark's was "shifting, sometimes not without grumbling from a few, from being an Anglican parish church and centre, to being more of a community-orientated place." With the shrinking population base of Anglicans, and so many resources "involved in keeping things going," to the extent that "we are choking on our structure," Varley looked to "new and creative ways of relating to other churches" as the way to go (15 January 2004).

Meanwhile, at St James' Anglican Church on the edge of the Queen's University campus, Rev. Bob Hales, now retired, said he did not know how to position St James'. "Anglican is as broad as you want it to be," he said. Describing himself as coming "from a very liberal school of thought," he recalled that after his arrival at St James' he realized "that it is far more conservative Protestant than I expected." Considering the influence of such predecessors as Desmond Hunt and Robert Brow, both prominent Anglican evangelicals having connections with the Inter-Varsity Christian Fellowship, perhaps Hales should not have been surprised. Queen's University sociologist David Lyon in his congregational history locates St James' from its beginnings in the 1840s within the evangelical stream of the Anglican Church (1995). Hales also relates that when he got to know the people in the congregation, he discovered "there are all sorts of theological thoughts here" ranging from very liberal to very conservative. In short, Hales reflected, "there's everything here ... I would have traditionalists call it evangelical and liberals see it as somewhat conservative, but we would probably be more liberal in the last twenty years." He repeated, "I don't know how to position us, to be honest with you." Hales felt that part of his role as priest at St James' was to "encourage the broadest spectrum as possible because you can grow from one another" (29 June 2004).

St James' has a ministry to Queen's students, extending back for many years, and continuing the earlier connections with the evangelical Inter-Varsity Christian Fellowship. Being a chaplain to Queen's students and to high-school students is the particular role of Val Michaelson, an ordained part-time youth minister at St James'. If St James' has university links, however, both St Mark's in Barriefield and St Paul's downtown on Queen Street have military connections. St Mark's, begun in 1843, originally served the families of men working at the naval dockyard at Point Frederick, now the site of the Royal Military College. Military families from the nearby Canadian Forces Base Kingston still attend St Mark's, and some of their children go to the Sunday School. St Paul's was built in 1845 "by army personnel" with money raised by the army. It is located just across Montreal Street from the Kingston Armouries, home of the Princess of Wales' Own Regiment and site of a military museum. St Paul's continues today as the "Regimental Church." The rector at St Paul's, David Ward – who retired in 2009 – described it as "our only inner-city church in the diocese," located "on the north side of the social barrier in Kingston." When Ward mentioned another division, this one "a divide in Kingston between mainline churches and evangelical churches," he was asked where St Paul's is positioned in relation to that divide. Without characterizing the congregation – though later he was to say that "most of the people in this church" opposed the blessing of same-sex marriages – he replied that he is part of a clergy fellowship consisting primarily of "ministers from evangelical and charismatic churches."

When a research assistant of Anglican background began the interview (2 September 2005) with the rector at St John's Anglican Church in Portsmouth, she referred to him as "Father Doering." Chris Doering asked to be called by his first name and said that most of the recent rectors at St John's had preferred that, explaining, "I think St John's in its history has always been a low Anglican church parish." Later he referred to St John's as "low evangelical," built to serve the families who worked at the shipyard and prison in Portsmouth, formerly a waterfront village west along King Street and still the site of Kingston Penitentiary and the Olympic Harbour. Doering thought that in even earlier days the rectors at St John's were customarily called "Mister" rather than by ecclesiastical titles, perhaps a reflection of the congregation's working-class origins. Of course, sometimes the use of titles depends as much on the individual priest in charge as on the character of the congregation, whether evangelical or Anglo-Catholic. Whereas Wayne Varley had told us that St Mark's in Barriefield was a blend of high and low, his successor was designated on the website of the Ontario diocese as "Major (Ret'd) the Rev. Canon E.T. Reynolds, CD, KTJ," and signed himself "Father Eric." Reynolds' military, ecclesiastical, and educational backgrounds, as former senior chaplain of the Royal Military College and invested into the Sovereign Military Order of Jerusalem, or "Knights Templar," would probably incline him more to the use of titles. His impressive list of degrees, provided with his profile on the diocesan website, include BA (Hons), University of Waterloo; MA, Laval University; B.Th., Laval University; JCB, St Paul University; BCL, University of Ottawa; JCL, St Paul University; MCL, University of Ottawa; and D.Min. candidate, St Paul University (Diocese of Ontario).

Chris Doering, who has a Queen's University bachelor's degree in English and history and a degree in education, did one year of theological studies at Queen's Theological College before finishing his M.Div. studies at Wycliffe College at the University of Toronto. "I went to an evangelical Anglican college in Toronto and many of us debated if we'd be called 'Father.' And it's just not something that I personally choose to be called," he says. Still, while the degree of formality does differ according to the priest's preferences, it might also depend on the parish setting. At the more sacramental Christ Church on Sydenham Road, where the current rector, Blair Peever, is a 2002 Wycliffe College graduate, he is introduced on the website as "Father Blair." His predecessor had a military background. Whereas Eric Reynolds' photo on the St Mark's website showed him standing in the church, arms outstretched, fully robed, and wearing a stole, Doering said that at St John's he wears his stole but no robe at the more contemporary service at 9:15 on Sunday mornings. Doering's previous appointment was at St George's

Cathedral, where he learned to "understand the importance of liturgy being done well to honour God." He summed up: "I believe, as Jesus teaches, it is what's in the heart that matters, not the externals. I believe that the externals of Anglicanism serve us well when they match what is in the heart. When they are not matching what is in our heart then they become an idol that we worship." Even if the congregation at St John's, because of its low-church evangelical character, is "not big into the ritual, not big into the flair," they are "big into outreach" (interview, 2 September 2005).

At Christ Church on Sydenham Road the rector, Edward Dallow, said: "To the best of my knowledge we have fourteen different denominations represented in this parish. So, although we do things in the Anglican way for the most part, there are fourteen different [denominations]. My own wife is Dutch Reformed, my daughter-in-law is Roman Catholic, her children are Roman Catholic, my son who just moved here with his family – his wife is United Church, my son is an Anglican, and their little six-and-a-half year old goes to a Roman Catholic school" (interview, 14 May 2004). Chris Doering reported that denominationalism, at least as evident from his vantage point at St John's, was decreasing: "We have a group of people here who couldn't tell you what it means to be Anglican." These people, which he estimated as the majority of the congregation, "were not Anglicans before" but had come there because the church meets their spiritual needs. Doering said, "I'd rather have them tell what it means to be Christian and deal with the Anglican stuff later." He further described the diversity of the congregation: "And because of my predecessor's [Terry McNear's] personal style and spirituality, there is a group of people here who are charismatic. So they are big into the working of the Holy Spirit – speaking in tongues, prophetic utterances, all that sort of stuff. Even though I had no experience with that when I came here, I was open to it because I try not to limit what the Holy Spirit can do. I was definitely uncomfortable with it. My comfort level has increased greatly. We see that not so much on a Sunday morning, but on Wednesday night service here, people do pray in tongues, sing in tongues – I've heard all that sort of stuff. So we are very diverse in that way" (interview, 2 September 2005).

Though Bill Clarke at St Luke's made a case for the uniformity of worship among Anglican churches in Kingston – he likened churches in the diocese to branches of Tim Hortons – variations do exist. Because the bishop appoints the priest to a parish church in the Anglican Church, the congregation has less say than in other Protestant churches who usually "call" their own minister, even though that call normally must be ratified. Bob Hales, then at St James', described the appointment process: "In the Anglican church the bishop appoints. He just doesn't say 'You're going there.' He first of all would say, 'Are you interested to be put there?' And I'd say, 'I'm interested.' And then I get interviewed by a group of people from the church, and they say to the bishop, 'Do you think this guy can be our priest or not?' And the bishop says, 'Yes.' And if he is still prepared to appoint you, and you are prepared to go, then you are appointed" (29 June 2004). If the parish committee should refuse the priest named by the bishop, then the bishop would offer another candidate. This process would continue until the parish agreed with the bishop's selection. This method of assigning clergy, somewhat more hierarchal than a call to an individual issued by a congregation, may provide some protection against a parish church assuming a particular character – by becoming too strongly evangelical, for instance. At the same time it means that a parish cannot have a priest "imposed" on them by the bishop as the process seeks a balance between the wishes of the parish and the candidates proposed by the bishop.

Consider, in this regard, the apparent differences occurring within St Mark's and at St John's with their respective succession of rectors. The Anglican order of worship is set, either in the older Book of Common Prayer, or BCP, or in the newer, inclusive-language Book of Alternative Services, or BAS. Though the Book of Alternative Services sparked a debate within Anglicanism between traditionalists – or "Prayer-Book Anglicans" – and modernists, it and the weekly Eucharist have become the norm at the major worship service in most Anglican churches since the BAS's introduction in 1985. Wayne Varley noted that at St Mark's the Eucharist is celebrated at their only service every Sunday, where the Book of Alternative Services is used: "We are very sacramental ... There are no services of Morning Prayer and things like that." Morning Prayer, with less frequent communion, was the staple of the Book of Common Prayer. On the other hand, at St John's there are three services of worship on Sunday morning, at 8, 9:15, and 11. At 8 and at 11, the Book of Common Prayer is used; at 9:15 a contemporary worship service is provided at which no books are used and everything is projected on a screen. Doering remarks, "We are the only church that has a full contemporary worship on Sunday morning, and I think we are the only church that still offers the Book of Common Prayer at a main service at 11. [In] most Anglican churches in this diocese, the Book of Common Prayer, which is the older book, is at 8." Even given the restrictions in choosing between the Book of Common Prayer and the Book of Alternative Services, as Bob Hales of St James' commented, "There are lots of ways of doing fixed liturgies."

When we interviewed Michael Oulton, he was the rector at St Peter's Anglican Church on the Bath Road along the water heading west toward Picton. Oulton came from Atlantic Canada and is married to a United Church minister. He has, therefore, an outsider's view of the character of the

Ontario Diocese of the Anglican Church of Canada, and of ecumenicity as practised in Kingston. Asked whether St Peter's was low or high church, he said, "I think this church very much mirrors this diocese. I think this diocese was formed out of – more out of – the evangelical tradition in the Anglican church so you'd call it more of a low-church style of worship that stresses proclamation, and stresses community service, stresses very strong influence on biblical teaching and those sorts of things." In that assessment Oulton was anticipating the impression we would gather in later interviews with other Anglican clergy. He went on to say that this Anglican evangelicalism was "one of the things that I had to grapple with when I came here from one of the dioceses in Nova Scotia – I tend to come from a more Catholic background within the church." As did other rectors, he affirmed his conviction that "the diversity of the church is what makes it strong." Given that, and despite his own background, he felt – perhaps like Doering adapting to people speaking in tongues at St John's – that it was up to him to adjust: "So, I had to join them, and we worked together on particular things. And, there are some things that we do that I smile at – and swallow – and do because I know it's important for a number of people. We have at our Sunday services Morning Prayer, and I have to smile – a lot – when I'm doing that service because to me a eucharistic-centred worship is critically important" (23 October 2003).

Despite Bill Clarke's metaphor of Kingston's Anglican churches "serving virtually the same thing every Sunday" like Tim Hortons, there clearly are differences from one parish to another. As Bob Hales noted, there are differing ways of doing fixed liturgies. Yet, nonetheless, the common liturgies, whether Morning Prayer from the Book of Common Prayer or the Eucharist from the Book of Alternative Services, are standard, and provide a pattern, leaving little room for an individual cleric to innovate or to change the accustomed manner of worship. That fact makes it possible for a sacramental rector like Oulton to function in a low-church setting such as St Peter's, and for a congregation to accept a new incumbent without much adaptation. The Anglican Church seems able to contain the vast differences represented in the parishes and their clergy. In the United Church, by way of contrast, the idiosyncrasies of a particular minister can be much more damaging because the Ministry of the Word – preaching – is more central, and because the liturgy can be altered to a larger degree. The theological stance of the minister and the interpretation placed on biblical texts can be highly influential. If what Oulton called "biblical teaching and those sorts of things" are at the fore, as they are at First Baptist Church, then deciding what the Bible says on particular points can be very divisive, as it was at First Baptist (see below in this chapter).

Perhaps too the more hierarchical style of the Anglican Church leaves less for individual clergy to do in decision-making on a grand scale. Oulton gave an example of some people at St Peter's who were painting woodwork in the church "and they were fretting about all of the discussion around same-sex marriage and ... what's going to happen to the church. Are we going to go into schism?" (In 2003 the Archbishop of Canterbury had established the Eames Commission to examine ways of preventing a split in the Anglican Communion after the appointment in the United States of an openly gay bishop and the blessing of same-sex unions in the Canadian Diocese of New Westminster.) Oulton's response to the group's worries was: "I don't know. All I know is that you're painting that baseboard and I've got an appointment in a little while." But he continued: "Because the other thing that I believe is if you pick up a paintbrush, or you do whatever you're doing because of your love of God, that Jesus means something to you and you're doing that, [then] that is your gift, your offering." With a kind of reversal of the usual contemporary maxim, his advice was, "Don't sweat the big stuff because there's bigger powers at work here than us." For him, a focus on the immediate tasks meant being able to relax in some trust that God could unite all of these tasks in some larger purpose. As he phrased it, "Accept the fact that all I'm supposed to do is to paint that baseboard today, or do this appointment, or see the next person that I have to see this afternoon, and because I'm doing it in the name of Christ, which is the most important thing to do" (23 October 2003).

In many of the interviews conducted at Anglican churches in Kingston from 2003 to 2005, two themes recurred: abuse at Indian Residential Schools and same-sex marriage. Regarding the first matter, the website of the Anglican Church of Canada outlines the church's efforts to achieve reconciliation and healing for First Nations peoples as a response to the injustices that occurred at the twenty-six schools the church administered between 1820 and 1969. The 2007 Indian Residential Schools Settlement Agreement amended the 2003 version of the agreement reached by the Anglican Church; it was that earlier agreement that figured in our interviews. The original commitment of the Anglican Church of Canada of $26 million was reduced in 2007 to $16 million, and the contribution of the Ontario Diocese from $1.1 million to $667,000. But in 2004 the Anglican churches in Kingston were struggling to raise the money toward their share of the settlement fund. St Mark's, with 120 families on the roll and a weekly attendance of seventy to eighty people, was initially committed to raising $4,200 in each of five years. St Luke's was expected to raise $28,000 over the five-year period.

The second issue, that of same-sex relationships, began to affect the Anglican Church in the 1970s, and will probably continue to do so for some years. In many ways Canadian Anglicans find themselves in an in-between position. Unlike the Roman Catholic Church, another worldwide church, the Anglican Church has no centralized authority such as the Vatican whose directives are binding upon churches in all of the different countries where the denomination is found. The Archbishop of Canterbury is not an Anglican pope. Because the thirty-eight provinces of the Anglican Communion are autonomous, each with its own primate – that is, bishop or archbishop – the Archbishop of Canterbury can, at best, offer spiritual leadership through the implement of persuasion. Unlike, say, the United Church of Canada, the Anglican Church of Canada is not simply a national church, and therefore must consider how its decisions affect churches in other countries that are also part of the international Anglican Communion. The greatest growth of the Anglican Communion has been taking place in African countries where the churches are quite conservative. A decision by the Anglican Church of Canada to allow their priests to bless same-sex unions could lead to a split in the worldwide communion. As Ron Graham summarized the matter in 1990, "The Anglican leadership does not revel in going to the barricade as the United Church moderators appear to, nor does it share the Catholics' style of coming down on the flock like a ton of rocks. It lets the United Church take the heat on the left for being the avant-garde of social and political transformation; it lets the Roman Catholics take the heat on the right for being the rearguard of authority and tradition; and, when the heat dies down, it comes down the middle looking composed and conciliatory" (225).

In other ways, however, Anglicans still find themselves in this sometimes difficult middle position two decades later. Some would want to have their clergy officiate at same-sex marriages. Others want to preserve the traditional understanding of marriage as existing exclusively between a man and woman. The Anglican Church of Canada has declined to solemnize same-sex marriages and instead moved the discussion to the blessing of same-sex "unions," that is, same-sex civil marriages that have occurred outside the church. In using the nomenclature of "union," the Anglican Church might seem to avoid the issue of whether the term "marriage" should be reserved for the relationship between a man and a woman. However, the consequence, frequently, is to offend both those who are more liberal and who believe that the term "union" relegates committed gay and lesbian relationships to some second-class status and those conservatives who are affronted by their church giving any kind of recognition to relationships they regard as sinful. Liberal Anglicans might be suspected by some of an incremental strategy whereby same-sex unions are a first step toward same-sex marriages.

What does it mean for an Anglican priest to "bless" a relationship or union? Chaplains are sometimes called upon to bless a college football team or the planting of a tree. A report by a task force of the Episcopal Diocese of Vermont, the "Blessing of Persons Living in Same-Gender Relationships," points out that at ordination "priests receive the authority to 'pronounce God's blessing' ... To do so is not to be the agent of blessing, but it is to recognize and name that which already shows forth as a sign of God's grace and presence – or it is to ask for God's grace and presence. Blessing is thus profoundly relational, for it is asking God to be in a relationship of grace with a person or persons. In offering to bless those making a covenant of Holy Union, the church is not blessing a sexual relationship or particular sexual behavior. It is blessing a couple who manifest in their life together the grace of God" (Diocese of Vermont). In parallel fashion, a Canadian Anglican, Rafe Mair, observes, "Neither the church nor its priests bless anything. They ask God to bless – a very different thing indeed. From time immemorial Anglican priests have asked God's blessing on warships and all who sail in them, knowing that given any provocation those ships will kill people" (2008). At St George's Cathedral a service has regularly been held for the Blessing of the Animals, a common Anglican practice held on the feast day of St Francis of Assisi, when people bring their pets to church. As one priest in Arkansas observed, "My gay friends are very sensitive about the notion that we've been blessing animals for years and find it so difficult to bless their relationships" (Episcopal News Service). All of these considerations would seem to minimize what it means for an Anglican priest to bless something, or someone, or a relationship.

The commission reporting to the primate of the Anglican Church in Canada in 2005 understood the "same-sex unions" under consideration to refer to "committed, adult, monogamous, intended lifelong, same-sex relationships which include sexual intimacy." The scriptures, this "St Michael Report" noted, say nothing about that kind of relationship between people of the same sex. Given that strong definition of a committed same-sex relationship, the analogy to marriage becomes apparent: "Any proposed blessing of a same-sex relationship would be analogous to a marriage to such a degree as to require the Church to understand it coherently in relation to the doctrine of marriage." The commission further stated that "blessing" a civil union has the effect of recognizing it as a Christian marriage, or Holy Matrimony (Anglican Church of Canada). With that statement, any softer interpretation of blessing unions was swept aside.

The mandate of the commission was to determine whether blessing same-sex unions was a matter of doctrine. They said it was a matter of doctrine, but not a matter of "core doctrine" such as could split the church – that is, that no one could remain an Anglican without affirming support of same-sex marriages. Perhaps anticipating the objection that blessing same-sex unions would follow a cultural trend accepting gay and lesbian relationships, the commission observed that "the challenge facing the church is to see our cultural norms through the eyes of Christ and then, out of allegiance to him, to promote those norms that honour him and renounce those that do not." The church in the course of its history had changed its mind, the commission noted, about things that it once had sanctioned – slavery, civil rights, and the cultural assimilation of aboriginal peoples.

The General Synod, meeting in June 2007, approved the findings of the commission's St Michael Report that blessing same-sex unions was a doctrinal matter. It then addressed a motion that would have given individual dioceses the authorization to bless same-sex unions. The motion was passed by the clergy and by the laity but defeated by the House of Bishops by a vote of twenty-one to nineteen; for the motion to pass, all three groups would have had to approve it. Probably the bishops were wary of being subject to the same disapproval levelled by Canterbury against the Episcopal Church in the United States after its decision to bless same-sex unions. In seeking to maintain the unity among Anglicans the world over, this result probably deepened the divisions within the Anglican Church of Canada. Because the Anglicans had deferred this discussion from its previous meeting in 2004 while it awaited its commission's report, the result was deeply disappointing to people on both sides of the issue. The matter was taken up once more at the 2010 Synod where it was agreed not to take any legislative action but to continue the discussion.

A "Chronology of the Same-Sex Debate in the Anglican Church of Canada" on the Anglican Journal website presents a confusing welter of movements, task forces, statements, studies, conferences, forums, synods, meetings, commissions, declarations, networks, deferred decisions, reports, agreements, and panels. A digest of all these events boils down to something like this: After the Diocese of New Westminster in British Columbia began to offer same-sex blessings in 2003, four dissenting parishes left the diocese to join the Anglican Coalition in Canada, under the jurisdiction of the Archbishop of Rwanda. By the summer of 2010 the Anglican Coalition in Canada had grown to thirteen parishes, most of them in British Columbia (Anglican Coalition in Canada). After the General Synod in 2007, three more dioceses – Ottawa, Montreal, and Niagara – asked to have their bishops perform same-sex blessings. By 2008 ten churches had decided to leave the Anglican Church of Canada and to join the church of the Southern Cone, an Anglican province that includes six South American countries, and whose primate offered to accept Canadian Anglican churches in dispute with their dioceses or the national church. Some disputes about possession of church buildings were being taken to court to settle questions of ownership when congregations left the Anglican Church of Canada.

Another dissenting group, the Anglican Essentials Canada, wanted to keep the Anglican Church of Canada within the worldwide Anglican Communion by recalling the church to the historic principles of its constitution, the Solemn Declaration of 1893. For this group, as for succeeding movements such as the Anglican Essentials Federation and the Anglican Communion Alliance, same-sex blessings are understood as indicative of a general departure from the Bible and the Anglican tradition (Anglican Essentials Canada). One of these succeeding groups, the Anglican Essentials Federation grew from the earlier Essentials movement, then becoming the Anglican Communion Alliance (Anglican Communion Alliance). Among other flashpoint issues, concerns were expressed about an appointment by the Bishop of Ottawa, one of the dioceses seeking to perform same-sex blessings; a female priest from Massachusetts who had married another woman in a civil ceremony there was made incumbent of an Ottawa parish. On the other side of the same-sex issue stands Integrity Canada, founded in 1975 as "a national network of organizations and friends working toward the full inclusion of gay and lesbian people in the life of the Anglican Church of Canada." In October 2007 Integrity Canada asked the House of Bishops to end its moratorium on same-sex blessings (Integrity Canada).

Same-sex marriages, civil unions and blessings, and the ordination of gays and lesbians have all become, as one Anglican priest told us, part of one large "burning issue." The Anglican Church of Canada has attempted to have what another priest referred to as "a reasonable conversation," and yet this perplexing and divisive matter still remains unresolved after several decades. By contrast, as we shall see below, the conservative turn taken by the Baptist Convention of Ontario and Quebec in its uncompromising stand shut out liberals from any continuing conversation among Baptists. For liberally – or even moderately – inclined Baptists, the possibility of further dialogue seems to have ended, despite the opposing efforts of a group known as the Gathering of Baptists. The Anglicans continue to be caught up in a debate that has local, national, and international reverberations, and that may already have gone on too long. Yet Anglicans have numerous options: to separate and join another province, or, for individuals, to become part of a minority fellowship within the national church or to leave their congregation for another nearby Anglican church perhaps more congenial to them. For Anglicans of whatever views, there are alternatives available within worldwide Anglicanism.

The United Church, however, is assumed to be free of the responsibility for maintaining worldwide connections and inherited traditions because of its being a comparatively young Canadian denomination that originated with the Union of 1925. Even though various denominational pasts were brought into the United Church, there seems to be a greater freedom to settle issues pertaining to gays and lesbians as part of ongoing efforts to address matters of social justice. There are no centuries-old historic positions, of the kind available to Anglicans, to which more traditional members can call the United Church to return – no orthodoxy to recover beyond what might be represented in the somewhat conservative, and recent, 1925 Basis of Union – nor are there international connections that affect the way the United Church of Canada can act. While Christians within the church may have felt the position taken on gays and lesbians to be a betrayal of what the Bible says, the possibility remains for an individual congregation to exercise its own policies as determined by the session.

Perhaps by biding its time, the Anglican Church may yet be able to capitalize on its breadth, its consultative processes, and the ongoing changes taking place in Canadian society about gays and lesbians. A 2006 *Maclean's* magazine poll entitled "What We Believe" points out how in the three decades following 1975 the percentage of Canadians approving of blacks and whites marrying increased from 55 per cent to 94 per cent (*Maclean's*). In the same vein, attributed by Reginald Bibby to a greater sense of compassion, approval of same-sex relationships has increased in Canada from only 28 per cent of Canadians in 1975 to more than two-thirds by 2006. Interestingly, Bibby says that mainline Protestants in Canada share similar views with their counterparts in the United States; so do evangelicals. However, whereas one-third of Americans identify themselves as conservative Protestants or evangelicals, only 8 per cent of Canadians do. That proportion skews acceptance of homosexual relations to the extent that only 38 per cent of Americans are approving.

In Bibby's 2004 study, "Religion and the Same-Sex Debate," he makes a distinction between those who "approve" same-sex marriage and those who "accept" it. He also compares the views of regular participants within faith groups with those who are less active. For instance, 25 per cent of Roman Catholics who attend church at least monthly approve of gay marriages; 55 per cent of Catholics who attend less frequently approve. Among Canadian evangelicals, the approval rates are much lower: 6 per cent of active conservative Protestants agree with gays and lesbians marrying, though among their less active counterparts 35 per cent approve. If one looks more broadly at gay and lesbian relationships – not marriages – they are approved *and* accepted by 8 per cent of active evangelicals. When they were asked if they *accept* such relationships even if they do not *approve* of them, that percentage went up to 17. Among mainline Protestants about 45 per cent approve of same-sex marriages, a figure that remains the same whether they are more or less active (Bibby 2004a).

Several conclusions could be suggested from these statistics. First, among evangelicals the degree of acceptance of gays and lesbians is much lower. The self-definition of the Baptist Convention of Ontario and Quebec – and accordingly that of First Baptist Church in Kingston – as evangelical, expressed in its affiliation with the Evangelical Fellowship of Canada, might account for the negative position taken by Baptists. Further, seeing oneself as evangelical, as some Anglicans and Anglican congregations do, creates a divide even within a supposedly mainline Protestant denomination. Sam Reimer, who contends that there is a common evangelical subculture that spans the Canadian-American border, says that "evangelicals maintain group boundaries through their theological and moral orthodoxy" (2003, 47), the area of family values in particular playing a large role in their strict morality. In interviews with evangelical pastors, Reimer learned that they were much more likely to preach sermons about traditional morality, including topics such as drugs, sex, violence, the media, and family breakdown, than on social-justice issues, politics, or the environment. Citing an American survey among evangelical college students, Reimer points out that the classic moral boundaries formerly employed to define proper Christian behaviour have changed: "Playing pool or cards, dancing, going to movies, smoking, and drinking alcohol are no longer seen as intrinsically wrong by the majority of young evangelicals, unless carried to excess." Despite such changes, the prohibitions against various forms of sexual conduct, especially premarital, extramarital, and homosexual acts, continue to be as strong as ever (89).

A second conclusion might be drawn from the statistic that 45 per cent of mainline Protestants, whatever their level of church attendance, approve of same-sex marriage. While generalized "Protestant," and perhaps puritanical, attitudes about sex undoubtedly linger, parishioners who regularly find themselves in worship services are not being greatly influenced toward even more conservative views by their clergy or co-religionists. Disapproving or non-accepting views toward gays and lesbians may be held by a slight majority of mainline Protestants, but not at a level much different from the rest of Canadians. About one-fifth of Canadians are from the four mainline Protestant denominations. Within those mainline churches, 83 per cent of the people are either United Church or Anglican. In effect, then, the overwhelming majority of mainline Protestants in Canada are from the two denominations that have already been grappling with the debate about same-sex marriage, whether resolution has been reached or not. They have been in denominations where strong dissenting views have been expressed against the overall trend toward acceptance. Whether they are regular or inactive attenders, their views remain identical with the other group. Does that allow one to wonder whether mainline Protestant attitudes have not been much affected in churches rocked by these debates?

A third conclusion is also suggested by statistics from Bibby's Future Families Project (2004b). Roman Catholics, who might be expected to take a conservative view on matters relating to homosexuality, display a surprisingly favourable view toward same-sex marriage. The 55 per cent of inactive Catholics who approve of same-sex marriage is a higher percentage than the 45 per cent of inactive mainline Protestants who approve. That figure is surprising, because here Roman Catholics differ sharply from evangelical Christians with whom they share, for instance, a strong stance against abortion. One might thus conclude that Canadian Catholics, the largest religious group in Canada, are part of the Canadian mainstream in a way that evangelicals are not. Either that, or else Catholics with respect to their thinking about same-sex marriage at least, feel able to take a position contrary to the one taught and promoted by their church at large. Again, perhaps they have become "inactive" Catholics in part because of their disagreement with the church's positions.

PRESBYTERIANS

Between the censuses of 1991 and 2001, the number of Presbyterians in Canada showed a steep decline to just more than 400,000 people, amounting to a minus 35.6 percentage change. By way of comparison, the United Church and Anglican Church each showed a decline in percentage of about 8 per cent. In contrast, Roman Catholics increased by about 5 per cent, and Baptists by a full 10 per cent. Furthermore, the median age of Presbyterians was the highest of all religious groups in the 2001 Census at 46.0 years, about nine years older than the median age of Canadians at large. Anglicans and United Church members are not far behind the Presbyterians at about 46 years, whereas Baptists and Roman Catholics, groups whose percentages are growing, are under 40 years. In the light of these statistics, the conclusion that Presbyterians are dwindling in number and aging as a denomination is inescapable.

Yet many notable Canadians have been Presbyterian, and their church has played a prominent role in Canada's history. Canadian prime ministers Sir John A. Macdonald and W.L. Mackenzie King were both Presbyterians. Canadian fiction written in English during the twentieth century is sometimes said to be characterized by small-town Presbyterianism, beginning with the works of Lucy Maud Montgomery and Ralph Connor and continuing through the novels of Hugh MacLennan, Margaret Laurence, and

Robertson Davies (see Osborne 2004, 5; cf. James 1998, 22–8). Davies went to Sunday School at Presbyterian churches in Renfrew and Kingston, and later attended Kingston's St Andrew's Presbyterian Church. Eventually he left the Presbyterian Church to become an Anglican. His complaint was that, although he admired the Presbyterians' firm theological stance, he disliked their didacticism and strictness and "resented the doctrine of predestination" (Grant 1994, 187–8). His biographer says, "It seemed to him unfair that though you might have been damned before the foundation of the world, you still had to behave like one of the elect on the chance you were predestined for everlasting life" (ibid.). While predestination is frequently maligned and misunderstood, its intention is to emphasize God's sovereignty and absolute supremacy above mere human endeavours and decision-making. When I asked Lincoln Bryant, minister at St Andrew's, about the doctrine and its effect in his life, he replied, "Because of my view of the sovereign nature of God – in fact on Sunday coming up I'm going to be preaching about 'Thy will as it is in Heaven' – I have a strong view that things don't happen by accident. That God is in control of the universe and that that God can be trusted even when we don't understand, even when we're puzzled by it, distressed by what happens. There is that thread that can be followed. So I supposed I would say yes, I was predestined to be a Presbyterian, predestined to be the minister at St Andrew's in Kingston" (Cogeco interview, 16 March 2005).

The Presbyterian Church in Canada is a denomination that continued as Presbyterian after the amalgamation that formed the United Church of Canada in 1925. Two of the founding denominations, Methodist and Congregationalist, entered the United Church en masse on the decision of each of their parent bodies. Presbyterians, on the other hand, put the issue to a vote in each congregation, with about a third of the churches in Canada deciding to continue as Presbyterians. As H.H. Walsh states, "many of the more prosperous Presbyterian congregations had thrown in their lot with the continuing Presbyterian church, while the overwhelming majority of the poorer or mission churches had joined the union" (1956, 303). Because these wealthier congregations that remained as Presbyterian were also larger, about half of the former Presbyterians – that is, 872,428 people – remained in their denomination at the time of the 1931 Census. As the census figures of 2001 reveal, in seventy years the membership of the Presbyterian Church in Canada declined to less than half. In Kingston, Chalmers Presbyterian, having already been joined by First Congregational Church in 1922, voted in favour of Union by a vote of 261 to 47. Cooke's and Zion Presbyterian churches also opted to enter Union. At St Andrew's Presbyterian the members voted 334 to 47 to continue as Presbyterians (Osborne 2004,

329). Though in congregations where the vote was close, one imagines a large departure of members on the losing side that would deplete the church, in Kingston congregations where the nay vote was small, these dissenters – at Chalmers, for instance – could simply have exchanged their seats for those in nearby churches if they wished.

Today Kingston has three congregations belonging to the Presbyterian Church in Canada. The oldest and largest, St Andrew's, at the corner of Clergy and Princess streets, is one of the centrally located churches whose history has been tied up with that of the city from the nineteenth century on. The other two Presbyterian churches were built in the west end around the same time as suburban churches of other denominations were being begun (see chap. 1). Strathcona Park Presbyterian Church, on McMahon Avenue in the area just north of Princess Street and east of Portsmouth Avenue, was dedicated in 1958 (see Cossar 2008; Osborne 2004). St Andrews' contributed several thousand dollars over a number of years to support the new congregation. In 1965 Trinity Presbyterian in Amherstview was built, in the far west end area of the city that saw the establishment of Edith Rankin United and St Peter's Anglican churches at about the same time.

Lincoln Bryant refers to St Andrews' as one of "the three founding churches of Kingston" given a grant of land early in the nineteenth century along with St George's and St Mary's (interview, 31 March 2004; cf. Osborne 2004, chap. 3). Bryant believes these three churches have a "unique spiritual role" and "collective responsibility" in the city, and spoke of how their clergy discussed this mission. He also stated that his church was "instrumental in the founding of the University." Despite his view that "Queen's University explicitly renounced us fifty or so years ago," he affirms that "at a spiritual level there is a connectedness that still exists and that's part of why we pray for Queen's University." In 1841 Queen's College was established in Kingston for the education of Presbyterian clergy and for the more general education of others. Then, in 1912 Queen's Theological College was formally separated from the university, becoming an independent though affiliated college (Roche 1972, 31). This decision, a result of the wish to secularize and nationalize the university, was "characterized by mutual understanding and cooperation between the two parties involved" (Roche 1972, 11). Although this separation formally ended Queen's University's Presbyterian connection, Brian Osborne writes that "the close ties between Queen's and St Andrew's transcended these legalisms and were to survive throughout the balance of the century" (2004, 263). For the congregation of St Andrew's today, a strong sense of their historical ties with the university and Kingston continues.

The responsibility of St Andrew's within the community is demonstrated in various ways, according to Bryant. In 2004 it provided about one

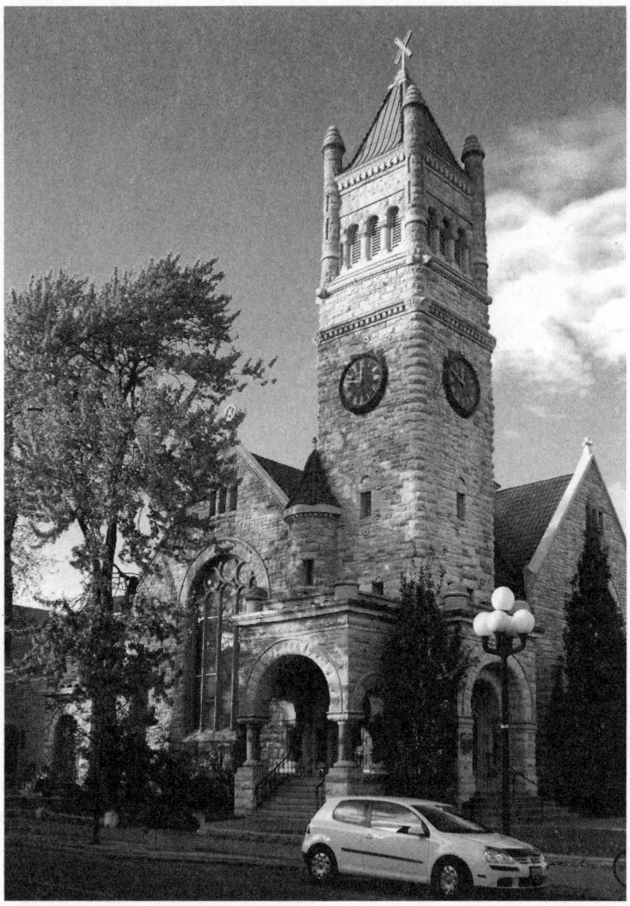

St Andrew's Presbyterian Church

hundred meals a week through its volunteer program that has served dinner on Sunday nights, all on a budget of about $4,000 annually. The church has offered classical music concerts and hosted events during the Buskers Festival in the summer. It also provides parking space and some electricity for a soup truck, operated by a group of churches through the winter months. In part due to its strategic location, across the street from Tim Hortons, St Andrew's attracts sizeable numbers of young people, especially those who are homeless, to its front steps and lawn – as Bryant points out, the only lawn in downtown Princess Street. He feels that those frequenting these areas outside the church represent the outcasts and marginal people toward whom Jesus directed his attention: "Jesus would hang out on our front steps." At the same time, this tolerant and welcoming approach, Bryant laments has led to the church's being "taken advantage of by the professional criminal element in the city, and so we're a major drug trafficking centre and a prostitution centre" (interview, 31 March 2004). The church had to increase exterior lighting and provide their custodian with a sharps container for used needles. It was decided, on legal advice, to empower the local police to "move people along" under the Trespass Act, in particular those known to be involved in criminal activity (see chap. 10 for St Andrew's handling of a related example).

Bryant, as a longstanding minister of a major downtown church, has had to balance his own evangelical leanings with the demands of being in a mainline denomination and having a role in the community. Some Presbyterian churches in Canada have ties with the Evangelical Fellowship of Canada, and some Presbyterian clergy have closer connections with pastors in evangelical congregations than with other clergy in United, Roman Catholic, or Anglican churches. Bryant observed that "there is no such thing as a Kingston Ministerial [Association], which is very unique in Ontario." He went on to mention his own affiliation with "a conservative evangelical group called the Christian Leaders Fellowship that meets for prayer; we have breakfast once a month" (interview, 31 March 2004). He has taken a master's level course on spiritual direction at Toronto's conservative Tyndale Seminary, yet he has also participated in eight-day and forty-day retreats following the Spiritual Exercises of Ignatius of Loyola at the Ignatius Jesuit Centre in Guelph, Ontario (Cogeco interview, 16 March 2005). In effect, his eclectic spirituality has brought him into contact with evangelical Protestants and with Roman Catholic practices.

Summing up the decades since Church Union in 1925, Bryant stated that the Presbyterian Church and United Church, in many respects similar politically and theologically at the outset, "have come apart" to the extent that today they "really have little connection." Presbyterians have moved "a little bit to the right" while the United Church "has moved significantly to the left," he estimated, citing the New Curriculum of the 1960s and the issue of sexual orientation and ministry in the 1980s as factors. While the United Church occupies a broad spectrum, the band occupied by the Presbyterian Church is narrower and more toward the right. Furthermore, Bryant stated, when one surveyed the half-century of service of the past three ministers at St Andrew's, himself included, "the leadership of this church has been on the right end, the conservative end – if you will, the literal end of the theological spectrum." Later on in the interview he mentioned that "what comes up on my radar screen is people leaving the United Church and wanting to come here, people leaving here and maybe moving to Polson Park Free Methodist Church for some reason or other" – perhaps indicative of shifts among

First Baptist Church

Presbyterians toward the evangelical end of the scale. Yet the church's national magazine, the *Presbyterian Record*, reports that "forty ministers from the Presbyterian Church have joined the UCC since 1985, while 10 United Church ministers have become Presbyterian since 1990" (MacLachlan 2008). Those figures may suggest that Presbyterian clergy may be more liberal than their parishioners, or else that they see the larger United Church body as a better place for them to exercise their professional ministries.

BAPTISTS

Baptists are the third-largest Protestant classification in Canada, and the only one among the top eight Protestant groups that did not show a percentage decline between the censuses of 1991 and 2001. The third-largest Baptist church in Kingston, the one closest to the mainline Protestant churches and the lone local affiliate of the relatively moderate Baptist Convention of Ontario and Quebec, is First Baptist Church, located downtown at the corner of Johnson and Sydenham streets. Kingston's other three Baptist churches, all of them more conservatively evangelical, are Bay Park Fellowship Baptist Church, which is a member of the Fellowship of Evangelical Baptist Churches in Canada formed in 1953, and two independent churches, the Bible Baptist Church and the Bath Road Baptist Church. Given the range of churches that refer to themselves as Baptist even within Kingston, and their differing affiliations, one cannot easily picture Baptists as a single, unified denomination. Not all Baptists are in association with one another, and even affiliated congregations differ.

The major distinction made among Ontario's denominational Baptists is whether they are "Convention" Baptists, like First Baptist Church, or "Fellowship" Baptists, like Bay Park Baptist Church. Congregations within the Fellowship of Evangelical Baptist Churches in Canada have a greater degree of autonomy within their denomination and a more conservative statement of faith – including, for example, a belief in the existence of Satan – than those within the Baptist Convention of Ontario and Quebec, sometimes referred to Convention Baptists. That having been said, the First Baptist Church website announces that it belongs "to the mainstream evangelical faith" and includes among its memberships and affiliations the Canadian Council of Churches, the Evangelical Fellowship of Canada, and the Canadian Baptist Ministries. As chapter 3, on evangelical churches in Kingston, indicates, a number of issues that might seem minor to an outsider's eye frequently are highly significant in a church's own self-definition. Even the meaning of the term "evangelical" is subject to a variety of interpretations. The current minister at First Baptist, Kevin Smith, understands "mainstream evangelical" as a designation typifying evangelical churches that accept women in roles of leadership. In a letter to CBC Radio's *Cross Country Checkup* Smith writes: "I switched denominations twenty years ago to the Canadian Baptist family because my views solidified in favour of women in ministry" (19 February 2006).

The question of what defines a Baptist is also somewhat complicated. In general, Baptists practise believer's baptism, performed with very few exceptions by total immersion. Smith has served on the Baptist Distinctives and Polity Advisory Team of the Baptist Convention of Ontario and Quebec (BCOQ). Notably, the first among the "Baptist Distinctives" listed on the First Baptist website is "Believer's Baptism by Immersion" (First Baptist Church a). The statement specifying that "the qualification for baptism is not a matter of age but of faith" indicates that spiritual regeneration precedes baptism. While infant baptism by sprinkling water over the baby is usual in most Catholic and mainline Protestant churches, in the Baptist Church infants and children clearly cannot be baptized because the candidate for baptism must "be old enough to understand the decision of faith in Christ and must have made that decision before he or she is baptized."

Though total immersion is the norm, exceptions can be made for someone with a "physical handicap, under the direction of a doctor." The youth pastor at First Baptist, Josh Mutter, said that candidates for baptism are taught in a course "why we believe that we baptize by immersion only – we won't sprinkle, we won't pour." Then he recalled an exception: "Well, we might pour in a certain instance where somebody is unable to be baptized by immersion; we took a Gatorade bucket and poured it over a guy in a wheelchair this summer because immersion just wasn't possible" (interview, 24 November 2006). Even the manner in which the exception is phrased here suggests that full immersion is a crucial symbolic act and the norm for this sacrament. This particular "Baptist distinctive" is not necessarily unique among evangelical churches, however, because it is practised by the Pentecostal, Christian and Missionary Alliance, and Free Methodist churches considered in chapter 3.

Baptists hold strongly to the ideal of congregational autonomy, so that no other church or denominational organization can claim authority over a particular local church. This standard of freedom is upheld in a number of areas, such as the separation of church and state. As applied to individual believers, spiritual freedom means that all are regarded as competent to interpret the Bible for themselves. For Baptists, statements of faith are always subordinated to the authority of scripture. As Kevin Smith's presentation of the Baptist Distinctives explains, "Although Baptists have repeatedly followed other groups in summarizing their convictions in 'confessing the faith' for apologetic and instructive uses, these have been seen as valid and helpful only to the extent that they succinctly reflect scriptural teaching." Smith, in an interview, stressed that First Baptist Church in Kingston "is quite a diverse congregation, so you have people reflecting a lot of diversity of points of view"; it is "a church that likes to think out loud and likes to think things through," he says (interview, 15 January 2004).

The website for First Baptist includes "A Short History of First Baptist Church at Kingston, Ontario, 1840–2002" (First Baptist Church b). Drawing on various sources, and with assistance from others, this account was largely prepared by George Rawlyk before his death in 1995 and then edited and updated by David McLay, an active Baptist layman and long-time physics professor at Queen's University. A postscript to the church's history mentions the diversity of First Baptist, partly attributed to the lack of other nearby Convention Baptist churches, and also to Kingston being "the site of three post-secondary institutions of learning, a number of federal prisons and several branch plants of well-known transnational companies." These factors contribute to the range of "cultural, economic, linguistic, racial and theological" representation within the congregation. The postscript concludes: "Diversity concerning the authority of scripture was a factor in the crises of 1966 and 1993. This has become clear to the congregation as a whole." In addition to these factors contributing to the variety within this congregation, the Baptist principle of individual competency, according to which each person has the right "to deal directly with God through Jesus Christ" and whereby "each person by faith, becomes his/her own priest before God," may result in differences in the interpretation of scripture. Such differences cannot always be settled by referring to a doctrinal or credal statement.

First Baptist Church may readily be included among Kingston's other mainline Christian churches having roots in the nineteenth century. Comparable to such neighbouring churches as St Mary's Roman Catholic Cathedral, St George's Anglican Cathedral, the formerly Presbyterian Chalmers United and the formerly Methodist Sydenham Street United churches, and St Andrew's Presbyterian Church, First Baptist stands as a flagship church of the BCOQ and the oldest representation of Baptists in Kingston – though perhaps the use of terminology that suggests the precedence of one church over others is un-Baptist. Like the others, it is housed in a limestone structure which, while perhaps less monumental than some, is nonetheless impressive, architecturally significant, and strategically located. Notable Kingstonians such as the Calvins of Garden Island, nineteenth-century shipbuilders and timber dealers, were counted among its congregants. The family of Olive Diefenbaker, second wife of Canada's thirteenth Prime Minister, were members. Syl Apps, famed hockey player with the Toronto Maple Leafs, and later an MPP, was active in First Baptist Church for many years. Queen's University faculty members continue to be among the members, including David Bonham, who has been chair of the congregation and a vice-principal at Queen's. The noted Canadian historian of Christianity, and especially of the Baptist tradition, George Rawlyk, was a member at First Baptist. Like most mainline Protestant churches, First Baptist has a tradition of learned clergy. The minister from 1981 to 1990, Mark Parent, holds a Ph.D. from McGill University and later became a cabinet minister in the provincial legislature of Nova Scotia.

The kinds of outreach and social programs sponsored by the church are similar to the ones offered by other mainline Protestant churches, aiming at service to the community with no intention to evangelize. In comparison with other congregations he had known, Kevin Smith characterized First Baptist as "very activist, I would say extremely activist" (15 January 2004). The Helen Tufts Nursery School was opened in the hall next door to the church in 1966 to assist children needing a bridge for entrance into primary school. In 2007 this nursery school was still serving sixteen children of preschool age on weekday mornings. In 1968 the separate but similarly named Helen Tufts Tutorial Friendship Program was established. Staffed entirely by volunteers, it continues for about sixty school-age children from disadvantaged Kingston families. First Baptist offers this program in association with Sydenham Street United Church, located a short block away. The children, aged six to twelve, are teamed with university and college students for tutoring assistance and friendship, meeting with their "buddy" at either First Baptist or Sydenham Street on Monday or Thursday nights.

In 1978 Project Reconciliation began to use the church's basement as part of a ministry of outreach to offenders, parolees, and their families. Project Reconciliation exists primarily to reintegrate recently released offenders into the community. In the early 1980s this ministry became a chaplaincy partner of the Correctional Service of Canada, and in April 2007 began operating under the name Kingston Community Chaplaincy. Among its various projects, it offers a lounge and resource centre that is open on a drop-in basis for several hours daily. Its mission includes the development of partnerships with other faith groups, both locally and in other regions, especially where no comparable services exist. The long-term duration of these programs in support of needs in the community displays the congregation's commitment to outreach. Another significant venture has been the church's refugee sponsorship, in particular of Salvadorean and Iranian refugees. That ministry to Hispanic families in Kingston continues with the appointment of an outreach minister to Portuguese families in 2004, Francisco Brandao, who had previously served at First Baptist in the early 1990s.

In 1966, the year of the first "crisis" at First Baptist mentioned on its website, the United Church of Canada was in the midst of adopting its New Curriculum, intended to modernize all the levels of Christian education for all ages. Part of the climate of the mid-1960s is shown in the books by Pierre Berton and others calling for a new, updated, and honest kind of Christianity (see chap. 1). One of the common worries was that clergy in their preaching were not helping to educate their congregations about developments in biblical scholarship that had been a part of their own theological education. Instead, they were often suspected of concealing their own understanding of the Bible and promoting a discrepant awareness by speaking as if they shared with their parishioners a common interpretation of particular passages. It might be less hassle, for instance, when preaching about the wedding at Cana, to allow those in the pews to assume that the preacher believed that Jesus performed a literal miracle and transformed water into wine, rather than offering a more "naturalistic" interpretation. At its worst such avoidance was seen as intellectual dishonesty, at best as employing a metaphorical interpretation that did not unnecessarily unsettle anyone's more literalistic views.

Given the aspiration of the United Church of Canada to be not just a "united church" but a "uniting church," it is hardly surprising that its efforts toward modernization amidst its ecumenical endeavours were affecting other denominations. Throughout the 1960s, possible union with the Anglican

Church was much in the air, though that eventually broke down despite United Church willingness to accept episcopal ordination. In Ontario, Baptists had been using, since 1936, a hymnary almost identical to that of the United Church. In 1964, describing similarities with the United Church liturgy among in Baptists in Ontario, Gerald Harrop wrote, "In fact, Baptist worship, especially in the older urban churches and the newer suburban churches, is hardly distinguishable from worship in the United Church of Canada" (qtd in Wilson 2001, 11). Baptists had also been using United Church Sunday school materials until the introduction of the New Curriculum, when older Baptist controversies over the Social Gospel and the "Higher Criticism" – that is, literary analysis of the origins and authorship of biblical texts – were rekindled. The New Curriculum, writes Robert S. Wilson, "rapidly decimated the United Church Sunday Schools and precipitated a break with the Baptists" (2001, 12). Wilson, using the kind of language evangelicals often adopt to dissociate themselves from more liberal churches, says that, because the United Church of the 1960s "was increasingly being led by the Canadian culture," more conservative Baptists distanced themselves from such tendencies toward theological liberalism (12). Surprisingly, perhaps, the New Curriculum affected First Baptist Church in Kingston, despite the fact, as the church's website points out, "the controversial curriculum was never adopted or even advocated by the Christian Education Committee." That very indecisiveness had the consequence of driving some members of First Baptist in one of two opposite directions, to a more conservative Fellowship Baptist church or to a more liberal United church: "Some people joined the new Bay Park Baptist Church, partly because the curriculum had not been rejected outright; others joined St Margaret's United Church because the curriculum had not been adopted" (First Baptist Church b). Parallels can be seen in other Christian congregations and denominations, where similarly divergent views about interpreting scripture have resulted in divisions.

The "Short History" on the First Baptist website refers to a second schism in the congregation that took place in 1993, again attributed to differences over the authority of scripture. Wilson describes conservative shifts taking place in the Baptist church about this time. He points out, for instance, how McMaster Divinity College, the major Baptist theological seminary in Ontario, in the 1980s "moved toward the mainstream of evangelical Baptist life." Wilson continues, "For a significant period before that, many of the pastors in BCOQ had chosen to go to more conservative schools" (2001, 13); and, in fact, many Baptist Convention clergy were graduates of such Bible colleges as Ontario Theological Seminary or Regent College rather than the Baptist Acadia or McMaster universities. George Rawlyk speaks of "an obvious shift in the Convention toward a conservative evangelical direction," bringing about appointments at McMaster Divinity School in the 1980s of a conservative chairman of the board and a conservative principal (1996, 45–6). Previously regarded by conservatives as a "bastion of modernism," the school became "increasingly evangelical." Whereas the Baptist Convention of Ontario and Quebec had been the most liberal branch of the Baptist church within Canada, and Kingston's First Baptist Church probably the most liberal congregation within that Convention, now First Baptist was experiencing the effects of this swing to the right. Throughout the 1980s this shift had begun, and in the 1990s divisions set in, partly as issues around sexual orientation came to the fore as they did in other denominations and churches.

In 1988, about the time of the United Church's statement on sexual orientation and ministry, the Assembly of the BCOQ had passed a resolution affirming "that the Biblical ideal for sexual relationships is within a permanent monogamous heterosexual union." The resolution went on to state: "Homosexual sexual expression clearly deviates from this Biblical pattern, and is strongly condemned in Scripture. We therefore assert that homosexual behaviour is unacceptable in the sight of God, since it is contrary to Scriptural principles of morality and family life" (BCOQ). Despite homosexual practice being regarded as sinful, the Assembly urged acceptance of gays and lesbians rather than condemnation and rejection. The document goes on to say, in a statement that, as we shall see, is somewhat remarkable for Baptists, "We believe that the good of society is served by upholding heterosexuality in law and public policy." The BCOQ also expressed its regret that sexual orientation had been included within the Human Rights Codes of the provinces of Ontario and Quebec as a prohibited basis of discrimination. That action, this Baptist body felt, had the effect of elevating sexual orientation to the same status as such "morally neutral" characteristics as race, religion, age, and sex, and of opening the door to the legitimizing of gay and lesbian sexual behaviour.

In 1985 a survey showed that about two-thirds of people affiliated with the Anglican, United, or Presbyterian churches regarded "two adults of the same sex having sex relations" as "always wrong" or "almost always wrong" (Bibby 1987, 155). Conversely, more than 30 per cent of people in those churches would not have held that strongly negative view. By the mid-1990s about half of Canadians favoured same-sex marriages, possibly a more difficult issue on which to get a positive response. Same-sex marriage, after all, presumably posed a greater threat to the traditional heterosexual understanding of marriage than same-sex "unions," more easily accepted if they were not seen as equivalent to "marriages." While no figure is given for Baptists, it would be fair to assume that some people within a congregation having the history and diversity of First Baptist would have been accepting of same-sex relationships in 1985. By 2004, however, Kevin Smith told interviewers for the Religious Diversity in Kingston project that in his congregation "we would have people from all different perspectives, but I think it is safe to say the vast majority would be opposed to same-sex marriage."

After the Baptist Convention of Ontario and Quebec resolution of 1988, recognition of gay and lesbian rights within Canada had progressed to the point that by 2003 court decisions in British Columbia, Quebec, and Ontario legalized same-sex marriages. The rest of the country was becoming more accepting in its attitudes as well, and same-sex marriage legislation was passed in Parliament and the Senate in 2005. A 2006 free vote in Parliament to re-establish the traditional definition of marriage was lost. In the midst of this movement toward the legislation of same-sex marriage, the reaction of the Assembly of the BCOQ in 2003 had been again to pass a resolution opposing same-sex marriage and declaring sexual relations of gays and lesbians to be sinful. Clarifying the position of his congregation, Smith wrote that "while there are probably a handful of Baptist churches across the country which have affirmed same-sex marriage either openly or discreetly, they are very rare." At First Baptist Church the congregation unanimously supported the Convention's position and "affirmed monogamous heterosexual marriage." Smith reported that "there was not a contrary vote" but suspected that "some who may have been opposed may have stayed away" perhaps because they did not like conflict or stress (personal communication, 12 April 2008).

The cherished Baptist principle of the freedom and autonomy of the individual to interpret the Bible does seem to have been constrained at First Baptist, a congregation that reportedly has "people from all different perspectives" on the same-sex marriage issue. Perhaps the expression of contrary views was inhibited by the Baptist Convention's conservative theological position that permitted no latitude in the interpretation of biblical passages assumed to proscribe same-sex relationships. Individual competency appears to have been abrogated when it came to the interpretation of these thorny parts of the scriptures. Within the BCOQ, an organization known as the Gathering of Baptists, founded in 1993, expresses its "concern for the pastoral needs of gay and lesbian people, and their families, who are or have been members within Baptist churches" (Gathering of Baptists). The group affirms the Baptist principles of soul liberty and freedom of interpretation, while upholding "fidelity in our relationships, particularly our sexual relationships." The Christian community, they state, "must welcome believers and seekers who come, without regard to social or physical status, gender, age, or sexual orientation." In 2003 the BCOQ Council passed its resolution restricting marriage to heterosexual couples and stating that "sexual intercourse is to be confined to one man and woman in marriage" (BCOQ). While affirming "the dignity and value of all persons regardless of sexual orientation," this resolution prohibited Baptist gays and lesbians from any means of sexual expression. They were given no choice but to be celibate on a lifelong basis. In the light of this action, the Division of Pastoral Relations within the BCOQ further recommended that "in the event an accredited pastor/chaplain/counsellor officiates or participates in a same-sex marriage, his/her permanent registration to perform marriages shall be revoked and all future requests for a registration to perform marriages will be dealt with on a case-by-case basis" (BCOQ). Responses from some individuals and from some Baptist congregations objected that these actions violated the principles of soul liberty, freedom of conscience, and the autonomy of individual churches.

Ray Hobbs, a retired professor of Old Testament from McMaster Divinity College and a member of the Gathering of Baptists, was among those questioning the BCOQ's directive, partly because it violated Baptist principles and partly because of the improper process and lack of debate involved in its adoption. In papers on the Gathering of Baptists website, Hobbs criticized the operative hermeneutical assumptions used in arriving at conclusions about biblical teaching on marriage and sexuality. "As with most moral and ethical issues," Hobbs said, "the Bible invites dialogue rather than offers directives, and this is simply because there are several sides to a topic." He expressed the fear held by others that in joining the Evangelical Fellowship of Canada, Convention Baptists had simply adopted EFC positions: "EFC policy has become BCOQ policy, especially in the matter of the place of gays and lesbians in the fellowship of the church. EFC's aggressive support of anti-gay moves across the country has not sat well with many who favour a more open and understanding approach to the matter" (Gathering of Baptists).

To suggest, as the First Baptist Church website does, that "diversity concerning the authority of scripture was a factor in the crises of 1966 and 1993" may misrepresent the central issue. It is not that members at First Baptist had differing views about the authority of the Bible to the extent that some affirmed it and some did not. After all, as the Baptist Distinctives, in the clause on the Primacy of Scripture found on the First Baptist website, announces, "For Baptists, the Bible is the final authority in matters of faith and practice." Baptists also "maintain that the Spirit speaking through the Bible must always be given preeminence in Christian life, although tradition, reason, and experience are not to be discounted." Further, this article on scripture states that "in the present the Spirit continues to be involved in the understanding and application of Scripture to each succeeding contemporary situation by means of illumination." All Baptists, even in the midst of these controversies, share a common conviction about the authority of the Bible. Baptist diversity exists about what the Bible means or how it is to be interpreted with respect to particular issues.

The Spirit, then, appears to be directing different Baptists in different ways on these matters. The principles of the Baptist Distinctives affirm that "each person [is] morally responsible for his/her own nature and behaviour," and that "Baptists ideally are champions of the cause of religious liberty." Such principles would allow, presumably, for differing interpretations, or at least for debate about what the Bible says. As J.R.C. Perkin, then president of Acadia University, observed in a sermon preached at First Baptist Church in 1990, "It is far from self-evident that contemporary Baptists are true to their traditional distinctives." He explained: "True, there is a clear recognition of the centrality of scripture; it is less clear that various interpretations are permitted and welcomed. Traditional admiration of scholarship has been replaced by a suspicion of academic enquiry which at times comes dangerously near anti-intellectualism" (Perkin 1991, 58–9).

Even more surprisingly, not only was the Baptist Convention imposing the norms of heterosexuality for its own clergy and laypeople, with its directives as to marriage and sexual conduct, but it was also calling upon the government to uphold "heterosexuality in law and public policy." Although other religious bodies were ordaining gays and lesbians, or were at that time asking the government to legalize same-sex marriages, the Assembly in 2004 passed a resolution "that the BCOQ continue to oppose all efforts by any court or legislative body to validate or legalize same-sex marriages" (BCOQ). This resolution appears to contradict the Baptist principle of the separation of church and state, as well as that of "individual competency" by which "Baptists believe that no group or individual has any right to compel others to believe or worship as they do." Of course, no "compulsion" as such was involved, though what the BCOQ was asking the government to do would have the effect of preventing clergy of other churches from performing legal same-sex marriages. Although the fear was often raised by those opposing same-sex marriage legislation that clergy would be forced to perform gay or lesbian marriages in contravention of their beliefs, most churches realized the status quo would be preserved – that is, that no clergy or religious organizations would be forced to marry anyone that they do not wish to marry.

Whether First Baptist Church in Kingston could have found some means to maintain its diversity – with regard to biblical interpretation, for instance – amidst the tendency in the parent denomination toward greater conservatism is debatable. During the 1990s, baptism – and therefore membership at

First Baptist – was refused to a woman when it was learned that she was a practising lesbian. By that time, almost everyone would have had a friend, family member, or colleague who was gay or lesbian, and would have known of their struggles and difficulties in living out and expressing that orientation. The application of measures and principles that must have seemed harsh or illiberal to people who thought they belonged to a moderate Baptist church was difficult for them to accept. As it happened, members, some of them lifelong Baptists, left First Baptist. Whereas conservative United Church members or Anglicans who disagreed with their denomination's decision to ordain gays or lesbians or to bless same-sex unions left their churches or formed dissenting groups, among the Baptists it was the liberal contingent who felt that they had lost their church home. For Baptists in Kingston, no other possible congregation remained for them within their own denomination.

"MAINLINE" NO MORE?

To describe a church or Christian denomination as "mainline" is in some respects not to say very much except to observe that these are the churches of most Canadians. In Kingston, where stability and continuity in matters of religion are still much in evidence – and where the historic connections of families with particular congregations persist over many decades – mainline churches have a lengthy history and solid presence. Notwithstanding their deep roots, these churches no longer enjoy the eminence locally or nationally that they once did. Their congregations are dwindling, their buildings are not always situated close to the homes of most of their congregants, and, simply as the result of their openness, adaptability, and relatively low demands upon their members, they no longer have the hold upon people's allegiance that they once had. Their position of power and prestige on the local scene is much diminished. Few of their members would count themselves as "religiously active." The views of their clergy – whether from the pulpit or in public forums – are no longer as readily heeded.

One could say that the continuing presence of Roman Catholics, United Church members, Anglicans, Presbyterians, and Baptists is assured. However, the great heyday of these churches is in the past. All of these denominations are faced with the challenges of a wide spectrum of belief and practice among their parishioners – and their clergy too. Some mainline Christian congregations in Kingston – for example, St Paul's Anglican, St Andrew's Presbyterian, and First Baptist Church – might count as being evangelical. The mainline Christian churches have not all adapted and changed at the same pace and in the same direction, as their differering responses to the great contemporary issue of same-sex relations and marriage illustrate. It would be fair to say that these churches, in their various ways, are attempting to steer a course between concerns thought to be the traditional focus of religion – personal morality and the individual relationship to the transcendent – on the one hand, and the demands of social justice and contemporary relevance on the other. To overemphasize matters of private religion is to be locked into the past and to be cut off from the world; to move in the direction of engaging political and social issues is to run the risk of becoming indistinguishable from the environing culture.

3 Protestant Evangelicals: Pentecostal, Christian and Missionary Alliance, Free Methodist

EVANGELICALISM IN CANADA TODAY

Toward the end of almost every interview for the Religious Diversity in Kingston project, researchers asked, "What is the defining characteristic of your congregation's way of being religious?" In some respects this is a "market niche" kind of question, about how one religious group differentiates itself from others. If the interviewee hesitated, we might rephrase the question in a comparative fashion, inviting comments about why a person would affiliate with this particular group in preference to some other, perhaps nearby, group. What makes St John's by-the-Gas-Station different from All People's Fellowship? Surely this kind of question occurs to anyone at all curious as to why, for instance, three United churches were situated in downtown Kingston within a stone's throw of one another. When most of the Christian churches in any city represent varieties of conservative Protestantism, how are they to be distinguished? On what basis does a person choose one over another? Perhaps this question is raised in the mind of a non-participant more often than an attendee who would be aware of the doctrinal and liturgical nuances among various worship sites, or who would know of their specific histories. Similarly – while acknowledging that the parallel might seem to be trivial – someone who does not eat fast food might wonder about the differences among hamburgers at A&W, McDonald's, Wendy's, Burger King, or Harvey's. In the same vein, what is the difference among the pizzas or Chinese food offered at any number of restaurants? Aficionados of fast food could surely explain and with appropriate nuances defend their preference.

Hannah Dick, following Paul Bramadat, has dealt with this issue of differentiation with respect to religious clubs on the Queen's University campus (see chap. 9). In the face of so many competing options, how does one particular group stand out? If there exists more supply than demand, how does a faith community capture attention and market share, especially in a secular context where religion itself may be perceived as marginal? At the same time, promoting religious pluralism means emphasizing common goals in interfaith endeavours to exhibit a unified front against a secular world indifferent to religion. Though religious groups compete for clientele and market share, it is sometimes advantageous to make common cause – much like otherwise competing real estate firms who share space in newspaper supplements or otherwise draw public attention to what they do and its implied significance. Religious people, it might be observed, often seem to spend more time differentiating themselves than finding common ground. A colleague once joked that for Presbyterians to join forces with other Christians was considered a sign of weakness. Nonetheless, some boundaries do become blurred over time, as historically differentiating issues fade or are muted while others become more pressing.

John G. Stackhouse Jr attempts to define the character of Canadian evangelicalism in the twentieth century by focusing on the institutions and organizations that typify it – especially higher education in the form of Bible colleges, seminaries, and liberal arts programs, the Sermons from Science pavilion at Expo 67, such student groups as the Inter-Varsity Christian Fellowship, and the Evangelical Fellowship of Canada. Stackhouse identifies the common ground held by Canadian evangelicals, showing how from the 1960s to the 1990s "transdenominational evangelicalism began to develop institutional resources to take advantage of the new openness of society and the declining strength of the mainline churches" (1993, 112). This kind of collaboration represented something new among evangelicals, often strongly individualistic, as they began to recognize the importance of the church and not just of the individual believer. Stackhouse identifies the agreement represented in transdenominational evangelicalism as marked by "doctrinal orthodoxy, personal piety, and evangelism" (1993, 112–13). As an instance of what evangelicals in Canada believe, he offers the "generic" statement of faith from the Evangelical Fellowship of Canada (1993, 179).

The seven doctrinal principles of the Evangelical Fellowship of Canada, listed by Stackhouse in 1993, have seen little change in their current iteration on the EFC website today (Evangelical Fellowship of Canada a). There, according to the first principle, the Bible is agreed to be "divinely inspired, infallible, entirely trustworthy," a more moderate definition of the authority of scripture than saying it is "inerrant" or "literally true" or "literally true, word for word" (see Rawlyk 1996, 120–3, 204–5). Surveys cited by George Rawlyk show that a large percentage of Canadian Protestant evangelicals uphold the historical accuracy of the account of creation given in the Bible, and, perhaps less surprisingly, the historicity of the record of Christ's life as given in the Gospels (1996, 122). The Evangelical Fellowship's statement of faith goes on to affirm, second, that there is one God in three persons. The third clause contains a number of affirmations about Jesus Christ, ranging from his Virgin Birth and sinlessness to his vicarious death and bodily resurrection. Fourth, salvation is possible only through "the merits of the shed blood of Jesus Christ received by faith apart from works." The fifth and sixth clauses state the work of the Holy Spirit and the nature of the Church, though in quite general terms. Finally, seventh, there is a statement about eschatology: "Ultimately God will judge the living and the dead, those who are saved unto the resurrection of life, those who are lost unto the resurrection of damnation." Though Christ's "personal return in power or glory" was affirmed in the third article, no specification is made in the seventh as to whether this return is the stricter, and frequently more pessimistic, premillennial return in which the Second Coming of Christ precedes his reign of thousand years or the more general, and sometimes metaphoric, postmillennial version (Evangelical Fellowship of Canada a).

In a last book before his death following a car accident, Rawlyk also examined Canadian evangelicalism in the 1990s, concentrating on surveys of attitudes and beliefs, together with numerous case studies of individuals. He wrote his book during the winter of 1994–95 in Charleston, South Carolina, thinking that would be a "suitable and congenial religious environment" and a good vantage point from which to consider Canadian evangelicalism. Soon after his arrival, he says, "I was afraid I had made a terrible mistake": "I was repelled by much of what I read about religion in the local papers, what I saw on television, and what I heard when I visited the local churches" (1996, 3). Rawlyk, a Queen's University historian known for his major studies of revivalism and evangelicals, as well as for his own Christian socialism as a member of the New Democratic Party, reacted in a strongly negative way to the growing influence and outspokenness of the religious right in America. In his efforts to distinguish Canadian evangelicalism from its American counterpart, and to show the greater degree of accommodation in Canada, he employed his customary grassroots approach, trying to understand Canadian evangelicalism from the bottom up by paying close attention to the voices and stories of individual believers. In contrast to Stackhouse's approach, Rawlyk questions whether contemporary persons of evangelical faith in Canada have much contact with the institutions set forth as central in Stackhouse's study (1996, 135).

A third study of evangelicals, Sam Reimer's book *Evangelicals and the Continental Divide* (2003), argues that a common evangelical subculture extends throughout North America. Reimer locates four distinctive emphases by which evangelicals are identified: (1) conversionism, or an emphasis on changed lives and salvation; (2) biblicism, that is, belief in the authority of scripture; (3) crucicentrism, or Christ's sacrificial work on the cross; and (4) activism, that is, that faith leads to action in the world (2003, 153). He concedes that the last area, that of activism, remains the weakest – and weaker in Canada than in the United States. The problem partly arises from the differing meanings of activism, ranging from evangelism, or sharing the Gospel with others, to behavioural standards, especially having to do with sexuality and the family, to performing acts of generosity and kindness to others. Among evangelicals, "good works" remain suspect because salvation comes from faith alone, though the fruits of that faith should be manifest in one's deeds. These identifying markers set the boundaries of who is an evangelical and who is not, such that evangelicals can recognize one another according to whether they acknowledge having been "born again," accept the authority of the Bible, and have been saved by Christ, through whom alone salvation is possible.

The Evangelical Fellowship of Canada has grown in significance and changed its emphasis – if not its doctrinal principles – over the last decade or so. From the twenty-seven denominations that Stackhouse mentions as having been a part of the EFC in 1989 (1993, 173), denominational affiliates have now increased to forty, though some of them are very small or difficult to distinguish from others similarly named. Among the largest or most prevalent evangelical denominations listed are seven Baptist denominations, four Mennonite denominations, three Pentecostal denominations, the Christian and Missionary Alliance, the Christian Reformed Church, Free Methodists, the Wesleyan Church, and the Salvation Army. Other members include individual congregations such as Kingston's Calvary Bible Church; educational institutions, in Ontario including Redeemer University College, McMaster Divinity College, and Tyndale University College and Seminary; and dozens of ministry and mission organizations that include the Billy Graham Association, the Scott Mission, the Gideons, Jews for Jesus, Inter-Varsity Christian Fellowship, and World Vision Canada (Evangelical Fellowship of Canada b).

One of the Kingston congregations belonging to the EFC, the Calvary Bible Church on Nelson Street, provides an example of the faith, emphasis on conversion, and activism characterizing contemporary evangelicals. The church gave sanctuary to a woman threatened with deportation to China after she had served a sentence for manslaughter. Kwai Kwan Zhao, or Lucy Lu, as she was better known, had been sentenced to prison for ten years after the death of her husband in Toronto in 1985, when she was a recent immigrant. Lu maintained her innocence, claiming that she was persuaded to plead guilty after legal complications in two earlier trials had resulted in a hung jury and a mistrial. She was released from the Prison for Women after serving less than three years of the sentence but was to be returned to China, where she was likely to be executed for the crime. She was offered refuge in the Calvary Bible Church in November 2000 and was able to go free sixteen months later after a torrent of public support won her a temporary reprieve from the deportation order. One church member, Bob Hawkins, championed her cause and provided employment in a shoe store he owned. Lu married another member of the Calvary Bible Church, Daryl Gellner. In 2007 she won landed immigrant status (*Whig-Standard*, 19 March 2002, 13 March 2007).

Indicative of its greater activity in recent years in the area of public policy, the EFC website identifies several areas of concern to evangelicals, for example, "seeking to uphold care for the vulnerable, religious freedom, sanctity of human life, marriage and family, and freedom of conscience." The fellowship is more active in its interventions to the federal government and the courts as well. In March 2008 the website listed, under the heading "Social Issues," a recent bill to raise the age of sexual consent, protection for "unborn victims of crime," opposition to advance polls being held on Sundays, opposition to assisted suicide, and opposition to removing the Lord's Prayer from the Ontario Legislature. On this last item, the president of the EFC did not urge exclusive use of the Lord's Prayer, as some were doing on the basis that Canada is a "Christian country" (Evangelical Fellowship of Canada c). Reluctant to see people compelled to recite the Lord's Prayer, Bruce J. Clemenger suggested in a letter to the *National Post* newspaper that it "could be retained as other provinces have done while providing for other expressions" (15 February 2008). (The possibility of rotating prayers from various faiths at such meetings is considered in chapter 10.) Other letters written by EFC officials – to newspapers, for example – over the past few years have addressed topics similar to those already mentioned, such as same-sex marriage, abortion, funding for religious schools, and threats to religious communities' freedom of expression.

The election of the Conservative Party in 2006 to a minority government, with Stephen Harper being spoken of as "a born-again prime minister," raised fears that Ottawa would emulate President George W. Bush's Republicans and their ties with the religious right in the United States. Stories of Canadian "theo-con" lobby groups domiciled in the shadow of Parliament Hill, or of the possibility of the government holding a free vote on same-sex marriage, increased such concerns about policy being driven by religious convictions. The most serious possibilities – for example, that a dispensationalist theology that interprets Israel in light of biblical prophecy might influence political decisions – are raised in journalist Marci McDonald's extensive article, and the subsequent book arising from it, about the connections of the Harper government to the extreme views of the religious right (2006). In her 2010 book, *The Armageddon Factor,* McDonald sees conservative Christians spurred on by visions of theocracy and apocalypse to create a Canada in which "non-believers ... have no place, and those in violation of biblical law, notably homosexuals and adulterers, would merit severe punishment and the sort of shunning that once characterized a society where suspected witches were burned" (qtd in the *Globe and Mail*, 21 May 2010).

In general, though, Canadians seem reluctant to follow the American example, loathe to abandon their social safety net to the ministries of faith-based groups. The Evangelical Fellowship represents relatively moderate evangelicals, not extreme right-wing Christians, and, even if they are stronger advocates of family values than of environmental issues, few of its members would likely view environmental catastrophe as the prelude to the biblical apocalypse and Second Coming. Their broadly inclusive view of evangelicalism is seen in their relatively moderate statement of faith, and in their estimate that 19 per cent of Canadians – 12 per cent Protestants and 7 per cent Roman Catholics – count as evangelical. This breadth is necessary to retain their large base of support and to operate as an umbrella organization parallel to the Canadian Council of Churches. Further, in the last few decades, higher education has increased among conservative Christians to the extent that they are less protective of their faith and more willing to be open to complexities. The proliferation of conservative Protestant churches on Kingston's religious landscape reveals a range of options, beliefs, and styles of worship. If a local evangelical church is part of a parent denomination, that denomination is likely to subscribe to the statement of faith offered by the Evangelical Fellowship of Canada. Some free-standing churches and "house" churches in Kingston – that is, congregations having no denominational affiliations – might also identify themselves as evangelical, apart from their own statements, by their membership in the Evangelical Fellowship of Canada.

A recurrent assertion of difference we heard from evangelical churches was the affirmation that "we believe in the Bible," as if to say that competing churches – even other conservative Protestant ones – choose not to believe it. William Sloane Coffin, the great American liberal Protestant, said in one of his sermons, "The great differences in the world are never between people who believe different things, but between people who believe the same things and differ in their interpretation." This phenomenon of believing the same things, but believing them differently, as Wayne Hilliker of Chalmers United Church paraphrased Coffin's remarks, marks the strongly individualistic faith of Protestants, especially evangelicals (interview, 3 October

2003). The remainder of this chapter examines some of the many examples of evangelical Protestantism in Kingston, mainly within the most prominent denominations of evangelicalism. The survey begins with the largest evangelical congregation, the Kingston Gospel Temple. Then, an independent church, Third Day Worship Centre, founded by former pastors of the Gospel Temple, illustrates the separation and schism common among conservative Protestants. Finally, consideration of some of the congregations within the Free Methodist and Christian and Missionary Alliance denominations shows something of the range of contemporary evangelicalism.

SOME KINGSTON EXAMPLES

Kingston Gospel Temple

The Kingston Gospel Temple, Kingston's largest evangelical church, was one of earliest churches within the Pentecostal Assemblies of Canada, founded in 1919. In 1920 the Kingston Gospel Temple was listed as one of twenty-seven assemblies in the *Canadian Pentecostal Testimony*. Pentecostalism in North America usually traces its origins to the Azusa Street revival in Los Angeles in 1906. The meetings in a small wooden hall, under Afro-American leadership, were characterized by ecstatic worship, enthusiastic singing, acts of healing, and speaking in tongues. What has been termed "the Azusa Street revival of the north," which also took place in 1906, occurred at the Hebden Street Mission in Toronto, often taken to be the beginning of Canadian Pentecostalism (see Wilkinson 2009, 84). These "Holy Rollers" attracted the scorn and censure of the more staid Christians of the day who looked askance at what appeared to them to be unseemly displays. For some, the manifestations occurring there were interpreted more as the work of the Devil than an outpouring of the Holy Spirit echoing the birth of the early Church in Acts 2:4. In the words of the King James Version, "And they were all filled with the Holy Ghost, and began to speak with other tongues, as the Spirit gave them utterance." Still, the emphasis on religious experience and emotional expression in Christianity, or in religions generally, for that matter, is nothing new. Pentecostalism represents a recurring motif in religious revival movements. John Wesley, who inaugurated what must be the most successful evangelical revival ever in the British Isles, said in the eighteenth century, "The emotions must be stirred to their depths, at frequent intervals, by unaccountable feelings of compunction, joy, peace, and so on, or how could you be certain that the Divine touch was working within you?" (qtd in Lewis 1989, 18–19).

Kingston Gospel Temple

The mammoth Kingston Gospel Temple is the oldest and most successful of the three Kingston churches belonging to the Pentecostal Assemblies of Canada, or PAOC. The other two are Evangel Pentecostal Church, located in the city's Rideau Heights area between Montreal and Division Streets, and City Christian Centre, a 1997 church plant from the Kingston Gospel Temple, further to the west on Woodbine Road. Another church, New Life Centre on McEwen Drive, is a United Pentecostal Church, a denomination that began its organizational history in 1916 after a split from other Pentecostals over the "oneness" of God. In contrast to the Pentecostal Assemblies of Canada, United Pentecostals believe that the trinitarian concept of God as existing in three persons obscures the biblical emphasis on God as one (see United Pentecostal Church International). United Pentecostals, therefore, do not use the traditional trinitarian phrase at baptism, despite the injunction of Matthew 28:19, again, as expressed in the King James Version: "Go ye therefore, and teach all nations, baptizing them in the name of the Father, and of the Son, and of the Holy Ghost." They argue that "name" is here used in the singular, and that these words were never intended to become a ritual formula. Like all other conservative Protestants, United Pentecostals set forth and defend their position on these issues with a consideration of all the biblical verses, especially from the New Testament, applicable to the case. What is at stake in these disputes, and the intricacies of the arguments used, is frequently lost on outsiders. Probably a major reason why the United Pentecostal Church does not belong to the Evangelical Fellowship of Canada is the view of God expressed in the second article in the EFC Statement of Faith, "There is one God, eternally existent in three persons: Father, Son and Holy Spirit" (Evangelical Fellowship of Canada a).

The Kingston Gospel Temple announces itself as a "Bible-based, Christ-powered, Spirit-empowered church." In keeping with the evangelical tradition's stress on doctrine, it displays a statement of faith on its website (Kingston Gospel Temple). Peter Hubert told a reporter in 1990 that the Kingston Gospel Temple did not post the name of the Pentecostal Assemblies of Canada, the parent denomination, in front of the church because "the temple's pastors feel they are not there to draw any particular group but to reach out to whoever will come" (*Whig-Standard*, 2 November 1990). The church's website includes a preamble stating that the Pentecostal Assemblies of Canada "stands firmly in the mainstream of historical Christianity. It takes the Bible as its all-sufficient source of faith and practice, and subscribes to the historic creeds of the universal church. In common with historical, evangelical Christianity, it emphasizes Christ as Saviour and coming King."

When evangelicals use such words as "mainstream," "historical" or "historic," and "universal," they are staking their claim to be acknowledged as continuing, or restoring, the major emphases of the church from its New Testament beginnings. The sentences including these words quoted above from the Kingston Gospel Temple's website identify a common theme shared among most conservative Protestant churches that claim to represent the central character of Christianity from the biblical period to the present. In some respects, this declaration of centrality is asserted against so-called mainline churches, seen as liberal innovators who do not share their high view of biblical authority or else have abandoned the teachings and traditions of the church for modern interpretations or compromises with the surrounding secular culture.

One of the pastors at the Kingston Gospel Temple in 1990, Gary Nettleship, was careful, as evangelicals often are, to distinguish his view of the Bible from that held by more liberal Christians: "In terms of scripture, I think it would be safe to say that understanding that the Bible contains history, poetry, prophecy, teaching, parables, all of that, we take it as a literal interpretation. Some would say the Bible contains the word of God, we say it is the word of God, in its entirety." He then continued, giving an example of what "a literal interpretation" does not include: "This doesn't mean that they take it literally in the sense of 'If your eye offends you, pluck it out'

[Mark 9:43], because Jesus spoke in parables, told imaginary stories and spoke in hyperbole and exaggeration" (*Whig-Standard*, 2 November 1990). The problem of course is that biblical literalism is impossible. Metaphor is excluded when every word should be read as if it were a statement of fact, like a mathematical equation or a statement such as "the sky is blue." Jesus's words "I am the vine, you are the branches" (John 15:5) cannot be interpreted literally. As Gary Nettleship's example illustrates, even a biblical literalist knows that not all parts of the Bible are susceptible to literal interpretation. Part of the problem is that "literally" has come to mean the opposite of its literal meaning: "literally" often means "figuratively," as when someone says "I literally jumped out of my skin" or "I literally died laughing." The word has become used as a way of saying "metaphorically," or as an intensifier. Evangelicals who say that they take the Bible literally probably are reaching for a way of affirming that they take its authority seriously, or that they do not soften hard sayings by regarding them as historically conditioned or merely symbolic.

The Kingston Gospel Temple's Statement of Faith specifies the significant particulars of Pentecostalism, especially "the distinctive position that speaking in tongues is the initial evidence when Christ baptizes in the Holy Spirit." The statement emphasizes some other positions of the Pentecostal Assemblies of Canada, such as practices of tithing and healing, belief in angels and demons, teachings about marriage and divorce, and most extensively, in Article VIII, its position about "The End of Time." Under that heading, Pentecostal teachings such topics as the Present State of the Dead, the Rapture, the Tribulation, the Second Coming, the Final Judgment, and the Eternal State of the Righteous are all dealt with in detail.

The Kingston Gospel Temple, moving westward from earlier downtown locations, was built on its present site on Princess Street near the intersection of Sydenham Road in 1988. The church owns a large parcel of land there, in total fourteen acres stretching to Taylor-Kidd Boulevard on the south, with the buildings and parking lot comprising the four-acre section of the "church campus." The church has undergone several expansions and renovations at its current site, with plans in the future to erect a Christian seniors' home on the property. Construction was completed in recent years on an addition including a gymnasium/auditorium, commercial kitchen, and "fireside" lounge. When the downtown Grand Theatre was closed for several years prior to its reopening in 2008, the Kingston Gospel Temple, as the largest venue in Kingston for concerts, hosted performances by the Kingston Symphony. The symphony continues to perform there on occasion, as do other groups. According to a newspaper article published when the facility was new, the sanctuary accommodates twelve hundred people, and another six hundred in the balcony (*Whig-Standard*, 12 February 1988). The assistant pastor, Ashley Arnold, said in a 2004 interview that attendance at Sunday morning worship services was seven or eight hundred people (29 January 2004). In a subsequent interview, just as the symphony was about to begin its use of the facility, he explained that a request for use by groups outside the church "goes before myself and other pastors and then to the board, and we decide whether it is beneficial to our church or not." Pastor Arnold indicated by way of example that "a rock band who stands against our morals, or what we believe as a church, they would not be allowed here" (11 August 2005).

A major part of the ministry at the Kingston Gospel Temple is its music, an emphasis that continues the expressive emotionalism of Pentecostalism generally. As Frank Burch Brown points out, drawing on the work of Martha Bayles, the earliest manifestations of rock and roll music came out of the environment of Pentecostalism, in its turn heavily influenced by Afro-American music such as rhythm and blues. "Elvis Presley, Jerry Lee Lewis, and Little Richard," Brown remarks, "all grew up in the Pentecostal church and sometimes made highly conflicted, guilt-ridden alterations of its music" (2000, 246). The Gospel Temple's website has included mentions of about two dozen groups and individuals who have given concerts at the church, covering a full range of the genres of Christian popular music, especially southern gospel, country music, rock, and choir music. Their respective websites convey something of the variety provided by these performers, almost always highlighting their Christianity, no matter how "secular" they might appear at first glance. Performers pitch their efforts to a segment of the Christian music market and, often, to a specific target audience. For example, Gold City offers four-part harmony gospel music; Paul Baloche plays electric guitar; Jaci Velasquez is a Christian Latin singer; Cheryl Dunn is a country music artist; Juno winner Amanda Falk addresses her music to teenage girls; Brian and Laura Dugas are a Canadian gospel husband-and-wife team; Thousand Foot Krutch is a Canadian Christian hard rock band; Michael English of PraiseFest Ministries invites fans to join him on a "Christian Cruise;" a group called "God Rocks" specializes in "Energizing Kids with the Good News;" the Oak Ridge Boys are "all born-again, Bible-believing Christians." In keeping with the Gospel Temple's emphasis on family values, at several points during our interviews Pastor Arnold mentioned previous and planned visits by such wholesome children's entertainers as Mary Lambert and Fred Penner for community concerts – this in addition to the other performers whose music has specifically Christian content. As well, on film nights the church has screened such movies as Mel Gibson's *The Passion of the Christ* or Michael Apted's *Amazing Grace*, about the life of William Wilberforce.

Kingston Gospel Temple directs much of its efforts to youth ministry, partly fulfilling this role for its two sister churches in the city, Evangel Pentecostal Church and the City Christian Centre. Because of the large, well-equipped space and available seating, some local high schools have held their graduation exercises at the KGT. The church has sixteen Sunday school classrooms and hosts mid-week programs for children and youth, and other activities and meetings for young adults and younger couples. Arnold describes his own "portfolio" as directed at those "forty and under," especially young married couples. He estimates 35 to 40 per cent of the congregation to be under thirty-five years of age, and 25 per cent under twenty-five (interview, 29 January 2004). A bus with capacity for about two dozen passengers collects students from the Queen's campus, about six kilometres distant, for Sunday morning worship. The church has a reputation among evangelical students at Queen's as being one of three or four in the city especially hospitable to them, and "safe" to worship at, in the sense of being congenial to their beliefs. "Protecting our congregation," says Arnold, "is our number-one priority" (11 August 2005). Earlier in that interview he referred to a decision about whether or not a rock band would be allowed to perform at the church facilities: "We obviously need to protect our church family first."

Protection of the family and youth as a value also affects decisions about what stance the Kingston Gospel Temple takes on contentious issues of the day. In 1986, when it was at its earlier location on Brock Street, a visiting evangelist from the United States preached on "Rock, Ruin, or Redemption: The Dynamic Christian Alternative to Demon-Dominated Rock." The evangelist, Dan Peters, was part of the large rallies in the United States at that time where recordings of contemporary rock were being burned. Rock music, Peters is reported to have said, led to "homosexuality, marijuana smoking, suicide, sado-masochism, venereal disease, pre-marital sex, teen-age pregnancy, anti-war sentiment, and the breakdown of the nuclear family" (*Whig-Standard*, 23 May 1986). Rock lyrics, Peters continued, encouraged "masturbation, violent sex, incest, the murder of parents and worship of the devil." He also maintained, drawing upon a paranoia of the day, that rock music, when played backwards, revealed "subliminal satanic messages." Of course, the 1980s saw widely shared opposition from more mainstream culture to the graphically violent and sexually explicit lyrics of many songs then popular, especially those by Judas Priest, Def Leppard, AC/DC, Prince, Twisted Sister, Madonna, and Black Sabbath. For the evangelical subculture, the threat posed by some areas of western secular culture explains, in part at least, the development of Christian alternatives in music, films, books, and other forms of entertainment.

Kingston Gospel Temple has hosted other events allowing conservative Christians to join forces in protection of their values and of the family. In 1989 an anti-abortion rally took place at the present Princess Street location, with five hundred people from fifty conservative Protestant and Roman Catholic churches taking part. A large white cross was erected in front of the church – an anti-abortion symbol, said Father Karl Clemens of St Paul the Apostle Roman Catholic Church, in memory of "the innocent children who have shed their blood and died" (*Whig-Standard*, 23 October 1989). Those attending this rally were met by opposing forces in the form of pro-abortion activists from Queen's. The same position against abortion was evident in the Gospel Temple's support of the Kingston Crisis Pregnancy Centre (later renamed the Kingston Pregnancy Care Centre) located in the downtown St Paul's Anglican Church. Since 1989 this centre has provided "information, counselling, pregnancy tests and aid to pregnant teens and women facing an unplanned pregnancy" (Kingston Pregnancy Care Centre). Because of earlier references on its website to "crisis pregnancy," the purpose of the centre might be misinterpreted – and perhaps such ambiguity is deliberate – as a resource offering services to women wanting to terminate a pregnancy by means of an abortion. Like similarly named centres elsewhere in other North American cities, frequently associated with churches and with Birthright International, the Kingston Pregnancy Care Centre offers alternatives to abortion. The earlier version of the website specified that the centre does not offer abortion referral; the current website does not make that clear. Rather, the centre indicates that it offers post-abortion counselling and adoption counselling. The Gospel Temple, in company with other, especially conservative, churches in the city, supports the centre financially and with donations of family items and baby clothing.

In contrast to the two above-mentioned events of the 1980s rallying opposition to contemporary secular rock music and abortion, it appears that the Gospel Temple today sometimes prefers to couch its message in more positive terms and to provide alternatives to aspects of secular culture that it regards in a negative light. Among the causes it has supported are Canadian troops, Martha's Table (a downtown facility providing meals for the needy), and, as a sign in 2006 outside the church proclaimed, "the State of Israel and Its Right to Exist." This backing of Israel, though, may not be as positive and as disinterested as it first appears. The church's website has listed theological and biblical reasons why Christians should support the state of Israel. After President George W. Bush announced in his State of the Union address in January 2008 a plan for a Palestine Liberation Organization state by the end of the year that would "take away Judea and Samaria from Israel," the Gospel Temple sought support for a petition in this "battle between lightness and darkness, between politics and prophecy." The link to a campaign to "Save Jerusalem" opposed the Bush plan as a "conspiracy" and a "betrayal" that overturned the understanding of some Christians of the establishment of Israel and the reunification of Jerusalem as fulfillment of biblical prophecy.

The support of Israel, and of Jews, on the part of evangelicals comes partly from a supersessionist theology whereby Judaism prepared the way for Christianity. Interpreted by way of covenant or dispensationist theology, Old Testament prophecies about the return of Israel are fulfilled in Jesus' Second Coming, sometimes accompanied by a conversion of Jews to Christianity. The Pentecostal Statement of Faith includes an article on the Second Coming: "The return of Christ to earth in power and great glory will conclude the great tribulation with the victory at Armageddon, the defeat of Antichrist and the binding of Satan. He will introduce the millennial age, restore Israel to her own land, lift the curse which now rests upon the whole creation, and bring the whole world to the knowledge of God" (Pentecostal Assemblies of Canada). In 1991 Peter Hubert, at that time the pastor of the KGT, connected the events taking shape during the crisis in the Persian Gulf as part of the "countdown" to Armageddon. He expected Armageddon to occur in this generation, with the final war to take place in a valley in Israel (*Whig-Standard*, 16 January 1991).

This evangelical support of Israel is carried one step further by dozens of organizations existing worldwide and grouped under the heading of Messianic Judaism. Their supporters claim to be Jewish while accepting Jesus – in Hebrew, Y'shua – as their messiah. They incorporate some Jewish practices and the celebration of Jewish holy days into their Christian faith. However, Jews everywhere, and the State of Israel too, regard these groups as Christian missionary organizations aiming at the conversion of Jews. Nevertheless, the Canadian website of the largest such group, Jews for Jesus, asserts that "because we are a Jewish mission and not a mission to Jews our approach is Jewish" (Jews for Jesus Canada). The contention that it is possible to be both Jewish and Christian is rejected by most Jews who would regard anyone claiming to be a "Jewish" Christian as, at best, a former Jew. As opposition to Jews for Jesus has grown over the last decade or so, including a counter-missionary group named Jews for Judaism that shadowed Jews for Jesus missionaries in Toronto, some conservative Christians have dropped their support of groups aiming at the conversion of Jews. This dispute, and the accompanying withdrawal of much evangelical support, may account for the apparent disappearance of the local Messianic Jewish Fellowship, as well as any mention of a connection with such organizations on the heavily revised Gospel Temple website in 2010.

Between 1985 and 1995 several stories on the Kingston Messianic Jewish Fellowship appeared in the *Kingston Whig-Standard*. In 1991, on their sixth anniversary, the newspaper reported that about twenty-five to thirty Messianic Jews met monthly at the Kingston Gospel Temple. "All but two or three of the group are gentiles (non-Jews)," said their leader, Andre Vanderwerff, who declared that they joined "because they love the Jewish people." The Gospel Temple's pastor, Peter Hubert, in a sermon preached at this sixth anniversary service, is reported to have observed that "the horrors of the Holocaust could easily happen again, if people are complacent about anti-semitism" (*Whig-Standard*, 29 November 1991). Though this Messianic Fellowship was promoted as a bridge between Jews and Christians, and to tell "Christians they should love Jews," clearly a major aim was also to facilitate, by means of this bridge, the passage of Jews into Christianity.

A theology of supersession, or replacement, is held by Christians who find something problematic in the continuing existence of Judaism as an independent religion having its own integrity. If Jesus of Nazareth was the messiah anticipated by Jews, why was he rejected by Jews? Of course, even to phrase the question in such a way assumes that Judaism awaits exactly such a messianic figure as Jesus represents for Christians. The group Jews for Jesus displays that assumption when it plainly states its raison d'être: "We exist to make the Messiahship of Jesus an unavoidable issue to our Jewish people world-wide" (Jews for Jesus Canada). However, as Rosemary Ruether indicates, the New Covenant that provides salvation and fulfilment for Christians ought not to be universalized to the extent that it abrogates the Mosaic Covenant or becomes the paradigm of the Jewish religion: "Christians must be able to accept the thesis that it is not necessary for Jews to have the story about Jesus in order to have a foundation for faith and a hope for salvation" (1974, 256). For dialogue between Christians and Jews to take place on any kind of even footing, Christians must surrender their version of Jewish history and understand Judaism as a parallel and equal religion.

Third Day Worship Centre

About a decade after Peter Hubert became senior pastor at the Kingston Gospel Temple in 1990, he emerged as the assistant pastor at the recently opened Third Day Worship Centre less than a kilometre north on the Sydenham Road. Hubert's former youth pastor at KGT, Francis Armstrong, was now the senior pastor at Third Day, a church that Armstrong had founded. The two men knew each other in Alberta when they were pastors together at a church in Leduc in the 1980s. When Hubert, then forty-two, came to the Gospel Temple from Edmonton, he invited Armstrong, aged

Third Day Worship Centre

twenty-nine, to join him (*Whig-Standard*, 2 November 1990). At the time Hubert was interviewed in 2003, the Sydenham Road site still carried the name Frontline Worship Centre, stemming from an earlier phase when Armstrong established a new church by that name in a storefront location in 1997. In effect, the two men reversed roles: whereas in 1990 Peter Hubert had invited Francis Armstrong to join him at the Kingston Gospel Temple, now Armstrong invited Hubert to become the assistant pastor at the Frontline – soon to be Third Day – Worship Centre. The site acquired in 2002 includes a renovated school building of about 12,000 square feet, sitting on five acres. In 2003 there were plans to open a nursery that eventually would become a day care centre, after which a kitchen would be added.

Hubert, who explained in 1990 that the Kingston Gospel Temple played down its denominational affiliation to appeal to a wider group, indicated in 2003 at the Third Day Worship Centre that both he and Armstrong had wanted to move into a new phase of "post-denominational" Christianity. While Third Day is part of the larger Pentecostal tradition, it remains independent of either the Pentecostal Assemblies of Canada or the United Pentecostal denominations. Hubert emphasized that the message or doctrine had not changed; rather, the difference resides in the church structure that means "we are pastor-led and not board-led" (interview, 19 November 2003). This change, he stated, is in agreement with the Bible: "We feel it is a violation of the Word of God that the Board has as much power and authority as they do. I think a pastor-led church is the right way." He also suggested, probably thinking of his former affiliation in the PAOC, that denominations tended to become too liberal.

Ashley Arnold, describing the process of finding a new pastor at the Gospel Temple, said that a search committee made up of representatives from the board and congregation would invite a prospective senior pastor to preach at the church. Then their nomination would be put to a vote of the members of the congregation itself. Normally 80 or 90 per cent of the congregation would have to be in favour of the new appointment. Arnold also explained that the senior pastor could then invite a compatible assistant pastor to join him, as Hubert did Armstrong at the Gospel Temple. It appears, though, that from the "post-denominational" perspective of the Third Day Worship Centre, this style of governance put too much power in the hands of the congregation. At Third Day, Hubert stated, "I am now able to do what I want to do. In a denominational church, to be elected by the congregation, I didn't always have the chance to do that" (interview, 19 November 2003). The Third Day Worship Centre has an appointed board of directors, as well as "a bylaw and a constitution," reportedly referred to in cases of dispute. Other leadership is in the form of "a number of volunteer pastors. We also have prayer counsellors."

The Third Day Worship Centre's website does not publish its constitution or bylaws and says little about specific aspects of the method of governance of the church. A few years after the relocation to Sydenham Road, the website then made it clear that the pastor's leadership is primary and that the board must be in agreement with the direction that leadership provides: "The structure we want to make possible is where the Pastor is the visionary leader with healthy accountabilities. The Board of Directors must have the same vision as the Senior Pastor, and cannot have their own agendas. Two visions bring division. There must be room for dialogue, but there must not be place for division. Too many churches are struggling and distracted with leadership issues. We believe that a paradigm shift is necessary in the Evangelical Church world, and we believe that the model we have set up helps Pastors to lead their churches in a more relevant and focused way." Over time the church's website has become less specific about these issues of governance and leadership, offering instead various versions of an unfolding vision being revealed to the pastor (Third Day Worship Centre a).

The Third Day Worship Centre identifies itself as "the flagship church of Third Day Fellowship of Canada," including churches in Gananoque and New York State, and as "a member of Open Bible Faith Fellowship." Open Bible Faith Fellowship at one time listed Armstrong on its board as "Senior Pastor/Apostle," though that list later changed. The term "apostle" apparently refers to one who is sent to establish churches. Hubert describes himself as "more of a pastor," whereas Armstrong is "more of an apostle." Open Bible Faith Fellowship identifies itself as "a charismatic, Bible-based fellowship" that began in Ontario and has grown in seven years to include more than 125 churches in North America and abroad. Even for unique, one-of-a-kind, or free-standing churches it is important to demonstrate some kind of linkage, if not to a denomination, then to an organization, however loose, in order to maintain their tax-exempt status.

Third Day Worship Centre emphasizes its ministry to youth, estimating that "approximately 60 per cent of the congregation are between the ages of sixteen and forty" (Hubert, interview, 19 November 2003). Attendance at morning services on Sundays was estimated at 300 to 350 and, in the evening, 200 to 250 people. Even at services on Wednesday nights, they have "easily" about 150 people. All these numbers are reported to have increased, according to more recent estimates by the church on its website. In 2003 a Bible School was established at the church with twenty-six full-time and part-time students attending. Young people are sent out from the church internationally to do mission work. Using Third Day's own television broadcast facility, services are televised on the Miracle Channel. Music too plays a large part in the ministry.

Video-streamed podcasts of sermons from Third Day show strummed electric guitar chords accentuating climactic points in the energetic and forceful preaching of Pastor Armstrong – "I don't have a lick of notes, but I have the Holy Spirit." Armstrong's expository sermons, in which he takes a biblical passage, then expands and applies it, are typical of Pentecostalism. His preaching is accompanied with gestures, repetitions, and direct queries such as "Amen?" or "Somebody help me now," or "Are you here?" or "Does anyone hear me now?" He sometimes cocks a hand behind his ear to encourage the congregation's response. Interrupting himself at various points, he might tell how a congregant has been healed or invite someone to stand up to receive a blessing or himself speak in tongues. After coughing, he might remark, "The enemy is attacking my throat like you would not believe." Or, "I'm havin' trouble under this anointing preaching this." He recounts his conversations with God in such words as "I'm just tellin' you what he said to me," or "Here's what he said."

The Third Day Worship Centre shares some emphases and affiliations with the Kingston Gospel Temple. It too has supported Martha's Table and the Kingston Pregnancy Crisis (now Care) Centre. Pastor Hubert expressed appreciation for what the Family Coalition Party, a pro-life political party in Ontario, is doing. He also affirmed the work of an organization to support Israel, Christians for Israel – distinct from the American-based Christians United for Israel. Christians for Israel sees "the return of the Jewish people to Israel as the clear fulfilment of biblical prophecy and a major 'Sign of the Times' – one that points toward the soon Coming of the Lord Jesus Christ who, for Christians, is the promised Messiah of Israel" (Christians for Israel). Hubert described how he had been in touch with Daniel Elkin, rabbi at Beth Israel Congregation, offering "to come sometime to tell their congregation that we are very sorry about what happened to the Jewish people about fifty, sixty years ago and we would love to be friends with them." He added, though his words left it unclear whether it was the offer or the visit that had been accomplished, "We've done that. That's very important to us." Hubert indicated that "blessing Israel as a nation and God's plan for the Israel people is very important to us." While not necessarily in agreement with all of the politics in Israel, he says, "God in his words is very clear that he's got plans for Israel and the Jewish people. Jesus is a Jewish Jesus by the way. So our hearts are very tender there" (interview, 19 November 2003). Despite the friendship and openness expressed in these words, again this relationship is undeniably one-sided, with Christians imposing their understanding of Judaism on Jews and seeking to incorporate them into their view of Christian eschatology.

In 2003 Hubert spoke against same-sex marriage as an example of how Canada was abandoning the biblical principles on which the country was founded. At that time, our interview touched on the imminent passage in Parliament of Bill C-250, which amended the existing legislation against hate propaganda to include inciting hatred on the basis of sexual orientation. Some Christians opposed that bill on the grounds that it might prohibit preaching on various biblical passages interpreted as condemning homosexual behaviour. In April 2005 Conservative Member of Parliament Stockwell Day addressed a rally at the Third Day Worship Centre opposing the same-sex marriage legislation that the Liberal government was presenting in the form of Bill C-38. Several hundred people attended the rally. Day, part of a national organization to defend the traditional definition of marriage as between a man and woman, was met by about fifty protestors, some holding placards stating that his opposition to the bill was motivated by hatred. Those organizing the rally pointed out that they were not opposed to gays or lesbians; their interest was in celebrating the institution of marriage (*Whig-Standard*, 14 April 2005).

Charismatic Christians include Pentecostals and others who experience and make use of particular spiritual gifts in the contemporary church. Within the Pentecostal tradition, the charismata, or "gifts of the spirit," referred to in 1 Corinthians 12 and elsewhere – especially prophecy, healing, speaking in tongues, the interpretation of speaking in tongues, and the discernment of spirits – were understood as intended not just for the early church but for present-day Christians as well. Pentecostals have sometimes been criticized by other charismatics for what is seen as an overemphasis on *glossolalia*, or speaking in tongues. In its Statement of Faith, the Third Day Worship Centre states that the "Baptism in the Holy Spirit" provides "the gifts or enablement of the Holy Spirit ... This experience is distinct from and subsequent to the experience of the New Birth and is evidenced by the initial physical sign of speaking with other tongues as the Spirit of God gives utterance" (Third Day Worship Centre b). The teachings of the Pentecostal Assemblies of Canada – and therefore of the Kingston Gospel Temple – offer something almost identical as a parallel clause in their Statement of Faith.

The understanding of *charisma* has become highly problematic today, when almost any salesperson or politician or celebrity having an attractive personality, a persuasive tongue, or the least degree of charm gets called "charismatic." The sociologist Max Weber has also defined charisma in a manner relevant to this discussion, using it to designate a particular kind of power resting on a leader's exceptional gifts and personal authority. He distinguished this kind of charismatic authority from "traditional authority" and from "rational-legal authority" (1947, part 3, 324–423). Traditional authority may be legitimized by inheritance, as in a monarchy, while rational-legal authority depends on a constitution or the rules of the state. A religious charismatic leader possesses gifts given by God. When I interviewed Peter Hubert for *Profiles: People of Faith*, he was careful to point out the need for an emphasis on morality and integrity: "We are strong teachers of character, character, character. As a matter of fact, I'll even give you a one-liner: 'Charisma without character is catastrophe.' Those are the three C's" (Cogeco interview, 6 October 2004). In putting things in this way, Hubert was recognizing the precarious nature of charismatic leadership, which can be transitory, especially if based solely on the personality of the leader.

Weber also indicated that charismatic authority inevitably develops toward routinization, becoming either the traditional or rational leadership type as the group becomes incorporated into society. Charismatic leadership is often revolutionary and unstable, and succession to the next leader becomes problematical, often unplanned. As applied to Pentecostalism, which arose after all in the atmosphere of revivalism in the early twentieth century, spontaneity and the free exercise of the gifts of the Spirit tend to become bureaucratized and regulated in the Pentecostal denominations. The restrictions of a denominational organization partly led to the Third Day Worship Centre presenting itself as post-denominational, favouring the liberty of a spiritually gifted pastor over the limitations imposed by a congregational board or procedures established at denominational headquarters. Yet even the Statement of Faith at Third Day codifies the Baptism of the Holy Spirit and speaking in tongues, institutionalizing what began as a charisma or spiritual gift. The denominational relatives of the Third Day Worship Centre, the Pentecostal Assemblies of Canada, and the United Pentecostals, of course do the same thing. While controls and accountability are said to be present in this post-denominational church, it is unclear exactly what recourse a disgruntled congregant might have in a dispute with the pastor, except to leave the church. Further, how the succession of leadership in the next generation of such a church is to be assured is unclear. Central to Weber's analysis of charismatic authority was the relationship between followers and the leaders, who must maintain their backing to continue in the leadership role.

Scholars of religious studies generally regard charismatic leaders in religions as unpredictable, because they are not bound by traditions or by rules. Hans Mol, a Canadian sociologist of religion, in writing about the difficulties of Doukhobors in Canada in contrast with the relative success of Hutterites, both of them communal groups, points to unchecked individualism and charismatic leadership as a weak point. Doukhobors, says Mol, tended to divinize their leaders. That created problems when one leader turned out to be a gambler and alcoholic, or another called a stop to sexual intercourse, or yet another made disastrous business decisions. In such cases, Doukhobor society splintered (1976, 103–16). In the city of Kingston, then, the future of the Third Day Worship Centre, a currently successful post-denominational church bent on expansion, depends on whether it can preserve its charismatic energy – that is, its emphasis on free exercise of the gifts of the Spirit – while its leadership inevitably becomes routinized over time.

Christian and Missionary Alliance

The Christian and Missionary Alliance Church has Canadian roots. Its founder, A.B. Simpson, was born in Prince Edward Island in 1843, educated at Knox College in Toronto, and became the minister of Toronto's Knox Presbyterian Church in 1865. He moved to a pulpit in New York City in 1879, and soon after left that church to begin a mission that in the 1880s became the present Christian and Missionary Alliance Church. The Canadian body became autonomous in 1981, and today has 251 churches with 45,000 members. Unlike the Pentecostal churches, the Missionary Alliance does not teach that speaking in tongues is an inevitable or necessary sign of baptism by the Holy Spirit. Rather, the Alliance denomination, perhaps remembering that Simpson began his new work after being filled with the Holy Spirit, has the view that the Spirit may bestow various gifts on the church and on individual believers. One article describes the Alliance position on spiritual gifts as "Expectation without Agenda" (Christian and

Missionary Alliance). As its name indicates, the church strongly supports mission work, at home and abroad.

The Christian and Missionary Alliance Church has three congregations in Kingston. Kingston Alliance Church is the original and oldest congregation; Bayridge Alliance Church is a recently relocated church near the Cataraqui Town Centre, the city's largest shopping centre; the third is the Kingston Chinese Alliance Church in the Brock Street premises vacated by the Kingston Gospel Temple after relocation to its present site (see chap. 5). The oldest, the Kingston Alliance Church, is located at Palace and Bath roads just beyond the old Traffic Circle at what used to be Kingston's western edge. It was built there "around 1959," according to the pastor, Paul Silcock, on land that had been a farmer's field: "There was nothing here" (interview, 22 January 2004). Today, with the expansion of the city even further westward, this church is now more central to the city core than it used to be. The church is within the same block as a branch of the public library and the YMCA and across the Bath Road from the city's oldest Canadian Tire Store.

Statistics from the 2001 Census show that the Christian and Missionary Alliance is a smaller denomination nationally than the various branches of Pentecostalism. It has about 66,000 members as compared with the Pentecostals' 370,000. In the light of these figures, Pentecostal denominations have a large share of the Canadian population – only 40,000 less than the declining Presbyterians and about 40,000 more than the reported number of Jews. Whereas Pentecostal membership dropped by 15 per cent between 1991 and 2001, the second largest decline among Protestant denominations after Presbyterianism, the Christian and Missionary Alliance denomination grew by 12 per cent in that period. John G. Stackhouse Jr, attempting in 2003 to account for this drop among Pentecostals, suggested that as the Pentecostal Assemblies of Canada has "'cooled off' and become more generically 'evangelical,' it is no longer as attractive to 'hotter' Christians who then migrate to the Vineyard or to nondenominational pentecostal/charismatic churches" (Stackhouse 2003). If that pattern is to be found in Kingston, then Pentecostals may well have gravitated with pastors Armstrong and Hubert to the new post-denominational – and arguably "hotter" – Third Day Worship Centre.

The Kingston Alliance Church has a smaller roster of members and attendees than the largest evangelical churches in the city. In January 2004 the pastor, Paul Silcock, estimated the size of the congregation at 104 members, though he said about three hundred people "would call this church home." He explained that, while attendance at service on a Sunday morning would be 150, "unlike other churches, our membership is lower than our attendance." This pattern of a congregation's size exceeding its actual membership is seen at Bethel Church, an evangelical congregation located downtown on Johnson Street near the corner of Barrie (see chap. 6), raising the difficulty of explaining why at these churches that should be the case, in contrast to, say, Roman Catholic, Anglican, and United churches, where membership greatly exceeds attendance. Perhaps the membership standards are higher, and numbers lower, because evangelicals demand more commitment than do other denominations – the expectation of tithing, for example. Alternatively, perhaps allegiance to their denomination or congregation is not as strong among evangelical Christians who may move from church to church more readily, either in search of more inspired preaching from another pastor or because of doctrinal disputes.

The Kingston Alliance Church accepts what the pastor referred to as "a responsibility to the city of Kingston and to the people of Kingston." The Storehouse of Hope, located in the church building, collects used clothing and other items for people in need. These things, along with a hot meal, are provided on Mondays and Wednesdays from noon until 3 PM: "People can come in and they can come downstairs and browse all the clothes." Silcock estimated that about one hundred people come on each of these days to "meet somebody, talk to somebody, have something to eat, hang around, leave. Whatever." He emphasized that there are "no strings attached – there is no [worship] service with that." Rather, he says, "the primary purpose is to provide people with their physical needs with so many people who are homeless, hurting, or poor" (interview, 22 January 2004). Kingston Gospel Temple used to have a similar clothing drive, but with fewer numbers of people using this assistance, perhaps due to their location, the Gospel Temple refers potential clothing donations to the Kingston Alliance Church. Though the role of the Storehouse of Hope "would identify our church in the community more than anything else," Silcock stressed that the church's "highest purpose" in Kingston "is to see people come to know Jesus Christ."

Silcock referred to a split that occurred in the congregation in about 1990, long before his time there, "that really took a large section of the church – it was gone." The departure of the senior pastor "terribly devastated the congregation." He continued, "It deeply wounded the congregation ... It was a horrible thing." While he did not mention any names, it was Dr Charles Seidenspinner, pastor of the Kingston Alliance Church in the late 1980s, who became pastor at the independent Calvary Bible Church on Nelson Street after his departure. As a way of dealing with the hurt that still lingered many years later, specific apologies were sent by the Alliance Church to the former members, seeking their forgiveness. In addition, the two churches exchanged letters to clear up the differences. The Calvary Bible Church had originated as the Grace Bible Church, begun as a church plant by Bethel Church. In time Grace Bible Church cut its ties with the Associated Gospel denomination and became independent. Seidenspinner, who died in 1998 at the age of eighty-six, had been a prominent evangelical leader in the United States and Canada and a president of the Evangelical Fellowship of Canada. He was pastor of many churches and president of several Bible colleges, including the non-denominational Southeastern Bible College in Birmingham, Alabama from 1945 to 1958, and the United Missionary Church's Emmanuel Bible College in Kitchener, Ontario, from 1972 to 1975.

Chris Walker, at the time associate pastor at Bethel Church, referred to members who left Bethel for the Calvary Bible Church, and identified another parallel instance: "Bayridge Alliance Church which has now just purchased the Duffus Funeral Home out there came out of this church [i.e., Bethel], not happily, I understand." He said that Bethel "has been known as a congregation that has had integrity in its leadership, for a long period of time – relatively free of major pathologies." Walker's view was that that division at Bethel "did not seem to provide a 'sickness unto death' for this congregation" because the church's leadership "staunched the flow of blood at that time enough to heal well and to move on" (interview, 4 November 2003). Bayridge Alliance Church, as it eventually came to be known, originated as a group of twenty or thirty Christians from Bethel who began meeting at St Lawrence College in 1972 to establish Ebenezer Bible Church. Soon they acquired property and became Bayridge Bible Church, a congregation within the Associated Gospel Church, the denomination of Bethel Church, which they had previously left. In 1979 the Bayridge Bible Church changed denominations once more, joining the Christian and Missionary Alliance, which Pastor Dan Baetz regarded as "fairly close in doctrine" to Associated Gospel (interview, 5 February 2004). The Bayridge Alliance congregation views the manner in which the strategically located property on Gardiner's Road came to them as an act of providence, despite its tragic circumstances. The family-owned Duffus Funeral Home was offered for sale after a highly publicized case in which Teresa Duffus was sentenced to prison for impaired driving causing death in 2001. The former funeral facility, whose business dropped off precipitously after the accident, was easily renovated by the Bayridge Alliance congregation for its new use as a church.

In effect, then, the story of the Christian and Missionary Alliance Church in Kingston displays a number of departures and unions. A congregational split at the Kingston Alliance Church resulted in people departing for the Calvary Bible Church where their pastor assumed leadership. Calvary Bible Church had begun as an Associated Gospel church planted by Bethel. Also within the Associated Gospel denomination, a group from Bethel – itself formerly Congregational – became the Bayridge Church, which in turn joined the Christian and Missionary Alliance denomination. A third congregation, the Kingston Chinese Alliance Church, which began in 1976 as an independent organization named the Kingston Chinese Evangelical Church, joined the Christian and Missionary Alliance in the early 1980s. In 1985, when the Kingston Gospel Temple moved from its location on Brock Street, the Kingston Chinese Alliance Church bought that property from the Pentecostals. Pastor Paul Silcock said that, considering the Christian and Missionary Alliance denomination on a national basis, most of their churches in Canada would, like the Kingston Chinese Alliance Church, be comprised of ethnic congregations (see chap. 5).

Evangelicals might be more prone to moving in this way from one congregation or denomination to another, a phenomenon that Reginald Bibby and others have termed "the circulation of the saints." Free Methodist pastor Robert Boutilier perhaps inaccurately identified it as a specifically local phenomenon when he mentioned "this really transient mentality of the church in Kingston." Boutilier said: "It's kind of like a smorgasbord: when this one is running hot, I'll plug in there, and when it's not, I'll go to the next one" (interview, 5 July 2004). In Kingston as in other places, some Christians have moved elsewhere to follow local trends, to discover a more congenial congregation, to find a more dynamic minister, or, sometimes, because of disruptions. While more common there, this "church-hopping" or leave-taking is not exclusively a phenomenon restricted to Protestant evangelicalism. Brian Osborne, in his history of St Andrew's Presbyterian Church in Kingston, deals in part with the ministry of Max V. Putnam from 1958 to 1976 during some of the church's most successful years. Putnam was a popular and an attractive personality; he became moderator of the Presbyterian Church in Canada. Just ten months after his wife died early in 1971, "he advised Session of his intention to marry a recently divorced member of St Andrew's" (Osborne 2004, 405). After the marriage took place a year later in October of 1972, divisions increased at the church. Some elders resigned, while other members left the church. Between 1970 and 1976 the congregation suffered a 20 per cent decline in adherents and members. The minister's remarriage, too hastily arranged and to a divorcee, became something of a local ecclesiastical scandal to a degree hard to imagine a generation later. The local problem was made worse by the fact that the national church had no guidance to offer to St Andrew's, lacking any firm position on the remarriage of divorced persons. The larger context, namely, other difficulties that the Presbyterian Church in Canada generally was experiencing during this period, exacerbated the local issue. Putnam's ministry at St Andrew's disintegrated, and he departed at the end of June 1976 for a pulpit in Australia.

While Chris Walker maintains that "you can get along with a sociopath [as pastor], but you can't get along without an excellent secretary," the "difficult" minister – or the departure of a member of the clergy under difficult circumstances – can divide a congregation and leave long-lasting wounds. At Sydenham Street United Church the minister of twenty-seven years, Rev. William Hendry, became ill and left on disability in 1999; but the pastoral relationship with this beloved long-term minister "unravelled and became very conflicted, and it just got worse and worse." A five-year hiatus ensued, with people "fighting with each other" and "eruptions at meetings." Hendry's successor, Elizabeth Macdonald, summed up: "There's still work to be done to deal with this former minister, who's very angry, who's threatening legal action. It was very, very messy and many people were hurt in the process" (interview, 27 January 2004). Of course, other departures from and by various congregations of the United Church of Canada were rife surrounding the decision in 1988 that sexual orientation was not a barrier to ordination (see Dickey Young 1990). In 2007 and 2008 entire congregations were leaving the Anglican Church of Canada, this time over another matter, the blessing of same-sex unions within the Anglican Church.

In the late 1980s St George's Anglican Cathedral in Kingston suffered a major, nationally publicized scandal over the sexual abuse of dozens of boys by their world-renowned choirmaster, John Gallienne. Two of his victims committed suicide. These criminal assaults took place over a period of fifteen years and were known to church officials as early as 1976, but Gallienne had promised to reform. In the early 1990s he served a sentence in federal prison after pleading guilty to more than twenty sexual offences. Some parishioners, especially those whose children were among the victims, accused St George's of failing to take any meaningful preventive measures, despite its knowledge of the acts Gallienne was committing, and also of not providing adequate counselling for the victims. Judge Richard G. Byers observed at Gallienne's trial that because of "a failure to protect these children from further harm ... the list of victims is longer than it should be" (qtd in Swainson 1991, 271). Some members of the church picketed the sidewalk in front of St George's on Sunday mornings, demanding justice and acknowledgment by the church of its lack of action. The effects of Gallienne's actions have continued to linger at St George's and in the city. After Gallienne's release from prison, he moved to Ottawa with his wife and subsequently took up work as a choirmaster there, contravening a church ban on continuing his musical leadership. In April 2010 he was charged with another case of sexual abuse by a complainant who had not come forward during the 1980s.

While the case of John Gallienne is beyond doubt the worst that has come to light in the history of religions in Kingston, many other congregations have been torn apart by scandals and controversies. One begins to think that any congregation that has not suffered a major split or disruption over one issue or another in its history is fortunate indeed. Sometimes the leadership of the church is to blame; on other occasions a congregation becomes lacklustre for no apparent reason and people leave. Whereas departures by members from congregations in the nineteenth century seemed more often to take place after doctrinal disputes, today's churchgoers, perhaps acting more in their role as religious "consumers," will take their business elsewhere for a variety of other reasons based on preferences and inclinations that are not always related to matters of theology, church governance, or denominational practice.

Free Methodist

The Free Methodist Church is a much smaller denomination nationally than the other evangelical churches dealt with in this chapter. Free Methodists are concentrated in central Canada, with only twenty-nine of their 150 Canadian churches west of Ontario. About 7,500 people are members of the Free Methodist Church in Canada, with perhaps another 5,000 adherents, echoing the Missionary Alliance profile of having more attendees than members at worship services. In view of these figures, Free Methodists in Kingston have a strong local presence, according to census figures, with a total of 1,700 people in four congregations. A major reason for its relative prominence comes from the nineteenth-century strength of Free Methodism in eastern Ontario. However, as with the other denominations considered already, its history is again marked by schisms, some reunions, and, sometimes, further divisions.

The Free Methodist Church, with its origins in the United States, was termed "free" because, under the leadership of B.T. Roberts in the 1860s, it opposed slavery, secret societies, and charging rent for the better pews in churches. When other Methodist groups merged in 1884 to become the largest denomination within Canadian Protestantism, the Free Methodists stayed out. From the standpoint of those charting the mainstream of Methodism in Canada, with the United Church understood to continue the tradition of Charles and John Wesley, Free Methodism is marginal. Neil Semple's massive *The Lord's Dominion: The History of Canadian Methodism*, presented as "a comprehensive history" and "an important standard reference book" for Canadian Methodism, mentions the Free Methodist Church on only a half-dozen of its 450 pages (1996). Semple states that the Free Methodist church "was heavily bound to its American parent until after World War II and was never able to convince Canadians that it was the true inheritor of the mantle of Canadian Methodism" (445).

Because of its high degree of relevance to the local situation, the history of the Free Methodist Church in Canada is worth sketching out here. By the

1880s it had a dozen preaching points and a few hundred members. They emphasized, together with such other groups as the Salvation Army, the "holiness movement" as an expression of John Wesley's teaching about Christian perfection, developing it into a doctrine of complete, or entire, sanctification. Free Methodists, then, picked up the experiential and conversionist dimensions of Wesley's thought and combined those emphases with personal morality to a much greater degree than did the other currents of Methodism. As mainstream Methodism shared more of the aims of the Social Gospel Movement with its goal of transforming society, the holiness movement churches maintained their position that the way to change society was to convert individuals. Ralph C. Horner, an ordained Canadian Methodist, began his evangelistic preaching in the late 1880s, initially with Methodist support and blessing. By 1895 he was deposed for what was regarded as excessive emotionalism at his revival meetings, held particularly through the Ottawa Valley, and because he was not amenable to the church's discipline and authority over him. Horner began the Holiness Movement Church of Canada, which he left in 1916 to join the Standard Church of America (Semple 1996, 221, 445). To bring things full circle, in 1959, by the action of the Conference meeting in Kingston, held at the Colborne Street Free Methodist Church, the Free Methodist Church in Canada merged with, or perhaps in some sense reunited with, the Holiness Movement Church. As the website of the Kingston Standard Church indicates, a local Standard congregation was established in 1918, with two successive church buildings downtown, after the revival meetings of Rev. J.G. Nussey in McBurney Park. Since 1975 it has been in its present setting on Sydenham Road, just north of 401. While retaining its name, in 2003 the Kingston Standard Church became part of another denomination, the Wesleyan Church, when the Standard Church of America merged with the Wesleyans (see Kingston Standard Church).

The Kingston Standard Church presents itself as situated within the Canadian evangelical tradition and, more specifically, as coming from the Methodist tradition. Pastor Peter Rigby explained that, when people ask about the Standard Church, "I say that we're the Methodist side of the United Church." He went on to say their "founder was a Methodist evangelist" who held tent meetings with ten thousand people in attendance in the 1890s. Contrary to Semple's version, Rigby affirms that "we come from that tradition and look back to, you know, John Wesley, who came out of the Anglican tradition. So that's how we see our roots, and how we connect ourselves." Asked about the relationship of the Standard Church with other churches, Rigby stated, "There used to be what they called the Canadian Holiness Federation, and in that Federation were Free Methodists, Nazarenes, Wesleyans, Standard, Salvation Army. And we think of them as sister denominations, if you want. There's a great deal of crossing back and forth between clergy. When, you know, one denomination has an opening [for a pastor] and they can't find someone, they'll come from the Frees, or the Wesleyans, or sometimes the Salvation Army" (interview, 27 February 2004).

To return to the Free Methodist churches in Kingston, Polson Park Free Methodist Church, while not the oldest among the four or five existing congregations, is the major church among them. In a paradoxical way, it has had a role as both child and parent in relation to another church: it is the daughter of a downtown church that later, when that congregation fell into decline, it in turn nurtured back into a new role. The former Colborne Street Free Methodist Church, Kingston's oldest Free Methodist church, is now the NeXt Church. In 1959 that Colborne Street church "planted" (to use the customary language of church development) a new congregation in Polson Park, one of the residential areas then beginning to be established at the city's western boundaries. The area of Polson Park lies between Johnson Street and Bath Road, west of Portsmouth Avenue. Meanwhile, says Pastor Brian Pritchard of the Polson Park church, "the old Colborne Street church slowly went down. It was more geared for people in the community who moved away, and gradually it was getting low in numbers." Faced with Colborne Street's closing, the Polson Park church decided, "No, let's take hold of it and put in a young congregation and serve who's currently in that area." That decision led to the birth of the NeXt Church, a church (re)planted by Polson Park, which itself had originally been planted by Colborne Street. As Brian Pritchard put it, "the pastors who are there, used to be here ... it was like a daughter church to us, and so we put it in" (20 November 2003). He emphasized that, as a separate congregation of the Free Methodist Church of Canada, the NeXt Church is fully independent of Polson Park.

Polson Park Free Methodist Church, after fifty years of existence, has evolved into a large facility. The sanctuary can accommodate 225 worshippers, and that many again can be seated in the fellowship hall to the rear of the church. There is office space for three pastors and secretaries. The large parking area is available to be used by others when not occupied by parishioners. A day-care facility, West End Children's Centre, was established in 1978 as part of the church's community outreach and has almost fifty children. As Pritchard says, the church "wanted to be able to serve the social needs of the community, as well as serve God." After extensive consultation with people in the neighbourhood and with city officials, they built a skateboard park for teenagers adjacent to the church and provided $50,000 worth of equipment. Polson Park equipped this skate park not primarily for their own young people but because there was no other satisfactory facility available in the city. Pritchard estimated that whereas seniors comprise about 40 per cent of the congregation, only 10 per cent would be teenagers. The church also sponsors an alternative Halloween event called a "Hallelujah Party," during which young people, under the supervision of adults, collect items for a local food bank. This terminology avoids the negative connotations of evil and witchcraft that "Halloween" has for some evangelicals.

While personal evangelism and missions abroad continue to be centrally important to the work of the Free Methodist Church in Canada, the denominational website shows its efforts to position itself more at the centre of Canadian evangelicalism rather than to the right. Through the early 1990s, Free Methodists in Canada went through a series of steps to establish their full independence from the more conservative American parent denomination, culminating with the four Canadian regional offices being centralized into one office in 1995. With their independence, Free Methodists in Canada have become increasingly able to define themselves in a relatively more moderate way and to recover some of the earlier emphases on social justice that they surrendered to mainstream Methodism in the late nineteenth and early twentieth centuries. The website of the Canadian Free Methodists now includes position papers on the poor, the environment, social justice, human rights, HIV/AIDS, and "homosexual behaviour" – distinguished from homosexual inclination. On the last item, this website, borrowing a statement from the Christian Reformed Church on the pastoral care of homosexual individuals, puts the need for chaste relationship under the same requirements as for other single Christians, providing no possibility of a sexual relationship. But departing from a more right-wing view that would single out homosexual acts as the worst of all sexual sins, this paper suggests that "sermons should refer to a wide variety of sexual sins and give examples of God's grace and comfort to people who struggle with brokenness" (Free Methodist Church a). A section of resources on "Eastern Thought and the Gospel" includes the Bhagavad Gita and books by Thomas Merton and the Dalai Lama (Free Methodist Church b). Other sections deal with organ and tissue donation, cloning, stem-cell research, and end of life care, all of them carefully presented, with thoughtful discussion, references, and a final position offered.

About as far west as one can get within the current city limits lies the Kingston West Free Methodist Church, built in 1982 and also begun by the Colborne Street Free Methodist Church. Situated on Woodbine Road, Kingston West has had some difficulty identifying what the needs of the community are: "We're kind of out at the end of a dead-end road," its pastor, Mike Hogeboom, told us. "We found it difficult to actually get more involved in our community" (interview, 3 August 2004). There are no homeless people in the region; the schools were not in need of breakfast programs; but the church did employ a youth pastor when it was suggested that more needed to be done for young people.

Asked about how he saw other churches not in the evangelical tradition, Hogeboom responded that "it concerns us when churches would choose to become more relevant to the culture – become more driven by the culture – than to be guided by what we say is God's Word." As "the prime examples for us," he cited "the issue of homosexuality and abortion." He was worried that interfaith dialogue would result in a "watered-down, less than satisfactory perspective by putting us all together in the same pot." He felt it was important to be straightforward about what it means to be Christian, "to communicate our message with more clarity, so it is not blurred by so many voices and opinions." In general Hogeboom sensed that "the spiritual temperature is decreasing." He saw religious diversity as resulting in "confusion," bringing about a "mosaic" and "hodgepodge" of religions, with a vagueness about what the Bible means.

Coincidentally, an evangelical website for gay Christians includes an article entitled "Straight Teacher Asked to Step Down Because She Will Not Condemn Gays!" that refers to the Kingston West Free Methodist congregation. The organizer of the website, Mary Pearson, a lesbian mother living in the Kingston area, tells how her daughter, Lauren Min-Pearson, was asked to leave her volunteer position working with teens at the Kingston West Free Methodist Church because she would not condemn gays. Min-Pearson, "a committed born-again Christian," took the scriptural position that she must not judge, and decided to resign. It is possible, of course, that her mother's website with its full and candid discussions about born-again gays and lesbians, mostly contrary to the Free Methodist position and ethos, drew the church's attention to Min-Pearson, or that what was asked of her has been misinterpreted (Christian Gays). Whatever circumstances might lie beyond this matter, this account dated May 2001 preceded the Free Methodist Church in Canada adopting its official position on homosexual behaviour in 2005, including its affirmation of "the church's historic commitment to the deep worth of all persons." That position also reminded Free Methodists of their "responsibility to minister in love to those of homosexual behaviour or inclination" (Free Methodist Church in Canada a).

Yet another local congregation, the Butternut Creek Free Methodist Church, began, as its pastor Robert Boutilier told us in 2004, "about eleven, twelve years ago as a church-planting initiative from the Polson Park Free Methodist Church." Boutilier recounted how Polson Park sent twenty or thirty couples from their own church to begin a new one in Pittsburgh Township east of the Cataraqui River, taking the name of a subdivision in that area, Butternut Creek Estates. They met for a time at the LaSalle

Secondary School on Highway 15 north of the junction with Highway 2, but after a few years the congregation had decreased to about twelve people. "At that time, the church had dwindled backwards" (interview, 5 July 2004). In 1997 Boutilier moved the congregation a kilometre north to St Martha Catholic School, and in doing so decreased the rent they were paying from $900 per month to a more manageable $160. The fact that Boutilier was a "bivocational" pastor who worked full time as an engineer with the Ministry of Transport also helped to cut expenses. Within six months Butternut Creek had achieved financial independence from Polson Park. Soon the congregation had increased to sixty or seventy people, but then the school space was needed by a nearby Roman Catholic Church "bursting out at the seams and looking for a place to do an alternative service." Butternut Creek moved again in 2001. Its third location was three interchanges further west on Highway 401 at le Centre Culturel Frontenac/Frontenac Cultural Centre on Dalton Avenue, a gathering place for Kingston francophones, and especially for their performances and artistic presentations. At that new site Boutilier was able to increase the size of the congregation to over one hundred people.

Though in 2004 Butternut Creek had $70,000 or $80,000 saved in a building fund, Pastor Boutilier said that "our philosophy at this point in time is to spend money on people, not on buildings." Because he wanted to avoid "putting a lot of debt load on the backs of the people in the church," other possibilities than a usual church building were under consideration. Among the options were leasing a facility or various buildings in different parts of the city "for a multi-faceted, multi-component style of ministry," or buying a large "executive-style home" that could be turned into apartments for seniors, or purchasing a large tract of land with a worship facility and "outdoor soccer pitches and baseball diamonds and ponds stocked with trout" that "plugs into the community." Boutilier was also considering "an emotional wellness facility" for people with mental illness who "cannot function in society" but who are not admissible to a psychiatric ward. Already he and his congregation were providing temporary housing in such situations for two-week periods when a need arose. Among the other ventures underway was a "mini food bank," with two volunteers from the church renting a van to drive to Toronto once a month and pick up dry foods from the Salvation Army for storage in a garage and distribution as needed.

While the Butternut Church has the goal of serving the community in some manner, among the particulars in "this sort of macro vision of the whole thing," many possibilities remain to be implemented. Pastor Boutilier has obvious energy, enthusiasm, and a knack for organization. He reported a negative experience as pastor of a country church when one member of the board committed a "serious breach of trust, as bad as it gets." Due to "politicking behind the scene," on the night that a crucial vote was held, people appeared who were "on the roll" of the church but whom Boutilier had never seen before – they "hadn't walked in the door for five or ten years." That experience, he said, "made me gag," and made him realize that such a procedure was not what God had in mind. When he first became pastor of Butternut Creek, he received permission from the Free Methodist bishop to allow him to try an experiment with church leadership. He asked the bishop and his congregation to trust his vision and model for the church, and says, "Seven years down the road there hasn't been any split. This is because we don't vote on things."

After three months of attendance at the Butternut Creek services, people are asked to go through classes and become members. In spite of that, members do not vote and there is no board. More than 90 per cent of the adult attendees are members: "We ask people to commit to unity, and we ask them to commit to expressing their views and opinions, but we ask them to do that in the context of unity. We also ask them to commit to hospitality and fellowship and spiritual growth and development." While Boutilier relies on the Free Methodist Statement of Faith for doctrinal direction, those who become members of Butternut Creek are not asked to join the Free Methodist Church in Canada, only to commit themselves to the direction and vision of this local church. Clearly this model allows freedom for congregational experiments while maintaining a loose association with the denomination. Someone with Boutilier's zeal and vision is given scope to develop a new church without creating a new competing church of another denomination – or of no denomination – in the process. While issues around questions of dispute resolution and the succession of leadership and the role of the denominational authority and structure may have remained, no split has occurred in the church or in the denomination. In fact, in 2007 Butternut Creek took steps toward fuller incorporation within the Free Methodist denomination. In April 2008 the congregation took a lease on what was to become their fourth location, the former Kingscourt United Church, which had closed a few months earlier. In March 2010, having purchased the property, Butternut Creek Free Methodist Church celebrated the launch of their new home and permanent worship site (*Whig-Standard*, 19 March 2010).

Another Free Methodist church "plant" is experimental in a slightly different way. Deliberately informal – the time of the Sunday service is posted as "around 11" – in 1997 Kingston's original Free Methodist Church on Colborne Street was reborn as the NeXt Church. The "X" in the church's name, written that way on the building's exterior signage and in its publications, perhaps signifies Generation X, referring to Douglas Coupland's 1991 novel about young people who were then "twenty-somethings," born roughly in the first half of the 1960s. On the other hand, perhaps the capitalized "X" is the Greek letter Chi that abbreviates the name of Christ or simply – and more cryptically – the unknown factor. The name of this re-established Free Methodist Church on Colborne Street recalls Charles Trueheart's 1996 article in the *Atlantic Monthly* entitled "Welcome to the Next Church." Trueheart characterized this new church, in a list that has "asterisks and exceptions," as consisting of: "No spires. No crosses. No robes. No clerical collars. No hard pews. No kneelers. No biblical gobbledygook. No prayerly rote. No fire, no brimstone. No pipe organs. No dreary eighteenth-century hymns. No forced solemnity. No Sunday finery. No collection plates." While the prime examples of these new ventures are "mega-churches" in the United States, they also include middle-sized and small examples. Trueheart's influential essay characterizes the worship within these "next" churches as involving various forms of multimedia, gathering "a flock of previously unchurched or unhappily churched people by being relentlessly creative about developing forms of worship – most symbolically and definingly, music – that are contemporary, accessible, 'authentic.'"

Many of the other markers of the next-church movement as described by Trueheart are evident in Kingston's NeXt Church, and to some extent in other evangelical churches in this chapter: the building's often unremarkable architecture, the emphasis on serving the community and on creating its own community, reading (or translating) the culture, music that is contemporary and relevant, an interest in sports and teams, giving people what they want, programming for people in their twenties, identifying people's "gifts" and encouraging volunteerism, and downplaying the connection with a denomination. The NeXt Church began as a small-group non-denominational gathering of thirteen people in 1997 that grew to 158 in a year. The pastor, Al Doseger, one of the church's founders, said that the difficulty was not in attracting people but in retaining them: "We didn't realize that we were going to be a transient church." Their biggest challenge, Doseger says, is to understand the members of the church family in the context of North American consumerist culture. "If your needs aren't met here, you'll just go somewhere else and have your needs met. So that's a challenge to figure out, you know, how to best serve the people that come" (interview, 7 November 2005).

The NeXt Church "became a bit of a harbour for those that didn't fit into church. We became a bit of a refuge for those that were either burnt or hurt by church." Some are young people who found no one else of their age in their previous congregation, while others, according to Doseger, "had no kind of church background." He speaks of the flock at Colborne Street as "a ragtag bunch of people – those with church history and those without ...

I like the fact that we have haves and have-nots and, you know, rich sit beside poor, and hurt sit beside people that seem to be healed." While the demographics of the congregation had changed, in 2005 the dominant age group was estimated as between twenty-four and forty. Young families made up a large part of the congregation, with children present too. Queen's University students, again a transient population, were also beginning to come in greater numbers. However, Doseger wanted the church to draw people from the immediate surrounding area and have an impact there. The church has regularly held a neighbourhood picnic in the nearby McBurney Park where they served "over nine hundred hamburgers and sausages." Doseger goes on to describe how at this party "we put a band on the stage and … rubbed shoulders with the very people that live in our neighbourhood." He said he would be worried if the church became predominantly for students from the university about a kilometre south, and he would also worry if people began to arrive at their services mostly in their cars: "We don't want to be a guest in this neighbourhood." That, he thought, was one of the factors contributing to the decline of the old Colborne Street Free Methodist Church – its people mostly came by car from elsewhere in the city.

Even since the NeXt Church was established, there has been a noticeable change in the degree of gentrification occurring on the nearby streets. Perhaps that factor partially led to a new satellite church being planted by the NeXt Church about a kilometre north, in a more working-class area on Russell Street, just off Division. The site had formerly been the Resurrection Community Church at Kingston, associated with the Congregational Christian Churches in Canada, a gathering of autonomous evangelical churches that began about two decades ago. Its succcessor, begun by one of the pastors at NeXt, was called simply "Rustle," a pun on the street's name, and its online blog was headed "Rustle: Goings on at the Ranch." When the Rustle pastor, Brandon Shillington, was ordained in February 2008, the country-and-western theme continued in a gathering at Rustle that included a cake inscribed "Ordained Wrangler" (see Rustle).

The NeXt Church website, nextchurch.com (a fortunate acquisition of a desirable domain name) is clean, contemporary, and generally establishes its playful relevance: "If NeXt were a photographer, we'd focus on letting everyone in on God's big secret – I'm changing everything and you're invited" (NeXt Church). The site is almost devoid of faith statements, doctrinal positions, and credal formulations; instead, there are announcements of events and programs, podcast sermons, MP3 recordings of the music from the services, links to blogs by members, and albums of photos posted on the flickr.com website. Only rarely does the website give any hint of the Free Methodist connection. As Al Doseger puts it, "If you asked the broad majority of our church whether or not we're Free Methodists, I think ... they'd kind of look at you like a dog staring through a screen door." The NeXt Church, though planted by Polson Park Free Methodist Church, began as non-denominational and then associated itself with the Free Methodist Church in Canada: "We fell backwards into this denomination. We found they really fit us, and we encouraged that, so they helped us fulfil the dreams we thought God had for us." One of the consequences of this association, as Doseger himself learned more about Free Methodism, was that the NeXt Church changed from never having a service of communion to its becoming a regular institution: "Now we do it once a month because ... it's part of our rich heritage." In keeping with this grassroots approach, in spring 2008 the church was having meetings to make decisions about its method of governance.

Another alternative place of worship, parallel to the NeXt Church, emerged with the establishment of the Café Church in September 2007 in the Wellington Street Theatre at the corner of Johnson Street: "It's funky. It's caffeinated. It's Church like you've never experienced it before. It's relaxed. It's for people who live, work and play in Downtown Kingston." This handsome gothic building was built in the nineteenth century as the Congregational Church. After 1925, when Church Union occurred and the building became available, it was the home of the Masonic Lodge for many years until reconfigured as a theatre space. Ironically, perhaps, more than eighty years after it last operated as a church, this old limestone structure once again provided a space for Christian worship, though only temporarily. Two years later, in September 2009, the Café Church moved to 259 Ontario Street next to a Subway sandwich shop. The pastor of the Café Church, Steve Fritz-Millett – who wears a "Jesus Is My Home Boy" t-shirt and red-laced sneakers – describes the place as "God's living room." He is retired from the military and working as an engineer, while studying part-time at the Tyndale Seminary in Toronto for a career in ministry. Fritz-Millett says that the idea for this venture was first suggested to him by Doug Martin, then pastor at Bethel Church located four blocks up Johnson Street. Whether the Café Church is a plant by Bethel Church, or how this ministry is supported, is unclear. As in the case of the NeXt Church, the ties of an alternative worship space with a sponsoring church or parent denomination tend to be muted. As Fritz-Millett says, "We're trying to demystify Christianity and kind of strip away the spiritual baggage" (*Whig-Standard*, 19 July 2008).

STANDARDIZATION AND INDIVIDUALIZATION

Any full and comprehensive account of all of the evangelical churches in Kingston, especially those not affiliated with a denomination, would have to include literally dozens of other congregations, most of them having less than one hundred members and adherents. In addition to the Calvary Bible Church, barely mentioned here, another independent Baptist church – the Bible Baptist Church – two congregations of the Church of Christ, as well as the Kingdom Seed Fellowship, the Pilgrim Holiness Church and the Kingston Mennonite Fellowship, the Kingsway Outreach Centre, the New Life Centre, the Seventh-day Adventist Church, and the Church of God of Prophecy, all have (or have had) a presence in Kingston. Other groups exist in an embryonic state as house churches and might never become more than that. Others appear, and then silently disappear, perhaps because they were conceived as experimental ministries or church plants that did not take root.

This plethora of contemporary evangelical churches might best be understood as an example of modern or postmodern differentiation. That is, these churches situate themselves in some space other than that controlled by the large overarching narratives of denominationalism; they represent a process of detraditionalization that celebrates individual choice and freedom from large ecclesiastical bureaucracies. Such churches choose instead to focus on their own stories of origin in preference to historical antecedents that reach back into the mists of Christian history. They represent, as Steven Connor has said in a discussion of the French philosopher of postmodernism, Jean-François Lyotard, "a shift from the ruffled majesty of grand narratives to the splintering autonomy of micronarratives" (qtd in Heelas 1998, 7). They want to organize themselves in their own way, free from domination by a central authority. They often begin – as Francis Armstrong and Robert Boutilier and Al Doseger illustrate here – with a pastor who experiences the call of God to start a new work in a new setting. Sometimes these pastors have become dissatisfied with congregations or boards who do not share or support their vision. Alternatively, these independent churches might originate from a small gathering of Christians meeting in temporary or borrowed space who decide the time has come to grow larger. Or else a new need, not otherwise met in the community, is perceived and identified. Less often, a group splits off from an existing congregation and goes on its own after a bitter dispute arises, sometimes of a personal kind, at other times over a doctrinal matter.

James Beckford uses a restaurant analogy not unlike the one with which this chapter began. In a consumerist society, people are pressured to make certain lifestyle choices as a way to construct their individual identity, with definite benefits promised as a result of their choices. Many contemporary restaurants, Beckford points out, "belong to transnational corporations; and their menus reflect hybridized and standardized notions of taste." Though the menus may seem to offer great variety, this range of freedom to choose may be only an illusion: "The appearance of diversity and choice masks underlying pressures toward standardisation." Diners are free to choose from among the items offered on the menu – but are also restricted in those choices. In modernity, Beckford argues, individualization and standardization, or liberty and discipline, are "mutually implicated." In the same way, as applied to religion, late modernity has "weakened the hold that traditional, communally oriented, ascriptive religious ideas used to have on many people's lives." While "subjective, self-regarding, elective ways of practising religion" grow and flourish, there is a concomitant pressure to "conform to various collective criteria and standards regarding the acceptable forms of religion" (2003, 213). Amongst conservative Protestant churches in Kingston, that kind of unity under the larger evangelical umbrella defines what is acceptable, directed, say, by the kind of faith statement that the Evangelical Fellowship of Canada provides. At the same time, these Christians are free to select various modes of worship, denominational affiliation, and church governance and liturgy that allow them to find a church that fits with their particular segment of the culture, or in accordance with their own preferences as to music, language, message, and community.

4 Proselytizing Groups: Salvation Army, Mormons, Jehovah's Witnesses, Brethren

MISSIONIZING IN PUBLIC

To chart the histories of the mainline Christian and Jewish places of worship in Kingston, and to consider where they have been located since their arrival here, and why they may have subsequently relocated (see chaps. 1 and 2), does not of course tell the whole story. The account of Protestant evangelicals in chapter 3 principally dealt with churches having a denominational parent, whether Pentecostal, Christian and Missionary Alliance, or Free Methodist, and a presence in Kingston going back a century or more. Those evangelical churches represent faith communities that do not belong to the Big Three Christian denominations, nor to the Big Five; neither are they Jewish. While they have adapted somewhat to the surrounding culture, becoming more "mainstream" in a sense, and while they have also incorporated social concerns into their respective missions to society, they continue their longstanding emphasis on conversion and personal salvation, family values, and relatively high demands made on their members. The four groups dealt with in this chapter – the Salvation Army, the Church of Jesus Christ of Latter-day Saints, the Jehovah's Witnesses, and the Brethren Assemblies – have also been present in Kingston for a long time, and they share some characteristics with evangelicals. But these missionizing or proselytizing groups distance themselves from society to a greater degree – and from other Christian churches too – with public declarations of theologies that are sometimes exclusivistic or unorthodox.

Some sociologists of religion, following Max Weber, use a typology of church-denomination-sect to classify religious groups. The utility of this scheme has diminished under the circumstances of religious pluralism, and because New Religious Movements (NRMs) tend to fall beyond the proposed continuum. For instance, Canada has never had – or at least never had for very long – a representative of the "church" type, that is, no "state church" comparable to the Church of England, holding a kind of religious monopoly. Denominations are well represented in Canada; indeed, every religious group considered thus far in this book could be considered an example of the denominational type. Sects are breakaway groups usually formed in protest against the parent denomination from which they have departed. Baptists and Methodists – and even early Christianity, considered as a sect of Judaism – are examples of groups that were once sects but subsequently became denominations, a pattern that the Protestant evangelicals of chapter 3 exhibit. The four faith communities designated as "proselytizing groups" in this chapter could be considered as examples of sects, with the exception that the Salvation Army has now attained denominational status. Especially in their beginnings, each of these groups appeared as novel or radical in their opposition to the world around them, and were frequently attacked or ridiculed by mainline Christians as heretical. They became known for public professions of faith or witnessing, for seeking converts, and for their desire to reform or purify the existing Christian church.

The Salvation Army, the Church of Jesus Christ of Latter-day Saints, the Jehovah's Witnesses, and the Brethren Assemblies all eventually established permanent places of worship outside the downtown core but still reasonably close to the city centre. Today they have all moved still further away from the centre to the suburbs. Moreover, from their first appearance in Kingston or continuing in evidence today, these groups have made an impact on the downtown or on the mainline churches. Though each of these proselytizing groups claims a place within Christianity, two of them, the Mormons and Jehovah's Witnesses, are considered by some other churches not to be genuinely Christian because they hold beliefs thought to be heterodox. At the very least, these two groups are non-trinitarian, with origins in Christendom. While the Salvation Army and the Brethren might easily be included among the evangelical Christian groups explored in the preceding chapter, they are dealt with separately here because of their lengthy tradition of public missionizing. The Salvation Army, when it first appeared in Kingston, quickly became notorious for its open-air preaching, brass bands, evangelizing in taverns, and Hallelujah weddings. The Brethren movement was established to recover the simplicity of early Christianity as revealed in the New Testament, an emphasis still seen in their mode of worship and style of life today. The Jehovah's Witnesses and the Mormons are probably the best-known examples of groups in North America that engage in door-to-door proselytizing. Further, the theologies of the Witnesses and Mormons are exclusive, because claims to absolute truth set them apart from other faith communities within the Christian church, even from ones that are theologically conservative.

SALVATION ARMY

Of these four faith communities, the Salvation Army and the Brethren bear the closest comparison with other Christian denominations, especially those toward the conservative end of the theological spectrum. The Salvation Army since its founding in the mid-nineteenth century has adapted more fully to secular culture than the Plymouth Brethren, or the Brethren Assemblies, have. Brethren still maintain a separatist stance toward secular culture, and somewhat toward other Christian churches as well. The pastors at Kingston's Salvation Army Citadel – formerly downtown, now on Centennial Drive – are a husband-and-wife team, Majors Wil and Catherine Brown-Ratcliffe. In a 2004 interview Wil Brown-Ratcliffe described the origins of the Army's presence in the city, in terms largely consonant with more standard histories, beginning with the 1880s: "A lady who came from the States was a Salvationist – with a team of people came here – and began to preach on the square just behind City Hall. From that, I guess, they began to rent out dance halls and other facilities" (interview, 20 July 2004).

By 1882 the characteristic and often colourful public preaching of the Salvationists had begun elsewhere in Ontario, in Toronto and London, led by Army members from Britain. They were known for their "tumultuous all-night meetings and rowdy parades" (Marks 1996, 140), their quasi-military uniforms and brass bands, and their "blood-and-fire" sermons directed especially toward the working class. At an early stage during their presence in Canada, in 1883, workers at three of Kingston's major factories had established Salvation Army prayer meetings for themselves (144). From its beginnings in England under William and Catherine Booth, the Army was avowedly egalitarian, offering leadership roles to women in a way that mainline Christian churches did not. In Ontario in the 1880s fully 60 per cent of the officers were women, most of them coming from towns and villages of less than five thousand people (178).

The "lady from the States" was twenty-year-old Captain Abbie Thompson from Brooklyn, New York. Thompson ushered the Salvation Army into Kingston in January 1883 and began her year-long campaign against sin, alcohol, and corruption. She became "the darling of eastern Ontario," Terence Cottrell writes (1999), her meetings attracting such luminaries as Sir John A. Macdonald and the principal of Queen's University, Rev. George Monro Grant. Abbie Thompson's name became the inspiration for the christening of a yacht and the naming of a bar of soap (*Whig-Standard*, 16 January 2002). The curate of St George's Anglican Cathedral, Dr Henry Wilson, was one of those saved, an experience he describes in terms that bear the marks of a classic account of conversion: "I found myself one night kneeling at the penitent form of the Army, pleading for pardon and peace, and needing both, as much as the drunkard on one side of me and the lost woman on the other. I saw myself as never before, a poor lost soul, just as much as they, so far as the need for a new heart and a right spirit was concerned" (qtd in Hird 2008).

Wilson began to praise the Army's work in his sermons at the cathedral; he appeared on the platform at their Kingston meetings, and he participated at services in Hamilton and Toronto. Further, in a move that would have counted as a giant step forward in embracing other faith groups at the time – and perhaps even as an example of the nineteenth century's furthest reach toward interfaith cooperation – he brought Salvation Army converts to St George's for communion, all the while championing the compatibility of the Salvationist faith and Anglicanism. The controversy fomented by Wilson split the congregation of St George's and resulted in his being fired. He ended up in New York, where he became associated with the Christian and Missionary Alliance, at that time an interdenominational parachurch organization (Cottrell 1999; see Hird 2008 and Knowles 1991). This church was later to become an evangelical denomination within the Christian church, its membership in Canada today exceeding 100,000 (see chap. 3).

After her work in Kingston ended, Abbie Thompson was married in Newburgh, New York, to another Salvation Army officer, also named Thompson, who was second-in-command among American Salvationists. The *New York Times* reported the wedding in terms that convey the standard view of the day: "Major Moore [head of the Army in the United States] and about a thousand other 'cranks' were here, and held a 'holiness convention,' ate a 'hallelujah banquet,' and indulged in the usual idiotic performances attendant upon meetings of the Salvation Army" ("Two Salvationists Married," 28 August 1884). The trio of scare quotes alerted the reader, if any alert were needed, to the disapproval of the *Times* at such goings-on.

Today the early street-theatre of revival meetings and hallelujah weddings is long gone. More than a century after its beginnings, a banner prominent at the top of homepage of the official website for the Salvation Army in Canada proclaims itself as "the largest non-governmental provider of social services in Canada." While many still associate the Army with its original mission of "soup, soap, salvation," directing itself to feeding, clothing, and evangelizing the down-and-out, it has also evolved into a Christian denomination. Major Wil Brown-Ratcliffe says that "many just think that the Salvation Army is a social organization ... they don't know it's a church" (interview, 20 July 2004). He points out that whereas their outreach program addresses the social and financial needs of people "living on the edge," the congregation that worships at the Citadel "isn't always from that pool."

As he explains, "Most of the people who worship here are from the middle class and upper-middle class." The fact that the Salvation Army was not initially conceived as a separate Christian denomination partly explains why it still does not offer its members baptism and communion, although it permits them to seek those sacraments elsewhere. In many other ways the Salvation Army is a conservative evangelical denomination with community service central to its mission. The absence of baptism and communion has brought some criticism from other conservative Christian churches with whom it is otherwise allied theologically. Some of them, says Brown-Ratcliffe, because of the emphasis on social outreach, might see the Salvation Army not as a legitimate church but "as a glorified organization with a conscience."

Brown-Ratcliffe discussed the Citadel's relationship with the wider community beyond the congregation. He explained the mission of the church: "Our vision has always been bottom-line evangelical ... How does it relate then to what we do in the community? For us, it's always for those who have difficulty, who are down and out. They need more encouragement in their life to realize that there is more to life than day-to-day. We focus a lot of attention there." He outlined the Citadel's support for the Harbour Light Centre, the connection with Salvation Army Correctional and Justice Services, and the Supervised Access Program. The Army also runs a Community and Family Services Program, as well as Tenant Assistance. Its day camp for children is "heavily subsidized." Other activities for which Salvationists are well known include coordinating Christmas hampers, holding an annual Thanksgiving meal attended by three or four hundred people, and collecting money at Christmas. They give out vouchers to those in need, and coordinate a large food bank supported by various organizations. While Brown-Ratcliffe says, "We don't make any bones about the fact that the Salvation Army was invented as an evangelical tool," he also emphasizes that no pressure is put on people, although they do take the opportunity to publicize their religious programs to those they have helped.

After a long history of having its major worship space close to Kingston's downtown, the Salvation Army has moved from its old Citadel, a red brick building with a flat roof that contrasts with the pitched roofs of other nearby Protestant churches. As so frequently has occurred with downtown churches, the lack of available parking was one reason for the move; so was the size of the sanctuary. When the Alfred Street building was filled to its 250-seat capacity for worship, extra chairs had to be brought in to accommodate the overflow. The new location, with double the space, is on a four-acre parcel of land at the corner of Taylor-Kidd Boulevard and Centennial Drive, in the newly developing suburban area of Stonebridge. Though the date was pushed back several times, it finally opened officially in January

Salvation Army Citadel

2010. While Brown-Radcliffe thought in 2004 that "we'll keep this building here downtown and there'll be new ministry development here as a result" (interview, 20 July 2004), the Alfred Street building was eventually sold.

The Stonebridge suburb consists of relatively upscale and newly built homes. The area is close to Kingston's largest shopping centre, big-box retail stores, schools, restaurants, cinemas, and a public library. Preparatory to moving into this area, the Army conducted an online "Neighbourhood Survey" that asked in part, "What programming do you think would serve our community best?" Other questions sought information about how long residents had lived in the area, who was in the household, and whether they attended a church regularly. It is noteworthy that the Salvation Army should have situated its new Citadel in a relatively middle-class neighbourhood and used the Internet to survey its possible constituency rather than employing the older methods of public evangelism or door-to-door visits.

In general, old-style Christian missionizing by means of public preaching and door-to-door canvassing has had its day, as have unannounced visits to parishioners by clergy. One summer in the early 1960s, Tom York, a Canadian novelist and United Church minister, and his wife, Lyn, conducted such an old-fashioned door-to-door survey for the United Church in the then-new subdivision of North Whitby: "Each day we were visiting, visiting, visiting. Walking the streets and knocking on doors." York emphasizes their youthful zeal in this "block-by-block, beachhead-by-beachhead campaign, with desolate stretches and skirmish lines" (York 1978, 148). Aside from those they verified to be Roman Catholic or Anglican or Baptist, "everyone else was fair game," until fifteen hundred people were identified among "the nominally United and the unchurched families (with the evangelicals operating as a fifth column) in whom we were most interested" and who would form the core of the fledgling church (149). This kind of visitation was the last vestige of an era that was effectively ending, when front-door visits by strangers on behalf of a religious group would, to any great extent, be welcomed by a householder. In those days it was still possible to find someone at home in the daytime, usually a mother looking after children. Moreover, the assumption then was that pretty well everybody belonged to one church or another, and no offence was were entailed in asking which one. At worst, a debate with the town atheist might ensue.

While Statistics Canada figures from 2001 show a decline nationally of 21.9 per cent in the Salvation Army's share of the Canadian population from 1991, the Kingston congregations of the Army appear to be thriving, as their expansion shows. If part of the reason for the national decline is an aging membership, then Kingston's congregations show a healthy proportion of young people, many of them, when it was at the old location, drawn from nearby Queen's University. At that time Brown-Ratcliffe identified a lack of people in their forties at the Alfred Street Citadel. While some of the young adults likely disappeared from the congregation with the Citadel's relocation – though plans were being made to run one or more buses to bring people to the new location – perhaps their place has been taken by those in early middle-age currently missing. This group has become notoriously difficult for many churches to hold on to, in the generational space between young marrieds with small children and older folk and retirees.

In the early twenty-first century, public presentations and meetings held by the Salvation Army are far less frequent and flamboyant than those in the nineteenth, and more often held on behalf of those in need than to preach a message of salvation. If Salvation Army members make door-to-door visits, they are not for the purposes of evangelizing but rather for fundraising, for example, for its Red Shield campaign held in May. Even that method of fundraising has lately been discontinued in Kingston, as hiring professionals to organize it has become too expensive. The other widespread visible public presence of the Salvation Army is the Christmas Kettle campaign, utilizing what Brown-Ratcliffe calls "the bubbles that people put money in," set up with bell-ringers in shopping centres and stores to assist the needy during the Christmas season. When asked about the receptivity of Kingstonians to different religions, Brown-Ratcliffe replied with an account of the sole surviving public presentation by contemporary Salvationists, akin to the evangelism of the early days, though in a much subdued form. The outdoor worship event takes place near the very area of City Hall and the Market Square where the initial Army presence in Kingston was evident: "Generally speaking, there's certainly an openness spiritually in the city. Interestingly enough, on summer Sunday nights we take an hour from 6:30 to 7:30 down in Confederation Park. The Salvation Army sponsors music, and we use our own music and invite Christian artists to come in. We read a Bible passage and we pray, and this is in a public forum. There's a certain receptivity and no negative feedback at all for using a public square. We are not saying that 'you have to believe this.' We are saying, 'This is what we believe and we celebrate our faith.' Our religion is certainly guaranteed by our Constitution, but certainly there's an openness." (This kind of religious activity in the public sphere, together with other examples of public religion, is taken up in greater detail in chapter 10.)

CHURCH OF JESUS CHRIST OF LATTER-DAY SAINTS

The Mormon Church, or the Church of Jesus Christ of Latter-day Saints, to give the group its official name, is similar in size to the Salvation Army in Canada, with 101,805 members as compared with the Army's 87,790. Each group comprises about 0.3 per cent of the Canadian population. While the Army's share has declined nationally, that of the Mormons increased between the 1991 and 2001 censuses by 8.4 per cent. The median age in the Mormon Church is 28.7 years, contrasted with Salvationists' 39.3 years.

Like the Army, Mormons have been present in the Kingston region for well over a century. Richard E. Bennett describes Kingston as one of the first areas visited by early Mormon missionaries: "By October 1830, converts to the Church were teaching the gospel to family and friends in Canadian cities and towns less than 200 miles from Palmyra, New York," the place where the fourteen-year-old Joseph Smith received his first vision in 1820. "Between 1830 and 1845," Bennett continues, "LDS missionaries labored in Upper Canada (now Ontario) and the more easterly Maritime Provinces of British North America ... Brigham Young, Parley P. Pratt and Orson Pratt, John E. Page, and even the Prophet Joseph Smith visited and preached in Upper Canada during these early years. Some 2,500 Canadians joined the Church in Kingston, Earnestown, Toronto, Brantford, Mount Pleasant, North and South Crosby, and elsewhere." Despite this early success, emigration and falling away from the faith left "only seventy-four Mormons in all of Upper Canada" (Bennett 1992).

Byron Johnston, president (or "bishop") of the Cataraqui Branch in the Kingston District of the Mormon Church, stressed the importance of Kingston in their early history: "Right from when the church was reorganized in 1830, there was a quorum, or a group of twelve apostles, back then from the first known recorded time when they had first met outside the US ... a number of them, the largest body of apostles, was in Kingston at one time" (interview, 5 December 2004). Canadian Mormon converts journeyed with their American counterparts to Illinois and then to Utah in a westward exodus, a consequence of the persecution they experienced in the east. Johnston reflects that "a lot of very prominent church leaders right from day one literally came from this area" and that their descendants now live in western Canada and United States.

Because of this emigration and other factors, the presence of the Mormon Church in the Kingston area, as in the rest of Upper Canada, declined through the latter half of the nineteenth century. By the end of World War II, Mormon membership in Kingston had diminished to one lone individual (Prete 2002, 36). In the early 1950s attendance increased to between ten and twenty people in the third-floor rented space at the corner of Montreal and Princess Streets (37). As attendance picked up to thirty, and then to sixty, the Kingston Mormons moved successively to the near north side of Kingston, first to the Ukrainian Hall and then to the Polish Hall. They purchased their own building at 362 Alfred Street from the Seventh-day Adventists after the Adventists moved to Calvin Park in 1966. In 1974 the Mormons bought a piece of land at the corner of Battersea and Unity roads north of the city, where a building was completed in 1977 after extensive fundraising efforts. This building has subsequently been enlarged. At Christmas 1977 the local branch first performed the outdoor nativity pageant, the event for which the Mormons in Kingston would come to be best known (47–8).

The annual pageant is one of the major ways that the local branch of the Church of Jesus Christ of Latter-day Saints – the name often used in full to distinguish this body from other breakaway groups – establishes its connection with the community. For three decades it has been staged out-of-doors with live animals, attracting many visitors over four nights in December. As Byron Johnston stressed, "We do a live re-enactment of the trip of Mary and Joseph into Bethlehem and so on. The Christmas story, I guess. That has really been quite ... a cultural thing for the city of Kingston. We have thousands of people come to that, where people remember coming to it as a child. It is a ritual, a tradition, that they come and do that as part of the Christmas season" (interview, 5 December 2004). This annual Christmas event is a way of recentring and normalizing itself in the public mind, of suggesting to what might be an otherwise sceptical community that theirs is a regular and respectable Christian denomination, not a fringe sect focused around strange beliefs. The Salvationists, on the other hand, use their downtown concerts as in days gone by, as a form of entertainment that also serves their aim to spread the Christian gospel.

Though both the Mormon pageant and the Salvation Army concerts at Confederation Park are outdoor, public events, one crucial difference is that

Church of Jesus Christ of Latter-day Saints

the nativity pageant is conducted on church, not municipal, property. As Johnston says, the Christmas event makes a three-fold declaration to the community: "There is a Mormon Church in Kingston; that Mormon Church is at Glenburnie; and, thirdly, Mormons are Christians, they believe in Jesus Christ, and I guess we want to send that message." The pageant attracts public and media attention at a time of the year when the holiday spirit enhances receptivity to the Mormons' message. Local newspapers have regularly featured somewhat light-hearted stories about the rented or borrowed animals, ranging from the difficulty of locating the requisite animals, to a donkey who developed stage fright, or a camel that fell ill and required a veterinary visit (Crosbie 2003). The Mormons want to establish themselves as Christians partly in reaction to those who challenge their belief in modern prophets, in modern revelation, and in other books of equal authority with the Christian Bible. Johnston explains the sacred texts of the Mormons: "Our scriptures ... would include more than the Holy Bible – the Old Testament and New Testament. There is also the *Book of Mormon* and a book called *The Doctrine and Covenants* and another book called *The Pearl of Great Price*. Those four constitute the standard works of the church."

People know well that Mormons rely on out-of-town missionaries for their proselytizing activities. When Laurie Gashinski interviewed four young Mormon missionaries temporarily in Kingston from Utah, Arizona, Montana, and Alberta, they spoke more candidly about their faith than a local official might. The language they employed was typical of evangelical Christianity, with stock phrases such as "sharing the Gospel," "serve the Lord," "our Heavenly Father is preparing people," and "invite them to come to Christ" (7 June 2005). One of the four, Sister Pederson, spoke of what was distinctive about the Mormon Church: "Well, the biggest two things that make our church different from the others is, one, modern revelation and another is priesthood authority direct from God." The official Mormon website (see LDS) describes their belief that after the time of the original apostles the ability to provide true teaching of the Gospel was taken from the Church, in a period known as the Great Apostasy, until it was restored to earth through Joseph Smith. As well as upholding this continuing revelation, Mormons are distinguished from other Christian denominations by their rejection of original sin and by their performing baptism on behalf of the dead. The local branch president explained this latter practice: "Every living soul needs to be baptized in order to qualify to return to God. That can't happen because some people have not had the opportunity of hearing, accepting, and being baptized. So, we believe in vicarious ordinance for those who have not had that opportunity." Johnston gave the example of a woman whose father had died without being baptized: "In the temple a person is baptized in behalf of someone who has passed away" (interview, 5 December 2004).

Another of the missionaries to Kingston, Sister Andrews, expanded on the uniqueness of the Mormon faith: "There is one church that Jesus Christ established when he was on the earth and we believe that our church is his church. He leads his church through revelation to a living prophet. Jesus Christ lives and he loves us and through the prophet, Joseph Smith, his church was restored. In our church we have the same organization of prophets and apostles and we have the priesthood authority from God to be able to perform ordinances so that his children can return to him" (interview, 7 June 2005). Christians attempting to preserve their own standards of orthodoxy object precisely to this kind of affirmation or claim – that there is a written scripture, the *Book of Mormon*, having divine authority together with the Bible, that the revelation of God in Jesus Christ is continued in a specific prophet, Joseph Smith, and that the Mormon Church is the only true church. On the other hand, it may be presumptuous or risky – and probably even "unchristian" – to deny to any group the right to call themselves Christian.

The young missionaries interviewed referred to the rules governing their behaviour while they were proselytizing in Kingston. Elder Cole said they had to be careful due to "false accusations" against them. They could not be alone with persons of the opposite sex, nor have physical contact with them other than shaking hands. They also had to restrict their contact with children and could not watch movies or television, listen to the radio, go on dates, or swim. Asked about the last prohibition, Elder Cole explained to

Laurie Gashinski: "This is a university town, and a lot of the girls dress immodest, I guess you could say. Pretty revealing, and it's not something we try and involve ourselves in at all. It's hard when you've got girls flashing themselves around everywhere. These bodies are special, and when we look at you ladies, we want to see a daughter of God. We don't want to see your flesh and bones sticking all around. That's one thing, as a missionary that you try to really stay focused." These rules – which may, after all, have become stricter in recent years – governing out-of-town missionaries do not seem to apply to local Mormons, or perhaps not when they are in the company of other Mormons. When two or three hundred Mormon youth attended a weekend mission conference at Queen's University in 1967, the program included "swimming, dancing, sports and a sunrise testimony meeting" (Prete 2002, 42).

Apart from the difficulties and challenges posed by the secular culture in which they found themselves, away from the proximity of the Mormon Church in their homes in the western United States and in Alberta, one missionary related with sadness that when people "reject a message that they know is true, that has to be the hardest thing in missionary work that I've found." They also reported their work in Kingston to be more difficult than in other areas where they had served, a problem attributed to the activity of Jehovah's Witnesses who "have been everywhere around this town." One of the elders spoke of a man they had visited who was "just very rude to us about three times" until, upon discovering they were not Jehovah's Witnesses, he invited them in. The young Mormon's assessment of Jehovah's Witnesses was that "they slow it down a bit because they are a very pushy kind of people." He continued, "But nothing will stop the work from progressing no matter what because we believe that this is it. This is the real thing. They can do all that they want, like any church, but they won't stop us."

Notwithstanding their determination and commitment, the young missionaries disclose some of the difficulties inherent in any front-door proselytizing. Pastors at the Bath Road Baptist Church when interviewed provided some additional perspective on the matter of Kingstonians' receptivity to representatives of religious groups on their doorstep. When this independent Baptist Church was founded in the 1950s, its first minister, Rev. Samuel Dempster, rented a hall, advertised, and visited over a thousand homes, but saw only ten people show up for an initial meeting (Bath Road Baptist Church). Pastor Troy Irwin explained in an interview in 2004 that subsequent attempts by the church to go from door-to-door and hand out a pamphlet with information about the church did not succeed either: "Most people feel that that's an intrusion, whether it's door-to-door salespeople or Jehovah's Witnesses, or if there's something that's turned people off, that format is not well-received ... I would say that out of every ten doors, nine people are not overly thrilled that you're on their doorstep" (5 March 2004). Despite these visits being "non-confrontational," Irwin is identifying a resistance to an unexpected knock from a stranger on one's door that may be local to Kingston – or to eastern Ontario – or may be, more likely, a sign of contemporary mores that regard any such solicitations as an infringement of privacy or at least an inconvenience. Others among these four proselytizing groups have experienced similar discouragement and unfriendliness.

JEHOVAH'S WITNESSES

Randy Nicoles, who spoke on behalf of Jehovah's Witnesses in the Kingston area, was asked about how local members of their faith viewed Kingston. He expressed appreciation for the religious freedom that Jehovah's Witnesses enjoy now in Canada, in contrast to past persecution when they were banned for a period in the 1940s because of their perceived opposition to World War II: "And so Kingston is good in that way, in the sense that we can worship in the way we feel we should by the scriptures." To be a Witness of Jehovah requires that "you go out and talk to others – it is a responsibility all Jehovah's Witnesses have." In the Witness tradition, "those who go out door-to-door and engage in the public ministry" are termed "publishers." While Nicoles acknowledged that publishing "may not be appreciated by all in the sense that they want us coming to their door," he emphasized, "we do have that right." The task of doorstep missionizing is believed to be helping people in the community, "and it's nice to be able to do that freely" (26 January 2004). While the days of official persecution in Canada have ended, it still continues elsewhere in the world. Witnesses refer at their meetings to forms of less overt "persecution" in the form of the rejection or hostility they experience in the secular world at large, and during their door-to-door publishing.

Publishing or public proselytizing on the doorsteps of households has been the traditional activity of all Jehovah's Witnesses. The website of the Watchtower Society, the main legal entity and parent organization of the Jehovah's Witnesses, stresses the importance of going from house to house to share their teachings: "Today, where it is possible, Jehovah's Witnesses endeavor to call at each home several times a year, seeking to converse with the householder for a few minutes on some local or world topic of interest or concern. A scripture or two may be offered for consideration, and if the householder shows interest, the Witness may arrange to call back at a convenient time for further discussion. Bibles and literature explaining the Bible are made available, and if the householder desires, a home Bible study is conducted free of charge. Millions of these helpful Bible studies are conducted regularly with individuals and families throughout the world" (Jehovah's Witnesses a).

Jehovah's Witness Kingdom Hall

James Penton, a historian at University of Lethbridge and a former Jehovah's Witness, outlines how the practice of publishing developed further to include the setting of quotas and goals and the reporting and recording of publishing activities on at least a monthly basis: "The publisher will fill out a report slip detailing the number of hours in which he or she engaged in 'the service,' the specific amounts of literature placed, the number of return visits made on interested persons, and the number of 'home Bible studies conducted'" (1985, 247). Specific requirements, such as ten hours each month, are sometimes set, and charts are posted in the local Kingdom Hall, though these demands have sometimes been modified or dropped altogether. Nonetheless, every publisher is expected to maintain a regular and accurate record of publishing activity. One of the primary roles of the elders in a local Kingdom Hall is to encourage and direct this work of preaching, which remains central to the mission of Jehovah's Witnesses.

At the time of the 2004 interview with Randy Nicoles, there were three Kingdom Halls in Kingston: on Mack Street, built in the 1950s, on Butler Street, and on Development Drive, where two congregations shared the space. These three Kingdom Halls show a movement from an area close to the downtown to the northern part of the city, and to the growing residential areas in the west end. Shortly after the interview was conducted, the Kingdom Hall on Mack Street, closest to downtown, was sold for use as a day-care centre. Nicoles found a photograph that he estimated – and probably overestimated – as dating from the 1920s, showing a small group of six to eight individuals meeting in Kingston. The name "Jehovah's Witnesses" was not used until 1931, after a schism developed in the early movement, dating from the 1870s, when followers of Charles Russell were known as the "Bible Students' Association" (see Penton 1985). Kingston's Witnesses met in private homes for several decades before the first Kingdom Hall was built on Concession Street. Nicoles, who has lived as a Witness in the Kingston area from childhood, said that there was initial opposition to

Kingdom Halls being built in a neighbourhood because of "misconceptions about who we are, what we are, what we are going to do in the community." However, he maintained that once the Kingdom Halls were established, people appreciated their presence. He offered the view that "the community is more open now" because there are "so many different religions out there." As a result of this diversity, "people tend to be a little bit more relaxed. They are not as frightened of different religions that they may have been in the past."

Although this Jehovah's Witness spokesperson agreed with the Salvation Army major about the degree of openness in Kingston to religions, the two groups differ in the relative importance of evangelism and social service. Whereas the Salvationists see meeting human needs as their principal imperative, the Witnesses put the presentation of their message first. Asked about local endeavours conducted by the Jehovah's Witnesses such as food banks or disaster relief, Nicoles explained that these efforts would be secondary to "Bible educational work" through which they could affect communities by building stronger individuals and families. Though Witnesses might help as volunteers, and because "we do feel it is our obligation as citizens of the community to help out when we can," he stressed that "most of our energy and most of our focus is on Bible education."

Statistics Canada reports the number of Jehovah's Witnesses in Canada in 2001 as 154,750, a percentage drop of 8.1 per cent since 1991 to 0.5 per cent of the population nationally. The official Jehovah's Witnesses website reports 112,705 Witnesses in Canada, 21,155,159 hours of "preaching," and 1,947 baptisms in 2009. The lower number of Witnesses in 2009 may be explained by the fact that the 2001 Census presents the number of Canadians self-reported as Jehovah's Witnesses, whereas the lower Watchtower Society figures represent the number of publishers reported by the Kingdom Halls in Canada. Each publisher in Canada would have spent 188 hours preaching in 2009, or an average of 3.6 hours each week. That means 10,866 hours of preaching were required for each convert (Jehovah's Witnesses b). Fifty-six publishers working for one year are necessary to bring about the baptism of one individual. Locally, one Witness likened these efforts to long hours of panning for gold during which very few nuggets are found.

While the Witnesses accept some of the doctrines that conservative Christians believe – as does the Church of Jesus Christ of Latter-day Saints – major exceptions stand out. They are not trinitarians, instead believing that there is one God from whom Jesus Christ is separate and to whom he is inferior. They believe that the Second Coming began in 1914 with a heavenly battle, and will soon end in a battle of Armageddon by which Christ's millennial rule will be inaugurated. These and other theological details are perhaps less well known by the general public than Witnesses' refusal to accept blood transfusions, or the fact that they do not celebrate Christmas, Easter, and birthdays, or that they do not engage in politics or serve in the military. Instead of paid clergy, Witnesses have local elders who are male. Like Mormons, Witnesses regard homosexuality and abortion as wrong without exception. In contrast, the Salvation Army position on both matters is more nuanced. They accept abortion under some circumstances, and stress pastoral care for a woman who has had an abortion. The Salvation Army recognizes that same-sex orientation is a reality, opposing those who demean such individuals. However, the Army calls for celibacy on the part of those whose sexual expression is inclined toward members of their own sex (Salvation Army). Addressing the matter of women in leadership positions in the Church of Jesus Christ of Latter-day Saints, Bishop Byron Johnston told interviewers, "Women do not hold the priesthood." Mormon priesthood is officially defined as "the power and authority of God, given to men on earth to act in all things for the salvation of God's children." Like the Mormon Church, whose authority is centralized in Salt Lake City, Jehovah's Witness doctrines and beliefs emanate from the headquarters of the Watchtower Bible and Tract Society in Brooklyn, New York.

For the interview in the Kingston area, Randy Nicoles was selected by the Witnesses to speak on their behalf. While it was the practice of the Religious Diversity in Kingston project to provide, by means of its website, the questions to be asked in the interview, advance preparation was especially important for the interviewee in this case. Nicoles brought to the interview written answers already prepared in response to the questions. By the same token, religious instruction that takes place in the Kingdom Halls adheres closely to the materials provided by the Watchtower Society. James Penton describes the congregational sessions as "highly formalized and directed question-and-answer studies" that encourage participation from all members, and that often "take on the atmosphere of a public-school class" (1985, 241). The rehearsal of prepared answers to particular doctrinal questions is common. Spontaneity and improvization are not encouraged. James A. Beckford has studied how accounts of their conversions given by Jehovah's Witnesses are constructed according to "a logic of congruence linking the features of the conversion account to, among other things, the group's ideological rationale" (1978, 260–1). That is, individual experience is interpreted in the light of a pattern, in keeping with the need to fit one's own spiritual transformation to the template sent out from the Watchtower Society. Although interpreting one's own experience according to the pattern of co-religionists is not unique to Witnesses, this group stresses a high degree of conformity to its teaching and, as is apparent in their literature, allows for little deviation.

Kingdom Halls are often erected in a few days by volunteer labour provided by Witnesses – sometimes in Witness parlance called a "hall build" – some of whom travel significant distances to assist. The building is functional and modest, completed according to a standard plan, marked by simplicity and unadorned with the kinds of religious symbols one might expect in a place of worship. Some fourth-year students at Queen's University who elected to visit Kingdom Halls in Kingston and Napanee reported similar styles of architecture, interior design, and worship service. Their fieldwork observations suggest that uniformity in the layout of the Kingdom Hall facilitates a sense of the familiar when Witnesses visit from out of town. It also prevents local variations or innovations in architecture or design that might lead to other departures from approved teachings. The building is usually one storey, featuring a slightly elevated podium with a microphone and a stand for the speaker who leads a lecture or seminar for the first hour. The second hour involves a discussion of readings from *The Watchtower*, often in a question-and-answer format. The meetings are organized and disciplined, and the members friendly and warm. Hymns are sung to piano accompaniment, either live or recorded. Facing the podium are rows of stacking, folding, or otherwise moveable chairs. The New World Translation Bible and Jehovah's Witness hymnals are available to visitors or congregants who did not bring their own. Displays of literature are set out. Washrooms and bulletins are located at the back of the centre or downstairs.

As with the LDS Church, Witnesses tend to dress modestly or in a formal or sombre manner for their services of worship – skirts or dresses for women, for example, and shirts and ties for men. Visitors are asked to respect that practice and to come wearing appropriate attire. By way of contrast, at the Salvation Army services those adherents who are not officers, and who therefore do not wear the Salvation Army uniform, tend to be dressed in everyday clothes ranging from jeans and sweatshirts to simple or patterned skirts. "There's no dress code," states Major Catherine Brown-Ratcliffe (Chiang 2005), but no extravagance in dress is generally observed. Also evident at Salvation Army services, in contrast with the use of lone piano accompaniment at Jehovah's Witness meetings, is the continued exuberant presence of brass instruments for traditional hymns, together with guitars and drums for contemporary worship music. The website of the Salvation Army, Ontario Central Division, explained the variations – in contrast to Witness uniformity of practice – among their church ministries: "Some Corps worship in a traditional manner, incorporating the contemporary style to varying degrees, while other Corps/Community Churches embrace a variety of contemporary elements, as they display their unique personality in corporate worship. Uniforms and brass bands are still important to the identity of many Corps, while informal attire and worship teams express the culture of others. Many of the Corps in this region also mirror the multicultural nature of their neighbourhoods, reflecting the model of the early Church, 'uniting people of diverse backgrounds with a message of love and hope'" (link expired). The Army maintains the tradition begun by its founder, General William Booth, who regarded all music as sacred when put to a sacred purpose. "Why should the devil have all the best tunes?" Booth demanded to know. For the Church of Jesus Christ of Latter-day Saints, the Mormon Tabernacle Choir remains, as it has since its beginnings in 1847, the centrepiece of their musical tradition, typified as "so familiar, so American, that its Mormon foundation is sometimes forgotten" (Barry 2007). The choir has performed at five presidential inaugurations and thirteen world's fairs (Mormon Tabernacle Choir).

These three faith groups vary as widely in their attitudes toward higher education as they do about the role of musical expression. In the Salvation Army, becoming more a part of mainstream Canada, as the major at the Kingston Citadel explained, means more middle and upper-middle class Canadians among the members. Salvationists today include professionals and those who are university educated, some of whom have gone on to graduate studies. The Mormons too value university education. Klaus Hansen, who studied to the master's level at Brigham Young University and completed his Ph.D. at Wayne State University, was a member of the history department at Queen's University over several decades. His major book was *Mormonism and the American Experience* (1981). Leroy Whitehead, for a time bishop of the Kingston LDS branch, was a professor in the Queen's University Faculty of Education, where he served for a time as an associate dean. The current bishop has a master's degree in finance, and has continued in his studies at the Ph.D. level. By contrast, the Jehovah's Witnesses do not encourage higher education, though as James Penton, himself a history professor and former Witness, states, "the society has never placed an absolute ban on university attendance" (1985, 273). Still, Penton argues, little has changed since the days when Witnesses were counselled not to send their children to school past high school graduation. Practical studies such as carpentry and mechanics for boys and secretarial skills for girls are encouraged (271). An article on the Jehovah's Witnesses official website addresses the question, "What kind of education can make your life a success?" and concludes that only "the education that true Christianity provides can free a person from vices and an immoral lifestyle." People are directed to "Jehovah's Witnesses in your neighborhood [who] will be happy to help you to receive such valuable education" (Jehovah's Witnesses c).

As this comparison of the Salvation Army, the Church of Jesus Christ of Latter-day Saints, and the Jehovah's Witnesses shows, all three faith groups, despite their nineteenth-century origins as well as early exclusivist and high-demand characteristics, have adapted to their surrounding cultures in different ways and to different degrees. Salvationists have continued their efforts at engaging with secular culture and employing contemporary means in their central task of ameliorating human needs, while Witnesses resolutely adhere to their characteristic front-door methods of proselytizing. Mormons, meanwhile, maintain the distinctiveness of their doctrine and message while undertaking to engage with the communities in which they live or to which they are sent as missionaries.

BRETHREN ASSEMBLIES

The Brethren are a numerically small Protestant group with about 5,500 members in Canada, a precipitous decline of 37.3 per cent between the 1991 and 2001 censuses. The Brethren must be distinguished from the Brethren in Christ, an Anabaptist group also present in Canada, and originating in Lancaster County, Pennsylvania. The very name of the group is itself a contentious issue. Many of the members refer to themselves simply as "Brethren," originating from the practice of calling one another simply by "Brother" or "Sister," eschewing the use of ecclesiastical titles. Sometimes they want to be known simply as "Christians." In general, it seems that the term "Brethren Assemblies" is used in preference to Plymouth Brethren. The latter name is the one usually applied to them by outsiders, but refers to only one of several places where they originated – Plymouth, England. This reform movement within the church in the early nineteenth century began more or less spontaneously in a number of cities including London, Dublin, and Plymouth.

The Brethren have perhaps sixty congregations in Canada. In Kingston their home for almost eighty-five years since 1925 was a plain, well-kept white clapboard building, the Union Street Gospel Chapel, one block west of the Queen's University campus. Their preference for simplicity is set forth in the architecture of their place of worship and its name, which follows the Brethren practice of naming a local church after its location – for example, Main Street Gospel Hall or Centre Road Gospel Chapel. The Union Street site had previously been known in its history as a Brethren place of meeting as a "Gospel Tabernacle" and then a "Gospel Hall"; they avoid calling their place of worship a "church."

Like other evangelical congregations in the older part of the city, the Kingston's Brethren Assembly in Kingston has recently moved to the suburbs, to a location on Malabar Drive near Centennial Drive, a kilometre south of the new location of the Salvation Army Citadel. Unlike the Salvation Army, and in keeping with Brethren practice, the Kingston Chapel does not engage in fundraising activities: "We don't believe in that. We believe if people are going to do it, people should contribute freely from what God has given to us and should return to him and give it back." Though they do not actively seek donations, even at their worship services, the Brethren do provide a regular account of their expenses and gifts to make their needs known to those in the assembly. Like the Mormons and the Jehovah's Witnesses, Brethren Assemblies have no paid clergy – nor even any "clergy" as such, because they do not accept ordination.

The history of the Brethren, like that of the Mormons and of the Salvation Army, extends back to the nineteenth century. The Brethren began as a movement in the United Kingdom to purify the existing church with a return to the simplicity of early Christianity. They saw many practices within the church that seemed to be badly in need of reform, or that deviated from the standards of early Christianity, or which had become merely hollow routines and ritualized. Like the Salvation Army, those Christians who later became known as Brethren did not initially see themselves as a Protestant denomination, nor as anything more than a movement meeting in people's homes. In fact, denominationalism was one of the aspects of nineteenth-century Christianity that they were opposed to as they tried to overcome the differences between various churches. A simple sign outside the Union Street Gospel Chapel read, either by way of factual announcement or perhaps as a kind of injunction, "Christians Gather Here."

When asked in 2004 about the affiliation of the Union Street Gospel Chapel, Elder Bill Graham replied, "While we are an autonomy in ourselves like other evangelistic churches, we are associated with the Brethren movement throughout the world" (interview, 16 August 2004). The Brethren have been referred to as "fundamentalists"(see Grainger 2008), an accurate term if it means returning to the fundamentals of the faith such as the core teachings of the New Testament or upholding the Bible as inerrant, but inaccurate if it evokes the dogmatism and militancy associated with contemporary fundamentalism, especially in some American forms of Christianity. They have also been termed literalists, which again may be on the mark if one keeps in mind that a certain degree of selection and interpretation is involved in accepting the "literal" truth of the Bible (see chap. 3). In 2007 an editor at *Esquire* magazine, A.J. Jacobs, caused a degree of media stir and pubic interest with his book *The Year of Living Biblically*. In it, Jacobs, a Jewish agnostic, detailed his conflicts and struggles in his year-long dedication to adhere to biblical injunctions: "To obey the Ten Commandments. To be fruitful and multiply. To love my neighbor. To tithe my income. But also to abide by the oft-neglected rules: to avoid wearing clothes made of mixed fibers. To stone adulterers. And, naturally, to leave the edges of my beard unshaven (Leviticus 19:27). I am trying to obey the entire Bible, without picking and choosing" (3–4). In a similar way, what the Brethren of the 1820s wanted to do was to return to the simplicity of early Christianity as presented in the New Testament and extricate themselves from the creeds and doctrines that were creating divisions in the church of the day.

Referring to the then-proposed move to Malabar Drive near Centennial Drive, one of the elders at the Gospel Chapel thought he could predict the name of the new building with some confidence: "I know that it is going to be Malabar, because it is the name of the street. We were going to call it Malabar Bible Chapel; some would like to call it Malabar Bible Church, or something else. I have a feeling that it is going to be Malabar whatever" (interview, 16 August 2004). The application to erect a church on the building lot was approved by City Council on 6 May 2003. Actually, by the time Kingston's Planning Committee approved the site plan on 17 September 2009, the name had been changed to the Meadowbrook Bible Chapel. The Brethren chose to adopt the pleasantly neutral and pastoral name of nearby Meadowbrook Park rather than using the perhaps too foreign name of the street deriving from a region of southern India. As mentioned in chapter 10, some evangelicals are wary of the associations evoked by certain street names.

Because there are no ordained clergy, Bill Graham explains, "I do the pastor's work to a certain extent." The local Brethren are "governed in the assembly by elders – we have three elders and three deacons. Deacons look after the main upkeep of the church, the elders are responsible for shepherding the flock and looking after the spiritual aspect and needs of the assembly." Invited preachers from other places come to participate sometimes, and "also some of us would share and speak on the platform on a Sunday, either in ministry or evangelization" (interview 16 August 2004). The Breaking of Bread – that is, a communion service – is held every Sunday. Worship is informal and non-liturgical. Women must have their heads covered in accordance with 1 Corinthians 11, and they do not "offer audible worship," in keeping with 1 Corinthians 14:34, "Let your women keep silence in the churches: for it is not permitted unto them to speak" (KJV). Women may, however, join in the singing of hymns. The Brethren understanding of scripture "precludes women leading the congregation in prayer and assuming the role of a teacher in the church gatherings," but they may evangelize among other women, conduct Bible study classes for women, teach women and children, and engage in "other ministries which do not require them to exercise authority over the man," according to a brochure supplied by the local Brethren. (For more on women in positions of religious leadership, see chapter 8.)

What other biblical principles, then, do Brethren uphold? A single authoritative answer is difficult to arrive at because this movement does not centralize authority, nor does it publish doctrinal statements. Shawn Abigail, a Brethren Christian living in Ottawa, works in information technology and has assembled the website BrethrenOnline.Org. One section, entitled "'Plymouth Brethren' FAQ," begins with the qualifier that "at almost every point in this FAQ, you will find Brethren churches that will disagree or differ. Variation is even greater between different countries." A list of widely held tenets comprising their doctrinal position includes aspects that would be widely shared among many evangelicals: verbal and plenary inspiration of the Bible, trinitarian beliefs, believers' baptism by immersion, ministry shared among believers, evangelistic witness, an eschatology summarized by Abigail as "pretribulational, premillennial, and dispensational," and unstructured meetings. The Brethren are sometimes credited with having introduced Dispensational Theology, a form of premillennialism detailing a succession of eras in God's dealings with humanity culminating in a Jewish restoration (Abigail 2006).

Because of the absence of a central authority and the autonomy of local meetings – and, sometimes, the presence of strong personalities – Brethren have experienced many disputes and divisions. In 1848 the first major split occurred, resulting in two groups, the Open and the Exclusive Brethren. John Nelson Darby, one of the early leaders of the Brethren, led the Exclusive group, known later as "Darbyites." Due to compromises they felt were taking place, Darby and his followers upheld the principle of a greater degree of separation from the rest of the world, including separation from other Christians. The Exclusive Brethren remained in the majority throughout the nineteenth century; today the Open Brethren are the majority of the movement. After Darby's death in 1882, Frederick Raven soon became leader of the Exclusive Brethren. Following his death in 1903, Raven was succeeded by James Taylor Sr, who in a few more years was succeeded by his son.

Further divisions occurred among the Exclusive Brethren, to a degree and of a kind almost beyond an outsider's comprehension. Garrison Keillor, the author of *Lake Wobegon Days* and host of the radio show *A Prairie Home Companion,* spoke in a 1999 interview with David Brady in Britain about his Exclusive Brethren upbringing in Minnesota. Keillor conveys a picture of the complexity of the divisions and resulting animosities: "Our group was known as the Booth Brethren, to distinguish us from the Ames Brethren, after a particularly disastrous split in 1948. Most of my father's family went with the Ameses and we went with the Booths. It was the result of an argument over the Glanton Brethren, who were in fellowship with us, whom the Ameses accused of harbouring Raven tendencies, or at least of not proving themselves to be clear of Ravenism, and so when some Brethren refused to cast out the Glantons on the basis of these accusations, the accusers broke off with us." Asked by Brady what he missed about the Brethren way of life, Keillor responded, "I have many fond memories of growing up in the meeting. Of the gentleness of people, of the transparency of their faith, of their devotion to the Word and to Scripture study. I don't miss the humourlessness, the lure of legalism, or the snares of the invisible liturgy" (Brady 1999).

Elder Bill Graham dates the Brethren in Kingston from about 1870 when some Brethren, apparently from Ireland, arrived in town and began to evangelize. That their presence raised concerns among other Christians in Kingston is indicated by a sermon preached by the Anglican bishop of Ontario, John Travers Lewis, at St Paul's Church on 6 March 1870 and entitled "Heresies of the Plymouth Brethren" (microfiche, Queen's University Library). For a time there was a common assembly meeting at the Orange Hall until in 1901, as Graham puts it, "some of them broke." These Open Brethren left the assembly and began to meet elsewhere, first in a home and then in other locations, until the Union Street building was purchased in 1925. Graham says the Brethren bought the building from the Baptists, although local Seventh-day Adventist history mentions their ownership of the space at that time. The website of First Baptist Church in Kingston states that the Union Street Baptist Church existed for twenty years after 1897, thus allowing for a brief hiatus of a half-dozen years when it was probably owned by the Adventists (First Baptist Church b).

Student visitors to the Union Street Gospel Chapel report being warmly received as observers. They were asked, though, not to participate in communion unless they were "born-again Christians." An Exclusive Brethren meeting would not, of course, have been willing even to include unknown visitors in their fellowship. Two female students visiting the Kingston meeting felt they were the focus of attention toward the end of the service when an elder prayed that "those who have not found Jesus in their lives and who have not realized that they have been saved, may not leave this place without finding the Lord." Graham indicated that there were "sixty-five people in the church as members," and that usually about one hundred attend the 11 AM service, known as "Sunday School & Family Bible Hour." The 9:30 AM service is the Breaking of Bread, or communion, advertised in front of the building as "The Lord's Supper." Observers report that there appeared to be more people between the ages of twenty and forty than is usual at church services elsewhere. Graham commented that there were ten or fifteen university students in the congregation, but that the twenty children between the ages of three and fourteen in Sunday School represented a decline from the 1930s when there were several hundred. After their relocation the Brethren planned to publicize their presence in the new neighbourhood and to provide programs for children not possible in the space on Union Street.

Perhaps as an expression of the movement's history of separation, the Kingston Brethren do not engage in cooperative or common endeavours with other evangelical churches, nor do they advertise in local media. They do support a radio program, *Family Bible Hour International*, prepared in St Catharines and broadcast to eastern Ontario and northern New York State from Cape Vincent, New York. Other forms of outreach include a prison ministry, hospital visits, and regular services at a home for the aged, Rideaucrest. Graham commented that the elders felt that not enough had been done lately to provide a ministry directed toward the community and were discussing the best way of doing so in future. Referring to the terrorist attacks of 9/11, he also displayed more of the Brethrens' ongoing sectarian tendencies and worldview: "I do see and believe that there's another event just around the corner. We are going to see people in North America turning once again to Christianity and seeking the word of God. We've gone away and the consequences are there and we are turning our backs on them" (interview, 16 August 2004).

DOES PROSELYTIZING WORK?

While many Christian conservative denominations are overtly evangelistic, and all Christian churches see "evangelism," however they define it, in some sense as part of their mission, these four groups intended as a major part of their early mandate to strive in an active way to make converts. Each had a high degree of early visibility resulting from their radical message, their methods of proselytizing, their theological distinctiveness, and their separation from the surrounding culture – or at least certain aspects of it. The Mormons and Witnesses in particular claimed a new, contemporary revelation that set them apart from existing Christian denominations and that became the motivating force for developing an exclusivist position. Jehovah's Witnesses and the Church of Jesus Christ of Latter-day Saints regard their respective faiths as the only possible true religion.

Because from its earliest appearance the Salvation Army utilized popular aspects of contemporary culture in the presentation of their message – brass bands, contemporary gospel songs, uniforms, and so on – their adaptation to the world around them has been the most thoroughgoing of all these groups. In other Ontario cities, the Army has recently been developing a style of high-tech electronic worship service especially geared to the tastes of young people – what has been sometimes termed "Gen-X" worship. Due to its mission, its engagement with the world, and the populations to whom it ministers, the Salvation Army has adapted the ways of spreading the Christian Gospel to the social milieu. If the Army's future is at all in doubt, it may be due to the result of the loss of its distinctiveness, or to a bifurcation between those who are the recipients of its social mission and those for whom it is their church home. Major Wil Brown-Ratcliffe had in mind this last-named split when he contrasted the social-economic strata of these two groups. Moving their Citadel from a somewhat seedy – or at least dated – downtown site to a newly built worship centre in a middle-class suburb may further drive a wedge between these two groups of "clientele." The Army may be taking another step toward becoming just another evangelical church with a mortgage in the suburbs: in short, more a denomination than a sect.

Ironically, the Salvation Army might well suffer the same fate as the United Church and other liberal Christian denominations. As Peter Beyer puts it, "Beginning with the rise of the Social Gospel, the Anglicans, Presbyterians, and especially Methodists/Uniteds allowed their 'product line' to lose much of its supernatural character and thus its identifiable religiousness. As long as this liberalization could be styled as the 'Christianization' of Canadian society in the face of industrialization, urbanization and massive immigration – the idea of building 'His Dominion' – liberal Protestants kept up their membership and regular participation." However, Beyer maintains, "the failure of this effort, which gradually became manifest in the post-war era, left those denominations with little effective product to offer their affiliates: hence the decline, especially among the most socially oriented of the churches, the United Church" (2006, 85).

The evangelical counterpart of this liberal or mainstream phenomenon would be the loss of a slightly different kind of distinctiveness. The Salvation Army, for example, had a reputation for preaching a message of salvation on the street corners and in the taverns. It was known for its conversionist emphasis on redemption from sin. In its early days in Kingston, that message and presence rocked the staid Anglicans whose curate knelt publicly and received salvation. Now the Army is viewed more as a social service agency whose activism is focused on direct involvement in meeting human needs in various forms. Other forms of Protestant evangelical Christianity too have gone more middle class, become politically active, and achieved greater social respectability. The Salvation Army no longer stands apart as it once did, challenging the environing culture even while using some of its methods.

Mormons and Jehovah's Witnesses retain the distinctiveness that has been part of their original message from their nineteenth-century beginnings. Their "product line" – in the phrase used by Beyer, in keeping with contemporary analyses that apply metaphors from the business world and marketplace to religion – retains "its supernatural character and thus its identifiable religiousness." The central theology of the Church of Jesus Christ of Latter-day Saints asserts that the angel Moroni delivered gold tablets to Joseph

Smith containing a new revelation that was the *Book of Mormon*. The Jehovah's Witnesses also adhere to beliefs that set them apart from other Christian groups. They believe that blood is sacred, that "Jehovah" – an inaccurate rendering of the Hebrew tetragrammaton – is the proper name for God, that Jesus died not on a cross but a "torture stake," and that after an imminent Armageddon an immediate resurrection will follow. Witnesses reject the classic Christian views of the Trinity, and refuse to celebrate the usual religious holidays of the Christian calendar. Like Mormons, they are patriarchal in church leadership and home life.

What does it mean for a religious group to retain its supernatural character, in effect preserving its separateness by upholding a view of the world distinct from that held by the rest of culture? In *Under the Banner of Heaven* Jon Krakauer details how in the early 1980s Ron and Dan Lafferty, members of a fundamentalist Mormon sect acting according to the directives of a divine edict, killed their sister-in-law and her infant child. Krakauer takes this instance of religious fanaticism as a means of raising questions about the nature of belief. Because of Ron Lafferty's bizarre behaviour at the trial, expert testimony was sought about his mental competence. Was he psychotic or delusional because he believed that evil spirits were trying to invade his body or because he heard voices speaking to him? Noel Gardner, a psychiatrist from the University of Utah, testified that these notions were part of what Lafferty had learned as a child, and consistent with the beliefs of millions of ordinary religious people. He drew on such examples as the in-dwelling of the Holy Spirit, transubstantiation, and the Virgin Birth to illustrate that many Christians adhere to views that may not be rational but are not the result of psychosis. Gardner himself had been brought up in a fundamentalist family, whose members believed that the seventeenth-century Irish Bishop James Ussher's chronology was correct: the world was created in six days about six thousand years ago. He recalled his father scoffing at museum displays, claiming that their methods of dating were a deception of the Devil. Another expert witness, the forensic psychologist Stephen Golding, testified along the same lines: "Almost every religious belief system that I know of is made up ninety per cent of things that are articles of faith and cannot be reduced to fact" (Krakauer 2003, 381). Golding and Gardner agreed that, while Lafferty's views were extreme, they were not a symptom of illness. Nonetheless, most people holding positions such as Lafferty's do not end up murdering others.

If the product line of a faith community originates from something that cannot be interpreted except as a supernatural revelation, then anything approaching or even suggestive of a total deconstruction compromises the very foundations of the tradition. In *The Protestant Era*, first published in 1948, theologian Paul Tillich argued that Protestant Christianity's basic principle is justification by faith alone, a view that allows for the most radical kind of questioning of churches or scriptures or creeds. This "Protestant Principle," Tillich said, "contains the divine and human protest against any absolute claim made for a relative reality, even if this claim is made by a Protestant church" (1957, 163). In this view, because God alone is absolute, no sacred system can exist. Nor can human beings claim to possess divine truth. A thoroughgoing application of this principle stands against any centralized authority, whether exercised by the Vatican or the Watchtower Bible and Tract Society or the successors of Joseph Smith in Salt Lake City. Justification by faith alone relativizes any claims to divine authority that usurp the absoluteness of God.

The Brethren too, having been split in the past by disputes about how "open" they ought to be to outsiders in the world around them, continue to face the recurring and vexing issue of the adaptation of any religion to the conditions of modernity: How far can such adaptation go without becoming an unacceptable compromise that loses the distinctiveness of the original message? While they use computers and the Internet, and send their gospel message over the airwaves by radio, they also continue to insist that women remain silent in church and cover their heads with scarves, as Paul prescribed for the church in Corinth in the first century of the Common Era. Brett Grainger (2008) describes how on a Sunday in 1988 he was memorizing a scene from Beckett's *Waiting for Godot* for a high-school class, while his Brethren grandfather, who had spent his entire adult life studying Bible prophecy, was convinced that on that very day the Rapture would occur, when the Lord would come again in glory.

A faith group that aims at retaining or augmenting its membership through proselytizing faces difficult challenges. Reginald Bibby, a sociologist at the University of Lethbridge, conducted studies of between sixteen and twenty evangelical churches in Calgary over several decades beginning in the 1960s. He discovered that only about 10 per cent of the new recruits to these churches came from outside the evangelical community. Most, about 70 per cent, came into these churches through "reaffiliation" – that is, before their arrival they were already members of other Christian churches who transferred to a new church. Another 20 per cent came in by "birth" – that is, they were the children of evangelicals. Proselytism accounted for the remainder. While the rate of reaffiliation remained quite stable, the increase in the rate of adding new members through proselytism went up from 9 per cent in 1966–70 to 13 per cent in 1976–80 and to 15 per cent in 1986–90 (1993, 40–2). Bibby argues that because increased success in proselytism corresponded with a decreased pool of children being born to evangelical members, adding members from outside the evangelical community was the only way to survive. Nonetheless, their success in proselytizing was at best limited, amounting to only between 1.3 and 2.9 previously unchurched outsiders being added by each church each year (42). Bibby has little confidence that the methods of evangelism employed by conservative Protestant churches are working very well.

Even more aggressive methods of proselytism such as the door-to-door "publishing" employed by Jehovah's Witnesses bring very modest results. If it takes more than fifty publishers working for a year to achieve one conversion, amounting to almost 11,000 person-hours, that exceeds the investment in practice time necessary for success that Malcolm Gladwell expounds in *Outliers*, according to his now-fabled "10,000-hour rule" (2008, chap. 2). Logging that number of hours, requiring an entire lifetime of effort for one publishing Witness, gets accomplished by early adulthood for one of Gladwell's successes, such as hockey players, Bill Gates, or the Beatles. When James Penton calculated that in 1983 it required more than 3,600 hours of publishing work "to produce *each* new active Witness" (243), perhaps success then came more readily. Studies cited by Penton (243), consonant with Bibby's research, indicate that most Witnesses do not join the faith as the result of door-to-door evangelizing. "Informal witnessing" involving such other contacts as relatives, neighbours, or at work or in school is more effective. The success of Mormons in increasing their numbers through conversion undoubtedly comes as the result of more intensive and concentrated activity. Mormon missionaries spend up to two years in full-time proselytizing between the ages of nineteen and twenty-five. More than fifty thousand young Mormons are serving in this capacity around the world at any given time. One evangelical Christian website estimates 4.6 converts per Mormon missionary in 2004, a considerable drop over the previous fifteen years, but more significantly, doubts that a third of those converts will remain active in their new faith (Mormon Info). These figures on conversion to the Jehovah's Witnesses or the Church of Jesus Christ of Latter-day Saints tell us nothing about whether these new recruits were previously unchurched – that is, whether they came into their new faith community from a previously "secular" life.

The research of Bibby and others casts further doubt on the effectiveness of the efforts of proselytizing groups such as the Salvation Army, the Brethren Assemblies, Jehovah's Witnesses, and the Mormons. Some of these faith groups are finding that their membership numbers, or their faith group's percentage of the population, is decreasing as time goes on. If they do hold their own, or even increase in size, it appears that those gains will come at the expense of other faith groups whose members will "switch" – the term is Bibby's. Many of these switchers, says Bibby, "are simply continuing their patterns of high participation elsewhere" (1993, 36). On the other hand, the major shift made by switchers is into the category of those who state that they have "no religion." In all, Bibby makes a strong case that religious affiliation remains constant from one generation to the next, and that Canadians do not move very far from the religious tradition into which they were born. While Anglicans might become United Church or Baptists become Pentecostals, religious identification remains close to the tradition of one's parents and grandparents. Mainline Christians do not augment the ranks of conservative Protestant denominations to any large degree. Yet, notwithstanding these obstacles, the imperative to proselytize and seek converts by such traditional means as public professions of faith and door-to-door visits remains strong.

5 Ethnic Christianity: Protestant, Eastern Christian, Roman Catholic

RELIGION AND ETHNICITY IN KINGSTON

One of the greatest enhancements to the religious diversity of Kingston is the contribution of Christian churches characterized by their respective ethnicities. The range includes sizeable congregations with large church buildings of their own, others occupying house churches or storefronts or other rented or borrowed space, and still others meeting within the sanctuary or even the basement of another existing church. Some ethnic congregations – Roman Catholic ones, for instance – are part of a larger denomination, but their liturgies are often conducted in the first language of the congregants. Some groups, such as the Greek Orthodox and Ukrainian Catholics, declare their ethnic origins in their very names. Others, such as the Lutheran and Christian Reformed churches, while they may have begun as churches more or less transplanted from the countries from which their members emigrated, have lost many of their associations with a particular ethnicity or culture.

In the 1980s, Hans Mol, a sociologist of religion at McMaster University, published a trio of what he termed his "F and F" books: *The Fixed and the Fickle* (1982), on New Zealand, *The Firm and the Formless* (1982), on Australian aboriginals, and *Faith and Fragility* (1985), on religion in Canada. Each was an application of his "identity theory" of religion earlier developed in his *Identity and the Sacred* (1976). "From a social-scientific point of view," Mol says, "religion is constantly attempting to make whole (or render fixed, firm, faithworthy) that which may fragment (or be fickle, formless, fragile)" (1985, 1). In that light, religion may either reinforce existing loyalties and connections – as Anglicanism and Catholicism did for British and French settlers in Canada – or it may transform allegiances and facilitate adaptation to new cultural realities – as it was to do, and is still doing, for countless subsequent waves of immigrants. Religion, as Northrop Frye has said in a somewhat different context, may serve either a conservative or a revolutionary function. It can preserve identities or it can transform them. Religion helps make people good citizens who obey the state and its laws; it also brings a transcendental focus into view that rallies them to challenge and question what the state tells them to do.

Mol begins the section on "Religion and Ethnic Groups" of his *Faith and Fragility* with a statement stressing religion's conservative role: "Wherever migrants settled in the new world, their religion functioned as anchors of the past or as shelters from culture conflict" (1985, 63). Applying this theory directly to Canada, he observes that when members of ethnic groups immigrating to Canada spoke neither English nor French, "their religion almost always proved to be the strongest preserver of each particular foreign language and culture" (66). He goes on to consider each of Canada's largest ethnic groups, according to the numbers available to him from the 1981 Census. In descending order they are: Germans, Italians, Ukrainians, Dutch, Scandinavians, Poles, and Jews. In some respects Mol's analysis of more than twenty years ago serves our purposes well. These ethnic groups are, for the most part, well represented in Kingston by immigrants who arrived here in the generation after World War II.

A Statistics Canada table showing data from the 2001 Census presents comparative figures for the ethnic origins of 142,765 people in greater Kingston. Several preliminary points about this table need to be made: first, people could make single or multiple responses, identifying one ethnic origin or several; second, they were allowed to select "Canadian" or "American" as their ethnicity; third, the unfortunate confusion of religion and ethnicity is here continued when "Jewish," probably best given as a descriptor of one's religion, is allowed as an ethnic origin – strange, in that, after all, Jews come from various countries. As one works down the Statistics Canada table for the ethnic origins of Kingstonians, coming after those declaring themselves to be English, French, Scottish, Irish, or Welsh, are 12,500 people who identify their origin as German, 8,110 as Dutch, 4,470 as North American Indian, 3,950 as Italian, 3,410 as Polish, and 3,335 as Portuguese. These figures correspond fairly closely with Mol's listing of major immigrants groups in Canada from the 1981 Census. When those reporting Swedish (810) or Norwegian (775) origins are added in, then at least 1,585 Kingstonians count themselves as having Scandinavian roots, Mol's fifth largest ethnic group. In Kingston, the next four groups – after the 3,335 Portuguese – are 2,555 people who identify themselves as Ukrainian, 1,770 as Chinese, 1,290 as East Indian, and 1,035 as Greek (Statistics Canada). Beyond these groups already mentioned, no other ethnicity was reported by more than one thousand people in the city.

According to a Canadian Press story, 90 per cent of third-generation Canadians consider themselves as Canadian, at least in part. Among second-generation immigrants, more than half originated from Europe, while "first-generation immigrants were most likely to identify themselves as Chinese, East Indian, Filipino or Vietnamese" (*Toronto Star*, 2 April 2008). Of course, immigrant groups are not equally represented in Canadian cities. Kitchener, with a population of 410,000, has 93,325 people of German ancestry, about the same proportion of Greeks as Kingston has, but with a higher percentage of Portuguese. Kingston has a higher proportion of people of Dutch background than does Kitchener. Saskatoon, with a population of 220,000, has – like Kitchener – almost one-quarter of its citizens reporting German roots but a lower percentage of people of Italian, Portuguese, or Greek ancestry than Kingston. In Saskatoon the proportion of Ukrainians and Scandinavians is much higher than in Kingston, following the pattern of immigration to the Prairies. With these statistics informing us of the relative presence of various ethnic groups in Kingston, let us turn to examine their presence in specific churches and denominations.

ETHNIC PROTESTANT CHURCHES IN KINGSTON

St Mark's Evangelical Lutheran Church

While those of German descent represent the largest group by ethnic origin in Canada, most German immigrants arrived here before World War II. Their adaptation and assimilation into Canada was hastened by the two world wars, with the resulting challenges to their loyalties, as well as by the comparative closeness of their own cultural backgrounds to the Canadian context. Though some major German settlements existed in Canada, Germans immigrants did not necessarily seek them out. If they were of Protestant background, they easily affiliated themselves with a United Church congregation where no Lutheran church was available.

In Kingston seventy Protestants, mostly Germans and Danes, established a Lutheran congregation here, marking a major step that was to lead to the building of a church in 1957. For a number of years the fledging St Mark's Lutheran Church used the facilities of the Seventh-day Adventist Church until their own building at the corner of Victoria and Earl streets was ready. Like other Kingston religious groups in the 1950s – Beth Israel Congregation, for instance – St Mark's established itself in the residential area just to the west of Queen's University. Unlike some of the other churches in the neighbourhood – Union Street Gospel Chapel and the Salvation Army come to mind – St Mark's seems intent on staying in that location, despite the usual limited parking space. A list of the pastors associated with St Mark's over its history of more than fifty years, many of them graduates of Waterloo Lutheran Seminary, shows the Germanic connections of most: Harry N. Lossing, Alfred Kramer, Everett Mossman, Earl Albrecht, Roy Baumgart, Eric Reble, Ken Gies, David Pfrimmer, Giselta Nolte, Bruce Schenk, Ralph Dipple, Stephen Scheidt (see *Whig-Standard*, 20 April 1990 and 18 November 2000). A newspaper article announcing the arrival of Rev. Stephen Scheidt in 2000 mentions that "the congregation has many members whose family origins are in Denmark, Estonia and Germany" (*Whig-Standard*, 18 November 2000).

The parent denomination of St Mark's, the Evangelical Lutheran Church in Canada, or ELCIC, should not, despite its name, be considered among churches identifying themselves as "evangelical" in the popular and contemporary sense of the word (see chap. 3). Contemporary evangelicalism embodies such common features as those named by Sam Reimer: conversionism, biblicism, crucicentrism, and activism (2003, 153). A separate, more conservative denomination, the Lutheran Church–Canada, or LCC, is indeed "evangelical" in terms of this understanding but has no congregation in Kingston, though there are reports of a small group of their adherents meeting periodically in borrowed space. This evangelical group was formed in 1988 by Canadian congregations affiliated with the Missouri Synod of the Lutheran Church. They preserve a conservative evangelical emphasis, opposing women's ordination and same-sex relationships. By comparison, Canadian members of the Evangelical Lutheran Church in Canada are, rather, "evangelical" in the more generalized Protestant meaning of the term that is applied to the tradition that comes from the Reformation and, for Lutherans especially, from Martin Luther's emphasis on justification by grace through faith.

The Evangelical Lutheran Church in Canada – the denomination of St Mark's – belongs to the Canadian Council of Churches but not to the Evangelical Fellowship of Canada. In fact, the denomination might be recognized for several reasons as belonging among the mainline Protestant denominations (see chap. 2). While their bishops passed a motion in 1989 that opposed the ordination of gays and lesbians – and that decision remains in force – the ELCC is presently considering its position on human sexuality, and in particular whether to bless same-sex unions. In May 2008 a married gay man, Lionel Ketola, was ordained in a Lutheran church in Newmarket, Ontario, by an American Lutheran denomination despite the concerns raised by his Canadian synod (*National Post*, 14 May 2008). In 2001 Canadian Anglicans and Lutherans both agreed as denominations to enter into closer ties, approving a Full Communion agreement. Finally, the general view that Lutherans are to be considered among other mainline Christian denominations is signalled by its inclusion among the so-called PLURA churches, that is, the Presbyterian, Lutheran, United, Roman Catholic, and Anglican denominations.

Because St Mark's is the only Lutheran church between Gananoque and Napanee, its stand-alone character has doubtless contributed to its persistence. There is no other nearby church belonging to either the Evangelical Lutheran Church in Canada or the Lutheran Church–Canada to which members of St Mark's can conveniently go, should they depart in the event of a dispute or theological disagreement. To be a regularly participating Lutheran in the Kingston area means to go to St Mark's. Another feature sustaining the congregational life of St Mark's is its proximity to the Queen's University campus. A student visitor to St Mark's in 2002 reported a congregation of about 130 people in attendance, of whom ten or twelve were students. In 1998 St Mark's passed a resolution to support a campus ministry directed toward Lutheran students at Queen's, St Lawrence College, and the Royal Military College, as well as other students who attend the church. About six students were estimated to have attended St Mark's regularly in 2007–08. This ministry includes a meal for students after church on the last Sunday of the month (St Mark's Evangelical Lutheran Church).

Probably the single most obvious respect in which the ethnic origins of this church have been maintained is in two special Christmas services offered on two evenings in December for many years, one in German and the other in Danish (see *Whig-Standard*, 4 December 1987 and 29 November 1985). Conducted by visiting pastors, these services are reported to be appreciated by elderly members and provide a nostalgic link with an earlier identity. Hearing the German and Danish languages again "reminds the older ones of that part of them they left behind in Europe when they came to Canada" (*Whig-Standard*, 4 December 1987). In 1987 the Danish service was celebrated at St Mark's on 13 December, St Lucy's Day, an important feast day for Scandinavian Christians. During the service a girl representing Lucia, wearing a crown of four lit candles, led a procession of younger children carrying candles. In recent years most participants at these special services appear to have come from beyond the 130 families affiliated with St Mark's, or from outside of Kingston.

Bryan Hillis concludes that "Lutheran identity in Canada is evolving and is not limited by the original Scandinavian and German ethnicities which accompanied it" (2008, 277). Hillis, who interviewed Lutheran clergy in 2005, reports that "to a person, even those who had a strong sense of their own ethnic background and that of the church agreed that the ethnic heritage of their congregations was not a significant part of their congregational life" (260–1). Among the 950 congregations belonging to the two major Lutheran denominations in Canada, the Evangelical Lutheran Church of

Canada and the Lutheran Church-Canada, only twenty-two churches remain where services are still conducted in German (281n33). Today, when Lutheran worship services are conducted in languages other than English, the languages heard are increasingly Asian ones – Cantonese, Mandarin, Korean, and Vietnamese. Lutherans continue their tradition of welcoming newcomers to Canada, though now these arrive from parts of the world outside of Europe.

Christian Reformed Church

The Christian Reformed Church in Canada traces its theological lineage to the Reformation teachings of John Calvin rather than to Martin Luther, therefore sharing much in common with Presbyterians (see chap. 2). The Christian Reformed Church is a bi-national denomination including one thousand congregations in the United States and Canada, with its headquarters in Grand Rapids, Michigan. In the two decades after World War II, about 750,000 people left the Netherlands, and 38 per cent of that number came to Canada. The Christian Reformed Church website refers to the influx of Dutch Calvinists to Canada in the early 1950s, then describing their differences in terms of "life experience, mindset, and moral and religious values" from Christian Reformed members in the United States. The distinction claimed is that "Dutch Canadians tended to focus their spiritual energies on working out the social ramifications of the gospel, not on personal piety" (Christian Reformed Church a). Nonetheless, our research involving the two Christian Reformed congregations in Kingston would suggest that personal piety is as high on the agenda here as are the social dimensions of the Gospel. As Stuart Macdonald points out, Dutch immigrants had a different understanding of Christianity from that of other Protestants in North America after World War II. Their vision included "the establishment of distinctively Christian institutions," especially schools, just as they had in the Netherlands, because they did not feel that existing Canadian schools were adequately Christian (2008, 181).

First Christian Reformed Church, located on the near-north side of Kingston in the Kingscourt area, was established, like St Mark's Lutheran, in the early 1950s. When that congregation became too large, a second congregation, Westside Fellowship, was established about 1984 in the residential west end. Of the two, First Christian Reformed remains largely identified with Dutch ethnicity, whereas at Westside the congregation is more ethnically mixed. While the Dutch would comprise the largest single ethnic group at Westside, they do not predominate. Like St Mark's Lutheran, First Christian Reformed continues to have in its congregation some of the charter members from its beginnings in 1950. Sid Ipma, an interim student pastor from Michigan during the summer of 2005, spoke about First Christian Reformed with the candour and objectivity of a visiting outsider: "This is still primarily a Dutch-background church. And that's going to display some of its weakness – it's very inward-focused in terms of what it desires to do, and what it needs on a Sunday. It can't be classified as the most welcoming for somebody coming from a different background. I'll still hear comments made in Dutch, and for the next generation that's extremely alienating, and for someone who's not from a Dutch background you're always going to feel like an outsider then, because you're not in on the little jokes" (interview, 13 July 2005).

Services at Christian Reformed churches in Canada were rarely conducted in Dutch because the acquisition of English was deemed important to facilitate the transition to Canadian life. Hans Mol, himself of Dutch background, says that although the Christian Reformed Church does not sacralize Dutch identity, it does sacralize family life, looking to the local church as the safeguard of its members' purity (1985, 76). Sid Ipma said that "right thinking," and the conviction that "there's a right way to do things," characterizes Dutch Calvinists. Pastor Ed Visser of the Westside Fellowship described how the church's elders might visit one of the members whose conduct was considered to be unchristian – "That's probably the most severe kind of decision that elders would be involved in" (interview, 3 March 2004). While drinking is not prohibited, if drunkenness were reported of someone, the elders might point out to the person that "that behaviour is inconsistent with the Gospel and with following Christ." They could forbid the individual from participation in the Lord's Supper, or from presenting children for baptism, "because you're not living in a Christian way." Their role in such situations is to encourage the person to be a disciple of Christ in all areas of life.

Visser stated that "in the denomination itself, there is a strong emphasis on scholarship, education, campus ministry." The initial task in Kingston, he said, "was getting the church established and getting the day school going. That was their first priority." First Christian Reformed Church established the Calvin Christian School on Wright Crescent in 1963 to ensure a Christian education for their children apart from the "secular" Ontario Public School system, though it was then still widely regarded as implicitly Protestant. Calvin Christian School was relocated to Woodbine Road in 1992 as the Kingston Christian School, open to children of all backgrounds and creeds. The school website states: "Kingston Christian School is distinctive in daily providing a solid academic environment where Christ is honoured. KCS teaches children that God is important in all things and that they have a role to play in God's universe." The difference from "secular" schools is seen is such statements as "We feel privileged to celebrate the true meaning of Christmas and Easter and to pray openly in school" (Kingston Christian School). On the Queen's University campus, a Christian Reformed campus ministry operates out of Geneva House on Frontenac Street, with a Reformed chaplain, currently Steven Kooy (see Geneva Fellowship; cf. chap. 9).

The Westside Fellowship has more than two hundred members, described by Visser as "quite a mix," economically, religiously, and ethnically. "Some are Italian, some are from India, some Dutch," he says, and they come from various backgrounds and traditions – "some Baptist, Anglican, some no background." By contrast, Sid Ipma felt that some of the families at First Christian Reformed "have been part of the leadership right from day one," and have difficulties surrendering that role: "What you find, especially with an immigrant population, is you'll get these personalities that are go-getters, they're forthright, they're going to make a new life for themselves. And so they come to a new country and they're trying to carve out that new life for themselves ... When you're starting a church, that crowd remains in leadership for many, many years, which is unusual. If you have a church that's been around for two hundred years, your leadership is going to be a little bit more spread out. So, yeah, there's that unofficial leadership that's been here for fifty years, and now they're seventy – they were twenty when they got here, and they're seventy now" (interview, 13 July 2005).

Pastors Ipma and Visser both described situations in which tragic splits had occurred within the Christian Reformed Church, especially over issues such as female ordination or women acting in other roles of leadership. Ipma thought such disputes were often exacerbated by the independence of Dutch immigrants, their Calvinist work ethic, and the determination to push their own approach. He said that when you put two people like that "head-to-head," and when they both want to get their way, "it can be ugly." Visser felt that the Christian Reformed denomination "is impoverished" because of disputes over theological correctness, especially about non-essentials. Visser suggested that some Reformed Christians might say, "Look, if you take two godly individuals and put them in a room with the same scripture, they would come out with different positions on different things." He described how the Christian Reformed Church in North America, a denomination of 300,000 members, lost about 40,000 members in the argument "about whether it's right or wrong to open the office of elder, deacon, minister, and evangelist to women." On this matter, in Visser's home church in Hamilton, "which was a fairly large immigrant church, they split right down the middle ... and basically ended up with two impoverished debt-ridden congregations that fought in courts for about two years. It was just awful." The fallout, he lamented, went on for decades, dividing families and friends over the role of women in the church – not on such essentials as who Jesus Christ is, or the authority of scripture, or the church's mission. Despite all that, he emphasized, "we're not a judgmental group," and concluded that what it means to be a member of the Christian Reformed Church is "to take seriously ... being a follower of Christ, being a disciple of Christ." Stuart Macdonald observes that "in the Christian Reformed Church, religion functions in a way similar to an ethnic identity, in that it acts as the touchstone for a group of people." By that he means that "it is the particular understanding and shape of the Calvinist tradition that has been transplanted to Canada, and this, more than language and ethnicity, has made the Christian Reformed Church distinctive" (2008, 197).

Kingston Chinese Alliance Church

Bruce L. Guenther states that "more than 26 per cent of the Chinese in Canada identify themselves with some form of Christianity." He adds that "this group represents the fastest growing and most dynamic component of the increasingly diverse world of evangelical Protestantism in Canada" (2008, 379). The Chinese, while not as abundant as the other groups previously considered, are still among the top ten most numerous ethnic groups in Kingston and the city's largest visible minority. Along with St Mark's Evangelical Lutheran Church and First Christian Reformed Church, the Kingston Chinese Alliance Church, or KCAC, represents a third Protestant ethnic group having its own church building. Because two other Christian and Missionary Alliance churches exist in Kingston, the Kingston Chinese Alliance Church, unlike the Evangelical Lutherans, is not the lone local representation of the denomination. There is less likelihood of its moving beyond its ethnic origins with the passage of time in the way that Westside Fellowship has, because its ethnicity is declared in its very name. The Kingston Chinese Alliance Church also differs from St Mark's Lutheran and First Christian Reformed – which do not conduct worship in either German or Dutch – in that its main Sunday morning service at 11 is conducted in one of the two major Chinese languages. Pastor Kong Lo described how he alternates Mandarin and Cantonese from one Sunday to the next, with translation into the other language provided (interview, 2 November 2003). The Kingston Chinese Alliance Church, however, distinguishes itself from what it refers to as the "typical Chinese church" by also offering a 9:30 AM service in English, and, as the website states, "Our English congregation is led by students for students targeted specifically toward students!" (Kingston Chinese Alliance Church).

Kingston Chinese Alliance Church

Due to the mobility of the student population, the church has more attendees – estimated by the pastor at 140 or 150 at the two services each week – than it does members. Students, however, are not the church's sole focus. Pastor Lo related how the church provides a place for seniors from Mainland China to gather on Tuesdays: "They don't know much English. They cannot read or speak and they don't go out. They are pretty isolated. So it is good they gather here." Aside from some gatherings with other Kingston churches, especially the other Alliance churches, and some joint events with the local Korean church, the Kingston Chinese Alliance Church mostly serves the Chinese in Kingston. Though they sponsored two Vietnamese families in the late 1970s, "by and large," says Lo, "we focus more on our ethnic community."

The Kingston Chinese Alliance Church, in distinction from St Mark's Lutheran or First Christian Reformed, dates its origins back to the mid-1970s, not the early 1950s. Many of the younger congregants are second-generation Chinese, born of Chinese parents but growing up speaking English and adopting Canadian values that may create generational problems. Lo talked about his awareness of this problem between parents and children, pointing out to them in his sermons "some of the things in this cultural environment that we have to monitor carefully." Chinese parents, he thought, "are more attached to their kids; it is harder to release their kids." Asked how he thought the Chinese population of Kingston might change over the next ten years, he said he believed that any change would be incremental, not large. Summing up, he said, "Queen's is a main attraction for a lot of Chinese students. We get boomlets. We got Hong Kong immigrants in the early to mid-1990s. Now we receive a lot of Mainland immigrants. A lot of these Mainland immigrants from China have young children. Ten years from now, Mainland Chinese children will be coming to Queen's. Maybe fewer people will be church-oriented, as Hong Kong families seem to have a higher proportion of churchgoers. This is going to change the dynamic of the church, for better or not."

Kingston Korean Presbyterian Church

The Kingston Korean Presbyterian Church, mentioned by Pastor Kong Lo as sharing some events with the Kingston Chinese Alliance Church, began meeting at Cooke's-Portsmouth United Church in Calvin Park on Sundays at 2:30 PM in September 2005. In addition to their Sunday services the Korean Christians use the Cooke's-Portsmouth facilities for services of morning prayer and for other events. Prior to their move to there in 2005, the Korean Presbyterians met at Polson Park Free Methodist Church, located just to the west across Portsmouth Avenue, until the growth of other Free Methodist activities made it less easy to accommodate the Koreans. When Assistant Pastor Brian Pritchard was interviewed at Polson Park Free Methodist, at a time when the Korean Presbyterians were still using space there, he described the Kingston Korean Church as "a plant direct from Korea" (interview, 20 November 2003). While he clarified that the Korean Presbyterians were not under the Free Methodist denomination, "years ago they were looking for a place to have church, and our senior pastor at that time offered them a place, and they have continued to grow at this location." He said that the Koreans attending the services were "scattered around the area, coming as far away as from Belleville and Brockville, and even some across the border come in, because there wasn't a large population of Koreans right here." The central location, in Kingston and with easy access by car, worked well for them. Both Polson Park Free Methodist Church and Cooke's-Portsmouth United Church are located on major streets and have large parking lots.

Lincoln Bryant, minister of the downtown St Andrew's Presbyterian Church, spoke of efforts made there to welcome Korean students of Presbyterian affiliation from Queen's: "Korean Presbyterian Christians are often very devoted to denomination and to faithfulness at worship. And partly because of the fact that we're Presbyterian, they come here. And I've also heard that partly because of the nature of my voice they come here

– because I speak slowly and clearly, and it's a good place to learn English" (interview, 31 March 2004). Another attraction of St Andrew's might be its proximity to campus, whereas Cooke's-Portsmouth is about a half-hour walk for most students. This trend also replicates a pattern at the Kingston Chinese Alliance Church and elsewhere. In contrast to the practice of their parents, second-generation Chinese and Korean students prefer to worship in churches where the services are conducted in English. That might also be true of Korean and Chinese students who come to Queen's as international students. Perhaps one of the reasons why the Kingston Chinese Alliance Church sends a van around to take students to their Sunday services, even though the distance of the church from campus is not particularly great, is to encourage their attendance at that church rather than seeing them drift away to other churches – non-ethnic ones – popular among evangelical students. Especially when they are away from home, studying in another city, young people are free to seek out another church whose worship style is adapted to their youth culture, or to be in the company of peers.

The example represented by St Andrew's Presbyterian Church – of a large downtown mainline Protestant church drawing in foreign students or having a ministry to specific immigrant groups – is also seen at First Baptist Church. There refugee sponsorships and assistance to immigrants have been a large part of the congregation's outreach ministry, especially to people from Iran, Brazil, and El Salvador. A Hispanic congregation was founded in 1989 and continued for a time under Pastor Ruth Kennedy, who was raised in Bolivia. In the early 1990s a Portuguese congregation began to meet at First Baptist under the leadership of the Rev. Francisco Brandeo. After returning from Brazil in 2004 where he had been serving as principal of a Baptist Bible college, Brandeo was appointed as outreach pastor to Protestant Portuguese and Brazilian families. An undated comment on the First Baptist website discloses the continuation of the pattern seen among other ethnic groups: "In the last two years, the Portuguese services of worship have been terminated although Bible study and prayer in Portuguese continues. This is partly a consequence of children of Portuguese and Brazilian families wishing to function in English and not in the language of their parents" (First Baptist Church b).

Afro-Canadian Congregations

This examination of ethnic Christianity within Protestant groups in Kingston concludes with the examination of two Afro-Canadian congregations, Faith Alive and the Church of Pentecost. While Faith Alive has been well established as a house church on Alfred Street near the corner of Princess for a number of years, the Church of Pentecost is a mission that is in town periodically and whose continuing status is uncertain.

The figures from the 2001 Census show that 4.7 per cent of Kingston's population consists of visible minorities. That is not a large percentage, especially in contrast with Toronto's 37 per cent, or even Windsor, London, Hamilton, or Kitchener with about 10 per cent. The percentages of South Asians and of Chinese in Kingston is about equal, at 1.1 per cent each of the city's population, while blacks are listed as 0.6 per cent (or about 850 people). To have a lower percentage of blacks than Chinese is unusual among smaller Ontario cities.

Student visitors to the Faith Alive worship services reported between twelve and thirty-five people in attendance at various times between 2003 and 2006. Paul and Faith Browne, an Afro-Canadian couple, are co-pastors. With the assistance of their children, they provide much of the music that is central to their worship. Most of those in attendance appeared to be visible minorities, including students from African and Caribbean countries, as well as an Asian woman on at least one occasion; some of the regular congregants are Caucasian. The ages of the congregation members ranged from young to middle aged. Two student participant-observers visiting Faith Alive on 16 October 2005 described a service: "The first forty-five minutes ... were very lively, consisting of music – sung by [the female co-pastor] and accompanied by her young son on drums, a woman on the piano, two young people with tambourines, a young man operating technical equipment, and a woman providing background singing. The congregants were very vocal in their praising, often shouting, dancing, clapping and exclaiming such things as 'Praise Jesus!' There was a lot of opportunity for members of the congregation to participate in the session, not only in singing, but, for example, by getting up before everyone and declaring what they were thankful for at the beginning of the service in the form of testimonials." On another occasion a man at the back of the small church augmented the musical accompaniment by playing a harmonica. The emphasis of the entire worship services is largely on thanksgiving and praise. The students who provided these observations, both Roman Catholics of European descent, said that "the people at Faith Alive were incredibly friendly and hospitable." A number of years earlier, students from the same class who chose to visit Faith Alive on one Sunday as part of their course requirements voluntarily returned several times throughout the academic year, taking friends with them, because they enjoyed the experience.

The website for Faith Alive International Ministries describes itself as "a full Gospel, Evangelical Ministry preaching the uncompromised Word of God." The Kingston Faith Alive church also indicates that it belongs to "the

Ministers Fellowship of Canada," presumably the same as Ministers Fellowship International, a network of pastors and leaders of independent churches who share a similar evangelical theology and purpose (Faith Alive a). The international website does not, however, include Kingston's Faith Alive in its "Church Locator" section (Ministers Fellowship International). Faith Alive Church also includes a day school on the premises for Grades 1–12, using the curriculum of the Accelerated Christian Education Canada, which meets the requirements of the Ontario Ministry of Education (Faith Alive b).

The Church of Pentecost, far from being a local and unique congregation like Faith Alive, is a worldwide organization in sixty countries, having more than thirteen thousand churches with 1.7 million members. The Church of Pentecost Canada, begun in Toronto in 1990 and based there, in December 2009 reported having eighteen churches in five provinces, with 4,120 members (Church of Pentecost Canada a). According to an earlier version of the website, "Small branches are being planted in Thunder Bay, Kingston, Windsor, and Halifax." That list later changed, and Kingston no longer appeared. In 2003, when I first became aware of the presence of the Church of Pentecost in Kingston, they were meeting in the Press Room at the Portsmouth Olympic Harbour. Walking through the facility one Sunday morning, I saw their sign in the hall – though I heard their singing first – and looked into the open door of a room with its small congregation of mostly black people, worshipping enthusiastically. One of my students, a Bermudan of Pentecostal background, visited the group on several occasion during the fall and reported the observations from this fieldwork. The nucleus of the group consisted of about six regular congregants, with one of them providing leadership, under the direction of an overseeing pastor from Montreal. Attendance at worship averaged about seven people, some of them Caucasian, but a larger number met on Sunday evenings at the home of the lay leader. At that time, many of those who attended the Sunday evening meeting were from other churches, and were interested in what the Church of Pentecost might have to offer but were not yet ready to commit themselves to become members.

The background of the Church of Pentecost is a fascinating instance of what might be termed postcolonial missionization. The Church of Pentecost was founded in the British colony of Gold Coast in West Africa – now Ghana – by Rev. James McKeown (1900–89). McKeown had arrived in Africa in 1937 as a missionary from the Apostolic Church in the United Kingdom. According to present-day members of the Church of Pentecost, he was unwavering in his determination to indigenize the Ghanian mission. With nationalism and decolonialization rising, he founded the Ghana Apostolic Church in 1953, which in turn was to become the Church of Pentecost in

1962. Ghana had become independent in 1957. After his death in 1989 a tribute was paid to McKeown's memory by Prophet M.K. Yeboah, then chairman of the Church of Pentecost: "He was a man of God from Ireland. He was obedient to his God and loved the African. He spent over forty years an African. This man of glory had no halo of glory round his devoted head. No luster marked the sacred path in which his foot-steps trod. Yet holiness was graven upon his thoughtful brow. And unto God unto alone, his high-borne Soul would bow" (Church of Pentecost Canada b). In effect, then, this church from Ghana, once the destination of missionaries from Britain, and now site of the international headquarters of the Church of Pentecost, sent missionaries to Kingston in a kind of reversal of the colonialization process.

EASTERN CHRISTIANITY IN KINGSTON

Father James Griggs, the priest in charge of the St Gregory of Nyssa Orthodox Parish, one of the congregations in the Orthodox Church in America, provided a description of the space used by his church in the downstairs of Christ Church Anglican in Kingston. Though St Gregory of Nyssa is Orthodox, it is not strictly an ethnic church. Despite that, Griggs's description is clear enough and general enough to apply to other Orthodox churches. He pointed out that in "the nave of the church itself, where people who are gathered to worship, traditionally we would stand" (interview, 15 November 2005). In most Orthodox churches in North America, however, there are pews placed for seating. He continued, "And then there is the sanctuary, which is divided from the nave of the church with an iconostasis, a screen, a stand that holds icons, images, of Christ, of the Mother, his Mother, Mary; and here we have John the forerunner, the Baptist; and St Gregory the Bishop of Nyssa, who is the patron of the parish: he was St Basil the Great's brother. And inside the sanctuary is the Holy Table, the altar table, as well as … another table, the altar of preparation, or table of preparation where the bread and wine are prepared for the Eucharist liturgy."

Following these details of the arrangement of the space, Griggs went on to outline the liturgy, describing it as "almost a dialogue between what the priest is doing in the sanctuary and what the people – either the people or the choir, or a chanter – are doing in the nave of the church. And there's movement between the sanctuary and the nave of the church." Clarifying the purpose of the iconostasis, he said, "The screen is not meant to wall the people off from what is happening inside and make it a big mystery, but it is a – what would you say? – a window into the reality of God's revealing of himself to his creation, his interaction with his creation, and the movement of the people of his creation, their movement into closer and deeper relationship with him and participation in the life of the Holy Trinity. That is probably the most basic capsule I could give you to describe why it's arranged the way that it is. And it finds its roots in the Temple worship of Jerusalem originally" (interview, 15 November 2005).

Dormition of the Theotokos Greek Orthodox Church

The Greek Orthodox Church most readily comes to mind one when thinks of Eastern Christianity in Kingston, in part because Greeks, though less numerous than people of Ukrainian descent, are such a sizeable ethnic group in the city. In addition, their church building downtown on Johnson Street across from Kingston's public library is a visible monument to their existence. Even on the larger national or global stage, the Greek Orthodox Church is a large presence and readily identifiable. As Myroslaw Tataryn, a Ukrainian Catholic priest, writes, "Historically, Greeks are the ethnic group most strongly associated with Eastern Christianity." The flourishing of the Byzantine Empire imposed "a strong Hellenic facade on relatively autonomous, local, indigenous forms of Christianity." Other Orthodox churches were assumed to be "Greek," an assumption that continues in Canada, Tataryn argues (2008, 299). In the early twenty-first century the Greek Orthodox Church in Kingston included 190 families in the city and surrounding area. The Dormition of the Theotokos Greek Orthodox Church is a red brick structure originally erected in the nineteenth century and purchased from the Baptists in 1962. The priest, Father Theologos Drakos, observed, "Our church is rather different than what a Byzantine-style church is. The typical church has a dome, and you'll see that the icons are actually painted all over the walls. It is actually very different than this" (interview, 20 November 2003).

The Greek Orthodox community in Kingston "started in the '50s, if not a little earlier." Because it was small at that time, this congregation at first used St George's Anglican Cathedral for the sacraments, and for regular services had to travel either to Ottawa or to Watertown, New York. With the acquisition of a building, a priest began to serve the local church: "Back then they used to go through priests very quickly. They used to come from Greece, spend some time here, and go off to Toronto or Ottawa." Theo Drakos was born in Calgary in 1974 of Greek immigrant parents. His father was an Orthodox priest before him. After graduating in history from the University of Toronto in 1995, he entered the Holy Cross Greek Orthodox School of Theology for his seminary studies. Holy Cross, in Brookline, Massachusetts, is the only Greek Orthodox seminary in North America. After being married and ordained in 1998, Father Drakos began what was to develop into a comparatively lengthy period of service – more than a decade – at the Greek Orthodox Church in Kingston.

Greek Orthodox Church

Drakos related that, although his parents' generation was Greek-speaking, younger people tended to speak English. As the censuses of 1961 and 1971 indicate, through the 1960s the number of Greek immigrants in Canada doubled to about 125,000 and then levelled off (Tataryn 2008, 300). By 2003, Drakos observed, more of the families in his congregation were marrying non-Greeks: "Mixed marriages are almost unheard of fifteen, twenty years ago. Now we have about 90 per cent mixed marriages. Last year it was almost 100 per cent." By comparison, "in Toronto, the marriages are 50–50, because there are a lot more Greeks." The 2002 movie *My Big Fat Greek Wedding* revolves around the crisis when a Greek woman, played by Winnipeg-born Nia Vardalos, decides to marry outside Chicago's Greek community. Filmed in Toronto, this romantic comedy was a box-office success and popular favourite. Measured by the degree of marriage outside the ethnic group, or exogamy, assimilation may take place more quickly in Kingston than in larger communities. Although the Kingston church operates a Greek school (like the one referred to in *My Big Fat Greek Wedding*), attendance has become less than a main concern. As Drakos comments, "It used to be a priority. Now, my generation that went to Greek school were forced to go to Greek school. My kids – we don't force them to go to Greek school; it is not a priority." In the Greek Orthodox Church overall, less Greek is being spoken lately, partly as a result of the influence of younger priests. Because the liturgy is conducted in Ancient Greek, very few of the Greek-speaking parishioners are able to understand it. Drakos feels that because "the Orthodox Church has always been a missionary church, it used the language and customs of the people, and so on and so forth." He is not concerned about that kind of adaptation.

Many immigrants and their descendants probably share the confusion as to what they inherit from their ethnicity and what from their Christianity. Bramadat and Seljak allude to the witticism of Jacques Grand'Maison to the effect that French Canadians in the 1950s were unsure whether they were following the religion of their culture or the culture of their religion (2008, 20). Father Drakos, asked about the "Greek" aspect of what it meant to be Orthodox, commented that because theirs is "an 'ethnic church' – our own fault – we sort of closed our doors, kept everything quiet." In his view, Greek ethnicity may in fact obscure a larger view of Orthodoxy and its role: "We believe the Orthodox Church is *the* Church, and everybody else sort of moved away from it." The Orthodox position on the history of the Christian Church is that the Roman Catholic Church split from the Orthodox Church, "and everything else sort of came from the Catholic Church." For Drakos, because the Orthodox Church is the original Christian Church, others have to return to it. Its role, unfortunately, has become more that of preservation – "We have actually become a defensive church" – and of attempting to draw other traditions back to the centrality that it represents. This position creates some problems in ecumenical endeavours, notwithstanding the welcome, the teaching, and the careful explanations Drakos provides to visitors to services at the Kingston church. Although he participated in interfaith services after 9/11 where the sacraments were not involved, he said that if a member of his congregation were to marry a Roman Catholic, "we do not allow the Catholic priest to come here and do a service or do a service with us." Neither can Orthodox priests participate at a Roman Catholic church: "We are very strict in those things because we are not in the same boat." Even at joint services of prayer there needs to be caution in participating with churches favouring same-sex marriages because "we are trying to preserve the truth."

St Mena Coptic Orthodox Church

Statistics Canada data show 126,200 Ukrainian Catholics at the 2001 Census, and 32,720 Ukrainian Orthodox Christians. In contrast, there are only 10,285 people affiliated with the Coptic Orthodox Church in Canada, but that number represents a doubling from 5,020 recorded in 1991. In Egypt, where more than 80 per cent of the population is Muslim, the majority of the Christian remainder is comprised of Orthodox, or Coptic, Christians. While one or two families, often transient, of Coptic Christians have been in Kingston since the 1960s, they began to meet as a small congregation in homes by the mid-1970s. In the mid-1990s they rented the Morgan Memorial Chapel in Queen's Theological College, paying $50 each time. In 2003 they moved to their own quarters, where they were to stay for seven years – a double storefront in a plaza off Development Drive, in the west end of Kingston, with the monthly rent increasing to $2,000.

An outside sign reading "St Mena Coptic Orthodox Church" spanned both halves of the two adjoining stores. The left side of the storefront, the entrance to their rented space – officially the narthex – was where the community gathered and met socially after their worship services. The right-hand side was carefully arranged for their liturgical needs, equipped with about six rows of oak pews on each side and icons placed across the front and side walls. Following the usual Orthodox practice for the arrangement of sacred space, a wooden panelled wall, or iconostasis, with three curtained openings divided the nave where the congregation sits from the sanctuary where the priest administers the mass. Dr Wagdy Loza, a psychologist who works for Correctional Service Canada, and who spoke to us on behalf of Kingston's Coptic Christians, modestly described St Mena as "a typical poor Coptic church, not an expensive one," of the kind one would find in Montreal or Toronto (interview, 4 August 2005). Despite this distinction, which really speaks more to the scale of the endeavour than to its appearing impoverished, this space was fitted at great trouble and with ongoing expense to become a liturgical site dedicated to their needs and according to accustomed patterns.

Loza's account of Coptic Christianity revealed his pride in its antiquity, origins, and status. He spoke of the proximity of Egypt to Jerusalem, of the flight of the Holy Family to Egypt as recorded in the Gospel of Matthew, and of the establishment of the church in Alexandria by St Mark in the middle of the first century. Referring to the Council of Chalcedon in 451 CE, and the split over christological issues that divided the Egyptian Church from the Eastern Orthodox and western churches, Loza said – here offering a different view from that of Father Drakos – that Coptic Christians like to think of the Greek Orthodox Church as a subsect of the Coptic Church. When the Lozas' daughter was married before the acquisition of the space on Development Drive, the Coptic priest would not conduct the ceremony in an Anglican Church. Instead, her wedding was held at the Greek Orthodox Church downtown. Intercommunion with other Christian groups, even Orthodox ones, is a difficult issue, as the preceding section on the Greek Orthodox Church shows. A Coptic Christian woman in Kingston married to a Roman Catholic could not receive the Eucharist in her husband's church, nor was a Coptic deacon permitted, with apologies from the priest, to take communion in the Ukrainian Catholic Church. Loza said this difficulty is "a sticky point" for the parties involved, commenting that the "Coptic Church is one of the most rigid and most conservative [churches], and they like to keep it this way."

St Mena Coptic Orthodox Church has at most sixteen affiliated families, including several from Napanee and Belleville. Loza stressed that the core group of supporters consists of only seven or eight families, and that even for Easter services the maximum attendance at worship, including children, would be a maximum of thirty-five or forty people. Clearly, maintaining their religious community is a struggle for such a small number. Loza said that "if you have thirty families, forty families, you will have a full-blown church – it's no problem": they could own their own church building and employ their own priest. But the Coptic Christian group in Kingston has remained at about the same size, and since many of them are professionals, especially doctors in Kingston for a residency, some come and then leave for elsewhere. As it is now, their services are held every two or three weeks, when they can get a priest to come to Kingston from Ottawa, Montreal, or Toronto. While the future of Coptic Christianity in Kingston depends on maintaining a critical mass of dedicated families, despite their children moving away, Loza felt that the attachment of young people remained strong. He said his nephews and nieces in Montreal "are more Copts than their parents."

Having mentioned another Orthodox group, St Gregory of Nyssa, that had used a storefront space and now uses the basement of Christ Church Anglican, Loza summed up the importance of having a dedicated space for worship: "It's just, you want a place, that's what it is. So, what do you do? And you are not rich, you don't have money, so what do you do? You buy?" He laughed. "You rent whatever you can." Despite that resignation in 2005 to the existing realities, by 2010 Kingston's Coptic Christians had succeeded in purchasing a building of their own, located closer to Highway 401 at 1281 Midland Avenue.

St Gregory of Nyssa Parish

As pointed out at the beginning of this examination of Eastern Christianity in Kingston, the St Gregory of Nyssa Parish, while it is Orthodox, is not an ethnic congregation. Part of the Orthodox Church in America, or OCA, it is one of twenty member parishes in Ontario, most of them in Toronto and the surrounding region. Gregory of Nyssa is one of 220 parishes of the Orthodox Church in America, established in the last two decades or so, that use English in worship and are not ethnically based. Originating from the activity of

Russian missionaries in Alaska late in the eighteenth century, eventually this Orthodox denomination grew to include seven hundred parishes in Canada, the United States, and Mexico. As we have seen already in the consideration of other Orthodox churches, Orthodoxy offers various competing possibilities, rather than a single Orthodox church in a particular region – that is, "multiple, overlapping jurisdictions based on ethnic background" (Orthodox Church in America a).

Until the early 1960s the Orthodox Church in America was known by the unwieldy name of the Russian Orthodox Greek Catholic Church of North America. Now most parishes employ English. The Orthodox Church in America has become autocephalus – that is to say, self-governing, free of administration from Moscow, and having its own primate, Seraphim, the bishop for Canada, who resides in Ottawa. In October 2010 it was announced by the Orthodox Church of America that Archbishop Seraphim had taken a leave of absence after claims about sexual misconduct (Orthodox Church in America b). Newspaper reports referred to allegations involving two ten-year-old boys in Winnipeg almost thirty years earlier (*National Post*, 29 October 2010). In November 2010 Seraphim was charged with two counts of sexual assault (*Globe and Mail*, 25 November 2010).

The parish of St Gregory of Nyssa deserves inclusion here not as an exclusively ethnic representation of Eastern Christianity – though there are various ethnicities in the congregation – but due to its connections, especially through the priest, Father James Griggs, with other Orthodox churches in the area. Further, Griggs's description of the arrangement of the liturgical space provided above applies to those other churches as well, indicating their commonality. St Gregory originated as a house church in the late 1970s when William P. Zion, a professor in religious studies at Queen's and formerly an Episcopal priest, became a priest in the Orthodox Church of America and took the religious name Father Basil. After Zion's death, the local congregation of the Orthodox Church in America continued with a remnant of about a dozen people dependent on visiting priests until the arrival of Father Griggs in the mid-1990s. When Christ Church, the Anglican Church in what used to be the village of Cataraqui on the Sydenham Road, built its new parish centre just to the north of the nineteenth-century limestone structure, space became available in the basement of the original church building. The St Gregory of Nyssa Orthodox Parish, which had been meeting in the John Deutsch Centre at Queen's University and then in a rented store, converted the basement area of Christ Church for their use in 2001.

Ed Dallow, the priest at Christ Church, outlines how the arrangement came to be when the small Orthodox congregation found that their rent at the strip mall was about to be tripled: "That would have caused them considerable difficulty. So Father James and I are acquaintances. He came and looked at our facilities and decided the old church would be helpful for him, but only the lower level which was the parish hall. The upper level has pews, and he couldn't put the iconostasis up there and change all of that architecture. He asked if they could use the lower level and rebuild that into an Orthodox setting" (interview, 14 May 2004). The Anglicans negotiated a reduced rent to allow St Gregory's congregation to move in. Dallow continued: "So, rather than having to pay three times as much, they in fact were coming in at 50 per cent at what they were paying at the present time. It's been a remarkable association." Griggs and his family were also able to move into the nearby stone rectory, which was not being used by Christ Church.

Father Griggs, who has a half-time position looking after the Greek Orthodox Church in Brockville, spends two Sundays each month at St Gregory of Nyssa, where the attendance grew to thirty or forty people. One family was from Belleville, "a second-generation Greek couple and their kids who came here because they wanted their kids to understand the liturgy – because it's served in English here" (interview, 15 November 2005). As their children grew older, they began to go to the Greek Orthodox Church in Belleville. Others have come from New York State, from Brockville, and from Sharbot Lake to the north of Kingston. Griggs says that a Greek woman, who admitted to not having much education, remarked, "I understand more now in English that I ever understood in Greek." Among the other congregants Griggs enumerates those who are "Russian, Serbo-Croatian, we have one family from South India, one family from Eritrea, we have Egyptian people from time to time. So it's sort of, again, an ebb and flow ... What else? Who am I missing? Romanian ... Greek ... I think that probably covers it." While the Orthodox Church in America, then, is not ethnic, it does cater to a number of ethnicities among whom orthodoxy is prominent. As Griggs puts it, "The one thing that they have in common is that English is at least the second or third language that everybody has."

Ukrainian Catholic Church

Myroslaw Tataryn, a Ukrainian Catholic priest, writes in an essay that people assume he must be Orthodox because he is married. "No," he explains, "I am in fact a Catholic in union with the Pope." Then he further complicates things when he adds, "But we maintain Orthodox traditions, so we have married priests" (2008, 287). The liturgy celebrated by Ukrainian Catholics is similar to the Orthodox liturgy, but they accept Roman Catholic dogma even while existing as a separate ecclesiastical jurisdiction from Rome.

Ukrainians have been in Canada for well over one hundred years, with most immigration having occurred by the time of World War II. Many settled in western Canada, where there were persistent difficulties in obtaining the services of a priest. As a result, and because of proselytizing activities, many Ukrainian Catholics became Orthodox or Protestant. Hans Mol has pointed out that between 1931 and 1981 Ukrainian Canadians "belonging to the Roman Catholic Church increased from 11.5 to 17.5%, those belonging to the United Church from 1.6% to 13.4%, those belonging to the Anglican Church from 0.3% to 3.8%" (1985, 73). As the religious options available increased, and with people moving to cities, their active affiliations declined, with the result that for Canadian Ukrainians ethnicity has become a greater preserver of identity than religion.

This background to the Ukrainian experience in Canada might help explain why Kingston's Ukrainian Catholic Church, sometimes known as the Ukrainian Greek Catholic Church, is smaller than the local Greek Orthodox Church. The Ukrainians have never had a resident priest, despite existing as a congregation in Kingston for more than fifty years and there being in the city more people of Ukrainian than of Greek background. Furthermore, because the greatest period of Ukrainian immigration occurred much earlier than Greek immigration, their assimilation into the mainstream of Canada was that much further advanced. The beginnings of Kingston's St Michael the Archangel Ukrainian Catholic Church go back to 1949 when visiting Ukrainian Catholic priests began to perform the liturgy in the St James' Chapel of St Mary's Cathedral. Their church continues to be housed in a building acquired in the 1950s on the near north side of Kingston at 472 Bagot Street; a parish hall was subsequently added.

A local leader in the Ukrainian community and professor of political geography at the Royal Military College, Lubomyr Luciuk offered a tribute in the newspaper after the death of Jules Charles Emil Riotte in 2000. Luciuk recalled Father Riotte's influence on local Ukrainians when he served in Kingston as a priest, commuting twice monthly from Toronto between 1959 and 1975. "For many of his Kingston years," Luciuk writes, "I was his altar boy. I was not originally enthusiastic. Father Riotte changed that. He had a habit of having lunch with parishioners after celebrating the divine liturgy. He became a regular guest at my parents' table. Imagine someone describing the religious views of first-century church father Origen, or the politics of Byzantium's emperor Justinian and his somewhat rakish consort, Theodora, or Edgar Cayce's revelations about Atlantis and reincarnation, while enjoying the Sunday bucket of Kentucky Fried Chicken, and you'll appreciate our enthrallment" (*Whig-Standard*, 15 June 2000).

Born in Dresden in 1901, Riotte became a pastor in the Evangelical Lutheran Church, then converted to Roman Catholicism, and eventually became a Ukrainian Catholic priest. Luciuk describes the sometimes violent enmity that existed after World War II among feuding groups consisting of "four distinctly Ukrainian and Ukrainian-Slavic ethnic organizations in Kingston" (1980, 101). Though these differences were not immediately settled with the founding of the parish, Luciuk writes that eventually Father Riotte was "largely successful" in resolving some of the conflicts (113n28).

Tataryn cites a study showing, based on 1971 Census data, that only about half of Ukrainian Canadians were at that time affiliated with either the Ukrainian Catholic or Orthodox Church. Analyzing 2001 Census figures, he estimates that "the percentage of adherents is in reality well below 50 per cent and probably around a maximum of 25 per cent" (2008, 296). Early in the twenty-first century a minority of Canadians of Ukrainian descent identify with either of their two traditional churches, and identification with other Ukrainians has decreased too, the result of exogamy and loss of language. A history of Roman Catholics in Kingston includes a section on St Michael the Archangel Ukrainian Greek Catholic parish, acknowledging the Ukrainian church's separateness from Roman Catholics but explaining that "in practice they work together and enjoy sharing their mutual spiritual heritages" (McKinnon et al. 2002, 48).

ETHNIC ROMAN CATHOLIC CONGREGATIONS IN KINGSTON

Among the various Roman Catholic communities and cultures singled out for special mention on the website of the Archdiocese of Kingston are the following: "There is a Portuguese parish in Kingston, and there are apostolates to Hispanic, Ukrainian and Polish communities, as well as ministries to youth, to prisoners, to the deaf and to the aged and infirm" (Archdiocese of Kingston). The Portuguese parish is Our Lady of Fatima Roman Catholic Church, located at 588 Division Street, and served by Rev. Manuel Tavares. The Spanish community is served by Deacon Orlando Diaz at St John the Apostle Church at 88 Patrick Street. Mass in Spanish is conducted every second week at the St James' Chapel of St Mary's Cathedral. The Ukrainian Catholic Church, dealt with just above under Eastern Christianity, is on Bagot Street. The Polish Apostolate, Christ the King, meets under the direction of Rev. Wieslaw Chochrek in the St James' Chapel at the cathedral. Finally, a francophone congregation, St François d'Assise, has its own church building at 512 Frontenac Street, under the administration of Rev. Robert Masters. Notably, these congregations are all clustered close to the older part of downtown Kingston, either for the sake of centrality or to be close to where their respective congregants live.

Hans Mol says that the conflicting claims of ethnic and national identities have not often been an issue within Canada, though services in foreign languages were sometimes suspended when loyalties were tested during the two world wars. Within Roman Catholicism, bishops sometimes had to deal with the wishes of ethnic parishes for more resources or greater autonomy, especially when such claims conflicted with the church's larger aims (1985, 63). As with other Christian denominations examined here, within the second generation of Catholic children in immigrant families the preference is often to worship in English rather than in their ancestral languages.

Other factors too determine whether Catholic immigrants seek ethnic continuity through establishment of their own parishes or follow the route of assimilation into the larger church. In Kingston, though Italian immigrants are slightly more numerous than those of either Polish or Portuguese background – each of the three groups having between three and four thousand people reporting one of these backgrounds – Italians have never had their own church or priest. Italians, who mostly arrived here in the 1950s, tended to identify themselves with particular regions within Italy rather than the country as a whole. In other cities, Italian national identity was forged in Canada with the establishment of particular organization or Little Italies, or else through pan-Italian loyalty to soccer teams in World Cup matches. My Italian neighbours, who have lived in Kingston since the 1950s, relate that they occasionally entertained visiting priests from Italy in their home. In one respect the family has resisted the church, exerting their independence when their children were going to be distributed among several different Separate – or "Roman Catholic" – schools. They chose instead to keep them together and send them to the "Protestant" public school a short walk down the street. Later they continued in the Kingston Collegiate and Vocational Institute, or KCVI, rather than going to Regiopolis-Notre Dame, the Catholic high school. While they remain staunchly Roman Catholic, for them the preservation of family unity trumped a Catholic education.

La Paroisse St François d'Assise

The francophone church in Kingston, La Paroisse St François d'Assise, originated during the 1950s among about one hundred people arriving in Kingston from Alberta, Saskatchewan, Quebec, other places in Ontario, and various parts of Acadia. Obviously an ethnic – though not an immigrant – congregation, St François d'Assise took root in Kingston from le Club Champlain, the francophone cultural association. Yet conducting worship services in French at this church, especially fifty years after it was founded, arises more from the wish to preserve language and culture than from any deficiencies in English among the parishioners. The strikingly simple yet beautiful little white-stuccoed church was designed by architect Wilfrid Sorensen, son-in-law of the artist André Bieler (1896–1989; Biéler, who emigrated from Switzerland to Quebec where he built his reputation as a painter, came to Queen's University as a professor of art in 1936 and lived in Kingston until his death). The church's website quotes from Léopold Lamontagne's *Kingston: Son Héritage Français*, which points out how the Roman arches of the church pay a nostalgic homage to pre-Gothic European models: "Cet ensemble architectural très modeste donne l'idée d'un petit cloître du moyen âge en plein cœur de la ville" (Paroisse St-François d'Assise).

Students who visited a service at St François d'Assise commented that French and English were spoken about equally by the parishioners. They were told that in many of the attending families one spouse is francophone while the other is anglophone. Younger people attending were students in one of the local French elementary or secondary schools, or at the university. Among those present were a family from Haiti and several other black congregants. A special service was conducted on the day that the students were there, the feast day of St Francis of Assisi. The congregation filed outside to the courtyard to sing and pray before returning inside in a procession. The priest, Bob Masters, was born in Rouyn-Noranda in northwestern Quebec. Ordained in 1995, Père Masters served as a priest in several Ukrainian Catholic and Roman Catholic churches before coming to St François d'Assise in 2003. In general this francophone parish fulfils Canadian ideals of providing a space for the language and culture of one of the two founding nations within this multicultural nation.

Our Lady of Fatima Portuguese Parish

Our Lady of Fatima Portuguese Parish was established in 1978, with mass initially being offered in Portuguese at the St James' Chapel at the cathedral. The Portuguese language still predominates in the church just off Division Street, tucked away almost out of sight behind a car dealership and completed in 1980. Because labour was contributed by the members of the Portuguese community, many of whom were skilled in building trades, the church was constructed for the cost of the materials (McKinnon et al. 2002, 43). The parish's third priest, Father Antonio Pinheiro, was appointed in 1984 and retired from the parish on 15 October 2010.

In 1989 Murray Hogben described in the *Whig-Standard* a unique citizenship ceremony held in Kingston when eighty-four Kingstonians who had emigrated from Portugal became citizens (*Whig-Standard*, 17 April 1989). The presiding officer said that this kind of "all-one-group citizenship ceremony was 'something new.'" Some of these Portuguese-Canadians, who had been in Kingston for thirty years, found that to participate as a group helped to overcome shyness or nervousness about this citizenship ceremony. The article also estimated the size of the Portuguese community at the time as consisting of seven thousand people from twelve hundred families, three-quarters of them from the Azores. The history of the Roman Catholic archdiocese refers to six thousand Portuguese in Kingston in 1980 (McKinnon et al. 2002, 43). Even though the Portuguese continue to be thought of by many as the largest ethnic group in Kingston, the 2006 Census figures show that those who identify themselves as having Portuguese ethnicity number just over three thousand, far behind those identifying German or Dutch connections and slightly less than those of either Italian or Polish background.

An article by Carlos Teixeira reflecting on Portuguese-Canadians in the early 1990s identifies the special challenges and difficulties they faced. Most Portuguese immigrants had little formal education and lacked job skills. They tended to live together in Portuguese neighbourhoods in Canadian cities – as they did initially in Kingston – in quite large family units. Teixeira describes their communities as close-knit, and often more conservative than they would have been in Portugal itself, frequently having little association with other cultural groups. The preservation of language and Portuguese institutions were important values, together with religious festivals and customs promoted by the church. Teixeira sums up: "The survival and integrity of Portuguese neighbourhoods and communities in Canada in the long term may be problematic. The reasons are many: the decrease in immigration; dispersion of first-generation Portuguese to different parts of the city and to the suburbs; internal and external threats to the community, such as replacement by other ethnic groups; inner-city revitalization/ gentrification, which displaces ethnic communities; and redevelopment projects and rising housing prices. All these factors may contribute to the expected gradual integration and/or assimilation into Canadian society" (Teixeira n.d.). In the light of this account, a possible explanation for the decline among those identifying themselves as having Portuguese ethnicity in Kingston is that among the second-generation a major break has occurred from the community, especially in comparison with the tight ties maintained by their parents.

Father Leo Byrne at St Paul the Apostle, Kingston's largest Roman Catholic Church with some three thousand families, was asked about the ethnic make-up of his congregation in the west end. He commented about the church and ethnicity in Kingston generally, "There's a large, if I could start, Portuguese background. Our Lady of Fatima Church on Division Street. I was stationed at St John's, corner of Patrick and Quebec, almost forty years ago. That's where the Portuguese community lived. They've obviously grown in forty years, and their children have moved out here and had children. So I run into the same. There's a large community from them." Father Byrne added, "A lot of the Portuguese, for example, don't go to Our Lady of Fatima, because they either marry people who don't speak Portuguese or that kind of thing" (interview, 30 October 2003). Writing about the citizenship ceremony in 1989, Murray Hogben commented on the changing directions among Kingston's Portuguese in recent years: "Most of the men are in construction work but some have spread out into other careers, such as architects, engineers, lawyers, business people and a group is now studying at Queen's University" (*Whig-Standard*, 17 April 1989).

Father Charles Gazeley of Holy Family Roman Catholic Church was asked about the ethnic makeup of his congregation. Holy Family is situated about two kilometres north of Our Lady of Fatima, toward Highway 401 in the north end of Kingston off Weller Avenue. Gazeley, who had been at Holy Family for ten years, commented that "there are a number of Portuguese people in the area." He elaborated, "There are a few Italians. There are a few of other European nationalities. I'd say other than the strictly Canadian Kingstonians, the largest number would be Portuguese in the area, as far as I know. Some of them attend the Portuguese church but some of them come here" (interview, 26 November 2003). He explained that first-generation Portuguese immigrants "tend to go to Our lady of Fatima, but when they intermarry with others who don't speak Portuguese they tend to come here because they only speak Portuguese at Our Lady of Fatima." At the mass at Holy Family on Sunday evenings, depending on how many Portuguese-speaking congregants are in attendance, the practice is to say at least part of the rosary in Portuguese. They might alternate with English, or "if everyone there is Portuguese they might say the whole thing in Portuguese. But generally speaking it's a mixture."

Christ the King Polish Apostolate

In 2003, Father Gazeley mentioned that a few years earlier a priest who came from out of town had conducted the mass in Polish once each month at Holy Family Roman Catholic Church: "But now they have established their own little community in Kingston and so they have mass every Sunday at St James' Chapel at the Cathedral." Off to one side and slightly to the rear of the property occupied by St Mary's Cathedral stands the Chapel of St James, named after James the Apostle. Consecrated in 1890, the chapel is described on the website of the Polish Apostolate: "The Chapel of St. James Boanerges [from the reference in Mark's Gospel to James and John as 'sons of thunder'] enchants with its stained glass windows, its beautifully sculpted front altar, effigies of former Bishops and Archbishops and its intimate interior" (Christ the King Polish Apostolate a).

The website provides a history of Polish Catholics in Kingston from the beginnings of the Polish National Association of thirty people in 1940. By the latter part of the 1940s other associations of Poles had formed, and a priest from Montreal would journey to Kingston to celebrate mass at St John the Apostle Church. Though various efforts were made to provide more regular services, it was not until the 1980s with the rise of the Solidarity movement that more Poles came to Kingston and a congregation became viable. Under communism, borders had been tighter and international mobility was discouraged. In 1994 Father Henryk Kociolek became the first spiritual pastor, and when by 1996 the congregation had grown to sixty families, the Polish Apostolate was founded. Today the congregation comprises about one hundred families under the leadership of Rev. Wieslaw Chochrek. Mass is celebrated in the St James' Chapel twice weekly in Polish, with the main service at noon on Sundays (Christ the King Polish Apostolate b).

Mariola Gozdek, who arrived in Kingston from Poland and now works as a lay pastoral associate at St Mary's Cathedral, said that coming to Canada from a country where 95 per cent of the population is Roman Catholic was "different, but I have to say it was a very positive experience." Married to a non-Catholic, she said she appreciates the contact with other religious traditions: "We are working toward the unity. We see this was what we have in common and we build on that. I have handled a few interdenominational dinners from the [Providence] Spirituality Centre, and my eyes were opening to all of those people coming there, and there was no real difference among us! I mean in the sense that we came ... to form a community. To build on this, what we have in common. We keep in touch and this is what we are doing now. Every once in a while those Christian unity prayers, this is, this is beautiful" (interview, 24 March 2004).

IMMIGRANTS AND CHRISTIANITY

The presence of these ethnic congregations in Kingston partly illustrates trends that can be seen in almost any Canadian city. Immigrants bring with them their religious traditions from their respective countries of origin. To have a place to worship in one's first language and in association with others from the same ethnic group functions to preserve identity, one of the two major roles – sometimes opposing each other – that Hans Mol (1985) recognizes for religions. That is, the transition to a new place is facilitated by organizations that help maintain continuity. The way in which various feast days and ethnic festivals are celebrated in particular churches demonstrates Mol's point. In time, with the acquisition of English and with intermarriage, these connections can dwindle in importance for Canadian-born children of immigrants. Perhaps especially in a city the size of Kingston – as we saw with the Greek Orthodox Church, where most marriages are taking place to non-Greeks – some earlier connections may lose strength or disappear. Then, too, ethnic groups differ in terms of the importance of employing religion to maintain traditions. Undeniably, among Chinese Christians, for instance, their language, ethnicity, and culture are not supported by the presence of Christianity in mainland China in the manner that Portuguese or Poles would experience in their homelands. Despite those obstacles, the Kingston Chinese Alliance Church provides a space for elderly Chinese to associate and converse, even if Christianity is not their religion.

Mol alternatively sees religion as exercising a transformative rather than conservative role. That is, religion, rather than preserving existing traditions, may help introduce new ones and thus assist in the process of adaptation. For example, the Christian Reformed Church, by conducting its services in English rather than in Dutch, facilitated its members' adjustment to the requirements of Canadian life. One of the marks of the success of such adjustment is that in the Westside Fellowship, the second church in the Christian Reformed denomination to be built in Kingston, people of Dutch descent do not constitute the majority of members. The original Christian Reformed congregation was named First Christian Reformed Church. However, Ed Visser of Westside has said that "because Kingston wasn't overloaded with immigrants" – in contrast to Edmonton, for example, where one might find First, Second, and Third Christian Reformed churches – "there'll never be a 'Second Christian Reformed Church'" in this city. Though the denomination continues, its Dutch connections have become muted. The name, Westside Fellowship, reflects its location in the western part of the city rather than its relationship to a sister church of the same denomination.

Using the example of Greek Canadians, Bramadat and Seljak comment that they "are now far freer to choose the features of communal Greek identity that suit their individual tastes." They might adopt a "pick-and-choose" approach, as so many other Canadians do, to their religion and their culture. As part of their existence in a multicultural Canada, they might also incorporate into their lives aspects of other cultures than their own. "Imagine," Bramadat and Seljak continue, "a Greek Canadian who adopts both Buddhism and vegetarianism and who marries an African Canadian atheist" (2008, 19). Such a person forging an individual identity is less at risk of suffering the rejection of family and friends than in earlier times, they suggest.

Over time the ethnicity of particular Christian congregations may tend to lose its salience, as we saw in the case of St Mark's Lutheran Church. Today the German and Danish roots of the founding members in St Mark's remain in evidence only to about the same extent that St Andrew's Presbyterian is predominantly Scottish – that is to say, as an aspect of the church's heritage, but not largely visible. Even having said that, it should be pointed out that the Scots do not embody a single ethnicity, and that from its beginnings in Canada Presbyterianism was comprised of several ethnicities. In nineteenth-century Kingston, after all, there were two Scottish Presbyterian churches and one Irish Presbyterian church. As immigrant identity wanes in significance in succeeding generations, the importance of ethnicity in a church originally connected with that group declines correspondingly. Again, the Christian Reformed Church may have succeeded so well in facilitating the adjustment of its members to Canadian life that its ethnic characteristics become less important than some other features. Stuart Macdonald points out that Dutch immigrants joining the Christian Reformed Church in North America might have had, contrary to other North American Christians, no compunctions about drinking or smoking, yet they could not understand why greater efforts were not being made to establish Christian schools (2008, 180–1). As their church accomplished its bridging function for its members to their adopted country, new roles developed. Mol points out that the church sacralizes family life – which is, after all, not exclusively a Dutch characteristic. Meanwhile, other more obviously ethnic traits of what it is to be Dutch are put aside, and the Christian Reformed denomination takes on the task of preserving and continuing theological characteristics of its Calvinist tradition.

The continuing role of an ethnic Christian church after the first generation of immigrant members may be developed in various ways. A Christian Reformed church, such as Westside Fellowship, might acquire more generically evangelical characteristics – though maintaining its theological distinctives – rather than continuing to be specifically ethnic. To the extent that they exercise a conservative role of preserving and protecting identities, it might be, too, that ethnic churches become part of the evangelical wing of Christianity rather than the mainstream. As well, ethnic churches, especially when formed in the homelands of their members as the result of missionary outreach, place a strong priority on evangelization. In Kingston the congregations at Faith Alive and the Kingston Chinese Alliance churches especially emphasize evangelism and missions. Macdonald comments that Koreans, the largest ethnic minority within the Presbyterian Church in Canada, came into the Canadian church just as it was declining precipitously in numbers – 35 per cent between the censuses of 1991 and 2001 (see chap. 2). A Korean interpretation of this decline might be that Canadian Presbyterians failed to emphasize evangelistic endeavours to the extent that the Koreans themselves did. Their response was to pursue their own mission work, in Canada and overseas, independently of the national church. Further, as Macdonald writes, "the Korean church brought a different heritage from Korea, in theology, approach to scripture, and the place of women in their churches" (2008, 186). These particular distinctive factors emphasized by Korean Christians, central as they are to the self-characterization of evangelicals, may continue to have a role in shifting Canadian Presbyterianism away from the place it has traditionally occupied within mainstream Christianity.

Without question, most of Kingston's Christian churches originated to some extent as immigrant churches, especially if one looks at their nineteenth-century roots. Whereas then those roots were European – and continued to be so through most of the twentieth century – today's immigrants arrive in Canada increasingly from Asian countries. Chris Walker, formerly pastor of Bethel Church, spoke of the changes he had seen taking place within the Christian church, and specifically in Kingston: "When I was growing up prior to 1975 there seemed to be a very insular approach to being a Christian – being a part of a large family. Everyone looked alike, sounded alike, and agreed on things that are accepted. It was certainly the case in this part of the world where I grew up, very eastern Ontarian, very typically North American for the day" (interview, 2 August 2005). At Bethel, because that church – "an old-style congregation" – served a largely student population, Walker saw changes taking place over each student generation, a period of three or four years. Even in a small city such as Kingston the multicultural nature of Canada was becoming evident: "That multicultural reality has brought the world to us, rather than us going to the world ... I'm stunned that when I came to Bethel [in 1997], there may have been – let me be generous – twenty Asian students, almost no African students. That has profoundly changed, as you have observed yourself." By 2004, he estimated, a typical Sunday-morning congregation at Bethel during the academic year was comprised of "half, two-thirds" visible-minority students. Because it takes time for such changes, accelerated as they are at Bethel, to trickle down within Kingston at large and to its other churches, he also thought that this kind of profound transformation would become visible in the city as a whole. The effects of immigration and multiculturalism, he felt, would mean that in the future Christianity in Kingston would become more Asian and African, less European. In 2009 Walker left Kingston to become a pastor at Ottawa Mandarin Wesleyan Church in Kanata, Ontario.

The contributions of immigrants to the lives of churches have spread through most churches and denominations. Despite their characterization as predominantly white, or aging, almost all Kingston churches have at least one immigrant family among their regular attendees. Increasingly that presence reminds Christians that their religion is not European, nor is it white.

For some churches, such as First Baptist, opening their doors to immigrants and refugees has become an important aspect of their life and mission. Some ethnic churches use facilities that exist primarily to house other congregations, pointing the way for others to possibilities of stewardship in the sharing of ecclesiastical space. In addition, the very location of ethnic groups and churches within the city, most of them near its core, creates a diversity and vibrancy in the downtown that would not otherwise be there. Several ethnic parishes began in St James' Chapel at St Mary's Roman Catholic Cathedral, temporarily using that space until having their own dedicated building became viable. The Roman Catholic diocese provides denominational continuity as well as affording such start-up opportunities. After the children of immigrants move to other parts of the city and become more assimilated into the Canadian mainstream, they can maintain their Catholicism as their connections with older customs and languages weaken, and after leaving the confines of a downtown ethnic parish. In all, ethnic Christianity, far from ghettoizing a kind of Old World – or, in its contemporary manifestations, Third World – religion, opens new possibilities for other groups with longer histories in Canada to consider.

6 Liberal Religion: Quakers, Reform Jews, Unitarians

WHAT IS "LIBERAL RELIGION"?

The three groups considered in this chapter – Quakers, Reform Jews, and Unitarians – are all instances of what could be termed "liberal religion." They extend, and in a sense champion, the tendencies of some of the mainline Christian churches away from dogma and toward social activism (see chap. 2), just as the proselytizing groups of chapter 4 extend the missionizing and conversionist tendencies of the evangelical Protestants of chapter 3. The term "liberal" with regard to religion refers not so much to politics as to belief. In point of fact, the category of belief is considered by religious liberals to be marginal or irrelevant to their kind of faith. They uphold freedom of conscience and seldom require subscription to the verbal formulations of doctrinal creeds. Quakers, Reform Jews, and Unitarians do not actively encourage conversion to their faith. To the contrary, their respect for the autonomy of the individual and the free exercise of conscience might even allow their congregants to remain within another faith tradition at the same time as allying themselves with one of these liberal traditions.

If creeds, doctrine, dogma, and belief are not a priority for groups that are religiously liberal, it might be said that their focus is more on the human spiritual quest and human action. The "seven principles" of the Unitarian Universalists represent an example of the kinds of standards and values espoused by religious liberals:

1 The inherent worth and dignity of every person;
2 Justice, equity and compassion in human relations;
3 Acceptance of one another and encouragement to spiritual growth in our congregations;

4 A free and responsible search for truth and meaning;
5 The right of conscience and the use of the democratic process within our congregations and in society at large;
6 The goal of world community with peace, liberty, and justice for all; and
7 Respect for the interdependent web of all existence of which we are a part. (Unitarian Universalist Association)

Notice that none of these seven principles says anything about the nature of God or of ultimate reality in any traditionally religious sense. The emphasis is entirely upon the human, with nothing about any transcendent dimension – unless, of course, "the interdependent web of all existence of which we are a part" may be taken as a this-worldly form of transcendence. Indeed, it might be wondered how these religious liberals might be said to be "religious" in any respect whatsoever, much less how they can be understood to be an aspect of "God's plenty." The answer, as I suggested in the introduction, is that "God" may be taken to stand for, as Tillich said, whatever is of ultimate concern – or as Philip Hallie has termed it: "The word *God* means the object of our undivided attention to the lucid mystery of being alive for others and for ourselves" (1994, 293). With that, Quakers, Reform Jews, and Unitarians deserve inclusion among the diversity making up God's plenty, however cautious they themselves might want to be about naming the divine.

Issues of space, so important to the major downtown churches in the nineteenth century, arise among these liberal groups, often as a matter of principle, or because these groups have quite minimal liturgical requirements. They do not require a dedicated sacred space for worship in which to display the religious symbols appropriate to their tradition. In that respect they differ greatly from, say, the Orthodox groups – for example, the Greek Orthodox Church, St Gregory of Nyssa Parish, or St Mena Coptic Orthodox Church – considered in the preceding chapter. Some time will be spent at the outset of this chapter – and though the succeeding section may seem digressive, I hope its relevance will become clear – in exploring some of the challenges and opportunities afforded by a dedicated downtown worship space owned by the congregation. To that end, two congregations, Sydenham Street United Church and Bethel Church, which could have been dealt with earlier when mainline churches or Protestant evangelical groups were considered in chapters 2 and 3, respectively, are examined here in some detail. Seeing how these two churches struggle with managing and using the real estate they own and occupy raises the question of renting as an alternative.

TO RENT OR TO OWN

Of these three groups, Reform Jews and Quakers have no facilities exclusively dedicated to their use, opting instead to use rented space or rooms otherwise available to them in the community. Both Reform Jews and Quakers have remained for most of their history on the Queen's University campus, reflecting their links with that community. Neither group has plans to erect a synagogue or meeting-house, nor to purchase an existing building, though the Quakers have lately begun to rent space from another liberal religious group, the Unitarians. The Christian Scientists for many years had their own building on Mowat Avenue, but as their membership aged and numbers dwindled, they sold it to the Girl Guides of Canada. The Quakers briefly attempted to rent space from the Guides but that arrangement fell through. The Unitarians – more properly referred to as Unitarian Universalists – also met for many years in a room at the university, and before that in five or six other places both on and off campus. They purchased a building in 1999 at 214 Concession Street, still close to Kingston's downtown.

Other faith groups began their respective histories, usually in rented quarters, in Kingston's downtown – consider the four "proselytizing" faith traditions of chapter 4, the Salvation Army, the Church of Jesus Christ of Latter-day Saints, the Jehovah's Witnesses, and the Brethren Assemblies. They moved progressively away from the core area of downtown, first acquiring their own buildings in the nearby residential areas between Queen's University and the former Kingston Shopping Centre, where none of the four remains today. All of these groups purchased vacant land further out and, like so many other religious groups, moved away from the commercial and business centre of the city, near to the residential regions in the western suburbs.

What difference does it make to a congregation's life and presence in the community if they do not have a place of their own? One might wonder, for example, whether a religious group can thrive and persist in rented quarters with the same vitality as it would in its own building. On the other hand, being free of mortgage payments, not to mention building maintenance, insurance, and heating costs, may allow a congregation to attend to other purposes – for example, to direct themselves to other ministries or service to the community or the world. Monsignor Donald P. Clement, rector of St Mary's Roman Catholic Cathedral, one of the largest of Kingston's downtown churches dating from the nineteenth century, spoke in a 2004 interview of the "problems with having structures like this because money goes into the structure itself that we'd like to have go into the programs" (interview, 24 March 2004). The cathedral's insurance premiums were about to rise to $79,000 a year, and the costs for electricity and heating were already

$50,000 annually. A few years earlier St Mary's had to undergo renovations costing $7 million after snow and rain got inside the double-wall construction and began to destroy the limestone exterior. Over the past years scaffolding for exterior work has also been visible at St George's and St James' Anglican churches, at Queen Street and Chalmers and Sydenham Street United churches, and at St Andrew's Presbyterian Church, to recall some notable examples.

These downtown churches, and many others besides, could not survive were they not exempt from paying property taxes, a benefit that they receive because, like hospitals and schools, places of worship are viewed as existing for the public good. Some might interpret this exemption as an unfortunate means by which the government promotes religion while depleting a city's tax base. Others would argue that people with an active religious affiliation have been shown to be good citizens and philanthropists. The rate of charitable giving and volunteer work for the actively religious – including donations and volunteerism beyond their own religious group – exceeds that of others in society. As Kurt Bowen found in a survey for Statistics Canada, while only about one-third of Canadians are religiously active, that group contributes almost two-thirds of all charitable donations, including 42 per cent of the money raised for secular causes (Bowen 1997). Still, how a religious property is put to use, whether for the benefit of the few who worship there or for the entire community, could determine whether their tax exemption will continue in the future.

Elizabeth Macdonald, minister at Sydenham Street United Church – sometimes referred to as "the Cathedral of Methodism in Upper Canada" – spoke of the costs of renovation work both inside and out for their mid-nineteenth-century building. Designed by architect William Coverdale, the church stands in the front ranks among the city's many historically significant buildings. Macdonald mentioned the enormous cost of hiring the skilled people to repoint old stonework and identified the congregation's dilemma: "It continues to be a source of ongoing debate and real soul-searching for us because the money we spend on the building could be used to support ministries" (interview, 27 January 2004). Yet, as she states, "this building is widely used by the community." As part of the church's social outreach, space is offered either free or for a nominal sum "to groups like AA and AlAnon and the Helen Tufts Nursery program." Other groups such as the six Cantabile choirs "make their home here" and are considered as "partners" in the building, rather than "tenants." In sum, Macdonald saw the use of the church in terms of Christian stewardship: "So we have had to move from looking at this building as being *ours*, for our use – i.e., the congregation – to understanding that we are responsible for this historic

Sydenham Street United Church

building which is a wonderful community resource, and how do we make the space available sometimes for ongoing use, sometimes for occasional use, so that the community can have the full benefit of this fabulous building."

Sydenham Street United Church has become increasingly popular for concerts, especially when the downtown Grand Theatre was closed for several years for renovations. As outlined in a "Joint Needs Assessment" report prepared in March 2007, rental of the sanctuary – "the fourth largest venue in Kingston" – and other rooms in the church brings in as much as $45,000 annually (Sydenham Street UC a). Now the congregation, still conscious of its longstanding ministry of music but self-described as "an aging population with some middle-aged congregants," is facing repairs to the organ estimated at $175,000. Attendance at worship has declined since the 1960s, when the size of the congregation had already decreased to between four hundred and six hundred people at two services each week. In 1996 attendance averaged two hundred people at a single Sunday morning service, declining further to about one hundred in 2005. Student visitors from Queen's University to worship services in the fall, usually in October, estimated – with an element of subjectivity, to be sure – 150 people present in 2002, eighty in 2005, and only thirty or forty in 2006. The declining birthrate, and the decrease in the number of young families at the church, has meant fewer baptisms – an average of about two or three annually between 2001 and 2005 – and the absence of a Sunday school or nursery (see Sydenham Street UC a). Over the decade from 1996 to 2005, congregational givings averaged about $200,000 annually, with deficits between $60,000 and $80,000 in each of the last five years that had to be made up from the endowment fund.

In the light of these fiscal realities, the members of the Joint Needs Assessment Committee were preparing a recommendation about whether to hire a new staff associate, and with what duties if hired, after the retirement of the person who had filled the position over many years. Despite the decline in the congregation's size due to secularization and changing demographics, and despite the burdensome expense of maintaining the church's presence in the downtown, the report also reveals more than a dozen active committees and many programs ministering to the needs of the community. In various ways this church retains its traditional emphasis on issues of social justice and outreach. Nonetheless, at this juncture it was reconsidering its vision and mandate and how to allocate its resources – for example, whether "to seriously invest in using our building as a resource to the community" – and how to choose priorities among such various possibilities as pastoral ministry to the members of the congregation, local outreach, and international missions.

In many respects the situation faced by Sydenham Street United Church today parallels that of Beth Israel Synagogue at its Queen Street location fifty years earlier. Most of the congregation's members lived not in the inner city neighbourhood where their building is situated but in an area some distance to the west. When Sydenham Street's "Needs Assessment" compared the addresses of its members with those of two other nearby United churches, Queen Street and Chalmers, or with other United churches such as Cooke's-Portsmouth, Princess Street, and St Margaret's, the conclusion was that "the churches all appear to draw members from the same geographical areas and are not exclusive to their respective settings" (Sydenham Street UC a). The "parish" model, whereby a congregation drew its members from surrounding neighbourhoods, exists no more. In many ways, then, the challenge is how the Sydenham United Church members are to maintain their building, and to provide services and ministry, in a downtown neighbourhood distant from where most of them live. Sharon Cohoon, minister of Christian Education and Pastoral Care at Chalmers United Church, summed up the problem faced generally by Kingston's United Church congregations: "We are, in my view, with buildings and all that, we are hugely rich. We are numbers poor. And that's a huge issue. And we have continued to put our money into upholding structures instead of upholding ministries, and that's not healthy" (interview, 13 February 2007).

A few blocks away, at 314 Johnson Street near Barrie, stands the evangelical Protestant, red-brick Bethel Church, a straightforward, ordinary-looking building with no steeple surmounting it, and almost unique among downtown churches for its adjacent parking lot shared with the law office next door. The funeral home across the street allows churchgoers to park in their lot. Bethel also owns the houses at 318 and 324 Johnson Street, renting them out at present but perhaps having an eye to possible future use of the properties by the church itself. Bethel Congregational Church began its history in 1874 but stayed out of the union that resulted in the new United Church of Canada in 1925. Bethel chose to remain independent until in 1949 it became affiliated with the evangelical Associated Gospel Churches of Canada. The church building has undergone numerous additions and renovations in its history, especially since the early 1960s.

By 2002 on each Sunday morning during the academic year Bethel's sanctuary – smaller than Sydenham Street's – was serving about a total of 550 worshippers at three morning services at 8:15, 9:45, and 11:15. In 1994, two years after the arrival of Bethel's senior pastor, Doug Martin, the church went from one Sunday morning service to two when students began to attend in greater numbers. Over the next decade three services became necessary. By 2007, however, in the immediate interim after Martin's departure, Bethel returned to offering two Sunday morning services at 9 and 11. When there were three services, the first two were geared mostly toward students from nearby Queen's University, augmented somewhat by students from the Royal Military College and St Lawrence College. The third service remained more traditional.

Participant-observation confirms the preponderance of students at Bethel's worship services. Student researchers visiting Bethel between 2003 and 2006 estimated 150 to 200 people in attendance at each service, the majority being of postsecondary student age. In 2005 two visiting students noted that "the church was packed for the 8:15 AM service, including the balcony seating," while another student at the same early service three weeks later counted 150 congregants. Even at the 11 o'clock service in 2006 "the church was completely filled" with about two hundred worshippers, about 70 per cent of whom appeared to be students, according to one observer.

Changes to the sanctuary show Bethel's adaptation to student worshippers. Many students were reportedly drawn to Bethel by its senior pastor's strong reputation as a dynamic preacher. The usual furnishings of Protestant worship space, such as pulpit and lectern, have been replaced with a sound system and a stage for musicians and their instruments.

Chris Walker, who in 2003 had been associate pastor at Bethel for six years, estimated the "core congregation" of regular Kingston residents at between 200 and 250 (interview, 4 November 2003). He explained that over the span of one month – that is to say, in "a month of Sundays" – 200 to 250 different core members would be in attendance at worship. Not all of these non-student regulars would be weekly attenders; some might attend only once in the month. Bethel Church was finding itself, in Walker's words, "student-driven," and while that focus posed a challenge – "student populations are not rife with dollars and cents" – for the most part the members of Bethel favoured committing a major part of their energy and resources to student ministry while retaining the usual evangelistic emphasis on world missions. Walker thought that many of the longstanding members found the student-centred and intergenerational nature of Bethel Church "sexy," enhancing the "perceived vitality of the congregation." Core members living in the suburbs were willing to drive downtown because of the energy and life that nearby students brought there.

Evangelicals attend church more often than do mainline Protestants, with an average rate of giving about four times higher, at least in the United States. The congregation at Bethel is roughly the same size as Sydenham Street United's. Bethel has fewer difficulties meeting its annual budget, even though, as Walker acknowledged, the congregation faces some financial challenges. In 2006, weekly contributions at Bethel averaged $6,535, or about $340,000 annually, working out to about $12 being placed by each attendee on the offering plate each week (see Bethel Church). The 2002–03 annual report records 130 members at the church, of whom ninety-seven are "active." For the year ending 30 April 2003 the offerings contributed in envelopes provided to church members users totalled $267,000, with an additional $20,000 in "loose offerings" at services. In 2003 Bethel built an addition costing $750,000, and in 2006, the average weekly receipts for the repayment of the building loan were $995, amounting to about $52,000 annually. If the situations might be compared, for example, by ignoring what students might contribute, it appears that the rate of giving at Bethel is at least twice per member what it is at Sydenham Street. At Sydenham Street two hundred contributors are donating $200,000, whereas at Bethel 130 members in 2003 contributed $267,000, or more than $2,000 per member. The United Church of Canada's website estimated the annual average contributions per member nationally in

2006 at just below $1,000, a figure that squares with contributions from Sydenham Street's members. Comparing donations nationally in these two denominations fifteen years earlier, United Church members then each contributed $301, while Associated Gospel members – the tradition with which Bethel Church is affiliated – each contributed $1,478, one of the highest levels in the country (Bibby 1993, 108).

It is important to realize, though, how misleading such comparative statistics may be. A "donor" might be a household unit of two or more people using a single offering envelope, while a "member" might be a person who never contributes financially, or who, as Bibby would put it, is affiliated but non-attending. Furthermore, some churches and denominations are more willing to retain inactive or non-contributing members on their rolls than others. The difference in the relative size of these denominations in Kingston also affects a comparison of per capita rate of giving. For example, Statistics Canada figures for the 2001 Census show just seventy-five people in Kingston reporting their religion as Associated Gospel, whereas more than 17 per cent of Kingstonians are United Church. Some members at Bethel not included in that figure of seventy-five people could be among the 6,140 Kingstonians reporting themselves as generically "Protestant," or among the other 2,330 declaring themselves as simply "Christian." Many evangelical Christians in particular consider themselves to be "post-denominational," stressing their own identity as Christians or as Protestants while remaining suspicious of institutions or structures beyond the local level – and sometimes even there. "Religiously active" people have been defined as those who attend worship at least once per month. Mainline Protestants, while much more numerous in Canada, represent about the same proportion of the religiously active as do Conservative Protestants in the Canadian population, that is, 20 per cent as compared with 18 per cent. Roman Catholics comprise 43 per cent of the religiously active in Canada outside Quebec (Bowen 1997). In the early 1990s Bibby spoke of an "imminent crisis" based on figures available at that time and estimated that by 2015 "on any given Sunday there will be three conservatives in the pews for every mainline Protestant" (1993, 105).

The Joint Needs Assessment Report for Sydenham Street United Church notes that none of their members lives in the four areas in the northern part of the city – Williamsville, Kingscourt/Novelis, Rideau Heights, and Marker Acres – where the average family income in 2001 is $42,000, more than $25,000 below the city's overall average. Instead, Sydenham Street "draws the bulk of its current urban membership from the immediate surrounding area, the area to the West, the districts to the Northwest and from the area to the East" – four parts of the city where the average family income is

$66,000, $72,000, $60,000, and $93,000, respectively (Sydenham Street UC a). Members of the Sydenham Street congregation, therefore, live in comparatively well-to-do areas of Kingston. Chris Walker, reflecting on the diversity and geographic distribution of Bethel's membership, noted that about half of those in leadership positions at Bethel live beyond Highway 401, in semi-rural places perhaps even less affluent than the four northern parts of the city proper.

While the majority of students at Queen's University are probably affiliated with one of the mainline Christian denominations, it is likely that few of them would count as religiously active. On the other hand, in the past decade or so, the evangelical student presence at Queen's has become much more visible, with groups such as Navigators, Inter-Varsity Christian Fellowship, or IVCF, and Campus for Christ – formerly Campus Crusade for Christ – providing opportunities to continue their associations with other evangelicals while away from their home churches, and to swell the ranks of Kingston's conservative Protestant churches. Bethel has become one of several churches (St James' Anglican on the campus itself, the NeXt Church, and the Kingston Gospel Temple are the others) that have become known by word of mouth as churches hospitable to evangelical Christian students. In addition, the Chinese Alliance Church, a few blocks from campus, serves the needs of some evangelical students of Asian descent. Conservative Christian students from Queen's have been using the sanctuary at Bethel on a monthly basis for a "Praise and Power" service, about which Chris Walker remarked, "They just come and use their space. We had nothing to do with it. I mean, it's not a Bethel event, frankly, but we let them do that. It's been packed every Sunday so far" (interview, 4 November 2003). Walker continued, "There's a lot of cross-referencing between us and the campus ministries. Sure, why not? You know there is a great church you can go to if you are part of IVCF, Campus Crusade, or whatever. And once they come, they see themselves. They see the vitality, they love it, and they stay." Walker also lamented in 2003, prior to Bethel's expansion of its space, that their existing facilities are "maxed out a good number of the nights each week" so that "we have not reached out beyond our walls ... because of a lack of resources, energy, money, and everything else." In sum, he said, "we are so hamstrung from our own lack of space that we wonder if we should defer any requests coming our way."

The situation at Bethel, then, is a striking contrast with Sydenham Street where there is room to develop more use by the community, and where the available facilities are provided to groups or rented out, and whose sanctuary is used to only part of its capacity at its single Sunday morning service of worship. While Bethel Church is focused on active participation of hundreds of students, youth involvement at the nearby United churches has dropped off. Whereas Sydenham Street United had in the past shared a tri-church youth group and senior Sunday School classes with its two closest United Church neighbouring congregations, Chalmers and Queen Street, neither of these ventures continues any longer. At Queen Street United Church, Sunday School in the 1940s was attended by four hundred children, whereas the entire congregational roll before its closing in 2008 consisted of 150 members (Schliesmann 2008). The congregation at Queen Street, having spent $500,000 in 2001 to repair the bell tower, finally decided to offer the building for sale seven years later when it became evident that further costly repairs were necessary.

In contrast to the long history of building ownership by Sydenham Street United and Bethel churches, other groups worshipping in Kingston's downtown have got by for years without a place of their own. Quakers, Reform Jews, and Unitarians have used rooms at Queen's for a long time. In 1999 the Unitarians finally purchased their own building, and in 2007 the Quakers began to rent space from them, while the Reform congregation continues, as it has for more than twenty years, to meet in a lounge on campus. The Kuluta Buddhists, who once held their meetings on campus, moved to a rented house in the suburbs in the late 1990s but now have their own dedicated space in the centre of the city's downtown. Quakers, Reform Jews, and Unitarians pride themselves on being "non-credal" – that is, characterized by openness and lack of dogmatism when it comes to requiring a statement of faith or beliefs from their members – and as we shall see, are often similarly casual about their spatial needs. Their liberalism is seen, as in the case of Sydenham Street United Church, by their strongly activist positions on contemporary social issues, especially same-sex marriage. In addition to these various factors, non-credal religions generally have a weaker hold on their members than, say, the proselytizing faith groups examined in chapter 3. High-demand congregations need dedicated space because they expect their members to return for other activities between their weekly worship services. Most religious liberals discharge their formal religious duties, such as they are, in an hour or two each week when they gather together. Otherwise, they experience no great disjunction between their religious lives and their roles as citizens.

THOUSAND ISLANDS MEETING OF THE RELIGIOUS SOCIETY OF FRIENDS

Bert Horwood, a retired professor of experiential and outdoor education at the Queen's University Faculty of Education, continues in his seventies as an avid canoeist and lover of the outdoors. He grew up in the town of

Pembroke in the Ottawa Valley, attending a YMCA camp and the United Church. The United Church remained as his affiliation throughout much of his later life until "eventually the mental reservations just outweighed the reasons for going." As he explained, "I could belt out a hymn like the best of them, and the Protestant hymnody is a marvellous collection of poetry and music, but a lot of the Wesleyan words are just – to me, they're just sheer nonsense. And I mean there comes a time when my intolerance for nonsense gets high enough that I can't do it anymore" (Cogeco interview, 10 November 2004). He explored various nature-based religions such as Paganism, Wicca, and Native traditions. He says that for him with First Nations religious traditions and with Daoism and Buddhism, "there is a question of integrity that eventually comes up" because they originate in other cultures and are based on other languages.

In Wicca, Horwood found it "really hard to escape the sort of early childhood influence of Christianity and my recall of many, many, many sermons and Sunday school and all those sorts of things." Eventually, in the 1990s the experiential and undogmatic discipline of a Quaker meeting provided for him a place where, as he puts it in the language many other converts use, "I just felt very much at home." Though "this profound experience of silence of others where one could be entirely in communion in the presence of others with the god within as well as the god without" did not resolve all his "uncertainties and issues," he found that Quaker practice "was supportive of the search" (ibid.). The website for the Kingston Quakers offers a quotation, dating back to 1908, from Caroline Stephens that expresses the ideal of a mystical and nonverbal apprehension of God in silent worship: "In the united stillness of a truly 'gathered' meeting, there is a power known only by experience, and mysterious even when most familiar" (Thousand Islands Quaker Meeting). The function of humour within religious traditions stands as a topic all its own, but the self-deprecating jokes that faith communities tell about themselves are frequently revealing. One of the jokes on a Quaker website cites a bumper sticker that says, "I'm not a member of an organized religion. I'm a Quaker." That very lack of emphasis on creeds, combined with the encouragement for one to search in silence, is typical of Quaker practice.

Horwood has served as the clerk and later, recording clerk, of the Thousand Islands Meeting of the Religious Society of Friends, better known as Quakers. Like the Brethren and other groups, the Quakers have no clergy, and there are few positions or offices in a local meeting. In keeping with Quaker egalitarianism, Horwood has been assiduous in pointing out to interviewers that he is not representing or speaking on behalf of the local meeting of the Society of Friends, nor is he their leader. In his interviews in 2003 and 2005 with researchers for the Religious Diversity in Kingston project while the Quakers were still meeting on the university campus, Horwood was asked in particular about the history of Quakers in Kingston, about their requirements for a meeting space, and about the nature and style of their meetings. For about ten years Kingston's Quakers met in the Ban Righ Centre, a meeting place and resource centre for mature women students on the Queen's campus. In return for the use of space there on Sundays, they gave an annual donation to the Ban Righ Foundation.

Horwood said that Kingston's Quakers are a small group who, before settling into Ban Righ, "tended to use people's homes, or they would try a place on campus." The Thousand Islands Meeting of the Religious Society of Friends seems to have begun with two or three people in the 1950s, eventually growing to a congregation averaging about twenty people in October 2002, when student researchers visited them. Horwood stated that the attendance in 2005 had ranged between about thirteen and thirty, with the higher number having "stimulated the need of moving to new quarters." At times like that, some had to sit on a table, the floor, or the arm of a chair, in a manner not suitable for the usual circle arrangement of a Quaker meeting. Due no doubt in part to their traditions of simplicity, Horwood said Quakers "are not disposed to, and without a great tradition of, property ownership." While acknowledging that Quakers have been "gently proud of their old meeting houses," he said that "they haven't been like some Christian denominations where the building is kind of the focus" (interview, 7 December 2005). Because a number of the members and attenders, to use a Quaker distinction, are in their seventies and eighties, and without younger families to take on maintenance chores or to pay to have them done, "at the moment there is no burning desire to build or own."

Two years earlier, in another interview, Horwood had been asked for his views about the religious landscape of Kingston. In keeping with the Friends' reputation for direct speech and the plain truth, he was critical of the number of Kingston's church buildings, citing the example of the United churches downtown: "I am immensely troubled by the amount of limestone that is piled up. There are three United churches located all within a few blocks of each other. I have no idea of the internal workings of those organizations. It is astonishing that there are three United churches within such a small area. Each is struggling to maintain their fabric and maintain their organization in their pride. There is kind of a parochial pride. I think that is a weakness" (7 November 2003). Apart from environmental or stewardship arguments for closing partly empty churches, Horwood relates social-justice concerns to another, more contemporary, downtown building project, an arena, suspected by some as being erected principally to accommodate the local hockey team, though capable of being used for concerts and other events. In several letters and articles in the local newspaper Horwood decried the nature of the facility and the process leading to its construction. Having set forth his own highest priorities for the city as "poverty, child well-being, and homelessness," he wondered, "What would it say of us to have a hockey Taj Mahal with beggars at its doors?" (*Whig-Standard*, 17 May 2004). Debates about buildings turn once more to the alternative issue of programs for people.

Discussions in a religious group about where to situate itself, whether in dedicated space or space that is rented or shared, are governed by many factors, some related to the group's traditions and liturgical needs, some specific to the local social context, and others coming from members' preferences. In some respects the needs of the Religious Society of Friends are quite minimal, and the common room in the Ban Righ Centre on Queen's University campus served them well. Most seem to have found the surroundings well suited to their meetings, which emphasize a direct experience with the spirit of the divine – the "inner light" – in their worship, mostly proceeding in an atmosphere of silence until someone is moved to speak. During this waiting in expectation in an "unprogrammed" meeting, the entire hour might pass in silence. However, at Ban Righ some of those present found the art hanging on the walls not entirely conducive to silent meditation. Quaker meeting houses tend to have unadorned walls and basic furnishings. Also, at certain times of the year, for example, during Homecoming weekend – when bagpipes were being played nearby, especially if the pipes were out of tune and the selections were limited to a few repeated songs – or during the welcoming ceremonies for incoming students, there was sometimes distracting noise from outside the building. On at least one occasion the chanting of a Buddhist group simultaneously using other space in the centre disturbed some of the Quakers.

In 2006 the Kingston meeting moved to the Unitarian Church on Concession Street, and changed the time of their worship from Sunday morning to the afternoon. In addition to more space, they wanted better facilities for children. The hope to relocate in the former Christian Science Church on Mowat Avenue collapsed when liability and insurance concerns prevented the Guides from renting to them. The area in the Unitarian Church serves them well, because the chairs can easily be moved into a circle, kitchen facilities are available for their monthly meal, and a room was already set up downstairs for child care. Unitarians do not normally place religious symbols or icons in their worship space, a practice that accords well with the Friends' own ideal of plainness. Traffic noise from busy Concession Street caused disruption of the silent meetings for some. To help block out that noise, pieces of styrofoam were temporarily placed in the front windows during meetings.

At first glance the Society of Friends might seem comparable to the Brethren dealt with in chapter 4, both groups having begun as movements to reform and to purify the Christian church, the Friends in the seventeenth century under George Fox, and the Brethren in the early nineteenth. Both opt for simplicity in their style of worship and in the architecture of their buildings. Neither group has clergy; both have had devastating schisms in their histories. While the Brethren remain centrally and avowedly within the Christian faith, the non-credal stance of the Quakers has largely moved them away from normative Christianity of late. A Brethren assembly is organized and directed almost exclusively by scripture, whereas Friends look to direct inspiration and personal revelation. Both tend to be non-violent pacifists. While Brethren outreach is focused principally on spreading the Christian gospel and winning converts to Christ, Quakers stress social justice. They are engaged today in tasks of alleviating hunger and homelessness as well as meeting the needs of prison inmates.

The number of Quakers in Canada is not large, estimated at 1,129 members in 1995, 57 per cent of them in Ontario, at twenty-two different meetings (Quakers Canada a). The 2001 Census showed a larger number, 2,975 people nationally claiming "Quaker" as their religion, thirty-five of them in Kingston. Such discrepancies between a religious group's own membership numbers and census figures reflecting self-reporting individuals have cropped up already in this book, and are dealt with later in this chapter in connection with the Unitarians. In the 1870s there were 7,000 Quakers in Canada, mostly in rural parts of Ontario. Pickering College, a boarding school dating from 1842 and located in Newmarket, north of Toronto, was founded by Quakers. Further, the former Quaker boarding school sixty kilometres west of Kingston in Prince Edward County, where Quakers were at one time the largest religious group, is now the museum in the town of Wellington. Among the twenty or so meetings listed in Ontario, there are Quaker groups in Toronto and Windsor and London and Ottawa, but also, surprisingly, in such obscure places as Ilderton, Annan, Killaloe, Hastings, and Codrington. Asked about the prospects for the Kingston meeting of the Religious Society of Friends, Bert Horwood said, "Given the lack of youthfulness, I can't see a long-term future for a Quaker community here. It pains me to say that."

REFORM JEWS: CONGREGATION IYR HAMELECH

Chapter 1 referred to the origins of Kingston's Reform Jewish congregation in the mid-1970s when a group of more liberal Jews, mostly professors and other professionals, decided to meet on their own rather than with the "umbrella" synagogue, Beth Israel, that accommodated Orthodox practice and whose members were mostly business people. According to Justin Lewis, then part-time rabbi of Congregation Iyr HaMelech (Hebrew for "the City of the King" and thus a reference to Kingston), "There was an attempt to make the Orthodox congregation more liberal on the part of some members, to have more of a role for women in the services and so on, and it didn't go over with enough of the members. And a group then formed a separate congregation" (interview, 22 October 2003).

The "advantages to being a congregation without walls" cited by Rabbi Lewis include being free of "the headache of a mortgage or maintenance or all those things that congregations with a building have to deal with." Though Iyr HaMelech once had a building fund and a committee and had considered the purchase of one property chosen from among several, they finally decided against it. After that "things more or less stalled," as members who had wanted a building gave up that possibility, though with some disappointment, while others who felt that it was not a priority turned to what in their view were more important concerns. Congregation Iyr HaMelech usually meets in a lounge on the fifth, uppermost floor of John Watson Hall, the tallest building on the low-rise Queen's University campus. The Whalley Room, named in honour of English professor, scholar, and humanist George Whalley, is the regular Shabbat morning place of worship for the Reform Jews of Kingston. With the installation of new seating when the lounge was refurbished, Lewis commented, "I think we have the most comfortable chairs of any congregation I've been to." The south-facing windows afford a view of Lake Ontario, "and we often arrange the chairs to take advantage of that view of the lake, so that is part of our experience."

For most of the Shabbat services "we get about ten people … sometimes it's up to twenty or even thirty, sometimes not." Lewis says the congregation estimates its size at about seventy households, or 150 people, if those who have some connection with the congregation are counted – for example, "people who come regularly who are not members as such." Though there are some young families with children, "we have a middle-aged to elderly crowd." While there are teenagers amongst them, "right now we're mainly missing the university student demographic." The peak attendance for the High Holy Days has been about 130 people. On Rosh Hashanah and Yom Kippur, when the congregation needs more room, the congregation relocates, sometimes to the Policy Studies building on campus and sometimes to the Kingston Public Library. Because Iyr HaMelech has been "from its beginnings largely a congregation of academics," Lewis feels that a campus location or even one closer to downtown is important to members. When the Whalley Room cannot accommodate larger numbers, some miss its familiar surroundings. Parking on campus is readily available and free on weekends, a bonus for any religious group, considering that lack of parking has prompted others to move away from the downtown.

The Iyr HaMelech congregation is liberal in its theology and practices and welcomes "Jews of all kinds." Lewis observed that "our congregation does not have a dogma or set of practices that you have to subscribe to to belong." In Jonathan Franzen's novel, *Freedom*, an older man explains to a college student the accommodating aspects of Judaism: "I think for a young person today it ought to have a particular appeal, because it's all about personal choice. Nobody tells a Jew what he has to believe. You get to decide all of that for yourself. You can choose your very own apps and features, so to speak" (2010, 269). The Wikipedia entry on Jewish humour has a joke, illuminating the liberalism of Reform Judaism, in which Orthodox, Conservative, and Reform rabbis are asked whether one is supposed to say a *brokhe* – that is, a blessing – over a lobster, food not normally eaten by observant Jews. The Orthodox rabbi doesn't know what a lobster is, the Conservative rabbi doesn't know what to say, and the Reform rabbi asks, "What's a *brokhe*?"

The Iyr HaMelech Congregation website states that membership is "open to all Jews and their families, including non-Jewish family members. Non-Jews interested in conversion to Reform Judaism or who are dedicated to participating in Reform Judaism are welcome to join as members." While the participation and roles of non-Jews in the congregation has been discussed, Lewis says, "my own view is to be as open as possible." Someone married to a non-Jewish partner would probably feel more at home at Iyr MaMalech than at the more Orthodox congregation, Beth Israel, despite its status as an "umbrella" synagogue. Persons who had converted to Judaism through the Reform or Conservative movement might find that they or their children were not recognized as Jews at Beth Israel. As observed in chapter 1, there have been debates about issues of Jewish identity between members of the two congregations.

Lewis himself converted to Judaism in his mid-twenties and brings to his adopted religion the enthusiasm and fresh perspective that converts often exhibit. Though he is married to a Jewish woman, that marriage came about later and was not his motivation for becoming a Jew. He had been brought up in the Roman Catholic background of his mother, while his father had been a Protestant who eventually chose to become a Quaker. Partly because in his childhood family he had lived with "religious difference and the possibility of religious exploration," Lewis investigated various religious options including Hinduism and Wicca. After a period as an agnostic, he found himself attracted to many things about Judaism, such as "the relative lack of dogma, the intellectual nature of the Jewish tradition and the intellectual openness, the encouragement to question, to delve in and to learn further" (Cogeco interview, 13 October 2004). Though he had not initially intended to become a rabbi, he wanted to be an informed layperson, and soon found himself in the position of being asked to teach and interpret Judaism to others, including Jews. Because his rabbinical studies were at the Academy for Jewish Religion, an independent rabbinical school in New York, he notes that he is not a member of the Association of Reform Rabbis and lacks "the kind of union protection" that a member of that association might have.

In his role as the rabbi in Congregation Iyr HaMelech, Lewis practises rituals symbolizing the human connection with nature, such as going outside and blessing the moon after Yom Kippur. He claims that this is part of the classical Jewish tradition, and not something that most Reform rabbis would do, but then "most Jews themselves are not familiar with their own tradition." He continues, "It's one of the great heartaches and at the same time one of the great opportunities for me as a rabbi and for many rabbis that we are serving a people who by and large don't know their own heritage, and we're trying to open doors to that heritage and just to express and make available some of the richness of Jewish thought and Jewish ritual" (ibid.). The ritual of blessing the moon, something Lewis does personally every month, seems in some respects parallel to the Neopagan practice of "drawing down the moon," the title of a book by Margot Adler. Though his earlier interest in Wicca might partially explain his affinity for the practice, Neopagan practitioners summon the power of the goddess into themselves, whereas Lewis understands blessing the moon in relation to the history of the Jewish people: "As the moon is growing, we bless her to continue growing more radiant and we identify ourselves with the moon in our own waxing and waning as a people historically and spiritually and personally."

A Reform Jewish congregation is governed by its own board, approved by the congregation as a whole at its annual meetings. Large issues are raised and debated at general meetings. While at Congregation Iyr HaMelech no major divisive issues have arisen, there have been discussions about the matter of a building, dissatisfaction with the religious school, the choice of a prayer book, and politics relating to Israel and the Palestinians. Lewis said that within Judaism the congregation has the final power, and can hire or fire the rabbi within the limits of their contract: "If there was a dispute between me and the congregation, it would come down to whether they thought it was still worth keeping me or whether they wanted to terminate my contract, or, of course, whether I was willing to compromise" (interview, 22 October 2003).

While he thought that future growth or a higher profile for the congregation would come slowly, if at all, Lewis summed up the current state of Iyr HaMelech in a largely positive manner: "The congregation as a whole is fairly satisfied with what they've got. They have a religious school, there are services to go to whenever they want to – and once a week is enough for anybody in this community. There are quite a number of opportunities for Jewish study. Again, enough. We have a lecture a couple of times a month between the study sessions that I do with the congregation and the Jewish Studies lecture series. That's plenty for this community. I think most people are fine with how things are."

KINGSTON UNITARIAN FELLOWSHIP

The Kingston Unitarian Fellowship is a member congregation of the Unitarian Universalist Association, thereby combining the two traditions of Unitarianism and Universalism. The Canadian governing body, the Unitarian Council of Canada, preserves its autonomy from the Unitarian Universalist Association, to which only individual congregations belong. While the local Kingston Unitarian Fellowship supports "Unitarian Universalist principles," and while some would consciously identify themselves as "UUs," many members refer to themselves simply as Unitarians.

Kingston's Unitarians, who have been meeting together since 1954, were led by lay people for forty years before they employed their first minister. Until 1999 they had no building of their own, getting together either in one another's homes or in various rented places. Like Quakers and Reform Jews, Unitarians are non-credal, but perhaps more consciously and avowedly undogmatic than either of the other two groups. They began their history within the Christian Church but eventually became separate from it. Unitarians trace their origins – at least in terms of spiritual, if not organizational, ancestry – to the Spanish physician and humanist Michael Servetus who in the sixteenth century was executed for challenging the doctrine of the Trinity. The Unitarian movement began more formally a century later in Poland and spread from there.

Contemporary Unitarianism values freedom of conscience and religious pluralism, drawing on the collective wisdom of all religions rather than viewing itself as a denomination or offshoot of Christianity. A longstanding emphasis within the tradition has been a two-fold doctrinal rejection, of the concepts of the Trinity, which Unitarians saw as a post-biblical innovation, and of original sin, which Unitarians and Universalists claimed misrepresented the mission of Jesus. Kingston's Unitarians describe themselves as looking "for their inspiration not only to the humanist tradition but to the world's many faith traditions" (Kingston Unitarian Fellowship). Their official statement about the "Seven Principles" – readily viewed on almost any Unitarian website – characterizing this congregation and the broader tradition, makes no reference to God. Among the six sources from which Unitarians draw is a reference to "direct experience of that transcending

Kingston Unitarian Fellowship

mystery and wonder, affirmed in all cultures" (Unitarian Universalist Association). Otherwise, most of the values they propound relate to the nature of humanity and of the human community, the quest for justice, the importance of free inquiry, and the role of reason. A student visitor to a Kingston Unitarian Fellowship service in 2006 observed that there was no reference to, or invocation of, a deity apart from the words of one of the four songs that were sung: "Instead, the language of the service was directed towards the congregants and appealed to personal insight rather than an external supernatural source."

Religious jokes, especially ones that traditions tell about themselves, here again provide clues about characteristic foibles or significant differentiating factors within traditions. Websites of several Unitarian churches in Canada have been circulating "Unitarian" jokes along these lines: Why did the Unitarian cross the road? To support the chicken in its search for its own path. Or, how can you tell a Unitarian? You can't; they know it all already. Or, once again, the question about how many Unitarians it takes to change a light bulb yields this answer: "We choose not to make a statement either in favour of or against the need for a light bulb. However, if in your own journey, you have found that light bulbs work for you, that is fine. You are invited to write a poem or compose a modern dance about your personal relationship with your light bulb. Present it next month at our annual Light Bulb Sunday Service, in which we will explore a number of light bulb traditions, including incandescent, fluorescent, three-way, long-life and tinted, all of which are equally valid paths to luminescence" (First Unitarian Church of Victoria).

In the 1960s Donald Mathers, a professor of systematic theology at Queen's Theological College, perhaps having in mind his experience in the United States a few years earlier, said that Unitarianism was more like a hall than a room: it was good for getting people out of the Christian church, or for getting people into the Christian church, but it wasn't a place you could stay. Today that observation ceases to be true, because Unitarianism may be chosen as a destination, as one's religious home. Rev. Kathy Sage, minister at the Kingston Unitarian Fellowship since 2001, said, "We have Pagans, or we have people who practice Buddhist meditation, but the majority of our members simply consider themselves Unitarian or Unitarian Universalists" (interview, 27 April 2004). According to its website, the "Kingston Unitarian Fellowship is not unusual among Unitarian Universalist congregations in numbering among its members people of diverse religious backgrounds, people who identify their current understanding as humanist, rationalist, Christian, Jew, Buddhist, or pagan, to name only a few" (Kingston Unitarian Fellowship).

The number of members in the Kingston congregation is about 130, with approximately sixty to seventy-five people attending weekly services. Sage estimated that there are 5,500 Unitarian Universalists in Canada (interview, 27 April 2004), a figure that corresponds with the Canadian Unitarian Council's total of 5,107 members as reported by their congregations for 2006 (see Canadian Unitarian Council). Statistics Canada figures show about triple that number with 17,480 individuals reporting themselves as Unitarians in the 2001 Census, a growth of 5.7 per cent since the 1991 census. The Census has 355 self-reported Unitarians living in Kingston. These discrepancies might be explained along similar lines as with other religious groups: more people regard themselves as Unitarians than those who actually have official membership in a congregation. A further possible reason is that an anarchist streak among some Unitarian Universalists might deter them on principle from taking out membership in a religious group, even while they are attending and contributing. Sage suggests that with only forty-seven Unitarian congregations in Canada, many people live at some distance from a congregation: "There are twenty [people] at least in Prince Edward County – two or three people drive over – but it is too hard to keep it up." As with any religious group, it is possible that when people move, they do not like the new congregation as much as the one they left: "So they do not join or attend that UU congregation, but on Stats Can they still identify as Unitarian" (personal communication, 27 November 2007). Sage says, "There are people from different perspectives who *discover* us, who think 'Oh, that's how I think!'" She finds, however, that Unitarians face the challenge of how to define themselves while remaining open. "You can't convert to Unitarianism, you *discover* you're a Unitarian." Once a person begins to say, "That's like me, that's how I approach the world, I want to know more," then they formally decide to affiliate – "but we never call it converting" (interview, 27 April 2004).

Anyone is eligible for membership in the Kingston Unitarian Fellowship who is in agreement with their four "Leading Principles," having to do with the exercise of private judgment in matters of belief, rejection of creeds, freedom to hold diverse views, and the commitment to truth, integrity, democracy, and the greater good. Kingston members are expected to affirm and promote the Seven Principles that all Unitarian congregations have agreed to support. Since Unitarianism has its roots in Protestantism, Statistics Canada continues to describe Unitarians as a "Protestant" form of Christianity. This categorization groups Unitarianism in the same larger group as Jehovah's Witnesses and the Church of Jesus Christ of Latter-day Saints, both of whom would accept being included there, though other Christians might not agree, and Quakers, some of whom probably would object to being counted as Christians. Sage was clear that Unitarians are not a Christian denomination, despite what some people might think. They do not belong to the Canadian Council of Churches whose member churches share with Unitarians concerns for matters of faith and justice and interfaith cooperation. Churches belonging to the Canadian Council of Churches differ from Unitarian Universalists because they "believe in the Lord Jesus Christ as God and Saviour, according to the Scriptures," and "seek to fulfill together their common calling to the glory of one God, Father, Son and Holy Spirit" (Canadian Council of Churches). Sage says that while individual Unitarians might consider themselves Christians, "no individual is asked to hold any particular [theological] belief" and neither is the parent body (interview, 27 April 2004).

By way of contrast, Canadian Quakers, like Unitarians in declaring themselves to be non-credal, do belong to the Canadian Council of Churches. Reportedly no other Quaker group belongs to the World Council of Churches. Canadian membership in the Canadian Council of Churches came about somewhat anomalously when in the 1950s a secretary of the Canadian Yearly Meeting described liberal Quakerism as sharing the experience of the universal Christ found in all religions. Leaders in the Canadian

Council of Churches at the time felt that view counted as "Christian." The question of whether the Religious Society of Friends consider themselves to be Christian inspires a lot of internal debate because some individuals count themselves as atheists or humanists or universalists. One member of the Thousands Islands Meeting described herself as "Christ-centred but led by the Light." Some Friends, who like Unitarians are not required to be exclusive in their allegiance to one religion, actively associate themselves with other faiths such as Buddhism or Islam. Nonetheless, the sub-group known as the Conservative Quakers of Canada asserts that they have retained the Christian beliefs of the founders of the Quaker movement. They maintain, "Like the earliest Christians, we believe that God is accessible to everyone – now, today, here – and that Jesus Christ, the Logos, the Word of God, the Inward Light, is willing to teach us individually how to come to Him and how to live our lives" (Conservative Quakers of Canada). The Conservative Quakers point out, however, that such views are not to be taken as a comprehensive statement of beliefs or a credal formulation.

POSITIONS ON SAME-SEX MARRIAGE

Not unexpectedly, a religious group's position on same-sex marriage has become a guarantor of its orthodoxy or, alternatively, as is here the case, an indicator of its liberalism. The Quaker stance with regard to same-sex marriage was set forth at the Canadian Yearly Meeting in 2003. Affirmed in the context of Quaker views on social justice and human rights, the stated practice for same-sex marriage parallels that for any other marriage: "In a Quaker Meeting, couples whose marriages have been approved by a local Meeting marry each other in the presence of the community without officiating clergy." The local meeting makes the decision as to whether same-sex marriages generally are to be conducted, as well as in particular cases (Quakers Canada b). On behalf of Kingston's Quakers, Bert Horwood laid out the general position of Quakers in Canada and then described the practice decided upon in the local meeting: "Here in Kingston, Thousand Islands Meeting has long been on record as being willing to receive applications to marry from same-sex couples in its membership. Such applications would be received and processed in exactly the same way as if the couple were heterosexual. The marriage application is approved when the couple are found to have established that spiritual bond and commitment to a loving relationship. Their marriage to each other under the care of the meeting is sanctioned and proceeds at some convenient time and place. The sex of those marrying isn't relevant to the process, and the joy of the community in the event is equally great" (*Whig-Standard*, 23 February 2005).

When Pamela Dickey Young, then head of Religious Studies at Queen's University, addressed the topic of same-sex marriage at the time of a free vote on the issue in the House of Commons in 2006, she listed Canadian faith groups whose official positions supported same-sex marriage. Those included the United Church of Canada, the Quakers, the Metropolitan Community Churches, Reform Judaism, and the Unitarians. The Metropolitan Community Church – which, if it had a Kingston representation, would have been considered in this chapter – was founded in 1968 as "the world's first church group with a primary, positive ministry to gays, lesbians, bisexual, and transgender persons." Among the five Ontario centres having Metropolitan Community Church congregations, the closest one to Kingston is in Belleville, eighty kilometres to the west. Sydenham Street United Church is one of twenty-one United Church congregations in Ontario that has declared itself to be "affirming," that is, actively working for "the full inclusion of gay, lesbian, bisexual, and transgender people in the church and in society" (Affirm United). Outside these affirming congregations, some of the comments, quoted below, from Elizabeth Macdonald raise questions about how widespread is the application of liberal principles within the United Church of Canada with respect to same-sex marriage.

Sydenham Street United Church on its website homepage indicates its status as a "liberal, affirming congregation." Later, a section on marriage at the church states: "Same-sex couples are as welcome to be married here as heterosexual couples. We celebrate marriage as an institution in which two people – a woman and a man or two women or two men – can live their love and their life-long commitment to each other. We seek God's blessing on all those who marry, so that they may live the vows they make on their wedding day" (Sydenham Street UC b). Macdonald said that a vote was taken in May 1999 in which 80 per cent of the members at Sydenham Street were in favour of becoming an affirming congregation. She thought that inclusivity was the defining characteristic of the church's way of being religious, which meant not just welcoming gay and lesbian people but being inclusive on a broader basis as well: "So that you walk in on any Sunday morning and you'll be able to see different generations, different family compositions, different lifestyle, different orientation" (interview, 27 January 2004). She clarified the difference between the "gay-positive" stance taken by the United Church at large, and many of its congregations, and what it meant to be an affirming congregation within the United Church of Canada: "'Affirming' means you've gone through the process and you have been recognized by Affirm United and you've made a public declaration that you are a safe and welcoming place, and therefore you can be held accountable. All these other gay-positive churches don't say it out loud, so when there are experiences of homophobia or heterosexism, there's no way to really address it, because they haven't made the commitment that they're going to be affirming." She gave the example of a United Church congregation she had served in Richmond Hill which, while generally supportive of gay and lesbian individuals, was unhappy with their denomination's support for gays and lesbians being able legally to adopt a child. Alternatively, another congregation might support a civil union of two people of the same sex but be uncomfortable with same-sex marriage. She also mentioned a case in which a church outside Kingston accepted a lesbian couple until a child was born to them. At that point baptism was refused: "So they came here and they were warmly welcomed and their baby was baptized." Being an affirming church, Macdonald said, meant the full integration of gay and lesbian people into the community, and having them serve in a number of different capacities.

Wayne Hilliker, minister at the nearby Chalmers United Church, explained that, while Chalmers supports same-sex marriage, it has decided not to be an affirming congregation, "because our mission statement has in it the phrase 'Welcome, All Who Come' and we decided that we'd rather have that than identify a particular group that we say we're going to especially welcome." He added that "there is a danger of then becoming a single issue church, perception-wise," which he suggested had happened at Sydenham Street (interview, 3 October 2003).

A student researcher visited Sydenham Street in the fall of 2002 at Elizabeth Macdonald's first service, when the chair of the congregation introduced her and her partner. Those present that Sunday morning did not know – at least not officially – when they selected her from among many applicants, that she was lesbian. Reportedly there were only positive responses when her sexual orientation was made clear that morning. In an interview Macdonald confirmed "it's true that the congregation wasn't informed that I was lesbian, but it's also true that I came and my partner was introduced with me on the first Sunday." She explained the role of human rights and the sequence of events as she was hired and presented to the congregation, in "this weird time where everybody wants to do things right":

> In the search process, it's a violation of human rights to ask about orientation. It's a violation to ask how old a person is; it's a violation to ask whether they're married, what their orientation is. And, therefore, from the candidate's point of view, you really would have to really want to bring it up, because the process is structured in a way that those questions don't get asked, and if they do get asked, it is said they're inappropriate. And so candidates are encouraged to be consistent, because it undermines the process if we say you can't ask any questions about

> whether you're married, except the married people are going to talk about their husband and wife. Like that really undermines it. So today in the United Church in the search process, whether you're a candidate or a committee, you're basically told you have to be really, really careful, that you not venture into these areas that violate human rights. And when a candidate is presented to the congregation, it is even more important that human rights not be violated. So, if the search committee knew, then it would be inappropriate for them to say, "So-and-so is gay or lesbian; so-and-so is married with three kids ..."

Macdonald also felt that disclosure is important once the minister is in a pastoral relationship with the congregation, at which point "you share your life and you're open."

In the United Church as with the Quakers, each congregation has a great deal of autonomy and independence. Not all congregations would follow the church's official policy. As Macdonald puts it, the United Church "takes stands nationally, but doesn't impose – well, for the most part doesn't impose – national policies on local congregations, but will encourage local congregations to mirror the policies and procedures that the national Church has committed itself to." Within the United Church of Canada it is actually the session, or equivalent body, within each congregation that establishes the policy on conducting marriages. That might be discussed at meetings, sometimes even with a congregational vote, but unless the session has committed itself to be bound by that vote, it sets the policy. A general policy might result whereby the minister may perform marriages only for members or adherents of the congregation. Alternatively, the session might require that each case be brought before it. With regard to the case of gay or lesbian couples, one session might permit them to be married inside the church but not outside it, while another session would allow same-sex marriages to be performed outside the church but not within it. Yet another session might allow same-sex marriages both inside and outside the sanctuary whereas another might forbid the minister to perform all such marriages.

John Young of Queen's Theological College, who provided these four different possibilities, could immediately come up with instances of three of these options "without thinking hard" and was "reasonably sure" he could find an example of the other option by doing "some checking around" (personal communication, 27 November 2007). Judy MacGillivray, interim minister at Calvary and St Matthew's United churches, two congregations that she "would classify as evangelical and certainly more conservative," said there was firm opposition to same-sex marriages being conducted by their minister, whether inside the church or elsewhere: "They are saying no and that is not an option." At Calvary, she said, she asked the session "about a couple of young fellows who would like to be married, and the vote was definitely no." She added that although the congregation "held firmly to their old beliefs," they asked her to find another church where the couple could be married by a minister: "They cared enough for the people to make things right for them" (interview, 14 May 2004).

Before Justin Lewis arrived on the scene, the Reform Jewish congregation already "was pro same-sex marriage for its members" (interview, 22 October 2003). The two previous rabbis, Barbara Borts and Ed Elkin, had both conducted same-sex marriages before they were recognized by law in Ontario. Lewis's position has been an important aspect of his own understanding, as "a basic fundamental question of social justice." Pamphlets displayed outside his university office set forth a Jewish position on this issue, presenting it as his own and the congregation's stand. His contract with the congregation included his ability to perform same-sex weddings: "I've made very clear my stand on that and tried to build that into the congregation's sense of itself." The pamphlet, entitled "Information on Same-Sex Marriage for Members and Friends of Congregation Iyr HaMelech," explained that the view of justice held by Reform Jews leads them to reject certain aspects of Jewish tradition, for example, on matters of gender and of sexual orientation. Decrees in the classical rabbinic literature, Lewis pointed out, were negative toward the sexuality of gays and lesbians.

As Lewis puts it, "the Reform movement does have positions, but it also recognizes a rabbinic freedom of conscience. So ultimately it's the individual rabbi and the congregation" (interview, 22 October 2003). Reform Judaism allows the individual rabbi to decide whether to perform same-sex unions. In keeping with this arrangement, then, what is negotiated and settled by a congregation contractually with one rabbi might change with the next, according to positions taken by that rabbi or by the members. After Lewis's departure from Iyr HaMelech, the website no longer mentioned same-sex marriages, and his successor as rabbi did not conduct them. When Lewis was still in Kingston for a time after ceasing to be Iyr HaMelech's rabbi, he was available to conduct same-sex weddings. After he left for Winnipeg in 2008, it became necessary for anyone seeking such a marriage conducted by a rabbi to travel elsewhere.

The percentage of Unitarian congregations who are "welcoming" is much greater than the proportion of "affirming" congregations in the United Church of Canada. The purpose of these designations, and the process leading to them, appears to be similar in both religious groups. Of forty-seven Unitarian congregations in Canada, at the end of 2007 thirty-six had become Welcoming congregations or were in the process of becoming so. The website for the

Canadian Unitarian Council announced late in 2010 that 99 per cent of Unitarian members in Canada belong to welcoming congregations who have completed a program of the Unitarian Universalist Association and voted to welcome the membership and participation of those who are lesbian, gay, bisexual, or transgendered (Canadian Unitarian Council a). Unitarians seem to regard the issue of same-sex marriage as something long since settled and no longer a matter for debate. While it would be difficult to find in Canada a Unitarian speaking out against same-marriage or homosexuality in general, in the United Church these questions still spark debate.

At the Kingston Unitarian Fellowship, Rev. Kathy Sage conducts marriages and other rites of passage for members, as her covenant with the congregation stipulates. Two lay chaplains are available to conduct ceremonies for weddings, memorial services, or the naming of a child for people in the larger community who are not Fellowship members. The lay chaplains are selected by the congregation and approved after a period of training; the position is renewed annually for up to six years. Sage was asked whether being within a "welcoming congregation" precludes a lay chaplain from opting out of performing a same-sex wedding on the basis of conscience. As with other groups considered here, and other Unitarian congregations, the Kingston Unitarian Fellowship establishes its own policies about the services conducted by the minister or a lay chaplain. As Sage explained, the kind of person selected to be a lay chaplain would be someone who represented the Unitarian tradition well and who would "be asked to marry persons of different faiths, traditions, cultures, and backgrounds." Because the Kingston Unitarian Fellowship had voted to become a welcoming congregation, lay chaplains would be expected to conduct same-sex weddings on the same basis as other weddings: that is, they should not discriminate against any group of persons, though they might turn down a particular request deemed inappropriate or unsuitable. While the exercise of one's conscience is an important value within Unitarianism, someone who felt unable to conduct a wedding ceremony for people of the same sex would not be a good candidate for a lay chaplain position, nor a good representative for the congregation (personal communication, 28 November 2007). In fact, not just a lay chaplain but anyone holding such views would be unlikely to feel at home in a Unitarian congregation.

HAS LIBERAL RELIGION A FUTURE?

A Unitarian Universalist congregation within Canada such as the Kingston Unitarian Fellowship will likely present, despite its stated openness and acceptance of diversity, a generally unified front. While consciously striving to be undogmatic, people who are Unitarians – or for that matter, Quakers and Reform Jews – will largely agree with one another and have their views settled with regard to many issues. Someone with a right-wing position in politics generally, or taking a conservative view on specific topics such as immigration, gun control, capital punishment, abortion, or sexual orientation, would not be very comfortable in such a group. It is difficult to imagine a free-ranging debate on these questions involving full representation from all sides among Unitarians. Probably part of realizing that one is Unitarian, along the lines that Sage described the process, involves discovering that one feels at home among people holding progressive social views, and who are also liberal and non-credal in matters of religion.

The Kingston Unitarian Fellowship provides a home for religious liberals, in a congregation consisting mostly of spiritual and secular humanists. Probably that identification is crucial for understanding the nature of the diversity treasured by Unitarian Universalists. A Unitarian congregation is unlikely to provide the kind of fellowship or spiritual home sought by someone whose way of being religious focuses on a deity outside of space and time, such as the God of traditional supernatural theism. The Canadian Unitarian Council characterizes Unitarianism as "a gathering point for those who reject creeds and dogmas in favour of an open and unfettered exploration of religious traditions" (Canadian Unitarian Council b). Among the named "sources" for Unitarian Universalist tradition – placed alongside "Humanist teachings" and "spiritual teachings of Earth-centred traditions" – are "Jewish and Christian teachings which call us to respond to God's love by loving our neighbour as ourselves" (Canadian Unitarian Council c). Although Unitarians stress that the religious quest is very much an individual matter, with respect for one's conscience, clearly that search operates under the aegis of a particular ethos. "Openness" does not necessarily extend equally to everyone, and "diversity" does not mean that all individuals will feel at home in this tradition. Unitarian Universalists perhaps emphasize the scientific and rational more than other liberal religious traditions do. One could almost say that they are characterized by a paradoxical dogmatism about being undogmatic, as they follow a line of questioning and debate and discussion in the attempt to frame and to state principles, yet without wanting those principles to emerge as a "creed."

By way of contrast, the religious liberalism of Quakers expresses itself in inwardness and a silent waiting upon the "light." Theirs is an experiential quest that rarely expresses itself in verbal formulations. While Unitarians are anxious to state that they are not Christians and why, Quakers are mostly content to accept their origins within Christianity – and their continuing association with Christian churches through the Canadian Council of Churches

– as a matter of ambiguity that does not demand to be cleared up. As one member of the Thousands Islands Meeting of the Religious Society of Friends put it, "Certainly the logic that, due to our membership in CC we must all believe the definition of Christianity given, is flawed. We are members of FUM [Friends United Meeting] too, and do not subscribe to its homophobia and credal efforts in bringing up the Richmond Declaration" (email, 2 December 2007). The Richmond Declaration, dating from 1887, contains "those fundamental doctrines of Christian truth that have always been professed by our branch of the Church of Christ" (Friends United Meeting). It was estimated that few members of the Thousand Islands Meeting would be "true blue trinitarians, and probably only a very few more ... would insist on the special Godhead and Sonhood of Jesus" (personal communication, 2 December 2007). While some members have obvious regard for the origins of the Religious Society of Friends within the Christian Church, and others have a special regard for the person of Jesus, many see the connection of the Quaker tradition with Christianity as a matter of history, but not necessarily something that they have to decide about appropriating as individuals.

Reform Jews, on the other hand, are also clear about their roots and the larger Jewish tradition of which they are a part. As Justin Lewis expressed it, they want to identify with being Jewish in a formal way, and find a way to participate in that tradition, while rejecting certain aspects that are contrary to contemporary experience. Although converts who have joined the religious group without having grown up within it are relatively common throughout the Society of Friends and Unitarian Universalists and Reform Jews, most converts to Reform Judaism, notwithstanding the example of Lewis himself, would join as the spouse of a Jewish partner. Selecting Reform Judaism from among a range of other religious possibilities that in Lewis's case included Hinduism and Wicca is a rather unusual route to take, especially given the difficulties and barriers put in the way of someone seeking to become Jewish. It is doubtful that those who find their place within Unitarianism would regard Reform Judaism as an attractive option: the responsibility to take on a tradition and a peoplehood is too much a burden for a freethinking outsider to assume. Certainly someone like Bert Horwood with "mental reservations" about theological language and religious discourse would find it too difficult to demythologize the terminology deriving from ancient Israel and rabbinic materials, to become an authentic follower without having the Hebrew language, or to identify oneself with an essentially monotheistic tradition rooted in a unique historical experience.

All three groups considered in this chapter provide opportunities for those who are uncomfortable with religious creeds and dogmas to continue in association with a faith community without having to assume too much theological baggage. While the research of Reginald Bibby and others tends to show that people stay quite close to the religious traditions in which they grew up, some members of these groups offer different stories. Many of the people speaking in this chapter of their experience as Quakers, Unitarians, and Reform Jews came to these faith groups from other religious traditions. They have left behind the religions of their respective childhoods and taken on new commitments and affiliations. The phenomenon of non-credal religion may be examined on several other contemporary fronts. The Canadian Centre for Progressive Christianity, following its American forebear, enumerates eight points that largely match the kinds of principles set forth by Quakers and Unitarians. Drawing upon the work of John Spong, Robert Funk, Dominic Crossan, Marcus Borg, Matthew Fox, Don Cuppit, and a long list of others – and in Canada influenced by the thought of Anglican journalist and author Tom Harpur – Progressive Christianity aims at making Christianity contemporary by regarding the Bible as a human document and by refusing the categories of the supernatural and the miraculous. As Gretta Vosper, a United Church minister and graduate of Queen's Theological College, expressed it at the inaugural meeting of the Canadian Centre for Progressive Christianity in 2004, "We have been called by those who have found too many of the Bible's moral messages, in the light of the call to love one's neighbour, worse than irrelevant, but actually life denying" (Canadian Centre for Progressive Christianity; cf. Vosper 2008). Rebekka King, a doctoral candidate at the University of Toronto who has been studying Progressive Christianity, wonders whether this effort to strip away outmoded metaphors and supernatural references in scripture and hymns and creeds and liturgies might amount to a "new literalism" that pays too much attention to verbal formulations without an appreciation of metaphor. Surely someone who recites the traditional form of the Apostles' Creed – with such lines as the ones affirming that Jesus Christ was "conceived by the Holy Spirit," or "descended into hell," or "sits at the right hand of God the Father Almighty" – does not confront the choice of having either to believe those words literally or to stop saying them.

While it is understandable that a person such as Bert Horwood might eventually find the struggles of continuing to use outmoded metaphors just too great, to such an extent that the alienation from the tradition becomes unmanageable, mainstream religions in Canada do accommodate a diversity of beliefs and practice. As a parallel instance, consider Bibby's claim that very few Canadians exclusively engage in such New Age practices as tarot cards, astrology, dream analysis, and meditation because "New Age thought seems to function as a supplement rather than a substitute for traditional faiths" (1993, 52). His argument is that most Canadians continue to be Roman Catholics or Protestants, in part because these groups have practised "menu diversification." Bibby says that "today's Roman Catholic, Anglican, or United Church member therefore has the option of being detached or involved, agnostic or evangelical, unemotional or charismatic. As a result, there's no need to switch" (1993, 57–8). Probably many Roman Catholics and Protestants think much as Quakers and Unitarians and Reform Jews or Progressive Christians do, but feel that their faith communities continue to provide a place for them. Professor and author David Helwig, writing as a self-professed agnostic who sang in the choir at St James' Anglican Church, asked: "What am I doing here, an unbeliever among believers, a detached observer at the solemnities of prayer and eucharist?" (1984, 132). Unable to find a satisfactory way of "believing," he remained an agnostic, though perhaps a "reverent" one, positioning himself outside the liturgies that he joined principally in song.

To some extent, religious liberals exhibit what is known as "seekership," defined in 1965 by J. Lofland and R. Stark as "floundering among religious alternatives, an openness to a variety of religious views, frequently esoteric, combined with failure to embrace the specific ideology and fellowship of some set of believers" (qtd in Campbell n.d). This characterization is somewhat negative, including such pejorative language as "floundering," "esoteric," and "failure." Those who affiliate themselves with Reform Jews and Quakers and Unitarians may have previously found "the specific ideology and fellowship" of other groups, perhaps Orthodox Judaism or mainline Christianity, too restrictive and confining. Those within such liberal faith communities demonstrate openness to various religious alternatives, sharing the conviction that truth is to be found in all religions. They also provide for an individual's religious quest as something that continues and progresses. To that extent, Donald Mathers' comment that Unitarianism is more like a hallway than a room remains apt. Nonetheless, seekers are usually affiliates of "esoteric" New Religious Movements that are themselves rather short lived.

The Religious Society of Friends and Unitarianism and Reform Judiasm are not "new" religions, but their demographics do raise questions about their ability to survive. Their rather loose belief structures and low demands may not have sufficient hold on people growing up within these traditions, or choosing to belong to them, for them to persist. Bibby indicates that people tend to come into religions by being born into them, not by conversion. Children growing up in families where liberal religious views are held may not themselves feel any need to affiliate with a faith community when they become adults. Instead, they might decide to identify themselves as among the large number of young adults who define themselves as having no religion. Another alternative, to be dealt with, for example, in chapter 8, is religious eclecticism: that is, cobbling together one's own religion – or "spirituality" – from a variety of sources without having an exclusive allegiance to one tradition. After all, someone having no single-minded commitment to one particular faith tradition is unlikely to subscribe to a single creed or dogma. That may well become the characteristic postmodern way of being religious (see James 1999).

7 Diversity of Religions: Islam, Bahá'í, Hindu, Sai Baba, Sikh

RELIGIOUS DIVERSITY IN KINGSTON: IS THERE ANY?

When one of the researchers for the Religious Diversity in Kingston project, a master's student from Toronto, told her father about the work she was doing, he queried, "Religious diversity in Kingston? Is there any?" In some ways that is an excellent, challenging question to raise. Census data from 2001 show that visible minorities in greater Kingston comprise less than 5 per cent of the population, numbering 6,735 out of 142,770 people, whereas in Ontario as a whole visible minorities amount to almost 20 per cent – and in Toronto about 37 per cent. About 12 per cent of Kingston's population is foreign born, as contrasted with Toronto's 44 per cent. In Kingston, then, there are not many people who are, to use the language by which Statistics Canada defines visible minorities, "non-Caucasian in race or non-white in colour."

Because no religion is monolithic or homogenous, religious diversity does not depend solely on race or colour. Consider the immense variety displayed in the various forms of Islam, for example (see Bramadat and Seljak 2005, 13–14). Moreover, people from similar racial or ethnic backgrounds may practise a variety of religions. One of the results of diversified immigration is the kind of multiculturalism that increases the numbers of immigrants representing visible minorities (see Germain 2004). A further problem occurs when religion is viewed as more or less inseparable from other aspects of cultural practice, or is subsumed under those other aspects. Then religion might not be studied or reported as a distinctive phenomenon in itself. Yet another issue arises when the categories used by census-takers are not familiar to respondents. The largest visible minority group in Kingston consists of the Chinese, but their "religion" remains largely invisible and unreported because people of Chinese descent in Canada do not think of themselves as Buddhist or Confucian or Taoist. It has been suggested that the reason almost 60 per cent of Chinese in Canada identify themselves as having "no religion" results from the absence of any such category as "Chinese religion" (see Lai, Paper, and Paper 2005). Another factor contributing to the invisibility of the religions of Asian immigrants is what Bruce Matthews terms "the insularity and exclusivist particularism of ethnic Buddhist communities" (2002, 129), among them Thai, Cambodian, and Vietnamese. That is to say, their religions are not shared with other ethnic groups and function out of the sight of most other Canadians.

Frequently whether a particular city counts as fully diverse or representatively multicultural gets measured against the standard set by Toronto, Montreal, or Vancouver (see, for example, Derouin 2004). These three cities were the destination of more than 70 per cent of the immigrants coming to Canada during the 1990s (Justus 2004). Recent immigrants – in fact, 90 per cent of them – have preferred to live in a metropolitan area, though results from the 2006 Census are revealing that more immigrants selected smaller cities than in the past. Kingston, however, ought not to be compared with the three great metropolises, nor even with such larger centres as Ottawa-Hull, Calgary, Edmonton, Hamilton, Winnipeg, Kitchener-Waterloo, Windsor, or London, all of which have foreign-born populations of about 20 per cent. Many more properly comparable (because closer in size) cities such as Saskatoon, Regina, Sudbury, Thunder Bay, Saint John, Sherbrooke, or Quebec have a lower proportion of foreign-born inhabitants than Kingston's 12.4 per cent. An exception is Abbotsford, BC – roughly the same size as Kingston – where 22 per cent are foreign born. Notably, 80 per cent of immigrants to Abbotsford in the 1990s were Asian, with about 60 per cent of them born in India – a phenomenon described as a continuation of "a longstanding pattern of South Asian settlement in that region" (Justus 2004). It might be questioned whether a large number of recent immigrants from a single part of the world, such as India, living in a small Canadian city expands representation of a full range of multicultural variety in that city.

What, then, of religious diversity as such considered apart from country of origin, ethnicity, or the representation of visible minorities? Remember that about 77 per cent of Kingstonians are Protestants or Roman Catholics; in Toronto these two major Christian groups amount to only 58 per cent of the city's population. Whereas in Kingston Jews and Muslims – each group having less than a thousand adherents reported – together add up to just 1.2 per cent of the population, in Toronto they are 15 per cent of the whole. Kingston has only 475 Buddhists, 465 Hindus, and 130 Sikhs, again an under-representation as contrasted with Toronto. The only dedicated space for any one of these three groups in Kingston is the Kuluta Buddhist Centre, part of the Kadampa tradition, consisting mostly of western followers of this adaptation of a branch of Tibetan Buddhism (see chaps. 8 and 9). The majority of these practitioners of Kadampa Buddhism are not of Asian descent, nor is their ancestral religious tradition usually Buddhist. Bruce Matthews remarks in his essay "Buddhism in Canada" that not only practitioners of Asian Buddhism but its observers and scholars will mostly be outsiders: "It is likely that non-Asian Buddhists will continue to dominate the field of Buddhist interpretation and studies" (2002, 133). While the Kuluta Buddhist Centre adds to the religious diversity of Kingston, at least in one sense, its members and adherents probably reflect the ethnic makeup of the city of Kingston. So, the question remains: Is there any? – religious diversity in Kingston, that is. Furthermore, what constitutes religious diversity?

Intrinsic religious diversity within a group might be more prevalent within congregations in small- and medium-sized cities in Canada than in larger metropolises. Kingston's Muslims are a case in point. The Islamic Centre of Kingston – not termed a "mosque" – exists for the benefit of all Muslims in the city and surrounding area. The local Muslim community is comprised of Sunnis and Shi'ites and some Ismailis, all representing various countries of origin and speaking different languages. As a result of their small numbers – again, less than a thousand – they must stress amidst their own diversity a central shared Islamic unity. As was the case among Kingston's Jewish population a century earlier (see chap. 1), among Muslims in Kingston no subgroup can afford to go its own way. Meanwhile, on the Queen's University campus, as many as a half-dozen different Muslim groups exist for students – the large majority of them coming from outside Kingston – who want to continue the specifics of their own practice of Islam while temporarily resident in the city to attend university (see chap. 9). Within the Islamic Centre of Kingston the intrinsic religious diversity of a community of Canadian Muslims is exhibited in one single location in a manner not possible in a bigger city.

MUSLIMS IN KINGSTON

When data were released from the 1991 Census showing that the number of Muslims in Canada had more than doubled since 1981, dramatic predictions ensued to the effect that nationally Muslims would someday outnumber Presbyterians. While Presbyterians had dropped to 636,000 in 1991, they still surpassed Muslims by more than two to one. By 1991 Muslims had increased to 253,000 from less than 100,000 a decade earlier. One telling difference was that only 3 per cent of Muslims were over age 65, and 44 per cent were under 25. Presbyterians, meanwhile, were an aging denomination, with almost 20 per cent of their members over age 65 and only

27 per cent under age 25. At the time hardly anyone thought that in the decade to follow this situation would change so quickly.

The 2001 Census showed that the number of Presbyterians had further declined to 410,000, while the number of Muslims had burgeoned to 580,000. Even by the mid-1990s Islam had overtaken Judaism as Canada's largest non-Christian religious community. The 2001 Census also revealed that some groups other than the three monotheistic traditions of Judaism, Christianity, and Islam had increased to about 300,000 people: Buddhists (300,000), Hindus (297,000), and Sikhs (278,000) were now approaching the number of Jews in Canada (330,000). By 2001, then, Muslims outnumbered every other religious group in Canada except for Anglicans, Baptists, Lutherans, Roman Catholics, and the United Church of Canada.

The Islamic Centre of Kingston is located on the west side of Sydenham Road, about five hundred metres north of Highway 401's Exit 613. The location would once have been thought to be at some distance from downtown Kingston, as was certainly the case before the city's amalgamation or at the time when the land was purchased in the mid-1980s. Though now within the municipal boundaries, it remains in an area on the outskirts where city begins to turn into country. Today the Islamic Centre stands at one end of a three-kilometre stretch of Sydenham Road extending from Princess Street to just north of Highway 401. This portion of road, serving as a major route of access to Highway 401, or to the villages and cottage country lying north of the city, has become a somewhat concentrated cluster of religious sites. From south to north they include the Kingston Gospel Temple on Princess Street, about four hundred metres west of Sydenham Road; then, Cataraqui United Church, more or less opposite Christ Church Anglican, both of these mainline churches dating from the nineteenth century and both just a few hundred metres north of the Princess Street intersection; next, the recently built Parish Centre for the Anglicans, surrounded, as is Christ Church itself, by the massive Cataraqui Cemetery that extends some distance along the east side of Sydenham Road; then, across on the west side of the road, the Third Day Worship Centre, an evangelical church in an expanded former pubic school; then, just on the east of Sydenham Road after the overpass crossing Highway 401, the Standard Church, in this location for about thirty years; and, finally, a little further north and on the west side of the road, the Islamic Centre of Kingston.

Writing some years ago in their newsletter, *The Bond*, Hafizur Rahman, then president of the Islamic Society of Kingston, summarized their history. He wrote how in the early 1960s Kingston's Muslims consisted of foreign students, some Queen's University faculty members, and some medical residents at the hospitals. Other recollections have the Muslim community in

Islamic Centre of Kingston

Kingston at that time even smaller than Rahman suggests. Originally from Egypt, Moustafa and Fatma Fahmy arrived in Kingston in 1965 so that Moustafa could take a position as an engineering professor at Queen's University. Fatma Fahmy recalls, "We were the first family here, but there were maybe three or four students" (Noble 2006). The only Muslim religious gathering was the organization of prayers, supplemented with occasional social events on the university campus. Nothing had changed greatly by the 1970s except that the presence of children brought about the establishment of a weekend school to teach Arabic and Islam. With the increase of Kingston's Muslim population in the 1980s, the Islamic Society of Kingston was formally established, and by the mid-1980s land had been purchased for a building. Construction on the Islamic Centre began in 1995, with the new building being opened in 1996.

Designed by Carleton University architect Guizar Haider, when it was built the centre was acclaimed as the only mosque between Toronto and Montreal. It was erected not just as a mosque where the Muslim community could pray, but as a community centre where Muslims could socialize with one another and to which others could be invited. Haider described the building as an "eclectic" borrowing of "forms from around the world" adapted to the regional landscape. Because the ground at the site is solid limestone, an unexpected further adaptation became necessary: no basement was constructed, and the first floor became larger than initially intended (Hogben 1996). The building was constructed on the location of the former barn of W.R. Aylesworth, used since 1950 for livestock auctions.

While the planes of the centre's roofs incorporate the shapes of typical Canadian barns and sheds, this "regional homage" is surmounted by a symbol new to Eastern Ontario, the dome of the minaret. Non-Muslim student visitors typically report being strongly impressed by the design of the prayer room – in this religion where the rising and setting of the sun are so important – with its windows and skylights providing natural lighting during the day. At night, or when the sun is setting, the structural metal framework of columns and girders supporting the roof is lit in such a way that the shadows cast on the floor are reminiscent of the shadows of palm leaves that might be seen on the floors of mosques in Asia or North Africa.

Mohammad Saleem said that those attending the Islamic Centre, where English is the language used, are "from all over world": "People come from Africa, people come from Asia. Some are from South America – North America, of course – and some are from Europe. The majority are from the Middle East and South Asia. You have some from South East Asia too. So it is from all over." He continued, "We put a lot of emphasis that while we are here we are nobody but Canadians – Canadian Muslims. That is what our identity is. We tell our children, and we emphasize ourselves, that we are Canadian Muslims. That's it. What we had back home, that was back home, but what we are here is Canadian Muslims. We are from different backgrounds and so forth and so on but ... we remain attached to the mainstream. We are able to define ourselves like that" (interview, 17 February 2004). Contrasting the Muslim community's presence in Kingston in 2007 with its early days, Hafizur Rahman observed that now the Islamic Society of Kingston includes "more permanent residents," many of them Canadian-born, who have come to Kingston to stay. More Muslims have made Kingston their destination in Canada and thereafter remained in the city, a contrast with the earlier transient Muslim population, especially students and medical residents, who tended to be in Kingston for only a few years before moving elsewhere (Harrison 2006a).

When Mohammad Saleem was interviewed during the time that he was the society's president (17 February 2004), he was asked about the degree of acceptance for Muslims in Kingston. Referring to the negative reactions to Muslims elsewhere after the attacks of 9/11, he emphasized that "we have found [that] overall people in the Kingston community reacted positively toward the Muslim community. And we value that. There were a couple of minor incidents, but nothing big. Overall, the response was very, very good." He said that generally relations with the community have been positive and "people have been friendly." Children from the neighbourhood are welcome to play in the centre's parking lot and encouraged to use the basketball net installed there, the only restriction being that they are asked not to play around the entranceway because of the stairs. Saleem stressed – using phrases such as "we haven't found any trouble," "we don't find any problem," and "I have never heard any complaint" – that the association of Kingston's Muslims with other members of the community has been largely free of negative events.

Kingston's Muslim community, by hospitably opening their doors, can take much of the credit for their high level of acceptance within the city. Less than three weeks after 9/11, the Islamic Centre of Kingston held its first open house on a Sunday afternoon, inviting the community "to tour the centre and to meet some of the Muslims in the city and surrounding area" (*Whig-Standard*, 29 September 2001). Saleem remembers that "we had a very big crowd because people wanted to know more at that time, under the circumstances." The event has been repeated, and "since then it's been a regular feature – a lot of people come and drop in." Another way in which the centre welcomes the community is by holding international bazaars – "and one of the main attractions is the food." Saleem explains, "Food starts from every part of the world. So the people come and we have food and books and so forth and so on. That's a very good attraction" (interview, 17 February 2004).

At the bazaars the public can tour the site, purchase books and crafts, have their hands painted with henna, and watch the men at prayer. The real interest and attention, though, is largely focused on the row of food-laden tables, where visitors line up alongside members of Kingston's Muslim community to be served food by the women who have prepared it and are available to explain the dishes. The role played by food, as in a case such as this, has become increasingly appreciated and studied as a way of accessing the faith traditions of others. Professor Michel Desjardins of the Department of Religion and Culture at Wilfrid Laurier University brings food into his classes "to change the mood, generate different forms of learning, and prod students to connect food and religion." As he puts it, "For the great majority of people religion is not primarily about verbal teachings; rather, it is about lived community. And lived community is rooted in food" (Desjardins 2004). Corrie E. Norman, in her article "Savoring the Sacred: Understanding Religion through Food," outlines how the foodways of other faiths open up the realization that religion is much more than belief. The roles of ritual, community, and the body move to the fore, as well as, perhaps most significantly, the frequently unnoticed participation of women who are "often the religious experts when it comes to ritual foodways" (Norman 2003).

KINGSTON'S CARTOON CONTROVERSY

Fasting practices further underline the relevance of food to religions. Denying oneself food for a period of time has ritual and symbolic significance. Widespread through many traditions, it may be a means of self-purification and enhancing spiritual awareness, or obedience to the obligations of the religion. Riad Saloojee suggests that to fast during Ramadan reminds Muslims of their mortality, of their connection with the hungry of the world, of their ability to transform ingrained habits, of the need to control one's consumption – and, most of all, to establish a focus on the divine (*Whig-Standard*, 23 October 2004). Just after the beginning of Ramadan – a week before Saloojee's article appeared – the *Whig-Standard* had published a cartoon by Aislin of the *Montreal Gazette* that gave hurt and offence to Kingston's Muslims. The cartoon, inspired by media accounts predicting an impending increase in violence in Iraq, showed a man reading a newspaper and saying to a friend, "Holy Moley! How sick is that? It says here that, with it being Ramadan, any suicide bombers who blow themselves up will get extra points from all the radical Islamist groups." The response of the man's friend is: "You mean like Air Miles?" (*Whig-Standard*, 16 October 2004). As an editorial in the *Whig-Standard* later explained, Aislin "got the idea from watching a CBC-TV report about how suicide bombers would be considered super-martyrs if they did their killing during the Muslim world's holy time of fasting and reflection." When letters began pouring in from members of the local Muslim community demanding an apology, the editorial page editor, Paul Schliesmann, called these objections a distortion of the paper's ideas and opinions and asked, "Why should we apologize for a cartoon that condemned those who would kill in the name of religion?" (*Whig-Standard*, 27 October 2004).

In Kingston the publication of this cartoon, the letters in response to it, and the statement of defence from the newspaper revealed a great gap in understanding existing within Kingston. To be sure, by comparison, the uproar a year later resulting from the publication in a Danish newspaper of cartoons depicting the Prophet is more easily seen as blasphemous or insensitive or arising from Islamophobia. Many Muslims do not regard visual representations of Muhammad as permissible. Aislin's cartoon was defended on the grounds that there was no attack on Islam or Muslims generally, and certainly no caricature of Muhammad, but rather a satirical exposé of extremists who kill in the name of Islam. Nonetheless, for many readers this cartoon reawakened the stereotypes and prejudice, especially rife since 9/11, depicting Islam as a religion of violence. Some of the letters from Muslim Kingstonians pointed out – as did Mohammad Saleem's – the insensitivity of "associating terrorism with one of the basic spiritual obligation[s] of Muslims," that is, of fasting during Ramadan. Saleem also emphasized, "The Muslim community in Kingston condemns terrorism in all forms and shapes" (*Whig-Standard*, 29 October 2004). In the same vein, Moustafa Fahmy, in a brief letter, spoke of the insensitivity shown to Muslims by the cartoon, and affirmed Ramadan as "the most blessed month of the year, a month for spiritual development, kindness to the poor and appreciation of all of God's blessings." He too called attention to the fact that "Islam condemns in the strongest terms the killing of innocent people" and cited the Qur'an, where to kill a single innocent person is akin to killing all humankind (*Whig-Standard,* 23 October 2004).

Probably most non-Muslim observers wondered why members of Kingston's Islamic community would take such offence. Anybody familiar with Aislin's cartoons over the years would know that this was not the first time he got into hot water for satirizing religious foibles. A Pakistani Queen's University student who decried the depiction of Islam in the cartoon as "cowardly," "highly disturbing," and "blatantly anti-Muslim," asked, "What would have happened if you made fun of another faith, one more widely represented in Canada?" (*Whig-Standard,* 19 October 2004). In the past, however, Aislin had lampooned George Bush's war-mongering conservative Christianity. He also caricatured the stupidity of the "Troubles" in Northern Ireland in a picture of two apes, one Protestant and the other Catholic, with a caption about this being the extent of evolution there. Canadian politicians above all, as well as the general public, would know that there is nothing unmentionable or sacred for this Montreal cartoonist, and no subject, especially not religion, that is off limits as fodder for his often biting, even vicious sketches. Despite such considerations, the Canadian Islamic Congress filed a complaint with the Quebec Press Council against the *Montreal Gazette*'s publication of the Aislin cartoon. The complaint read in part: "False identification of Ramadan – the holiest month of the Muslim year – with terrorism is offensive in the extreme. It is, in fact, hate literature. Would a cartoon denigrating and falsifying the faith disciplines of Lent, Advent, or Yom Kippur pass the Gazette's editorial scrutiny?" (Canadian Islamic Congress).

The Islamic Society of Kingston, as letters from members were at pains to remind people, had made repeated and generous efforts to reach out to Kingstonians and to build bridges of understanding. Muslims in Kingston could not comprehend why the first mention of Ramadan in the local newspaper during October 2004 should be a negative and critical one – that was the "insensitivity" to which they objected. David Feltmate, a Ph.D. candidate at the University of Waterloo researching the topic of religion and humour, comments that "what is a simple joke to people in a position of power and established dominance, is to the marginalized group a reminder of their status as not fully accepted into society." One of the worst fears of a minority group would be that the host community could casually make them or their religion the object of a joke. The kind of seemingly offhand jab represented in the Asilin cartoon reminded Kingston's Muslims that, despite all their efforts for understanding and acceptance, they are not part of the mainstream. As Feltmate points out, "North American Muslims are highly self-conscious about their marginal status ... The terrorist stereotype is one they have to work doggedly against because it is constantly reinforced through mainstream media. While Aislin and his readers may think that he was 'just joking' and that he was just attacking terrorists, Muslims are well aware that there is no clear cut line between Muslim and terrorist in the popular imagination" (personal communication, 9 December 2009).

Moreover, if the butt of the cartoon's humour was simply Islamic terrorism, the *Whig-Standard* failed to balance this critique with any positive story about Ramadan or about Kingston's Muslim community as they entered a period so significant in their religious life. As Mohamed M. Bayoumi said, "We should care for one another rather than offend one another." He reminded the paper's readers of their open houses and of visits to "schools, churches and service clubs to enhance our understanding of one another." He spoke too of how, just a few days before the cartoon's appearance, local Muslims erected a display to educate people about Islam and the meaning of Ramadan. They had also held a bake sale in support of the Kingston General Hospital (*Whig-Standard,* 19 October 2004).

The feeling, then, was one almost of having been betrayed by the neighbours to whom Kingston's Muslims had tried to reach out. Saleem, in his role as president of the Islamic Society of Kingston, reminded people of how they had "worked with other faith groups, charitable organizations, correctional services, academic institutions, hospitals, the city administration, provincial and federal politicians, peace groups, the media and individuals to promote harmony and peace in this community." He added: "We regularly extended cordial invitations to all, including the *Whig-Standard*, to attend our open-house events" (*Whig-Standard,* 29 October 2004). In return for their generosity and efforts at creating positive relations, the Muslim community of Kingston felt that they had treated unfairly.

Diversity within Islam

To represent fully the context of the Aislin cartoon incident, two further points need to be made. First, as suggested above, the publication of the cartoon at the outset of Ramadan came at a time when local Muslims expected to be the recipients of the community's good wishes and support. Instead, the local newspaper featured a story praising the efforts of other faith communities. On the same Saturday that the cartoon was published, the *Whig-Standard* ran a front-page article running to more than a thousand words, and also relating, ironically, to food. This piece chronicled the growing demand on the city food banks, with 5,400 meals served monthly at ten soup kitchens, "many of which are located in churches." In addition, eight hundred hampers were being distributed each month by the Partners in Mission Food Bank, an organization begun in 1984 by the Religious Hospitallers of St Joseph in fulfillment of the Christian mandate to feed the hungry (see Mooy 2007). The story, detailing the growing need and the role of volunteers, concluded with a fact box naming "Kingston's 10 church-based meal providers and the people they feed" (*Whig-Standard,* 16 October 2004). At the outset of Ramadan, then, a positive front-page account in the weekend paper praising the efforts of Kingston's Christians was juxtaposed with an editorial-page cartoon about Islamicist extremists. Much of the dismay, then, on the part of members of the Islamic Society of Kingston was at the absence of any positive mention of their Muslim faith as they entered Ramadan, given its importance for them and their efforts at building good relations with the larger community. A positive story relating to Ramadan by Riad Saloojee of the Canadian Council on American-Islamic Relations appeared in the *Whig-Standard* a week after the cartoon appeared and the controversy already had erupted.

The second factor in assessing the Kingston reaction to the Aislin cartoon is the role of self-critique within Islam. As became clear in the fall of 2005 when the Danish cartoons appeared, the western ideal of the right to exercise free speech, and critiques of Islam in the media along the same lines as criticism of any other religious group, collided with the Islamic imperative to defend the faith against its enemies and against ridicule. When the Aislin cartoon in the *Whig-Standard* was discussed in a senior undergraduate seminar of students from various religious backgrounds – or none – at Queen's University, they generally agreed that this particular publication was unwise. One of the reasons offered was that – unlike some branches of Christianity, where in principle nothing is beyond critical examination or debate, and unlike Judaism where disputation is at the very heart of their theological method – Muslims feel themselves to be part of a global unity in which an offence against one is an offence against all. When Jews are criticized, paradoxically Jewish humour often operates by means of self-deprecation, often internalizing and playing upon the very terms of the critique. As an example, consider the 2006 movie *Borat* in which Sacha Baron Cohen employs the stereotypes of anti-Semitism apparently to lampoon Jewish hypersensitivity about the possibility of anti-Semitism (see James 2008).

Further, the western Enlightenment's principles of critical examination and historical consciousness, deeply ingrained in the contexts of western Christianity and of Judaism, have not played as large a role in Muslim experience. True enough, a few Christians picketed the movie theatre in

Kingston at the screening of the controversial Martin Scorsese film *The Last Temptation of Christ* in 1988. And there were vigorous debates, some of them local, about the depiction of Jews in *The Passion of the Christ* (2004), or of the Catholic Church in the *Da Vinci Code* (2006) or in *The Golden Compass* (2007). Even though in most of these cases the film was less objectionable than the book on which it was based, there were marked differences within the religious communities themselves about whether the content or presentation was offensive, and to what degree. No single unified response was to be heard. But when a young Muslim at a Kingston interfaith gathering in the 1990s stated that he would defend his religion in the same way he would defend against an assault on his mother or sister, the point was lost on most Christians and Jews in the room, some of whom might be as likely themselves to be in the forefront of any questioning or critique of their own faith. This young man was expressing the "lesser jihad," according to which he was prepared to struggle in the defence of Islam when the faith is under attack. (The "greater jihad" requires that each person struggle within themselves to do what is right and good.)

Even to attempt a characterization such as this, distinguishing self-critique within Islam from that within other religions, oversimplifies complexities. Many followers of various traditions feel obliged to remain silent on issues they might personally feel strongly about, for the sake of preserving unity. As British author Karen Armstrong emphasized in a discussion at the Parliament of the World's Religions held in Barcelona in July 2004, those occupying the moderate centre within faith communities must speak out lest the only voices heard be those of extremists. Still, some Jews who have misgivings about Israel's policies with regard to Palestinians may feel they have to stifle them. Further, Christians with doubts about the historicity of Jesus or the resurrection, or who interpret these core teachings of Christianity metaphorically, may find it wise or politic to remain silent about them. With that in mind, suggestions that Islam is monolithic or unified can only be upheld by ignoring the debate and ferment within the Muslim community or the diversity that Islam exhibits.

In Canada an online blog cleverly named mooselim.ca (now disappeared, having apparently migrated to Facebook and Twitter) explored various sides of issues within Islam ranging from the meaning of jihad and hijab to shariah law, terrorism, and multiculturalism in Canada. As another example, the hit CBC-TV sitcom series *Little Mosque on the Prairie*, displays in comic form a range of Muslim practices and beliefs and personalities in a small prairie town. The writer of the series, Zarqa Nawaz, a Canadian Muslim woman of Pakistani background, also directed an hour-long National Film Board documentary *Me and the Mosque* (2005), in which she dealt with issues about equal access for women in Canadian mosques. Another controversial and outspoken Canadian Muslim woman, Irshad Manji, self-described as a "Muslim refusenik" who defends the diversity of Islam, calls upon Muslims not to "clam up and conform" but to "protest the ideological occupation of Muslim minds" (Manji n.d.). A refugee to Canada from Idi Amin's Uganda, Manji wrote the book *The Trouble with Islam Today* (2003) and made the film *Faith without Fear* (2007). The director of the Moral Courage Project at New York University, she speaks in strong personal terms as a Muslim woman. Other books on contemporary Islam are appearing in their scores, covering from various viewpoints topics such as politics, theology, feminism, ecology, social movements, terrorism, and human rights.

As one interview in the series *Profiles: People of Faith* on Kingston's local cable channel, I spoke with Professor Sylvat Aziz of the Department of Fine Art at Queen's. She was born and grew up in Pakistan and comes from a Muslim background. During our interview she was dressed casually in white running shoes and cotton pants, a T-shirt and vest. Her hair was uncovered, though she said that sometimes in Pakistan she covers her head as "as a sign of respect': "If I'm meeting an elder or my grandparents I do veil" (Cogeco interview, 20 October 2004). Thinking of her teaching on Islam and art, as well as the veiled figures and Islamic themes that appear in her work "Transformations" from her *Peripheries* exhibition, I asked her whether as a practising artist she saw herself as an exponent of Islam. Aziz answered that although her "work does express issues in Islam ... it does not do it in a monolithic kind of way." Instead, she views her art as "very much a comparative study, so issues in Chinese history and religions, issues in Christianity and Judaism, are equally important to posit reality between Islam and the other major religions and philosophies." Even though she asserts that Islam is "the bedrock ... because that's where my experience is," her art "interacts with the other philosophies and ideologies as well." She continued: "I do not think I am an apologist for Islam because I feel no reason to be one. One in every five people in the world are Muslims so I think there is enough critical density there for me to be excused from this" (20 October 2004).

When I asked her what kind of Muslim she was and whether she was a Muslim feminist, Aziz also declined that role: "I am a Muslim all right, but I think there are very many better people than me to take up the cause of feminism in Islam." She went on to say that she focuses her energies on understanding the workings of the World Bank and debt service, on viewing the world in the light of class, privilege, and economic status, especially in terms of "foreign policy between the first and developing worlds." She affirmed, "My engagement is in that area rather than in the area traditionally ascribed to the feminist domain." Yet she was also emphatically positive about her experience of Islam as a woman: "I don't think any religion would respect my intelligence like Islam does. No religion in my opinion would give me common sense as much as Islam does ... It gives me permission to talk to my God, absolutely, without any intermediaries. No other religion gives me that option. I am not confined to a place to worship. I am responsible for my own good and bad, completely. I am absolutely independent in that ... God tells me, 'I have given you the ability to do right and wrong – you choose.' That can be a little daunting, but it's exhilarating as well" (20 October 2004).

Mohammad Saleem spoke of how in the Islamic Society of Kingston, in keeping with the central emphasis in Islam, the effort is to find a moderate or middle way between extremes. Some of these – for example, having men at prayer with heads uncovered, holding social gatherings with both men and women together, and welcoming the presence of women on committees – may diverge from the practices people were used to in their countries of origin. In such matters as "what dress a women wears when she comes to prayer," or "what type of scarf she is to wear or not to wear in the hall," these decisions are left to a woman, so long as "modest dress" is worn, a requirement that applies to both women and to men. Saleem stated that while these questions of accommodating people's preferences might pose a challenge, such challenges have been met: "We manage all right without any big problem" (17 February 2004).

Islam in the Canadian Context

Among those interviewed for *Profiles: People of Faith* were Alia and Murray Hogben. They met and fell in love while both were both students at Carleton University in the 1950s. Alia was born in Burma of Indian parentage into a Muslim family and had lived in Japan, India, Europe, and Canada with her Muslim parents. Murray converted to Islam in 1957, having grown up in Canada in a Presbyterian family. Their life together encompasses fifty years of living as Muslims in Canada, beginning in Toronto among a small group of Muslims from different backgrounds and ethnicities before there was any Islamic centre there. Later in the 1960s, Toronto Muslims were to buy a downtown Presbyterian church whose members were aging and moving away – a prophetic irony, given later trends among the numbers of the respective adherents and comparisons of the future fortunes of Presbyterians and Muslims in Canada. Today, as Alia Hogben explains, "what's happening in Toronto, from what we understand, is because the number of Muslims has increased, groups are breaking up into ethnicities or languages." They find the Muslim community in Kingston retains its intimacy and cohesiveness: "Here the nice thing is that it's similar to the one in Toronto when we first started because everyone gets together there – Arabs and Bengalis, Indo-Pakistanis, and some Africans. So it's very nice" (Cogeco interview, 1 December 2004).

The Hogbens, like many couples who have been together many years, are so much in tune that each is able to complete the other's sentences and expand on the other's thoughts. Alia was explaining that, when she grew up, for her family there were no sectarian distinctions, and that such inclusiveness continues in Kingston today: "If someone was a Muslim, they were a Muslim and it was broad-mindedness and tolerance and not only that but a sort of active acceptance of differences that I grew up with." Murray continued, "I guess I've grown into that and that's why we don't make any – we're theoretically Sunni Muslims because that's what we are." Alia added, "I don't even think we talk about that," and Murray went on, "but we don't distinguish the sectarian aspect because Islam is very complicated by its sectarian side but, like Alia just said, anyone who says they're Muslim – that's just fine by us – we're not going to question, that's up-to-God kind of thing, and get on and do whatever we have to do – not make distinctions of race or religious affect."

Alia Hogben stated that in her role as executive director of the Canadian Council of Muslim Women she had done a lot of work in relation to the controversy around Muslim family law in Ontario. While some groups were advocating the application of *sharia* law, the women's council took the position that "we're here in Canada and that Canadian laws should apply to us, as women, as Muslims, as Canadians." The council, Alia said, doesn't see "a reason why other forms of law should be brought into Canada." Issues of Muslim family law "can adversely affect women's equality rights," and these have not been resolved in Muslim-majority countries where they are practised: "Some of the practices are not so positive for women, and so we're querying why we need to have any other law in Canada." After this interview took place, legislation was passed in Ontario in 2006 that provided for faith-based arbitration, but not in a legally binding manner. That is, couples could seek advice from religious experts relating to issues of family law such custody and divorce, but the laws of the province would finally govern such disputes. The website of the Ministry of the Attorney General for Ontario summarizes the situation: "Nothing in Ontario law prevents people from turning to a religious official or someone knowledgeable in the principles of their religion to help them resolve their family dispute. However, if that person made a decision based on religious principles, the decision would not be a valid family arbitration award under the law. Both spouses could comply

Prayers at the Islamic Centre

with the decision voluntarily, but the decision would not be enforceable if one of the people involved took it to court. The court may only enforce awards made in arbitrations conducted exclusively under Canadian law" (Ministry of the Attorney General).

The hiring in 2006 of the first imam in Kingston, Abu Noman Mohammad Tarek, stands as an important landmark in the life of the Muslim community here. The new imam, in addition to leading prayers and offering guidance to the Muslim community, was expected to fulfil a major role as an educator who would be knowledgeable about Islam and could communicate to other Muslims as well as to the wider community. When Imam Tarek was interviewed by the Religious Diversity in Kingston project just a few months after his arrival, he spoke of his preference at this stage of his life for Kingston over Montreal, where he had also been offered a job. Kingston, he said, was comparable in size to Oakville, where he had been living previously. In this relatively small community he would have an opportunity to know his surroundings better and to be involved in all aspects of the work of the *masjid* – that is, a place of prayer permanently dedicated to Allah. In Toronto he had been assisting another imam in a secondary role. He also was pleased to be amongst educated Muslims including, he was told, three or four doctors, in a place where the university would afford him the opportunity for further study. Tarek had completed an honours degree in Bengali literature and a master's degree in Islamic law in his native Bangladesh. After 2001 he came to Canada to complete a degree in computer science at Acadia University, where he performed some of the religious duties for the community in Wolfville, Nova Scotia (interview, 31 January 2007).

Amongst his other activities at the Islamic Society of Kingston, Tarek taught Islamic studies, Arabic, and the Qur'an to children four or five evenings per week and at a weekend school held on Saturdays, and conducted at least four *halaqas* – that is, "knowledge circles," or gatherings – for teaching each week. The community wanted to use Tarek primarily as an educator, not as an administrative leader. Only twenty-seven at the time of his appointment, Tarek said that he was satisfied with this role: "I'm so young, so I can't lead the community" (Harrison 2006b). Joan Montgomerie, in an online article in *Peace* magazine, explores the preparation and training of imams serving in Canada, principally at the eighty or ninety mosques in the Toronto area (Montgomerie 2007). Imam Abu Patel told her that imams do not get the kind of training that ministers, priests, and rabbis receive. Most of the imams in Toronto are volunteers, and, according to Imam Hamid Slimi of the International Muslims Organization of Toronto, "there are fewer than ten full-time imams for 450,000 people in the GTA." He maintains that the resulting lack of religious leadership leads to disunity. Because most imams receive their education abroad, those interviewed agreed that it would be beneficial if, like other clergy, imams were to have an undergraduate degree in humanities followed by seminary education. That kind of background might help leaders in Islamic centres to bring together faith and social concerns.

Tarek, whose own studies in Bengali literature provide exactly the studies in the humanities that Mongomerie's article saw as important, emphasized the role of education as important in Islam, directed both within and outside the community. He spoke of how young people in Canada, where freedom of speech is valued, are able to challenge what their parents tell them. What children are told about the teachings and duties of Islam must be accurate and supported by sources in the Qur'an and Sunna. Tarek gave the example of a boy arriving at the Islamic Centre with his mother, who told the child that he was not to wear his shoes inside. After the boy protested and continued to insist, his mother at last informed him, "Allah said not to go into the *masjid* with shoes." With that, said Tarek, the boy "stopped because he is scared of Allah." Yet, as Tarek asks, "Did Allah say to never go into the *masjid* with shoes? Never ever." Though the community would wish to keep the centre clean, maintaining this standard by misinforming children about religious obligations as a way of ensuring their compliance eventually results in a loss of parental authority: "The children then say, 'Okay, Mother, show me where Allah says this.'" Tarek therefore finds it important to impart "the right message with the proof." This practice "is good for our community and our nation as well." Especially with teenagers, and in matters relating to dress, music, and dating, he says, it is crucial to distinguish between the core teachings of the faith and cultural conventions that some might assume to be part of the religion, or that are particular to the place from which parents emigrated.

In December 2007 Canadian news media were filled with accounts of the death of a Mississauga Muslim teenager, Aqsa Parvez. The young woman's father and brother were eventually convicted of second-degree murder. In newspaper reports her friends said Aqsa enjoyed dancing, photography, and fashion. She had been unwilling to conform to family edicts about wearing the hijab, or headscarf, and had been changing into western-style dress en route to school. The sixteen-year-old was estranged from her strict family and was living with a friend at the time she was killed; she had returned home to retrieve some belongings. Much of the debate in the press was about the adaptation of Islam in the West, or about conflicts between cultural and religious values, or about the customs held by immigrant parents – Aqsa's parents were from Pakistan – colliding with those of their Canadian-born children. Because older brothers were reported to be involved in enforcing their father's dress code, speculation arose early on that this might be a case of an "honour killing" resulting from the patriarchy allegedly intrinsic to some religious traditions. Imams explained at various press conferences that whether a young woman wears the hijab or not should be her decision. In June 2010 Aqsa's father and brother pleaded guilty to second-degree murder.

The issue involved here was initially explained more in terms of intergenerational domestic violence, a matter of parenting and child abuse, than of religious conflict (see El Akkad and Wallace 2007). Anver N. Emon, a professor of Islamic law at the University of Toronto, poses the following question to people who have to come to Canada from traditional communities: "Is it realistic to think that we can leave our homes, come to a new country and not expect changes in the way we and our children construct our identity?" (2007). The question he asks of Canadians in general is: "How might we create a climate where newcomers can openly participate in our society and culture with limited angst, while we celebrate together in what all of us bring to our shores?" While Emon identifies injunctions in "the historical Islamic tradition ... that require a woman after the age of majority to cover herself" with some kind of veil, he says that his research has not located "any punitive sanction against a woman who chooses not to veil that could even remotely explain Mr. Parvez's alleged actions" (ibid.).

There is, to be sure, a perennial aspect to disputes that arise from a conflict between parental values and norms and teenagers' wishes to conform to the subculture of their peer group. These conflicts have for a long time been played out in disagreements about dating, curfews, dress, and the use of drugs and alcohol. Today such clashes are if anything even more heightened, because the norms of teenage social networks play a greater part in shaping patterns of behaviour. Frequently in families with two parents, both work outside the home, increasing the time teens spend without the direct influence of a parent. Heavy use of cell phones and computers increases the time spent in communication with peers. Among the children of immigrant parents the addition of disparities from the prevailing milieu of the host culture in religion, mores, and language raises the stakes, making such clashes even more difficult for both sides to negotiate or resolve.

An honour killing has been thought to occur in another case too, even more puzzling and shocking, this time within Kingston's city limits. Three family members – a married couple, Mohammed and Tooba Shafia, and their eighteen-year-old son, Hamed – were accused of the murders in June 2009 of four women and girls whose bodies were found in a submerged car in the Rideau Canal. Three of the victims were the Shafias' teenaged daughters, while the fourth was the first wife of Mohammed Shafia. The alleged perpetrators and the slain women and children were all Muslims from the Montreal area who had originally lived in Afghanistan before moving to Montreal from Dubai several years ago. The murders took place while the group was travelling in two cars and passing through Kingston en route to their shared home in Montreal. There were some reports from family members living in Europe that "honour" may have been involved in these killings too. Though little evidence is available because of publication bans as the case goes to trial, the family had reportedly felt disgraced by the relationships of their eldest daughter. Tragically, these kinds of events illustrate the scrutiny that Islam in Canada is subject to, and the assumptions that are made about the role of religion in cases where other, more proximate, reasons are worth examining too.

BAHÁ'Í FAITH IN KINGSTON

As is the case with the other four faith communities considered here, the Bahá'í faith has its roots outside the western world, as well as being, at least in part and in its origins, a religion of immigrants. It also has a unique relation to Islam. A monotheistic religion, it was founded in Persia in the mid-nineteenth century by Bahá'u'lláh (1817–92), understood by Bahá'ís as the culmination of God's progressive revelation and the most recent in a line of messengers that include Abraham, Krishna, Zoroaster, Moses, Buddha, Jesus, and Muhammad (Bahá'í Faith). The Bahá'í faith is still regarded in Iran, where it is the largest religious minority, as a heretical sect of Islam. Subject to persecution in many predominantly Muslim countries, Bahá'ís consider their faith as "the youngest of the world's independent religions," to quote from their local website (Kingston Bahá'ís). The United Nations has repeatedly expressed concerns about human rights in Iran, and in March 2009 the Canadian Parliament passed an all-party resolution condemning the persecution of Bahá'ís in Iran (Bahá'í World News Service). Bahá'ís resist vigorously the characterization of their religion as a syncretic blend of earlier religious traditions, or as a continuing offshoot of Shi'a Islam, pointing out the parallel problems in identifying Christianity, two thousand years after its beginnings, as a sect of Judaism.

While India has the largest number of Bahá'ís (more than two million), Canada is one of many countries throughout the world where Bahá'ís live. They numbered 14,730 in the 1991 Census and reached 18,020 in 2001, an increase of more than 20 per cent. Lynne Sitar, the local contact person, says that there were Bahá'ís in Kingston from the 1940s (interview, 10 March 2004). Especially in the decade of World War II, this missionizing movement, whose teachings and background would be considered unusual in Canada, was not well received. Will Van den Hoonaard comments in his book on the history of Bahá'ís in Canada that "between 1898 and 1948, some 555 Bahá'ís lived in eighty-four locales across Canada." Because in most of these places they lacked any visible structures, Bahá'í teaching had little impact on Canadian society (1996, 292). The Kingston Assembly was formed in 1953 and incorporated in 1973 when the local Bahá'í community had become large enough to elect the requisite nine members. Currently more than sixty Bahá'ís live in Kingston, with an attendance of about thirty when they meet, usually in one another's homes. Although worldwide there are seven major Bahá'í Houses of Worship, in places the size of Kingston, Bahá'ís generally follow the practice of meeting in members' homes, in rented places, or in local centres.

The numbers in Kingston fluctuate, according to Sitar, as "Bahá'ís tend to be pretty mobile," especially because they "travel a lot to different communities to help out." In the local group are people from Australia, Spain, and Africa. Prayers are held in various languages – some members speak Persian; some are French-speaking. Many are here only for a brief time while they are students at Queen's University. Bahá'í students at Queen's attest to the importance for them of finding and relating to local Bahá'ís while at university. (See chapter 9 for the Queen's branch of the Campus Association for Bahá'í Studies). Lynne Sitar is listed on the website of the Queen's University International Centre, under the heading "Religious and Spiritual Support," as one of nine contact people on the University's Interfaith Council and to aid students in "Finding people who practise your religion." (See Queen's University International Centre; on the Interfaith Council, see also chapter 9.)

Bahá'ís are highly visible at interfaith events. As their website explains, because religion is one, with all faiths originating from the same divine source, "the worldwide Bahá'í community has, since its earliest days, articulated in interfaith activities religion's essential unity, thereby working to promote harmony among the world's faiths and their followers" (Bahá'í Faith). For example, when an interfaith service was held at St Andrew's Presbyterian Church in 1991 to mark the 150th anniversary of Queen's University, Bahá'ís were among the seven groups reading prayers. The others were from Native, Hindu, Islamic, Sikh, Jewish, and Christian traditions (*Whig-Standard*, 17 October 1991). Bahá'ís also tend to be represented on committees organized to promote diversity, or where there is representation from various faith traditions, and at gatherings having participants from different religions. These activities fit with their stated aims: "Canadian Bahá'ís, in large cities and small towns, and from every conceivable background are dedicated to the creation of a worldwide society built on principles of justice and unity, characterized by the elimination of racial and religious prejudice, and the equality of women and men – where diversity is celebrated and the arts, sciences and a love of learning is encouraged" (Bahá'í Community of Canada). Central to Bahá'í teachings are the principles of the unity of God, the unity of religion, and the unity of humankind. In that light, it is hardly surprising that a longstanding member of the Kingston Bahá'ís, a retired management consultant from Ottawa, Jim Atack, has served as president of the Kingston Area Race Relations Association (*Whig-Standard*, 26 May 2005, 15 December 2003).

Many of the more progressive Bahá'í tenets, as developed in Canada and the West, according to Van Den Hoonaard, were formed within the cradle of liberal Protestantism (1996). These principles fit well within the context of modern western democracies: the equality of men and women, the celebration of diversity and multiculturalism, the elimination of prejudice, the emphasis on peace, and the promotion of science and higher education. Many of these positions that became central to Bahá'ís enabled the spread of the faith in the West because the original sacred texts had not been translated from Persian and Arabic. On the other hand, the Bahá'í tradition also enjoins upon followers quite strict codes and obligations such as obligatory daily prayer, a nineteen-day fast in March, the prohibition of alcohol and illicit drugs, strictures against homosexuality and premarital sex, the shunning of excommunicated members, and a ban against Bahá'ís joining political parties.

Press reports and scholarly articles have from time to time dealt with the difficulties of more liberal Bahá'ís who have found what they claim to be an increasingly conservative Bahá'í leadership to be too restrictive of their individual freedom and expression. Ira Rifkin reported one such debate on the Religion News Service in February 1997 in an article, "Critics Chafe at Bahá'í Conservatism" (qtd in McGlinn 2010), outlining how some members of what they understood to be a liberal faith were objecting to an increasing authoritarian leadership attempting to return the tradition to greater orthodoxy. Another essay asked why controls on the behaviour and speech of members should have increased at the same time that the Bahá'í faith wanted to portray itself as liberal (Cole 1998). Todd Lawson, a Bahá'í and Islamic specialist who is a professor at the University of Toronto, defends the Bahá'í position in terms of a need for consensus. He maintains that the Bahá'í stance – namely, that where there is no unanimity, the majority rules – does not amount to "totalitarianism." Lawson says, "The Bahá'í faith posits a non-confrontation version of problem solving. My view is if you opt out of that mode, that's your prerogative. But there are others who take a longer view of things ... Bahá'í ideals are extremely demanding" (Bahá'í Library Online; link expired).

The Bahá'í religion could be examined from a number of perspectives, though perhaps only partially from any single one. Given its relatively recent beginnings approximately 150 years ago, it could be seen as a New Religious Movement (NRM). Indeed, it shares some of the features common among NRMs, such as placing relatively high demands on its followers. It might also be examined as a minority religion similar to other alternative traditions chosen by women (see chap. 8). Among Bahá'í members women tend to predominate, their numbers in Canada at times approaching 75 per cent (Van den Hoonaard 1996). Bahá'ís also actively seek to advance their faith, though not in the door-to-door manner characteristic of Mormons and Jehovah's Witnesses. Instead, in order to make themselves known, Bahá'ís favour involvement in public platforms related to social concerns of peace and justice, or in the visible settings that interfaith gatherings provide. For instance, a representative from the Kingston Bahá'í group – along with spokespersons from three or four other traditions – was part of a panel on religions and health care presented at Hotel Dieu Hospital. Despite the relatively small numbers of Bahá'ís in Canada, they achieve by these means a relatively high degree of public recognition. Representatives make themselves available to speak in courses in Religious Studies at Queen's University. The department also received a request from a Bahá'í delegation to teach a course dedicated to Bahá'í studies, a request that was difficult to accommodate given the size of the department and considering the relative paucity of academic attention afforded to the Bahá'í faith alongside other religions.

Finally, from some perspectives at least, the Bahá'í religion appears to be worthy of inclusion together with other instances of liberal religion (see chap. 6). Their emphasis on the unity of humankind and of all religions, combined with their focus on promoting peace and combating prejudice, may seem to align Bahá'ís with Unitarians and Quakers. Yet their position on homosexuality, their restrictions on political involvement, and the demands placed on members for annual fasting and obligatory daily prayer appear to be more comparable to the requirements placed on individual followers by more conservative faith traditions. Similar to that of some Christian evangelical or Catholic students, the reaction to the social environment of the university displayed by Bahá'ís at Queen's (see chap. 9) reflects their wish to withdraw from a milieu viewed as hostile to the practice of their faith. Regardless of their historic – and perhaps continuing – relation to Islam, the Bahá'í faith has been treated here in accordance with their desire to be seen as an independent religion. Because of its origins outside European – or what might be called "Judaeo-Christian" – culture, the Bahá'í tradition is recognized here as adding to the extrinsic diversity of religions in Kingston.

HINDUS IN KINGSTON

Hindus in Kingston present a case somewhat parallel to that of Muslims in the city: their small numbers require that sectarian distinctions be put aside for the sake of maintaining their community. Kamala Narayanan estimated that of perhaps 150 families in Kingston with origins in India, about two-thirds would be Hindu (interview, 11 July 2005). The 2001 Census reports 460 Hindus in the greater Kingston area. The remaining non-Hindu Indian families might include as many as thirty or forty families of Christians from Kerala. In addition, Narayanan said that some of the Indians in Kingston were Muslims or Sikhs – numbering together about 125 – and a few might be Parsis. All these groups were regarded as part of the Indian community: "We feel very proud about the fact that we have so many different religions in the country like in India." Some of Kingston's Hindus are from countries other than India, such as Burma, Pakistan, Bangladesh, Guyana, Fiji, and Sri Lanka.

Kamala Narayanan has been a member of the local association of Indians since she began to work in the Queen's University library in 1979. For much of her time in Kingston she has been a member of the Queen's Interfaith

Council operating from the Chaplain's Office (see chap. 9), and the informal contact person for students from India arriving at the university. Narayanan has been generous in being available to come and speak to classes in religious studies about Hinduism. The Gitanjali group, as the local Indian association informally calls itself, was formed in the mid-1970s: "It started off as just a few people gathering, getting a picture of one of the deities," she says, "meeting in one person's house." For a time the group was able to book a room free of charge at St Lawrence College, an arrangement that had advantages because some of those interested in attending meetings might be reluctant to go to someone's home and intrude upon their private space.

Asked what image was used at their gatherings, Narayanan said it did not really matter because any symbol or picture resembling one of the Hindu deities would be "enough to start any kind of group relating to the Hindu faith, so it doesn't have to be any particular deity at all." Having a temple devoted to a particular deity, she continued, could only happen in India. She explained, "We are not going to be like in India where you could say, 'Okay, I belong to a certain kind of community and I go to this temple and this is my temple, or this is my temple that my family was associated with and my ancestors were associated with. And I only go here and I won't attend any other temple.'" Asked about the possibility of having a temple for Hindus in Kingston, she replied that such a measure would create divisions and factions, especially once a leader was brought in who might have specific ideas about deities and worship practices not widely shared in Kingston. Meanwhile, Hindus in Kingston wanting specific rites travel to Toronto to visit a temple there or bring in a priest from elsewhere for special occasions (interview, 11 July 2005).

The present practice of meeting informally in people's homes has been in place amongst Kingston's Hindus for several decades, requiring flexibility and adaptation. In India Vaishnavas would not normally have anything to do with another sect, such as Saivites, that did not have Vishnu as its main deity. Narayanan pointed out that "in India they could do that, but it's impossible to practise that same thing over here." As another example, some of the Hindu families in Kingston who are used to silent meditation might disagree with the singing of hymns when the group meets. Yet part of the customary devotions of the majority includes the singing of a hymn: "And when we sing it, we are singing it all together and it's kind of loud, with all those bells and everything, because we are actually pretending that we are waking up the deities. We are invoking their presence into us" (personal interview, 11 July 2005). Maintaining the unity of the religious group demands that minorities within it do not insist on their own theologies nor on their preferences in worship.

Narayanan also explained that while some families in Kingston follow a particular guru located elsewhere, there is no single figure in a position of authority for all of the Hindus in Kingston. She mentioned that one local couple might go to California to consult their guru who was visiting there from India. Within Kingston there are other smaller groups who follow a particular guru. One of these, the Sai Baba group, is dealt with later in this chapter; another, comprised of followers of Sri Chinmoy, is considered in chapter 8. When needed, priests are brought to Kingston, usually from Toronto, for special occasions. But as Narayanan pointed out, "the priests are very busy, and sometimes you have to book them up to a year in advance for a wedding." Although a priest might come for a particular emergency, "If we needed a priest for a funeral, sometimes they aren't available." On occasion local Hindus might arrange for a priest to perform a ceremony when they buy a new house or car or open a business. There are also those, she explained, "who believe that the priest is the medium to reach to God."

In general the picture Narayanan conveyed in answer to specific and sometimes detailed questions from interviewer Lisa Pim, herself knowledgeable about Hinduism, involved distinguishing between what might occur in India and what was possible in Kingston. When Pim asked about Kali and Durga, or about a Ganesh temple, or about the Bhakti movement or International Krishna Consciousness, Narayanan would describe the distinctions between Hindus from Bengal or Bangladesh, or differentiate Arya Sammaj from the Brahma Sammaj, or elaborate on how Shiva's son, Kartikeya, is revered in the south of India. In general, though, the story she conveyed of Hindus in Kingston – evident as well among Muslims – underscored the need for adaptation and flexibility. She mentioned how the names of the sacred rivers of India, especially the Ganges, were altered in Canada with references in hymns to, for example, Lake Ontario, even though of course it appears nowhere in Hindu mythology. As she explained, Hindus in Canada "have the flexibility of changing" such references "because it doesn't make sense to talk all the time only about where we came from, which is India." She added, "You have to think about the future," because few Indians in Canada – and especially not their children – would be going back to India to live.

Religions of course are changed and modified in various contexts, especially as practitioners move from one country where their faith might be shared by the majority to another where it is a minority tradition. Kingston's Hindus, part of a larger local community of people of Indian background, exhibit the need to compromise, to put aside unessential differences for the sake of the greater good, and to be willing to adapt to local exigencies. The adaptation of Hindus to life in Canada, emphasizing their diversity and flexibility, is well described by authors Sikata Banerjee and Harold Coward (2005, 30–51).

SRI SATHYA SAI BABA CENTRE OF KINGSTON

Kingston's Sri Sathya Sai Baba Centre is one of twelve hundred such centres around the world that follow the teachings of the Indian guru Bhagavan Sri Sathya Sai Baba, born in South India in 1926. His teachings, fundamentally Hindu in nature, affirm that "all human beings are inherently divine" and that "all religions are facets of the same Truth." The emphasis of Sai Baba on a basic unity is evident in four principles: "There is only one religion, the religion of Love. There is only one language; the language of the Heart. There is only one race; the race of Humanity. There is only one God, and He is Omnipresent" (Sri Sathya Sai Baba Organization in Canada). Each Sai Centre houses a library of resources and provides a meeting place for devotees of Sai Baba.

The Sai Baba Centre in Kington began in the early 1980s. The president, Rekha Vyas, together with long-time member Anju Acharya, both of them women, was interviewed by Lisa Pim (7 December 2005). In keeping with the Sai organization's principles of gender equality, Vyas succeeded three previous leaders, all of them male. The president does not function as a spiritual guide, but holds responsibility for facilitating the group. Vyas described the other governance positions in the centre, including "an education coordinator" and "the spiritual coordinator who will run the study circles." The membership of the centre in Kingston has grown slowly in the last few decades with increased immigration from India and other places where Sai Baba worship is more common. Advertisement must be by word of mouth alone, especially since proselytizing is forbidden. The followers of Sai Baba in Kingston have always worshipped in people's homes, in part because their numbers are small – perhaps thirty-five to forty members. They are not planning to develop a separate, permanent meeting place. People often travel to Ottawa, where there is a developed centre, or to Toronto.

The ethnicity of the members of the Sai Baba group is predominantly Sri Lankan and Indian. Though they speak English, many of the prayers are in Sanskrit and Hindi. The age groups range widely, from children, to teens, to adults of all ages including seniors. Those attending the meetings are generally women, many of them housewives who wear traditional clothing such as the sari. A children's meeting time is scheduled during the week, as well as a youth group for teens, a study group, and the weekly meetings when the *bhajans*, or the devotional songs by which the worshipper feels closer to the divine, are sung. Members also participate in charity work, giving food baskets to several institutions.

A Queen's University student visitor described how at the meeting people went barefoot on a floor covered with white cloths. A small altar table displayed a picture of Sai Baba, with such offerings as apples and bread. After the service people ate these offerings and also stayed to chat and have tea. The highly participatory service was "very lively," with different people taking turns singing the bhajans. No particular bhajans were scheduled to be sung; rather, a number was displayed to show the person who chose next from among the thousands of bhajans possible. Though the bhajans are all found in a book, those present sang from memory. Once everyone was seated on the floor, the singing began without introduction. The first song, about Ganesh, was sung by a boy about eight or nine. The next songs featured Hindu gods, though some were addressed to Sai Baba alone. The rhythmic, lyrical, and loudly sung bhajans were accompanied with clapping and a few people playing instruments such as the tambourine. The hour of singing was followed by a period of about fifteen minutes of silent meditation, partly guided by the leader. Then the president read for about fifteen minutes from a book about the nature of life and existence. After the service, once people got Indian sweets and chai tea from the kitchen, they continued informally in conversation for about another forty-five minutes.

Both of the interviewees, Vyas and Acharya, agreed that Sai Baba "draws you to him" (interview, 7 December 2005). One may subscribe to any other religion and also follow Sai Baba, since "all religions are one, all gods are one." As well, a person of any class, region, or ethnicity may pray to Sai Baba, an accessibility augmented by the fact that donations are never asked for. As Vyas notes, "we even have people in their twenties – people that are in Queen's University that come and attend the bhajan." The presence of more women than men is explained by the fact that men "believe but they don't necessarily have the time." Neither Acharya nor Vyas grew up in the Sai Baba faith but rather came to it later during times of crisis in their lives.

Acharya and Vyas also spent some time discussing Sai Baba as leader and Sathya Sai Baba's previous incarnation as Shirdi Sai Baba. Though he has never been outside of India, Sai Baba's role is similar to that of the guru Sri Chinmoy: both leaders have miracles and exceptional powers attributed to them. Much of the discussion with Acharya and Vyas about Sai Baba paralleled what Paramita Jarvis and Janet Faubert said of Sri Chinmoy (see chap. 8). All four women depict their spiritual leader as childlike, expressing a very personal, intimate relationship with him, explaining their experience as one of being "drawn" to him.

The Sai Baba group's relationship to the Kingston community illustrates how aspects of the overall mission of Sai Baba followers to help or feed people continue locally, for example, in making up Christmas baskets for patients in psychiatric units. In this vein, Acharya and Vyas discussed the work of the larger Sai Baba organization, pointing out the existence of a free hospital in India. For the Kingston community, the Sai Baba group has a youth group and "a bahbi class which is mainly for children, and that runs pretty much like a schooling system." The character of the Sai Baba group derives from the larger organization: "We don't try to denounce anybody. I think that appeals to me the most," Acharya explains, again emphasizing the inclusive nature of the group in accepting all religious paths. When asked about conflict resolution, Vyas says, "We have never come across a dispute as such. We discuss things as a group. And we ask for [Sai Baba's] guidance." Acharya also points out that "there are very strict guidelines," so that disputes do not arise. Indeed, most details of the organization are run by the central authority of the Sai Baba International Organization.

Asked whether Kingston is supportive of the Sai Baba group, Acharya made the interesting comment, as if to use the occasion to declare the group's independence in the local context, that "we don't need their support as such." The use of English is obviously one example of an adaptation to the Canadian scene. While specific religious aspects of Kingston were not discussed, Acharya did note that "we are very blessed because we have a very small town" where all the people can attend the meetings with ease. In bigger cities, she pointed out, "everyone can't go and accommodate all people and stuff." Asked about the future of Sathya Sai Baba, Vyas thinks that "it will just grow" all over the world.

KINGSTON SIKH CULTURAL ASSOCIATION

According to the 2001 Census, Sikhs are the fifteenth largest religious group in Canada, with total numbers of 278,000. The Sikh population worldwide is estimated at twenty million people, almost all of them with ties to the Punjab in India. That affinity of a faith tradition and a particular place strongly links religion and ethnicity within Sikhism (see Mahmood 2005, 52–68). The 2001 Census put the number of Sikhs in Kingston at 130, a number that, as we shall see, far exceeds the estimate that the community itself gives of its size.

The Kingston Sikh Cultural Association offers an instance of one Kingston religious organization with roots in another country that has not grown but rather has declined as a result of shifts in the local population. Avtar Gahir, the leader of the association, began the interview with RDK researcher Joe Green by describing their history (interview, 29 November 2006). While the community may date back over forty years, Gahir explained that Kingston Sikhs began meeting formally around 1978 when an older couple was visiting their son who was a doctor. The couple taught Sikh worship to some others. There were about thirty Sikh families in Kingston then: "Most of them, I think, were in the taxi driver business, and some of them were doctors, professors at the university and so on." Initially the members met in people's homes, although soon the group grew too large and moved to the cafeteria at St Lawrence College, despite the hard floors that made their worship a bit uncomfortable. Then, following a decrease in the number of Sikhs in Kingston approximately twenty years ago and eventually to its present size of about ten families today, members began meeting in their houses again. Gahir explained that from the beginning the Sikh Association had been host to Muslim and Hindu families from India as well as Sikhs. Though Sikhs are generally known for their openness and hospitality, at its beginnings, more than five hundred years ago, Sikhism distinguished itself from Hinduism and Islam, especially in having no priesthood and by abolishing such requirements as pilgrimages or fasting.

The community of Sikhs in Kingston includes only two men who are baptized, or *khalsa*, an order created in 1699. Khalsa Sikhs are individuals who have been initiated according to a special ceremony and who wear the "Five Ks:" *kesh* or uncut hair for men, protected by a turban; the *kanga* or wooden comb; the *kaccha* or specially designed underwear; the *kara* or iron bracelet; and the *kirpan* or strapped sword. A Sikh, though, is anyone – even without having been baptized – who embarks on the Sikh path of learning and adheres to the code of conduct (see Sikhism). Khalsa Sikhs, termed by Gahir "complete Sikhs," are those who have felt ready to make their declaration to live their lives to the full extent of Sikh teaching as decreed by the tenth guru.

Gahir went on to describe how people's homes are transformed for worship ceremonies, which occur on a monthly basis. They rotate among three or four different houses, adapting each space as necessary to make it into a *gurdwara*, a Sikh temple. The room used for Sikh worship must be dedicated to the holy text, elevated above everything else. The Sikh scripture, the Guru Granth Sahib, became the leading spiritual guide for the Sikh religion after the death of the tenth living guru, Gobind Singh, who died in 1708. In effect, then, the Sikh sacred scripture became the eleventh and final guru, succeeding the line of authority established by the ten early Sikh gurus who were human beings. It is customary for Sikhs to refer to their scripture as "the guru." As Gahir put it, "In our believing this is our living guru, our teacher. We treat the book as a human being." Gahir also explained the religio-historical significance in the worship space of having a canopy and fly swatter: "Considering that the Guru Granth Sahib is a living guru for us, we do not want any debris to fall or insects or whatever to fall and then be killed when we close the book." He noted too the requirement to cover the floor with white sheets – shoes are removed – and that all entering the room cover their heads.

As well, Gahir discussed the musical aspect of worship and the importance of hymns, usually accompanied by a harmonium and tabla – though the local group lacks a tabla player. He explained that the couple who originated the group had played both instruments between them, but their departure left local Sikhs without a tabla player. Gahir then bought a keyboard with a rhythm section to accompany their hymns, but he remarked, with a laugh, "If you find us a new tabla player, he will be most welcome to come and join us. It really doesn't matter what instrument you play, you know, the emphasis is less on the music and more on what is being sung – the meaning of what the hymns are about." He also stressed that the hymns are sung in their original language, though the accompanying explanation could be in English: "If I want to explain the meaning of the hymn, I will explain it in whatever language I want to. But when it is sung in the gurdwara, then it is what the gurus wrote." However, when Joe Green commented that at a service he attended one of the Hindu women present also sang a hymn, then Gahir explained it was permitted in such a case that "she would sing something that someone has written in praise of the god." This practice seems to be a local accommodation for he added that "we do not object to that, although strictly in other gurdwaras there is a protocol that you only sing in the temple what the gurus wrote or the contemporaries wrote."

In terms of advertising their gatherings, Gahir reflected, "We thought at one time that we would advertise on Channel 13, the Kingston community channel ... but we have felt that in our case that if a ceremony is held in my house, people who know me, they will come." As a result, word-of-mouth is the only means of advertising, because outsiders to the community, likely to be deterred by the lack of a public place of worship, would not respond to advertisements in any event.

Gahir emphasized the community's small size and explained the resulting crossover between the Kingston Sikhs and Hindus: "Normally we find that, especially when we are celebrating a particular day like Baisakhi, or some other popular days like that, a lot of the Hindu families also come and join us." He says that some Hindus attend regularly: "There have been occasions when we have had a gathering and there are more Hindu families than Sikh families." Sikhs are also invited to local Hindu events. Punjabi and English are the primary languages employed in worship, and English translations have recently been used in an attempt to draw younger members of the community to worship. Hymns are all sung in their original language, however. There is low participation by children as well as by students, who have their own weekly meetings led by one of the community members. Gahir explained the sex ratio: "There are more women, more females to males. And the females generally come basically because they are the ones who have prepared the food." He also mentioned that the community members are fairly affluent.

Gahir then went on to discuss the governance of the group, which appears to be informal. He says, "Although we were saying when we signed the paper that I was the leader, I think I only say I am the leader because, at the moment, I conduct the ceremony from beginning to end." He explained how he assumed this leadership role twelve years previously and points out that when leadership changes, it does not alter worship at all. His particular focus is attempting to get Sikh children more involved in the community. Leadership positions are recommended based on the needs of the community – there is no official election process. When asked about disputes and their resolutions, Gahir said, "I don't know if we have ever had a dispute. I think that if our community was three times as large, we probably would have had a dispute." He elaborated, explaining that people are willing to compromise: "Because the community is so small everybody knows that if something goes wrong the whole thing will fall apart and we do not want it to fall apart." However, technically, "What the gurus said was that, if a dispute of that kind arises, then five khalsas should discuss it and make a ruling. Then everybody abides by it."

In terms of the Sikh relationship with the broader Kingston community, Gahir strongly emphasized interfaith dialogue and charitable donations. On interfaith events, he said, "If there is a forum where various religious people are getting together to air their views, I have my name in various circles." He highlighted several interfaith events and services, observing – in accordance with Sikh views – that "we are all praying to the same God – it's, you know, the parts may be different." Such gatherings demonstrate that "what we are doing is not unique." The Sikh community has donated money to many causes including disaster relief – the flooding of the Red River in Manitoba, the 2004 tsunami, and Kingston's 1998 ice storm – as well as the local food bank, highlighting the importance of giving, even from this small Kingston group. In this vein, Gahir discussed the importance of sharing food in the Sikh tradition and the significance of the *langar* meal: "This has come all the way from the gurus, that is why every ceremony we have, there is always a meal that is served. Any gurdwara – Toronto, Montreal, especially the large centres – you can go any time and ask for a meal. They will not ask you who you are, what you believe in, why you are here, or anything like that. We feel that this is what comes in our teachings."

Gahir emphasized as well Sikh solidarity with other Indians in terms of multicultural or national events, not wishing to assert a separate Sikh nationality: "Although when we talk religiously we talk of the Gurus, we talk of the Shivas, we talk of the hymn singing, we are from a certain section of the subcontinent. But when it is a national problem we are no different from the Hindus or the Muslims or the Parsis." Nevertheless, the 1984 attack on the Golden Temple at Amritsar, the most holy place for Sikhs, conducted by the Indian military to remove Sikh separatists, was a significant event for the local Sikh community. Gahir also mentioned an interfaith prayer session held in response to the worst act of terrorism in Canadian history, the bombing of an Air India flight in 1985 by Sikh terrorists in which 329 people died, 280 of them Canadians. When asked about the defining characteristic of the local Sikh community, Gahir emphasized the social bonds between members, suggesting, "I think that they feel that getting together like that they are – they feel as if they are in the homeland."

Gahir spoke favourably of Kingston to interviewer Joe Green, hinting at the fact that minority religious groups can be heard and made visible in the small city. The size of the city also allows many Sikhs to participate in meetings because they do not have far to travel. While he suggested that the Sikhs have not been affected by other religious groups in the city, Gahir spent much time discussing the value of interfaith services. However, he also said, "I don't think that gathering of various religious leaders or people should affect other religions. I think that the opportunity is that you discover things. What other religious groups are doing." Gahir described Kingston as a microcosm of Canadian diversity.

One thread running throughout this interview was the configuration of religion and ethnicity for the local Sikh community. Indian ethnicity seems to be the primary means of self-identification and communal organization in Kingston, and the boundaries between the Sikh and Hindu communities appear to be fluid. One significant marker of this is the inclusion into Sikh worship of non-traditional hymns contributed by Hindu women. While such hymns are not typically suitable in gurdwaras, they are nevertheless an acceptable part of Sikh worship in Kingston. At the same time, however, Gahir emphasized the uniform nature of the Sikh tradition around the world as one unaffected by local cultures. The tie to Indian cultural and ethnic identity is therefore asserted to be quite strong. This connection between religion and ethnicity is further solidified by the name of the group itself, Kingston Sikh Cultural Association. Not just the inclusion of "cultural" in the group's title but the way they worship helps them feel tied to "the homeland."

UNITY AMIDST DIVERSITY

All of the groups examined in this chapter – Muslims, Hindus, Sai Baba followers, Sikhs, and Bahá'ís – provide examples of the full array of diversity, both within the religious landscape of Kingston and internally among their own numbers. That is, they exemplify both extrinsic and intrinsic religious diversity. They are all faith traditions whose growth in Canada – though they may have been present here for a longer time – has especially flourished in the past few decades and brought each one to greater prominence. None of them would have been very visible on Kingston's religious scene prior to the 1960s. Though Sikhs and Hindus have a history in Canada that goes back well over a century, the increase in their numbers and their national presence has been dramatic in the last few generations. Muslims too, not only nationally but in Kingston, have become a major force in Canadian religion in the last two decades and, for better or worse, have received increased attention in the first few years of the new millennium after 9/11.

Kingston's religious diversity through most of the first century after Confederation was evident almost exclusively in the plethora of Christian denominations and sects in the city – always with the dominance of the Big Three or the Big Five Christian denominations among them, and with the addition primarily of one or two hundred families of Jews. Diversification among Kingston's religions in those early years was a matter of theological distinctions now long since become mostly irrelevant, even among their adherents. There were, to be sure, some ethnic and national differences evident among, say, Irish Catholics or Scottish Presbyterians – or within Presbyterians between the Scots and Irish. Over time, though, such distinctions dwindled in importance. Diversity within Christianity emerged again in earnest after World War II with new immigrants arriving in Canada from Europe. (See chapter 5, on ethnic Christianity.)

The five religious traditions examined here all represent the faith communities of immigrants to Canada that originated in countries that lie elsewhere than in Europe. Their religions are other than Christianity or Judaism. In size these groups range from almost one thousand members down to only thirty or forty. In terms of antiquity, Islam and Sikhism are relatively old monotheisms, more than five hundred years old. Hinduism's history extends back even further. On the other hand, the Sai Baba group – and the Bahá'í faith too – might be described as New Religious Movements, even granting the difficulty of such terminology for Sai Baba because of its ancient roots within Hinduism. Sai Baba and the Bahá'í faith, like other such movements as Sri Chinmoy or Krishna Consciousness, represent a trend evident for several decades, of religious options with origins in the east now available to westerners.

In their degree of openness to one another, and to the larger community of Kingston, all five faith traditions have made impressive contributions toward high standards of citizenship and social integration. Each has pitched in on causes ranging from the local to the national and the international. They have contributed to food banks and hospitals, and to relief for victims of natural disasters. As part of interfaith gatherings, to which they have enthusiastically contributed, they have wondered whether there is a mechanism within religions that can help to overcome poverty. They have also opened their doors of their places of worship – even when those are in their homes – in gestures of hospitality and acceptance and mutual understanding. They have been anxious to be received and accepted by their neighbours, usually with no motive to thereby augment their own numbers.

Perhaps what is most unusual, especially for those whose view of religions might have been soured by discordant divisions, is the degree to which these groups help one another out and contribute to the flourishing of one another. To step back and fully appreciate the extent and manner of this cooperation, one inevitably contrasts the theological and historical distinctions – and overt name-calling and competition – so often evident among Christians. A Roman Catholic woman cannot receive the Eucharist alongside her Protestant husband. Christians frequently emphasize their differences from other Christians or are unable to make common cause. Christian clergy in Kingston have met together only infrequently as part of the same ministerial association. Among the groups examined in this chapter we heard of occasions when at the local Sikh gurdwara there are sometimes more Hindu than Sikh families present. A Sikh might say, "No matter how you pray or what you do, we are all praying to the same God," or might declare – in terms that almost any devotee of any faith ought to assent to – that sharing what one has is at the heart of religion. Here ecumenicity and inter-religious practice is a lived reality.

Perhaps as a result of their small numbers, the members of these five communities of faith appreciate what religions have in common and stress that commonality. Because they cannot afford internal dissensions that would split and divide their small communities, they find ways to overcome differences and focus on essentials. Moreover, as people whose religious belief and practice is often strange in the eyes of their new neighbours, they have made efforts to understand and to be understood. They achieve the acceptance they enjoy among others in the community by first demonstrating their acceptance and understanding of one another, both their co-religionists and those with whom they share ethnicity, if not religion.

The practice of their religious traditions shows adaptation and accommodation. They change the language of their hymns and liturgies to English for the benefit of their own young people whose first language is English. They do this also in order that outsiders might understand them. They are willing sometimes to surrender some of the particulars of their own practice so that others might worship with them. Sometimes they even alter the very symbols of their religion to adapt them to the Canadian setting. In all of this it is interesting that among the Muslims, Sikhs, Hindus, Sai Baba followers, and Bahá'ís, it seems that people are brought together in their religious practice and in their liturgies. On the theological or theoretical level there would be much to divide them, if they were to discuss it. In the mid-1990s, while living in Japan for five months, I heard a lecture given by the abbot of a Zen temple in western Kyoto. He spoke of how a group of monks from the temple had travelled to Italy to share their experience of meditation with a group of Benedictines, so that these Buddhists and Roman Catholics could learn from each other. His comment was that inter-religious practice was more effective in bringing people together than inter-religious dialogue.

8 Women's Roles in Religions: Mainline Denominations and Alternative Spiritualities

MAINSTREAM TRADITIONS AND WOMEN

The changing roles of women in various aspects of society, especially over the past generation, have also made their impact felt on religion. Both popular and academic research has uncovered the oft-neglected involvement – and, regrettably, the exclusion too – of women in religious groups and communities throughout the past and, in some quarters at least, continuing into the present. In terms of providing roles for women, religions have more often been conservative than revolutionary. As former American President Jimmy Carter, speaking at the Parliament of the World's Religions held in Melbourne, Australia, in December 2009, said, "It is ironic that women are now welcomed into all major professions and other positions of authority, but are branded as inferior and deprived of the equal right to serve God in positions of religious leadership. The plight of abused women is made more acceptable by the mandated subservience of women by religious leaders" (Carter 2009). While new venues and possibilities for women to practise their religion and to exercise roles in leadership have been emerging, in Kingston as elsewhere, the most visible presence of women in most faith communities continues to be in their roles as supporters and attendees. Typically, an interview with the religious leader of a local congregation takes place with a male representative. Except for several female United Church clergy and a few others, by far the majority of the interviews conducted for this project were with male religious leaders.

As those doing field research in faith communities have suggested, to discover what is going on behind the scenes, one has to get into the "kitchens" of religious traditions and talk to the women, not just as a way of hearing women's voices but of uncovering otherwise hidden aspects of the community. Fortunately for this project, the series of interviews conducted for the

Cogeco television series *Profiles: People of Faith* focused more on the individual religious journeys of men and women in Kingston, and half of those twenty-four interviews included women. The interviewees were relating the details of their own spiritual biographies, of their upbringings and subsequent practice, rather than speaking as representatives of particular religious groups – even when in some cases they happened to be in a leadership role. Those television interviews play a large role throughout this chapter in illustrating how women have charted their own religious journeys, especially as they have left the confines of organized or mainstream religions.

In the course of the investigations conducted among Kingston's religious groups over several years, when the questioning turns to demographics and the makeup of a congregation, invariably it turns out that women outnumber men. Sometimes this preponderance of women is explained by their being more "spiritual," at other times, in an aging congregation, by the fact that women live longer than men. Even if the clergy occupying the pulpits and conducting the liturgies have traditionally been men, it has often been the case that women were the ones who kept things going in churches and synagogues and temples. By preparing and serving food, maintaining and decorating the sanctuary, teaching in Sunday schools and looking after nurseries, organizing various sales and special events for fundraising, women in general have provided a supportive structure, usually behind the scenes and invisibly, without which their faith communities could not operate. Increasingly women are participating more in religious services, reading scriptures, welcoming congregants, offering prayers, even though they do not usually occupy the main leadership role in their congregation.

Ordained female clergy are most often found in the United, Anglican, and Unitarian churches, as well as in Reform Jewish congregations (see, for example, the interviews with Elizabeth Macdonald and Kathy Sage, chapter 6). Kingston currently illustrates that tendency. Of fourteen United Church congregations in the city, four or five have in recent years been served principally by women, and in two or three others women are part of the ministerial team, sometimes as diaconal ministers or as lay associates. With vacancies in some of the city's United churches, and impending amalgamations, the staffing situation is changing frequently. To have a woman serving as the primary or sole religious leader in a city congregation is relatively new, even in the United Church. When women began to be ordained in larger numbers it was not easy for them to land a post in a city congregation, except as an associate. As a result, many began their ministries – as male clergy used to do – in rural churches where, paradoxically, conservative traditions and expectations that to be a minister was a man's job could make life particularly difficult for them. Because for many women ordained ministry was a second career or was initiated after establishing a family, they might find it more difficult to relocate to a remote area with other obligations or spousal employment limiting their mobility.

Tracy Trothen (2003) shows how, from the beginning of the ordination of women in the United Church in 1936, greater obstacles were placed in their way than in the case of men. Because women were expected to raise children, if a woman was of child-bearing age and married – or even expecting someday to be married – in practice it was highly likely that she could not be ordained. The same conditions were basically upheld by the United Church's General Council in 1948 with the decision that a woman could not serve as an ordained member of the clergy unless she was able "to give herself wholly to the work of the ministry," a condition that in effect excluded mothers (ibid., 28–9). In the 1950s ordained women were supposed to exercise different ministries from their male counterparts – in keeping with their traditional roles as caregivers, mostly directed toward children and youth. It was not until the United Church General Council met in 1964 that women became officially eligible to be ordained after they were married (35).

Late in 2009 the list for the Anglican Diocese of Ontario included ninety active clergy having parish affiliations. Of those, about twenty are women, judging by their given names and in the absence of other identifying details such as a photo. The Diocese of Ontario, centred in Kingston, is not contiguous with the boundaries of the Province of Ontario but consists of five counties in eastern Ontario. The eight ordained Anglican women who have principal charge of parishes in the diocese are mostly situated in towns and villages in rural eastern Ontario. As anyone knowing the area can confirm, these are places where the prevailing ecclesiastical culture remains relatively traditional and where the resistance to a woman as a clergyperson might be expected to be higher. Two female Anglican priests have recently become the incumbents of major parishes. In 2008 Barbara Robinson, who has a doctorate from the University of Ottawa, was appointed rector of St Paul's, Brockville. In September 2009 Mary Irwin-Gibson was installed as the dean of St George's Cathedral in Kingston, the most prominent church in the diocese. The remaining Anglican female clergy are in honorary, associate, or assistant positions in churches in Kingston, Belleville, or Picton and elsewhere, or they may be serving in youth ministry or as military or hospital chaplains.

At Congregation Iyr HaMelech, Kingston's Reform Jewish congregation, a female rabbi, Michal Shekel, succeeded Justin Lewis in 2007. Further, the Kingston Unitarian Fellowship is currently served by Rev. Kathy Sage (see chap. 6). Thus, as one might expect, within Christianity and Judaism, the religiously liberal denominations are the ones more likely to include women in professional ministerial roles as ordained clergy.

The various religious groups considered in previous chapters include some that continue the patriarchal traditions of religion. Roman Catholic churches as well as Protestant evangelical ones exclude women from assuming most clergy positions. When one conservative evangelical church was moving from Kingston's downtown to the suburbs in the 1980s, a female member of the congregation was not given a place on the all-male building committee, despite her experience in owning and managing rental property. In the Roman Catholic Church, one of the seven sacraments is that of Holy Orders, that is, ordination to the priesthood or diaconate. Only men are ordained, though women may serve as nuns or sisters in religious orders. St Mary's Roman Catholic Cathedral lists nine male priests and deacons as "staff and clergy," or as being "in residence."

Our interview in 2004 at St Mary's Cathedral was with the then-rector, Monsignor Donald Clement, and with Mariola Gozdek, the lay pastoral associate, who is not a member of a religious order and therefore not a nun or sister. Mrs Gozdek, who is married to a non-Catholic, came to Kingston from Poland and assists with the ministry to the Polish congregation, Christ the King Polish Apostolate, whose services are held at the St James' Chapel at St Mary's. She also coordinates various ministries and study groups at the cathedral, preparing people for the sacraments and leading the program Rite of Christian Initiation for Adults. Monsignor Clement said, "It's a blessing to have someone like Mariola," adding that the contribution of women to the church's ministry is "invaluable because they have gifts that we just don't have" (24 March 2004).

Especially in western countries where gender equality has become increasingly valued, Orthodox Jews and most Muslim groups are generally seen as being inhospitable to contemporary women. As well, Jehovah's Witnesses, Mormons, and Brethren Assemblies (see chap. 4) prohibit women from assuming positions within the church that would mean exercising authority over a man – a disruption of what is thought to be the divinely ordained order of things. In these traditions a woman is not allowed to teach a man. Strictly adhering to Paul's directives in 1 Corinthians 14:33, with the injunction that women must keep silent in churches, means a complete ban not just on preaching or "ruling" – that is, acting in the capacity of an elder – but even exclusion from leading public prayers at worship.

The application of this kind of exclusion of women is a perennial hermeneutical emphasis in conservative Christianity. A consideration of Paul's instructions on these matters led Benjamin B. Warfield to the conclusion that "the prohibition of speaking in the church to women is precise, absolute, and all-inclusive." Warfield stated that "the difference in conclusions between Paul and the feminist movement of today is rooted in a fundamental difference in their points of view relative to the constitution of the human race ... To the feminist movement, the human race is made up of individuals; a woman is just another individual by the side of the man, and it can see no reason for any differences in dealing with the two." In case the references here to "the feminist movement" mislead anyone, because they sound so current (well, perhaps excepting the phrase that assumes a women's place is "by the side of the man"), Warfield, principal of Princeton Seminary from 1887 to 1921, was writing these words in *The Presbyterian* in 1919.

SISTERS OF PROVIDENCE OF ST VINCENT DE PAUL

Founded in Kingston in 1869, the Sisters of Providence of St Vincent de Paul stand as an unusual example of a religious congregation of women. Despite their being the only religious order founded in this city, their archivist, Sister Gayle Desarmia, says that their earlier "low-key" approach has meant that "Kingstonians never knew about us" (interview, 11 February 2004). From their beginnings the Sisters of Providence have carried out a special mission to the poor and destitute, varied and adapted to respond to the needs of the times. In the 1930s the sisters acquired a thirty-three acre property, known as Heathfield, on Princess Street just west of Macdonald Boulevard, for their motherhouse. The original villa with its extensive grounds dates back to the 1830s and was for a time the home of John A. Macdonald when he was prime minister. When purchased, Heathfield was a farm. An official history of the Sisters of Providence rightly describes its present appearance, after the planting of trees, cultivation, and landscaping, as having been transformed into a "parkland" (Electa 1961, 61). Today the property accommodates the offices of the administration and leadership team that governs the congregation, a retirement home for the sisters, and the Providence Spirituality Centre with its contemporary chapel, designed and renovated in 1999–2000. Other offices on the premises listed by Sister Desarmia are "the archives ... our Justice and Peace Office, our Ecology and Environment Office, our Associate office, our Elector Resource Centre, and then we have some sisters – besides the retirement community – who live here and work here or some of them work out in the city" (interview, 11 February 2004).

The leadership of the congregation, consisting of the superior general and three councillors, is elected to serve the congregation for a term of three to six years. The mandate for their leaders, following a consultative "consensus model of shared decision-making," according to a directional statement of 2007, is "to plan the future use of our resources using an inclusive process, honouring our ethical responsibilities, especially to the poor, protecting the integrity of creation and providing inspiration for our future legacy" (Sisters

Heathfield, Sisters of Providence Motherhouse

of Providence a). The major endeavour of the Sisters of Providence at the time of the interview in 2004 was the Providence Continuing Care Centre, the largest health network in southeastern Ontario, consisting of four sites: the retirement home, St Mary's of the Lake for rehab and chronic care, mental health services in Kingston's former psychiatric hospital, and a chronic care hospital in Brockville. After more than a century of involvement in such work, in 2006 the congregation's operation of health care institutions was transferred to the Catholic Health Care Corporation of Ontario (see Ross 2007, 210). Over the years their work in Kingston has included group homes for orphans, single mothers, and Latin American people in Kingston, and accommodation for students at the Newman House residence on Queen's campus. Additionally, there are ministries to prison inmates, a clothing depot, and hospitality centre.

In a highly public and visible aspect of their ministry, since the mid-1990s the Sisters have a led a silent noon-hour vigil outside the Kingston City Hall. This vigil was instituted to draw attention to the plight of the poor following cuts in social programs. Because this situation has not been alleviated, the weekly vigil continues. On Good Friday 2004, though a cross was centrally featured on the front steps, the silent vigil was expanded into a special interfaith gathering including speeches from the rabbi of Beth Israel Congregation, the monsignor of St Mary's Cathedral, and the president of the Islamic Centre. At about this time a controversy raged about the anti-Semitic aspects of Mel Gibson's film, *The Passion of the Christ*; Canada's oldest Jewish day school in Montreal had been firebombed on the eve of Passover; and in Toronto acts of vandalism and arson had been perpetrated on Jewish and Muslim sites. These events were "all the more reason," said Jamie Swift, co-director of the Sisters of Providence Justice and Peace Office, "to reach out to the Jews and Muslims of Kingston with a message of hope and peace" (*Whig-Standard*, 8 April 2004). At the vigil Mohammad Saleem, president of the Islamic Centre of Kingston, said, "We people of faith, we people who believe in peace, should raise voice against brutality [throughout the world]" (ibid., 10 April 2004). Four hand-held signs, one word each, spelled out the motto "We Stand In Hope." Rabbi Daniel Elkin, holding a sign protesting genocide, stood beside two of the sisters who supported the six-foot wooden cross plastered with newspaper clippings about poverty. Other signs protested war, especially the conflict in Darfur.

In October 2005 the block of downtown Kingston on which the City Hall and Market Square are situated was completely circled by a white banner made of fifty bed sheets sewn together by two of the sisters, held up at intervals by supporters, and labelled with such declarations as "Make Poverty History," "Poverty Is Political," and "Peas on Earth" (Ross 2007, 193). In October 2009, in an event called Climate on the Line, City Hall was again encircled, this time with a makeshift clothesline strung at intervals with laundry. This occasion, part of the International Day of Climate Action (see 350.org), was the subject of a four-minute video by Clarke Mackey of the Queen's Department of Film and Media. That kind of involvement in issues related to social justice, which also include violence against women and ecological concerns, has made the Sisters of Providence increasingly better known in the Kingston area.

The Providence Spirituality Centre hosts various programs and retreats on its beautiful, partly wooded property on Princess Street. The scheduled retreats are of several different kinds, intended to be open to anyone, and ranging from those, directed or guided, that focus on seasons, sacred art, or particular topics, to private retreats arranged outside the formal schedule. The programs have included such series as Stillness in the Spirit, led by one of the sisters, which provides on instruction of quieting the body "through yoga exercises and Christian breathing meditation." A program for seniors is centred on ecospirituality, while other topics include book discussions (one featuring the popular Christian novel by William P. Young, *The Shack*), reflections on Advent, or talks on cybersafety and abuse by police and technology experts. Sister Kay Morell conducts classes in T'ai Chi Chih – she is the first accredited instructor in Ontario – and in art therapy.

The Sisters of Providence, like many other religious orders, especially in North America, have enthusiastically embraced the reforms of Vatican II and adapted their mission to contemporary needs. Ellen Leonard outlines the changes taking place in religious congregations in Canada during the 1960s and '70s, the outcome of developments within the church as a result of Vatican II, and beyond it due to feminist movements (Leonard 2007). Frequently, as indicated by their work in yoga, Tai Chi, and ecospirituality, the sisters have ventured into areas that do not always accord with traditional Catholic teachings. One sister was reported in a commissioned history of the Sisters of Providence to be practising "reflexology and reiki" (Ross 2007, 200). American nuns have been censured for similar work, for example, the use of Reiki healing techniques that seek to rebalance energy centres in the body. Reiki, which originated in Japan, was judged by the Committee on Doctrine of the United States Conference of Catholic Bishops to have "no support either in the findings of natural science or in Christian belief." The bishops declared in their guidelines issued 26 March 2009 that "for a Catholic to believe in Reiki therapy presents insoluble problems" (US Conference of Catholic Bishops). The *New York Times* reported in 2009 that the Vatican was undertaking two investigations, in which "each congregation of nuns will be evaluated based on how well they are 'living in fidelity' both to their congregation's own internal norms and constitution, and to the church's guidelines for religious life," according to Mother Mary Clare Millea, who was preparing a confidential report. Kenneth Briggs, author of a book about American nuns, has fears about this scrutiny from Rome: "It's an effort to bring about a re-establishment of a very traditional, very conservative set of standards for what convent life is supposed to be" (Goodstein 2009).

Sister Irene Wilson joined the Sisters of Providence as a young woman from the town of Perth in eastern Ontario, partly because she sought an active rather than a contemplative community – that is, she wanted a community whose purpose is for mission rather than mainly for prayer. After many years working as a teacher in different Catholic elementary and high schools, and following the dictate of Ignatius of Loyola that to be contemplative is to be active, Sister Irene became a spiritual director in the Providence Spirituality Centre. In an interview she reflected how spiritual direction, once reserved for those involved in the religious life, was now being made available to many different people as they are enabled to find God in their everyday lives (Cogeco interview, 27 April 2005). She endeavours to help people find their journey with God in their own histories, as well as identifying their "sin history," interpreted as consisting of the times when they have been "out of synch" with themselves, their families and their co-workers, and with God. This way of bringing together prayer and involvement in the world is characteristic of the Sisters of Providence in their adaptation to the changing needs of society.

Another venture at Heathfield, an heirloom seed sanctuary, shows the same trend. Established on the grounds in 1999 by Carol and Robert Mouck, this project preserves and stores seeds in a greenhouse and a portion of a barn. These seeds "are not genetically modified, [but] the good old-fashioned ones," Sister Gayle Desarmia emphasized. A group known as the Heirloom Seed Savers meets once a month, also holding "Weed Walks, Botanical Latin classes, celebrations of seasonal change (Equinoxes, Solstices), workshops and networking with various community groups concerned with sustainability" (Sisters of Providence b) and events tied in with Earth Day. In August they host an Heirloom Tomato Day, attended by three hundred people, at which varieties of tomatoes are displayed and made available for tasting. Sister Gayle added that apart from this special day "the Sisters get to eat some of the tomatoes, some of them are given to the Food Bank or wherever, shared with the poor" (interview, 11 February 2004). In 2008 the Sisters of Providence received a Sustainable Living Award in recognition of their work for the environment.

As Sister Gayle Desarmia explained, "We originally started as a diocesan congregation" under the jurisdiction of the bishop of Kingston, who prescribed what work they would do. Then the sisters "made the application to Rome to be under the Pope," and in 1953 the order was granted the status of a papal congregation. One of the practical consequences of this move was to eliminate the difficulties of working in many dioceses under different bishops – "each bishop has his own ways of doing things." "Being papal," Sister Gayle commented, "frees us up," though she also acknowledged "we are still in contact with bishops in each place" (11 February 2004). One might surmise that the independence from the local diocese enjoyed by the sisters allows them the freedom to pursue their mission and to engage in their ministries according to their understanding of the needs of the surrounding community and in keeping with their interpretation of what the church is saying. Yet Sister Gayle pointed out that new members are not joining their order in the numbers they once were: "There are a lot more opportunities for women to get involved and make contributions to societies now." She observes that at an earlier time, when roles for women were more restricted, "religion offered a venue where they could be administrators of hospitals, principals of colleges and universities" (ibid.). Religious orders, then, such as the Sisters of Providence of St Vincent de Paul, continue to allow Roman Catholic women opportunities for a different kind of service and mission within the church, often seeming to border on the subversive but always providing creative ways of ministering to social needs.

NADENE GRIEVE-DESLIPPE: "ONLY THE SUFFERING GOD CAN HELP"

While the ordination of women began to occur in the United Church of Canada in 1936, in the Presbyterian Church in Canada in 1967, and in the Anglican Communion by the mid-1970s, obstacles to women fully participating as ordained clergy or in other capacities of religious leadership continued, and in various ways they still remain. The removal of formal barriers does not immediately lead to acceptance. For Nadene Grieve-Deslippe, who grew up in an Evangelical United Brethren congregation in Hamilton, Ontario, the barriers were both internal and external. Though churches in the Evangelical United Brethren denomination were later to come into the United Church of Canada, they tended to be more conservative in their theology and practice than were most United churches of the day. Grieve-Deslippe says that in the 1960s her home congregation, where "men were men and women were women," was "conservative theologically, conservative politically." In that context of her youth, roles were defined by adults: "I was a teenager – sixteen, seventeen – just wondering what I was going to do with my life, and this thought of being a minister started to percolate. I just kept suppressing and dismissing it because I didn't think it was a woman's job. I didn't think it was for women" (Cogeco interview, 2 February 2005).

After her ordination in the United Church in the 1980s, she began her ministry at a pastorate in rural Manitoba as a single woman in her mid-twenties. She was the first female minister in that particular church – "they didn't really know what to do with me." As she matured, her own theological views changed too, with God becoming for her "less detached, less far away, maybe less transcendent." Her understanding of God, she says, "has moved from something very patriarchal, very male, to something decidedly more feminine. I certainly believe in a suffering God who weeps with us when we are broken and who dances with us when we celebrate and rejoice." That kind of change in thinking about the nature of God has been advanced and hastened by the presence of women in ministry. Older views that make the Christian deity more or less equivalent to Aristotle's "Unmoved Mover" emphasize the remoteness and transcendence of a God usually imaged and referred to as male. That God, as the Westminster Confession of 1646 puts it, is "infinite in being and perfection, a most pure spirit, invisible, without body, parts, or passions, immutable, immense, eternal, incomprehensible, almighty, most wise, most holy, most free, most absolute." On the other hand, the kind of "suffering God" that Grieve-Deslippe believes in is more related than absolute, and having "passions," shares in humanity's joys and troubles. The theme of divine suffering has been present in a muted form throughout the history of the Christian church, but in general divine impassibility – that is, the belief that God is unaffected, devoid of emotion, and not subject to change – was the classic theological position.

While there are many dimensions and aspects to any major shift in how people think and feel, or how theological ideas change, feminist theology and women's roles in ministry have helped enormously in bringing to the fore new understandings of the divine feminine, especially in making more concrete and relevant understandings of God as related rather than absolute. In many liberal Protestant seminaries today, women comprise more than half the student bodies. Studies have shown that they are far less concerned with the abstractions of theological doctrinal correctness than are their male counterparts. When Grieve-Deslippe speaks of God's participation in suffering, she speaks as a mother who watched her eldest daughter, Lesley, die of a rare form of liver cancer over the space of less than four months in 1997. At the same time she was the minister of Faith United Church in the eastern part of Kingston. During the season of Lent "this twelve-year-old child carrying the weight of this terrible burden of mortality, and doing it with grace and dignity" paralleled for her mother the image of Christ carrying the weight of the cross. As she put it in a newspaper piece, referring to the words of Job, "I don't believe literally that 'the Lord gives and takes away' but I have a figurative affinity to the notion" (*Kingston Whig-Standard*, 2 October 2002). In my television interview with her, replying to a question about how she viewed God's role in her child's cancer, she said, "I never thought that God willed it. If God didn't spare the sacrifice of God's only born son, I don't think that we can expect that we will all be spared or exempt. I choose to believe that God was – and is – as broken hearted as I am."

Grieve-Deslippe represents the insight most succinctly expressed by Bonhoeffer, himself killed by the Nazis: "Only the suffering God can help." A "high" view of God that asserts divine transcendence and absoluteness can be preserved intact only at the expense of divine relativity and involvement in the human condition. This sea-change in Christian theological thinking has been largely brought about, at least on the level of everyday and practical theology, by the presence of women in pulpits of churches. Female clergy have often been able to accomplish in their ministries an incorporation of their own experience as women into the process of theological thinking and have been able to bring that to their preaching and pastoral work.

Grieve-Deslippe served as minister at Faith United Church, a congregation without its own building, from its establishment in 1989 until 2007. Because this was a new church development inaugurated by Kingston Presbytery of the United Church of Canada, she felt that it was important to be inclusive from the beginning and to be open to everyone moving into the area. Almost the only church already existing in the part of Kingston that extends from the east bank of the Great Cataraqui River toward the town of Gananoque was St Mark's Anglican in Barriefield, whose facilities Faith United was eventually to use beginning in 1994. Prior to that, the people comprising this fledgling United Church congregation, from various religious backgrounds or even having "no church memory," met in a school gymnasium. In that context, Grieve-Deslippe relates, "the whole approach to communion was a sore spot for some" (interview, 19 May 2004). Conflict arose because she did not want to deny anyone, even children, the sacrament of Holy Communion. Though her husband was Roman Catholic, she was not allowed to receive communion in the Roman Catholic Church. As a result of that experience she decided she was not going to deny the sacrament to anyone: "Because we were in a school gymnasium and the children were there, we offered them communion." That was an offence to some members of the congregation, especially those whose church background was other than United Church.

A question about the Eucharist in a "mixed marriage," when one partner is Christian but non-Catholic, came up in an interview with Rev. Leo Byrne at St Paul the Apostle Roman Catholic Church in Kingston's west end. Father Byrne explained that when only those who are Roman Catholics are invited into Eucharistic Communion, "it certainly doesn't mean that others don't believe what we believe." Still, he said, "Roman Catholic tradition tends to be a bit in your face ... it's meant to grate. It's not meant to be easy." He compared the disunity in the Christian church to a family fight or disagreement: "You don't sit down to a meal and smile and pretend that everything's all right. You settle the fight and then sit down to the meal." To act as if the divisions do not exist would be dysfunctional, he thought. While he also acknowledged that others might see things differently – and maintain, for instance, that sitting down to the meal together could itself be a reconciling event – "at the present time it's not the Roman Catholic stance." Byrne felt that, given "the scandal of division" and disunity in Christianity, this rather uncompromising position – one that he was personally convinced of – might be necessary "to jog us after five hundred years of complacency." In a few isolated situations, such as in the far north of Canada where only a Roman Catholic Church exists, specific permission is given at times for, say, an Anglican or a Lutheran to participate in communion. Byrne summarized the matter of "closed" – as opposed to "open" – communion by acknowledging that mixed-marriage couples "bear the burden of disunity and they're meant to kind of spur us on." He concluded, "Because it's not their fault. I always tell them, it's like children of divorced parents, they didn't cause it but they're impacted by it" (interview, 30 October 2003).

In the United Church, allowing children to receive the elements during a communion service has become regular practice. In fact, the "Overview of Beliefs" on the United Church's website stresses inclusiveness: "The United Church invites all who seek to love Jesus to share in this family meal." This policy of openness is presented as following the example of Jesus in welcoming everyone regardless of age, for children are "full and welcome participants at the heart of each congregation" (United Church of Canada c). In Methodist churches – one of the denominations that founded the United Church in 1925 – children are regularly offered the communion elements, that is, the symbols representing the body and blood of Christ.

Grieve-Deslippe describes the controversy at Faith United about including children in communion as an early and painful learning experience in her ministry there. Though she acted out of her own sense of having been excluded elsewhere, and perhaps too as someone who as a mother wanted to see children encouraged to participate in communion services, no contravention of church polity was entailed. In a subsequent forum held with people at Faith United, a United Church representative explained the policy of an "open table," clarifying that for very young children the decision rested with their family. Today, Grieve-Deslippe feels that because she had not adequately discussed the issue in advance, difficulties arose, especially among those of Presbyterian or Anglican background, and that "substantial" wounds were left. "My learning from that is to be open, honest, and certainly not be controlling, and to view from the side rather than from the front, to learn from conversation and be collegial."

This issue could be examined from several different angles. In an earlier generation, receiving the elements of communion in the United Church of Canada was restricted to those who had been confirmed, usually in their early teens. The Report on Christian Initiation in 1984 made it clear that baptism, at whatever age it is performed, is the sacrament by which an individual enters the Christian community. The covenant that baptism represents, though a person might want to renew it from time to time, does not need to be repeated, nor does the rite of confirmation "complete" baptism. Confusion about the meaning and role of confirmation seems to continue, as a discussion on the United Church's Wondercafe website suggests. In all, there are in the United Church a variety of views showing differing interpretations about the meaning of baptism and confirmation with some people even questioning whether such rituals have any meaning at all.

This incident about children receiving communion reveals the fluidity and range of thinking within the United Church. Frequently clergy – and lay people too – do not know where they stand, or changes in policy at the level of the national church do not quickly filter down to the local level. In terms of procedure, the same conditions apply as in the case of whether a minister may conduct a same-sex marriage – the session is the body that decides what is to be done within each congregation. As Grieve-Deslippe has demonstrated in her handling of other issues that developed later at Faith United, collegiality and consultation are highly important in faith communities today. Even in more hierarchical and less egalitarian faith communities, the distinction between lay people and the clergy has in some measure broken down. Protestant ministers are much less likely to be wearing a clerical collar than they were a generation ago. They tend to be less authoritarian and less insistent on the use of ecclesiastical titles. With the tendency to see the particular expertise of the clergy as lying in the realm of the personal (see Philip Rieff's 1965 book, *The Triumph of the Therapeutic: Uses of Faith after Freud*), the conflicts of the individual are put at centre stage, while commitments and faiths are rendered more difficult. Today the objective nature of the Christian sacraments is frequently regarded as less important than the personality and performance of the presiding priest. In the fourth century CE the Donatist controversy concerned the validity of the sacraments received from the hands of an apostate or unworthy priest. Contrary to the teaching of Donatus, the church affirmed that the sacraments were valid whatever the moral character of the priest. Today, a couple wants the officiant to be someone who can tailor the wedding ceremony to their needs, or seeks a minister or priest who "knows them" to baptize their baby. Funeral services are becoming more personal and less often done according to a book of services. To that extent, female clergy who would bring the experiential, the personal, or the autobiographical into the ministerial role are participating in an alteration that goes beyond them and is characteristic of a change in what it means to be religious that marks this past generation.

WOMEN AND ALTERNATIVE SPIRITUALITIES: FIVE STORIES

In the late nineteenth century, when conventional religious leadership roles excluded women almost completely, the only option beyond conformity and adaptation was to develop one's own tradition or seek alternatives outside the conventional mainstream. At that time the Salvation Army was unique in offering opportunities for women. Lynne Marks reports that in the 1880s in Ontario more than half of the conversions to the Army, and more than half of its officers, were women (1996, 144, 169–70, 178). Part of the scandal the Salvation Army offered to the middle class of the day was the spectacle afforded by women preaching. Yet Marks claims that Catherine Booth, cofounder of the Army with her husband, William, issued "what was in many ways an explicitly feminist critique of male religious domination"

(170). These "Hallelujah Lasses," mostly from the working class, many domestic servants, also challenged the patriarchal ideal of the Victorian family.

Their exclusion from the mainstream of religious leadership in their time meant that women had to take their considerable energies and talents elsewhere, often to inaugurate their own traditions. The influential Madame Blavatsky (1831–91) was one nineteenth-century woman who, buoyed by the interest in Spiritualism (reportedly begun by the Fox sisters in the mid-1800s) and possessing abilities as a psychic and medium, founded the Theosophical Society. She was to have an effect on such authors as Yeats and Joyce, on leaders and religious figures such as Mahatma Gandhi and Rudolf Steiner and her own successor, Annie Besant, and on other progenitors of New Age thought. Aimee Semple McPherson (1890–1944) was a Canadian-born celebrity revivalist who began the Church of the Foursquare Gospel. As discredited as she later was, in some ways McPherson might be taken as a model of contemporary women in ministry: first, the content of her preaching, though sensational enough in form, was of a gentler kind than the usual fire-and-brimstone variety favoured by other evangelists; second, she broke down racial barriers and integrated her tent meetings. Mary Baker Eddy (1821–1910) discovered the principles of health, in large measure stemming from her own experience with religious healing, which led to her beginning the Church of Christ, Scientist.

Some women, it is true, remained solidly within the Christian church and found in it an outlet that was the counterpart to their home life. Lynne Marks notes that Alice Chown (1866–1949), whom she terms "an early-twentieth-century Kingston feminist," experienced her Methodist religion, at least in her early days, as "the poetry of her life" (Marks 1996, 29). Yet Chown too would later reject the church and develop a radical pacifist free-thinking standpoint. She would write about women's rights and the way in which institutions suppressed women (Chown n.d.). Of the books on my shelves passed down through the family, one of the oldest is my mother's copy of *Studies of Famous Bible Women*, published by Fleming H. Revell in 1925 and inscribed with my mother's maiden name. She would have owned it as a teenager in the late 1920s. The author, Henry T. Sell, D.D., begins his foreword: "This is a woman's age. She is coming into her right and taking the place which belongs to her" (5). Sell goes on to say that this "advanced position of woman" was being achieved because of the "widespread dissemination of Scriptural ideals and standards for women." The twenty-one portraits in this little book extend all the way from Eve, "The New Woman," to Lydia, "A Business Woman," with stops in between to cover Deborah, "An Able Leader of Men," the Woman in Solomon's Song, "The Single Standard," and the Woman of Samaria, "A Keen Questioner." Along the way such negative instances as Delilah and Jezebel are included, but the examples considered are primarily of women who are resourceful, faithful, influential, and possessed of common sense.

In the course of the Cogeco series *Profiles: People of Faith*, three of those interviewed – Elizabeth Greene, Kellye Crockett, and Joan Fast – were women who no longer maintained an active affiliation with the religious tradition in which they had grown up, Judaism, Roman Catholicism, and Mennonite Christianity, respectively. Each woman had developed an alternative way of being religious, either more or less on her own and through the experimentations of trial and error, or by coming into contact with an alternative spiritual practice such as Tarot reading, Wicca, religious dance, and yoga. Two others, Roberta Lamb and Janet Faubert, have been active in two of the most visible Kingston options outside the religious mainstream, the New Kadampa Tradition, a form of Tibetan Buddhism, and Sri Chinmoy, a Hindu sect. Each of these movements, having Asian roots and an identifiable founder-figure or guru, has spread and expanded principally in the West. Neither Lamb or Faubert, however, is exclusively devoted to either the New Kadampa Tradition or to Sri Chinmoy. Both women combine other religious modalities of a less formal and organized kind with these eastern religions.

The remainder of this chapter portrays and analyzes the stories of these five women, beginning with Lamb and Faubert. Their stories require more space than those of Greene, Crockett, and Fast because of their association with the specific religious communities of New Kadampa Buddhism and Sri Chinmoy. Having a larger place in the context of Kingston, those two religious groups require more description and explication. All five individuals, though, illustrate the ongoing adaptability and creativity in matters of religion typical of many contemporary women.

Roberta Lamb and the Kuluta Buddhist Centre

Roberta Lamb, an associate professor in the music department at Queen's University, represents an instance of a contemporary woman with an affinity for religion who finds ways of accommodating that affinity outside the mainstream of religious life. Lamb's focus is on music education – how music is taught in schools – and on gender issues in music. Cross-appointed to the Faculty of Education and the Department of Women's Studies, she has worked with the Symphony Association and local school boards, and been involved in the Queen's University Faculty Association.

Lamb grew up in the United States, where she went to the Episcopal Church – "it was High Church" – which her family attended. She sang in the choir and participated in a girls' youth group. In the youth group she was initially puzzled by a visiting woman who explained that, although she had the educational qualifications to be an Episcopal priest, she could not be ordained. Only after the fact did Lamb realize this was because she was a woman. Growing up in the 1960s, with the attention given to social responsibility, civil rights, and antiwar protests, Lamb "felt quite a disconnect between the religion that was practised in the church on Sunday and what was happening in the society." By the time she was sixteen, as a result of "distancing" and "teenage alienation," she found herself getting "further and further away from the actual day-to-day practice of that religion, even though it had seemed so important to me" (interview, 6 February 2006).

Though her churchgoing had ended, her reading of books on religion, including Christianity, continued into adulthood. Before the late 1980s, when she arrived to take up a position at Queen's, she had been meeting with other women at another university in Manitoba, exploring new forms of spirituality. It was a time when women felt themselves to be very much embattled, both in the larger society – the Montreal Massacre had taken place on 6 December 1989 – and on the Queen's campus. By 1990 Lamb and some other women had formed a women's circle, meeting every six weeks and conducting rituals coordinated with the solstices and equinoxes and quarter-holidays in between – "friends who got together and talked about things religious, and really [wanted] to find a women-centred way of doing it." They read Starhawk's *The Spiral Dance*, Zuzanna Budapest's *The Holy Book of Women's Mysteries*, and Barbara Walker's *The Woman's Encyclopedia of Myths and Secrets* to develop rituals based on their experience as women – all feminists, all lesbians, and all connected with the university. While the members of "The Circle," as they began to call it, never defined for themselves whether what they were doing was earth-centred spirituality, goddess worship, or Wicca, most of them had had "one or more negative experiences with Christianity, and that was the one thing we were clear we weren't doing." Marked by intimacy and intense discussions, the Circle by intention never grew very large and was never simply open to anyone who wished to come. Some of the participants moved from Kingston, and one person died of cancer; in 2006, three among the eight women participating in The Circle were from the original membership of more than fifteen years earlier.

By January 2003 Lamb and her partner realized that "both of us were wanting to increase what we were doing spiritually." Other members of their group did not wish to meet more often than once every six weeks. As part of a program of recovery from an illness, Lamb and her partner began to attend weekly meditation classes at the Kuluta Buddhist Centre. The centre, present in Kingston for about a decade, is part of the New Kadampa

Tradition of Buddhism, an international organization founded in England by Kelsang Gyatso in 1991. Whether the New Kadampa Tradition continues the ancient Kadampa traditions or is a sect that broke away from that school of Tibetan Buddhism is a matter of controversy. It can be described as a New Religious Movement which, like many others, is focused on a contemporary founder-figure, Kelsang Gyatso, while drawing much of its teaching from ancient roots. The Kuluta Centre, recently moved downtown to a tastefully renovated central location, represents the most prominent of several kinds of Buddhism available in Kingston, though, perhaps surprisingly, the New Kadampa Tradition is not mentioned anywhere in the 450 pages of *Wild Geese: Buddhism in Canada* (Harding, Hori, and Soucy, eds. 2010).

Two other Buddhist groups present in Kingston are worth mentioning here. Like the Kadampa Tradition, their members and followers too are western converts and practitioners rather than immigrants. A small, highly dedicated and disciplined Zen meditation group meets on the Queen's campus; three of its members also belong to the Montreal Zen Center. (In 2003 the teacher and director of the Montreal Zen Center, Albert Low, was the recipient of an honorary LL.D. degree at Queen's, initiated by the nomination of the three Queen's faculty members involved in the group; see Montreal Zen Center; also Peressini 2010). The third Kingston Buddhist group is Soka Gakkai International, another Buddhist New Religious Movement begun in 1930, with its origins and headquarters in Japan. Like the Zen group, Soka Gakkai International is most identifiable as a campus, not community-based, club, whereas the Kuluta Centre promotes activities at Queen's and in the Kingston community (see chap. 9.4). The Kuluta Centre, active, ambitious, and well-staffed for its outreach endeavours, holds meditation classes in area prisons and in such neighbouring towns as Napanee, Belleville, Brighton, and Brockville.

Roberta Lamb began her association with the Kuluta Buddhist Centre in the way most people do, with an introductory class in meditation leading to more regular classes. She progressed to festivals and retreats, and to the twice-weekly Foundation Program. By 2006 she was facilitating a noon-hour session in breathing meditation at the Ban Righ Centre, a house on campus that mainly serves mature female students at Queen's. In these sessions with a few students, she focused on breathing and on meditation as a way to reduce stress and calm the mind; she conducted no explicit teaching of Buddhism as such. Meanwhile, one of the nuns from the Kuluta Centre was giving regular, larger classes in meditation and Buddhist teaching at the John Deutsch University Centre. Lamb spoke at length about how she combines in complementary fashion the feminist spirituality of her Women's Circle with the Buddhist meditation and teachings of the New Kadampa

Kuluta Buddhist Centre

Tradition. Ironically, given her reasons for leaving the Episcopalianism of her childhood, she says that "Buddhism is still a patriarchal religion." However, after the passage of several decades, "it just didn't seem to be such a big deal anymore," and she has decided simply to take from the New Kadampa Tradition "what helps me."

One of the things she found helpful at the Kuluta Centre was the image of the Bodhisattva Tārā enshrined on the altar: "She's one of the very important ones ... she's a rescuer, she's also wisdom, she's just one strong lady there, right up there with the guys." At the same time, as an aspect of her own practice within The Circle, Roberta had dedicated herself to the Chinese goddess of compassion, Kuan Yin, or "Guanyin," during her self-initiation into a period of spiritual growth. At the Kuluta Centre she learned that Avalokiteśvara was the Tibetan Bodhisattva in male form from whom the Chinese Kuan Yin originated. For Lamb this transgendered and cross-cultural makeover signified that here was a Buddhist deity who illustrated that beings can be enlightened in female form. The New Kadampa Tradition as taught and practised at the Kuluta Centre afforded this kind of freedom of interpretation to complement what she was doing in The Circle with other women. Neither group was dogmatic, and "in each case, you are testing what you're practising with your own experience ... there's no danger of heresy." In a similar vein, Lamb summarized the New Kadampa Tradition to students at a forum on religious clubs on the Queen's University campus this way: "The Kadampa tradition is one that is based in a scholarly pursuit of a Buddhist mandate, and a practical pursuit, and I think both of those are what attracted me to it. The position is that through creating peace in one's own mind, we can create peace in the world ... The benefit for the community is that anyone can come to classes – it is not necessary to be a Buddhist to benefit from meditation. You can come and learn to meditate, and then take it where you want to. Whatever level of involvement you want is okay. You don't have to believe anything. You come and you take the classes and you sort of [relate them] to your experience" (Rels-451, 5 October 2005).

By incorporating two kinds of practice into her religious life, Lamb represents a contemporary trend that might not be unusual. Drawing on my observation of religions in Japan, where people follow several different traditions, I have written about how in Canada one's own religious practice – or what is more often called a "personal spirituality" – can also be cobbled together from various sources, but without combining these into a single unity. Religious dimorphism, or drawing upon religions selectively and situationally, may be the characteristic postmodern way of being religious, related, of course, to the "pick-and-choose" patterns of consumption of the marketplace (see James 2006).

Janet Faubert and Sri Chinmoy

Janet Faubert is another Kingston woman who has developed her own spiritual path, drawing on the techniques and resources of several different traditions. Faubert , who came to Kingston in 1995, works as a registered nurse in the Neonatal Intensive Care Unit at the Kingston General Hospital, a job requiring skill, compassion, and the ability to handle stress. Like Roberta Lamb, she practises meditation. Though Lamb began meditating in her fifties, Faubert has "practised a meditation method since I was in my twenties." To share the effectiveness of the meditation method she uses, Faubert has written a book, *Colours of the Spirit* (2007). She wanted to write a self-help book that would show "how to go about transforming a personality spiritually – how to systematically address inherent flaws of character" (email, 19 October 2005). Her method of meditating on colours involves understanding their particular meanings and properties. Using the physics of light, colour meditation is a way of connecting oneself with the divine energy of the universe.

Raised as an Anglican in northern Ontario, Faubert came to distrust organized religion. At age twenty, while a student at McMaster University, she took a course in meditation from PSI, or "People Searching Inside," as that New Age movement was known. She regards the fee of $129, paid from her "meagre student bank account," for the four-day course as "the best investment I have ever made" (Faubert 2007, xxx). Influenced by other forms of eastern thought such as Eckankar, a method of connecting with divine spirit through soul travel and dreams, PSI provided for her a way into meditation and into psychic experiences. It also introduced her to kundalini. She and the man who would later be her husband, Barry, went to India with 250 other PSI students to listen to several days of lectures from Gopi Krishna (1903–84). Gopi Krishna is credited, through his 1967 book, *Kundalini: The Evolutionary Force in Man*, with bringing to the attention of the West the significance of kundalini energy as a way of transformation. In this autobiography, republished in 1993 as *Living with Kundalini*, he wrote: "The phenomenon represents the attempt of a hitherto unrecognized vital force in the human body, releasable by voluntary efforts, to mold the available psychophysiological apparatus of an individual to such a condition as to make it responsive to states of consciousness not normally perceptible before" (Gopi Krishna).

As Faubert was herself to write later, Gopi Krishna described "how the energy-substance which is called kundalini in the Hindu tradition, chi in the oriental world, and the Holy Spirit in the Christian, rises from its dormant state at the base of the spine, to permeate the body." "This subtle, intelligent energy-essence," she goes on to say, "purifies and transforms the organs, nervous system, and brain" continuing "until the body is made stronger, the personality becomes balanced, and one's consciousness is permanently transformed (2007, 16). Faubert herself did not become what she describes as "kundalini active" until many years later, in 2000, by which time she had already become involved in the local Sri Chinmoy Centre. She had been looking for a group where she could continue her own observance of meditation. She was clear that she did not want Buddhism as the context for her meditation practice, in part because she felt the need for a guru.

As with Lamb's involvement with the Kuluta Buddhist Centre, Janet Faubert's connection with the Sri Chinmoy Centre needs some background. Sri Chinmoy (1931–2007) was a philosopher and guru, born in East Bengal. He experienced advanced states of meditation, and came to the United States in 1964. In lectures and poetry and books he encouraged his followers toward an expansion of inner consciousness and a unity with the divinity inside themselves. He promoted vegetarianism, physical fitness – sponsoring marathons for peace has been a prominent activity – and celibacy. The Sri Chinmoy Centre in Kingston was begun in 1991 by some members from Ottawa, where a centre had been established in about 1972. The leader of the Kingston group, Hladini Wilson, and her "right hand," Paramita Jarvis, had been with the Ottawa centre from the 1970s, and moved to Kingston on the instructions of Sri Chinmoy to begin a new centre. They share a Kingston house together, large enough to accommodate the centre's meditation classes and other needs. As Jarvis explains, "I have to say it gets very well used. And Hladini and I are both like nuns. We're very much like Buddhist nuns, or Christian nuns: we're celibate, and we practise our spiritual disciplines as the centre part of our life, you might say" (3 December 2005). Both women have grown children from their earlier marriages.

Jarvis says that about twenty women and ten men, mostly in their forties and fifties, are members of Kingston's Sri Chinmoy Centre. They are predominantly of European descent and from Christian backgrounds. The group at present includes three nurses – two of them being Faubert and Jarvis – and some teachers, while Wilson is an editor – "and then we have every level from lawyer and doctor right through to taxi driver." Commenting on the larger proportion of women involved in Sri Chinmoy, Jarvis reflects, "I think it's just the time in history right now that women are wanting to awaken spiritually; they're looking for spiritual fulfillment through many, many different paths." While people find their different pathways to God, she says, and the important thing is to go on this quest, "women are more aware of that than men right at this time, so there tend to be more women seekers." She stressed that most people come to the centre from their desire to learn about meditation. While Sri Chinmoy's own background was Hindu, he valued all religions. The teaching is not dogmatic, emphasizing the unity of all religions and attempting to enable people to fulfil themselves spiritually.

When Jarvis spoke of Sri Chinmoy, still living when this interview took place, she invoked his presence as a revered guru. She pointed to the very place in the room where he sat on visiting Kingston in October 1997. Asked if Sri Chinmoy's followers turn to texts to resolve a problem, she replied that "we would tend to go within" to find "inner guidance." She stresses that Sri Chinmoy's own writings emphasize "peace and harmony and oneness." She says that when she and Wilson "get into conflicts from time to time," as is inevitable because they are different people, "we both know one hundred thousand per cent that there is no way that Sri Chinmoy can be happy with us if we are in conflict with each other." It is as if the guru is internalized: "We both know that disharmony is not something that he values, and that he would not be happy, that it would painful to him, if there was conflict between the two of us. So, knowing that, it would give us extra motivation to come back to a harmonious state."

The *New York Times* article that appeared after Sri Chinmoy's death summarized his feats: "His followers said he had written 1,500 books,

115,000 poems and 20,000 songs, created 200,000 paintings and had given almost 800 peace concerts" (13 October 2007). At his concerts he normally performed on a dozen different instruments, and on one occasion is reported to have played 150 instruments. He said that he slept only ninety minutes each day. He advocated extreme physical activity as a means of self-transcendence. Using a special apparatus he publicly lifted such large objects as planes, trucks, a baby elephant, a sumo wrestling team, and two Mounties on horseback. In his seventies he performed a 256-pound wrist curl. These accomplishments, all cited on various websites devoted to him, were intended to inspire others to overcome their supposed limitations. The organization he founded became well known for its sponsorship of marathons, several of which have been held in Kingston. A free concert at the Kingston Collegiate and Vocational Institute was part of the 1997 Kingston visit.

In 1991, the year that the Kingston Sri Chinmoy Centre was founded, the *Kingston Whig-Standard* reported from 17 May to 24 May on the efforts made to have several international bridges over the St Lawrence River named after Sri Chinmoy. While some confusion surrounds the events, on 15 May 1991 there was a dedication at the Thousand Islands International Bridge, about sixty kilometres east of Kingston, in honour of Sri Chinmoy. The ceremony took place at the small thirty-metre Rift Bridge, the international portion between the several larger spans covering the total distance of fourteen kilometres between the American and Canadian sides of the river. Sri Chinmoy gave prayers and blessings, and about one hundred runners from the United States and Canada carried torches. Despite the three plaques erected referring to the "Sri Chinmoy Peace Bridge," Bridge Authority officials stated that the bridge was not being renamed, regarding this ceremony as one of several over the years performed by various groups. The newspaper referred to the bridge being opened in 1938 by Prime Minister Mackenzie King and President Franklin D. Roosevelt and originally dedicated "as a symbol of peace between Canada and the United States" (*Whig-Standard*, 16 May 1991).

Meanwhile, further downriver, a request from the Sri Chinmoy organization to erect plaques at either end of the Ogdensburg-Prescott International Bridge met with resistance. Officials were not keen to have the bridge rededicated or renamed, and felt that plaques bearing the inscription "Sri Chinmoy Peace Bridge" would be misleading. "Considering there's no plaque on the bridge now," the executive director said, putting a plaque on it would lead people to believe that "it's been renamed" (*Whig-Standard*, 17 May 1991). In the aftermath of the refusal at the Ogdensburg-Prescott International Bridge, officials of the Thousand Islands Bridge Authority had to clarify that, no matter what the plaques said, their bridge had not been renamed.

In 2007 a vegetarian restaurant, Lotus-Heart-Blossoms, described on its website as "a Sri Chinmoy enterprise," opened at 185 Sydenham Street in Kingston's downtown. The restaurant was established by Kim and Mark Mohan on the request of Sri Chinmoy, who also gave it its name (*Whig-Standard*, 27 October 2007). Many other Sri Chinmoy restaurants are found around the world, from New York to San Francisco in the United States, and in Canada including the similarly named Perfection-Satisfaction-Promise Restaurant in Ottawa. The *Whig-Standard* restaurant reviewer, Greg Burliuk, was told by Kim Mohan that the vegetarian "meats," such as veggie burgers, came from Oshawa: "We've found that the Seventh-day Adventists make the best vegetarian meats." The Seventh-day Adventist Church, whose members are also vegetarians, has its national headquarters in Oshawa.

The Lotus-Heart-Blossoms restaurant was situated during the three years of its existence in an attractive space a few doors from Princess Street, with large windows and a bright blue awning over the entrance. Most of the staff serving tables wore saris. Music by Sri Chinmoy was playing, pictures of him hung on the walls, and his books were displayed – and for sale. Despite all this, the Kingston restaurant was not to be regarded as "an indoctrination centre," as the reviewer put it. Not all of the servers and kitchen staff were followers of Sri Chinmoy. Before it opened, Paramita Jarvis explained that Kingston's Sri Chinmoy Centre would be housed within a large space in the same building. That space, described as being "down some stairs and across a little hallway," was formerly a showroom when the building was a furniture store. Even given this separation of functions, the restaurant closed on Wednesdays when the Sri Chinmoy Centre held its meetings. The restaurant closed permanently in August 2010, partly as the result of the costs in trying to run a labour-intensive vegetarian restaurant without the revenues that a liquor licence would have provided. Together with the Kuluta Buddhist Centre, the Sri Chinmoy restaurant for a time represented another downtown religious presence, in a highly visible storefront location, of a group having its roots in the East.

Since 2000 Janet Faubert has been attending the weekly meditation meetings at the Sri Chinmoy Centre on a regular basis. She says she needs the structure of a group within which to continue her meditation practices, whereas her husband, Barry, prefers to avoid religious organizations. As well, though Faubert wanted a guru and was inspired by Sri Chinmoy – "You know, so it isn't that I need to [have a guru], but [that] I like it and I like him" – her husband did not put himself under a guru's direction or guidance. She has also been involved in the organization of outreach and humanitarian endeavours of the Sri Chinmoy Centre, including bake sales, fundraising, peace runs, and distributing an educational manual to schools.

She emphasizes, however, that she must limit such activities – "I still have to be master of my own domain kind of thing" – and retain the spiritual independence that her husband values. She says that Sri Chinmoy is "accepting of any path," a freedom that allows her to incorporate her own strong interests in kundalini, and other practices too. In her home she has set up a space dedicated to her personal meditation, with a violet cloth and purple cushions, related to her colour meditations, and a candle. She reads poetry when she meditates. The main picture, known as "The Transcendental," is of Sri Chinmoy "in a high state of consciousness." There are other pictures of him too, and off to the side, photos of leaders of a Hindi sect that helped Barry with his practice.

In about 1978, when her three children were at the ages of ten years, five years, and eight months, Faubert presented them for baptism at a United Church in Ottawa. Though she had been brought up Anglican, and while she clearly has had her quarrels with Christianity, she had the children baptized at the church she had been attending – despite the fact, as she puts it, that "my husband wouldn't come. He does not believe in organized religion." She says that her children, now grown, have had their own religious experiences: "They all read spiritual books, they all believe in kundalini." About her own book, she says, "I give a whole picture of how you can take control of your life and live spiritually." Her spiritual practice has been continuous for more than thirty years, from the time when she first encountered meditation as a university student at age twenty. In *Colours of the Spirit* she writes that, during her youthful experience of church, "services seemed like the formal recognition of God," failing to satisfy her need for inner connection (Faubert 2007, xxiii). In her first chapter, "The Sorry Story of Religion," she expresses the view that "those who question … are beginning to understand that organized religion is superfluous" (8). She also believes that "religions are woven into the fabric of our lives," providing rituals for rites of passage, and that such "societal traditions are tethers of enormous strength" (5). Her position is that "we do not have to discard our religions, but instead search within them for pure spirituality" (12).

Like Roberta Lamb, Janet Flaubert is a religious eclectic who utilizes the religious practices from various sources – and of her own construction – but without being subject to the aegis or dictates of any single religious tradition. Probably neither woman would describe herself as "Christian" in terms of doctrinal practice or formal allegiance, yet they both maintain some connection, however tenuous, with the Christianity of their respective childhoods. Lamb feels that perhaps the visual component of the high Episcopalian religion of her childhood attuned her to the Buddhist statues before which she offers her devotions today. Faubert, meanwhile, has not entirely abandoned the Protestant traditions she grew up with, still appreciating the "cultural Christianity" of contemporary Canada, and its passage rituals such as baptism. Evidently both women insist on being in charge of their own spiritual paths and would not be willing to accept any limitations on practising as they see fit.

Elizabeth Greene and Tarot

Three other brief concluding examples might be offered of women who have developed their own ways of being religious, largely outside the confines of an organization or group. Elizabeth Greene, a professor and poet, was born in New York and completed her graduate studies at the University of Toronto in medieval studies and English literature before coming to Queen's in 1969. "The tarot cards said that if I must go to graduate school, it was better if I go to Canada and Toronto," Greene told a reporter (*Whig-Standard*, 19 June 2010). Greene played a major role in helping to establish women's studies at Queen's, as well as courses in creative writing. Much of her life has been directed by tarot cards, including her decision to retire in 2007 and devote herself to writing on a full-time basis. Her second book of poetry, *Moving*, was published in 2010. Its initial poem, "Magic," begins by referring to language as the tool of poetry, "the deck of cards I watch you shuffle." The poem concludes that the magic the poet possesses is "not tricks, not spells" but perhaps memory or "listening to stars, or settling for the truth of old drowned boots" hauled up from the deeps (2010, 1). In another poem, "Lost Luggage," as the travelling poet heads for Cairo, she draws as her "card for the day" the Seven of Swords – "the man in his olive tunic stealing five swords, slipping away." Later, in New York she discovers the card's meaning: "my bag was never loaded on the plane, mine and four others" (33).

Greene was raised in a Jewish family in Philadelphia, but, she emphasizes, the family was "very lapsed, lapsed Jewish." She explains: "I grew up almost totally without religion, but of course I did grow up Jewish. I wasn't part of a congregation, but most of my parents' friends were Jewish and I think my attitudes are Jewish. I certainly would describe myself as Jewish although someone else may throw up their hands in horror because I'm not part of a congregation; I don't go to synagogue." She says that what she thinks "she was looking for in Judaism was the mysticism and the ancientness." Greene, who is both jocular and intensely serious, spoke in our interview about the time at age eighteen when a friend of her mother read her fortune with a tarot deck: "And I found it very scary, which is probably one of the reasons why I don't ask for divination, but I found it very riveting" (Cogeco interview, 24 November 2004).

The seventy-eight cards of the various tarot decks have been in use in games in Europe since about the fifteen century. Their role in divination and prophecy developed several centuries later when they began to be associated with magic, mysticism, and the occult. Even today some decks continue these associations with the esotericism and magic, one deck, for instance, being connected with the influential occult practitioner Aleister Crowley (1875–1947). Tarot cards have also been linked by C.G. Jung to the archetypes for which he is famous. In her readings Greene incorporates the mythic patterns she encounters in literature, discovering the connections between tarot and Kabbalistic Judaism, and learning about the perils of seeking divination rather than resolving issues and looking for guidance. "The cards," she explains, "would take apart your set of circumstances and what you were dealing with, what the energies were, what the conflicts were, and then they would give you some guidance about how to proceed."

Greene describes her spiritual path as almost the reverse of that taken by Justin Lewis, who came to Judaism from a Christian background (see Cogeco interview, 13 October 2004; cf. chap. 6). Though without becoming a Christian, for several years she journeyed from her Jewish roots into medieval Christianity: "I love the English mystics; I love Julian of Norwich. I love medieval Latin poetry. I went to cathedrals whenever I could." She remarks that a tarot reading is a "religious act" for her and that she often prays before doing it – "that the reading will be accurate and helpful and provide guidance." She feels that reading tarot cards is about bringing healing to people. In answer to my question about to whom she prays, she replied: "Well, sometimes to God, sometimes to the Goddess, sometimes to whatever is up there, spirits. I think I am a pantheist" (Cogeco interview, 24 November 2004).

Kellye Crockett and the Sacred Source

Kellye Crockett, who has done Ph.D. studies in linguistics at Queen's, has owned and operated the Sacred Source Bookstore on Brock Street since 1999. When RDK researcher Megan Unterschultz began to study Pagan communities in Kingston, "the first place I was told to go was the Sacred Source Bookstore" (interview with Brendan Fox, 24 November 2004). Sacred Source, which Crockett prefers to identify as a "metaphysical" rather than "New Age" bookstore, is situated in a heritage block with some of the city's most prestigious businesses – Cooke's Fine Foods, Cunningham and Poupore Men's Clothing, Le Chien Noir Bistro and the adjacent Atomica Gourmet Pizza and Wine Bar with their outdoor patios, Trugs Flowers, and shops selling pet accessories and kitchen supplies. These establishments draw much of their business from tourists visiting Kingston's waterfront and the nearby City Hall and Market Square. Initially conceived as a place to provide "resources on different faiths," Sacred Source incorporates three facilities in one building. Downstairs is the retail area with "resources and books and so on – from healing, to auras and chakras, to tarot, to candles and jewellery and clothing" (interview, 12 April 2006). Upstairs is an area known as Brigid's Cauldron, described on a Pagan website as "a magickal, energy-sensitive environment which represents Wicca and other Pagan paths with positive, sacred intent" (WiccanWeb). Though occasionally circles were held in Brigid's Cauldron in the first year or so of the store's existence, it now serves as "sort of a one-stop information centre" for those wanting materials or books, or who are "curious about the Wiccan or other Pagan faiths" (interview, 12 April 2006). The third space is the meditation garden out back where circles were also held at the beginning.

In 2006 Crockett rented space around the block on Princess Street and inaugurated the Oasis Dance Studio, to be used for movement classes and other types of dance. She was already teaching six dance classes weekly, in addition to being in the store six days a week, offering tarot readings, and working on her thesis. In an interview about the practice of sacred dance, Crockett said: "Primarily dance has often been seen as a form of entertainment or a way to exercise or socialize, but in ancient times it was one way to achieve communion with the divine" (Cogeco interview, 3 November 2004). She teaches belly dance, involving "movements that come from the core part, the inner core," associated in women with the womb. Although belly dance "honours feminine sensuality and expresses that in very beautiful ways," she emphasizes that it is "not something to be denigrated or suppressed or eroticized." Rather, as an art form it "allows a woman to connect with ... the inner divine."

Kellye Crockett was raised "in a very Catholic family in Prince Edward Island." Her grandmother, "very Irish and very magical," believed in precognitive dreams and ESP: "She read tea leaves for people and I think she was seen to be quite eccentric by many of the town's people and was even known as the town witch." Though her grandmother "lived her life as a Catholic wife," and though there were always priests – one of them a relative who was a monsignor – coming to the house, she also gave people advice through divination. Crockett herself says that a fortunate result of this family environment was that her own psychic abilities were not suppressed: "Mine were allowed to foster and grow," and, in a subtle way, her grandmother's mantle was passed on to her. She recalls as a child "playing priest, as many children like to do," and she "always ended up being in the priest position, dispensing knowledge and communion ... I was quite disappointed to find out that I couldn't become a priest or a pope because I was a girl." This realization was partly what reoriented her toward the more egalitarian nature religions. In Wicca, she states, creative energy can be worshipped in the form of both God and Goddess: "So we see deity and divinity as being dual and equal."

Brendan Fox of the Pagan Federation in Kingston confirms that the interest used to come from "a very extreme number of women, but now it's getting to be more of a sixty-forty split" (interview, 24 November 2004). If in Wicca and Pagan traditions women are involved more than men, and if more women than men come through the doors of Sacred Source, Crockett explains that it represents a rebalancing of centuries of patriarchy in religion taking place. Her own success as a businesswoman and Wiccan practitioner testifies to her fairness and flexibility, to her measured and moderate approach, and to her ability to gauge the spiritual needs existing in the community, especially among women. With Sacred Source she has been able to create this niche at a level unmatched in many larger cities.

Joan Fast and Yoga

Another example of a woman developing a unique spiritual path derived from her own biography is Joan Fast, an instructor at the Yoga and Relaxation/Lila Centre on Princess Street in Kingston. A few years ago, the studio was known simply as the YRC, short for the Yoga and Relaxation Centre. The addition of the Lila Centre to its title appears partly to be an effort to add "the use of self-investigation tools, such as meditation and compassionate communication, as ways to increase both individual and global consciousness" to the centre's mandate. Probably a dozen or more Kingston venues offer instruction in yoga, including the athletic facilities at the university and the YMCA. The Yoga and Relaxation/Lila Centre is one of the places offering instruction in yoga that stresses alongside its physical and practical benefits its connection with the ancient tradition of Hindu spiritual discipline. Yoga, states the centre's website, "has the capacity to take us much more deeply into ourselves and … to a place of wisdom where the keys to peace and tolerance in the world reside" (Lila Centre; the earlier site, yogarelax.ca, is no longer active). Among the dozen teachers working at the centre, most have credentials in meditation or other areas of spiritual practice, and include a doctor, a Unitarian Universalist minister who also conducts singing workshops, and a retired biology professor who has taught at the Naropa Institute. In keeping with its dual emphasis on the spiritual in company with the practical or physical, the centre offers a 10 AM Sunday service "to bring a sense of joy and sacredness to your life … so that you can go out and share it with others!"

Joan Fast grew up in a quite strict Mennonite family on a fruit farm in the Niagara region of Ontario. She rebelled as a teenager against the restrictions placed on her – no dancing, no drinking, no hanging out with people who were not Mennonite – and dropped out of school after Grade 10. Still, her religious background deeply affected her. As early as age four, she recalls, "I was terrified if I died, I'd go to hell" (Cogeco interview, 9 March 2005). A few years later, she was among ten children trick-or-treating on a country road when the group was struck by a drunk driver's car – "he thought we were mailboxes, so he hit and he ran." She had shattered glass from the car's windshield thrown into her face, her sister had a concussion, another child had broken legs, and one girl was killed. She remembers an older sister later asking about the girl who died and her father saying that "he wasn't really sure, if someone is Catholic, whether they'd go to heaven."

In her thirties, after the breakdown of a marriage, Fast went to Japan to teach English. There, amidst an experience of stress and health problems – "Mennonite girl goes to Tokyo" – she was introduced to yoga by an Australian woman living in the same house: "Just that feeling of actually feeling my spine, and I think I just started to bring a lot more energy along my spine doing all those movements. But, like, I just remember feeling fantastic." Later, she went to the Kripalu yoga centre in Massachusetts where she experienced a transformation ritual in which, as she describes it, "I'm letting go of my past and moving into something new." The accompanying flood of energy she says was like the energy she gets from the practice of yoga, but "maybe a big hit of it at one time." A few years later, after her Kingston studio, the Yoga Loft, had begun to be successful as a business, she had another accident, falling thirty feet off a cliff during a workshop in New York State, when a rock she was sitting on – one that she had particularly singled out as a sacred spot for meditation – dislodged. She spent five weeks on her back in the hospital and was unable to teach for six months. Among all of the traumatic and ironic aspects of this event, she says that whereas yoga had taken her into her body, "this experience kind of put me out of my body, kind of made me more similar to how I was living my life when I was younger." In effect, her Mennonite upbringing required that she separate herself from her body; now the accident undid that integration of self and body that her practice of yoga had accomplished.

Relating these incidents to me (Cogeco interview, 9 March 2005), in her gentle, soft-spoken, and understated manner, what Fast was conveying through her story was a journey of healing and realization that in another venue – on *The Oprah Winfrey Show*, for instance – would have been showcased as a contemporary narrative of conversion and of triumph over adversity. On reflection, her story may be seen to contain the pattern of descent and rebirth, or of disintegration and reintegration, seen, for example, in Margaret Atwood's novel *Surfacing* (1972). It seems that falling off the cliff and the resulting injuries were both traumatic in themselves and also an instance of post-traumatic stress in which Fast experienced flashbacks of the childhood Halloween accident. During her convalescence, when she says, "I was in a very dark place," she found out that she had been the one who discovered many years earlier that her Grade Four friend had been killed. Part of Fast's extended process of healing was learning to re-enter and rediscover her own body, and to find once again that energy that had been sustaining her.

RESHAPING TRADITIONS

Syncretism, a somewhat pejorative term that implies combining two traditions into a third, newer tradition, does not quite describe the practice of the five women considered here who have ventured into alternative forms of religion. Pattana Kitiarsa, a scholar of Thai religion, uses terms like "religious hybridity" or "marketized spirituality" to refer to the development of local animistic spirit-cults alongside the prevailing Theravada Buddhism of Thailand, one aspect of the convergence of religion and capitalism (2005, 476). As religious authority becomes decentralized, Kitiarsa claims, hybridization is "taking place in the 'betwixt and between spaces,' where several religious faiths come together and where popular concerns over the impact of the market economy are channeled" (485). Wade Clark Roof describes this "spiritual marketplace" as the arena in which baby boomers in particular, each on their individual spiritual quest, draw on the bits and pieces of the religious fragments available to them to construct a religion (1999). What others, for example, Catherine Cornille, have termed "multiple religious belonging" may occur when someone draws upon other sources of religion, but sees them in the light of a single prevailing tradition (2002).

Nicole Libin, while a Ph.D. student at the University of Calgary, has written about how the self is constructed from various sources and how there is no such thing as a single authentic Jewish identity. In such a context, she says, "The possibility of Jewish hybridity," which includes such possibilities as a Jew practising Zen meditation, "emerges out of the genuine recognition of a lack of both essentialist Judaism and a static, singular self" (Libin 2006). "Perhaps we can recognize as an authentic Jew one who looks to aspects within the various traditions of Judaism to construct what is personally authentic to him or her self." One of the concerns sometimes voiced about religious seekership, especially when the individual self becomes the arbiter of authenticity, relates to the possibility of unbridled choice being ungoverned by any norms. Is something to be acclaimed as good solely because I choose it? Or is one religion to be preferred over another for personal reasons that cannot be questioned or debated?

Charles Taylor, whose book *Sources of the Self* Libin draws upon, argues in his CBC Massey Lectures (published under the title *The Malaise of Modernity*) that authenticity demands that individual choices transcend the self and be related to some larger horizon. unless they are to be completely arbitrary. Something must be significant for some reason beyond the fact that someone has chosen it. That is, some "background of intelligibility" (1991, 37), some defence and justification must be offered on the basis of values beyond oneself that can be appealed to and defended. As Taylor puts it, "Only if I exist in a world in which history, or the demands of nature, or the needs of my fellow human beings, or the duties of citizenship, or the call of God, or something else of this order *matters* crucially, can I define an identity for myself that is not trivial" (40–1).

Peter Emberley, a Carleton University political scientist and philosopher, charts in his book *Divine Hunger* the spiritual searchings of baby boomers, and says that "the most troubling feature" of their religious quest "is their tendency to think aesthetically and psychologically, but not metaphysically" (2002, 257). In a requirement that far exceeds the demands of Taylor's "background of significance," Emberley wants to install a metaphysical perspective on reality because reliance on "personal experience and feeling," or finding one's assurance in "a good story," cannot provide an index of truth. He argues that "this 'aestheticization' of faith may be appealing because it offers a powerful means of 'connecting' to religion – much faster than the painstaking setting out of reasonable arguments, or the longer road of spiritual disciplines – but it does not alter the fact that choice, feeling, or intense belief are no proof of a faith's concrete actuality" (258). As the five stories related here show, philosophical debates about such metaphysical questions as the nature of reality or proofs for the divine existence are mostly irrelevant today for many religious people. In the case of spiritual seekers, such as the women whose stories are dealt with in this chapter, a lack of interest in "reasonable arguments" or the truth status of religious claims is surely not because they want a spiritual "quick fix" nor is it to avoid religious hard work; the duration and intensity of their respective quests shows otherwise. Rather, the test of religious validity has moved more toward its experiential validity for these practitioners. That does not become mere subjectivism so long as they can provide reasons for and an account of their experience.

In his essay "What Is Happening to Religion?" sociologist James V. Spickard (2003) includes six "sociological narratives," each attempting an account of the current state of religious life in the United States. The fourth,

"Religious Individualism," outlines the shift from institutions to individuals as the place where religion is located: "Individuals now pick and choose among various religious options, crafting a custom-made religious life, rather than choosing a package formulated by any religious hierarchy" (14). Rather than accepting what religious leaders tell them, individuals now choose for themselves. According to this view, people might stay within a tradition even while they reject the core beliefs of that tradition, a demonstration of "the growing autonomy of religious believers" (16). Spickard, not entirely inclined to see this trend as a unique instance of postmodern individualism, suggests that religious eclecticism goes back at least several centuries, and that laity have often practised rituals not entirely consonant with orthodoxy. Folk traditions, for example, might be tolerated or overlooked, "so long as individuals adhered to such core practices as baptism and Holy Week duties" (16). In this respect, his fourth narrative, "Religious Individualism," does not provide a full account of contemporary religious change. Nonetheless, the novelty of this option might lie in its being exercised by those who choose to remain outside the aegis of any single religion, who do not, in other words, simply add to, or deviate from, the practices or beliefs of their core denomination – like the Jew who practises Zen.

For Roberta Lamb, for instance, no question arises of "cultic tolerance" for her practice of whatever rituals the members of her "Circle" might engage in; nor on the other hand is she restricted by her involvement in the New Kadampa Tradition of Buddhism. Rather, she takes from each of her two religious involvements what suits her. She told RDK researcher Hannah Dick that when a scheduling conflict arose between the twice-weekly meeting of the Kuluta Centre's Foundation Class and a meeting of her women's circle, she choose to go to The Circle because it gathered less frequently, only once every six weeks. She said that the teacher then resident at the Kuluta Buddhist Centre, Gen Thekchen, was comfortable with her choice. Yet, realistically, how could he take any other position? The Kuluta Centre mostly provides its programs on a fee-for-service basis; participants do not have to promise that they will not avail themselves of religious services elsewhere. If a group insists on being its practitioners' sole source for spiritual practices, such a requirement may be too great a demand. Claims for exclusive religious allegiance will not work with those seeking to augment or supplement their religious lives.

In the late 1970s one of the most popular books addressing the topic of women and religion was a collection of essays entitled *Womanspirit Rising* (Christ and Plaskow 1979). Often used in religious studies courses, and since overtaken by scores of other books published in the area, this classic text raised the issue of whether traditional theologies, given their patriarchal nature, were relevant to women. More specifically, could the past be reshaped or reinterpreted so as to include women's experience, or did new traditions have to be created? Amidst other parallel experiences of contemporary women in Kingston, many of whom have been able to find ways of exercising appropriate religious leadership, the stories of Roberta Lamb, Janet Faubert, Elizabeth Greene, Kellye Crockett, and Joan Fast stand as examples of how the religious upbringing of one's childhood informs the adult life. Though their adult practices may appear to be at some distance from the faith that was a part of their younger lives, their eventual religious resting-places are not necessarily contradictory or at complete odds with those early religious influences. Contemporary women in particular have been exemplary in forging new spiritual pathways, often on the peripheries and borders of organized religions, and have found ways of constructing a coherent way of integrating their own experience into a consistent religious life story. Despite historic and systemic exclusion from formal religious leadership roles, women have persisted in charting their own routes into alternative ways of being religious and living out their religious identities.

9 Religion in Institutions: Universities, Hospitals, and Prisons

A CITY OF INSTITUTIONS

One of the best-known characterizations of Kingston is that it is a "city of institutions" – most notably five federal prisons, the Canadian Forces Base, the Canadian Forces Joint Headquarters, Queen's University, the Royal Military College, and St Lawrence College, to say nothing of the various hospitals, secondary schools, and office headquarters that one would find in any city its size. A 2009 year-end newspaper supplement published by the Kingston Economic Development Corporation lists Kingston's largest public sector employers, ranging from CFB Kingston with 7,800 employees, and Queen's University with 4,200, through the health-care institutions and school boards and Correctional Services Canada, all with more than a thousand employees each. In contrast, among private sector employers only two, StarTek Canada and Invista Canada, with 1,200 employees each, have more than one thousand people on their payrolls. Kingston has never developed into a major manufacturing or industrial centre.

Some of the institutions serve a much larger population than the city's approximately 150,000 people. Hotel Dieu Hospital's website says that it provides "expert care to more than 500,000 people in the region" encompassing southeastern Ontario (Hotel Dieu Hospital a). Although Kingston soon lost its capital status when the federal government was relocated safely inland and northwards to Ottawa, and although its importance as the junction of shipping by water through the Great Lakes or the Rideau Canal has diminished since the nineteenth century, the city has achieved and retained its status as a "sub-capital" (Osborne and Swainson 1988, 245). That is to say, its facilities serve the needs of the surrounding region, including an area whose boundaries can, for some purposes, extend west to Oshawa or Toronto and east almost to Montreal and north as far as Ottawa.

Kingston's role as a regional sub-capital can be clarified in comparison with some other Ontario cities. Guelph, a city of about the same size or even a bit larger than Kingston, is about an hour's drive from Toronto, less than an hour from Hamilton, an hour and a half from London, and just a few minutes from Kitchener-Waterloo. All of these other places are larger centres of population than Guelph's 150,000 people. That means, therefore, that if hospitalization or specialized medical treatment is required, any one of these other cities provides the resources that might not be available locally or as an alternative to the 180-bed Guelph General Hospital. Further, the University of Guelph, a medium-sized comprehensive university of high quality, has an undergraduate population of more than seventeen thousand students, and two thousand graduate students. Even so, other universities are available nearby, such as Wilfrid Laurier University, the University of Waterloo, McMaster University, the University of Western Ontario and, of course, several more options existing in the larger Toronto area – for example, the University of Toronto, York, and Ryerson. In contrast, for a Kingstonian seeking comparable or alternative options for either hospital care or for university education, the closest facilities are in Ottawa, two hours away, or in Toronto, three hours to the west.

Some of the differences between Queen's University and, say, the University of Toronto or Laurier University became evident to me over several visits to these and other campuses over a period of many years. As a visiting professor at the University of Toronto, I realized how many students travelled by public transportation specifically for their classes and then left soon after to return home. The campus appeared to be relatively deserted at night. York University, of course, is known as a commuting campus that many students reach by car. Similarly, I was told that many students at Wilfrid Laurier live at home with their parents and drive up to an hour to reach the university. For others, Laurier has a satellite campus at Brantford. Things are different at Queen's University where most – the usual estimate is 90 per cent – of its fifteen thousand students come from outside Kingston, well beyond commuting distance, and about 90 per cent of that number is estimated to live in housing within walking distance of the campus. These facts alone, as we shall see, mean that student services are heavily utilized at Queen's, and that student clubs, including religious clubs, are a major feature of campus life. For instance, whereas students in Toronto from minority religious traditions can practise their faiths at home or in local places of worship that their parents attend, in Kingston, especially if no such facilities are available, campus religious clubs provide the necessary alternatives.

Students arriving at Queen's from across the country and from other countries bring to a Kingston a range of religious backgrounds hardly to be found among the permanent residents of the city. The same is true – perhaps even to a greater extent – among the more than three thousand students at the Royal Military College, now Canada's only military college, situated on its picturesque peninsular vantage point between Fort Henry and the La Salle Causeway. In 2002 the Protestant and Roman Catholic chaplains at the college arranged a multifaith religious service with the participation of the officer cadets, or OCdts, who read the prayers. The RMC news release of 4 October 2002 reported: "The military cadets to represent their religious traditions during this service are Fourth Year OCdt Bruno Bérubé – First Nations of Canada prayer; First Year OCdt Birendra Konara Ranasinghe-Bandara – Buddhist prayer; Fourth Year OCdt Alinah Espinas Cruz and Third Year OCdt Sébastien Hubert Allard – Christian prayer; First Year OCdt Ryan Edwards Thomas – Jewish prayer; Second Year OCdt Loay Mohamed Nabil Abd El-Beltagy – Muslim prayer; First Year OCdt Taryn Neelam Johal – Sikh prayer; and Second Year OCdt Dazius Mirza – Zoroastrian prayer." Captain Swavek Gorniak, RMC's Catholic padre, stated: "This celebration reflects the diversity and plurality of RMC and Canada as a nation." While the last-named prayer in this list was given by a Zoroastrian student, few if any Zoroastrian, or Parsi, families are living in Kingston, indicative of the religious diversity that students coming to Kingston for post-secondary education bring with them.

QUEEN'S UNIVERSITY: THE UNIVERSITY CHAPLAIN

One of the unusual aspects of Queen's University is the existence of a university chaplain, until recently a full-time position filled by an ordained member of the Christian clergy who is an employee of the university. There have been only two incumbents since the World War II, Marshall Laverty from 1947 until 1983, and Brian Yealland from 1983 to the present. With his partial retirement in 2008, Yealland continued the chaplain's work on a half-time basis. Both Laverty and Yealland, by accident more than intention, have been ordained United Church ministers. According to Yealland, the position at Queen's was established along the lines of a military chaplaincy. Laverty had been a chaplain during the war, and continued to use the familiar title "Padre" during his life at Queen's, where he became a well-known presence. Yealland describes the position as coming "into prominence following the Second World War when the university was welcoming a number of veterans back to Canada from the war effort, and finding ways to include them ... most of whom probably had experienced a fair amount of battle fatigue and the kind of trauma associated with seeing war" (interview, 27 September 2005). Describing Laverty's work as chaplain, Yealland continues: "So he guided this whole process from what began as a kind of an extension of care to veterans all through the '60s and '70s and into the '80s."

Initially the position made more sense when it was assumed that most students were Christians. Padre Laverty in most aspects of his role as chaplain would conduct what amounted to a service of Christian worship. He included a Christian prayer in various events in the life of the university – at convocations or meetings, at services for the installation of the principal, on Remembrance Day or at Christmas, or at the baccalaureate service for graduating students. Laverty visited students who were hospitalized and was available for drop-in counselling at his office prominently situated near the entrance to the gym. He also conducted, especially for current or former students, weddings in the chapel of the Theological College, baptisms, or, when necessary, funerals. He was legendary on campus for having a "photographic memory": provide him with your surname or hometown, and he would ask about someone you might know, or whether you were related to a particular individual, especially if that person had come to Queen's. Even in the 1960s the entire incoming first-year class would be entertained, in groups of forty or fifty, in the Laverty home on Albert Street over a succession of Sunday evenings. Laverty would introduce each new arrival at one of these gatherings to those already seated around the living room. These introductions became a tour de force – a recitation of a long list of names by the time the invitees had all arrived.

Yealland noted that by the time he became chaplain questions had been raised about "what sense would it make to take – to bring in – a professional religious person from a specific tradition for a university which is clearly becoming a pluralist institution." One of his early challenges was how "to be a resource to this diversity of religious groups." The Christianity of almost every member of the student body could no longer be taken for granted: "Certainly by the time I came into the position in 1983, you didn't make that assumption at all, and certainly you don't make that assumption now. You make the assumption that the vast majority of students are likely more on the secular side. And then there are a whole range of particular groups of students with a religious background – Protestant, Catholic, Muslim, Jewish, Hindu, whatever." The Interfaith Council, today made up of representatives from the groups Yealland lists here – and with Buddhist and Aboriginal representation added – was established to assist students in finding contacts for their particular faith. As well, this Interfaith Council came together and assisted at a memorial service in Grant Hall after 9/11, and again in January 2005 after the Asian tsunami: "We have developed the ability to form a prayer circle, to stand in a circle with each other and offer a prayer or a meditation or an offering in regard to a specific issue" (interview, 27 September 2005).

Aside from his role in being part of, or conducting, ceremonies in the university, Yealland says that his job involves "offering support, advice, encouragement, counselling – mediation on occasion – advocacy, for anyone in the community who needs that sort of support." Despite these efforts, he feels the chaplaincy is not as visible as it once was. Perhaps that is the inevitable result of the university becoming larger and more diverse, making it impossible for any individual to function as the kind of visible figurehead Padre Laverty was. Too, the expansion of various kinds of student services includes some of the work previously done by the chaplain. Student Affairs at Queen's today includes a range of services provided by a staff of 170, covering various facets of counselling, health and disability, residence life, career planning, day care, and athletics. With the increase of minority religious traditions at Queen's, students from within those traditions tend to seek out an advisor from their own faith group. As Haseeb Khan, the chair of the Queen's University Muslim Students Association, commented, the chaplain is "not the first figure" he would approach for issues about his faith. Though he said that Yealland had helped their group in several important ways, for personal issues related to Islam he would prefer to seek out one of the Muslim professors on campus (*Queen's Journal*, 30 January 2007). This kind of recourse to the expertise from mentors within one's own tradition, in addition to the growth of religious clubs on campus where peers provide their own alternative religious communities, has also affected the role of the university chaplain.

DENOMINATIONAL CHAPLAINS AT QUEEN'S UNIVERSITY

The denominational chaplaincies at Queen's University include the Roman Catholic and Christian Reformed campus ministries. Father Raymond J. de Souza is chaplain at Newman House, a large red-brick home on Frontenac Street west of the School of Business and the location of the Roman Catholic mission to campus. A few doors away, on Frontenac at the corner of Union Street, stands Geneva House, the home of the Geneva Fellowship Campus Ministry, whose director is Rev. Stephen Kooy, a Christian Reformed minister. Newman House and Geneva House conduct programs on their premises and rent out rooms to Queen's students. Both these chaplains are recent ordinands, de Souza in the Archdiocese of Kingston in 2002, and Kooy in 2007. Kooy had ten years' experience as a youth pastor in Ancaster, Ontario, before coming to Queen's. De Souza, who also serves a parish on Wolfe Island, completed two degrees at Queen's as well as graduate studies at Cambridge. In many respects he fulfils the role of the public intellectual, writing a weekly column for the *National Post* on varied topics from the perspective of his Catholic faith – collected with his other writings covering topics such as secularism, politics, and sexuality on his website (de Sousa).

A third campus ministry is conducted by Rev. Val Michaelson of St James' Anglican Church. This Anglican chaplaincy was previously centred at Canterbury House on Queen's Crescent and run by Sel Caradus, a math professor who became an Anglican priest. Because of the proximity of St James' Church, located, in fact, on campus, the Anglican ministry to Queen's students is now provided from the church. Aside from Bible study groups, the most prominent aspect of Michaelson's work is a regular Wednesday morning communion service, with visiting speakers, geared to students.

To these denominational chaplains could be added the paid staff of those campus religious clubs – for example, Queen's Navigators, and in the past, Campus Crusade for Christ and Queen's Christian Fellowship – who are also considered chaplains. Previously all these campus chaplains used to meet frequently, but as Yealland explained, "We haven't been meeting regularly like that in the last few years; there have been fewer of us, and we're, I guess, a bit more dispersed in what we do – not quite as focused on doing things in a coordinated kind of way." While they never operated as "chaplains" in any official capacity, at various times clergy and other people from such nearby churches as Chalmers United, St Andrew's Presbyterian, First Baptist, and Bethel churches "were interested in being a part of what was happening at Queen's," Yealland recalled (interview, 30 March 2007).

The Roman Catholic chaplaincy deserves extra attention due to its long history at Queen's. Two Newman Clubs were established in 1917 in Canada, the first at the University of Toronto and the second at Queen's a few months later. For much of the twentieth century when students were assumed to be either Protestant or Catholic, the spiritual needs of Roman Catholic students were served by the Newman Club, with masses specially provided at the St James' Chapel of St Mary's Cathedral. Catholics were a minority group in those early years, perhaps less than sixty students, according to an article in Queen's *Alumni Review* magazine (Spring 2002). Monsignor J. Gerald Hanley of St Mary's Cathedral was for many years the Roman Catholic counterpart to Queen's Padre Laverty. Like Laverty, Hanley was a fervent Queen's supporter – I recall him passing along the Golden Gaels football score during the procession of a fall convocation – and, like Laverty, is listed with a dozen other honorary members of the Alumni Association. Asked who founded or was most involved in Newman House from its beginnings – though the Newman Club is ninety years old, there has been a Newman House for fifty – Raymond de Souza immediately thought of Hanley, commenting that while "there may have been other people before him, he just happened to be part of it the longest, and was best known" (interview, 10 March 2006).

In an interview de Souza said that the biggest challenge for the Roman Catholic mission on campus is that "the university itself is very secular." Although "the chaplaincy officially gets along very well with the university ambience," he thought that "the ideas that animate the *Queen's Journal* or the lectures and so forth would be very secular, and often anti-religious" (ibid.). Judging by materials put out by "the university Student Health Centre or the AMS [Alma Mater Society], or orientation activities," he felt that the image conveyed is that for Queen's students "socializing would involve mostly alcoholism and promiscuity – that would be the two main things." In contrast to his impression of the dominant culture at Queen's, he noted that there are probably a thousand students who belong to Christian groups and who are not in that category. He thought that drinking and sexual activity may occur to a greater extent at Queen's than at other universities, and that Queen's faculty is "more hostile" and "more secularized" than elsewhere, with the result that "there are poor relations with the Catholic community."

Maintaining religious faith in a university environment that is, in some sense, secular is addressed by religious clubs, predominantly student-run, on campus. Hannah Dick, in a paper presented to the Canadian Society for the Study of Religion in 2007, dealt with how these clubs create their space in an atmosphere that is both officially secular and at the same time religiously pluralistic, promoting the co-existence of many different religious traditions. The following section expands on some of the arguments and illustrations offered in her paper, "Religious Clubs at Queen's University: Between Secularism and Pluralism."

RELIGIOUS CLUBS AT QUEEN'S: BETWEEN SECULARISM AND PLURALISM

Charles Taylor begins his hefty book of almost nine hundred pages, *A Secular Age*, with the question, "What does it mean to say that we live in a secular age?" (2007, 1). He goes on to inquire what this secularity consists of. While there may be debate over whether secularization – and what kind of secularization – is a feature of contemporary society (Swatos and Christiano 1999; Stark 1999), Paul Bramadat suggests that "if some (even merely institutional) form of secularization seems to be evident in North American culture in general, it is especially evident in the social and academic contexts of secular universities." For, as Bramadat continues, "Although most universities in North America began as outgrowths of Christian denominations, during the past century the majority of these institutions have become explicitly secular" (2000, 15).

At a university such as Queen's, the advocacy of religion – much less of a particular religion – in research or teaching contravenes the tenets of neutrality and objectivity that govern academic inquiry. For some years now such Christian vestiges as the Lord's Prayer have been removed from the university's convocation ceremonies. In 2007 Jason Laker, then dean of Student Affairs at Queen's, told a reporter from the student newspaper that universities do not know "quite how to handle religion." He attributed the difficulty to two things: "One is this notion that it's very esoteric, medieval stuff, and we're about rational thought and evidence. Another angle has to do with fear of litigation. The university does not want to run into a situation where they seem to be promoting religion in general or a particular religion" (*Queen's Journal*, 26 January 2007). Subsequently, the student government at Queen's, the Alma Mater Society, announced the formation of a Religious Issues Committee with the objective of understanding the different faiths represented on campus. One member of the student government said, "It will be a formal acknowledgement and will put religious identity on the radar within the AMS." He added, "I don't buy the argument that we live in a secular society" (*Queen's Journal*, 27 May 2008). Another member commented that it was necessary to counter the impression that the university environment is hostile to religion: "At a lot of universities, the atmosphere is extremely atheist so those who choose to believe in a religion are often made fun of or made to feel less intelligent for their beliefs ... That's discrimination."

Such views align with the conclusions of Conrad Cherry, Betty A. DeBerg, and Amanda Porterfield in their ethnographic examination of the state of religious practice on four American university and college campuses. They stated that post-secondary institutions in the United States have "become more optional and pluralistic" rather than more secular (2001, 294). The authors found that, while the study or practice of religion is no longer compulsory as it once was at some colleges, and while tolerance toward other religions is widely shared, American students "have never been more enthusiastically engaged in religious practice or with religious ideas" (295). At Queen's, a non-religious institution with Christian origins, both secularism and pluralism inform the religious landscape. Following Paul Bramadat's assertion that an evangelical club at McMaster University, Inter-Varsity Christian Fellowship, or IVCF, is on the "periphery" of the university campus (2000, 20), it is worth exploring the ways that religious clubs at Queen's resist marginalization and re-centralize religion in their members' lives by negotiating the secular and pluralist terrain of the campus. Interviews with club leaders and participants, supplemented with data from club websites and the Queen's University Archives, are used here to examine three areas:

the proximity of clubs to one another, possibilities for interfaith dialogue, and the challenges of the secular learning environment.

First, notwithstanding the means by which religious clubs distinguish themselves from one another, they stand relatively close together on campus. Despite its long-entrenched Christian heritage extending back to the 1840s, Queen's has an undeniable history of religious diversity. Indeed, many of the Christian groups extant on campus are contemporaneous with – if not more recent than – the other religious clubs associated with "minority" traditions such as Islam and the Bahá'í Faith. Jewish, Muslim, and Bahá'í students have maintained organizations on campus for at least the past fifty years. However, this diversity is not yet widely appreciated: the census of incoming students conducted by the university, which examines ethnic, socio-economic, and sexual diversity, does not inquire about religious affiliation. This omission provides one example of religion being marginalized on the secular campus to the extent that it is not part of the discourse of diversity that customarily revolves around issues of race and ethnicity.

Nevertheless, the campus is a microcosm for the religious diversity present in Canadian society at large, with representatives from various different religious traditions all sharing the same secular space available for their needs. For example, the Soka Gakkai International Club, or SGI, a Buddhist group with origins in Japan, was initially designated to share worship space with the Queen's University Muslim Students Association, or QUMSA, although this cooperation became impossible due to the prayer needs of both groups (SGI interview, 5 October 2005). Similarly, the Ban Righ Centre has been host to a number of campus religious clubs that have used the same space at different times (interviews with Campus Association for Bahá'í Studies, 30 September 2005, and Unitarian Universalist Club at Queen's, 3 October 2005). Quakers – a religious organization from the community using campus space – when meeting at Ban Righ experienced distractions from Buddhists chanting in the building at the same time (see chap. 6).

Religious clubs must also share the same venues and media on the campus for news and publicity. Various groups vie for visibility by putting up posters to promote events and meetings and by advertising through student newspapers. For the most part the groups are drawing their new members from the same pool of students. This competition for attention is further heightened at the biannual campus Clubs Night, when various associations set up displays to advertise to prospective members within the student body. The faith-based clubs are usually grouped together in one specified area, making "shopping" for religious clubs quite convenient. At the John Deutsch University Centre, religious diversity is evident when posters advertising a Campus for Christ meeting appear next to an ad for a QUMSA panel discussion on Islamophobia or to an interactive display on the Holocaust erected by Hillel.

Bramadat employs a theory of differentiation to explain the contemporary state of religion whereby "religion is not expelled from the larger social system." Rather, he says, "religion simply becomes more concentrated in a different part of an increasingly complex social system" (2000, 17). At universities, religion as a marginal phenomenon becomes concentrated in campus religious clubs (17–18). As Bramadat points out, in a pluralist environment – such as that at Queen's, where religion is "differentiated" – groups need to define themselves in opposition to one another (17). For example, Queen's Christian Fellowship, or QCF, began to assert a more "low-key" style of evangelism once Campus Crusade for Christ (later known as Campus for Christ and, still later, in Canada at least, as Power to Change Ministries) emerged at Queen's in the late 1990s (interview, 3 February 2006). One QCF member explains that this differentiation occurred naturally once the more assertively evangelical group appeared at Queen's and each club began to cater to a different facet of the Christian student populace. In an instance of conscious differentiation, the Unitarian Universalist Club at Queen's was established in direct response to the aggressive tactics employed by Campus for Christ in an attempt to create an alternative environment for discussing religious issues (interview, 3 October 2005).

There are at least nine non-denominational Protestant clubs at Queen's and three Catholic ones. Moreover, each has found a particular way of maintaining a distinctive identity in the face of so many options, though sometimes the denominational affiliations are muted. Morning Star Christian Fellowship appears to be centrally Christian with its claim, "Members of our group are inter-denominational; we believe that the Bible should speak for itself, allowing the Holy Spirit to guide us" (Morning Star). There is nothing explicit on any of the eight pages of the Morning Star website, each one featuring the official Queen's crest, that reveals the parent organization to be Seventh-day Adventist. One of the links provides a scant clue, however. It refers to vegetarianism, a feature of Seventh-day Adventist practice, and contains the initials SDADA, for the Seventh-day Adventist Dietetic Association. Campus for Christ has asserted itself as an aggressively missionizing group, the majority of whose members attend conservative evangelical churches, specified by the Campus Crusade for Christ representative as Bethel Church, the NeXt Church, or Kingston Gospel Temple (interview, 27 October 2005). More particular groups, such as Athletes in Action and Think, Inc., combine extracurricular activities, athletics, and drama, respectively, with Christianity. In the instances of the Korean Christian Fellowship, the Kingston Chinese Christian Fellowship, the Queen's Chinese Catholic

Community, and the Korean Catholics of Queen's, two marginalized aspects of identity, religion and ethnicity, have been aligned so as to differentiate further these clubs from other Christian groups on campus. The number of Christian clubs thus reflects the diversity of religious needs at Queen's.

This differentiation is present among non-Christian groups as well. The Thaqalayn Muslim Association was formed in 2001 as an alternative to QUMSA, where some Shi'a members felt their minority needs were not being met. As the co-founder of the Thaqalayn Muslim Association put it, "I decided to found a new organization that could cater to the educational aspects – the propagation of information of the Shi'a school of thought to the wider community at large, to the Muslim and the non-Muslim community" (interview, 1 November 2005). While this club purports to represent the views of all Shi'a Muslims, the presence of another Shi'a club, the Ismaili Muslim Students' Association, has caused the Thaqalayn club further to distinguish itself by representing the particular views of Ithna Ashari Muslims: "Our activities just really have been a bit different than what the QUMSA or what the Ismaili Students would do – so sort of filling a different niche in the community."

Other groups are too small or already too particularized to become further stratified. Though the Kuluta Buddhist Centre is present on campus, as well as a Zen meditation group, there is no general Buddhist club. The Soka Gakkai Club caters to members of Soka Gakkai International – a New Religious Movement that is an offshoot of Nichiren Buddhism – that has taken hold primarily in Japan. Soka Gakkai at Queen's attempts to re-centre itself by advertising public lectures, inviting students to come and "learn about Buddhism." For other groups, being non-differentiated can pose unique challenges. One past president of Hillel, the only Jewish students' organization at Queen's, emphasized the challenge of catering to Jewish students of differing affiliations and levels of adherence: "The sects of Judaism are based on affiliation, but every single Jew has their own way of practising, their own way of believing, and their own way of, you know, expressing themselves Jewishly, and their own way of considering themselves a member of the Jewish people" (interview, 27 September 2005). In effect, it appears that differentiation and particularity have become the norms on the pluralist campus.

Second, possibilities for interfaith dialogue are created amidst diversity and differentiation. Bramadat explains the tension that arises when a university that encourages diversity finds itself host to religious groups that do not share this pluralistic view (2000, 17–18). Chaplain Brian Yealland elucidates this tension when he remarks that "the counterbalance to the issue of diversity is the issue of particularity." Then he asks, "Who doesn't feel pluralist here?" Yealland mentions such chaplaincies on campus as the Christian

Reformed Geneva House and the Roman Catholic Newman House, as well as Queen's Christian Fellowship, Campus for Christ, and Navigators. "And so," he concludes, "here are these chaplaincy based groups that are fairly particular, and for the most part these days not moving towards pluralism or diversity" (interview, 27 September 2005). While the Campus Crusade for Christ spokesperson said that the Christian clubs on campus have an agreement not to proselytize among one another's members, members of non-Christian groups often remain viable targets (interview, 27 October 2005).

Vivian Lee, an RDK research assistant, has even suggested that there are adverse psychological effects from the presence of proselytizing groups like Campus for Christ. Lee argues that groups whose mandates directly contradict the pluralist concerns of the university should not be tolerated and that their harmful effects on the university populace need to be recognized. Queen's Alma Mater Society refused to fund a new group called the Gentlemen's Club because, as an organization open to males only, it was viewed as sexist. However, Lee states, "Campus Crusade's accusations and propaganda against students who they consider 'immoral' directly challenge students' freedom of dignity and freedom of religious pluralism" (paper, Rels-451, April 2003). In the fall of 2006 QUMSA had to defend itself against charges that it was exclusivist because, although many of its activities were open to non-Muslims, only Muslims could be elected to executive positions. The group pointed out that under the Ontario Human Rights Code exemptions were granted for groups such as theirs.

At Wilfrid Laurier University in 2007, a controversy arose from an opposite point of view when an application for official club status for the Laurier Freethought Society was denied. Interestingly, at Laurier the supposed atheistic secularism of the university was subordinated to the tolerant aims of religious pluralism. The refusal was based on the Freethought group's promotion of "a fulfilling life without religion or superstition." The accompanying explanation for the denial of status was: "While this university is indeed technically a secular institution, secular does not denote taking an active stance in opposition to the principles and status of religious beliefs and practices. To be clear, this is not meant to say that the promotion of science and reason are illegitimate goals. But due to the need to respect and tolerate the views of others, the Campus Clubs department is unable to approve a club of this nature at this time" (Frame Problem). The club's vice-president wondered in his online blog how his club could be denied official status on the basis of intolerance when the promotion of exclusive religious dogma by other clubs was permitted (Venovcev n.d.). Eventually, when club status was granted for the society, its acceptance was credited to the influence of wide media attention. The exclusion of such a campus club at Laurier seems anachronistic when one learns that a parallel instance occurred at Queen's University as long ago as 1949, when Paul Roddick, a war vet, tried to found the Queen's Atheist and Agnostic Society. Principal Wallace, apparently worried that such a club might be an affront to the "Christian traditions of Queen's" in the midst of a financial campaign, took steps to divert the issue until the fundraising was past (Roddick 2006, 27–9).

An alternative tactic to disallowing specific clubs is to promote interfaith dialogue in an effort to give each religious group on campus a voice. One student-run club on the Queen's campus, the Interfaith Council, seems to want to do just that, promoting interfaith discussion and understanding. In practice, though, most religious clubs do not participate in this group. For several years at least it was primarily composed of members of the Bahá'í and Soka Gakkai clubs who initiated a series of dialogues between their clubs: "We had speakers from the Kingston community on the SGI side and some from the Bahá'í group" (SGI interview, 6 October 2005). Both these groups tend to agree more than they disagree on religious and social issues. Far from fulfilling the interfaith aims of religious pluralism, it appears that meetings of the Interfaith Council were partly a means to promote their respective groups. After giving an invited presentation to a meeting of the Interfaith Council, I was loaned a copy of a promotional video by a Soka Gakkai member who wanted to make an appointment later to discuss SGI with me. In contrast, the largest and most visible clubs – including Campus for Christ, QUMSA, and Hillel – are less concerned with providing a voice to each group on campus than with the challenges of secularism and discrimination.

Interfaith dialogue may not in fact be the most successful way to negotiate the pluralist landscape at Queen's. In fact, such dialogue may lead to conflict when the proselytizing interests of some groups allow for the active recruitment of students who belong to non-Christian clubs. Instead, more needs to be done to map out the face of religious diversity at Queen's to determine whose views are being heard and made visible and whose are being overlooked. In this vein, the Queen's Interfaith Council recently conducted a survey of students' religious affiliation and perceived levels of religious accommodation at Queen's. Because Queen's collects no information of this kind, these data will be the first step toward determining representation and visibility. In addition, another identically named "Interfaith Council" – not referring to the student club this time but to a group comprised of representatives from various faith groups and organized from the Chaplains' Office – has compiled a calendar of important faith dates. By showing the festivals and holy days from various religions, the calendar identifies occasions when individuals might be absent from classes or work. It also serves to publicize the needs of pluralism and to encourage administrative and professorial support for different faith concerns. These attempts may prove to be more effective at promoting pluralism in the long term than efforts at interfaith dialogue or the prohibition of particular clubs.

Third, the challenges of secularism confront all religious groups on the university campus. One aspect of this challenge shared by members of every single religious group on campus is that of the secular learning environment. Indeed, the effects gained by participation in a campus religious club are predominantly related to the ability of these groups to negotiate a spiritual dimension in an otherwise secular environment. Bramadat mentions that evangelical students tend to "negotiate contracts" with the secular world around them to aid in their transition to university. He refers to the Inter-Varsity Christian Fellowship as "an alternative institution within an institution," providing assistance in coping with university life and offering religious counterparts to secular social events (2000, 21). His analysis of McMaster's IVCF group could also be applied to the Queen's context. For instance, George Rawlyk provides a case study of a young woman entering Queen's who had become a Christian with the assistance of her high-school teacher in her hometown of Hamilton. The teacher's own Christian faith had been strengthened during her university years by her association with Queen's Christian Fellowship, and she wanted to help ensure similarly Christian support at university for her student. The student sought out Queen's Christian Fellowship soon after her arrival at Queen's, though she was later to switch to Campus Crusade for Christ (Rawlyk 1996, 25–30).

As another example, QUMSA provides prayer space on the Queen's campus for Muslim students who must pray five times daily. This prayer space is easily negotiated between the administration and a campus group, where otherwise a Muslim student might have to pray individually and more explicitly in public – which he or she may not feel comfortable doing. In an interview, one QUMSA representative emphasized the club's role in arbitrating on behalf of Muslim students, highlighting both the provision of prayer space as well as the introduction of Halal food in the cafeteria (interview, 25 October 2006). Another important function of the group, he noted, is to petition on behalf of students who have exams that conflict with Muslim holidays. While the faith-dates calendar is a step in the right direction, clearly it has not fully eliminated the need for case-by-case negotiation by such groups.

One of the most important ways that campus religious clubs negotiate religiosity in the secular learning environment is by providing a community where religion is accepted. Queen's Hillel holds Friday night dinners for Jewish students, allowing them to retain some connection to their religious identity or culture and to form a community with other Jewish students. Hillel also aspires to create an environment on campus that is hospitable for the practice of Judaism, even for students who never participate in Hillel (interview, 23 September 2005). Their efforts toward increased understanding include promoting Jewish holidays and educating the Queen's community on Jewish faith and history. The Hillel mandate thus includes asserting a comfortable Jewish space on campus in the midst of secular learning and a plurality of other groups.

For Soka Gakkai Buddhists, daily chanting is a pivotal part of practising their faith. Moreover, chanting with others is considered more religiously effective than chanting alone. Daily morning sessions held by the club provide both a venue for public prayer as well as a community with which to chant, thus encouraging the enactment of religion on campus. Queen's club member Ben Jones remarked, though, that some practices might seem strange to other students: "Of course, it's also just a really different thing, if you go into a room and see people chanting to a scroll, it's sort of frightening and people will sort of shy away from that. So that's one of the concerns. And we've had people come to the group and then just become – and just not show up anymore. And we ask them, they just say, 'It's just too cult-like for me,' or something, and that's one of the problems, I think" (interview, 6 October 2005).

The Campus Association for Bahá'í Studies also seeks to create an alternative community. Members of this club are often challenged by the "party culture" at Queen's, and find in the club not only access to other Bahá'í students but also access to the Bahá'í Community of Kingston, to which the campus club is closely tied (interview, 30 October 2005). According to one member of this club, this community support provides an invaluable sense of comfort and belonging in an otherwise alienating secular context. It also provides an important connection to the Bahá'í Community of Kingston's public devotions, as there is no designated place for Bahá'í worship in Kingston. The member of the Campus Association for Bahá'í Studies we interviewed said that she did not know any other Bahá'ís in Kingston when she arrived at Queen's: "I went to Clubs Night, saw that they had a nice poster of the Shrine of the Báb in Haifa – and I was like, 'Oh, that's the Bahá'í group!' – signed up, and already you feel like you've known these people all your life. You know, you may not know them on a, you know, where they're from and what they like to eat and that sort of basis, but you already know that their central values and beliefs about a lot of things are exactly what you feel. And that's a real, real asset to have – in any circumstance, anywhere you go."

The challenges of secularism are faced by members of all religious clubs, both by Christian groups and those representing faiths other than Christianity. Like Inter-Varsity Christian Fellowship at McMaster, the

Queen's IVCF chapter, Queen's Christian Fellowship, provides alternative frosh week activities to counter the secular social events of the main campus (Bramadat 2000, 21; QCF interview, 3 February 2006). Indeed, most campus religious clubs hold alternative events throughout the school year, many of them having less to do with religious devotion as such than with fostering a social environment where activities do not conflict with theological or moral norms. Such activities enable club members to live within the university environment. As well, they can serve as a demonstration of their faith to outsiders. The representative for the Campus Association for Bahá'í Studies spoke of how they gave workshops, or "deepenings," to address specific topics such as alcohol and addictions because "Bahá'ís don't drink and don't consume anything that impairs judgment." On the day she was interviewed she said that that evening one of the members was "going to go over the reasons for this and pull from the Bahá'í writings to support why this is an important aspect of the Bahá'í faith" (30 September 2005).

Haseeb Kahn of QUMSA stressed the association's involvement in such events as the organization of an annual Fast-a-thon and in volunteering to assist with cleanup duties in high schools and elsewhere in the community: "Because it is in action where you can learn where one thing means and something does not mean. So that's what we do, we try to hold events, such as Fast-a-thon. We try to hold events – such as Islamic Awareness Week, documentaries, films, talks throughout the year – where we can provide information to the general Queen's population. And I keep on emphasizing this again and again, and I tell people, that everyone is welcome in our club space. Everyone is welcome to attend our prayer spaces, prayer services, any of our talks even though ... because it is obvious the prayer service is for Muslims, but that does not mean that non-Muslims are barred from it ... we cannot do our job unless we invite everyone to what we do" (interview, 26 October 2006).

Religious clubs also provide a safe place for religious identity to be expressed. As one member of the Queen's Catholics (later renamed the Newman Catholic Club) explains, "A lot of people will come to Queen's not ready to practise their faith or not even concerned about it at all, and then they'll start struggling in classes if they find something that is [the] exact opposite of what they believe – which happens a lot. A lot of classes and professors will be spouting off things that people don't always agree with, and they'll want somewhere to go to talk about it" (interview, 10 November 2006). During a panel discussion held in Religious Studies 451 a member of Campus for Christ made a similar statement about the role this club played in her personal exploration of religiosity: "Coming to Queen's, it was more like I had to make my faith my own. I decided for myself what I wanted to believe. Like, I didn't have my parents to be on my back, [asking] 'Did you go to church? Did you go pray?' and so it was a decision that I had to make myself. So having Campus Crusade as a fellowship, and knowing that there were other people going through the same things ... was really encouraging to me" (interview, 5 October 2005). Not only do campus religious clubs provide the resources and means for living a faithful life on campus, they also support students going through the process of religious self-discovery.

Some Christian clubs go one step further, actively combating secularism on campus through rigorous missionizing and by holding public events. For example, the hugely popular "Does God Exist?" debate series sponsored by Campus for Christ is advertised to the general campus population. This event is one attempt to recentralize religion on the secular campus by involving prominent faculty members in theological debate. Furthermore, by resisting secularism and providing a venue for religion, campus clubs are also promoting their own interests. Moreover, helping to maintain the faith of students in a time when religiosity usually declines (Madsen and Vernon 1983, 128) promotes the health of religions beyond the context of the university campus.

It would be a gross simplification to conclude that the administrative and academic secularism of a post-secondary institution inevitably leads to the secularism of that institution's students. At Queen's, religion continues to thrive and survive in multiple ways, aided to a large degree by the existence of campus religious clubs with a vested interest in promoting the religiosity of their participants. For the university, which must balance the two mandates of secularism and pluralism, as well as for the students who participate in these groups, these "institutions within an institution" occupy an important niche that fulfils a role far beyond the scope of the casual social club. Chaplain Brian Yealland concluded his follow-up interview with us in this way: "If we thought that religion was kind of dead in the secular university – forget it, not at all! And I think when you add into that the spirituality issue, the fact that the vast majority of humans, whether they define themselves as religious in any way at all, somehow see life as having a sacred element to it or a spiritual element to it ... there's a lot of life there" (30 March 2007).

CHAPLAINCY AT THE ROYAL MILITARY COLLEGE

The Royal Military College is situated on Point Frederick, just east of Kingston's downtown between the Great Cataraqui River and Navy Bay. Established in 1874 to train gentlemen for the military profession, RMC has sent its graduates to fulfil Canada's military obligations around the world for more than a century. In 1959 RMC was granted the power to confer degrees in the arts, science, and engineering. By the mid-1970s it became officially bilingual, and in 1980 women were admitted for the first time. When Collège militaire royal de Saint-Jean and Royal Roads Military College were closed in 1995, RMC became Canada's sole military college. Today it has developed beyond its more limited initial role to become a research university to educate officers for Canada's armed forces.

In many respects RMC is what sociologist Erving Goffman describes as a "total institution," that is, "a place of residence and work where a large number of like-situated individuals, cut off from the wider society for an appreciable period of time, together lead an enclosed, formally administered round of life" (1961, xiii). While Goffman chiefly has in mind prisons and mental hospitals, where the residency is involuntary, he comments that "every institution has encompassing tendencies." RMC is more encompassing than Queen's, though both are universities. Among the five categories of total institutions that Goffman enumerates, he includes among his fourth category such places as "army barracks, ships, boarding schools, work camps, colonial compounds, and large mansions from the point of view of those who live in the servants' quarters" (5). The Royal Military College is comparable to at least two of these examples – the army barracks and the boarding school – that are set aside the better to accomplish their task by confining the sleep and work and play of the residents to one setting.

Research assistant Joe Green interviewed Major Jean-Yves Fortin, the Roman Catholic chaplain at RMC, on 12 April 2007 about a year before Fortin's unexpected death on 3 May 2008. Padre Fortin characterized the environment on the campus of the military college as "isolated." Author Jane Urquhart, who has lectured at RMC and whose novel *Sanctuary Line* (2010) has an RMC grad as one of its characters, spoke at the Kingston WritersFest in September 2010 of the college as a "sacred place" because of the way it is set off from the outside world. As a self-contained and enclosed world, this military college does not have the presence of an array of religious clubs on its campus. Its two chaplains, one Protestant and one Roman Catholic, assume responsibility for the religious needs of this entire community. As Fortin said, "here we are in our own little world," distinct from the city of Kingston and even from the nearby Canadian Forces Base Kingston where regular members of the Canadian military work and where they live with their families. The clientele belonging to the academic environment at RMC, Fortin stated, consists "mainly of officer cadets and university students who are training to be junior and senior officers in the Canadian Forces." The two Protestant and Roman Catholic chaplains, whose positions were established at the college after World War II, "are also responsible for the personnel, civilian and military," who work there.

Funeral of Capt. Matthew Dawe, Royal Military College, 14 July 2007

Contrary to its otherwise cloistered nature, the military college in July 2007 held a funeral ceremony to which the wider community thronged. Two thousand people attended the service for Captain Matthew Dawe, an RMC graduate and Kingston boy who had been killed in Afghanistan. Matt Dawe was the youngest of four sons, all of whom followed in the footsteps of their father, retired Lieutenant-Colonel Peter Dawe. The crowd observed the progress of the hearse through the Memorial Arch, then joined in the service across the road in the athletic centre. In the ten days following Captain Dawe's death, along with that of five of his comrades after the explosion of a roadside bomb, accounts occupied the attention of local news media and received national press coverage as well.

The nearby Canadian Forces Base Kingston has its own chaplains – seven of them, according to Padre Fortin – who care for the larger population of the units stationed there. Fortin described the work of the Canadian Forces chaplains: "On every CF base there is a chaplain on duty twenty-four hours a day, seven days a week, for whatever situation can arise – emergency from families, death notice, spousal abuse, child abuse. Go help the MPs [military police] calm someone down. Husband or wife is on a ship and the other partner needs something." Fortin stressed that RMC and CFB Kingston are two different entities, although their chaplains share a common mission:

"To minister to their own, facilitate the worship of others, and care for all," whatever their religious affiliation (interview, 12 April 2007).

Given the all-encompassing character of the Royal Military College, its two chaplains have more duties and responsibilities for the religious needs of the entire community than their counterparts at Queen's University. For one thing, no other part-time chaplains and no other religious professionals from outside are based on or regularly serve the RMC campus. Further, there is less interaction by the students with the religious institutions of the city of Kingston. Fortin did comment, though, when he has taken Roman Catholic cadets to St Mary's Cathedral for special, apparently infrequent, occasions, they have always been welcomed. Sometimes the two chaplains, either together or singly, conduct an ecumenical service for both major Christian groups. Otherwise, they are obliged to accommodate the religious diversity within the student body, including those who are not Christian. On Remembrance Day, Fortin said, "even though I am a Christian chaplain I will pray in a manner that will not offend non-Christians." In 2002, due to the growing number of Muslims present at the college, a curtain was put up in the Roman Catholic chapel to hide specifically Christian symbols and to create a place for worship for Muslims. Though this space was mostly set up for the noon prayers of Muslims on campus, it is used by others as well, including Jews. Fortin summarized the situation: "Every Friday after noon prayers it is converted to an RC chapel, and every Sunday after Mass it is reconverted to non-Christian prayer space in order to accommodate everyone. We have adapted." Although in recent years the Canadian Forces at the national level have added a Muslim chaplain and two Jewish chaplains, Fortin carefully pointed out that "they are not chaplains for the Muslims and for the Jews." Again, he emphasized, repeating the statement of the chaplain's mission, "they are chaplains for the Canadian Forces where chaplains minister to their own, facilitate the worship of others, and care for all."

HOSPITAL CHAPLAINCIES

The practice of accommodation to those of various faith backgrounds by a chaplain is witnessed in many institutions. At the Hotel Dieu Hospital crucifixes still hang throughout the building, and a statue of Joseph stands at the entrance. The hospital's website emphasizes both the historic and continuing Christian connections of the institution and the breadth of its mandate to provide care. Its mission, "rooted in the Gospel of Jesus Christ, is to make visible the compassionate healing presence of God to all persons" (Hotel Dieu b). The hospital chaplain, Ed Shea, a Catholic layperson, commented that the biggest change there has been "the absence of sisters and priests on site." He went on to state, "People know it's a Catholic hospital, but we have a United Church person, an Anglican person, Lutheran – so we're trying to be as multifaith as possible" (interview, 6 December 2005). While the Pastoral Care representatives were at the time of the interview only from different Christian denominations, Shea said, "we make it known that we will get in touch with anybody else." Even if he happened to know something about a particular other tradition, he said, "I'd bring someone in. Usually they want to see somebody of their own faith." In 2005 the Christian chapel on the main floor just inside the Sydenham Street door was being used by a few Muslims who would leave their prayer mats there. In October 2009 the hospital's newsletter announced the opening of a new Multifaith Centre, as recommended by the Pastoral Care Advisory Committee: "Located on Sydenham 3 in space occupied many years ago by a small Anglican chapel, the Centre provides a sacred space for people of all faith traditions. A quiet and warm spot, the Centre will be decorated with simple wall hangings and will make available prayer rugs and other features such as the exact direction of Mecca for Kingston" (Hotel Dieu c).

At the nearby Kingston General Hospital, Bob Hunt, then director of Spiritual and Religious Care, explained that the chapel there had been renamed a spiritual centre "to embrace the fact that we are not solely a Christian community" (interview, 16 November 2005). He said that while morning worship is held there for Christians, "If you go down at the right times of day you'll find people from the Islamic faith, right, and also people from the Jewish faith. We also have sweetgrass ceremonies for folks ... So we try to make that space as open and as inviting as we can, and we do that by not having any symbols that are specifically religious that are left, but are placed in the appropriate places when, for example, at a Christian worship service is taking place, we do have a cross that we hang on the wall, but when that service is over we remove it and store it." The Spiritual Care Advisory Committee of Kingston General Hospital, Hunt pointed out, included representatives from the United, Anglican, and Roman Catholic churches, as well as from Muslim, Jewish, and Native traditions. He reported that displays were set up in the hospital during Passover and Ramadan. This kind of interfaith venture in spiritual care at Kingston General Hospital, Hunt observed, was shaped after the events of 9/11, when "we simply made a decision to provide a space for people to come together around that."

Jim Scanlon, a retired Anglican priest who served for many years at St John's Portsmouth, in 2005 described the newly renovated chapel at the Providence Continuing Care Centre, the former Kingston Psychiatric Hospital, as "ecumenical" (7 December 2005). He mentioned that Anglicans, the United Church, and Roman Catholics used the chapel, transformed from its earlier use as a cafeteria. The Worship Centre won a Best of Canada Design Award in 2004 – one of twenty-five interiors in Canada to receive the honour that year – for the project design done by the architectural firm of Mill and Ross in Kingston. Designer Jason-Emery Groen says that his "favourite feature" of the space is the five-metre high oak cross (not a "crucifix" as it is sometimes mistakenly designated) described as "the unquestionable focal point of the chapel" (*Whig-Standard*, 28 August 2004). Thus the chapel is not quite the "multifaith worship centre" that the *Whig* article depicts, a point not lost on one reader who wrote to the newspaper's editor. Phyllis Robbins noted that it might be difficult for "Muslims, Jews, Buddhists, Unitarians and others who don't follow Christian religions" to feel welcome in a worship area dominated by a cross. She concluded, "Interfaith chapels have certainly been created in many public spaces to serve all of the above in providing a respectful and worshipful space for members of any and all religions. This space, unfortunately – and regardless of the design kudos it has received – isn't one of those. At the very least, that fact ought to have been recognized" (*Whig-Standard*, 9 September 2004).

Whereas the Hotel Dieu and the Kingston General hospitals have provided generic religious space for multifaith worship, the recently designed chapel at the Providence Continuing Care Mental Health Services is specifically Christian. PCCC, along with St Mary's of the Lake and Providence Manor, has since 2006 been under the sponsorship of Catholic Health Care in Canada, which assumed that role from the Sisters of Providence of St Vincent de Paul in Kingston. The Sisters of Providence previously took over the management of the old Kingston Psychiatric Hospital from the Ontario government. Listed on the website of the Catholic Health Alliance of Canada among the "tangible signs" that should identify Catholic health-care organizations are "a culture that supports Christian ethical values and spiritual beliefs" and "the prominence of various Christian symbols," among which the five-metre cross in the PCCC worship centre could be counted (Catholic Health Alliance a). While continuing its mission to care for the sick, clearly the Roman Catholic Church wishes to ensure the Catholic dimension of its health care organizations and providers.

An essay by Michael McGowan on "Sponsorship of Catholic Health Care Organizations" deals extensively with these roles in the context of various changes with respect to their historic mission and in the light of canon law (2005). Unfortunately, no consideration is given to what it might mean for the Roman Catholic Church to care for people of other faiths, or of none. While other chapels, such as at the Royal Military College or at other health-care institutions in Kingston have been transformed into multifaith worship centres, or else such a space has been added to accommodate those whose religion is other than Christianity, those using the mental health services at the Providence Continuing Care Centre find themselves in an institution whose central religious space is obviously and exclusively Christian. In a partly analogous situation, Providence Manor in Kingston provides long-term care for frail seniors. Its website speaks more to Christian ecumenicity rather than religious pluralism: "Worship services are held in the Mother of Sorrows Chapel, a beautiful sanctuary built in 1898. Services and pastoral visiting are offered by clergy of different denominations. The faith of individuals is respected" (Providence Manor). In every room at Providence Manor there is a crucifix, though it can be removed if the resident wishes. At the time of writing, none of those staying at Providence Manor were members of a faith other than Christianity, but some of the residents were agnostics or atheists who might want to make that request.

The tradition of having a Christian chaplain care for the religious needs of everyone within an institution has of course been long established in places – such as hospitals, schools, prisons – where for much of their history little provision was made for people who were not of Christian background. With religious diversity, when such assumptions are no longer viable, Christian chaplains have sometimes expanded their duty of care, as we have seen. Occasionally the degree of accommodation to those of other faiths, or of none, has been restricted, ungenerously provided, or entirely absent. On some occasions the chaplain's position has been an opportunity for proselytizing or for the exercise of a kind of Christian triumphalism. A 1992 Memorandum of Agreement between the Government of Ontario and the Ontario Provincial Interfaith Committee on Chaplaincy set forth as one of its principles that "it is the responsibility of the Government ... to collaborate with the faith groups in ensuring the provision of spiritual and religious care to those in government institutions and transfer payment agencies, and appropriate access for those in care to representatives of the faith of their choice" (Ontario Multifaith Council). What that "appropriate access" to religious care might mean has obviously received a range of interpretations within Kingston institutions, both Catholic and non-Catholic ones.

With issues such as these in mind, in the mid-2000s Queen's Theological College, now the Queen's School of Religion, in partnership with the Ontario Multifaith Council established a new program leading to a master's degree or certificate in Spiritual and Religious Care in a Pluralist Society. While providing courses in Christianity, the program also includes courses about other religions and about pluralism within the Canadian context. This program was set up "for those who are preparing for work in a pluralist context, such as a hospital, home for the aged, nursing home, prison, university, the military, or parish nursing, and who are already trained in a faith tradition" (Queen's University School of Religion). While such initiatives represent a new direction in the awareness of religious pluralism and diversity, the unfortunate legacy of providing chaplaincy and religious care for minorities under the aegis of the majority religion of Christianity has persisted for a long time.

NATIVE RELIGIONS IN KINGSTON PENITENTIARY

Because of a high concentration of incarcerated First Nations offenders from all parts of Canada, it is probably safe to conjecture that more native religion is practised inside Kingston's federal prisons than anywhere else within the city limits. In addition, as James Beckford comments in connection with British prisons, "prisons offer a particularly clear demonstration of how struggles over the reification of religion occur in the context of relations of power" (2009). That is, within prisons the form of religion becomes fixed in shape, in contrast with its generally fluid nature. This concretized religion is more easily managed and regulated according to the policies of the state that administers penal institutions and manages their incarcerated populations. As a result of what Beckford terms this "reification of religion" in prisons – as well as religious discrimination against First Nations people throughout the larger society of Canada – the right of native peoples to the observance of their ancestral religious traditions within federal penal institutions was not easily achieved.

This section of the present chapter on religion in Kingston's institutions examines the abrogation of native religious traditions within federal penal institutions in Canada and recent attempts to rectify that injustice. Some additional preliminary commentary helps illustrate the longstanding, often officially sanctioned, marginalization of the religions of First Nations peoples in Canada. Lori Beaman (2006) has written about how the legal construction of freedom of religion excluded or ignored the religions of First Nations people. Examining case studies in the United States and Canada, she observes how courts have ruled against the sacramental use of peyote, procuring eagle parts for religious ceremonies, recognition of land claims and the protection of sacred space, the right to hunt or fish out of season, and cutting trees and camping in a park according to ritual and customary observance. These activities have not been afforded protection as instances of religious freedom, usually understood and interpreted from a narrowly Eurocentric or Christian standpoint. Because the colonizers extrapolated the meaning of "religion" from western examples focused on the individual in relation to the supernatural, the religious rights of Aboriginal peoples in

Canada have not been protected by the law. Far from being an isolable compartment of their cultures, the religions of First Nations peoples permeate the whole of their lives. They consider the natural world itself as a sacred cosmos. As Beaman comments, "Certainly a number of religions provide their believers with a world view that is both prescriptive and explanatory or interpretive, but the sacralization of the life-world remains almost the exclusive terrain of Native Americans" (230).

The general incommensurability of Christian and native worldviews is summarized by John Webster Grant in his magisterial book, *Moon of Wintertime*. The shock to the native psyche at the European arrival, he memorably states, must have been "comparable to that which we might feel if extraterrestrial beings set out to colonize the earth" (1984, 21). Grant says that for First Nations peoples the "ultimate religious symbol was the circle, represented in the campfire or the circuit of the heavens." Alternatively, he suggests, for Christians the comparable symbol might be "an arrow running from the creation of the world through God's redeeming acts in history to the final apocalypse" (24). Put baldly, whereas European religious views understand the divine-human nexus to be disclosed in God's mighty acts, in God's revelatory intervention in history, Aboriginal peoples understand human life as continuous with nature. Europeans little knew about what to do with a religion whose two main components were dreams and visions, and ceremonialism (Hultkrantz 1989, 3). As a result, the validity – and viability – of the religions of First Nations peoples in Canada has been denied by the European colonizers, including government prohibitions of such ceremonies as the potlatch and sun dance.

What Nino Gualtieri of Carleton University heard when he interviewed clergy in the Western Arctic in 1971 was that "prior to the advent of the Christian missionaries there was little, if any, religion among the native peoples" (1984, 122). Whether considered to be inferior, worn out, or nonexistent, the religions of native peoples were devalued. True, sometimes points of contact were sought and used to facilitate the task of missionization or assimilation, but such comparative enterprises were not informed by a desire for inter-religious dialogue, to say the least. The disparity between the senders and receivers of the missionary message made such reciprocity an impossibility (see Grant 1984, 261, 263). As Grant states, "If the measure of success is that most Indians have become Christian, the measure of failure is that Christianity has not become Indian" (262).

Census data show that a higher percentage of native people than non-native people are Christian in Canada. This fact is sometimes used to demonstrate the insignificance of native religious traditions, even – and perhaps especially – today. Although Statistics Canada allows census respondents to report several ethnicities, only one religion can be chosen. At the conference Interrogating Religion where an earlier version of this part of the current chapter was given (17–19 April 2009), Peter Beyer of the University of Ottawa observed that Statistics Canada had lost the utility of the concept of ethnicity by allowing multiple selections in the 2001 Census. StatsCan appears not to want to have the same thing happen in the 2011 Census with respect to the category of religion. Though this official restriction to a single response is reportedly a consequence of statistical simplicity and convenience, thereby offering another instance of the state's reification and control of religion, it also indirectly provides a governmental endorsement of the popular view that an individual can have only one religion. Theresa Smith reported from her studies in the 1980s of the Anishnaabe of Manitoulin Island that they practised both Roman Catholicism and their traditional native beliefs. Indeed, she maintains that their Anishnaabe traditions, though operating less consciously, were "held at a somewhat deeper level than the Christian beliefs" (1995, 36).

Given the requirement to report only one "religion," it is more than likely that Christianity becomes the religion of choice for census purposes. As a partial consequence, the ten thousand self-reported practitioners of native religious traditions comprise less than 1 per cent of First Nations people in Canada. I have elsewhere dealt with the difficulties, in the western world at least, of taking into account religious hybridity (James 2006), or else what has been called "multiple religious belonging" (see Cornille 2002). Further, as observed in chapter 5, the religions of Chinese people in Canada are not well accounted for in the options presented on census forms, where the available choices are restricted to such religions as Buddhist or Daoist or Confucian. Because they do not fit within the categories offered, most Chinese Canadians (58.6 per cent) simply state that they have "no religion" (see Lai, Paper, and Paper 2005, 104). As the examples of the religions of Japan and of First Nations people in Canada also illustrate, the exclusivities of western monotheisms provide a too narrow means of accounting for other ways of being religious.

The provision of religious services to native inmates in Kingston Penitentiary, one of Canada's federal prisons, illustrates these longstanding tendencies. Kingston, with nine prisons in or near the city, has a reputation as Canada's prison capital. Kingston Pen, or KP, opened in 1835, is one of eight maximum-security prisons in Canada. First Nations people are "over-represented" in Canada's prison system – a phrase that makes it sound like an achievement, as when Jews are said to be over-represented in higher education. Statistics from Correctional Service Canada show that "at the end of March 2007, Aboriginal people comprised 17.0% of federally sentenced offenders

North Gate, Kingston Penitentiary

although the general Aboriginal population is only 2.7% of the Canadian adult population" (Correctional Service Canada a). Moreover, as compared with non-native offenders, their sentences are longer, they spend more time in maximum security and segregation, and they have a higher rate of recidivism. The correctional investigator, Howard Sapers, in his annual report for 2005–06 attributed at least some of this disproportion to a "failure to manage Aboriginal inmates in a culturally responsive and non-discriminatory manner" (Sapers 2006). Religious freedom is often claimed by individuals or groups seeking exemption or accommodation with regard to a single aspect of their practices and traditions: Mormon sects practising polygamy, soccer players wearing the hijab, Sikh boys carrying the kirpan to school, Jehovah's Witness children refusing blood transfusions, or Christians using corporal punishment on their children. With respect to First Nations people, the issue is more the elimination of an entire religion from recognition as a religion.

The Correctional Service Canada website provides details through documents and reports about how religious and spiritual services are now made available to federally incarcerated offenders. While respect for freedom of religion is guaranteed, the security requirements of the institutions might limit the provision of services. Chaplains are hired according to the policies laid out in a memorandum with an Interfaith Committee on Chaplaincy, which mentions "the responsibility of chaplains to exercise their profession by upholding the belief and practice of their faith community within a multifaith setting, collaborating with representatives of religious expressions different from their own and seeking to provide pastoral care and chaplaincy services to persons of different faith communities with the same commitment as to members of their own community" (Correctional Service Canada b). Until a few decades ago First Nations offenders were considered to have their religious needs adequately met by existing Christian chaplains. Making native religions a subset of Christianity often meant that only on the recommendation of Christian chaplains could native elders be admitted to penal institutions. When they were admitted, they often suffered the indignities of having their medicine bundles seized and searched by unsympathetic guards; a pipe ceremony might be scoffed at by staff or other inmates.

In the early 1980s members of the Department of Religious Studies at Queen's University signed a statement to the effect that the religion practised by First Nations people was indeed an authentic and bona fide religion. That kind of measure was seen as necessary to counter the suspicions of Correctional Service Canada that it was synthetic or illegitimate – or perhaps a kind of New Age pastiche. Part of the difficulty in accommodating First Nations religions was the inability to identify a priest, imam, or rabbi who would function parallel to other religious leaders; there was no holy book or sacred text comparable to the Torah, Koran, or Christian Bible, no regular day or time for worship services such as the Sabbath or Sunday that could be specified. How could something be regarded as a religion without seminary-trained priests, a sacred scripture, or a regular Sabbath? "Imagine, no religion!" someone might say in parodic paraphrase of John Lennon. How were native religious leaders trained and credentialled, especially when they sometimes appeared to be self-appointed? What kinds of sacred substances for burning or smoking could be brought into the prisons, and how were these to be distinguished from illicit drugs? What ceremonies were normative, given the diversity of tribal cultures represented in federal institutions?

Efforts to recognize something as a religion begin with what is known and familiar, especially the religion of the majority, a part of the regrettable process of the reification of religion. Within a government bureaucracy such as Correctional Service Canada, points of contact may be sought from the well-recognized practices and principles afforded by the Christian Church. The features of a relatively unknown religion are accounted for or explained by reference to the particulars of another. A century ago, when the potlatch ceremony practised by First Nation's peoples on Canada's West Coast was under attack, it was defended on the grounds that "a strict law bids us dance," suggesting that God had bestowed this dance as an alternative to the scriptures conferred upon Europeans. Similarly, the peyote ceremony has been made by members of the Native American Church analogous to the communion service. Oral history is assessed for its accuracy and veracity in comparison with normative written versions. Theseus's Paradox raises questions for us about the limits to this process of replacing one feature by another, supposedly analogous, one. Theseus's Paradox asks if an object remains fundamentally the same when all of its component parts have been replaced. After Theseus returned from Crete, the Athenians preserved his ship by removing old planks and timbers and rebuilding it: Plutarch asks about the identity of the ship if all the pieces are eventually replaced. More simply, do I still have my grandfather's axe if I substitute a new handle, and then a new head? Is it the same religion if most or all of its distinguishing features are replaced by analogous ones?

Anyone who has worked through possible definitions of religion with an undergraduate class will know the propensity to typify religion as entailing such supposedly necessary conditions as belief, ethics, worship, ritual, sacred text, priesthood, and so on. When examples prove such attributes not to be necessary, then the next step is often to specify conditions considered to be sufficient – though not necessary – for a phenomenon to be a religion. After that, the definitional task often turns to broader considerations of world view or ideology, at which point, of course, it begins to looks as if anything can be a religion. The article in the 1967 *Encyclopedia of Philosophy* (Edwards 1967) proceeds through these phases and finally lists a number of "religion-making characteristics" – a distinction between the sacred and the profane, and so on – in the attempt to sidestep the futilities of definition. The more of these characteristics that are present, the more likely that something could be described as a religion. Of course, then the question becomes how many of these religion-making characteristics can be absent and yet the designation still be claimed. How much can be subtracted from an accepted model or standard while it yet remains a religion?

In an anecdote perhaps oddly relevant to our purposes here, my brother relates how he made applesauce muffins, experimenting with removing one ingredient after another. He used white sugar instead of brown, and then decided the recipe didn't need sugar. Because he didn't know what to do with a leftover egg yolk, he stopped putting in the egg white. Not understanding the difference between baking soda and baking powder, he put in neither. Milk became water. He cut out the cinnamon because his son didn't like it. Next, vegetable oil, an unwanted fat, was eliminated. Finally, he upped the amount of oatmeal and left out the flour. My brother comments, "Admittedly the taste and texture of the applesauce muffins had changed by this time. The kids decided we *had* reached the point that they weren't really muffins – and so called them 'nuffins.'" Perhaps, then, by this process of subtraction the religions of First Nations peoples become a "nuffin" religion.

That is, when so many of the familiar ingredients are taken away, little is left to identify what remains as recognizably a religion. This characterization is supported by the view that religions progress through various stages of development from primitive animism until they reach the sophistication of full-blown monotheism. As Sam Gill states, the term "primitive" in primitive religion gets in the way of understanding, because it put too great a gulf between us and them. He prefers to speak of "nonliterate" culture, thereby stressing its "oral and nonverbal aspects." Hoping to avoid the pejorative connotations of the word "primitive," Gill admits is still "unfortunate" that his alternative term, "nonliteracy," "must state the condition negatively" by referring to what they lack, that is, writing their language (1988, 7). Again we arrive at the point of fallout and confront the consequences of evaluating other cultures' ways of being religious by the normative standards of the West.

Let us turn to positive developments in this sketch. In the early 1980s a policy statement on the practice of "Aboriginal spirituality" was prepared for Canada's federal prisons by Joseph E. Couture, of Cree descent, a Ph.D. in psychology, and a former missionary. Couture rightly emphasized the primacy of ceremony among First Nations peoples rather than of "codification, dogma, or doctrine" (1983, 6). While stressing "the oneness of culture, spirituality, and religion" (11), he made no effort to specify shared theological principles of any kind, such as belief in the Great Spirit or Mother Earth. Rather, his position paper identified twelve "components" that he viewed as necessary "to enter into Aboriginal spiritual realities" in the context of the federal penal institution. These features include (1) elders, recognized by the community for their wisdom, and who function as master teachers, healers, medicine people, and sometimes as shamans; (2) gifts or powers possessed by elders; (3) feasting and sharing, especially when certain foods or tobacco are shared; (4) prayer, whether petition or thanks, by which the relationship to other powers is expressed; (5) fasting, an age-old tradition that is a form of prayer; (6) pipes, used by individuals and in groups; (7) sweat lodges, specially constructed for purposes of purification; (8) religious artifacts, ranging from eagle wings to shells and gourds; (9) herbs and incense such as cedar, sage, sweetgrass, tobacco, animal substances, or peyote; (10) diet requirements that may be local, seasonal, or spiritual in nature; (11) teaching/learning needs within an educational program prescribed by the elders, and including chaplains, social workers, and liaison people; and (12) spiritual advisors or native chaplains, provided when elders are not available (6–10). Such components, of course, correspond to widely shared aspects evident in the pan-Indian movement throughout native North America, and therefore represent commonalties. As a central operational principle Couture insisted that Correctional Service Canada accord to native religion "status and protection equal to that of other religions." He also sought to have acknowledgment of "the inherent and preferred right, retained by incarcerated Native inmates, or freedom to believe, express, and exercise their religion" (11).

The current situation within Canada's federal prisons is one in which access by native offenders to religious practices is vastly improved over what it once was. On 2 April 2008 I interviewed Tanya Michelin, the Aboriginal liaison officer at Kingston Penitentiary, where about seventy of the 420 inmates have Aboriginal ancestry. The programming offered to native offenders includes sweats and pipe ceremonies, weekly healing circles, and change-of-season ceremonies held four times each year. Perhaps most impressive is the fenced area, obviously widely regarded as a kind of sacred space, within the grounds of Kingston Penitentiary, which contains a permanently installed sweat lodge. In addition, procedures have been developed for the assessment of native elders, who must be free of a criminal record, have the recognition of their own community, demonstrate knowledge of native culture, and be suited to work within the prison. Most of them are over the age of forty, and some are above seventy. The "Strategic Plan for Aboriginal Corrections" protects native elders bringing sacred materials into the prison, as well as any inmates possessing such materials: "Security processes must respect the diverse cultures, traditions and practices of Aboriginal peoples. Security examinations of Aboriginal sacred objects will be accomplished in a manner respecting the spiritual nature of the objects and respecting the spiritual practices of the holder of those items." Consideration of Aboriginal social history is now part of the assessment conducted for the native offender. Over a five-year period beginning in 2000, almost $19 million was allocated toward release planning and enhancing the reintegration of native offenders into their communities (Correctional Service Canada c).

One innovation resulting from this initiative is evident at the Pittsburgh Institution, a minimum-security facility located at Joyceville, north of Kingston. There "native grounds," with a full-time native offender as groundskeeper, are situated overlooking the Rideau River. These native gardens provide the "three sisters" vegetables – corn, beans, and squash – as well as other traditional products such as sweetgrass, tobacco, cedar, and sage. The same site includes a shed, tipi, and sweat lodge for native offenders. These provisions are aimed at complementing other programs with the goal of "a culturally-relevant supportive environment conducive to healing" (*Dawagun Mikan* n.d.). The website for Correctional Service Canada includes a large section on "Aboriginal Initiatives," including a description of the establishment of eight healing lodges to assist with the reintegration of native offenders into communities (see Correctional Service of Canada a).

Asked whether any difficulties have arisen because of practices specific to one First Nations tribal culture conflicting with others that are "pan-Indian" – that is, more widely shared or more generically Aboriginal – Michelin acknowledged that sometimes problems had arisen, in particular with regard to the ten or twelve Inuit inmates. Nonetheless, she pointed out, the Inuit are united with other native inmates by drumming practices. Because their dietary customs are quite different from all other inmates, "country meat" is being provided for the Inuit offenders within Kingston Penitentiary – at the greatest distance from their home communities in the North – who also have access to an Inuit support worker. She reported no conflicts between native inmates practising Christianity and those following traditional practices. As one might suspect, given the importance of religion among prison inmates generally, Aboriginal offenders frequently begin to practise their own native religious traditions in a conscious way while incarcerated.

An audit in 2002 of the efforts to accommodate religious diversity within federal prisons concluded that the needs of the adherents of Aboriginal spirituality had been met relatively well. The major difficulty identified in the report was with the needs – especially the dietary requirements – of the 10 per cent of federal offenders who are neither Aboriginal nor Christian. Providing kosher and halal food, setting aside space for Wiccan ceremonies, and accommodating Rastafarian practices were specifically mentioned (see *Globe and Mail*, 13 January 2003).

In conclusion, then, an issue that remains – one with larger methodological and definitional implications beyond Aboriginal religions – has to do with the use of terminology referring alternatively to religion or to spirituality, sometimes differentiated as mutually exclusive. Many First Nations people refer to their traditional native practices as spirituality rather than religion, a view reflected in common popular understandings as well. Similar views are, of course, often heard by followers in many different traditions who, in preference to the term "religion," speak instead of their faith, or of finding the truth, or discovering a way of life.

In many circles "spirituality" is a nicer-sounding and less baggage-laden word than "religion." It is favoured, for instance, among groups who want to disavow their association with traditional institutional religion. That may account for the low reporting of Aboriginal religion on the census: you declare your religion but keep your spirituality private. Some groups want to assure people that their spirituality can be practised alongside a religion – Transcendental Meditation, for example, is not presented to prospective followers as a religion. The foregoing examination of Aboriginal religions within Canada, and within Canadian prisons, suggests that acceding to such terminological distinctions may hamper, perhaps needlessly, efforts to achieve official or legal recognition of some practices as religious. While there may be ignominious uses of the word "religion," and many reasons for seeking other terms of designation or description, and though there are instances where the application of the term is misleading or imperialistic or culturally insensitive, significant reasons remain for preserving its use. The late acknowledgment of native religious traditions within the context of Canada's federal prisons shows the limits of the narrow, popular, and inherited understanding of what religion is in a western context and how that can be a disadvantage for those excluded from its parameters.

CHAPLAINCY AND RELIGIOUS DIVERSITY

The problem evident in federal prisons when a chaplain from one denomination or religion is expected to meet the religious and spiritual needs of those from other faith traditions is common among institutional chaplaincies. In April 2008, when Lazer Danzinger was appointed as only the second rabbi since World War II to serve as a chaplain in the Canadian Forces, his battalion's senior chaplain commented, "We worship with our own, facilitate the worship of others, and serve all" (Runyan 2008). That mandate, paraphrased for the RDK interviewer by the Royal Military College chaplain Padre Fortin, sets a high standard for ecumenicity and pluralism when a representative from a particular faith tradition functions in a multifaith context. This kind of ideal – far from requiring that a chaplain represent a universalized "one-size-fits-all" religion amenable to everyone – means respecting and enabling the faiths of other people without muting or denying one's own. It means bearing witness to one's own faith without devaluing the faith of the other. To fulfil that requirement properly means, in many instances, surrendering the exclusive and prejudiced stances that some religions have held against other religions. It means recognizing that other faith traditions may, for those within them, be equally as valid as one's own. One denominational chaplain at Queen's University revealed that maintaining such a stance was very difficult – perhaps impossible – for a Christian, because "when you know that you have the truth," it is hard to attribute validity to the religion of someone else. In 1994, Bill Groningen, the Christian Reformed chaplain at Queen's University, affirmed the missionary imperative to spread "the unfolding story of Jesus which draws us into life everlasting" as "the best tale of life that can ever be told" (*Whig-Standard*, 21 January 1994).

The need for chaplains within institutions to be open and pluralistic varies according to the job description and context. For Canadian Forces chaplains, as we have seen, to "serve all" is part of the job requirement. Similarly, the Queen's University chaplain, Brian Yealland, has a responsibility to care for all those within the university, and not just members of his own religion. The same principle applies in "public" – or publicly funded – institutions such as hospitals, prisons, and nursing homes. The institutional chaplain whose position is funded by such a public institution has an overall responsibility to care for all of those who are under its care. Presumably some of those duties can be discharged by others when denominational chaplains are also present to care for their own members. For instance, the Queen's University chaplain knows that there is a Catholic or Christian Reformed chaplain on campus, or a faculty member available to advise Muslims, or that a particular campus club has a connection with its counterpart in the community. Most chaplains we spoke to stated that, if a need arose, they would readily call on a representative of another faith tradition for anyone under their care.

Some institutions, however – a Roman Catholic school might be an example – have their own explicitly religious character and focus as part of their mandate. Kingston's Regiopolis-Notre Dame, Canada's oldest English Catholic high school, founded in the 1830s, includes the following statement as part of its philosophy of education: "By inviting the individual to know Jesus Christ and His Church, the people of God, the students are called to be part of the Church's mission in the world" (see Regiopolis-Notre Dame). We were told in an interview that of 1,021 students at Regi-Notre Dame, three hundred did not indicate their religion. Some of these might be students attending the school from Asian countries as part of the school's international program. Of the rest, 683 stated they are Catholic, while the remainder – approximately forty – said they were Protestant. Emphasizing that "it's a Catholic school, I'm a Catholic priest," the chaplain, Father Dan Quackenbush, told us that "it's a requirement to go to Mass every month" and that each year students must "take one religion course in the two semesters." That required course "might be a philosophy course or a history of religions course, a world religions course" (interview, 16 June 2006).

My observation of religious studies majors at Queen's University who had graduated from Roman Catholic secondary schools in Ontario is that they were by no means narrow or rigid in their Catholicism. Rather, in a Catholic milieu at high school where they felt reasonably secure in their own religious background, they also developed a curiosity about the religious faiths of other people. Many reported that their high school courses in religion gave them an acquaintance with other religions that they chose to develop and explore further in their university studies. Father Quackenbush stated that his role in organizing religious activities as the school's chaplain is distinct from the teaching of religion within the curriculum, though he had sometimes been invited to classes. He thought that dialogue among people from differing religious backgrounds occurred in these classes. When he was asked to comment on "the defining characteristic, if there is one, of the school's way of being religious," he said there is "a deep abiding respect for the person in the school" and that "there's a real sense of community." The administration, he said, "go out of their way sometimes to accommodate the students here that come from especially difficult backgrounds."

The awareness of religious diversity in the wider community has done much to alter the role of the institutional chaplain, who can no longer assume that all those under his or her care will all share the same faith. People of various religions have become part of schools and universities and hospitals and prisons where only a generation before the religious composition had been quite uniform. That awareness of difference – and of the possibility of having no religion – has resulted in vast changes in the assumptions that chaplains bring to their tasks. Surely one of the great gains in cooperation and understanding that we have achieved is that clergy and faith representatives can respect the religious preferences, or lack thereof, of those outside their own traditions.

10 Religion in the City: Public Religion and the Religious Imagination

PERFORMING THE ACT OF RELIGION IN PUBLIC

A green awning above the stage shelters from the weather a vocal quartet and a half-dozen musicians with their traditional brass instruments. Behind them a large banner bearing the Salvation Army red logo proclaims "Sharing God's Love." In the background boats are moored in the municipal marina at Confederation Basin, with the nearby Shoal Tower and the blue expanse of water of Kingston Harbour stretching toward Wolfe Island and the St Lawrence River. "On summer Sunday nights," the major at the Salvation Army Citadel explains, "we take an hour from 6:30 to 7:30 down in Confederation Park," directly opposite the front of City Hall in the heart of Kingston's downtown. In this prime location the Salvation Army provides its music or invites Christian artists to participate: "We read a Bible passage and we pray – and this is in public forum. There's a certain receptivity and no negative feedback at all for using a public square." The major affirms that there is "certainly an openness spiritually in the city." This public demonstration of, and testimony to, their Christian faith "is certainly guaranteed by our Constitution" (interview, July 2004).

On 29 January 1883, 125 years earlier, Salvationists held their first meeting in Kingston, in Market Square on the other side of City Hall away from the waterfront (see chap. 4). On that occasion too there was a vocal quartet, and then four Salvation Army officers "knelt upon the snow and engaged prayer," according to the *British Whig*. That initial gathering, though, was considerably more raucous than its twenty-first century successor: "Revivalistic in style, the meeting consisted of enthusiastic singing, impassioned addresses against sin, fervent prayers for salvation, and frequent testimonies of the glory wrought by God in the lives of those saved" (Knowles 1991, 247–8). A second meeting the same day attracted fifteen hundred

Salvation Army at Confederation Park

spectators, including some hecklers. While that nineteenth-century arrival of the Salvation Army in the midst of public space in the city of Kingston was in the context of a Canada more or less thought to be Christian, their presence there today – albeit in a more subdued form – raises questions about the conditions and limits of the public practice of religion. What kinds of religious practice may be conducted in public space? Is a profession of Christianity permissible or acceptable to a degree that would not be extended to other religious groups?

During its centennial year of 1967 Canada was being transformed from a Christian country to a religiously pluralistic one (see Miedema 2005). Four decades later, Peter Beyer predicted that immigration from non-English and largely non-Christian parts of the world would mean, assuming persistence of the trends evident from 1981 to 2001, that "the religious landscape of Canada will continue to become more pluralistic, especially in favour of the three largest non-Christian worldwide religions, Islam, Hinduism and Buddhism" (2005). Yet, despite aging congregations and plummeting church attendance, the lineaments of something like a Christian culture linger in many Canadian towns and cities, reinforced by such measures as the observance of Good Friday and Christmas as statutory holidays, or Ontario's support of a Separate, or Roman Catholic, school system – and comparable measures in some other provinces – or the continuing vaguely theistic affirmations of God in the national anthem, the Charter of Rights and Freedoms, and prayers in Parliament (Biles and Ibrahim 2005).

The prophecy of inevitable and complete secularization has not been fulfilled. David Lyon cogently points out that instead of "no religion" we have "deregulated, reshaped, relocated, and restructured religion" (Lyon and Van Die 2000, 13). Religion has not disappeared from the public into the private sphere. The resulting situation has become far more complex than a simple bifurcation between those wanting more Christianity in the public realm and those who wish society to be free of all religion, or what in the United States has become a polarization of the religious right against the secular left. Most of the contributors to a collection of Canadian essays, *Recognizing Religion in a Secular Society*, argue from the assumptions of the three major western religions – and from such precedents as the mention of God in the Charter – for an enhanced role for presumably monotheistic religion in Canadian public life. No mention is made in the book of Sikhs, Buddhists, Confucians, or Hindus, or – except slightingly – Wiccans (Farrow 2004). Similarly, other scholarly considerations of "religion in Canada" have confined themselves to the statistical majority, that is, Christianity (see Hewitt 1993; Bibby 1987). Peter Emberley argues that maintaining references to God in the Constitution is not a matter simply of heritage nor recognition of historical roots but of metaphysics: "there needs to be a foundation of an incorruptible nature" (2002, 125). For him, religion is about reality and truth to be believed, not something to be dealt with psychologically, symbolically, or aesthetically (2002, 257–8).

Charles Taylor of McGill University, one of the co-chairs of the Commission on Reasonable Accommodation in Quebec, was a panellist on the topic "Rethinking Secularism" at the meeting of the American Academy of Religion in Montreal on 8 November 2009. Taylor said there were two broad types of normative thinking that represented the nature of secularist regimes. One, more hegemonic, is represented by France, and seeks to control religious boundaries. The other, represented by the United States, recognizes religious diversity. Amidst the principles of liberty of conscience, of equality for all, and – here the task of the Quebec Commission was especially apt – of providing an opportunity for all voices to be heard, neutral state institutions seek to honour freedom of conscience and to preserve neutrality, not just between religions but between religion and non-religion. The other panellists, José Casanova, Saba Mahmood, and Craig Calhoun, commented on secularism as an ideology and as statecraft, on individual and collectivist concepts of religious liberty, and on the ways that secularism is shaped by its religious context to the extent that a complete separation of religion from politics might not be possible.

Religious pluralism in Canada, largely the result of immigration, has meant that the stark alternatives of Christian hegemony versus secularism have been enriched and complicated by arrivals here who are, to be sure, Jews and Muslims, but Buddhists and Sikhs and Hindus, Zoroastrians, and Confucians as well. Various scholars have estimated the effects of immigration throughout the history of Canada on the prevailing patterns of religion. Keith Clifford has written of how, between 1880 and World War II, the Protestant vision of Canada as "His Dominion" was thrown into crisis by the massive immigration to Canada of "the Orientals and the Slavs" and by the religious beliefs and practices of "Mormons, Jews, Mennonites, Hutterites, and Doukobors" (1977, 28). Sociologist Hans Mol has examined the major immigrant groups of the twentieth century – Germans, Italians, Ukrainians, Dutch, Scandinavians, Polish, and Jews – maintaining that "old-country religion reinforced ethnicity all the more when the immigrant group and its members were marginal to Canadian culture" (1985, 63). Yet in 1993 Reginald Bibby could still write, rather dismissively and prematurely, that immigration had not much altered the religious makeup of Canada: "An examination of religious identification in Canada since the first census in 1871 through 1991 reveals that, for all the immigration that has taken place, the proportion of Canadians lining up with religions other than Christianity has changed very little" (1993, 22). He declares that from the standpoint of religion the Canadian mosaic is a "myth," and agrees with a *Maclean's* magazine survey that Canada is a Christian nation in name and in belief (26–7). While Bibby and others did not anticipate – or else did not fully appreciate – the impact of immigrants whose religion was other than Christianity, nonetheless earlier successive waves of immigration have each had their effect on religion in Canada. Their doctrines and worship and behavioural codes and rituals necessitate adjustments and accommodations on the part of Canadian towns and cities.

In the Montreal area municipality of Outremont, some Orthodox Jews wanted to fence their neighbourhood using a wire strung, almost invisibly, high between existing utility poles in order symbolically to demarcate an area for their Sabbath observances. This practice, known as *eruv*, was at first denied by Outremont in 2000 on the grounds that municipalities in Quebec were not permitted to allow the religious use of public space. In 2001, the Superior Court judge hearing the case took an opposing view, ruling that municipalities had a duty to accommodate religious practices when doing so would impose no hardship on others. The decision was acclaimed as a victory for the guarantees of religious freedom provided for in the Charter (Siemiatycki 2005). While such a case is unlikely to arise in Kingston – the number of Orthodox Jews is too small, nor do Jews live in a particular area of the city – Kingston nonetheless exhibits many of the tensions and adjustments exhibited in municipalities across Canada as the presence of diverse religious traditions affects the way in which school boards, city government, and municipal agencies conduct their business, often challenging the customary ways of doing things inherited from an earlier era.

The usual view is that Kingston represents the epitome of Upper Canada, especially its Anglo-Celtic customs and values (Osborne and Swainson 1988). Hugh MacLennan has depicted this Upper Canadian ethos in his novel *The Precipice*, set in the fictional town of Grenville during the 1930s, situated on the King's Highway between Toronto and Montreal on the shores of Lake Ontario. In MacLennan's Grenville, "Canada breathed out the last minutes of her long Victorian sleep" (1948, 3). Like almost every other Ontario town rooted in that past, its streets are "sweetened by names redolent of British colonial history: Wellington Street, Simcoe Street, Sydenham Avenue, Duke Street, Elgin Lane." As MacLennan so wryly and perceptively observes, in this matter of conferring street names, "Grenville was typical of its province," for "there was hardly a British general, admiral, or cabinet minister who had functioned between the French Revolution and the accession of Queen Victoria who was not commemorated in the name of a street, town, or county somewhere in Ontario" (13). Grenville's traditions, even in the period between the wars, was to continue to bear many of the characteristics of the nineteenth-century Protestant culture of the old Ontario that William Westfall has so ably described (1989).

Another renowned Canadian novelist, Robertson Davies, in his first trilogy set in the 1950s fictionalized – and satirized – Kingston under the name of Salterton, a small eastern Ontario city whose centres of civic power were the Anglican cathedral, the newspaper, the university and, to a lesser extent, the military college. A few years earlier, under the guise of the slyly ironic newspaper columnist Samuel Marchbanks, Davies offered a comparative description of Kingston in the 1940s: "As they are approached over water Quebec is noble, Montreal mighty, and Toronto strenuously aspiring, but Kingston has an air of venerable civilization which warms the heart; domes and spires, and the moral yet kindly outlines of its houses of refuge and correction give it a distinction of which any city might be proud" (qtd in Grant 1994, 93).

Those "domes" would of course include Kingston's City Hall and the architecturally similar St George's Cathedral, as well as Kingston Penitentiary, while the "spires" might refer to the Gothic architecture of Sydenham Street United Church or St Mary's Roman Cathedral, and Queen's University's Grant Hall. Moral, yes, but can the limestone features of a psychiatric hospital, homes for the aged, or prisons – "its houses of refuge and correction" – truly be said to be "kindly"? Kingston has not had the reputation of adapting rapidly to change, nor of being a city hospitable to outsiders or recent arrivals, though its size and location doubtless have more to do with a relatively small proportion of immigrants than overt unfriendliness. Yet, ironically enough, much of the city's religious and ethnic diversity comes from its hospitalized and incarcerated and student populations rather than from its permanent residents (see chap. 9).

How has the increased ethnic and religious diversity of the past generation, together with other changing practices, altered the face of religion within this mostly unilingual city? Further, how has the municipality responded to these changes? Geographer Brian Osborne shows that in the nineteenth century the fortunes of Kingston's major Presbyterian congregation, St Andrew's, were intricately bound up with the origins of Queen's University and the city of Kingston itself, in addition revealing much about the battles and vicissitudes within the Christianity of that era (2004). At least some of those sectarian struggles stemmed from different immigrant groups having religions not identical with those of earlier arrivals. The roster of ethnic Christian congregations considered in chapter 5 reveals far greater diversity within Christianity today in contrast with an earlier time when perhaps the greatest division imaginable was between Scottish Presbyterians and Irish Catholics.

In 1824 a Presbyterian funeral procession bearing a child's body – the son of one of the elders of St Andrew's – made its way toward the burial ground adjacent to St Paul's Anglican Church on Queen Street only to find the entrance blocked by Anglicans asserting their sole rites to inter the corpse. For the burial to take place, the Presbyterian minister had to defer to the Anglican priest. In 1843, and continuing for several more decades, a series of violent skirmishes erupted between Roman Catholics and Irish Protestants who were supporters of the Orange Lodge, culminating in a shooting death at the building site of the new Catholic cathedral. One outcome was a local split within Presbyterianism between Scottish and Irish factions. Today "Shannon's Cannon" – brought to Kingston, according to the inscription, "from the ramparts of Londonderry, Ireland where it defended Protestantism from 1649 to 1688" – sits on the lawn of St Andrew's Presbyterian Church, its barrel more or less pointed in the direction of St Mary's Roman Catholic Cathedral a few blocks away. In 1891, with temperance issues in the fore, the Presbyterians were objecting to the establishment of a new tavern across from their church at the intersection of Princess and Clergy – the same intersection, we shall see, where more than a hundred years later Presbyterians had to cope with street people using the church lawn or irreverent advertising in a storefront window. Internally, there were also debates among nineteenth-century Presbyterians about the celebration of the "'popish' festival" of Christmas, not that far removed from today's controversies around the meanings and observances attached to Christmas. Many of these battles within nineteenth-century

Christianity, so fully and ably detailed by Brian Osborne, parallel and foreshadow contemporary problems.

Even in the twenty-first century some of these issues – religious-secular conflict, inter-religious conflict, tensions among groups of immigrants or between more recent immigrants and long-time residents, the assumption of religious privilege on the part of an entrenched tradition – continue, though Presbyterians are less likely to be in the thick of them. Presbyterians have waned in relative size, importance, and influence in Kingston and in Canada over the past two centuries. Though Christians continue to have some of their most vehement quarrels with their co-religionists of other denominations and differing theologies, or even within their own churches, the growth of religions other than Christianity has created a new urban reality. Christian hegemonic assumptions are challenged by matters as various as recognizing the importance of Ramadan for Muslims (see chap. 7), accommodating the presence of various faith traditions in schools and hospitals and other institutions (see chap. 9 above), or decisions governing the distribution of explicitly Christian materials at public schools – for example, the shoeboxes prepared for Operation Christmas Child.

Prayers at Council Meetings

Though Jews have been present in Kingston since the nineteenth century, only in 2003 did the city elect its first Jewish mayor, Harvey Rosen. Rosen, at the time also the president of Beth Israel Congregation, announced as one of his first acts that there would be no religious dimension to the installation ceremony for the new council: "The simplest thing would be to eliminate it." The alternative, to have one or a number of clergy administer an invocation, prayer, or blessing at this multifaith council, was reportedly rejected as too "complicated" or "difficult" (Phillips 2003). The mayor's decision, while far from a unique response, was not the only option for altering existing practices, often persisting for a century or more, that assumed a uniformly Christian society.

In 1999 the Ontario Court of Appeal ruled in a case arising in another jurisdiction that the use of the Lord's Prayer, which tended to "impose a Christian moral tone on the deliberations of Council," violated religious freedom (Csillag 1999). The decision resulted from the efforts of one of the few Jewish residents of Penetanguishene, an Ontario town of eight thousand people, who felt pressured to stand and recite the prayer with others when he attended council meetings. Reportedly, he had even discarded the idea of running for council because of this practice. The court suggested as an alternative that the town "follow the lead of the House of Commons, where, since 1994, proceedings have opened with a moment of silence and a non-denominational prayer." Penetanguishene's mayor seemed not to comprehend the principles involved and issued a statement reporting that townspeople were having difficulty "understanding how one person can dictate what they can say or not say" (ibid.). Diana Eck, who since the early 1990s has headed up the Pluralism Project at Harvard University, argues that Christians need to discover ways of maintaining the truths they find within their own religion without denying the validity of other faith traditions for those practising them – "it is not fine for us to bear false witness against neighbors of other faiths" (2001, 24). She maintains that Americans must discover a form of "positive pluralism" beyond mere tolerance or recognition of the diversity of religions.

Even if the wishes of a majority cannot settle what mode of religious invocation might be used to open a city council meeting, neither can the objections of every possible minority be anticipated or satisfactorily accommodated. In 2001 the Ottawa City Council voted to retain its opening prayer – "Almighty God, let us work together to serve all our people" – despite its invocation of a "singular supreme being" that excluded atheists, non-theists, or people having no religious faith (Wheeler 2001). When a secular humanist objected that the council in nearby Renfrew violated his religious freedom with recitation of a prayer that named God, the court ruled against the objection. It is worth noting, as an aside, that such objections seem more often to come from atheists or secularists than from non-theists or non-monotheists such as Hindus or Buddhists or Confucians. Justice Hackland, citing parallel phrasing in the Charter, observed that the reference to God in a prayer as a source of values was not "a coercive effort to compel religious observance": "The current prayer is broadly inclusive and is nondenominational, even though the reference to God is not consistent with the beliefs of some minority groups. In a pluralistic society, religious, moral or cultural values put forward in a public governmental context cannot always be expected to meet with universal acceptance" (White 2005).

The question of how to "commit the act of religion in public," as someone has wittily phrased the issue, remains a challenge within a religiously diverse Canada. Members of a Roman Catholic order, the Sisters of Providence, have themselves demonstrated ways in which public multifaith ventures might be conducted. More than a decade ago they initiated a weekly silent vigil against poverty outside City Hall (see chap. 8). On key occasions representatives from other faith groups have joined them. On the tenth anniversary of their silent vigil, for example, there was an interfaith service with participation from Orthodox and Reform Judaism and various Christian denominations, as well as Quaker, Unitarian, Hindu, and Muslim representatives. While broadly inclusive representation might be unwieldy on every single occasion, other alternatives exist, such as rotating through a roster of participants, or drawing on a selection of prayers from various faith groups, or using an inclusive, more generic prayer.

Christmas and Seasonal Celebrations

In many parts of Canada old customs die hard, especially at particular seasons of the year. In Toronto several years ago the city came under fire when in an attempt at inclusivity the civic Christmas tree began to be referred to as a "holiday tree." A spokesperson for B'nai Brith Canada, as reported in a Reuters news story of 26 November 2002, opined that "to take a generic term, slap it on a symbol that really only has significance to one religion ... and then say we're being multicultural does not really fit." Common sense would seem to support the view that "whatever you call it, it's still a Christmas tree." Bernie Farber of the Canadian Jewish Congress added that he thought this renaming exhibited an excess of political correctness: "It's time to sort of get on with life, accept everybody for who they are and revel in their holidays as opposed to look for ways to deny people's holidays. It's just plain silly" (Rense 2002).

In Kingston in 2004 some objections were raised about a city employee who sent Christmas greeting cards to co-workers in City Hall. After the story appeared in the *Kingston Whig-Standard*, letters to the editor took up both sides of the issue, some seeing the gesture as a well-meaning expression of goodwill while others thought it was insensitive. Local religious leaders, including Jewish and Muslim representatives, in general have agreed that people should be free to extend whatever form of greeting they wish – though of course they cannot expect a religiously identical reciprocal greeting. In concert with contemporary practice, the City of Kingston made the decision to refer to December as the holiday season rather than the Christmas season, and to holiday hours rather than Christmas hours (Popplewell 2005). Nonetheless, as the city's website announced in December 2005, a "Christmas tree" remained, perhaps anomalously, in the office of Kingston's Jewish mayor, decorated by the H'Art Studio, a local organization for adults with intellectual and developmental disabilities. This "holiday" versus "Christmas" debate was greatly reinvigorated in 2005 when Boston seemed about to rename a Nova Scotian gift of a Christmas tree a "holiday tree." A similar fate of renaming threatened the tree at Rideau Hall. In both cases the threat was averted, according to an editorial in the *Ottawa Citizen*, when Boston's mayor and Canada's governor-general both opted for the more traditional nomenclature of "Christmas tree" that they themselves had grown up with (*Ottawa Citizen*, 29 November 2005).

Manger Scene at Confederation Park

While a municipal Christmas tree, especially if interpreted as secular seasonal symbol, or Christmas cards distributed by one city employee might be acceptable or at least excusable, a more explicitly religious representation such as a public manger scene may well cause offence. In the United States displays featuring the symbol of one religion have been prohibited in public places, because church-state separation forbids favouring one religion above another. A religious symbol might be acceptable if paid for privately rather than by public funds, or if one religious exhibit is "offset" by the symbol of a second religion – for example, placing a menorah alongside a crèche. In one Florida town, however, the town removed both displays when it was objected that placing a menorah beside a Christmas tree amounted to foisting the Jewish religion upon residents (Lithwick 2001).

In Kingston a nativity scene, owned, maintained, and stored by the city, is erected annually in Confederation Park across the street from City Hall. In 2002 Isabel Turner, then Kingston's mayor, contradicted a news report that its installation was going to be discontinued after some complaints had been voiced. The mayor announced, as reported on the city website, that council members had agreed to continue the practice. Following that announcement, the practice was still being continued as recently as December 2010. Turner also stated that "the majority of councillors want all creeds to be offered an equal opportunity to erect and display symbols of their faith that recognize important dates or events." These comments ignored the fact that the city itself, not a religious organization, had arranged the display of the manger scene. For such an "equal opportunity" to be truly equal, any other faith group should be able to ask the city to purchase a religious object appropriate to their tradition and have it erected, dismantled, maintained, and stored by the Parks Operations department at taxpayers' expense. Because such a request for equal treatment is unlikely to emerge from a minority religious group that has appeared only comparatively recently in the city, this civic presentation of Christianity has continued, as does the large Christmas tree erected in the nearby Market Square.

Close to the nativity scene is the outdoor stage where Salvation Army members have, as already mentioned above, continued to sing hymns and gospel songs. In other ways too religious groups have made use of public civic space. One church distributed flyers throughout their neighbourhood inviting people to join them in a nearby city park for food, refreshments, and entertainment. Whether this occasion served a missionizing or evangelistic purpose for the group rather than general service to the community or an opportunity to get acquainted, one can imagine that aggressive preaching or giving testimonials in parks or on street corners might today arouse objections, despite a general understanding that there exists the freedom in Canada to promulgate one's religion. Regulations governing the barricading of streets for parades or other events might affect religious organizations differentially. A group of Christians still gets approval to march down Princess Street carrying a cross from St Paul's Anglican Church to St George's Anglican Cathedral on Good Friday, but could the city similarly accommodate other religious organizations on their sacred days – especially if those are not statutory holidays?

People can be seen in public spaces in Kingston practising Tai Chi (whether or not it is accounted an explicitly religious practice), as they can in most other Canadian cities. Perhaps more notably, the Queen's University Muslim Students Association has held their welcoming picnic in September near the *Time* sculpture on Kingston's waterfront, accompanied with the offering of prayers in the usual position of prostration or *sajda*. A city park is a public area, and therefore "the public," including religious groups, may use it in any way, at any time, for any reason, without permission. So long as a group does not violate any municipal, provincial, or federal laws, cause damage to the park, or infringe on others' enjoyment of the space, they are free to use the city's public space. However, while it is not necessary for individuals and groups to seek permission from City Parks before meeting in Kingston's public parks, booking a park is highly recommended if a group wants to ensure use of the facilities in an uninterrupted manner. As with many procedures that lie in abeyance or remain unenforced, such booking "recommendations" can presumably be invoked as a means of control should the need arise – another potential example of the state enforcing a reified view of religion.

To gain the city's approval, a form must be completed with the name and purpose of the event – whether social, such as church picnics or reunions, or legal, such as weddings, or religious, such as prayer services and memorials. Applicants must provide proof of liability insurance coverage of at least $2 million. As the City Parks use permits specify, no one using a park may "stereotype or discriminate on grounds prohibited under the Ontario Human Rights Code" nor may they "promote or preach hatred or derision of any groups covered by section ii of this declaration." If any group is found to be discriminatory or inciting hatred, the city has the right to deny the booking, or to cancel an event in progress even if approval was not sought, and may deny any future requests from the respective group.

Monuments and memorials in public spaces play an essential role in fostering a sense of Canadian collective identity and a shared national history. They become the site of memorial ceremonies, as can be easily demonstrated at war memorials every Remembrance Day in towns and cities across Canada, when people come together to reflect upon the past, its meaning, and our collective loss. Such commemorations create a sacred space for this activity of shared religious and ritual observance. The Islamic Society of Kingston on its website publicly endorses participation by its members in Remembrance Day observances, together with an exposition of the Muslim view of war and peace. The only restriction on Muslim involvement is a caution against taking part in rituals that are specific to another religion. In general, though, such public gatherings have aimed at being inclusive and multifaith in nature. Even the aforementioned Sisters of Providence vigil held in front of City Hall on Good Friday a few years ago – on that occasion oriented toward world peace – included reflections by the rabbi of Beth Israel Congregation, the president of the Islamic Centre, and the monsignor from St Mary's Cathedral. Perhaps ironically, particular religious groups, often supposed to be at odds with one another, have often promoted interfaith cooperation far beyond anything that municipal governments have endeavoured to facilitate.

Memorials and Shrines

Shrines and memorials – even such practices as the lowering of a flag to half-mast – continue in an era often typified as "secular" as an expression of the human community's need to surmount the limit that death imposes (see Chidester 2002). Spontaneous shrines, more popular after the death of

Princess Diana or 9/11, are frequently set up at the scene of a road accident or of a murder, consisting variously of bouquets of flowers, written messages of condolences, or, if a child's death, toys or stuffed animals. Whether personal acts of remembrance, public displays of grief and loss, acknowledgment of human mortality, warnings of societal dangers, or defiant political statements – for example, with deaths due to drunk driving and gang-related shootings – these shrines represent positive and life-affirming responses, inherently religious because they seek to transcend the limits imposed by death. Such public expressions of the grief of private citizens, individually or en masse, are often constructed without the express permission or consent of the respective authority.

Sometimes families want a continuing memorial at the site, perhaps a lasting commemoration of their loved one, or to make a statement about unsafe streets or drunken drivers. A proliferation of crosses at a dangerous bend in a highway has for decades served as a more effective reminder to slow down than any warning sign could provide. However, an unauthorized wayside memorial might itself become a traffic hazard if drivers reduce speed unexpectedly to gawk. Responsibility for the maintenance of such sites as years pass, or when people move elsewhere, may also be a problem. While some memorials are maintained, or are renewed annually – often on the anniversary of the fatal incident – often they are left to their fates as crosses break down with age, and flowers wilt or fade over time.

Obviously, the practice of erecting shrines represents deeply meaningful human behaviour. What is a city to do when public space becomes sacralized due to the acts of a few citizens? Normally the City of Kingston requires an eighty-five dollar encroachment permit before the erection of any sign or physical object on public property. In the case of roadside shrines, despite the unauthorized nature of their presence, bylaw enforcement officers have an unspoken policy of leaving them intact as a gesture of respect to both the living and the dead, as long as pedestrian or vehicular traffic is not obstructed. Additionally, City Parks may ask for their removal if snow clearance or grass cutting is affected. Trees bearing memorial plaques in parks are a possible alternative, and have become a popular commemoration that also renews the urban canopy of foliage. In general, municipal officials informally recognize roadside memorials as private sacred spaces on publicly owned lands. Roadside shrines are an example of a policy grey area – neither legal nor illegal, neither written nor spoken. Likewise, when it comes to the private religious use of public spaces, the City of Kingston prefers a "live and let live" approach.

Regarding the scattering of cremated remains – strictly speaking, not "ashes," but compressed bone fragments, a much denser and more particulate substance – the city seems to have no clear answer. For all intents and purposes, the scattering of remains on public parks and waterways is sensitively overlooked within Kingston. Bylaw officers, City Parks employees, and funeral directors seem equally unaware of – or else benevolently ignore – the laws and regulations governing this practice. One memorial society based in Peterborough, Ontario, refers to cemeteries, private space, and crown land as possible areas for the scattering of cremated remains: "Cremated remains can be scattered just about anywhere, this contrary to what some cemetery salespersons say in an effort to sell cemetery plots and markers." While public parks are not mentioned, this society does state that it is "best not to scatter them on the ground where people will frequent" (Memorial Society of Peterborough). The Ontario Ministry of Government Services is in the process of replacing the Funeral Directors and Establishments Act and the Cemeteries Act with the Funeral, Burial and Cremation Services Act, which states at one place: "No person shall scatter cremated human remains at a place other than at a scattering ground operated by a person licensed under subsection (1) unless the person is permitted by regulation to scatter cremated human remains in such circumstances, at such a place or in such a manner as may be prescribed" (ServiceOntario).

As with the case of the erection of roadside or sidewalk shrines, presumably the permission to scatter the remains of a loved one is not generally sought beforehand. Families may opt to spread such remains discreetly on their own terms while the City of Kingston remains uninformed and unaware of the time and place of such practices. So long as the scattering of remains goes undetected, the city is tolerant of a custom that proceeds unhindered. Kingston does have a memorial bench and tree program in place, currently under revision with regard to placement, payment, and perpetuity. Citizens may purchase a bench or subsidize the planting of a tree in memory of a departed loved one. People sitting on a park bench, or whose dog visits a park tree, might well wonder if anything else was surreptitiously placed at this private sacred site. During the gathering of our research we learned of several individuals who had scattered a friend's or relative's ashes in a public place. We also heard of at least one funeral director who provided a film canister with a small portion of the cremains for scattering, while the larger part was left in the usual urn. The State of California, in part to alleviate the conflict people felt as they covertly scattered ashes in accordance with the last wishes of a departed person, has regularized the practice of public scattering. Cremated remains may be disposed of in various places, including at sea, under certain conditions or, with written permission, in public places where the practice is not prohibited. The major requirement is that such scattering must be done by a registered "cremated remains disposer" (California Code).

Concerns by city residents about the impact of religious practices on their city or neighbourhood might be aimed directly toward faiths that are new or unfamiliar, or that simply are representative of a minority tradition. In some cities the establishment of a mosque, meditation centre, or Hindu temple has led to protests. In Kingston in the early 1950s the Roman Catholic Church reportedly declined to sell property to a Jewish congregation wanting to relocate (see chap. 1). A few years earlier, in 1945, Ontario Justice Keiller MacKay had ruled against a restrictive covenant aimed at preventing the sale of property to Jews, on the grounds that it contravened public policy. MacKay stated: "If sale of a piece of land can be prohibited to Jews, it can equally be prohibited to Protestants, Catholics or other groups or denominations." He felt that "nothing could be more calculated to create or deepen divisions between existing religious and ethnic groups in this Province, or in this country" (qtd in McLachlin 2004, 19). One suspects that the citizens of a more secular society today might worry about the presence and practices of a Christian group as readily as those of any other religion. What of a Christian church situated in a mostly residential area providing a mission to the homeless, to street people, to psychiatric outpatients, or to ex-offenders? A church with a large bell or carillon, whatever the denomination, might not be readily tolerated by neighbours whose sleep is disturbed on a Sunday morning. Indeed, an anti-noise bylaw in Kingston has restricted the use of some ecclesial chimes and bells.

Religious Pluralism and the Public Sphere

The confident assumptions and predictions of a generation ago that increasing secularization would drive religion out of the public sphere have far from materialized. Despite an undeniable increase in an inner and private spirituality focused on the individual, the public manifestation of religion in a pluralistic society remains, demanding to be accommodated. Sometimes those who are unaffiliated seek to establish their shrines, scatter remains, or hold services in public spaces. As a result, the distinction between religious and secular has become difficult to uphold in contemporary Canada. Nineteenth-century Christians were concerned about the use of canals on the Lord's Day. As Marguerite Van Die writes, in the late Victorian era "national transportation systems of canals and railways ... moved people and goods more quickly and efficiently, but at the cost of being in operation seven days a week, thereby undermining the hallowed Protestant Sabbath" (2009, 7). Today stores stay open on Sundays, as do sports arenas, theatres, and other centres of commerce and entertainment. Illustrating the collapse of earlier rigid boundaries, one Kingston restaurant trades on the decline of the sacred with a sign that gleefully announces, "We confess! Our desserts are sinful," while a similarly designed sign outside a United Church dispenses maxims of secular advice such as "Never let failure go to your heart."

In 2004 signs in the window of a clothing store offended members of Kingston's largest Presbyterian Church across the street. The store, on the northeast corner of Clergy and Princess streets, posted an advertising banner in its windows showing a whirling vortex of water, a crown-of-thorns logo, and the words "gsus sucks." An adjacent banner read "lost in gsus." Perhaps members of St Andrew's Presbyterian Church upon leaving Sunday worship saw the banner and gave "gsus sucks" their most obscene meaning, that is, a reference to Jesus performing fellatio. Of course, the verb "sucks" has become simply a handy colloquial negative designation (Seth Richardson, *Slate Magazine*, 2 August 2006).

The tongue-in-cheek defence that "gsus," the brand name of the Dutch clothing company, Gsus Sindustries, was a reference to a "G suspended" guitar chord, and not a homonym of the name of Christianity's central figure, would do little to settle such a storm. After all, the company's website disclosed many more examples of allusions to Christianity – "Gsus is coming," "Gsus de f*ing Dutchman" walking on water, celebrity wearers as "disciples" – all an obvious effort to create brand-name recognition, instil edginess, and "create," in their words, "some rumble in the shopping streets." On a similar sign outside a store on Toronto's hip Queen Street West proclaiming "life's great, gsus sucks," the last word was obliterated by a tagger. Discussions raged on blogs about whether paying attention to the advertising only contributed to achieving its objectives. Is this generally irreverent approach after all only a form of juvenilia that is best ignored?

In Kingston, perhaps having in mind how Jews react to swastikas in public places, or how Muslims object to slights against the Prophet, objections were made by local Christians to the newspaper, to Kingston's Dutch consul, to the Downtown Business Association, and to the police – raising the possibility of these signs being an instance of hate crimes. A 2004 *Toronto Star* article about Gsus Sindustries stated that these were the only complaints brought against the company during its three years in Canada (*Toronto Star*, 29 July 2004). Lincoln Bryant, the minister of St Andrew's Presbyterian Church, says that he preferred to be guided by the biblical directive "to go to the person who has offended me" (interview, 13 April 2004). He approached the store's manager directly and brokered a compromise to remove the sign on weekends, and to seek a replacement from the company. When a second "lost in gsus" banner arrived, "gsus sucks" came down permanently, and the minister sent a thank-you letter.

The possibility of hate propaganda arose earlier in connection with the Aislin cartoon that offended Muslims (chap. 7). The Criminal Code specifies that wilfully promoting hatred against an identifiable religious group is a crime. If the statements are believed to be true, if their discussion is for the public benefit, and "if, in good faith, [the person] expressed or attempted to establish by argument an opinion on a religious subject," then a crime has not been committed (Media Awareness Network). Motivation obviously becomes a key issue here: the person must have intended to promote hatred against the group. On this basis it is difficult to argue that Terry Mosher or Gsus Sindustries are in the same category as such infamous Canadian hate propagandists as Jim Keegstra and Ernst Zundel, both of whom were convicted of hate crimes. But the basis on which native leader David Ahenakew, despite his remarks about Jews and the Holocaust, had an appeal against his conviction for a hate crime upheld is instructive. Ahenakew's angry and private confrontation with a reporter was the context of his anti-Semitic remarks, which were therefore interpreted as less than "wilful" and public promotion of hatred.

The ways in which religions maintain their roles within the municipal environment, and the extent to which religions contend or cooperate with one another, can in some respects be gauged by the history of St Andrew's Presbyterian Church. Coincidentally, in the late nineteenth century the congregation was concerned about the appearance of a new tavern at the same intersection. That century was marked by the aforementioned inter-religious confrontations, as with the Anglican Church over Presbyterian rights of burial in a churchyard, or by violent conflicts between Catholics and Orange Protestants at the site of the new Roman Catholic cathedral. Today Catholics and Protestants, as well as Jews and Muslims, live more or less amicably together. The proportion of Presbyterians has declined in the past century and a half, while the number of Muslims in Kingston today exactly equals the number of Jews. Nationally, the number of Muslims exceeds the number of Presbyterians by more than 40 per cent – 580,000 as contrasted with 410,000. Kingston's Presbyterians today find themselves confronting the enemy of secularism, feeling threatened by the way Christianity can be mocked or pushed aside in mainstream popular culture. In general, most people would readily understand the outrage of these Presbyterian Christians by these signs. Yet interestingly, while both Presbyterians and Muslims in Kingston have wanted to claim that they were the victims of hate crimes, there is no indication that these two faith groups gave support to each other in their shared experiences. An opportunity for a wider discussion of how religious groups are subject to blasphemous or insensitive remarks seems to have been missed.

Yet the changing demographics of religious pluralism have sometimes led to new alliances. On such contemporary issues as same-sex marriage, evangelical Protestants may find that they have more in common with Roman Catholics, or even Orthodox Jews or Muslims, than with liberal Protestants. Orthodox Jews seeking to establish a Hebrew Day School might also find more commonality with other faith groups wanting government funding for their religious schools than with Reform Jews. As Diana Eck says, "stories of interreligious encounter also remind us that our religious traditions are multivocal, that no one speaks for the whole, that we argue within our traditions about some of our deepest values, and that newfound alliances may be made across the political and religious spectrum" (Eck 2001, 384).

Kingston, like many other Canadian cities, tends to deal with the challenges posed by immigration and the resulting religious diversity, as well as changing contemporary practices, through trial-and-error modifications, informal accommodations, ad hoc adjustments, or alterations necessitated by formal legal tests more often than by undertaking deliberate and considered policy changes. In the absence of any coherent policy, age-old practices are allowed to continue as if Kingston were still uniformly Christian – which, of course, never was entirely the case. Opportunities are available to Christians that are not extended to other groups. If occasions do arise in which religious privilege or preference becomes too blatantly obvious or offensive, the expedient is often simply to banish religion altogether from the public realm – assumed to be "secular" – rather than trying to accommodate religious diversity.

When interfaith ventures are undertaken, they almost always occur at the initiative of the various faith groups themselves, not because the municipality has sought to provide a space for such cooperation or invited their participation. Surely providing a public forum in which the full range of voices existing in the community can be heard is one of the imperatives of civic government. Moral issues will arise in any community needing discussion in a public forum where religious diversity will be present, and in which, it is hoped, religious pluralism can be forged. As Eck maintains, "Pluralism is much more than the simple fact of diversity. Pluralism is not a given, but an achievement. It is engaging that diversity in the creation of a common society. Now, as then, the task is to engage in the common tasks of civil society people who do not share a single history or a single religious tradition" (2005, xiv). In almost any Canadian municipality, immigrant groups of differing religions and ethnicities are to be found, eager to share their traditions and to participate in this common task of creating a civil society. In many respects the need is for something like what Paul Bramadat urges, namely, "cultivating a pluralistic, multicultural, open society" of the kind most Canadians cherish in their best moments by making "much better use of the constructive and creative social capital generated by certain forms of religion" (2005, 214).

THE CITY AS A "DARK PLACE"

Kingston Transformation Network

Not all faith communities and centres of worship in Kingston support the kinds of interfaith ventures discussed above. Some assume there was a time when Canada was officially a Christian nation. For them Canada still is – or ought to be – a Christian nation. They want to continue that ascribed status. In their view the country has slipped into secularism and needs to be recalled to its rightful place as a society existing under God. The aims of religious pluralism, requiring that people of a particular faith acknowledge the validity of other traditions, is sometimes seen as a threatening or compromising of claims of absolute and exclusive truth. How can genuine inter-religious dialogue take place if one of the conversation partners believes, as a matter of unalterable conviction, that the other is wrong? The website of the Evangelical Fellowship of Canada puts forth as one of its aims to provide "a constructive voice for biblical principles in life and society." Among its guiding values is "a deepening understanding of the role and relevance of the Christian faith in a diverse society" (Evangelical Fellowship of Canada d). There can be little objection to such aims and values, so long as it is understood that not all members of Canadian society are Christian, and so long as Christians support the rights of other faith traditions to participate in discussions of principles and the role of religion in society from the standpoint of their own faiths.

A view of the role of religion in the public sphere entirely different from that of proponents of religious pluralism comes from the perspective of some Christians who see the city as a kind of spiritual battleground, where a high-stakes war is being waged between the forces of good and evil. Before detailing the practices such as spiritual mapping and "Strategic-Level Spiritual Warfare" employed in this "war," some clarification of the several associations of the often fragmented and disparate Kingston clergy – and the direction taken by one of these organizations – is required. The Christian Leaders Fellowship, with a mailing list of more than fifty names, has already been referred to as a group consisting mostly of evangelical pastors, joined by a few ministers from mainline churches. The Christian Leaders met for a dozen or more years every Thursday morning, having breakfast at Smitty's Family Restaurant on outer Princess Street on the first Thursday of the month and meeting at other locations for fellowship, prayer, and Bible study on the other Thursday mornings.

In 2006 Roger Rutter, a local businessman and pastor with thirty years' experience – for eleven years he also led a prayer network of business leaders – became the leader of the Christian Leaders Fellowship and took its members along an entirely new course. Rutter's own congregation, Prepare the Way Ministries, had no building though it was registered as a church – "it's really a calling, not a church" (interview, 24 April 2007). Rutter describes his congregation as "undercover": without a phone number, it works in small groups, and incorporates churches from "at least eleven different denominations." He indicates that his role, as leader and apostle of Prepare the Way Ministries, is to "oversee the intercession for the city." (The term "apostle," by the way, can have various meanings in evangelical circles: someone who founds or plants churches, a person who has oversight, or someone sent out on a special mission.) For Rutter, a change took place in his ministry – a new "calling" – when he became "just bored being a pastor." He resigned his post as pastor when he heard "a word from God to go downtown and pray." With this divine summons he began a new ministry involving the city of Kingston as a whole – to "see betterment in our community." In becoming the "director" of the Christian Leaders Fellowship, Rutter saw his role (though not all members would agree with his sense of this specific mandate) as bringing together a group of like-minded pastors and Christian businessmen to focus on a new related task "to engage all the spheres of influence in the city."

In 2006 the second of several "prayer summits" of Christian leaders was held at Camp Iawah, a Christian camp of several hundred acres situated on Wolfe Lake near the village of Westport, north of Kingston. Some of the prayer summits, including this second one, were led by Tom White, the American founder and president of Frontline Ministries, who introduced the term "transformation network" to this group of Christian leaders, mostly evangelical pastors but including a few from mainline denominations. White is portrayed on his website as "a recognized practitioner and expert in city transformation – building unity among leaders and churches to catalyze vision for more effectively reaching their communities." He is described as leading "an international ministry developing city-wide prayer movements, and teaching in the areas of spiritual warfare, intercession and strategic city-reaching." One of the special emphases in his work on spiritual warfare is how to deal with what is called "evil supernaturalism," battling the satanic influences in the city. White has also published many books, among them the following: *The Believer's Guide to Spiritual Warfare* (1990), *Breaking Strongholds: How Spiritual Warfare Sets Captives Free* (1993), and *City-Wide Prayer Movements: One Church, Many Congregations* (2004). Finally, White is billed as having "facilitated hundreds of Leaders Prayer Summits in the U.S., Canada, Japan, Russia, Australia and Israel, Europe, Sri Lanka, and India" (Frontline Ministries). Though any overt emphasis on spiritual warfare appears to have been muted at the Kingston meetings, by the end of the weekend prayer summit in February 2006 the decision was made to rename the Christian Leaders Fellowship the Kingston Transformation Network. The new leadership consisted of Roger Rutter, Ed Visser of Westside Fellowship, Peter Hubert of Third Day Worship Centre, Ken Bandy of Ellel Minstries Canada, and Bern McLaughlin of Living Stones Christian fellowship.

Rutter described what he understood himself to be bringing to the group: "The Christian Leadership Fellowship came to a point, last February, of '06, that leadership in the city by pastors to see a city change or anything effective in the city was not working. So they wanted to bring someone on who had more of an apostolic business approach, to see a little more peripheral vision and I was asked to be a part of it and then to take the lead of it" (interview, 24 April 2007). Rutter repeatedly emphasized that people involved in business and the marketplace needed to participate in the project of civic transformation to augment the pastors' approach, though once again it is clear that his vision was not shared by all other members of the group. Even after the renaming, the earlier Christian Leaders Fellowship still continued, though now nameless, alongside the new Kingston Transformation Network. Though it does not come into this present story, a third group, the original, long-dormant Kingston Ministerial Association, picked up again in 2005, quite independently of these developments in the other two groups.

Though the second "prayer summit" of Christian leaders at Camp Iawah proved to be pivotal, Tom White's earlier emphases on spiritual warfare were not a major focus there. What was presented and discussed among the pastors and religious leaders in February 2006 was a model of "Kingdom Governance of the Emerging City Church" that included a "royal priesthood" comprised of various groups within Kingston, ranging from campus ministries to the business community to ethnic leaders to chaplaincies in prisons and the military, and including the realms of arts and media. However, many of those attending already shared a vision of the city as a "dark place," especially as a stronghold of evil forces, and in need of "transformation." Online sources associate the use of the term with some contemporary evangelicals such as White. Its religious use among evangelicals earlier applied most immediately to the regeneration of the individual believing Christian, as in Paul's injunction in Romans 12:2, "Be ye transformed by the renewing of your mind." White's "working definition," part of his program for "Advanced City Reaching," as an article by Lynn and Sarah Leslie explains, includes "pervasive awareness of the reality of God, a radical correction of social ills, a commensurate decrease in crime rates ... supernatural blessing on local commerce, healing of the brokenhearted (the alienated and disenfranchised), and an exporting of kingdom righteousness" (Leslie 2005).

As part of a plan to bring spiritual revival to Kingston, the newly formed Kingston Transformation Network began to organize the hosting of an appearance by the Impact World Tour, an outreach campaign promoted by an organization of international Christian young people called Youth with a Mission, or YWAM. Pronounced "Why-Wham" (see YWAM Campaigns a), the organization is identified by scholar René Holvast as one of several that incorporate spiritual mapping into their programs (2009, 122). With the support of local churches – the sponsorship by the Kingston Transformation Network was not made explicit – the Impact World Tour involved over ninety events held during a period of eighteen days in the Kingston area, culminating in four massive rallies held at the recently completed K-Rock Centre, 3–6 April 2008.

The Impact World Tour entails old-fashioned mass evangelism presented under a new cultural guise: "The multimedia presentation is a high energy, entertaining adrenaline rush" (Impact World Tour a). One local pastor referred to this kind of evangelism as "Billy Graham on steroids." Videos on the IWT website portray teams of skateboarders, bikers, hip-hop artists, athletes exhibiting feats of strength, and costumed dancers performing at the free events. Several videos of the presentations in Kingston are available on YouTube, including one in which Roger Rutter states, "I have lived here forty-three years and we have never seen anything of this size, magnitude, spirit that would encompass all that God is doing. Tonight we have just again seen hundreds go forward. We have not seen that in all my life here. God is definitely doing something in our community" (YouTube a). The "tour stats" at the end of this five-minute video indicate that the attendance at the events in the Kingston area totalled 29,000, with 1,584 responses; these "responses" presumably are those who answered an altar call, filled out a card, or sought a counsellor. Another website claims that "over 40,000 people heard the gospel message in 3 weeks and over 3,300 people responded to the Gospel message" (Pursuit Canada). Yet another states, "Over 70% of all the recorded decisions for Christ were made by those 18 years of age and under" (YWAM Campaigns b). Statistics Canada figures show that in 2006 the population of Kingston comprised of young people between the ages of ten and nineteen years was under fifteen thousand. If only, say, three-quarters of the young people making a decision for Christ came from within the city, that means that between 8 per cent and 17 per cent of Kingston's youth was converted during the 2008 Impact World Tour in Kingston.

Despite this evangelistic focus, at only one place, buried on a single page amidst the promotions on the IWT website, is it revealed that this Impact World Tour with its "pumping, hearty-pounding beat" and "high energy, entertaining adrenaline rush" was in fact to be an evangelistic crusade targeting young people. The question is raised in the "About Us" section, "Is IWT Religious?" The answer provided is: "IWT staff are from a wide cross-section of international and local Christian communities – they do not adhere to any one set of Protestant or Catholic group traditions or beliefs. Rather, they are united by a simple faith, seeking to love God and others in speech and action and encourage others to do likewise" (Impact World Tour b). Some controversy arose in Kingston around the evangelistic intentions of the event being muted, and perhaps deliberately concealed. One woman writing to the local newspaper complained that the evening turned into a "preachfest": "My fiancé and six-year-old son attended, as my son is a fan of skateboarding. Half the show was non-religious entertainment, but it soon turned into preaching at the crowd. Children were targeted in particular; they were encouraged to come up and be 'saved.' My fiancé and many other parents quickly left with their children as the preaching and the crowd became more intense and began to turn into a scene seemingly plucked from the documentary *Jesus Camp*." She noted that the Christian theme of the event was hidden in the promotion: "It is wrong to aim evangelical antics at unsuspecting children. As parents, we have a right to know what we may be exposing our children's young and impressionable minds to" (*Whig-Standard*, 12 April 2008). In the following days several responses were published, suggesting, for instance, that those attending "should have known" what the event was about, or that in this age of media hype and sexualized advertising, a message about God's love ought to have been welcomed.

In a 2007 interview, about a year before the Impact World Tour, Rutter told an RDK researcher about his map of the city with some points of spiritual influence marked on it. He said that since about 1998 he had been practising "spiritual mapping" (described in further detail below) and "strategic intercession" with members of his congregation: "Many of the streets have been prayer-walked in the city." At one level, "prayer walking" might just mean going to a place that you want to pray for, as described in a Canadian Anglican online resource that compares it with pilgrimage (Anglican Fellowship of Prayer). Other interpretations, using military metaphors, speak of making a specific site a "target" for prayer, for instance, to expel demonic influences. For Rutter, the practice is of the more aggressive kind, a way of getting rid of negative forces or evil spirits. He described how when he maps the city spiritually, locating areas under demonic control or dark influences, "things move." He explained: "For example, psychic places. We've gone to psychic places, prayed. They've been gone within a week or two; they come up somewhere else." A little later in the same interview, he repeated many of the same phrases and expanded on the practices being portrayed: "We can map it, we can pray into it, and we can try to cast things out. We can do all those things. But once they're cast out, what's going to fill it? Do you know what I'm saying? And so that's where I think we need I think righteous people. We need change" (24 April 2007). Rutter was probably alluding to Luke 11:26, in which after an "unclean spirit" has been cast out of a man, the spirit returns to the place where he used to reside, and finds it clean and empty: "Then goeth he, and taketh to him seven other spirits more wicked than himself; and they enter in, and dwell there: and the last state of that man is worse than the first." Rutter is saying, then, that merely banishing evil influences from specific sites in Kingston is not enough – some positive replacement is needed to replace the evil that has departed. Expressing concern about "morals" in the city, Rutter offered as the replacement more Christian "righteousness." The Impact World Tour, with its goal to evangelize young people in the city and bring about conversions, would be a major means to fill these spaces with "righteous people."

Though in the interview we were initially exploring the phenomenon of spiritual mapping, it became clear that Rutter was more interested in advancing what he called "targeted intercession" or "strategic intercession." Spiritual mapping he regarded as something that had been done, and he wished to go on to the next stage. He reiterated, "If you don't fill the void with something, long-term it's left empty." He spoke of how he had gone with others and prayed around City Hall, a place where they frequently convened: "We went; we anointed with oil." He referred to other things they had done, such as burying crosses at certain locations and praying at Masonic Lodges, in order "that they would see the light." He emphasized that, as head of the Kingston Transformation Network, he was summoning everyone to the task of bringing "more righteousness in the city." He continued: "I mean, I just led the city-wide prayer summits – we just had thirty-four major leaders together for two days in February – and we're not doing our job."

Rutter mentioned additional specific sites in the city where intercessory prayer had been conducted. He and members of his congregation had gone to the area of Aberdeen Street near Queen's University, where a street party involving thousands of young people erupted into destructive behaviour during Homecoming in the fall of 2005. They had visited other places where violent acts had taken place, including a murder-suicide that had occurred in 2001 near the Zellers store at the Cataraqui Centre. Prayer walks had taken them to Pentecostal, Anglican, and United churches: "We've prayed for God's blessing on them. We're not praying for them to change; we're praying for them to see God. Because that's their choice."

Rutter's identification of spiritually dark places takes an unexpected turn in his interpretation of Kingston's prisons. Whereas others might reasonably choose a prison as a likely place to offer prayer in the effort to banish evil spirits, Rutter says that prison inmates are "really just people who have made a mistake." However, he continued, "we have a lot of people who have made mistakes that aren't in prisons." His conclusion: "I don't think the prisons are the big things here. I think the number one thing in this city is more occult worship, things like that – which is not seen." Because spiritual warfare is entailed, supernatural evil tends to be identified not so much as criminal activity as involving unseen powers, demonic forces, or other gods. Indeed, some evangelicals understand occult worship or evil spirits being involved in many current practices ranging from tarot cards, palm-reading, and astrology to Pagan use of spells and magic and including yoga, meditation practices, and eastern religions (see chap. 8).

For spiritual mappers and prayer walkers, the history of a particular street might be significant – perhaps like Aberdeen Street – or, alternatively, just the implications of a street's name – for example, Division or Concession streets in contrast with the positive or biblical implications of Union or Stephen streets – might make it the special target of prayer walks. Otherwise, what another pastor characterized as places where "spiritual slime" might be detected, such as occult stores and game stores, could also be regarded as "dark places." Rutter said that the Kingston police would claim the real danger to the city comes from psychic and occult practices rather than criminal activity.

The direction and emphasis of this new Kingston Transformation Network with its vision of Kingston as a spiritually dark place was at least partly divisive and schismatic. Some of those who became active in the new group had never been involved in its predecessor, the Christian Leaders Fellowship. In the aftermath of the Impact World Tour and the ensuing controversy, several people dissociated themselves from the Kingston Transformation Network. Some who had initially supported the group and its aims eventually drew back from it, aware that their own theology saw the world in rather different, less negative, terms. Before considering alternative Christian views of the nature of society and the world of culture, it is useful to get some additional background for the practices employed in Kingston as described above.

What Is Spiritual Mapping?

Early in the process of gathering our research for Religious Diversity in Kingston, one of the project's interviewers explained to a local member of the clergy that our aim was to "map" the religious landscape of the city early in the twenty-first century. The minister being interviewed pointed out how a parallel term, "spiritual mapping," had some currency in conservative Christian circles, and that to prevent confusion we should be careful about using such similar terminology. Using a quick sketch of Kingston, he explained that some Christians pinpointed on a map the strongholds of the enemy where evil resides and, conversely – though less often – the loci of divine power. An example of such an evil place was an alleyway beside a downtown McDonald's where drug deals were said to occur. In the Bible, God instructed people to search out the cities and places that they were about to enter for the purpose of identifying where the enemy was located. We were also told that the use of such "spiritual mapping," followed by focused prayer, had helped some cities, especially in the United States, to rid themselves of wicked influences.

Most of the available resources on spiritual mapping come from "insider" perspectives, especially on the Internet, written from an evangelical standpoint by Christian clergy for or against the practice. The major external academic treatment of the subject is René Holvast's *Spiritual Mapping in the United States and Argentina, 1989–2005* (2009) – significantly subtitled "*A Geography of Fear*" – that puts the phenomenon in decline at the time of writing. At the outset Holvast defines spiritual mapping as "the use of religious techniques to wage a territorial spiritual war against unseen non-human beings" (1). In effect, this practice involves the detailed cartography of a given place identifying particular points believed to be under the influence of the demonic. Strategic-Level Spiritual Warfare (SLSW) is employed after an area has been spiritually mapped, to pray for and engage in a spiritual battle with the identified demonic influences (Ediger 2000, 132). Gerry Ediger explains that C. Peter Wagner's version of SLSW "aims to locate, identify, and remove beings at the top of the demonic hierarchy" as identified by their nature and rank (127). Roger Rutter acknowledged that he had attended some of Wagner's conferences; the terminology he employed in our interview is consistent with that used in circles engaged in this kind of spiritual combat.

In the course of conducting spiritual mapping, a series of questions are asked about a given city. The website of Isaiah 54 Ministries includes such questions as: "What place does your city have in your nation's history?" "Was there a time when a new religion emerged?" "Under what circumstances did the gospel first enter the city?" "Have there ever been wars that affected this city?" "Have there been any traumatic experiences such as economic collapse, race riots, or an earthquake?" "Has there ever been a sudden opportunity to create wealth such as the discovery of oil or a new irrigation technology?" (Isaiah 54 Ministries). Another website offers alternative questions formulated according to its "watchdog methods": "What is the spiritual land like? Do we have camps or strongholds of pornography? Does our city have camps of homosexuality, alcohol abuse, drugs? Is our city held by strongholds of poverty, debt, maybe greed? What camps have joined forces in order to accomplish a greater work?" (Battle Axe Brigade). The answers to these questions help spiritual mappers to formulate a cartographical representation of spiritual forces in the city.

Once particular places under demonic control are plotted, the results are tabulated to determine patterns. For example, a website showing the spiritual mapping of Madras, India, explains that two Hindu Temples and a "Theosophical Society" line up and point directly to governmental headquarters. The authors conclude that this extrapolated line represents demonic control over the government: "Our court system is highly corrupt and the enemy has a clear control of the businesses (Revelation 18:3). The key is to *pray for all in authority* breaking any satanic influence over them (1 Timothy 2:1,2)" (Appius Forum). Once the important locations have been identified on a map, Strategic-Level Spiritual Warfare may be employed to counter these forces. An extensive breakdown of the process is provided on another website: "We will go to the location and pray in whatever way the Lord directs us. Sometimes we are impressed to anoint the ground or building with oil. Maybe we'll plant a Bible there" (Battle Axe Brigade). This account employs the language of warfare: "reconnaissance work," "the enemy," "behind enemy lines," "Battle Axe Brigade." Theologically, the practice rests on the belief in multiple "deities or evil spirits," accompanied with a view of a jealous God who "does not intend for us to 'serve and worship Him' as we live amiably in the midst of other gods." Its theology takes literally the rhetoric of spiritual conflict in a world where the Christian God is at war with other gods.

Arthur Moore explains that the term "spiritual mapping" was coined in 1991 by the president of the Sentinel Group, George Otis Jr, although "enthusiastic proponents say it is really the reprise of an old practice that can help propel the church toward fulfillment of the Great Commission" to go forth, preach the Gospel, and make disciples (Moore 1998; see also Ediger 2000). Ediger examines the history of Christian spiritual warfare and argues for the continuity of his methods with those of early Christianity: "A consistent linkage of overt, deliberate, and aggressive confrontation against the demonic with considerations of territory, human spiritual bondage, and evangelism seems to be evident" (2000, 136–7). In contrast, Kent Philpott, a Baptist minister in California, provides a sceptical account of the phenomenon, interpreting spiritual mapping as an extension of evangelism: "What could not be accomplished using sophisticated telemarketing strategies, spiritual mapping would. In fact, some of the same people who were instrumental in the promotion of the church growth movement are also deeply invested in spiritual mapping. C. Peter Wagner, perhaps the best-known figure in the church growth movement, has firmly entrenched himself in the spiritual mapping movement as evidenced in his books *Warfare Prayer* and *Breaking Strongholds in Your City*" (Spiritual Mapping). Philpott further explains that the movement was propelled by John Dawson's 1989 book, *Taking Our Cities for God,* where Dawson identified the importance of geographical areas and the demonic.

Wagner's Global Harvest Ministries and Otis's Sentinel Group, both non-denominational evangelical Christian organizations, were the chief proponents of these practices. Originating in the movement AD2000, Global Harvest Ministries was dedicated primarily to spiritual mapping and SLSW. Global Harvest Ministries became the United States Global Apostolic Prayer Network, or USGAPN, with its program to reinstate the United States as a Christian nation, developments briefly outlined in a letter from Wagner (2007). Otis's Sentinel Group shares a similar emphasis – "a Christian research and information agency dedicated to helping the Church pray knowledgably for end-time global evangelization and enabling communities to discover the pathway to genuine revival and societal transformation" (Sentinel Group). Before forming his organization in the 1990s, Otis worked as part of the Lausanne Committee for World Evangelization, a movement established by Rev. Billy Graham. The Sentinel Group has also made a series of films documenting communities in Colombia, Kenya, California, and Guatemala that were "transformed by God." In the interview with Hannah Dick, Roger Rutter referred to these *Transformations* videos documenting what happened in communities when churches united in prayer and almost the entire population became born-again Christians. In the videos it is maintained that God showed communities why darkness was so strong in their towns and how to pray against it, with the result that crime rates plunged, bars closed and became churches, occult worship dropped dramatically, and streets were renamed after biblical characters (YouTube b).

The Lausanne Covenant was a document created at the 1974 International Congress on World Evangelization when some 2,300 evangelicals came together from around the world (Lausanne Movement a). The covenant, signed by those present at the congress in an effort to increase worldwide evangelism, speaks in a section on "Spiritual Conflict" about the need to battle the powers of evil: "We know our need to equip ourselves with God's armour and to fight this battle with the spiritual weapons of truth and prayer. For we detect the activity of our enemy, not only in false ideologies outside the Church, but also inside it in false gospels which twist Scripture and put people in the place of God." The covenant also expresses the need to "permeate non-Christian society" (Lausanne Movement b). In the years after the explosion of interest in the issue of spiritual warfare, the organization issued several papers clarifying their position on the matter, which was to try to restore what they saw as a biblical perspective amidst distortions and excesses. For example, in a subsequent document entitled "Deliver Us from Evil," the Lausanne Committee for World Evangelization meeting in Nairobi in 2000 warned that "there seems to be little biblical warrant for a number of the teachings and practices associated with some forms of spiritual conflict which focus on territorial spirits" (Lausanne Movement c; cf. Holvast 2009, 334).

Today, spiritual mapping remains a highly controversial topic in Christianity – although perhaps less controversial than its application, Strategic-Level Spiritual Warfare (Moore 1998, 55) – and is embraced by some evangelical Christian organizations located primarily in the United States (see Ediger 2000; Moore 1998; Lowe 1998; cf. W3Church). During the fall 2008 election campaign in the United States, stories began to appear about the religious faith of Sarah Palin, running mate of Republican presidential candidate John McCain, in particular about her status as a Pentecostal Christian and "prayer warrior." To be sure, these stories were obscured somewhat by other details of Palin's life – her wardrobe expenses, her pregnant teenage daughter, her lack of knowledge about details of foreign policy, her frequent verbal gaffes and non sequiturs. Laurie Goodstein, a religion writer for the *New York Times*, wrote about Palin's lengthy connections with Christians involved in "spiritual warfare," characterizing the movement this way: "Its adherents believe that demonic forces can colonize specific geographic areas and individuals, and that 'spiritual warriors' must 'battle' them to assert God's control, using prayer and evangelism. The movement's fixation on demons, its aggressiveness and its leaders' claims to exalted spiritual authority have troubled even some Pentecostal Christians" (24 October 2008). The *Huffington Post* reported that Palin had been involved in the ministry of C. Peter Wagner as early as 1989 as a member of a prayer group in Wasilla, Alaska (2 November 2008). Though spiritual warfare and strategic prayer in a contemporary urban context might seem like extreme or marginal practices to an outsider, they represent an emphasis well known among evangelicals, and sometimes including sympathetic Christians from mainline denominations.

Spiritual Warfare in Kingston

Roger Rutter states that ultimately "spiritual mapping apart from strategic warfare is not effective. And strategic warfare without something in place to maintain the land – naturally and spiritually – is not effective." He did, however, view his spiritual mapping work of the previous decade as successful, paradoxically pointing to economic growth in the city as evidence. Spiritual mapping, then, is only the beginning of what continues to be a lengthy process of discerning and improving the physical and spiritual health of the city. While Rutter knows of no other person or group performing spiritual mapping on a long-term basis in the Kingston community, the concept is implicitly mentioned in a number of interviews by the RDK project with pastors of conservative evangelical churches. One minister noted with a chuckle that "there are also darker areas" in the city. Another described the negative side of Kingston's religious character: "Spiritually speaking, I think it is a darker place. I think that the Kingston people in general are not as receptive to religion ... I think it's the fact that we have several prisons around Kingston and just that dark presence – the presence of Satan – working at people's heart is bold and strong." However, he also had hope for the future of Kingston and its religious character, emphasizing the need "to be aware of the spiritual influences in the city and take measures to combat them – prayer, unity among church pastors."

At several occasions before and after the Impact World Tour events in 2008 Alistair Petrie came to Kingston bringing a similar vision of the church and the city. Petrie's Canadian-based Partnership Ministries is described as "offering programs in spiritual warfare, community diagnostics, intercessory prayer, healing and reconciliation in Christ" (Partnership Ministries). Petrie, who served as an Anglican priest in British Columbia for fifteen years, is known for using the tools of spiritual mapping and spiritual warfare in preparation for the transformation of cities. The titles of his DVDs illustrate themes already evident among other practitioners of spiritual warfare: *Doing Business the Kingdom Way*, promoted as "explaining how businesses can impact society with Kingdom culture," *Heal the Land*, and *Shout! For the Lord Has Given You the City.* In newsletters and videos on Youtube, Petrie suggests that in acts of terrorism, the earthquake in Haiti, dust storms in Australia, and financial turmoil in world markets God is shaking the world. The Partnership Ministries website refers to its links with such other groups as Global Harvest Ministries, Youth with a Mission, the Wagner Leadership Institute, and Ellel Ministries International, the last of these maintaining a centre for healing retreats and workshops near Kingston. In short, then, representatives of various organizations having connections with one another and advocating a particular view of the spiritual nature of the city were present in Kingston at various points in the first decade of the twenty-first century.

One local Christian website, Pray Kingston (praykingston.com), now discontinued, advertised an interdenominational prayer group that followed the Lausanne Covenant. Pray Kingston organized members of its network into "Lighthouses of Prayer" to perform Strategic-Level Spiritual Warfare: "A Lighthouse of Prayer is simply a 'household' of one or more believers praying specifically for the felt needs and the salvation of lost people within their perimeter of influence, whether it be the neighborhood, the workplace, or the school!" The City Christian Centre and Polson Park Free Methodist Church were the only local congregations identified as having official links to Pray Kingston. One Kingston minister characterized the area surrounding his church as one "where there is crime and there isn't light." Instead of simply praying for "dark" areas, the congregation actively helps people in these areas by providing food, shelter, and meeting other needs. Yet another pastor in his interview described spiritual mapping at length, although not necessarily agreeing with it. He would, however, seem to agree with the aims that the Impact World Tour were to bring to the city: "We believe that when Kingston has spiritual revival here and the spiritual temperature goes up, it will impact Ontario and Canada in a very positive way." The minister of one of the oldest congregations in the city explained that he is involved in directed prayer with a ministerial organization that "regularly prays for city council, the police department, the fire department, the hospitals, Queen's University, Royal Military College, St Lawrence, and so on. Because we believe that we have, if you will, a biblical imperative to pray for those who are in authority over us, and we believe that it is helpful that we pray for the institutions that are a part of our community. So a group of us meet at 7:00 every Thursday morning for an hour, and that's the focus of our prayer – the city."

Here confusion arises as to what exactly spiritual mapping or directed prayer amounts to. To what degree is praying for city council, or the city in general, engaging in spiritual battle with "the enemy"? After all, such language is a central part of mainstream Christian discourse. A generalized view of a struggle between good and evil is part of many Christians' view of the world. The metaphor of a spiritual battle with the enemy – or one envisaging a battle between light and darkness – is evident in many parts of the Bible. To extend that view to include demonic spirits inhabiting specific places would not be difficult for some believers, however theologically questionable it might be for others. Because evangelical pastors were steeped in and informed by a dualistic biblical vision that blended easily with the more aggressive forms of spiritual warfare, they were willing to rename their

Christian Leaders Fellowship and to accept at least some of the basic contours of the theology being propounded by Roger Rutter and others within the new Kingston Transformation Network. Under the direction of a core group of leaders, and responding to the impetus provided by Tom White at their second prayer summit, this group came together with a vision of spiritual renewal.

To set these issues in a larger context, consider some of the responses to spiritual warfare against territorial spirits from within evangelical circles (see, for example, Holvast 2000, 231–79). The website of the Christian Reformed Church in North America provides a link to a report from its "Committee to Study Third Wave Pentecostalism" presented to their synod in 2007 (Christian Reformed Church b). While the term "third wave" is said not to be in common use, the committee picks it up from Peter Wagner's book of 1988, *The Third Wave of the Holy Spirit*. The claim is that the first wave of Pentecostalism was the Azusa Street revival in the early twentieth century; the second wave occurred with the charismatic movement of the 1960s and '70s; the third wave – notice the increase in frequency – began in about 1980. Its four emphases include prophecy and hearing the voice of God; powerful prayer; healing ministries; and spiritual warfare and deliverance ministries – it is the last area that is relevant here. The thirty-two page report, while maintaining the evangelical approach of the Christian Reformed Church, offers a full and balanced consideration of this Third Wave movement, evaluating its various facets, offering various approvals and cautions, and providing advice for congregations and pastors.

Though sympathetic with some of the approaches and methods of the Third Wave, the Christian Reformed report sets the phenomenon in the context of its own Reformed theology, going back to Calvin and Augustine, which understands the world as the domain of God's sovereign work of redemption. That theology puts in perspective the attention given to demons, territorial spirits, or prayer warfare. The report calls into question the Third Wave's emphasis on the nature of evil, the role of demon possession, and their version of spiritual warfare, especially when the focus is largely on such areas as "the lure of pornography or the fight against abortion." The report offers this caution: "We ought therefore to be critical of those in the Third Wave who speak of spiritual warfare as though it were exclusively or primarily a matter of demon possession (perhaps more appropriately called demonization) and the casting out of unclean spirits in Christ's name. An unhealthy preoccupation with deliverance ministry and the occult is likely to distort the biblical understanding of all of human life as religion" (Christian Reformed Church b). It speaks of the dangers of sensationalism and the lure of elitism on the part of those claiming to be spiritually gifted.

On the specific matter of Strategic-Level Spiritual Warfare and the interest in territorial spirits – a focus with "little or no biblical basis" – this committee cautions against an "unhealthy interest in and overemphasis on the demonic." This well-informed theological evaluation of the movement sets the stage for our own larger consideration of how the city is envisaged from various religious points of view.

Amongst some other evangelicals – the Lausanne Movement, for instance – the concern is raised that an emphasis on territorial spirits, or demons inhabiting specific places, adopts the world view of religions other than Christianity. Animism, for example, holds the view that souls or spirits inhabit places and natural phenomena, as well as such other-than-human creatures as animals. Groups like the Kingston Dowsers, referred to in the introduction of this book, might be said to be at least partly animistic in their world view, seeing certain locales as charged with positive spirits and therefore sacred. Spiritual mappers and prayer walkers, in contrast, tend to view any spirits in the external world as evil. In the same vein, while casting out demons and breaking the stronghold of evil forces is the means to cleanse a place of such influences, Wiccans or Pagans draw a circle and invite the divine into specific areas. Brendan Fox of the Pagan Federation described the ritual to researcher Meghan Unterschultz: "So that's where your temple is: wherever you happen to be standing at the moment." He stated that when Pagans gather in a group, in order to remind them "about being in the presence of the gods," a circle is drawn: "And everything within that circle is considered to be sacred space, and a place where you commune with your God" (interview, 24 November 2004). Summing up his faith and the duties incumbent on him, Fox said, "You're supposed to express your faith in a positive, caring, loving, healing way . That's what you're supposed to be doing." Paganism, then, affirms both the world of nature and urban space because any place can be regarded as sacred. The language and theology of Neopagan groups such as Wiccans make them a target of spiritual mappers who believe in evil territorial spirits and "occult groups." In some respects, then, Paganism and spiritual warfare represent the furthest extremities of world-affirming and world-denying possibilities in a spectrum of views on how the world around us is to be evaluated in religious terms.

KINGSTON IN THE RELIGIOUS IMAGINATION

The two major sections of this chapter have considered, first, how Kingston takes religion in all of its pluralistic diversity into account today and makes – or fails to make – policy decisions to accommodate people of different faith traditions. From the other side of things, the sketch of spiritual mapping and directed prayer shows how some Christians view Kingston as a battleground between the forces of good and evil – though, in fact, their preoccupation seems mostly to be with the presence of evil. Here we have two opposing views of religion in the urban centre – what should be emphasized and strengthened, what should be avoided or reformed, and what the role of religion (especially of Christianity) ought to be.

Characterizations of the city offered by religious people through the centuries have gone through various renditions. Today these evaluations shift according to the relation between religion and the state and depending on whether governments are viewed as supportive of religion in one form or another. In a somewhat related vein, poet and critic W.H. Auden, in the published version of his lectures given at the University of Virginia in 1949, showed how the city could be viewed as both good and evil: "The natural desert is therefore at once the place of punishment for those rejected by the good city because they are evil, and the place of purgation for those who reject the evil city because they desire to become good" (1967, 14). In these opposed views the space outside the city is, alternatively, a place of exile for those expelled from it or a place for restoration for people needing respite and healing.

Is the city good, or is it evil? And, in contrast to what? While Auden makes the desert the symbolic opposite of the city, in a Canadian setting such as Kingston, that contrast is more likely to be expressed as the wilderness. Northrop Frye argues that nature in Canada has traditionally been understood as threatening, as the abode of demons, in contrast with the safety of the "garrison" where civilization and protection were afforded. Today, of course, these symbolic meanings tend to be reversed. The wilderness is revered as a place of purity, relatively free from environmental degradation (though less free from pollution than it used to be), providing relief from the ills and violence of city life. Escaping the city, whether for retreat or recreation or retirement, may mean for Kingstonians a cottage on a Canadian Shield lake to the north or the Thousand Islands to the east, a boat trip on the river or a ferry ride to Wolfe Island.

Spiritual mappers tend to contrast the earthly city not with the wilderness but with an invisible counterpart, the New Jerusalem in the heavens where God's kingdom will be established at the end of time. For some conservative evangelicals this present world remains in the grip of satanic forces whose evil presence can be located and charted. One website devoted to "spiritual warfare" explains that Christians are engaged in "warfare that involves the trickery and power of the devil, as opposed to a human battle. Even though human beings will certainly play a role in line with the schemes of the Devil, they are being used by these entities for the purposes of accomplishing evil.

Evil spirits are the true power behind those who oppose the things of God (knowingly or unknowingly)" (Spiritual Warfare). This kind of dualistic thinking, involving "truth and falsehood, love and hate, good and evil," sees what is real and enduring as invisible and beyond the earth, which is at best a temporary and preliminary arrangement. Those who see the city in the grip of principalities and powers and the rulers of darkness of course differ in their estimation of the degree of that grip of evil upon contemporary urban reality, and what should be done about it. Suffice it to say that at one extreme some believe the world is ruled by a darkness so pervasive and intractable that a final resolution can emerge only after a cataclysmic battle when God's kingdom is established.

Robert A. Orsi, introducing a collection of essays on "urban religion," outlines how "fantasies born of desire for (and fear of) the alien city overwhelmed the real lives of city people" (1999, 11). What he terms "the phantasmagoria of urban pornography," a reference to the dangers and depravity of the city, obfuscates the reality by ignoring other positive aspects, but functions as a necessary trope in the drama of Christian redemption. The city is depicted as dirty and other in order that God can redeem these filthy depths: "The dramatic and spiritual fulfillment offered by these Christian narratives of urban conversion lies in the power of grace to touch absolutely the darkest, most vile, and most inhuman corners of the city's sinfulness" (11). While Orsi's topographies employ more conventional loci of human sinfulness, especially in the dens of vice and iniquity characteristic of the moral underworld of the American inner city, contemporary deliverance ministries use a different cartography to locate invisible beings, demonic spirits, and other gods that inhabit an alternate reality. These demonic powers can so radically infect the city as to control its municipal government and deter its economic development. The "geography of fear" characterizing spiritual mappers fantasizes the realms of unseen principalities and powers that control the city on an imagined level beyond the usual strip clubs, adult video stores, casinos, and bars that comprise the filth of other, more conventional cartographies.

The best analysis of the various ways Christians relate God and the world is still to be found in H. Richard Niebuhr's classic book of 1951, *Christ and Culture*. There Niebuhr sets out five examples or types to illustrate the different ways that the two sometimes dissimilar entities of Christianity and civilization – or Christ and culture, or the church and the world – have been seen as existing together in some kind of relationship. Niebuhr's five types range between two extreme positions of radical Christianity and cultural Christianity – "Christ against Culture" and "The Christ of Culture." Between these two extremes he poses three intermediate positions, "Christ above Culture" or the synthesist position, "Christ and Culture in Paradox" or the dualist position, and "Christ the Transformer of Culture" or the conversionist position. This typology would situate spiritual mappers with the radical type of Christians who are antagonistic to culture and opposed to the world, understood as the realm of nature as contrasted with the realm of grace. Such a position, seldom held in its purest, most world-rejecting form, of course embodies ambiguities and contradictions. Radical Christians end up employing the very culture that they reject, just as spiritual mappers who see Satan active in Kingston make their livings as the owners of businesses within the city and pray for the mayor and council who govern it. Yet, oddly, they measure spiritual success in terms of municipal economic development. At the other extreme, in the more liberal position where Unitarians and Reform Jews and Quakers might be found, are those who are humanistic and affirming of human possibility while urging the reform of society to meet the needs of its weakest members. Their preference is for accommodation to culture, for reason over revelation.

Niebuhr is correct in saying that most Christians through the centuries are somewhere between these two extreme types. They find that God and the world are neither one-and-the-same nor diametrically opposed. Rather, Christ and culture are in some form of relationship, whether paradoxically, synthetically, or in the conversionist position preferred by Niebuhr. This middle position matches the view of the Christian Reformed Church, where culture is neither totally to be shunned nor is it the highest expression of God's intentions. Rather, culture is part of the rule of God in time that will be redeemed.

Charles Williams, the third and least well-known member of the Inklings, a trio of Oxford Christians most prominently represented by C.S. Lewis and J.R.R. Tolkien, has written about the city in the history of western culture. Williams – a poet, novelist, and critic – understands, like Augustine, the human city as a likeness of the heavenly city. His friend C.S. Lewis said that while most people would react to the sights of the streets of London with a feeling of chaos, "Williams, looking on the same spectacle, saw chiefly an image – an imperfect, pathetic, heroic, and majestic image – of Order" (qtd in Williams 1958, xivii). In a review of two books by Jacques Maritain and Nicolas Berdyaev, Williams expressed this central conviction, including the possibility of being "nourished," as he puts it, by one's enemies: "If *anthropos* has any meaning, if the web of humanity is in any sense one, if the City exists in our blood as well as in our desires, then we precisely must live from, and be nourished by, those whom we most wholly dislike and disapprove" (113).

A generally positive valuation of the city and of its possibilities characterizes much of mainstream Christianity of the last generation or so, beginning about the time of Harvey Cox's book of 1965, *The Secular City*. What Cox, at the time a young Harvard professor, was saying was in concert with much of the more liberal Protestant theology of the mid-1960s (see chap. 1). That is, a dualism of the supernatural and the natural, a division into the sacred and the profane, lacked credibility in the modern era. Cox was trying to emphasize that the so-called temporal world could no longer be understood in the late twentieth century against the backdrop of eternity; the earthly city could no longer be seen as constructed according to the pattern of the heavenly city, nor as prefiguring it. Instead, he argued, "in our day the secular metropolis stands as both the pattern of our life together and the symbol of our view of the world" (1965, 1). In Cox's analysis "the world is becoming more and more 'mere world'" (217), in contrast to, say, the spiritual mappers whose language and thought preserves the age-old distinctions, building upon the dualisms of God and Satan, good and evil, light and darkness, spiritual and material. In *The Secular City* human beings take on responsibility for this single world rather than relegating that responsibility to a divine power. Cox's conclusion speaks of a "transition ... from the age of Christendom to the new era of urban secularity" (268).

One of the ways of differentiating mainstream religious groups from New Religious Movements, especially those of the more extreme kind, is to consider the kinds of demands enjoined upon followers and adherents. In NRMs of the "high demand" type and tending toward exclusivism, there is a marked tension between being a member of the group and fitting into the everyday world. That is, the exclusivist group looks on the world as being in conflict with their ideals and projects. Followers are called on to separate themselves from their jobs, their families, and all concerns considered as "worldly." They are frequently expected to renounce all other ties and allegiances, or to meet them only minimally. At the furthest extreme are groups that require their members to leave the ordinary secular world and to live communally. In Canada, Hutterites and Doukhobors, and perhaps today, too, radical sectarian forms of the Mormon faith, are the best-known examples. Mainstream religious groups, on the other hand, find no great tension between their religious belonging and their functioning as regular members of their society. They attend worship, exercise their civic duties, fulfil family obligations, and earn their livings with no particular stress between these various parts of their lives.

People who ally themselves with mainstream churches, such as the Roman Catholic, United, Anglican, Presbyterian, and Baptist churches – and Canadian Jews and Muslims too – may have their difficulties with governments and the way their society is run and organized. While they work for various reforms, especially in the area of social policy, they do not view the state as evil or somehow inimical to their religion. In fact, the classic establishment position, represented in the Book of Common Prayer of the Church of England, is to pray for the monarch as the head of state and head of the church: "We beseech thee also to save and defend all Christian kings, princes and governors; and specially thy servant *Elizabeth our Queen,* that under her we may be godly and quietly governed: and grant unto her whole Council, and to all that are put in authority under her, that they may truly and impartially minister justice, to the punishment of wickedness and vice, and to the maintenance of thy true religion and virtue." This Anglican prayer derives from various places in the New Testament, which generally counsels compliance with authorities, as, for example, when 1 Timothy 1:2 urges prayers to be made "for kings, and for all that are in authority; that we may lead a quiet and peaceable life in all godliness and honesty." In the nineteenth century, even after the Anglican Church was no longer the established religion of Upper Canada, the continuing affinity of St George's Cathedral and Kingston City Hall remained embodied in their architectural similarities (see chap. 1). Though by no stretch of the imagination do they envisage a harmonious continuity of their churches and the municipal government, the spiritual mappers do take seriously biblical imperatives. It is their interpretation of the Bible and of the nature of evil that leads these radical sectarian Christians to go to City Hall in their prayer walks and to pray for the mayor and members of council. While their specific aim is to bring municipal government within the ambit of their particular religious views, they share with people of other faiths the effort to apply their faith perspective to their lives as citizens.

Extreme attitudes rooted in insecurities about the future, or based on a dichotomized worldview that locates evil forces in particular people or places or religions, are not going to disappear. Some Christians in Kingston with a radical view of what they would call "the world" pronounced with the utmost assurance that the most dangerous and evil powers in the city of Kingston were to be found today in cult practices, Paganism, or witchcraft – the last usually assumed to be equivalent to satanic worship – or, simply, in religions other than Christianity. Pagan Federation representative Brendan Fox referred to letters in the newspaper "saying that we make pacts with the devil," or have "rituals to open up the gates of Hell, for demons to come visit" (interview, 24 November 2004). The views of religious people who see evil as residing in the "other" are usually reinforced with millennial or apocalyptic teachings that interpret the world as infected with radical evil, soon to be ended by the intervention of a righteous God. Karen Armstrong has taught and written extensively about the current manifestations of fundamentalism, especially in the three western monotheistic religions. For example, in a lecture entitled "What Is Fundamentalism," presented at the

Intolerance and Fundamentalism Seminar at the London School of Economics, she spoke of the need to look beneath and decode "repulsive ideologies" (26 January 2005). Armstrong characterizes fundamentalists as wanting to withdraw from secular society, "in conscious defiance of the Godless world that surrounds them," and to reinstate religion in public life: "Some undertake a counteroffensive designed to drag God or religion from the sidelines to which they have been relegated in modern secular culture, and bring them back to center stage." While this campaign "is rarely violent," except in the Middle East or Afghanistan where violence pervades the society, fundamentalists are in revolt against a secular world seen as inhospitable to faith (Armstrong 2005). The theologies of spiritual mappers, prayer walkers, and those practising spiritual warfare verge toward these tendencies among fundamentalists.

At the furthest extreme, such fundamentalist views become religious violence for those who imagine the collapse of civil order and images of cosmic war. Mark Juergensmeyer argues that because "all religions are inherently revolutionary," any one of the major religious traditions can provide the imaginative and ideological resources for religious violence (2000, xii). He concludes that when violence accompanies religion, "it has much to do with the nature of the religious imagination, which always has had the propensity to absolutize and to project images of cosmic war" (241). Adherents of all faiths must assume the responsibility of standing apart from their extreme co-religionists and of refusing to allow them, by maintaining their silence, to speak for the entire tradition. Moderate Muslims must denounce Islamist terrorism, and moderate Christians must speak out when extremists preach intolerance and hatred against other religions.

Conclusion

Even in a city the size of Kingston, mapping the entire religious landscape is, of course, an impossibility. Limits have to be set. Any map involves selections and omissions, not always drawn according to fully enunciated principles. A map also fixes what is fluid and in transition. Some personnel, buildings, and other things have altered since the major research for this book was conducted, to the extent that recent changes are not fully reflected here. Accordingly, this book has its limitations, blind spots, highlighted themes, and even prejudices. At its completion the author remains aware that there may be deficiencies, or interpretations and emphases that are not fully elaborated or which can be misunderstood, and some topics and themes that may have been overdone. The conviction remains, after all of the interviews, through the reading of so many reports and statements, and as new developments emerge, that religion continues to be a vital force even in the midst of a society too easily dismissed as "secular." What, then, is to be said by way of summary about the religious character of Kingston?

Like almost any Canadian city of comparable size, Kingston is in some respects both religiously typical and religiously unique. Yet the ways in which it is similar to and different from other cities are salutary. Some years ago a report emerged that put Kingston in a second-place tie for having the most "average" weather among Canadian cities (*Whig-Standard*, 30 September 2003). That is, Kingston's climate with the annual mixture of sunny and cloudy, snowy and rainy, and hot and cold days was about at the Canadian average. Another comparative survey showed that its demographics, though with some variations, were in many respects also average. Perhaps Kingston might also be said to be a typical Canadian city in terms of its religions, especially in comparison with cities of about the same size. It stands amidst continuity and change, maintaining traditions going back more than 150 years, while witnessing recent phenomena unimaginable a generation ago. The large limestone downtown churches mostly continue as they were, with little in the way of visible changes. Yet in just the past few years, one has been sold to a developer; another, long fallen into disuse, has been renovated as a banquet and wedding hall; a third, for some time used principally as a theatre space, for a few years hosted a Sunday-morning café church.

The Lotus-Heart-Blossoms vegetarian restaurant operated by followers of Sri Chinmoy (see chap. 8) during its three years of operation stood near the top of the user-contributed reviews of Kingston restaurants on the TripAdvisor website. Who would have thought, before the Lotus-Heart-Blossoms' opening in 2007, that such an achievement, transitory though it might have been, would be attainable? Regrettably, though, the culinary excellence of this vegetarian restaurant did not reap commensurate financial rewards, and its doors closed in August 2010. But on the brighter side, amidst the closing in the downtown in 2009 of two venerable family owned and operated retail establishments – the S&R Department Store, and Source for Sports – Sacred Source Bookstore persists in these difficult economic times. While other storefront galleries and shops along and near Princess Street have appeared with "for lease" signs in their windows, the Kuluta Buddhist Centre remains and, to all appearances, continues to thrive. One rationale for these relative successes might be that the presence of Queen's University near to the city's core helps to provide a steady source of clientele for an alternative religious bookstore and a Buddhist mediation centre. In fact, as we have seen in chapter 9, the existence in Kingston of various institutions, whether academic, military, health care, or penal, increases the range of religious options available, both within those institutions and within the city.

Kingston's successful downtown, with its healthy balance of living space, venues for entertainment, picturesque waterfront, market square, and retail businesses has been praised as comparable to only a few other cities of similar size. In 2004, in an American planning journal, four researchers put Kingston, along with Victoria and Halifax, at the forefront of Canadian cities of between 100,0000 and 500,000 people (*Whig-Standard*, 21 July 2004). Between the 1950s and the 1980s, when other downtowns were being razed to build indoor shopping malls, Kingston's historic buildings remained largely intact. The newspaper story summarizing the research named such significant ingredients as "an active retail scene, a pedestrian-friendly environment, cultural activities, street-oriented retail, people on the sidewalks, employment, frequent transit, civic events, green space and well-preserved neighbourhoods."

While Kingston has been criticized over the decades as being inhospitable to developers and to newcomers, and has been seen as standing for older values reminiscent of all that is staid and resistant to change, paradoxically it also hosts a countercultural undercurrent. Partly due to the influx of students – and the wish of some of them to remain after their degrees are completed – as well as the opportunities for theatre, music, movies, and restaurants that would do credit to a larger city, the outlooks of those from elsewhere who bring with them different ideologies and habits of mind offset the somewhat conservative attitudes of long-time residents who embody an eastern Ontario ethos. There's a story about someone taking an elderly Kingston woman out for drive. The woman, in her eighties and a lifelong resident of Kingston, remarked when they drove north of Princess Street that "she had never been in that part of the city before" (Wise 1993, 184). If Kingston's great divide in socio-economic terms used to be the way Princess Street divided the north and south parts of the city, the great religious divide, in terms of the location of centres of worship, is now between the downtown and the residential west end. Kingston's religious sites have moved to the suburbs.

The religious landscape of Kingston mostly reflects its "typicality." Kingston has fewer Roman Catholics than Canada at large, but more United Church members and Anglicans. About one-third of Kingstonians are Roman Catholic, 17 per cent are United Church of Canada, and 13 per cent belong to the Anglican Church of Canada. One recent development ("recent" because it has just begun to be measured in the last few censuses) is that 17.5 per cent of Kingstonians report that they have "no religion." Whether that percentage of "religious nones" will grow, remain constant, or decline is anybody's guess. Given the large proportion of young people in that category, some sociologists such as Reginald Bibby predict that they will seek out membership in faith groups as they get older. My own sense of things – again, only a guess – is that the percentage stating they have no religion will continue to grow. Having a religion is not an expectation in Canada as it is in the United States, where to say that you follow no religion is more difficult. Nonetheless, and Bibby's research bears this out, even among my students who declared that they followed no religion, in the background there remained a distinct awareness of the religious allegiances of their parents or grandparents. While their own connection with those familial faith traditions might be lapsed or tenuous, they knew what they were and were not seeking another faith to replace it.

When a scheduled interviewee failed to arrive for the Cogeco television series, *Profiles: People of Faith*, Vivian Lee, a research assistant on the Religious Diversity in Kingston project, consented to my impromptu request to substitute as the subject for a taped interview. Despite its being unrehearsed and on the spot, Lee was articulate about her personal religious background, where she currently stood, and what religious options she had considered. Vivian, or Lee Wing-Hin, grew up in Hong Kong in a Chinese family with no formal religious connections. She began to go on her own to an evangelical Protestant Sunday School and eventually considered being baptized. During her teens Lee felt, "experientially," as she put it, that "God helped me through" much of her conflict with herself, her friends, and her family. Yet she observed that at about the same time "my Christianity started to shake, and eventually was non-existent because I felt that because so much of the Protestantism that I was exposed to, which was Conservative Evangelical, was based on beliefs I don't agree with." For her that kind of Christianity was based on "oppression of others and almost a sense of superiority, and the dichotomy of self and other separations that I didn't feel were necessary, or even correct when dealing with people" (Cogeco interview, 17 November 2004).

As time went on, Lee began to be interested in Buddhism, and to practise meditation, but was unable to discard her Christian background and experience of God. Reincarnation, for example, was in direct conflict with the Christian beliefs she had been taught: "Even though I don't believe in them staunchly now, they still have an effect on me." Though wanting to include a personal God, such as Christianity provides, she was also seeking a religion, like Buddhism, that is "egalitarian" because it stresses equality between humans and nature and animals: "It has to somehow reconcile God as a divine person, and nature, and myself, and politics in some sense." She feels that "in Christian culture humans are still, I think, regarded as more superior than a lot of non-human beings. That I find very hard to swallow."

Though Lee would probably formally have described herself as having "no religion," clearly she remains a religious person, or a person with religious inclinations, who wants a faith where her own experience and her convictions are integrated. In the meantime, she remains, perhaps, a religious eclectic or a seeker who has not yet arrived at the place she would like to be. While there is much in her spiritual journey that is unique – she was a religious studies major in university, after all, with a singular background – there are also aspects of her choices that are typical of contemporary young people. Perhaps in a few more years her story will look more like those of the five women considered at the end of chapter 8 – that is, women who grew up with some connection with an organized religious tradition but have ended up moving more toward alternative kinds of spirituality.

The range of Christian and Jewish options for worship in Kingston continues to be wide. Despite the general suburban drift, the mainline Christian churches are well represented both downtown and in the suburbs. The "umbrella" Jewish congregation, Beth Israel, as well as the Reform Jewish congregation, Iyr HaMelech, are centrally located and active. Evangelical churches are available, from many denominations or of the unique standalone variety and representing a wide range of practices and emphases. Some, such as the Free Methodist Church and Standard Church, continue a long presence rooted in eastern Ontario. Various ethnic Christian churches are represented throughout the city. The Islamic Centre of Kingston located northwest of the city was the first mosque between Montreal and Toronto. Kingston's Muslims have worked hard to become part of the religious and social fabric of Kingston, welcoming the rest of the community inside its doors at various times of the years. Minority faith traditions such as the Mormons and Jehovah's Witnesses have existed in Kingston for a long time, and continue in well-established places of worship.

Spatial problems play out in various ways among faith traditions in Kingston. In this city where numbers existing in many religious groups are small and likely to remain small, sectarian divisions and doctrinal disputes often have to be put aside in the interests of unity and cooperation, especially if one is, for example, Hindu, Jewish, Muslim, or Sikh. Less visible than many other groups, because they lack a dedicated worship site, are non-Christians of Asian descent, whether Chinese, Vietnamese, or Cambodian. Asian Buddhists tend to meet in homes or to confine their celebrations to cultural events at particular times of the year. Whereas in places like Ottawa or Toronto or Montreal they do have their own temples, in Kingston they lack the critical mass necessary for dedicated worship space. Still, it is surprising how a fairly large community, such as Hindus, continues over several decades without a temple. At the other end of the scale, it is impressive that a relatively small number of Coptic Christians have worked valiantly to maintain their own separate place of worship in rented spaces until they were able in 2010 to purchase a building of their own. The more numerous Hindus continue without a temple because their internal diversity mitigates whatever wish they might have for a common place of worship with an outside leader who might lead them into factionalism. Clearly there are groups for whom it is essential to establish a distinctive place of worship, whereas for others it is not.

Throughout the visits and research interviews conducted for the Religious Diversity in Kingston project, one surprising central theme was the persistence of issues of sexuality and gender. In unexpected places strong views about same-sex relationships continued to come to the fore. Should same-sex marriages or unions be conducted within a certain denomination or religious site? Can a practising gay or lesbian be ordained, or even accepted as a full-fledged member of a congregation? What position should governments and schools take on these matters? Same-sex relationships have emerged as the touchstone of both conservative orthodoxy and of religious liberalism in the past few decades. Within Christianity for many centuries, the most heated doctrinal disputes centred on trinitarian controversies, especially concerning the relationship of Jesus Christ to God the Father. Today questions of subordinationism and the like have ceased to be of burning interest to most Christians. On the other hand, Dr Ian Ritchie, an Anglican priest, says that for some more conservative Anglicans the real concern underlying the debate about same-sex relationships is the threat to orthodox faith. To compromise what is understood to be the traditional Christian view of marriage leads to other compromises, such as the divinity of Christ: "The question of the centrality of Jesus as 'the only Son of the Father' now seems up for grabs in so much of what is called 'liberal' theology" (personal communication, 14 January 2010). Though the ancient creeds central to Anglicanism do not say much about sexual ethics, they do carefully define the relationship between God the Father and Son. Because Pentecostals and other evangelicals might be said to be doctrinal rather than credal, for them questions about trinitarianism and the uniqueness of Christ are resolved by scripture – though admittedly interpreted in various ways with emphasis being laid on differing passages. In short, then, the debates about what is core doctrine or essential in Christianity persist in many quarters, provoked by issues of same-sex relationships.

Even if controversies about the nature of God continue in the background, what more obviously today divides denominations, or may precipitate people's decisions to leave the religion of their upbringing or seek out new traditions, is a disagreement about gay or lesbian orientation or practice. The fervour and divisiveness of that debate is not likely to subside any time soon. At the same time, for many people seeking to find a contemporary way of being religious, their sexuality has become for them the source of the sacred. That is, one's own experience of embodiment and the very physicality of being human demands to be integrated into one's spirituality, especially for those whose experience has been one of marginalization and exclusion. Notice, for example, how the current description for a theology course at Queen's University, Sexuality and Spirituality, situates these issues: "Examines sexuality as the foundation for any spirituality of relationship, while exploring the relevance of ethics, justice and the power of sexuality. The course addresses topics including intimacy, eroticism, gender, violence, sexual orientations and pleasure in relation to Christian theological reasoning" (Queen's University School of Religion b).

Occasionally there is a discrepancy between the declared teaching of a religion and the actual practice of some people within that tradition. For instance, many Roman Catholics use artificial means of birth control despite the official position of the church. Sometimes a split emerges between the clergy who are expected to uphold the authorized position and the laity who may be more liberal in their views. At other times, clergy within a tradition may hold more liberal views than parishioners. Not all United Church people, for example, agree with their denomination's view on same-sex marriage, as became clear in the case of two congregations in the north part of Kingston. The manner in which a faith community accommodates or deals with such dissent might help individuals decide whether they can continue to hold views at odds with the official teachings of their religion or denomination. At such times it is often convenient to resort to one's own personal spirituality where such convictions are held privately, while maintaining a nominal affiliation with the tradition.

In 2000 Eric Beresford, then coordinator of ethics and interfaith relations for the Anglican Church of Canada, wrote: "At this point it is interesting that the positions adopted by the Anglican Church of Canada have insisted on the moral significance and dignity of fetal life and on the importance of the rights and needs of women who are clearly recognized as the primary decision makers" (2000). Like the developing Anglican views on same-sex union, the Anglican position on the morality of abortion may be a moderate one, treading a line between the polarities of a "right-to-life" position and a "freedom-to-choose" position. Canadian Anglicans may be balancing these two poles, avoiding the dogmatism of either extreme. Perhaps this accommodating breadth may succeed in keeping conservative Anglicans, who might otherwise drift away or leave for other churches, within the Anglican communion. At St Paul's Anglican Church, rector David Ward allied himself with the evangelical Protestant clergy. Early in 2010 Ward was succeeded by Kris Michaelson, a graduate of Vancouver's evangelical Regent College. St Paul's, whose congregation, Ward told us when he was interviewed, would mostly oppose same-sex marriage, has housed the Kingston Pregnancy Care Centre, which takes an anti-abortion stance. The website for the Kingston Pregnancy Care Centre states that it works with Jewels for Jesus, a private Christian adoption agency.

This leaning toward evangelical Protestantism by an Anglican congregation – considered to be in the mainstream of Christianity (see chap. 2) – is indicative of how new alliances are occurring among some churches. Most of the other support for the Pregnancy Care Centre would come not from other Anglican congregations in Kingston but from Protestant evangelical churches, and perhaps from Roman Catholics. Shared positions, in this case socially conservative ones, may lead to the crossing of denominational boundaries to find like-minded Christians. This tendency also shows that doctrinal positions, once the stimulus to divisions and schisms, have become in some instances less weighty than they used to be. With the invitation from the Vatican in the fall of 2009 removing barriers for Anglicans to join the Roman Catholic Church, we see how some earlier obstacles have paled in significance as conservative Anglicans sought a place that would honour their preferences for a heterosexual male clergy and heterosexual marriage as the Christian norm. Accordingly, a new home emerged for disaffected Anglicans who felt that their church had drifted too far and stretched its historic position too much.

Yet if some religious groups are joining forces in opposition to social trends of which they disapprove – they would stress the preservation of traditional values, respect for life, and the integrity of the family – others are making common cause for positive reasons. When Rabbi Daniel Elkin of Beth Israel Congregation was interviewed in November 2003, he described how shortly after his arrival in Kingston he began an interfaith group of teenagers, including Muslims, Roman Catholic high school students, and United Church and Bahá'í young people, who "had a car wash and they raised over $500, which they gave to the Kingston Youth Shelter" (see also *Whig-Standard*, 29 June 2002). Within the first year of becoming Beth Israel's rabbi, Elkin contacted the Islamic Centre, and the board of Beth Israel had several meetings with board members from the Islamic Society of Kingston. Jews and Muslims in Kingston have been actively involved in interfaith worship and community work, ranging from participation in City Hall vigils organized by the Sisters of Providence – and a tenth anniversary service at their motherhouse on 16 October 2005 – to an interfaith service with nine hundred people in attendance held at St Mary's Cathedral on the occasion of the death of Pope John Paul II. Archbishop Anthony Meagher invited representatives from fifteen faiths to participate, saying in his homily that the late pope would have approved: "He was a bridge-builder, and I think we've built some bridges tonight that will last beyond tonight" (*Whig-Standard*, 6 April 2005). After Tony Meagher's death, Kingston's Multi-Faith Group continued under Monsignor Joseph Lynch, with participation from the Jewish, Bahá'í , Unitarian, and Christian faith communities (see Kingston Multi-Faith). A survey in 2006 showed a dramatic increase in the United States in participation in interfaith events after 9/11. More significant was the change in the participation in such events, from having been primarily ecumenical Christian gatherings to a point where now "minority faiths, such as Islam, are the most active in interfaith work" (*Whig-Standard*, 13 May 2006).

Interfaith participation can also lead to a backlash. In the United States. David Benke, a Lutheran minister, was called a heretic and terrorist because he prayed publicly at an interfaith service at Yankee Stadium a few days

Interfaith Vigil, Kingston City Hall, Good Friday 2004

after 9/11. Benke was vilified by other Lutheran clergy for being on the same platform with representatives of the Jewish, Muslim, Hindu, and Sikh faiths, thereby implying that Christianity was a religion no different from and no better than others. A petition from his co-religionists led to Benke's suspension from his denomination, though that was later rescinded. His response, part of a Public Broadcasting Service film, *Faith and Doubt at Ground Zero*, was, "Their belief is that the doctrine of the church does not allow a Christian to stand at the same podium with someone of another faith or everybody is going to get the same idea that all religions are equal ... If religion leads people to make these kinds of accusations at exactly the worse moment in American history, then what's underneath religion?" (PBS). Post 9/11, religion has been marked by both pronounced unity and increased differences.

Many traditions realize that it is time to join hands with one another, build bridges, and present an allied front against a world often perceived to be secular. At the same time, however, some religions distinguish themselves by stressing their differences from others. To use again the metaphors of the marketplace, in an economy where many different options present themselves to the consumer, it is often crucial to differentiate one's product from others. At the conclusion of each of the interviews for this project, we asked two related questions. The first was: "Has the presence of new and different religious traditions in Kingston affected your religious tradition?" The second was: "How do you think Kingston is changing as this new multi-religious reality starts to be visibly present?" The responses covered a wide range. In his response, Peter Rigby of the Kingston Standard Church affirmed the principle of freedom of religion, but went on to say, "Part of my religion is not to say that every religion is equal, and that we're all teaching the same thing." The mission of Christianity, he said, "is to reach people with the Gospel of Jesus Christ." He maintained that Christians "operate the same way" as do Muslims: "just as a Muslim will tell us about their faith and be happy if we convert to the Muslim faith" (interview, 27 February 2004).

Pastor Mike Hogeboom of the Kingston West Free Methodist Church said that the presence of new faiths in Kingston required that "we have to communicate our message with more clarity, so it is not blurred by so many voices and opinions" (interview, 3 August 2004). Harold Alston of Princess Street United Church thought the presence of other religions in Kingston was "extremely good" because "it makes us conscious of other stories besides our story." Alston said that it was essential to be "good neighbours" and to show "respect" to those of other faiths, but that did not, for him, mean "I surrender a sense of ultimate truth." Though he acknowledged the commonalties among Christianity and Judaism and Islam, he thought that he could be a witness to Christianity, even at a mosque or synagogue, without thinking that all three faiths are identical, despite their "family resemblance" (interview, 12 March 2004).

Elizabeth Macdonald at Sydenham Street United Church provided a different slant in her answer, especially cautioning against Christian hegemonic assumptions. She thought that co-existing amidst members of other faiths, as United Church people do in their workplaces and where they live, meant teaching about other faiths in worship services: "We have to become a lot more intentional, more aware, using the multifaith calendar, praying for other traditions at holy times, lifting them up, looking at some connections between these festivals." She also thought that religious diversity provided an opportunity "to see ourselves as 'other' in the eyes of more and more people in the community." Rather than assuming "we're the dominant religion," it is useful to assume that "we're the ones who are strange, we're the ones doing these odd things that people don't get, and may be a little anxious about, or suspicious of, or sceptical of" (interview, 27 January 2004). Macdonald's position emphasizes knowledge about the faiths of other people. She also stresses that in a world that may be indifferent to or ignorant of religion, one's faith needs explanation and interpretation, though not in a defensive or missionizing way.

When Lincoln Bryant at St Andrew's Presbyterian Church was asked about the effect of the presence of Jews and Muslims and Buddhists in Kingston, he replied, mentioning interfaith events, that "to me, those things are enriching." He continued: "But the reality is they're so small, or relatively small, as to be inconsequential. They don't sort of come up on my radar screen. What comes up on my radar screen is people leaving the United Church and wanting to come here, people leaving here and maybe moving on to Polson Park Free Methodist Church for some reason or other" (interview, 31 March 2004). Mohammad Saleem of the Islamic Centre of Kingston affirmed that "though people after September 2001 reacted in different ways, we have found overall people in the Kingston community reacted positively toward the Muslim community." He thought there were "positive changes," and that "exploring who lives here, what faith groups live here, what they do, how we are interacting .... all of these positive things could lead to more cooperation and integration between religious groups and working together" (interview, 17 February 2004). Daniel Elkin of Beth Israel strongly supported the presence of new and different religions in Kingston. Nonetheless, he commented that "it hasn't affected us," which he amended to, "I mean, we haven't given up our Judaism in that sense." He added, "We believe everyone is created in God's image and we have to be respectful of everybody." Among the opportunities that interfaith dialogue had opened up, he said, was the opportunity to speak on Judaism to one hundred eleventh and twelfth graders at Holy Cross Catholic Secondary School (interview, 3 November 2003). Joseph Lynch of St Joseph's Catholic Church emphasized as one of the "major, major changes" of the past forty years or so "the church's openness towards those of other faith traditions" (interview, 14 July 2005).

David Iverson of St Margaret's United Church was not prepared to give Kingston "very high marks" in interfaith ventures. Congregations in Kingston, in his view, were functioning as "separate entities" without many interfaith or even interchurch activities. He thought that the possibility of joining forces with other religions, realizing what they share, was widely recognized as valuable, but that active cooperation had not been undertaken to the extent it should. Iverson felt it was important to reach out to those of other faiths, for instance during their religious holidays, though he acknowledged that in extending such gestures many Christians "feel that you are somehow watering down who you are." He hoped that people in his own congregation could individually "open themselves up to be part of that search" for common ground alongside people of other faiths, "because it will not be done within any specific religious community" (interview, 15 July 2004). He saw that as a way of strengthening one's own religious identity.

The former British prime minister, Tony Blair, gave a course at Yale University on faith and globalization in the fall of 2008. Rather than religions being a matter of conflict and division, or a means of spreading "hatred and sectarianism," he wants to see them become synonymous with "reconciliation, compassion, and justice." Among the ten things Blair says that he learned from his exploration of the subject – for instance, that "religious faith matters," that "faith is not in decline," and that "the key to respect is understanding" – he maintains that organized religions ought to lift up and support the process of learning and educating themselves about the religious faiths and traditions of other people. Notwithstanding the differences among various religious creeds, Blair seeks an acknowledgment by people of various faith traditions of such common values as "the equal dignity and equal worth of every individual before God" (2008). The Tony Blair Faith Foundation declares its support for "respect, friendship and understanding between the major religious faiths." The foundation endorses organizing "simple, informal multi-faith activities to raise awareness and funds to support those of different religions who are working together … on a shared cause" (Tony Blair Faith Foundation). In Kingston this kind of attempt is evident in the participation of different leaders in interfaith services, in the efforts of the late Archbishop Tony Meagher to gather representatives of different faiths together, and in a host of other declared intentions and small initiatives to instil understanding and friendship among people of varying faiths. The challenge of interfaith relationships, raised in differing ways by almost every one of those quoted here, is how to bear witness to one's own religious faith while honouring the truth that others have found in theirs.

In the course of thinking about this conclusion I happened to pull down from my shelf a book that I hadn't looked at in many years, *Seven Rivers of Canada* by Hugh MacLennan. I turned to his chapter on the St Lawrence because of Kingston's location at the river's juncture with the Great Lakes and the Rideau Canal. After discussing its history, its significance as a transportation route, "the greatest inland traffic avenue the world has ever known" (1961, 69), and its role in the exploration of Canada, MacLennan goes on to estimate the great river's effects on the lives and characters of the people living near it, people he terms "Laurentian." He says Laurentian folk are "intricate," "not intellectual," but "complex." Then he asks, "Does it make any sense to say that a Canadian – not a Maritimer, not anyone west of Kingston – is apt to be a person so subtle that compared to him the average Englishman is an open book?" (76). Picking up the phrase I quoted in chapter 1 from Douglas LePan, about the voyageur as "Hamlet with the countenance of Horatio," he says that Kingston's favourite son, Sir John A. Macdonald, exemplifies that mixture of "Hamletian doubt and imagination" and "Horatian self-control and endurance" (77). Not taken seriously by either the Americans or the English because he was a colonial, Macdonald understood that Canada's independence rested in serving the interests of both those countries.

Summing up the character of Laurentian people, MacLennan says that they do not hate each other, but they hate "the frustrations resulting from the necessity of living an eternal compromise" (78). While he might have been thinking particularly of the French and English in Quebec, what he goes on to say applies to Kingstonians as well: "So it has come about that the Laurentian people, over the years, have acquired the art of looking at life with a sextuple vision – as individuals, as members of their own racial or religious group, as Canadian citizens, as North Americans always required to balance their own interests in a kind of invisible juggling act with their southern neighbours whom they deeply like, as cultural scions of the French and English archetypes, and finally as cold-hearted realists in an international society" (78). Now, I'm not sure where exactly Laurentia is, if it exists, and whether Kingston is fully a part of it, but rereading those words, written fifty years ago, I think I understand something of Kingston's religious character. How does someone – or a particular religious institution – in a city such as Kingston preserve all of the old allegiances and ties, the continuing traditions and obligations, while being open to the future, welcoming new groups and cultures, and co-existing with those whose presence may seem to relativize, and even to threaten, what is familiar and held dear?

In the last stages of writing this book, I met Stewart Fyfe, now retired from political studies at Queen's, on Clergy Street in front of St Andrew's Presbyterian Church, and we stopped to talk. Fyfe has a long memory of things in Kingston, going back to his arrival as a student in 1945. He told the local newspaper he thought that he had attended every one of the New Year's Day levees at City Hall since they were begun in 1973, Kingston's tercentennial year (*Whig-Standard*, 2 January 2010). He is active in the local historical society and is an expert on municipal government. When I told him about the RDK project, he said he thought that Kingston was "cosmopolitan" because of the types of people who came to Kingston and who live here; the many institutions based in Kingston bring so many different people to the city from outside – from prison guards and inmates, to doctors and patients, and to professors and students. Recalling, for example, the material of chapter 9, on religion in Kingston's institutions, I agreed that that seemed to be the case.

Fyfe went on to say that he thought that Kingston was "progressive conservative," not in the political sense but because the city is characterized by being both progressive and conservative. In 1972, when the federal riding of Kingston and the Islands elected an actual Progressive Conservative, they sent a so-called Red Tory, Flora MacDonald, to Ottawa, where she served for sixteen years. Though Kingston prides itself as the home of Canada's first prime minister – another Conservative – when it elected MacDonald, it was in the midst of forty years of Liberal representation; she was preceded by the Liberal Edgar Benson and followed by the Liberal Peter Milliken. Even politically, then, Kingston is "progressive conservative."

The conservative aspects of the city are sometimes too readily evident, and sometimes become fodder for anecdotal accounts. It used to be said that you had to have three generations of ancestors buried in the Cataraqui Cemetery before you could be reckoned as one of the "Old Stones," or even rightly call yourself a Kingstonian. Robertson Davies, in many ways a conservative with few progressive tendencies, acknowledged and embraced the stodginess of Kingston by characterizing his "Salterton" as "dreamy and old-world," "at anchor in the stream of time," and as a place whose "tranquility was not easily disturbed." People who use such adjectives as "quaint" of Salterton (or Kingston), Davies' narrator comments in defence, are those "whose own personalities are not strongly marked and whose intellects are infrequently replenished" (1951, 9). Some locals resorted to wringing their hands as their city council hesitated for decades about what to do with the piece of waterfront vacant land on Block D, while developers' proposals kept getting turned down. Many of the city's institutions – Queen's University, for one – have been similarly painstakingly slow to adapt to change, as universities so often are. The upside of that conservatism is found in such gains as the resulting preservation of its stock of old buildings, for instance. Was there ever a Canadian city so proud of its buildings as Kingston?

Since this book began with Kingston's geographical location and its buildings, let it end with its people. In thinking again about the "progressive conservative" character of Kingston, and Stewart Fyfe's comment that the cosmopolitanism of Kingston partly derives from so many people coming here from elsewhere, I reviewed the backgrounds of the two dozen "people of faith" I interviewed on television (see appendix D). A few – Sister Irene Wilson and pastor Chris Walker and educator Bert Horwood – were born and raised in eastern Ontario, though their education and professional experience took them elsewhere too. United Church ministers Nadene Grieve-Deslippe and Elizabeth Macdonald came to Kingston from the Toronto area, but they had worked in Canada's Far North or on the prairies. Theo Drakos of the Greek Orthodox Church was born in Calgary to Greek parents; after serving in Kingston for some years, in 2008 he left for Hamilton. Pentecostal pastor Peter Hubert was also born in Alberta, where he went to Bible college and was a pastor for thirteen years. Anglican priest Fergy Wilson graduated in forestry and worked in a wilderness park in northwestern Ontario before becoming a prison chaplain working with mentally disordered offenders.

Anishnaabe woman Georgina Riel, whose background was in social work prior to coming to Queen's to manage the Aboriginal student centre, grew up near Sault Ste Marie in northern Ontario.

Elizabeth Greene, a tarot card practitioner and poet, came from an American Jewish background and studied medieval Christianity en route to becoming an English professor at Queen's. Rabbi Justin Lewis, leader of the local Reform Jewish congregation, grew up in a nominally Christian environment in Toronto before converting to Judaism; he has now left Kingston for Winnipeg. Gen Kelsang Thekchen, for several years the resident teacher at the Kuluta Buddhist Centre prior to moving to Toronto, was a university student in Ontario before going to India and encountering Buddhism there. Joan Fast, a yoga instructor, was raised in a Mennonite Brethren home in the Niagara area and discovered yoga while teaching in Japan. Val Michaelson, now an Anglican priest and campus chaplain, studied in Montreal and Vancouver and also worked in Japan for a year. Lincoln Bryant, long-time minister at St Andrew's Presbyterian, grew up in a Presbyterian family in Edmonton and lived for a time in Sri Lanka (then Ceylon).

Alia Hogben, executive director of the Canadian Council of Muslim women, says, "I'm of Indian parentage but I was born in Burma, and lived in Burma, and then in India, and my father became a diplomat and we moved to Japan, then to Canada and then to Europe" (1 December 2004). Sylvat Aziz, a Muslim woman from Pakistan, who describes the "bedrock" of her artistic work as Islamic, emphasizes that "issues in Chinese history and religions, issues in Christianity and Judaism, are equally important to posit reality between Islam and the other major religions and philosophies" (20 October 2004). Kamala Narayanan, a Hindu from India who represents Indians on interfaith groups, has been in Kingston since the 1970s. Vivian Lee, a student in religious studies at Queen's, grew up in Hong Kong. David Fiske was an active Anglican in South Africa before encountering Maharishi Mahesh Yogi and Transcendental Meditation, and eventually practising and teaching Tai Chi. Daniel Elkin had experience as a teacher and chaplain, living in such places as "London, England, Montreal, just outside of Tel-Aviv, New York City, and Seattle, Washington" before becoming the rabbi at Beth Israel in Kingston. Major Ed Call, a Salvation Army officer with Freedom Ministries, also originated from Montreal, and worked in Regina, Saskatoon, and Halifax "pastoring churches, in drug and alcohol addictions work, homeless shelters, and with the thrift stores and recycling" (9 February 2005). Kellye Crockett came from a Roman Catholic background in Prince Edward Island, studied linguistics at Queen's, and developed her expertise in Wicca, tarot, and belly dance – including dance studies in Cairo with Dr Hassan Khalil (see Oasis). Finally, Tony Meagher, who came from Toronto

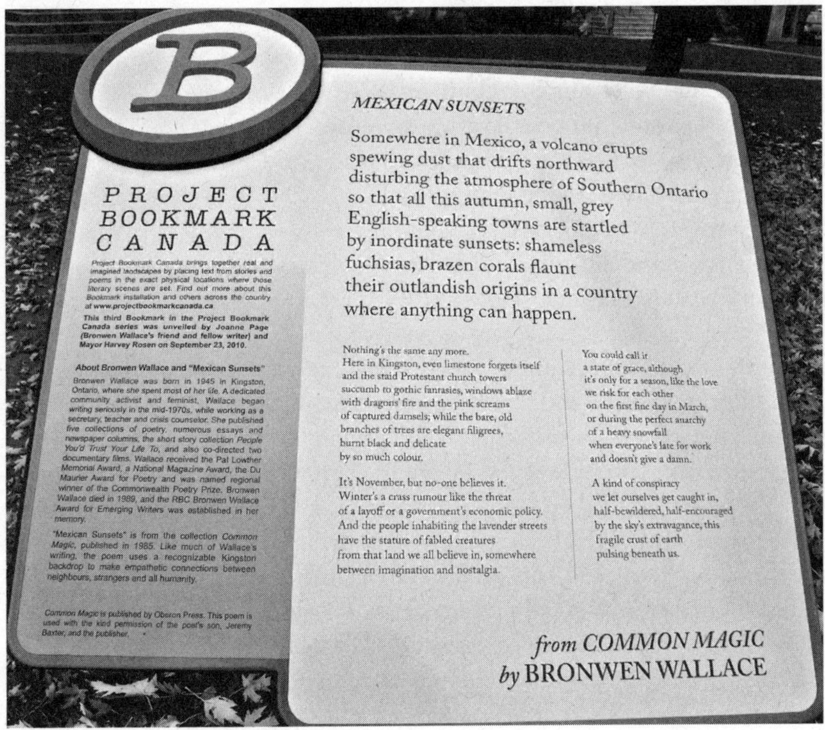

Bronwen Wallace's poem "Mexican Sunsets"

to be Kingston's Roman Catholic archbishop, travelled the world in various capacities, even making a trip to Rome just months before his death to witness a friend being made a cardinal.

On 23 September 2010, a short time after my conversation with Stewart Fyfe and a few metres away, a plaque was erected at St Andrew's Presbyterian Church displaying Bronwen Wallace's poem, "Mexican Sunsets" (1985, 23–4). The plaque was installed as part of an initiative that brings together words and landscapes: "Through a series of permanent markers bearing a fragment of text, Project Bookmark Canada reveals where our real and imagined landscapes merge, allowing the writers' words, images and characters to stir us (residents and visitors, pilgrims or passersby) in the very locations where the stories take place" (Project Bookmark).

"Mexican Sunsets" describes how the eruption of a volcano in Mexico colours the skies in southern Ontario: "so that all this autumn, small, grey / English-speaking towns are startled / by inordinate sunsets" (ll. 4–6). The poet imagines a transformation occurring in places like this Presbyterian church in Kingston's downtown:

Nothing's the same any more.
Here in Kingston, even limestone forgets itself
and the staid Protestant church towers
succumb to Gothic fantasies, windows ablaze
with dragon's fire and the pink screams
of captured damsels; while the bare old
branches of trees are elegant filigrees,
burnt black and delicate
by so much colour. (ll. 10–18)

But more than sunsets and buildings are altered. Changes in human attitudes and behaviour appear too as "the sky's extravagance" affects them. As ordinary and humdrum as people's lives might seem to be, potential for surprise and wonder persists just below the surface, ready to be summoned forth: "You could call it / a state of grace, although / it's only for a season" (ll. 26–28). At one level, then, the poem provides an example of how the global becomes local and how strange things from afar can appear here; at another, it's about how we are all connected in our common humanity. The poem displayed on a church lawn stands as a remarkable exemplar of the links between the literary and religious imagination in the city of Kingston as a poet's words and an ecclesiastical structure are brought together in a way that generates new associations and reflections. "Mexican Sunsets" beautifully represents how the hues of cosmopolitanism enrich the monochromatic greys of a limestone city.

Rabbis and priests and ministers and pastors; nuns and chaplains and ecclesial officials; artists and journalists and poets; students and teachers; librarians and government workers and private business owners – all these groups are represented in the interviews comprising *Profiles: People of Faith*. These two dozen diverse men and women, about the same number as those pilgrims whose stories were related by Geoffrey Chaucer in *The Canterbury Tales*, have had remarkable lives within their respective faith traditions and spiritual practices. Admittedly, they were selected for the Cogeco television interviews because their religious journeys were felt to be of interest, yet their stories could be augmented with those of many more people too who are included – and many more who are not – in the pages of this book. This survey of the range of religious beliefs and observances to be found in Kingston has canvassed only some of that rich array. The poet John Dryden said of Geoffrey Chaucer: "'Tis sufficient to say, according to the Proverb, that here is God's Plenty." Dryden was thinking not only of the assortment of pilgrims on their way to Canterbury in Chaucer's great poem but the richness of his portrayal of the medieval panorama in fourteenth-century

England. Taken all together these "people of faith" from a city in southeastern Ontario – along with so many others representing religious diversity in Kingston – at various stages in their respective pilgrimages early in the twenty-first century, exemplify "God's Plenty" too.

APPENDICES

APPENDIX A

Interview Questions

BACKGROUND

1 What is the background or history of your religious group in Kingston?
2 Did you worship somewhere else before?
3 Who founded this centre? Did you face any challenges when you first established this site?

DESCRIPTION OF THE CENTRE/PLACE OF WORSHIP

1 Please describe this religious centre or place of worship. Did it have a previous use?
2 How have you adapted, renovated, or rebuilt this centre to suit your religious needs?
3 How is your site publicized (bulletin board, bulletins, website, posters, Yellow Pages, newspaper)?
4 What facilities exist and what are their uses (additional worship room, basement, day-care, religious school, on-site kitchen, gymnasium or activity centre)?
5 Is this centre shared with another group? If so, how often do they worship on this site? What is your religious centre's relationship with that other group?

DEMOGRAPHICS

1 What is the ethnic makeup of the congregation here?
2 What languages are spoken here? Is there a dominant cultural or social challenge which you and your congregation face as a result of your ethnic makeup?

3 What is the dominant age group? Is there a relatively equal number of women and men? Do you feel this religious centre has a healthy population of young people in regular attendance?

GOVERNANCE

1 Has the leadership changed? Why and how did this take place? How has leadership change affected your group?
2 If a dispute arises in this religious group or congregation, how does it get settled? (For example, what if the leader's views conflict with the congregation, or the congregation with the parent body?)
3 Do you defer to and derive solutions from scripture or a holy text? If so, what process is followed to find a solution?
4 If there is a board, what is its role? Who is represented on the board, and how are its members chosen?

RELATIONSHIP WITH THE COMMUNITY

1 What role does this centre play in the city/community? (e.g., what is your mission in the community?)
2 Where does this religious centre interface with the community (Hadassah Bazaar, public lectures, socials)?
3 Are there any specific events which the Kingston community has come to appreciate and depend on (talent shows, suppers, etc.)?
4 Are there volunteer programs in your religious centre? How do they fit within your overall mission (outreach: helping/feeding/housing the homeless, book drives, bake sales, used clothing sales, etc.)?
5 What important events have helped to shape your group?
6 How have you dealt with them?
7 What do you think the city of Kingston looks like from your religious standpoint? (Is it supportive of your religion? Does it have a healthy social fabric? Is it a good place to raise religious children?)
8 Does your place of worship have any religious traditions that have changed or adapted to the local Kingston (or wider Canadian) context?
9 How has your congregation reacted and/or dealt with any changes in your tradition?

CONCLUSION

1 What is the defining characteristic of your congregation's way of being religious?

2 Has the presence of new and different religious traditions in Kingston affected your religious tradition?
3 How do you think Kingston is changing as this new multi-religious reality starts to be visibly present?

APPENDIX B

Religious Site Profile Template

(ADAPTED FROM HARVARD UNIVERSITY'S PLURALISM PROJECT)

Religious site name:
Tradition:
Religious site address:
Mailing address (if different):
Phone number:
Fax number:
Email address/website:
Contact name and title (not to be published):
Contact phone/fax number (not to be published):
Date religious site founded:
Religious leader and title:
Lay leader and title (not to be published):
Membership/community size:
Ethnic composition:
Affiliation with other communities/organizations, activities and schedule:
History (include brief background on the history of this group in this city, where they worshipped before, who founded the religious site, any challenges faced, etc.)
Demographics (who worships at the religious site – ethnicity, languages spoken, age groups, etc.):
Description of the religious site (physical description, what the centre was before, description of facilities and their use):
Religious site activities (include worship schedule, special events, programs for children, classes, group meetings, newsletters or other publications):
Other (any other qualities that make this religious site particularly interesting):

Researcher notes (referrals to other religious sites or organizations, follow-up requests)
Project notes (guidelines for future visitors, photographic notes, etc.):
Researcher:
Date:

APPENDIX C

List of Interviews Conducted

Sites and Groups Interviewed	*Interviewee*	*Date*
Aboriginal Liaison Officer, Kingston Penitentiary	Tanya Michelin	2 April 2008
Bahá'í Community of Kingston	Lynne Sitar	10 March 2004
Bath Road Baptist Church	G. Belyea/T. Irwin	5 March 2004
Bay Park Fellowship Baptist Church	Wally Mills	3 February 2004
Bayridge Alliance Church (CMA)	Dan Baetz	5 February 2004
Beth Israel Congregation (Jewish Orthodox)	Daniel Elkin	3 November 2003
Bethel Church (Associated Gospel)	Chris Walker	4 November 2003
Bethel Church	Chris Walker	2 March 2005
Bible Baptist Church	Randy Mumper	13 November 2003
Butternut Creek Free Methodist Church	Bob Boutilier	5 July 2004
Calvary/St Matthew's United Church	Judy MacGillivray	5 March 2004
Campus Association for Bahá'í Studies (Queen's)	Nicole Sabet	30 September 2005
Campus Crusade for Christ (Queen's)	Chris van de Vrande	27 October 2005
Cataraqui United Church	Christina Davis	13 July 2004
Chalmers United Church	Wayne Hilliker	3 October 2003
Chalmers United Church	Sharon Cohoon	13 February 2007
Christ Church Cataraqui (Anglican)	Edward Dallow	14 May 2004
Church of Jesus Christ of Latter-day Saints	Byron Johnston	5 December 2004
Church of Jesus Christ of Latter-day Saints	Four missionaries	7 June 2005
Church of the Good Thief (RC)	T. J. Boyle	n.d.
Cooke's-Portsmouth United Church	Terry Deline	16 January 2004
Dowsers	Barbara Caldwell	9 June 2005
Edith Rankin Memorial United Church	Mark Flemming	27 February 2004
Faith United Church	N. Grieve-Deslippe	19 May 2004
First Baptist Church	Kevin Smith	15 January 2004
First Baptist Church	Josh Mutter	24 November 2006

Sites and Groups Interviewed	*Interviewee*	*Date*
First Christian Reformed Church	Sid Ipma	13 July 2005
Frontline/Third Day Worship Centre	Peter Hubert	19 November 2003
Greek Orthodox Church	Theologos Drakos	20 November 2003
Holy Family Roman Catholic Church	Charles Gazeley	26 November 2003
Hotel Dieu Hospital Chaplain	Ed Shea	6 December 2005
Indo-Canadian Community Centre (Hindu)	Kamala Narayanan	11 July 2005
Islamic Society of Kingston	Mohammad Saleem	17 February 2004
Islamic Society of Kingston	Imam Tarek	31 January 2007
Iyr HaMelech Congregation (Reform)	Justin Lewis	22 October 2003
Jehovah's Witnesses	Randi Nicoles	26 January 2004
Kingscourt United Church	Gerri Butler-Preston	3 March 2005
Kingston Alliance Church (CMA)	Paul Silcock	22 January 2004
Kingston Chinese Alliance Church	Kong Lo	2 November 2003
Kingston Church of Christ	Richard Maddeaux	9 August 2004
Kingston General Hospital, Spiritual Care	Bob Hunt	16 November 2005
Kingston Gospel Temple (Pentecostal)	Ashley Arnold	29 January 2004
Kingston Gospel Temple (Pentecostal)	Ashley Arnold	11 August 2005
Kingston Sikh Cultural Association	Avtar Gahir	29 November 2006
Kingston Standard/Wesleyan Church	Peter Rigby	27 February 2004
Kingston Transformation Network	Roger Rutter	24 April 2007
Kingston Unitarian Fellowship	Kathy Sage	27 April 2004
Kingston West Free Methodist Church	Mike Hogeboom	3 August 2004
Kingsway Outreach Centre (Evangelical)	Andrew Belair	28 July 2004
Kuluta Buddhist Centre	Roberta Lamb	6 February 2006
NeXt Church (Free Methodist)	Al Doseger	7 November 2005
Newman House Chaplain	Raymond de Souza	10 March 2006
Orthodox Christian: St Gregory of Nyssa	James Griggs	15 November 2005
Pagan Federation (Wicca)	Brendan Fox	24 November 2004
Parish of Kingston North (Anglican)	Douglas Fox	15 December 2004
Polson Park Free Methodist Church	Brian Pritchard	20 November 2003
Princess Street United Church	Harold J. Alston	12 March 2004
Providence Continuing Care: Anglican Lay	Audrey Kilpatrick	15 December 2004
Providence Continuing Care: Anglican Priest	Jim Scanlon	7 December 2005
Quakers (Religious Society of Friends)	Bert Horwood	22 October 2003
Quakers (Religious Society of Friends)	Bert Horwood	7 November 2007
Queen Street United Church	Stephen McAlister	5 February 2004
Queen Street United Church	L. McKnight-Walker	23 October 2006
Queen's Catholics	Katherine Kelly	10 November 2006
Queen's Christian Fellowship (IVCF)	Lydia Cruttwell	3 February 2006

Sites and Groups Interviewed	*Interviewee*	*Date*
Queen's University Chaplain	Brian Yealland	27 September 2005
Queen's University Chaplain	Brian Yealland	30 March 2007
Queen's University Hillel Club	Ira Goldstein	23 September 2005
Queen's University Muslim Students Assn	Haseeb Kahn	25 October 2006
Queen's Religious Clubs, Panel, Rels-451	club representatives	5 October 2005
Regiopolis-Notre Dame Chaplain	Dan Quackenbush	16 June 2006
Royal Military College RC Chaplain	Jean-Yves Fortin	12 April 2007
Sacred Source	Kellye Crockett	12 April 2006
Salvation Army, Citadel	Wil Brown-Ratcliffe	20 July 2004
Salvation Army, Freedom Ministries	Ed Call	21 December 2004
Sisters of Providence	Gayle Desarmia	11 February 2004
Soka Gakkai International (Queen's)	Ben Jones	5 October 2005
Sri Chinmoy Centre	Paramita Jarvis	3 December 2005
Sri Chinmoy Centre	Janet Faubert	5 December 2005
Sri Sathya Sai Baba Centre	R. Vyas/A. Acharya	7 December 2005
St Andrew's by-the-Lake United Church	Jean Barkley	26 February 2004
St Andrew's Presbyterian	Lincoln Bryant	31 March 2004
St James' Anglican Church	Bob Hales	29 June 2004
St John's (Portsmouth) Anglican Church	Chris Doering	2 September 2005
St Joseph's Roman Catholic Church	Joseph Lynch	14 July 2005
St Luke's Anglican Church	Bill Clarke	17 March 2004
St Margaret's United Church	Dave Iverson	10 November 2005
St Mark's Anglican Church	Wayne Varley	15 January 2004
St Mary's Cathedral	D. Clement/M. Godzek	24 March 2004
St Mena Coptic Orthodox Church	Wagdy Loza	4 August 2005
St Paul's Anglican Church	David Ward	5 August 2004
St Paul the Apostle Catholic Church	Leo Byrne	30 October 2003
St Peter's Anglican Church	Michael Oulton	23 October 2003
Sydenham Street United Church	Elizabeth Macdonald	27 January 2004
Thaqalayn Muslim Association (Queen's)	Samil Chagpar	1 November 2005
Union Street Gospel Chapel (Brethren)	Bill Graham	16 August 2004
Unitarian Universalist Club (Queen's)	K. Im-Jenkins	3 October 2005
Westside Christian Fellowship (Reformed)	Ed Visser	3 March 2004
Zen Meditation Centre	Malcolm Griffin	n.d.
Zion United Church Outreach Ministry	Brian Yealland	6 February 2004

APPENDIX D

Interviews Broadcast in the *Profiles: People of Faith* Series

Twenty-four episodes of a weekly half-hour series of interviews with men and women in Kingston about their spiritual journeys were aired on Channel 13 Kingston, during fall and winter 2004–05. The series was a co-production of TVCogeco and the Department of Religious Studies at Queen's University.

Name	*Affiliation*	*Date*
Sylvat Aziz	Art professor; Muslim	20 October 2004
Lincoln Bryant	St Andrew's Presbyterian Church	16 March 2005
Ed Call	Freedom Ministries, Salvation Army	9 February 2005
Kellye Crockett	Sacred Source Book Store (Wicca)	3 November 2004
Theologos Drakos	Greek Orthodox Church	29 September 2004
Daniel Elkin	Beth Israel Congregation	26 January 2005
Joan Fast	Yoga and Relaxation Centre	9 March 2005
David Fiske	School of Tai Chi and Esoteric Arts	22 September 2004
Elizabeth Greene	Tarot card practitioner	24 November 2004
Nadene Grieve-Deslippe	Grace United Church	2 February 2005
Alia and Murray Hogben	Muslims	1 December 2004
Bert Horwood	Religious Society of Friends	10 November 2004
Peter Hubert	Third Day Worship Centre	6 October 2004
Vivian Lee	Religious Studies student	17 November 2004
Justin Lewis	Congregation Iyr HaMelech	13 October 2004
Elizabeth Macdonald	Sydenham Street United Church	15 September 2004
Anthony Meagher	Roman Catholic Archdiocese	2 March 2005
Val Michaelson	Anglican campus chaplain	23 February 2005
Kamala Narayanan	Hindu, Queen's Interfaith Council	23 March 2005
Georgina Riel	Four Directions Aboriginal Student Ctr	13 April 2005

Name	*Affiliation*	*Date*
Gen Kelsang Thekchen	Teacher, Kuluta Buddhist Centre	20 April 2005
Chris Walker	Bethel Church	27 October 2004
Fergy Wilson	Chaplain, Correctional Service Canada	30 March 2005
Irene Wilson	Sisters of Providence	27 April 2005

APPENDIX E

Letter of Information and Consent Form

LETTER OF INFORMATION

Queen's University
Department of Religious Studies
Theological Hall
Queen's University
Kingston, Ontario, Canada K7L 3N6
Tel 613 533-2106
Fax 613 533-6879

<date>

Dear <Religious Leader>,

This letter seeks your consent to be interviewed for our research project on Religious Diversity in Kingston. The interview should not take more than an hour of your time. The project aims at a total mapping of the religious landscape of Kingston, Ontario, early in the 21st century. We are compiling a series of about 100 profiles of religious groups, sites, and activities in Kingston, Ontario, to be made accessible on a public website. In the next phase various aspects of Kingston's religious terrain will be given further systematic examination and detailed analysis. After the conclusion of the three-year project a book on all of the various facets of religion in Kingston will be completed. We hope that this study will serve the people of Kingston and the religious groups of the city – as well as the usual academic audience.

This study is funded by the Social Sciences and Humanities Research Council of Canada and sponsored by Queen's University. Both institutions have strict guidelines for ethical research conduct, which the research team members are bound to follow to ensure that no harm will come to any of the participants. Please be assured that your participation in this project is strictly voluntary. The public nature of your position means that it is not possible for us to present the results of this interview anonymously; however, you will not be identified in any written report without your express written consent. The information gathered during this session will be kept strictly private and will not be used for any purpose other than the objectives of the research project, published in standard academic outlets available to researchers, students, policy makers, and the general public. While we do not wish to ask questions that are offensive or unduly invasive, you may refuse to answer any question with which you do not feel comfortable. You have the right to withdraw from the study at any time with no effect and to have any information about you removed from the study. The interview will be recorded by means of audio or videotape to assist us in analysis of the information. Queen's University guidelines require that all records of the interview be stored in a secure place for eventual archival preservation once the project has been completed.

Thank you very much for your participation in this project. Your contribution is a very valuable one, and will help to enhance our understanding of various aspects of religion in Kingston. Should you have any concerns, or require further information, please do not hesitate to contact Prof. Bill James, by telephone or at the above address. Should you have any questions concerning Queen's University ethics policy, please contact the Chair of the Research Ethics Board, Prof. William Morrow, or Chair of General Research Ethics Board, Prof. Joan Stevenson.

Yours sincerely,
William Closson James, Professor.

CONSENT FORM

Project Title: *Religious Diversity in Kingston*

Name of participant: ______________________________

I have read the letter outlining the terms under which I am participating in the above project and I have had any questions answered.
I understand that:

1 The purpose of the research project is to study religious groups, sites, and activities in Kingston, Ontario;
2 The interview will be recorded confidentially and for research purposes only;

3 My participation is voluntary and I am free to withdraw at any time;
4 The researchers have taken all precautions to ensure confidentiality;
5 I am aware that I can contact Professor Bill James of the Department of Religious Studies or the Chair of the Department's Research Ethics Board or the Chair of the General Research Ethics Board, with any question, concern, or complaint I may have;
6 I have been assured that reasonable steps have been taken to maintain privacy.

As a religious leader,
☐ I agree
☐ I do not agree
to be identified in the final research report.

☐ I agree
☐ I do not agree
to having the interviewed videotaped.

☐ I agree
☐ I do not agree
to having the interview recorded on audiotape.

(signed) ______________________________
(date) ______________________________

APPENDIX F

2001 Census, Kingston Religion

Census Product 97F0022XCB2001002

Title	*Total*
Total – Religion	142770
Catholic	43930
Roman Catholic	43760
Ukrainian Catholic	165
Polish National Catholic Church	10
Other Catholic	0
Protestant	66745
Adventist	135
Anglican	19160
Apostolic Christian Church	0
Associated Gospel	75
Baptist	2050
Brethren in Christ	70
Charismatic Renewal	75
Christadelphian	0
Christian and Missionary Alliance	305
Christian Congregational	10
Christian or Plymouth Brethren	35
Churches of Christ, Disciples	15
Church of God, n.o.s.*	25
Church of the Nazarene	10
Doukhobors	0
Evangelical Free Church	0
Hutterite	0
Jehovah's Witnesses	460

Title	Total
Latter-day Saints (Mormons)	500
Church of Jesus Christ of Latter-day Saints	500
Reorganized Church of Latter-day Saints	0
Lutheran	1285
Mennonite	50
Methodist Bodies	2140
Evangelical Missionary Church	100
Free Methodist	1700
Methodist, n.i.e.**	340
Mission de l'Esprit Saint	0
Moravian	10
New Apostolic	0
Pentecostal	1645
Presbyterian	2890
Quakers	35
Reformed Bodies	555
Christian Reformed Church	505
Canadian and American Reformed Church	10
Dutch Reformed Church	25
Reformed, n.i.e.**	20
Salvation Army	315
Spiritualist	20
Standard Church	210
Swedenborgian (New Church)	25
Unitarian	355
United Church	27920
Vineyard Christian Fellowship	0
Wesleyan	15
Worldwide Church of God	20
Non-denominational	190
Interdenominational	0
Protestant, n.o.s.*	6140
Christian Orthodox	1140
Antiochian Orthodox Christian	0
Armenian Orthodox	0
Coptic Orthodox	0
Greek Orthodox	780
Romanian Orthodox	15
Russian Orthodox	50

Title	Total
Serbian Orthodox	10
Ukrainian Orthodox	25
Orthodox, n.i.e.**	255
Christian, n.i.e.**	2330
Muslim	850
Jewish	855
Buddhist	475
Hindu	460
Sikh	125
Eastern religions	70
Baha'i	20
Jains	10
Shinto	0
Taoist	10
Zoroastrian	25
Eastern religions, n.i.e.**	10
Aboriginal spirituality	45
Pagan	190
Unity – New Thought – Pantheist	10
New Age	20
Scientology	15
Gnostic	0
Rastafarian	0
Satanist	0
Other religions, n.i.e.**	25
No religious affiliation	25480
Agnostic	165
Atheist	95
Humanist	10
No religion	24935
Other, n.i.e.**	275

* not otherwise specified
** not included elsewhere
Source: Statistics Canada

Bibliography

Abigail, Shawn G. 2006. "'Plymouth Brethren' FAQ." Shawn G. Abigail: Brethren Online. http://www.brethrenonline.org/faqs/Brethren.htm

Affirm United. "What Is Affirm United?" Affirm United. http://www.affirmunited.ca/AFFIRMPOSTER-8x11Handouts.pdf

Anderson, Scott K. 1988. "A Summer Walking Tour of Kingston Churches." *Kingston Whig-Standard*, 15 July.

Anglican Coalition in Canada. "Find a Church: ACiC Canada." ACiC Canada. http://www.acicanada.ca/find-a-church/

Anglican Church of Canada. "Report of the Primate's Theological Commission of the Anglican Church of Canada on the Blessing of Same-Sex Unions: The St Michael Report." The Anglican Church of Canada. http://www.anglican.ca/primate/ptc/smr-intro.htm

Anglican Communion Alliance. "Anglican Communion Alliance." Anglican Communion Alliance. http://www.anglicancommunionalliance.ca/

Anglican Essentials Canada. "Anglican Essentials Canada." Anglican Essentials Canada. http://www.anglicanessentials.ca/index.php

Anglican Fellowship of Prayer. "Prayer Walking." Anglican Fellowship of Prayer (Canada). http://www.anglicanprayer.org/resources/G-46-Prayer%20Walking_Web.pdf

Anglican Journal. "Chronology of the Same-Sex Debate in the Anglican Church of Canada." *Anglican Journal*. http://forums.anglicanjournal.com/timelines/ssb/

Appius Forum. "Strategic Level Spiritual Warfare Prayer." Appius Forum – Impact of Early Indian Christianity on India. http://appiusforum.net/mapping.html

Archdiocese of Kingston. "Home." The Roman Catholic Archdiocese of Kingston. http://www.romancatholic.kingston.on.ca/

Armstrong, Karen. 2005. "What Is Fundamentalism?" Intolerance and Fundamentalism Seminar, London School of Economics, 26 January 2005. http://www2.lse.ac.uk/publicEvents/events/2005/20041217t1358z001.aspx

Atwood, Margaret. 1996. *Alias Grace*. Toronto: McClelland & Stewart.

Auden, W.H. 1967. *The Enchafèd Flood: Or The Romantic Iconography of the Sea*. New York: Vintage Books.

Bahá'í Community of Canada. "The Bahá'í Community of Canada." The Bahá'í Community of Canada. http://ca.bahai.org/

Bahá'í Faith. "The Bahá'í Faith – The International Website of the Bahá'ís of the World." The Bahá'í Faith. http://bahai.org

Bahá'í Library Online. "Browse the Collection: Articles in Newspapers." Jonah Winter. http://bahai-library.com/Newspapers/

Bahá'í World News Service. "Canada's Parliament Condemns Persecution of Baha'is in Iran." Bahá'í World News Service. http://news.bahai.org/story/706

Bailey, Edward I. 1997. *Implicit Religion in Contemporary Society*. The Hague: Kok Pharos.

Banerjee, Sikata, and Harold Coward. 2005. "Hindus in Canada: Negotiating Identity in a 'Different' Homeland." In *Religion and Ethnicity in Canada*, ed. Paul Bramadat and David Seljak, 30–51. Toronto: Pearson Education Canada.

Barry, Dan. 2007. "Humble Voices Lifted, to Join a Glorious Throng." *New York Times*, 28 October.

Bath Road Baptist Church. "Church History." Bath Road Baptist Church. http://www.bathroadbaptist.com/about-us/church-history/

Battle Axe Brigade. "Spiritual Mapping." Battle Axe Brigade. http://www.battleaxe.org/spiritual%20mapping.html

Bauckham, Richard. 1984. "'Only the Suffering God Can Help:' Divine Passibility in Modern Theology." Themelios 9, no. 3 (April): 6–12. http://www.theologicalstudies.org.uk/article_god_bauckham.html

BCOQ (Baptist Convention of Ontario and Quebec). "Same-Sex Marriage Resources for Churches." Baptist Convention of Ontario and Quebec. www.baptist.ca/documents/About_Us/AU_CBOQ_Same_Sex_Marriage_Resources.pdf

Beaman, Lori G. 2006. "Aboriginal Spirituality and the Legal Construction of Freedom of Religion." In *Religion and Canadian Society: Traditions, Transitions, and Innovations*, edited by Lori G. Beaman, 229–41. Toronto: Canadian Scholars' Press.

– and Peter Beyer, eds. 2008. *Religion and Diversity in Canada*. Leiden: Brill.

Beckford, James A. 1978. "Accounting for Conversion." *British Journal of Sociology* 29, no. 2 (June): 249–62.

– 2003. *Social Theory and Religion*. Cambridge: Cambridge University Press.

– 2009. "Power and the Reification of 'Religion' in Prisons." Paper presented at the conference Interrogating Religion, University of Ottawa, 17–19 April.

Bennett, Richard E. 1992. "The Church in Canada." In *Encyclopedia of Mormonism*, Vol. 1, *Doctrine, LDS Differences*. http://www.lightplanet.com/mormons/daily/history/canada.html

Beresford, Eric. 2000. "Image of Tiny Hand Does Not Resolve Abortion Debate." *Anglican Journal*. 1 March. Link expired.

Berton, Pierre. 1965. *The Comfortable Pew: A Critical Look at Christianity and the Religious Establishment in the New Age*. Toronto: McClelland & Stewart.

Bethel Church. "Get Involved." Bethel Church. http://bethelkingston.com/get-involved/serve-in-kingston/

Beth Israel. "Our Back Pages: History." Beth Israel Congregation, Kingston, Ontario." http://www.kingston-bethisrael.ca/history.htm

Beyer, Peter. 2000. "Modern Forms of the Religious Life: Denomination, Church, and Invisible Religion in Canada, the United States, and Europe." In *Rethinking Church, State, and Modernity: Canada between Europe and America*, edited by David Lyon and Marguerite Van Die, 189–210. Toronto: University of Toronto Press.

– 2005. "The Future of Non-Christian Religions in Canada: Patterns of Religious Identification among Recent Immigrants and Their Second Generation, 1981–2001." *Studies in Religion/ Sciences religieuses* 34, no. 2: 165–96.

– 2006. "Religious Vitality in Canada: The Complementarity of Religious Market and Secularization Perspectives." In *Religion and Canadian Society: Traditions, Transitions, and Innovations*, edited by Lori G. Beaman, 71–91. Toronto: Canadian Scholars' Press.

Bibby, Reginald W. 1987. *Fragmented Gods: The Poverty and Potential of Religion in Canada*. Toronto: Irwin.

– 1993. *Unknown Gods: The Ongoing Story of Religion in Canada*. Toronto: Stoddart.

– 2002. *Restless Gods: The Renaissance of Religion in Canada*. Toronto: Stoddart.

– 2004a. "Religion and the Same-Sex Debate." Reginald W. Bibby: Papers, Pre-edited Articles, and Article Links. 10 December. http://www.reginaldbibby.com/images/Religion_Same-sex_Debate_Dec1004.pdf

2004b. *The Future Families Project: A Survey of Canadian Hopes and Dreams*. Ottawa: Vanier Institute of the Family 2004.

Biles, John. 2005. "Religious Diversity in Canada: In the Shadow of Christian Privilege." *Canadian Diversity/Diversité Canadienne* 4, no. 3: 67–70.

– and Humera Ibrahim. 2005. "Religion and Public Policy: Immigration, Citizenship, and Multiculturalism – Guess Who's Coming to Dinner?" In *Religion and Ethnicity in Canada*, edited by Paul Bramadat and David Seljak, 154–77. Toronto: Pearson Education.

Blair, Tony. 2008. "Faith and Globalization: An Alliance of Values." *New York Times*, 18 December.

B'nai Brith Hillel Foundation at Queen's University: Constitution. 1952. Queen's University Archives: Campus Clubs – Constitutions (II). Kingston: Alma Mater Society, Queen's University.

Bowen, Kurt. 1997. "Religion, Participation, and Charitable Giving: An Executive Summary." Canada Centre for Philanthropy. A 1997 national survey by Statistics Canada. http://www.givingandvolunteering.ca/files/giving/en/n-vc1sen.pdf

Brady, David. 1999. "An Interview with Garrison Keillor: 22nd February 1999." BAHNR 2: 34–9. http://brethrenhistory.org/qwicsitePro/php/docsview.php?docid=409

Bramadat, Paul. 2000. *The Church on the World's Turf: An Evangelical Christian Group at a Secular University*. New York: Oxford University Press.

– 2005. "Religion, Social Capital and 'The Day That Changed the World.'" *Journal of International Migration and Integration* 6, no. 2: 201–17.

– and David Seljak, eds. 2005. *Religion and Ethnicity in Canada*. Toronto: Pearson.

– and David Seljak, eds. 2008. *Christianity and Ethnicity in Canada*. Toronto: University of Toronto Press.

– and Matthias Koenig, eds. 2009. *International Migration and the Governance of Religious Diversity*. Montreal and Kingston: McGill-Queen's University Press.

Brodeur, Patrice C., and Susan F. Morrison. N.d. "Shared Sacred Space: New Religious Communities versus the Planning and Zoning Commission of New London, CT." http://www.pluralism.org/research/articles/brodeur_article.php?from=articles_index

Brown, Frank Burch. 2000. *Good Taste, Bad Taste, and Christian Taste: Aesthetics in Religious Life*. New York: Oxford University Press.

Brown, Robert McAfee. 1977. "The Holocaust as a Problem in Moral Choice." In *Dimensions of the Holocaust: Lectures at Northwestern University*, by Elie Wiesel, Lucy S. Dawidowicz, Dorothy Rabinowitz, and Robert McAfee Brown. Evanston, IL: Northwestern University Press.

Burwell, Adam Hood. 1849. *Summer Evening Contemplations*. Montreal: Lovell and Gibson. Published as an electronic edition in *Literature Online*. Cambridge: ProQuest Information and Learning Company, 2002.

California Code. "Article 6.5. Cremated Remains Disposers – California Business and Professions Code – Section 9740-9749.5 – California Code: Justia – US Laws, Codes, Statutes & Cases – Justia." US Laws, Codes, Statutes & Cases – Justia. http://law.justia.com/california/codes/2009/bpc/9740-9749.5.html

Campbell, Colin. N.d. "Cult." *Encyclopedia of Religion and Society*. Hartford Institute for Religion Research. http://hirr.hartsem.edu/ency/cult.htm

Canadian Centre for Progressive Christianity. "It's Time: Gretta Vosper." Canadian Centre for Progressive Christianity. http://elementsconference.ca/progressive/?page_id=447

Canadian Council of Churches. "History: Overview." Canadian Council of Churches. http://www.councilofchurches.ca/en/About_Us/history.cfm

Canadian Islamic Congress. "Islamic Congress Files Complaints with Quebec and Ontario Press Councils against Montreal Gazette and Ottawa Citizen,

20 October 2004." http://www.canadianislamiccongress.com/cic2010/2004/10/20/islamic-congress-files-complaints-with-quebec-and-ontario-press-councils-against-montreal-gazette-and-ottawa-citizen/

Canadian Society of Dowsers. "Associate Groups of CSD." Canadian Society of Dowsers. http://www.canadiandowsers.org/index.php?option=com_content&view=article&id=22&Itemid=24

Canadian Unitarian Council a. "Welcoming Congregations." Canadian Unitarian Council. http://www.cuc.ca/programs/welcoming_congregations.htm

Canadian Unitarian Council b. "Who We Are and About Us." Canadian Unitarian Council. http://cuc.ca/who_we_are/whoweare.htm

Canadian Unitarian Council c. "The Principles and Sources of Our Religious Faith." Canadian Unitarian Council. http://cuc.ca/who_we_are/principles/principles_sources.htm

CaraCo. CaraCo Development Corporation. http://www.caraco.net/

Carter, Jimmy. 2009. "Speech by Jimmy Carter to the Parliament of the World's Religions, Melbourne, Australia, 3 December 2009." The Carter Center. http://www.cartercenter.org/news/editorials_speeches/parliament-world-religions-120309.html

Catholic Health Alliance. "Resources: Health Ethics Guide." Catholic Health Alliance of Canada. http://www.chac.ca/resources/ethics/ethicsguide_e.php

Christ the King Polish Apostolate a. "Chapel." Polish Apostolate in Kingston. http://www.kingpol.org/chapelCA1.htm

Christ the King Polish Apostolate b. "History of the Apostolate." Polish Apostolate in Kingston. http://www.kingpol.org/chapelCA1.htm

Cherry, Conrad, Betty A. DeBerg, and Amanda Porterfield. 2001. *Religion on Campus*. Chapel Hill: University of North Carolina Press.

Chiang, Jack. 2005. "Growing Salvation Army to Build New Church." *Kingston Whig-Standard*, 1 November.

Chidester, David. 2002. *Patterns of Transcendence: Religion, Death, and Dying*. 2nd ed. Belmont, CA: Wadsworth.

Choquette, Robert. 2004. *Canada's Religions: An Historical Introduction*. Ottawa: University of Ottawa Press.

Chown, Diana. N.d. "Chown, Alice Amelia." *Canadian Encyclopedia*. www.thecanadianencyclopedia.com/index.cfm?PgNm=TCE&Params=A1ARTA0001604

Christ, Carol P., and Judith Plaskow, eds. 1979. *Womanspirit Rising: A Feminist Reader in Religion*. San Francisco: Harper & Row.

Christian and Missionary Alliance. "Spiritual Gifts: What Are Spiritual Gifts?" Christian and Missionary Alliance. http://www.cmalliance.org/about/beliefs/perspectives/spiritual-gifts

Christian Gays. "Straight Teacher Asked To Step Down Because She Will Not Condemn Gays!" Christian Gays. http://christiangays.com/articles/lauren.shtml

Christian Reformed Church a. "Historical Journey of the CRC." Christian Reformed Church: The Official Website of the CRCNA Ministries. http://crcna.org/pages/history_of_crc.cfm#Coming%20to%20North%20America

Christian Reformed Church b. "Committee to Study Third Wave Pentecostalism (Majority Report)." Christian Reformed Church: The Official Website of the CRCNA Ministries. http://www.crcna.org/site_uploads/uploads/resources/ThirdWavePentecostalismReport.pdf

Christians for Israel. "Vision." Christians for Israel, Canada. http://www.c4i.ca/Vision/23/0

Church of Pentecost Canada a. "About Us: Overview of the Church of Pentecost." The Church of Pentecost Canada. http://www.pentecost.ca/aboutus.html

Church of Pentecost Canada b. "Biography of Rev. James McKeown, Founder, The Church of Pentecost (1900–1989)." Church of Pentecost Canada. http://www.pentecost.ca/mckeown.html

Clifford, Keith. 1977. "His Dominion: A Vision in Crisis." In *Religion and Culture in Canada/Religion et Culture au Canada*, edited by Peter Slater, 23–37. Waterloo, ON: Canadian Corporation for Studies in Religion.

Cole, J.R.I. 1998. "The Bahá'í Faith in America as Panopticon, 1963–1997." *Journal for the Scientific Study of Religion* 37, no. 2: 234–48.

Committee of Architectural Review, Kingston, Ontario. 1971. *Buildings of Architectural and Historic Significance*. Vol. 1. Kingston, ON: n.p.

Congregation for the Doctrine of the Faith. "Considerations Regarding Proposals to Give Legal Recognition to Unions between Homosexual Persons." Congregation for the Doctrine of the Faith. http://www.vatican.va/roman_curia/congregations/cfaith/documents/rc_con_cfaith_doc_20030731_homosexual-unions_en.html

Conservative Quakers of Canada. "Our Beliefs." Conservative Quakers of Canada. http://www.quakers.ca/index.php

Cornille, Catherine, ed. 2002. *Many Mansions?: Multiple Religious Belonging and Christian Identity*. Maryknoll, NY: Orbis Books.

Correctional Service Canada a. "Aboriginal Initiatives." Correctional Service Canada. http://www.csc-scc.gc.ca/text/prgrm/abinit/who-eng.shtml

Correctional Service Canada b. "Chaplaincy Services, Documents and Reports: Memorandum of Understanding between the Interfaith Committee on Chaplaincy and the Correctional Service of Canada." Correctional Service Canada. http://www.csc-scc.gc.ca/text/prgrm/chap/mou-eng.shtml

Correctional Service Canada c. "Strategic Plan for Aboriginal Corrections." Correctional Service Canada. http://www.csc-scc.gc.ca/text/prgrm/abinit/plan06-eng.shtml

Cossar, Bruce. 2008. *Arise and Be Doing! Strathcona Park Presbyterian Church, Kingston, Ontario, 1958–2008*. Kingston: Strathcona Park Presbyterian Church.

Cottrell, Terence. 1999. "1883: Rise of Salvation Army Sparks Churchly Controversy." *Kingston Whig-Standard*, 7 April.

Couture, Joseph. 1983. "Traditional Aboriginal Spirituality and Religious Practice in Federal Prisons: An Interim Statement on Policy and Procedures." Prepared for Correctional Service Canada. Working Paper no. 1. Revised Draft no. 3.

Coward, Harold, John R. Hinnells, and Raymond Brady Williams, eds. 2000. *The South Asian Religious Diaspora in Britain, Canada, and the United States*. Albany: State University of New York Press.

Cox, Harvey. 1965. *The Secular City: Secularization and Urbanization in Theological Perspective*. New York: Macmillan.

Crysdale, Stewart, and Les Wheatcroft, eds. 1976. *Religion in Canadian Society*. Toronto: Macmillan.

Csillag, Ron. 1999. "Lord's Prayer Banned at Penetanguishene Council." *Canadian Jewish News*, 7 October.

Davies, Robertson. 1951. *Tempest-Tost*. Toronto: Clarke, Irwin.

– 1970. *Fifth Business*. Toronto: Macmillan.

Dawagun Mikan: Pathways Transition House. N.d. Brochure. Pittsburgh Institution. Kingston, ON.

Department of Justice Canada. Table of Contents, Criminal Code. Department of Justice Canada. http://laws.justice.gc.ca/en/c-46/index.html

Derouin, Jodey Michael. 2004. "Asians and Multiculturalism in Canada's Three Major Cities: Some Evidence from the Ethnic Diversity Survey." *Our Diverse Cities* 1 (Spring): 58–62.

Desjardins, Michel. 2004. "Teaching about Religion with Food." *Teaching Theology & Religion* 7, no. 3: 153–8. http://www.wlu.ca/documents/2320/TeachingAboutReligion1.pdf

de Souza, Raymond J. "A Collection of Articles and Publications." Father Raymond J. de Souza. http://fatherdesouza.ca/

DeVeau, Gary, and Eileen Koff. 2001. "Spiritual Mapping: Seeing Our World as God Sees It." *Transformations – Ourselves and Our Communities*. Middle Island, NY: Isaiah 54 Ministries. http://www.isaiah54.org/SpiritualMapping.html

Dewart, Leslie. 1966. *The Future of Belief: Theism in a World Come of Age*. New York: Herder & Herder.

Dick, Hannah. 2007. "Religious Clubs at Queen's University: Between Secularism and Pluralism." Paper presented to the Annual Meeting of the Canadian Society for the Study of Religion, Saskatoon, May.

Diocese of Ontario. "Clergy of the Diocese." The Ontario Diocese of Ontario, Anglican Church of Canada. http://www.ontario.anglican.ca/cgi-bin/newsscript.pl?database=clergy&record=74

Diocese of Vermont. "A Report to the Bishop and People of the Episcopal Diocese of Vermont from the Task Force on the Blessing of Persons Living in

Same-Gender Relationships – Executive Summary." Diocese of Vermont Home Page. http://www.dioceseofvermont.org/Orgs/TFonBlessings.html

Drache, Sharon. 1984.*The Mikveh Man: And Other Stories*. Downsview, ON: ECW Press.

Dueck, Gordon. 2009. "The Origins of Beth Israel, Kingston's First Synagogue." *Historic Kingston* 57: 26–31.

Eck, Diana L. 2001. *A New Religious America: How a "Christian Country" Has Become the World's Most Religiously Diverse Nation*. New York: HarperCollins.

– 2004. *A New Religious America: How a "Christian Country" Has Become the World's Most Religiously Diverse Nation*. San Francisco: Harper.

– 2005. "Foreword." In *Taking Religious Pluralism Seriously: Spiritual Politics on America's Sacred Ground*, ed. Barbara A. McGraw and Jo Renee Formicola, ix–xv. Waco, TX: Baylor University Press.

Ediger, Gerry. 2000. "Strategic-Level Spiritual Warfare in Historical Retrospect." *Direction* 29, no. 2 (Fall): 125–41.

Edwards, Paul, ed. 1967. *The Encyclopedia of Philosophy*. 8 vols. New York: Macmillan.

El Akkad, Omar, and Kenyon Wallace. 2007. "Teen Tried to Leave Strict Family." *Globe and Mail*, 12 December.

Electa, Sister Mary. 1961. *The Sisters of Providence of St Vincent de Paul*. Montreal: Palm Publishers.

Emberley, Peter C. 2002. *Divine Hunger: Canadians on Spiritual Walkabout*. Toronto: HarperCollins.

Emon, Anver N. 2007. "A Malignant Vestige of Tradition." *National Post*, 14 December.

Episcopal News Service Archives. "Arkansas: Bishop Allows Same-Gender Blessings as Pastoral Response." Episcopal Church. http://www.episcopalchurch.org/3577_76939_ENG_HTM.htm

Evangelical Fellowship of Canada a. "Statement of Faith." Evangelical Fellowship of Canada. http://www.evangelicalfellowship.ca/Page.aspx?pid=265

Evangelical Fellowship of Canada b. "Current Affiliates." Evangelical Fellowship of Canada. http://www.evangelicalfellowship.ca/Page.aspx?pid=384

Evangelical Fellowship of Canada c. "Social Issues." Evangelical Fellowship of Canada. http://www.evangelicalfellowship.ca/Page.aspx?pid=187

Evangelical Fellowship of Canada d. "Mission and Vision." Evangelical Fellowship of Canada. http://www.evangelicalfellowship.ca/Page.aspx?pid=264

Faith Alive a. "About Us: Who We Are." Faith Alive International Ministries. http://faim.ca/

Faith Alive b. "Faith Alive Academy." Faith Alive International Ministries. http://www.faim.ca/school.htm

Farrow, Douglas, ed., 2004. *Recognizing Religion in a Secular Society: Essays in Pluralism, Religion, and Public Policy*. Montreal and Kingston: McGill-Queen's University Press.

Faubert, Janet Elizabeth. 2007. *Colours of the Spirit: A Universal, Scientific, and Practical Guide to Self-Transformation*. Lincoln, NE: iUniverse.

First Baptist Church a. "Baptist Distinctives." First Baptist Church, Kingston Ontario. http://www.firstbaptistkingston.net/fbc/baptist_distictives.html

First Baptist Church b. "Church History." First Baptist Church, Kingston Ontario. http://www.firstbaptistkingston.net/fbc/churchHistory.htm

First Unitarian Church of Victoria. "Just for Laughs." First Unitarian Church of Victoria. http://www.victoriaunitarian.ca/hUUmour.php

Flynn, Louis J. 1973. "The History of Saint Mary's Cathedral of the Immaculate Conception, Kingston, Ontario, 1843–1973." CCHA *Study Sessions* 40: 35–40. http://www.umanitoba.ca/colleges/st_pauls/ccha/Back%20Issues/CCHA1973/Flynn.html

– ca. 1976. *Built on a Rock: The Story of the Roman Catholic Church in Kingston, 1826–1976*. Kingston, ON: Archdiocese of Kingston.

Frame Problem. "Waterloo, Ontario's Wilfrid Laurier University Denies Recognition to Campus Freethought Group." The Frame Problem. http://theframeproblem.wordpress.com/2008/02/01/waterloo-ontarios-wilfred-laurier-university-denies-recognition-to-campus-freethought-group/

Franzen, Jonathan. 2010. *Freedom*. Toronto: HarperCollins

Free Methodist Church a. "Statement on Homosexual Behaviour." Free Methodist Church in Canada. http://www.fmc-canada.org/en/who-we-are/position-papers/281-statement-on-homosexual-behaviour

Free Methodist Church b. "Eastern Thought and the Gospel." Free Methodist Church in Canada. http://www.fmc-canada.org/en/who-we-are/position-papers/277-eastern-thought-and-the-gospel

Frey, Christopher. 2009. "Enter the Holy Now: How African Pentecostalism Is Driving – and Commercializing – Global Christianity." *The Walrus* 6, no. 6 (July-August): 30–6.

Friends United Meeting. "About Friends United Meeting: Declaration of Faith." Friends United Meeting. http://www.fum.org/about/declarationfaith.htm

Frontline Ministries. "About Tom." Frontline Ministries. http://flministries.org/about/

Frye, Northrop. 1971. *The Bush Garden: Essays on the Canadian Imagination*. Toronto: Anansi.

Gashinski, Laurie. 2006. "Religious Diversity in Kingston." Panel Presentation for Religious Diversity in the City. Meeting of the Canadian Society for the Study of Religion, York University, 30 May.

Gathering of Baptists. "Statement of Affirmation and Welcome." Baptists Gathering in Integrity and Wholeness, Following the Example of Jesus. http://www.gatheringbaptists.ca/Welcome/

Geneva Fellowship. "Geneva Fellowship Home." http://geneva.queensu.ca/

Germain, Annick. 2004. "Religious Diversity: A Problem for Municipalities?" *Our Diverse Cities* 1 (Spring): 143–4.

Gill, Sam D. 1982. *Beyond "The Primitive": The Religions of Nonliterate Peoples*. Englewood Cliffs, NJ: Prentice-Hall.

Gladwell, Malcolm. 2008. *Outliers: The Story of Success*. New York: Little, Brown.

Goffman, Erving. 1961. *Asylums: Essays on the Social Situation of Mental Patients and Other Inmates*. New York: Anchor Books.

Gold, Raymond L. 1997. "The Ethnographic Method in Sociology." *Qualitative Enquiry* 3, no. 4: 387–402.

Goodstein, Laurie. 2009. "U.S. Nuns Facing Vatican Scrutiny." *New York Times*, 1 July.

Gopi Krishna. "Living with Kundalini." *Ecomall: A Place to Help Save the Earth*. http://ecomall.com/gopikrishna/livingwith.htm

Graham, Ron. 1990. *God's Dominion: A Skeptic's Quest*. Toronto: McClelland & Stewart.

Grainger, Brett. 2008. *In the World but Not of It: One Man's Militant Faith and the History of Fundamentalism in America*. New York: Walker & Company.

Grant, John Webster. 1984. *Moon of Wintertime: Missionaries and the Indians of Canada in Encounter since 1534*. Toronto: University of Toronto Press.

– 1988. *A Profusion of Spires: Religion in Nineteenth-Century Ontario*. Toronto: University of Toronto Press.

Grant, Judith Skelton. 1994. *Robertson Davies: Man of Myth*. Toronto: Viking.

Greene, Elizabeth. 2010. *Moving: Poems by Elizabeth Greene*. Toronto: Inanna.

Gresik, Alison. 2000. *Brick and Mortar*. Ottawa: Oberon.

Gualtieri, Antonio R. 1984. *Christianity and Native Traditions: Indigenization and Syncretism among the Inuit and Dene of the Western Arctic*. Notre Dame: Cross Roads Books.

Guenther, Bruce L. 2008. "Ethnicity and Evangelical Protestants in Canada." In *Christianity and Ethnicity in Canada*, edited by Paul Bramadat and David Seljak, 365–414. Toronto: University of Toronto Press.

Hallie, Philip F. 1994. *Lest Innocent Blood Be Shed: The Story of the Village of Le Chambon and How Goodness Happened There*. New York: HarperCollins.

Harding, John S., Victor Sogen Hori, and Alexander Soucy, eds. 2010. *Wild Geese: Buddhism in Canada*. Montreal and Kingston: McGill-Queen's University Press.

Harrison, Brock. 2006a. "Muslim Community Sets Sights on First Imam." *Kingston Whig-Standard*, 8 February.

– 2006b. "Kingston Islamic Society Hires Its First Imam." *Kingston Whig-Standard*, 30 August.

Heelas, Paul, ed. 1998. *Religion, Modernity, and Postmodernity*. Oxford: Blackwell.

Helwig, David. 1984. "Mere Self." *Canadian Literature* 100 (Spring): 132–8.

– 1986. *The Bishop*. Markham, ON: Viking.

– 2006. *The Names of Things: A Memoir*. Erin, ON: The Porcupine's Quill.

Henry, Fred. 2005. "Bishop Fred Henry – Troubled by Same Sex Marriage?" *Western Catholic Reporter*. 17 January. http://wcr.ab.ca/old-site/bishops/henry/2005/henry011705.shtml

Herberg, Will. 1960. *Protestant – Catholic – Jew: An Essay in American Religious Sociology*. New edition. Garden City, NY: Anchor Books.

Hewitt, W.E., ed. 1993. *The Sociology of Religion: A Canadian Focus*. Toronto: Butterworths.

Hillis, Bryan. 2008. "Outsiders Becoming Mainstream: The Theology, History, and Ethnicity of Being Lutheran in Canada." In *Christianity and Ethnicity in Canada*, edited by Paul Bramadat and David Seljak, 247–86. Toronto: University of Toronto Press.

Hird, Ed. 2008. "Dr Henry Wilson, Big Baby Brother." In *Battle for the Soul of Canada*. http://twgauthors.blogspot.com/2008/05/dr-henry-wilson-big-baby-brother-hird.html

Hogben, Murray. 1996. "Islamic Centre Gets Minaret: Mosque Is the Only One between Toronto and Montreal." *Kingston Whig-Standard*, 26 October.

Holvast, Rene. 2009. *Spiritual Mapping in the United States and Argentina, 1989–2005: A Geography of Fear.* Leiden: Brill.

Hotel Dieu a. "Home: Hotel Dieu Hospital, Kingston, ON." Religious Hospitallers of Saint Joseph of the Hotel Dieu of Kingston." http://www.hoteldieu.com/

Hotel Dieu b. "Leading the Way in Patient Care: A Snapshot." Religious Hospitallers of Saint Joseph of the Hotel Dieu of Kingston. http://www.hoteldieu.com/onepager082007.pdf

Hotel Dieu c. "Hotel Dieu Hospital Update, 2009 October." Religious Hospitallers of Saint Joseph of the Hotel Dieu of Kingston. http://www.hoteldieu.com/200910.pdf

Hultkrantz, Åke. 1979. *The Religions of the American Indians*. Berkeley: University of California Press.

– 1989. "The Religious Life of Native North Americans." In *Native American Religions: North America*, edited by Lawrence E. Sullivan, 3–18. New York: Macmillan.

Hutchinson, Roger. N.d. "Ecumenical Social Action." *Canadian Encyclopedia*. http://www.thecanadianencyclopedia.com/index.cfm?PgNm=TCE&Params=a1ARTA0002520

Impact World Tour a. "Greater Kingston: March 17–April 6 '08 ." Impact World Tour. http://www.impactworldtour.com/Groups/1000024090/Impact_World_Tour/locations/Canada/Kingston/Kingston.aspx

Impact World Tour b. "Greater Kingston: March 17–April 6 '08: About Us ." Impact World Tour. http://www.impactworldtour.com/Group/Group.aspx?ID =1000024110

Integrity Canada. "Integrity Canada: Gay and Lesbian Anglicans and Friends." Integrity Canada. http://integritycanada.org/integrity.html

Isaiah 54 Ministries. "Isaiah 54 Ministries." http://www.isaiah54.org/

Islamic Society of Kingston. "ISK – Home." ISK – Home. http://www.kingstonmuslims.net/

Iyr HaMelech Congregation. "Iyr HaMelech Congregation: Home Page." Iyr HaMelech Congregation. http://cd003.urj.net/

Jacobs, A. J. 2007. *The Year of Living Biblically: One Man's Humble Quest to Follow the Bible as Literally as Possible*. New York: Simon & Schuster.

James, William Closson. 1998. *Locations of the Sacred: Essays on Literature, Religion, and Canadian Culture*. Waterloo, ON: Wilfrid Laurier University Press.

– 2006. "Dimorphs and Cobblers: Ways of Being Religious in Canada." In *Religion and Canadian Society: Traditions, Transitions, and Innovations*, edited by Lori G. Beaman, 119–31. Toronto: Canadian Scholars' Press.

– 2008. "Borat and Anti-Semitism." *Journal of Religion and Film* 12, no. 1 (April). http://www.unomaha.edu/jrf/vol12no1/Borat.htm

– and Laurie K. Gashinski. 2006. "The Challenges of Religious Pluralism in Kingston, Ontario." *Canadian Journal of Urban Research* 15, no. 2, 50–66.

Jehovah's Witnesses a. "Ways They Use to Share the Good News." *Watchtower: Official Site of Jehovah's Witnesses*. http://www.watchtower.org/e/jt/article_05.htm

Jehovah's Witnesses b. "Statistics: 2009 Report of Jehovah's Witnesses Worldwide." *Watchtower: Official Site of Jehovah's Witnesses*. http://www.watchtower.org/e/statistics/worldwide_report.htm

Jehovah's Witnesses c. "What Is the Best Education?: What Kind of Education Can Make Your Life a Success?" *Watchtower: Official Site of Jehovah's Witnesses*. http://www.watchtower.org/e/20051015/article_01.htm

Jessup Food & Heritage. "Venue." *Jessup Food & Heritage/Fort Henry Kingston/Renaissance*. http://www.foodandheritage.com/index.php/renaissance.html

Jews for Jesus Canada. "About Us." *Jews for Jesus Canada*. http://www.jewsforjesus.ca/aboutus.aspx

Juergensmeyer, Mark. 2000. *Terror in the Mind of God: The Global Rise of Religious Violence*. Berkeley: University of California Press.

Justus, Martha. 2004. "Immigrants in Canada's Cities." *Our Diverse Cities* 1 (Spring): 41–7.

Kawamura, Leslie K. 1977. "The Historical Development of the Buddhist Churches in Southern Alberta." In *Religion and Culture in Canada/Religion et Culture au Canada*, edited by Peter Slater, 491–506. Waterloo, ON: Canadian Corporation for Studies in Religion.

Kingston Bahá'ís. "About the Bahá'í Faith." Bahá'í Community of Kingston. http://kingstonbahais.com

Kingston Chinese Alliance Church. "Our Mission." Kingston Chinese Alliance Church. http://www.kcac.ca/en/?page_id=74

Kingston Christian School. "About Us." Kingston Christian School. http://kingstonchristianschool.ca/about.htm

Kingston Gospel Temple. "Kingston Gospel Temple: Home." Kingston Gospel Temple. http://kgtchurch.org/about.php

Kingston Multi-Faith. "Kingston's Multi-Faith Group." kingstonmultifaith.ca/

Kingston Pregnancy Care Centre. "Kingston Pregnancy Care Centre." http://www.kingstonpcc.com/

Kingston Standard Church. "History." Kingston Standard Church: The Wesleyan Church in Canada. http://www.kschurch.ca/history.html

Kingston Unitarian Fellowship. "About Us: Our History." Kingston Unitarian Fellowship. http://www.kuf.ca/page18.html

Kitiarsa, Pattana. 2005. "Beyond Syncretism: Hybridization of Popular Religion in Contemporary Thailand." *Journal of Southeast Asian Studies* 36, no. 3: 461–87.

Knowles, Norman. 1991. "Irreverent and Profane Buffoonery: The Salvation Army and St. George's Anglican Cathedral, Kingston." In *St. George's Cathedral: Two Hundred Years of Community*, edited by Donald Swainson, 147–62. Kingston, ON: Quarry Press.

Koven, Merle, and Gini Rosen, eds. 1986. *From Strength to Strength: 75th Anniversary Commemorative Book*. Kingston, ON: Beth Israel Congregation.

Krakauer, Jon. 2003. *Under the Banner of Heaven: A Story of Violent Faith*. New York: Doubleday.

Lai, David Chuenyan, Jordan Paper, and Li Chuang Paper. 2005. "The Chinese in Canada: Their Unrecognized Religion." In *Religion and Ethnicity in Canada*, edited by Paul Bramadat and David Seljak, 89–110. Toronto: Pearson Education Canada.

Paroisse St-François d'Assise, la. "Bref historique de la paroisse." *La paroisse St-François d'Assise*. http://www.stfrancoisassise.ca/

Laurence, Margaret. 1974. *The Diviners*. Toronto: McClelland & Stewart.

Lausanne Movement a. "About the Lausanne Movement." *The Lausanne Movement*. http://www.lausanne.org/about.html

Lausanne Movement b. "The Lausanne Covenant." *The Lausanne Movement*. http://www.lausanne.org/covenant

Lausanne Movement c. "Deliver Us from Evil: Consultation Statement." *The Lausanne Movement*. http://www.lausanne.org/all-documents/consultation-statement.html

LDS (Church of Jesus Christ of Latter-day Saints). "Christ Organized His Church on Earth." *Church of Jesus Christ of Latter-day Saints*. http://www.mormon.org/restoration/

Lee, Vivian. 2004. "Puritanism on Campus: Queen's Campus Crusade for Christ." Term paper for Rels-451 at Queen's University.

Leonard, Ellen. 2007. "The Process of Transformation: Women Religious and the Study of Theology, 1955–1980." In *Changing Habits: Women's Religious Orders in Canada*, edited by Elizabeth M. Smyth, 230–46. Ottawa: Novalis.

Leslie, Lynn, and Sarah Leslie. 2005. "What Is Transformation?" Kjos Ministries. http://www.crossroad.to/articles2/05/sarah-leslie/transformation.htm

Lewis, I.M. 1989. *Ecstatic Religion: A Study of Shamanism and Spirit Possession*. 2nd ed. London and New York: Routledge.

Libin, Nicole. 2006. "Jewish Constructivism: Making Room for Hybridity." *Student Journal of Canadian Jewish Studies*. http://web2.concordia.ca/canadianjewishjournal/pdf/nicole_libin.pdf

Lila Centre. "Welcome to the Lila Centre – Kingston ON Canada." *Lila Centre – Kingston ON Canada*. http://www.lilacentre.ca/

Lithwick, Dahlia. 2001. "Crèche Test Dummies: Nativity Scenes on Public Lands Are Illegal, Rules the Supreme Court. Except When They're Not." *Slate*, 21 December.

Lowe, Chuck. 1998. *Territorial Spirits and World Evangelisation?* Borough Green, Kent, UK: OMF International.

Luciuk, Lubomyr Y. 1980. *Ukrainians in the Making: Their Kingston Story*. Kingston, ON: Limestone Press.

Lyon, David. 1995. *Living Stones: St James' Church, Kingston*. Kingston, ON: Quarry Press.

– and Marguerite Van Die, eds. 2000. *Rethinking Church, State, and Modernity: Canada between Europe and America*. Toronto: University of Toronto Press.

MacDonald, Mary Lu. N.d. "Adam Hood Burwell Biography (1790–1849)." *The Scribbler, The Canadian Review and Literary and Historical Journal, The Christian Sentinel*. http://www.jrank.org/literature/pages/7512/Adam-Hood-Burwell.html

Macdonald, Stuart. 2008. "Presbyterian and Reformed Christians and Ethnicity." In *Christianity and Ethnicity in Canada*, edited by Paul Bramadat and David Seljak, 168–203. Toronto: University of Toronto Press.

MacLachlan, Amy. 2008. "Ministers Mix It Up: Denominational Ties Are Increasingly Rare." *Presbyterian Record*, 1 May. http://www.presbyterianrecord.ca/2008/05/01/ministers-mix-it-up/

Maclean, Norman. 1976. *A River Runs through It and Other Stories*. Chicago: University of Chicago Press.

Maclean's. "Maclean's Poll 2006: What We Believe." *Maclean's.ca*. http://www.macleans.ca/article.jsp?content=20060701_130104_130104

MacLennan, Hugh. 1948. *The Precipice*. Toronto: Collins.

– 1961. *Seven Rivers of Canada*. Toronto: Macmillan.

Madsen, Gary E.. and Glenn M. Vernon. 1983. "Maintaining the Faith during College: A Study of Campus Religious Group Participation." *Review of Religious Research* 25, no. 2 (December): 127–41.

Mahmood, Cynthia Keppley. 2005. "Sikhs in Canada: Identity and Commitment." In *Religion and Ethnicity in Canada*, edited by Paul Bramadat and David Seljak, 52–68. Toronto: Pearson Education Canada.

Mair, Rafe. 2008. "Go in Peace, Church Dividers." *The Tyee: BC's Home for News, Culture, and Solutions*, 3 March. http://thetyee.ca/Views/2008/03/03/Anglican/

Manji, Irshad. 2003. *The Trouble with Islam: A Wake-Up Call for Honesty and Change*. Toronto: Random House.

– N.d. "The Book: *The Trouble with Islam Today*." Irshad Manji. http://www.irshadmanji.com/the-book

Marks, Lynne. 1996. *Revivals and Roller Rinks: Religion, Leisure, and Identity in Late Nineteenth-Century Ontario*. Toronto: University of Toronto Press.

Martin, David. 2000. "Canada in Comparative Perspective." In *Rethinking Church, State, and Modernity: Canada between Europe and America*, edited by David Lyon and Marguerite Van Die, 23–33. Toronto: University of Toronto Press.

Massey, Alexander. 1998. "'The Way We Do Things around Here': The Culture of Ethnography." Paper presented at the Ethnography and Education Conference, Oxford University Department of Educational Studies (OUDES), 7–8 September. http://www.voicewisdom.co.uk/waywedo.htm

Mathers, Donald M. 1962. *The Word and the Way*. Toronto: United Church Publishing House.

Matthews, Bruce. 2002. "Buddhism in Canada." In *Westward Dharma: Buddhism beyond Asia*, edited by Charles S. Prebish and Martin Baumann, 120–38. Berkeley: University of California Press.

McDonald, Marci. 2006. "Stephen Harper and the Theo-Cons: The Rising Clout of Canada's Religious Right." *The Walrus* 3, no. 8 (October): 44–61.

McGlinn, Sen. 2010. Sen McGlinn's Blog. "Evolving to Individualism and Reflections on the Bahai Teachings and Community." 10 January. http://senmcglinn.wordpress.com/quirky/footnotes-to-individualism/

McGowan, Michael. 2005. "Sponsorship of Catholic Health Care Organizations." *Catholic Health Alliance of Canada*. http://www.chac.ca/resources/otherresources_e.php

McKendry, Jennifer. 1995. *With Our Past before Us: Nineteenth-Century Architecture in the Kingston Area*. Toronto: University of Toronto Press.

McKinnon, Margie Ann et al., eds. 2002. *Springing from the Rock: A Portrait of the Archdiocese of Kingston, 1976–2001*. Kingston, ON: Roman Catholic Archdiocese of Kingston.

McLachlin, Beverley. 2004. "Freedom of Religion and the Rule of Law: A Canadian Perspective." In *Recognizing Religion in a Secular Society: Essays in*

Pluralism, Religion, and Public Policy, edited by Douglas Farrow, 12–34. Montreal and Kingston: McGill-Queen's University Press.

McLellan, Janet. 1999. *Many Petals of the Lotus: Five Asian Buddhist Communities in Toronto*. Toronto: University of Toronto Press.

Media Awareness Network. "Criminal Code of Canada Hate Provisions – Summary." http://www.media-awareness.ca/english/resources/legislation/canadian_law/federal/criminal_code/criminal_code_hate.cfm

Memorial Society of Peterborough. "A Funeral Consumers' Planning Information Service." Funeral Advisory and Memorial Society of Peterborough & District. http://www.myfuneralplan.org/ptbo.htm

Metropolitan United Church. "Metropolitan United Church – Our Story." Metropolitan United Church. http://www.metropolitanchurch.com/index.cfm?i=5936&mid=1000&id=110567

Meyer, Marion E. 1983. *The Jews of Kingston: A Microcosm of Canadian Jewry?* Kingston: Limestone Press

Michaels, Anne. 2009. *The Winter Vault*. Toronto: McClelland & Stewart.

Miedema, Gary Richard. 2005. *For Canada's Sake: Public Religion, Centennial Celebrations, and the Re-Making of Canada in the 1960s*. Montreal and Kingston: McGill-Queen's University Press.

Milot, Micheline. 2009. "Modus Co-Vivendi: Religious Diversity in Canada." In *International Migration and the Governance of Religious Diversity*, edited by Paul Bramadat and Matthias Koenig, 105–29. Montreal and Kingston: McGill-Queen's University Press.

Ministers Fellowship International. "Membership." Ministers Fellowship International. http://www.mfi-online.org/index.php?/welcome/membership

Ministry of the Attorney General. "Ministry of the Attorney General: Faith-Based (Religious) Family Arbitration." Ontario Ministry of the Attorney General. http://www.attorneygeneral.jus.gov.on.ca/english/family/arbitration/faith-based.asp

Mol, Hans. 1976. *Identity and the Sacred: A Sketch for a New Social-Scientific Theory of Religion*. Agincourt, ON: Book Society of Canada.

– 1985. *Faith and Fragility: Religion and Identity in Canada*. Burlington, ON: Trinity Press.

Montgomerie, Joan. 2007. "Islam and Education in Toronto." *Peace Magazine*, January-March, 13. http://www.archive.peacemagazine.org/v23n1p13.htm

Montreal Zen Center. "Welcome to the Montreal Zen Centre." Montreal Zen Center. http://zenmontreal.ca

Moore, Arthur D. 1998. "Spiritual Mapping Gains Credibility among Leaders." *Christianity Today* 42 (January 12): 55.

Mooy, Rob. 2007. "Partners in Mission Food Bank Unveils New Logo." *Kingston This Week* (November). http://www.kingstonthisweek.ca/ArticleDisplay.aspx?e=778361

Mormon Info. "Is the LDS Church Really the Fastest Growing Church?" Courageous Christians United. http://mormoninfo.org/news-info/news/lds-church-really-fastest-growing-church

Mormon Tabernacle Choir. "Choir Facts." Mormon Tabernacle Choir. http://www.mormontabernaclechoir.org/info/

Morning Star. Morning Star Christian Fellowship at Queen's University. http://morningstar.mstars.org/queens/

Next Church. "About." Next Church. http://www.nextchurch.com/about/

Oasis. http://oasisdancestudio.ca

Noble, Mark. 2006. "Muslim Community Celebrates Hajj." *Kingston Whig-Standard*, 10 January.

Norman, Corrie E. 2003. "Savoring the Sacred: Understanding Religion through Food." http://www.pluralism.org/affiliates/norman/savoringthesacred.pdf

Ontario Multifaith Council. "Memorandum of Agreement between the Government of Ontario and the Faith Groups of the Province as represented by the Ontario Provincial Interfaith Committee on Chaplaincy, December 3, 1992." Ontario Multifaith Council. http://omc.ca/memorandum.html

Orsi, Robert A. 1999. "Introduction: Crossing the City Line." In *Gods of the City: Religion and the American Urban Landscape*, edited by Robert A. Orsi, 1–78. Bloomington: Indiana University Press.

Orthodox Church in America a. "A History and Introduction of the Orthodox Church in America." The Orthodox Church in America. http://www.oca.org/MVhistoryintroOCA.asp?SID=1

Orthodox Church in America b. "News and Events: Archbishop Seraphim of Ottawa on Leave of Absence." The Orthodox Church in America. http://www.oca.org/news/2282

Osborne, Brian S. 2004. *The Rock and the Sword: A History of St. Andrew's Presbyterian Church, Kingston, Ontario*. Kingston, ON: Heinrich Heine Press.

– and Donald Swainson. 1988. *Kingston: Building on the Past*. Westport, ON: Butternut Press.

O'Toole, Roger. 2000. "Canadian Religion: Heritage and Project." In *Rethinking Church, State, and Modernity: Canada between Europe and America*, edited by David Lyon and Marguerite Van Die, 34–51. Toronto: University of Toronto Press.

– 2006. "Religion in Canada: Its Development and Contemporary Situation." In *Religion and Canadian Society: Traditions, Transitions, and Innovations*, edited by Lori G. Beaman, 7–21. Toronto: Canadian Scholars' Press.

Paper, Jordan. 1988. *Offering Smoke: The Sacred Pipe and Native American Religion*. Moscow, ID: University of Idaho Press.

Partnership Ministries. "About Us: Vision, Our Doctrine." Partnership Ministries. http://www.partnershipministries.org/about-us/vision/

Patrick, Jeremy. 2006. "Church, State and Charter: Canada's Hidden Establishment Clause." *Tulsa Journal of International and Comparative Law* 14, no. 1: 25–52.

PBS (Public Broadcasting Service). *Faith and Doubt at Ground Zero*. PBS Frontline. WGBH Educational Foundation, "The Question of Religion," http://www.pbs.org/wgbh/pages/frontline/shows/faith/questions/religion.html

Pentecostal Assemblies of Canada. "Statement of Fundamental and Essential Truths." Pentecostal Assemblies of Canada. http://www.paoc.org/about/what-we-believe

Penton, M. James. 1985. *Apocalypse Delayed: The Story of Jehovah's Witnesses*. Toronto: University of Toronto Press.

Perkin, J.R.C. 1991. "Denominational Distinctives: Traditional Characteristics of the Baptists." In *In Search of the Canadian Baptist Identity: Essays Celebrating the 150th Anniversary of First Baptist Church Kingston, Ontario, 1840–1990*, edited by George A. Rawlyk, 47–61. Kingston, ON: Alex Zander Press.

Peressini, Mauro. 2010. "Albert Low: A Quest for a Truthful Life." In *Wild Geese: Buddhism in Canada*, edited by John S. Harding, Victor Sogen Hori, and Alexander Soucy, 348–76. Montreal and Kingston: McGill-Queen's University Press.

Phillips, Annette. 2003. "Religion Removed from Council Ceremony." *Kingston Whig-Standard*, 19 November.

Pluralism Project. "Mission." *The Pluralism Project at Harvard University*. http://www.pluralism.org/about/mission

Popplewell, Brett. 2005. "Wither to Wish a Merry Christmas." *Kingston Whig-Standard*, 19 December.

Pray Kingston. 2002. "Lighthouses of Prayer." http://praykingston.com/aboutthemovement.php. Link expired.

Preston, Richard A. 1991. "The Garrison Church: The Military History of St. George's." In *St George's Cathedral: Two Hundred Years of Community*, edited by Donald Swainson, 15–26. Kingston, ON: Quarry Press.

Prete, Roy A., ed. 2002. *Legacy of Faith: Kingston and Area, 1830 to 2002*. Kingston, ON: Kingston Branch of the Church of Jesus Christ of Latter-day Saints.

Project Bookmark. "Imagine That." Project Bookmark Canada. http://projectbookmarkcanada.ca/imagine

Providence Manor. "Providence Care: Our Sites, Providence Manor." Providence Care. http://www.providencecare.ca/cms/sitem.cfm/our_sites/providence_manor/

Pursuit Canada. "Conference Worship Leaders: Antonio Baldovinos." The Pursuit Canada. http://www.thepursuitcanada.com/index.php?id=88

Quakers Canada a. "The Religious Society of Friends (Quakers): An Introduction." Canadian Yearly Meeting of the Religious Society of Friends. http://www.quaker.ca/ContactInfo/Intro/intro.html

Quakers Canada b. "A Minute of Record by Canadian Yearly Meeting. August 8, 2003." Canadian Yearly Meeting of the Religious Society of Friends. http://www.quaker.ca/concerns/SameSexMarriageMinuteCYM.pdf

Queen's University International Centre. "QUIC: Living in Kingston, Spiritual and Religious Support." QUIC: Queen's University International Centre. http://quic.queensu.ca/incoming/religion.asp

Queen's University School of Religion a. "School of Religion – Home." School of Religion, Queen's University. http://www.queensu.ca/religion/index.html

Queen's University School of Religion b. "Theological Studies: Degrees, Courses, Systematics and Ethics Courses." School of Religion, Queen's University. http://www.queensu.ca/religion/theology/grad/courses/systematics-ethics.html

Rawlyk, George A. 1996. *Is Jesus Your Personal Saviour? In Search of Canadian Evangelicalism in the 1990s*. Montreal and Kingston: McGill-Queen's University Press.

– ed. 1991. *In Search of the Canadian Baptist Identity: Essays Celebrating the 150th Anniversary of First Baptist Church Kingston, Ontario, 1840–1990*. Kingston, ON: Alex Zander Press.

Regiopolis-Notre Dame. "About RND: Catholic Philosophy of Education." Regiopolis-Notre Dame High School. http://www.reginotredame.ca/index.php?option=com_content&task=view&id=308&Itemid=237

Reimer, Sam. 2003. *Evangelicals and the Continental Divide: The Conservative Protestant Subculture in Canada and the United States*. Montreal and Kingston: McGill-Queen's University Press.

Remus, Harold, William Closson James, and Daniel Fraikin. 1992. *Religious Studies in Ontario: A State-of-the-Art Review*. Waterloo, ON: Canadian Corporation for Studies in Religion/ Corporation Canadienne des sciences religieuses.

Rense, Jeff. 2002 "Christmas Coming under Fire in Canada as Not PC: Have Yourself a Merry Little Holiday?" Jeff Rense website, Rense.com. www.rense.com/general32/christm.htm

Rieff, Philip. 1966. *The Triumph of the Therapeutic: Uses of Faith after Freud*. New York: Harper & Row.

Rifkin, Ira. 1997. "Critics Chafe at Bahá'í Conservatism." Religion News Service. 27 February. www.religionews.com. Link expired.

Robinson, J.A.T. 1963. *Honest to God*. London: SCM Press.

Roche, Edmund J. 1972. *Queen's Theological College Faces the Future*. Kingston, ON: Queen's Theological College.

Roddick, Paul M. 2006. *Hard to Believe: A Beginner's Guide to Heresy*. Victoria, BC: Trafford.

Roof, Wade Clark. 1999. *Spiritual Marketplace: Baby Boomers and the Remaking of American Religion*. Princeton: Princeton University Press.

Ross, Alec. 2007. *Walking in Hope, 1961–2006: History of the Sisters of Providence and St Vincent de Paul*. Kingston, ON: Sisters of Providence of St. Vincent de Paul.

Ross, Val. 2008. *Robertson Davies: A Portrait in Mosaic*. Toronto: McClelland & Stewart.

Rubenstein, Richard L. 1966. *After Auschwitz: Radical Theology and Contemporary Judaism*. Indianapolis: Bobbs-Merrill.

Ruether, Rosemary. 1974. *Faith and Fratricide: The Theological Roots of Anti-Semitism*. New York: Seabury.

Runyan, Joshua. 2008. "Canadian Rabbi Is Brigade's First since WWII." Chabad Lubavitch Media Center. April 22. http://www.chabad.org/news/article_cdo/aid/665937/jewish/Canadian-Rabbi-is-Brigades-First-Since-WWII.htm

Rustle. "Rustle: Goings on at the Ranch." Rustle. http://rustleranch.blogspot.com/

Saloojee, Riad. 2004. "Reflections on the Meaning of Ramadan." *Kingston Whig-Standard*, 23 October.

Salvation Army. "Gay & Lesbian Sexuality." The Salvation Army Canada and Bermuda Territory. http://salvationist.ca/about-us/position-statements/gay-lesbian-sexuality/

Sapers, Howard. 2006. "Annual Report of the Office of the Correctional Investigator of Canada 2005–2006, 16 October 2006." Office of the Correctional Investigator. http://www.oci-bec.gc.ca/comm/sp-all/sp-all20061016-eng.aspx.

Schoemperlen, Diane. 2001. *Our Lady of the Lost and Found*. Toronto: HarperCollins.

Sell, Henry T. *Studies of Famous Bible Women*. New York: Fleming H. Revell 1925.

Semple, Neil. 1996. *The Lord's Dominion: The History of Canadian Methodism*. Montreal and Kingston: McGill-Queen's University Press.

Sentinel Group. "Glowtorch: A Network of Light for Darkened World: An Online Service of The Sentinel Group." http://www.glowtorch.org. Replaces earlier link http://sentinelgroup.org

Service Ontario. "Funeral, Burial and Cremation Services Act, 2002." ServiceOntario e-Laws. http://www.ontariocanada.com/registry

Sikhism. "Sikh – Who Are the Sikhs?" Sikh.Net. http://www.sikh.net/Sikhs.htm

Siemiatycki, Myer. 2005. "Contesting Sacred Urban Space: The Case of *Eruv*." *Journal of International Migration and Integration* 6, no. 2: 255–70.

Silcox, Phillips A. N.d. *Unlock the Doors*. Toronto: United Church of Canada, Board of Evangelism and Social Service.

Simonds, Merilyn. 1996. *The Convict Lover: A True Story*. Toronto: Macfarlane Walter & Ross.

Simpson, John H. 2005. Review of Sam Reimer, *Evangelicals and the Continental Divide: The Conservative Protestant Subculture in Canada and the United States*. *Canadian Journal of Sociology* 30, no. 4: 550–2.

Sisters of Providence a. "Sisters of Providence Administration." The Sisters of Providence of St Vincent de Paul. http://www.providence.ca/about/administration.html

Sisters of Providence b. "Seed Sanctuary." The Sisters of Providence of St Vincent de Paul. http://www.providence.ca/seeds/

Smith, Theresa S. 1995. *The Island of the Anishnaabeg: Thunderers and Water Monsters in the Traditional Ojibwe Life-World*. Moscow: University of Idaho Press.

Smyth, Elizabeth M., ed. 2007. *Changing Habits: Women's Religious Orders in Canada*. Ottawa: Novalis.

Spickard, James V. 2003. "What Is Happening to Religion? Six Sociological Narratives." http://www.ku.dk/Satsning/Religion/indhold/publikationer/working_papers/what_is_happened.PDF

Spindler, George, and Louise Spindler. 1992. "Cultural Processes and Ethnography: An Anthropological Perspective." In *The Handbook of Qualitative Research in Education*, edited by Margaret D. LeCompte, Wendy L. Millroy, and Judith Preissle. San Diego: Academic Press.

Spiritual Mapping. "Spiritual Mapping: A Church Site to Stimulate Your Thoughts." Spiritual Mapping. http://w3church.org/SpiritualMapping.html

Spiritual Warfare. "Spiritual Warfare: The World, the Flesh, the Devil, and the Glory of God." http://battleinchrist.com

Sri Sathya Sai Baba Organization in Canada. "Who Is Sai Baba?" http://www.saicanada.org/docs/common/Who%20Is%20Sai%20Baba.pdf

Stackhouse, John G., Jr. 1993. *Canadian Evangelicalism in the Twentieth Century: An Introduction to Its Character*. Toronto: University of Toronto Press.

– 2003. "Census Canada." In *Sightings*. The Mary Marty Center for the Advanced Study of Religion, The University of Chicago Divinity School. 29 May. http://divinity.uchicago.edu/martycenter/publications/sightings/archive_2003/0529.shtml

St Andrew's by-the-Lake. "Welcome to St Andrew's by the Lake." St Andrew's by-the-Lake United Church. http://www.standrewsbythelake.ca/

Stark, Rodney. 1999. "Secularization, R.I.P." *Sociology of Religion* 60, no. 3 (Fall): 249–73.

Statistics Canada. "Market Research Handbook: Table 9.2: Selected Ethnic Origin, Census Metropolitan Areas, 2001." Statistics Canada. http://www.statcan.gc.ca/pub/63-224-x/2006000/4122859-eng.htm

St George's. "Welcome to St. George's." The Cathedral Church of St George. http://www.stgeorgescathedral.on.ca/

St Mark's Evangelical Lutheran Church. "St Mark's Community of Friends (SMCF): Student and Young Adult Ministry." St. Mark's Evangelical Lutheran Church. http://members.kingston.net/stmarks/SMCF.HTM

Swainson, Donald. 1991. "Afterword: Past Truths and Future Consequences." In *St. George's Cathedral: Two Hundred Years of Community*, edited by Donald Swainson, 263–74. Kingston, ON: Quarry Press.

Swatos, William H. Jr, and Kevin J. Christiano. 1999. "Secularization Theory: The Course of a Concept." *Sociology of Religion* 60, no. 3 (Fall): 209–28.

Sydenham Street United Church a. 2007. "Joint Needs Assessment: Final Report, March." Sydenham Street United Church. http://www.ssuc.org/jnac2007.pdf

Sydenham Street United Church b. "The Celebration of Marriage at Sydenham Street United Church." Sydenham Street United Church. http://www.sydenhamstreet.ca/special-services/57-weddings.html

Taoist Tai Chi. "What We Teach." International Taoist Tai Chi Society. http://www.taoist.org/content/standard.asp?name=whatweteach

Tataryn, Myroslaw. 2008. "Canada's Eastern Christians." In *Christianity and Ethnicity in Canada*, edited by Paul Bramadat and David Seljak, 287–329. Toronto: University of Toronto Press.

Taylor, Charles. 1991. *The Malaise of Modernity*. Toronto: Anansi.

– 2007. *A Secular Age*. Cambridge: Harvard University Press.

Teixeira, Carlos. N.d. "Portuguese"; "Multicultural Canada." *Canada's Multicultural Historical Resources Online*. http://www.multiculturalcanada.ca/ecp/content/portuguese.html

Third Day Worship Centre a. "Third Day Worship Centre Kingston Ontario Canada." Kingston Ontario Canada. http://www.raisethestandard.org/index.html

Third Day Worship Centre b. "Raising the Standard in Canada: Statement of Faith." Kingston Ontario Canada. Third Day Worship Centre. http://www.raisethestandard.org/about/statementoffaith.shtml

Thousand Islands Quaker Meeting. "Thousand Islands Meeting, Kingston, Ontario, Canada: Thoughts, Beliefs, Perspectives." Quakers: The Religious Society of Friends. http://kingston.quaker.ca/Quotes.htm

350.org. "2009: International Day of Climate Action (24 October)." 350.org. http://www.350.org/en/october24.

Thurlby, Malcolm. 1986. "Nineteenth-Century Churches in Ontario: A Study in the Meaning of Style." *Historic Kingston* 35: 96–118.

– 1990. "Church Architecture and Urban Space: The Development of Ecclesiastical Forms in Nineteenth-Century Ontario." In *Old Ontario: Essays in Honour of J.M.S. Careless,* edited by David Keene and Colin Read, 118–47. Toronto and London: Dundurn Press.

– and William Westfall. 1986. "The Church in the Town: The Adaptation of Sacred Architecture to Urban Settings in Ontario." *Etudes Canadiennes/Canadian Studies* 20, 49–59.

Tillich, Paul. 1957. *The Protestant Era*. Abridged ed. Translated by James Luther Adams. Chicago: University of Chicago Press and Phoenix Books.

Tony Blair Faith Foundation. "The Tony Blair Faith Foundation." http://tonyblairfaithfoundation.org

Trothen, Tracy J. 2003. *Linking Sexuality and Gender: Naming Violence against Women in the United Church of Canada*. Waterloo, ON Wilfrid Laurier University Press.

Trueheart, Charles. 1996. "Welcome to the Next Church." *Atlantic Monthly*, August 1996, 37–58. http://www.theatlantic.com/issues/96aug/nxtchrch/nxtchrch.htm

Tulchinsky, Gerald. 1992. *Taking Root: The Origins of the Canadian Jewish Community*. Toronto: Lester.

– 1998. *Branching Out: The Transformation of the Canadian Jewish Community*. Toronto: Stoddart.

– 2008. *Canada's Jews: A People's Journey*. Toronto: University of Toronto Press.

Unitarian Universalist Association. "Principles." Unitarian Universalist Association of Congregations. http://uua.org/visitors/6798.shtml

United Church a. "A Statement of Faith (1940) – The United Church of Canada." The United Church of Canada. http://www.united-church.ca/beliefs/statements/1940

United Church b. "A Song of Faith – The United Church of Canada." The United Church of Canada. http://www.united-church.ca/beliefs/statements/songfaith

United Church c. "Overview of Beliefs – The United Church of Canada." The United Church of Canada. http://united-church.ca/beliefs/overview#4

United Pentecostal Church International. "About Us." United Pentecostal Church International. http://upci.org/about.asp

United States Conference of Catholic Bishops. "Reiki Therapy Unscientific, 'Inappropriate for Catholic Institutions,' Say Bishops' Guidelines." United States Conference of Catholic Bishops: Office of Media Relations. http://www.usccb.org/comm/archives/2009/09-067.shtml

Valpy, Michael. 2006. "Canadians Praying in Private, Statscan Says." *Globe and Mail*, 3 May.

Van Die, Marguerite. 2009. "'What God Hath Joined…': Religious Perspectives on Marriage and Divorce in Late Victorian Canada." *Studies in Religion/ Sciences religieuses* 38, no. 1: 5–25.

Van den Hoonaard, Will C. 1996. *The Origins of the Baha'i Community of Canada, 1898–1948*. Waterloo, ON: Wilfrid Laurier University Press.

Venovcev, Anatoly. N.d. "Cosmopolitan." Cosmopolitan. http://acosmopolitan.blogspot.com

VisionTV. 2003. "Canada Ten Years Later: Still a Nation of Spiritual Seekers." 2003 Annual Survey on Faith & Spirituality. http://www.visiontv.ca/Programs/VisionTVAnnualSurvey.pdf

Vosper, Gretta. 2008. *With or Without God: Why the Way We Live Is More Important Than What We Believe*. Toronto: HarperCollins.

W3Church. "A Church Site to Stimulate Your Thoughts." http://w3church.org

Wagner, C. Peter. 1988. *The Third Wave of the Holy Spirit: Encountering the Power of Signs and Wonders Today*. Ann Arbor, MI: Servant Publications.

2002. "Global Harvest Ministries: Yesterday, Today, and Tomorrow!" *Global Harvest Ministries*. http://globalharvest.org

– 2007. "Global Harvest Ministries Evolves into 'Global Apostolic Network.'" CCNews Portal and Blogs. http://www.ccnews.org/index.php?mod=Story&action=show&id=2886&countryid=0&stateid=0

Wallace, Bronnen. 1985. *Common Magic*. Ottawa: Oberon.

Walsh, H. H. 1956. *The Christian Church in Canada*. Toronto: Ryerson Press.

Warfield, Benjamin B. 1919. "Paul on Women Speaking in Church, by Benjamin B. Warfield." Bible Research by Michael Marlowe. http://bible-researcher.com/warfield1.html

Weber, Max. 1947. *The Theory of Social and Economic Organization*. Edited and translated by A.M. Henderson and Talcott Parsons. New York: Oxford University Press.

– 1958. "The Sociology of Charismatic Authority." In *Max Weber: Essays in Sociology*, edited and translated by H.H. Gerth, and C. Wright Mills, 245–52. New York: Oxford University Press.

Weiss, David W., and Michael Berenbaum. 1989. "The Holocaust and the Covenant." In *Holocaust: Religious and Philosophical Implications*, edited by John K. Roth and Michael Berenbaum, 71–81. New York: Paragon House.

Westfall, William. 1989. *Two Worlds: The Protestant Culture of Nineteenth-Century Ontario*. Montreal and Kingston: McGill Queen's University Press.

– Louis Rousseau et al., eds. 1985. *Religion/Culture: Comparative Canadian Studies/ Études canadiennes comparées*. Vol. 7, *Canadian Issues/ Thèmes canadiennes*. Ottawa: Association for Canadian Studies/ Association des études canadiennes.

Wheeler, Carolynne. 2001. "City Council Keeps God in Its Prayer." *Ottawa Citizen*, 18 January.

White, Mervyn F. 2005. "Recent Ontario Decision Revisits Prayer in Government Proceedings." *Church Law Bulletin* no. 10, 30 April.

White, Tom. " Frontline Ministries." Frontline Ministries. http://flministries.org

Williams, Charles. 1958. *The Image of the City and Other Essays*. Selected by Anne Ridler. London: Oxford University Press.

WiccanWeb. "Pagan Address Book." WiccanWeb. http://www.wiccanweb.ca/index.php?module=pnAddressBook&func=viewDetail&id=41&formcall=edit&authid=bfeb5f15791d14f5284a57ed04ce3c8a&catview=0&sortview=0&formSearch=&all=0&menuprivate=0&total=62&page=1&char=O

Wiesel, Elie. 1970. *One Generation After*. New York: Avon Books.

– 1974. "Talking and Writing and Keeping Silent." In *The German Church Struggle and the Holocaust*, edited by Franklin H. Littell and Hubert G. Locke, 269–77. Detroit: Wayne State University Press.

Wilkinson, Michael, ed. 2009. *Canadian Pentecostalism: Transition and Transformation*. Montreal and Kingston: McGill-Queen's University Press.

Wilson, Robert S. 2001. "Patterns of Canadian Baptist Life in the Twentieth Century: Baptists in Canada Met in the Summer of 1900 in Winnipeg to

Organize an All-Canada Union." *Baptist History and Heritage*, Winter-Spring. BNET: CBS Business Network. http://findarticles.com/p/articles/mi_moNXG/is_2001_Wntr-Spring/ai_94160920/

Wise, S.F. 1993. "The Many Kingstonians." In *Written in Stone: A Kingston Reader*, edited by Mary Alice Downie and M.-A. Thompson, 183–90. Kingston, ON: Quarry Press.

York, Thomas. 1978. *And Sleep in the Woods: The Story of One Man's Spiritual Quest*. Toronto: Doubleday.

YouTube a. "IWT Kingston 08." YouTube. http://www.youtube.com/watch?v=GfoOp91JpY4

YouTube b. "Transformations: A Documentary Trailer." YouTube. http://www.youtube.com/watch?v=dBvxWl7jXro

Young, John. 1990. "Homosexuality and Ordination in the United Church of Canada: Two Congregations Respond." In *Theological Reflections on Ministry and Sexual Orientation*, edited by Pamela Dickey Young, 128–46. Burlington, ON: Trinity Press.

YWAM Campaigns a. "YWAM Campaigns – Impact World Tour." YWAM Campaigns. http://ywamcampaigns.com/

YWAM Campaigns b. "Impact World Tours – Kingston." YWAM Campaigns. http://www.ywamcampaigns.com/Mobile/default.aspx?group_id=1000011736&article_id=1000010272

Index

abortion, 208, 348, 362; evangelicals and Roman Catholics on, 63, 84, 92, 110; Jehovah's Witnesses and Mormons on, 133; Salvation Army on, 133

accommodation, religious, 320; chaplains and, 301, 304, 308; Commission on Reasonable Accommodation, 319; evangelicals and, 82, 144; among Hindus and Sikhs, 236–7, 240, 242, 246; by Muslims, 230; at Queen's University, 294; by Sisters of Providence, 256

Acharya, Anju, 238–40

Ahenakew, David, 333

Alston, Harold J., 365

Anglican Church of Canada parishes: Christ Church, 20, 50, 52–3, 161, 166–8, 216; Kingston North, 20, 50; St George's Cathedral, 5–6, 11–15, 24, 50, 52, 58, 65, 71, 105, 120–1, 162, 183, 250, 321, 327, 351, 354; St James', 15, 50–4, 183, 189, 211, 287; St John's (Portsmouth), 50, 52–5, 302; St Luke's, 20, 49, 50, 53, 56; St Mark's, 50–2, 54, 56, 259; St Paul's, 50–1, 78, 92, 140, 322, 327, 362; St Peter's, 20, 50, 54–6, 65; St Thomas', 20

anti-Semitism, 17, 94, 223, 224, 254, 333

architecture, of worship sites: Beth Israel, 20–1; Brethren, 136, 194; contemporary style of, 18, 21–3; Cooke's-Portsmouth, 23; in downtown Kingston, 3–4, 6–7, 71; evangelical churches and, 113; Gothic, 4, 12–15, 183, 321; Holy Family, 23; Jehovah's Witnesses, 134; Kingston Islamic Centre, 217–18; neoclassical, 14; primitive medievalism, 15; Providence Continuing Care Centre chapel, 302–3; Providence Spirituality Centre, 252; Quakers and, 192–3, 194; St Joseph's, 22–3

Armstrong, Francis, 94–100, 101, 116

Armstrong, Karen, 224, 354–5

Arnold, Ashley, 90–1, 96

Associated Gospel, 31, 102–3, 186, 188. *See also* Bethel Church

Atack, Jim, 233

Athletes in Action, 291

attendance at worship: in 1960s, 16–17; Anglicans and, 56; Bahá'ís and, 232; at Bethel Church, 186–7; Chinese Alliance and, 158–9; and church membership, 101–2; Church of

Pentecost and, 160; decline in, 16–18; Faith Alive and, 159; Jews and, 27–8, 195; at Kingston Gospel Temple, 90; Mormons and, 126; at Quaker meeting, 192; Roman Catholics and, 38; at St Gregory of Nyssa, 168; St Mark's and, 151; at St Mena Coptic, 166; at Sydenham Street United Church 184–7; at Third Day Worship Centre, 97
Atwood, Margaret, 5, 30, 278
Auden, W.H., 350
Aziz, Sylvat, 225–6, 370

Bahá'ís: Bahá'í Community of Kingston, 231–5, 244–6, 363; Campus Association for Bahá'í Studies (Queen's University), 290, 294, 296, 297; distribution of, 232; and interfaith activities, 233; and liberal Protestantism, 233–4; as NRM, 231–2, 235; origins, 232; proselytizing and, 232, 234–5; and women, 234
Bailey, Edward, xxvi
Bandy, Ken, 337
Baptists: Bath Road Baptist Church, 68, 129; Baptist Convention of Ontario and Quebec (BCOQ), 37, 60, 62, 69–77; Bay Park Fellowship Baptist Church, 68; Bible Baptist Church, 68, 116; Fellowship Baptists, 68, 69, 73; First Baptist Church, 37, 55, 62, 68–78, 140, 158, 179, 287
Barkley, Jean, 23–4, 46
Battle Axe Brigade, 343
Bayoumi, Mohamed M., 222
Beaman, Lori G., 215–16
Beckford, James, 116–17, 133, 305
Benke, David, 363–4
Beresford, Eric, 362
Berton, Pierre, 26–7, 72
Bethel Church: architecture of, 15; Asian students and, 178–9; attendance and membership, 101–3; Chalmers property and, 34; connection with Café Church, 115; origin and location of, 31; Queen's University students and, 287, 291; spatial and financial issues at, 186–90
Beyer, Peter, 9, 15, 24, 142, 307, 318
Bibby, Reginald W.: church attendance, 16–17; evangelicals, 104, 144–6, 188; religions of immigrants, 319–20; religious allegiance, 210–11, 358; "religious nones," 358; same-sex debate, 61–3, 74; United Church, 48
biblical literalism: 1960s and, 26; Brethren Assemblies and, 137; Robertson Davies on, 4; evangelicals and, 81; A.J. and, Jacobs 137; and Job, 258; meaning of, 88–9; miracles and, 72; Progressive Christians and, 210; spiritual mappers and, 343; St Andrew's Presbyterian and, 67
"Big Five" churches, 36, 118, 245
"Big Three" churches, 8–9, 20, 24, 30–1
Blair, Tony, 366–7
Blavatsky, Helena, 262
Booth, William and Catherine, 120, 135, 216, 261
Boutilier, Robert, 104, 110–12, 116
Bowen, Kurt, 183
Bramadat, Paul, 80, 288–9, 291, 292, 295; on pluralism, 334
Brandao, Francisco, 72, 158
Brethren (Brethren Assemblies), 30, 136–41; beliefs of, 139; as evangelicals, 119; exclusive nature of, 120 139, 140; as fundamentalists, 137; governance and, 138; history of, 137, 140; and naming chapels, 138;

outreach and, 140; schisms among, 139–40; women and, 138
Brown, Frank Burch, 90
Brown-Ratcliffe, Catherine, 120, 134
Brown-Ratcliffe, Wil, 120–4, 142
Browne, Paul and Faith, 159
Bryant, Lincoln, 64–8, 157, 332, 365, 370, 384
Buddhism: ethnic, 213–15; Kuluta Buddhist Centre, 33, 190, 214–15, 263–8, 271, 280, 292, 383; New Kadampa Tradition, 214, 215, 263–70, 280; Soka Gakkai International, 265, 290, 292, 294, 296; Zen Meditation Centre, 265, 292, 298
Burwell, Adam Hood, xvii
Bush, George W., 84, 92–3, 221
Byrne, Leo, 173–4, 259

Café Church, 32, 115, 357
Caldwell, Barbara, xviii
Call, Ed, 370
Calvary Bible Church, 32, 83–4, 102–3, 116
Campus Association for Bahá'í Studies. *See* Bahá'ís
Campus Crusade for Christ (Campus for Christ), 189, 287, 291, 293, 295, 298
Canadian Forces, 299, 301, 314–15; Canadian Forces Base Kingston (CFB Kingston), 51, 282, 299–301
Carter, Jimmy, 248
cartoon, by Aislin (Terry Mosher); and Muslims in Kingston, 219–22, 223, 333
Catholic Apostolic Church, xvii
chaplaincy. *See under* religion in institutions
Chochrek, Wieslaw, 170, 175
Chown, Alice, 262
Christian and Missionary Alliance, 100–6; Bayridge Alliance Church, 103–4; characteristics of, 100–1; Kingston Alliance Church, 101–4, Kingston Chinese Alliance Church, 104, 155–7, 158, 176
Christianity: in Canada, 7, 285, 317–20; Chinese and, 155, 176; and culture, 351–5; disunity of, 259, 322; eastern, 161–70; immigrants and, 175, 245, 320; interfaith relations and, 43, 64, 363–7; Islam and, 216, 223; Judaism and, 7, 93–4, 119, 223, 232, 274; liberal, 191, 211, 224; native religions and, 306–7, 309, 313; in nineteenth century, 7–8; Progressive, 47, 210; public religion and, 318–19, 327, 364; Quakers and, 194, 208–9; and secularism, 28, 72, 296, 333, 345; Unitarians and, 198, 201; women and, 250–1, 263–4, 272, 358–9, 370. *See also* ethnic churches in Kingston; evangelicalism; liberal religion; mainline Christian denominations. *See also* specific churches and denominations
Christian Science (First Church of Christ, Scientist), xx, xxv, 182, 193
"Circle, The" (women's spirituality group), 264–7, 280
Clarke, Bill, 49–50, 53–4, 55
Clemenger, Bruce J., 84
Clemens, Karl, 92
Clement, Donald P., 182, 251
Clifford, Keith, 320
Coffin, William Sloane, 85
Cohen, Sacha Baron, 223
Cohoon, Sharon, 186
Congregational Christian Churches, 114
Congregational Church, 8, 31, 44, 64; Bethel Church, 15, 31, 34, 103, 186;

First Congregational Church, 13, 15, 32, 44, 64, 115
Connolly, Joseph, 7, 13
Cornille, Catherine, 278, 307
Correctional Service Canada, 72, 165, 222, 282, 307–13
Coupland, Douglas, 112–13
Couture, Joseph E., 311–12
Coverdale, William, 7, 183
Cox, Harvey, 26, 353
Crockett, Kellye, 33, 263, 274–6, 281, 370. *See also* Sacred Source Bookstore
Crowley, Aleister, 273
culture: in Canada, 13, 250, 318, 321; evangelicals and, 91–2, 110, 113; evangelical subculture, 62, 82, 91–2, 113, 117, 341; immigrants and, 147–8, 164, 170–1, 176, 230, 235, 320; Jews and, 28, 295; mainline churches and, 37, 78–9, 88, 110, 118, 352–4; Mormons and, 129, 143; native peoples and, 306, 309, 311–13; nature religions and, 191; proselytizing groups and, 135–6, 141, 143; religion and, 48, 73, 79, 333, 351–5; Roman Catholics and, 303; Salvation Army and, 120, 134–5, 141, 142; Sikhs and, 244; Unitarians and, 199, 207; United Church and, 48, 73; youth, 158, 231, 288, 296. *See also* secular, the

Dallow, Edward, 53, 167–8
Danzinger Lazer, 314
Davies, Robertson: on Kingston, 3–4, 6, 321, 369; and Deptford churches, 36; and Presbyterianism, 64
Dawe, Matthew, 300
Day, Stockwell, 98
"death-of-God" theology, 25–8
Desarmia, Gayle, 252, 256
de Souza, Raymond, 43, 286–8
Dick, Hannah, 80, 280, 288, 344
Dickey Young, Pamela, 203
differentiation, religious: 50, 80–1, 115–17; campus clubs and, 291–2
diversity, religious, 213–14; chaplaincy and, 314–16; characteristics of, xxvi–xxvii, 214; Christian responses to, 110, 364–5; civic response to, 322, 334; definition of, 213–15; extrinsic, 235, 244; in institutions, 284, 290, 294, 301, 304, 313; intrinsic, 215, 244, 245. *See also* pluralism, religious
Doering, Chris, 52–3, 54, 55
donations, to churches: Bethel Church, 187–8; Brethren, 136–7; Copper Sunday, 11–12; Sydenham Street United Church, 185
Doseger, Al, 113–15, 116
Dowsers, xvi–xvii, 349
Drache, Sharon, 6
Drakos, Theologos, 162–4, 165, 369
Duffus Funeral Home, 103. *See also* Bayridge Alliance Church

Eck, Diana, 324, 334
Eckankar, 268
ecumenicity, 54–5, 246, 304, 314; of Christians and Jews, 11. *See also* interfaith relations
Eddy, Mary Baker, 262
Ediger, Gerry, 342–3, 345
Elkin, Daniel, 18, 98, 254, 363, 366, 370
Emberley, Peter, 48, 279, 319
Emon, Anver N., 230–1
ethnic Christianity: changes in, 176–7; growth of, 178; identity and, 175–6; multiculturalism and, 178; and religious diversity, 147–8; role of, 177–8. *See also* ethnic churches in Kingston

ethnic churches in Kingston: Christ the King Polish Apostolate, 170, 174–5; Church of Pentecost, 160–1; Dormition of the Theotokos Greek Orthodox Church, 162–4; Faith Alive, 158–60; First Christian Reformed Church, 31, 152–5, 156, 176; Kingston Chinese Alliance Church, 101, 104, 155–7, 158, 176, 177, 189; Kingston Korean Presbyterian Church, 156, 157–8; La Paroisse St François d'Assise, 170, 171–2; Our Lady of Fatima Roman Catholic Church, 170, 172–4; St Gregory of Nyssa Orthodox Parish, 161–2, 166–8; St Mark's Evangelical Lutheran Church, 149–52; St Mena Coptic Orthodox Church, 164– 6; St Michael the Archangel Ukrainian Catholic Church, 168–70; Westside Fellowship Christian Reformed Church, 152–5, 177. *See also under* individual churches

ethnicity of Kingstonians, 148; as compared with other cities, 149; Chinese, 148, 158, 159, 360; Danish, 149, 151, 176; Dutch, 148, 152–5, 176, 177, 320; German, 148–9, 150, 151, 176, 320; Italian, 148, 149, 154, 171, 173, 174, 320; Polish, 148, 170–1, 174–5, 251; Portuguese, 19, 72, 148, 158, 170, 172–4, 176

Evangelical Fellowship of Canada, 103; affiliates of 69, 83, 150; social activism and, 84–5; theology of, 76, 81–2, 88, 117, 335

evangelicalism: biblical authority and, 81–2, 85–6; characteristics of, 81–6; and Jews, 92–4, 97–8

Evangelical United Brethren, 44, 257

Fahmy, Fatma and/or Moustafa, 217, 220

Farber, Bernie, 325

Fast, Joan, 263, 281, 370; and Mennonite Brethren, 263, 277, 370; and yoga, 276–8

Faubert, Janet, 239, 263; and Christianity, 267, 272–3; and meditation, 267–8, 271–3; and Sri Chinmoy, 267–73

Feltmate, David, 221–2

First Christian Reformed Church. *See under* ethnic churches

Fiske, David, 370

Flemming, Mark, 46

food: religion and, 196, 219–20, 222–3, 238, 242, 249, 295, 313; food banks, 109, 111, 222, 243, 256, 347

Fortin, Jean-Yves, 299–301, 314

Fox, Brendan, 274, 276, 349, 354

Free Methodist Church, 32, 70, 83, 106–15; Butternut Creek Free Methodist Church, 35, 104, 110–2; Colborne Street Free Methodist Church, 31, 107–9, 112; history of, 106–7; holiness movement and, 107–8; Kingston West Free Methodist Church, 22, 109–10, 365; Methodism and, 106, 109; NeXt Church, 12, 31, 108, 112–15, 189, 291; Polson Park Free Methodist Church, 67, 108–11, 115, 157, 347, 366; Rustle Church, 114

Fritz-Millet, Steve, 115

Frontline Worship Centre. *See* Third Day Worship Centre

Frye, Northrop, 147, 350

Fyfe, Stewart, 368–9

Gahir, Avtar, 240–5

Gallienne, John, 105

Gashinski, Laurie, xviii, 127, 129

Gathering of Baptists, 69, 75–6
Gazeley, Charles, 43, 174
Gibson, Mel, 90, 254, 299
Global Harvest Ministries. *See* Wagner, Peter
Goffman, Erving, 299
Goodstein, Laurie, 245, 345
Gopi Krishna, 268
Gozdek, Mariola, 175, 251
Graham, Bill, 137–41
Graham, Billy, 83, 338, 344
Graham, Ron, 47, 48, 57
Grand'Maison, Jacques, 164
Grant, John Webster, 7–8, 306
Greek Orthodox Church (Dormition of the Theotokos): Coptic Church and, 165; dedicated space and, 181; ethnicity and, 147, 162–4; exogamy and, 163, 176; James Griggs and, 168; intercommunion and, 165–6; location of, 32, 162; Ukrainian Catholic Church and, 169. *See under* ethnic churches; *see also* Drakos, Theologos
Green, Joe, 240, 242, 244, 299
Greene, Elizabeth, 273–4, 281, 370
Gresik, Alison, 6
Grieve-Deslippe, Nadene, 49, 257–61, 369; child's death and, 258; on communion, 259–60; ordination of, 257; and suffering, 257–8; theology of, 257–8, 260–1
Griggs, James, 161–2, 167–8
Groen, Jason-Emery, 303
Groningen, Bill, 314–15
Gsus Sindustries, 332–3
Gualtieri, Antonio R., 306
Guenther, Bruce L., 155

Haider, Guizar, 217
Hales, Bob, 50–1, 53–4, 55
Hallie, Philip F., xxix, 181
Harper, Stephen, 84–5
hate crimes, 98, 221, 332–3
hegemony: Anglican, 11; Christian, 305, 318–19, 323; Church of England as "established church," 9
Helwig, David, 4–5, 211
Hendry, William, 105
Henry, Fred, 43
Herberg, Will, xxv
Hilliker, Wayne, 34, 85, 204
Hillis, Bryan, 151
Hindus, 20, 196, 209, 214, 216, 233; in Kingston (Indo-Canadian Community Centre), 235–7; liturgy of, 235–6; Sai Baba and, 238; Sikhs and, 241, 242, 243, 244, 245, 246; and unity in Kingston, 236. *See also* Sri Chinmoy; Sai Baba, Sathya
Hobbs, Ray, 76
Hogben, Alia, 226–7, 370
Hogben, Murray, 172, 174, 217, 226–7
Hogeboom, Mike, 109–10, 365
holiness movement, 8, 22, 30, 107–8, 121
Holocaust, 28, 94, 98, 291, 333
Holvast, Rene, 338, 342, 345, 348
"honour killing," 230–1. *See also* violence, religious
Horner, Ralph C., 107
Horwood, Bert, 190–4, 202, 209–10, 369
Hotel Dieu Hospital, 40, 234, 282, 301–3
Hubert, Peter, 337, 369; at Kingston Gospel Temple, 88, 93; at Third Day Worship Centre, 94–100, 101
humour, religion and, 25, 81, 191, 196, 199–200, 221–3
Hunt, Bob, 302

Ignatius of Loyola, 67, 255
imams, training and role of, 228–30

Impact World Tour, 338–41, 346–7
Indian Residential Schools, 56
interfaith relations: after 9/11, 164, 363–4; backlash against, 363–4; Bahá'ís and, 233, 234; chaplaincy and, 304, 309, 320–3; common goals and, 81, 233, 245–6, 292, 294–5, 363–4, 366–7; differentiation and, 81, 110, 292, 294; and ecumenicity, 38, 121; Jews and, 363–4; Muslims and, 224, 363–4; pluralism and, 294, 334–5, 363; at Queen's University, 233, 235, 285, 290, 294–5; Roman Catholics and, 38–9, 43, 366; Sikhs and, 243–4; Sisters of Providence and, 253–4, 324, 328
Inter-Varsity Christian Fellowship (IVCF): Paul Bramadat on, 289, 295; and evangelicalism, 81, 83; Queen's Christian Fellowship (QCF), 287, 291, 293, 296–7; and St James' Anglican Church, 51
Ipma, Sid, 153–4
Irwin-Gibson, Mary, 250
Isaiah 54 Ministries, 342–3
Ismaili Muslim Students' Association, 292
Iverson, David, 19, 22, 366
Iyr HaMelech congregation. *See* Judaism, Reform

Jarvis, Paramita, 239, 269, 271
Jehovah's Witnesses, 130–6, 360; beliefs of, 119, 132–3, 137, 143; dress and, 134; education and, 135; Kingdom Halls, 134, 182; music and, 134; as Protestants, 201; "publishing" by, 129, 130, 131, 145, 234; statistics, 132; and women, 133, 251
Johnston, Byron, 125–30, 133
Jones, Ben, 296
Judaism, 7–8, 10, 27–9, 101, 320–1, 359–60; B'nai Brith Canada, 325; Canadian Jewish Congress, 325; city council and, 323; as ethnicity, 148; evangelicals and, 83, 93–8, 334; and humour, 223; numbers, compared with Muslims, 214, 216. *See also* Judaism, Orthodox; Judaism, Reform
Judaism, Orthodox (Beth Israel Congregation): Centre St, 16, 17–18, 20–1; and interfaith events, 38, 253–4, 328, 363, 365–6; at Queen St location, 10–1, 15–16, 185, 331; "umbrella" character of, 18, 29, 194, 196, 359
Judaism, Reform (Congregation Iyr HaMelech): 29–30, 194–8; as liberal religion, 180–2, 209–10, 211; same-sex marriage and, 206
Juergensmeyer, Mark, 355

Kahn, Haseeb, 297
Kawamura, Leslie, xxv
Keillor, Garrison, 139–40
Ketola, Lionel, 150
King, Rebekka, 210
Kingston, city of: as "average," 356–7, 358; character of, xviii, xxvii–xviii, 5, 282–4; as "dark place," 335–49; demographics of, 16; and literary imaginations of religion, 3–6; location of, xv–xvi; "progressive conservative" aspects of, 338, 368–9; 321, 369; religious architecture in, 4; religious character of, 3, 315, 346, 356, 358, 368; visible minorities in, 159, 213–14
Kingston Alliance Church. *See under* Christian and Missionary Alliance
Kingston Chinese Alliance Church. *See under* Christian and Missionary Alliance

Kingston Economic Development Corporation (KEDCO), 282
Kingston Gospel Temple (Pentecostal), 86–94; and clothing drive, 102; as compared with Third Day Worship Centre, 97, 99; denominationalism and, 95; earlier location of, 101, 104; evangelical students at, 189; former pastors at Third Day Worship Centre, 94–5; location of, 216
Kingston General Hospital: 9, 40, 267; spiritual care at, 302–3
Kingston Pregnancy Care Centre (Kingston Crisis Pregnancy Centre), 92, 97, 362, 405
Kingston Sikh Cultural Association. *See* Sikhs
Kingston Standard Church (Wesleyan), 107, 216, 360, 364–5
Kingston Transformation Network, 335–42, 348
Kingston Unitarian Fellowship, 32, 198–202; diversity and, 207–8; future of, 207–12; history of, 198; membership of, 200–1; non-credal aspects of, 201; same-sex marriage and, 207; and seekership, 211; theology of, 198–200. *See also* Sage, Kathy
Kingsway Outreach Centre (Evangelical), 116
Kitiarsa, Pattana, 278
Kooy, Stephen, 154, 286
kundalini, 268, 272

Laker, Jason, 289
Lamb, Roberta, 263–7, 272, 280–1; Episcopal Church and, 263–4; Kuluta Buddhist Centre and, 263–7, 280; "The Circle" and, 264–7, 280
Latter-day Saints, Church of Jesus Christ of, 118–19, 125–30, 145, 320; beliefs of, 128, 132, 141, 142–3; education and, 135; history of, 125–6, 182, 360; missionaries in Kingston, 127–30; nativity pageant, 126–7; as Protestants, 201; women and, 133, 251
Laurence, Margaret, xv–xvi
Laurier Freethought Society, 293–4
Laverty, Marshall, 284–7
Lawson, Todd, 234
Lee, Vivian (Lee Wing-Hin), 293, 258, 370
Leonard, Ellen, 255
LePan, Douglas, 4, 367
Leslie, Lynn and Sarah, 338
Lewis, C.S., 352
Lewis, Justin, 194–8, 206, 209, 250, 274, 370
liberal religion: 24, 28–9, 30, 37, 180–212, 352–5; Anglicanism and, 51, 57; Bahá'ís and, 233–5; Baptists and, 60, 73–4, 78; characteristics of, 180–1, 207–12; diversity within, 207–10; evangelicals and, 88, 96, 142, 334; future of, 207–12; non-credal aspects of, 180–1, 201–2; Progressive Christianity and, 210; Quakers and, 190–4; Reform Jews and, 194–8; 198–202; same-sex relationships and, 202–7, 361–2; spatial issues and, 181–90; Unitarians and, 98–202; United Church and, 44–9, 205; women and, 250, 258
Libin, Nicole, 278–9
Lo, Kong, 155–7
Lotus-Heart-Blossoms Restaurant, 33, 271, 357. *See also* Sri Chinmoy
Lower, Arthur, 7

Loza, Wagdy, 165–6
Lu, Lucy (Kwai Kwan Zhao), 83–4
Luciuk, Lubomyr, 169–70
Lutheran Church: as PLURA church, 36. *See also* ethnic churches in Kingston
Lynch, Joseph, 38, 363, 366
Lyon, David, 51, 319

Macdonald, Elizabeth, 105, 183, 203–5, 365, 369
MacDonald, Flora, 368–9
Macdonald, John A.: burial place of, 20; homes of, 17, 252; as "Laurentian," 367; as Presbyterian, 63; Salvation Army and, 120
Macdonald, Stuart, 152, 155, 177–8
MacKay, Keillor, 331
Maclean, Norman, xxviii
MacLennan, Hugh, xx, 27, 63, 321, 367–8
mainline Christian denominations: 36–79; Anglicans, 49–63; Baptists, 68–78; definition of, 36–7; 78–9; numbers in Kingston, 36–7; PLURA churches, 36–7, 150; Presbyterians, 63–8; Roman Catholics, 37–43; same-sex relationships and, 60–3; social justice and, 37; theology of, 37; United Church, 44–9
Mair, Rafe, 58
Manji, Irshad, 225
Marks, Lynne, 261–2
Martha's Table, 92, 97
Masters, Robert, 170, 172
Matthews, Bruce, 214, 215
McAlister, Stephen, 44
McDonald, Marci, 84–5
McGowan, Michael, 303–4
McKendry, Jennifer, 14–15
McKeown, James, 160–1
McLaughlin, Bern, 337
McPherson, Aimee Semple, 262
Meagher, Anthony, 39–43, 373, 367, 370
Messianic Judaism (Jews for Jesus), 83, 93–4
Methodist Church. See "Big Five" churches; Free Methodist Church
Meyer, Marion, 10–11, 15, 18, 29
Michaels, Anne, 6
Michaelson, Kris, 362
Michaelson, Val, 51, 287, 370
Michelin, Tanya, 312–13
Miedema, Gary Richard, 318
Millea, Mary Clare, 255
Mol, Hans: on charismatic leadership, 100; on Christian Reformed Church, 153, 177; identity theory of, 147–8, 170–1, 175–6, 320; on Ukrainian Catholics, 169
monotheism, 25, 209, 216, 231, 245, 307, 311, 319
Moore, Arthur, 343–4
Morell, Kay, 254
Mormons. *See* Latter-day Saints, Church of Jesus Christ of
Morning Star Christian Fellowship, 291
My Big Fat Greek Wedding, 163
Muslims (Islamic Society of Kingston): diversity of, 222–7; growth of, 215–16; history of in Kingston, 216–17; Islamic Centre of Kingston, 216–19; origins of in Kingston, 218; unity of in Kingston, 215
Mutter, Josh, 69

Narayanan, Kamala, 235–7, 370
native religions (First Nations religions; religions of Aboriginal peoples), xvi, 191; and Anglicans, 56, 59; and census, 307; characteristics of, 307, 309,

311–12; and Christianity, 306, 309; at Kingston Penitentiary, 305–14; at Queen's University, 285, 370; religious freedom and, 305–6, 308; at RMC, 284; as "spirituality," 313–14
nature religion: animism, 311; Christianity and, xvi–xviii, 349–50; Kellye Crockett and, 276; Bert Horwood and, 191; Vivian Lee and, 359; Justin Lewis and 197; native religions, 306. *See* Dowsers; native religions; Wicca
Nawaz, Zarqa, 224–5
Neopaganism. *See* Wicca
Nettleship, Gary, 88–9
Newman Club, 287–8
New Religious Movements (NRMs): Bahá'ís and, 234; characteristics of, 234, 353; as esoteric, 211; seekership and, 118; Sai Baba and, 234, 245
Nicoles, Randy, 130–6
Niebuhr, H. Richard, 351–2
"no religion," census category of: 146, 212, 309, 319, 358–9; and Chinese in Canada, 214, 307

Orsi, Robert A., 351
Osborne, Brian, 9, 64–5, 104, 322–3; and Donald Swainson, 7–8, 16, 282, 321
Otis, George, Jr, 343–4
O'Toole, Roger, 8–9, 36
Oulton, Michael, 54–6

Paganism. *See* Wicca
Palin, Sarah, 245
parking: Bethel, 186; Beth Israel, 21; Cooke's-Portsmouth, 157; Islamic Centre, 218; Polson Park, 108, 157; Queen's University, 195; Salvation Army, 122; scarcity downtown, 7, 34, 150; St Joseph's, 22; St Margaret's, 21
Parvez, Aqsa, 230–1
Peever, Blair, 52
Pentecostalism: 101, 361, 348; characteristics of, 88–9, 90, 97; and charisma, 98–100; origins of, 86. *See also* Kingston Gospel Temple; Third Day Worship Centre
People Searching Inside (PSI), 268
Perkin, J.R.C., 77
Peters, Dan, 91
Petrie, Alistair, 346
Philpott, Kent, 344
Pinheiro, Antonio, 172
pluralism, religious: chaplaincy and, 304–5, 314; common goals of, 81; early form of, 7; Diana Eck on, 334–5; in Kingston, 319–20, 324, 331; NRMs and, 118; public religion and, 318–35; religious clubs at Queen's University and, 288–98; Unitarians and, 198
Pluralism Project (Harvard University), xxi–xxii, 324, 380–1
postmodernism, 116, 212, 267, 280
Power, John, 7, 32
Power, Joseph, 7, 13
Presbyterian Church of Canada, 63–8, 156–7. *See also* St Andrew's Presbyterian Church
Pritchard, Brian, 108, 157
proselytizing (proselytism): 118–19, 180, 182, 190, 304, 320; Bahá'ís and, 232; Brethren and, 136–41; effectiveness of, 144–6; and evangelicalism, 118–19; and exclusivity, 141–4; Jehovah's Witnesses and, 130–6; Mormons and, 125–30; Queen's University clubs and, 293, 294, 298; Sai Baba and, 238; Salvation Army and, 120–5; time spent in, 145

Providence Manor, 304
Providence Spirituality Centre, 175, 252, 254, 255
Pugin, Augustus, 12–13
Putnam, Max V., 104

Quackenbush, Dan, 315–16
Quakers (Thousand Islands Meeting of Religious Society of Friends). *See under* liberal religion
Queen's Catholics (Newman Catholic Club), 297
Queen's Interfaith Council, 233, 285, 294
Queen's Navigators, 287
Queen's Theological College (Queen's School of Religion), 52, 65, 165, 200, 205, 210, 304–5
Queen's University Chaplain. *See* Laverty, Marshall; Yealland, Brian
Queen's University, denominational chaplains at, 286–8. *See also* de Souza, Raymond; Kooy, Stephen; Michaelson, Val
Queen's University Hillel Club, 291, 292, 294, 295–6
Queen's University Muslim Students Association (QUMSA), 286, 290, 292–7, 327

Rahman, Hafizur, 216–18
Rawlyk, George A., 70–3, 81–2, 295
Regiopolis-Notre Dame High School, 171, 315–16
Reiki, 255
Reimer, Sam, 62, 82, 150
religion and nature. *See* nature religion
religion in 1960s: 26–31, 113, 348, 353; and mainline churches, 36; and United Church, 48, 67, 72–3, 123, 184, 257
religion in institutions: 31, 70, 222, 282–317, 323, 357, 368; chaplaincy and, 314–16; Hotel Dieu Hospital, 301–2; Kingston General Hospital, 302; Kingston Penitentiary (native religions), 305–14; Providence Continuing Care Centre, 302–3; Providence Manor, 303–4; Queen's University, 284–98; Regiopolis-Notre Dame, 315–16; Royal Military College, 298–301
religion, public: 318–35; Christmas and seasonal celebrations as, 325–8; and cremated remains, 329–30; memorials and shrines as, 328–35; prayers at council meetings as, 323–5; and public policy, 334–5; religious pluralism and, 331–5. *See also* pluralism, religious
Religious Diversity in Kingston (research project): methods of, xviii–xxviii, 80, 133, 213–15, 342, 360
religious hybridity (eclecticism; dimorphism; multiple religious belonging): 116, 212, 267, 272, 278, 280, 307
Reynolds, Eric T., 52
Riel, Georgina, 370
Rifkin, Ira, 234
Rigby, Peter, 107, 364–5
Riotte, Jules Charles Emil, 169–70
Ritchie, Ian, 361
Robbins, Phyllis, 303
Robinson, Barbara, 250
Robinson, J.A.T., 25–6
Roddick, Paul, 294
Roman Catholic parishes: Christ the King (Polish Apostolate), 170, 174–5, 251; Church of the Good Thief, 6, 15, 18, 38; Holy Family, 18, 23, 43, 174; Our Lady of Fatima, 19, 170, 172–4; Our Lady of Lourdes, 19;

St François d'Assise, 19, 170–2; St James' Chapel, 169–70, 172, 174–5, 179, 251, 287; St John the Apostle, 18, 170; St Joseph's, 18–19, 22–3, 38, 366; St Mary's Cathedral, 13, 38, 169–70, 174–5, 251, 253, 287, 301, 328, 363; St Paul the Apostle, 19, 92, 173, 259
Roof, Wade Clark, 278
Royal Military College (RMC): 1, 51–2, 282–4, 347; chaplaincy at, 298–301, 303, 314. *See also* Fortin, Jean-Yves
Ruether, Rosemary, 94
Rutter, Roger, 336; and "dark places," 341; and Impact World Tour, 338–9; and Kingston Transformation Network, 337, 348; and spiritual mapping, 339–40, 346; and Transformations videos, 344

Sacred Source Bookstore, 33, 274–6, 357. *See also* Crockett, Kellye
Sage, Kathy, 200–8, 249–50
Sai Baba, Sathya. *See under* Hindus
Saleem, Muhammad, 218–20, 222, 226, 254, 366
Saloojee, Riad, 220, 223
Salvation Army: 8, 30, 83, 107–8, 111, 120–5, 136, 149, 370; on abortion and same-sex relationships, 132; conversionist emphasis of, 142; denominationalism and, 119, 142; dress and, 134; history of, 32, 137, 141, 182; music and, 126, 134–5; public religion and, 119–21, 122, 124–5, 126–7, 317–18, 327; social activism of, 122, 124; women and, 261–2
same-sex marriage (same-sex relationships; same-sex unions): 360–1; Anglicans and, 49, 51, 56–61, 105, 362; Baptists and, 74–8; Reginald Bibby on, 61–3; Canadian views of, 74–5; evangelicals and, 84, 133, 334; Greek Orthodox view of, 164; Kingston Unitarian Fellowship and, 206–7; liberal religion and, 190, 202; Lutherans on, 150; Elizabeth Macdonald and, 205–5; mainline churches and, 62–3, 78–9; Reform Jews and, 206; Roman Catholic Church and, 41–3, 334; Sydenham Street United Church and, 203; United Church of Canada and, 44, 49, 105, 362
Sapers, Howard, 308
Scanlon, James, 302–3
schism, 30, 86, 105–6, 116, 165, 246, 322, 362–3; Anglicans, 56–8, 121; Brethren, 139, 144, 194; Christian Reformed Church, 154–5; First Baptist Church, 73; Free Methodism, 106; Jehovah's Witnesses, 131; Kingston Alliance Church, 102–5; Kingston Transformation Network, 341; Pentecostals, 87, 94–100
Schoemperlen, Diane, 5
secular, the (secularism; secularity; secularization): Brethren and, 120; Christianity and, 26, 88, 90–3, 153–4, 183, 333–4, 355; Harvey Cox on, 26, 353; humanism and, 37, 208, 324; Jehovah's Witnesses and, 130, 145; Judaism and, 28; liberal religion and, 24; David Lyon on, 319; Mormons and, 129, 145; Queen's University and, 43, 65, 285, 288–98, 319, 328, 331, 335, 356, 364; religion and, 26, 81; and sacred, 13, 15, 25, 323, 331–2; Salvation Army and, 136; society as, 185, 289; Charles Taylor on, 26, 288. *See also* culture
seekership, 211, 278–9

Seidenspinner, Charles, 102–3
Sell, Henry T., 262–3
Sentinel Group. *See* Otis, George, Jr
Seraphim (Kenneth William Storheim), 167
Seventh-day Adventist Church, 116, 126, 140, 149, 271, 291. *See also* Morning Star Christian Fellowship
Shafia, Mohammed, Tooba, and Hamed, 231
sharia law, 227–8
Shea, Ed, 301–2
Shekel, Michal, 250
Shillington, Brandon, 114
Sikhs, 20, 214, 216, 235, 240–4; ethnicity and, 243, 244; governance of, 244; history in Kingston, 240–1; interfaith relations and, 243, 244, 245–6; liturgy and, 142–2
Silcock, Paul, 101–4
Sisters of Providence of St Vincent de Paul: 252–6; functions of, 252–3; governance of, 252, 256; health network and, 253; noon-hour vigil of, 253–4, 324, 328, 363–4; programs of, 254
Sitar, Lynne, 232, 233
Smith, Kevin, 69–71, 75
Smith, Theresa, 307
social justice: evangelicals and, 62, 79, 109; liberal religions and, 185, 192, 194, 202, 206; mainline churches and, 36–7, 46–7; Sisters of Providence and, 252; United Church and, 25, 47, 61
Soka Gakkai International (SGI). *See under* Buddhism
Sorensen, Wilfrid, 171–2
Spickard, James V., 279–80
spiritual mapping, 335, 338, 339, 340, 342–9; as evangelism, 344
spiritual warfare, 335; Christian Reformed Church and, 348; as directed prayer, 347; evil supernaturalism and, 336, 341; 343, 345–6, 349, 355; Lausanne Covenant and, 344–5; as mainstream practice, 347–8; Pray Kingston and, 347; spiritual mapping and, 342, 343; "Strategic-Level Spiritual Warfare" and, 335, 342, 345, 347, 349; targeted intercession and, 340
spirituality, 212; aboriginal, 311, 313; ecological, 254–5; Janet Faubert on, 272; feminist, 264–5, 267; marketized, 278; religion and, 298, 313, 314, 331, 359, 362; sexuality and, 361
Spiritualism, 5, 30, 262
Sri Chinmoy, 263; Centre in Kingston, 267–73; compared with Sai Baba, 237, 239; and renaming Thousands Island Bridge, 270; as NRM, 245. *See also* Faubert, Janet; Lotus-Heart-Blossoms Restaurant
Stackhouse, John G., Jr, 81–3, 101
St Andrew's Presbyterian Church, 9, 12, 71, 177, 183, 370; Gsus Sindustries and, 322–3; interfaith events and, 233, 365–6; Korean Presbyterians and, 157–8; as mainline church, 63–8, 78; "Mexican Sunsets" at, 371; Max V. Putnam and, 104; Shannon's Cannon at, 322
supernaturalism: 199, 210, 305, 353; and belief, 142–3; decline of in 1960s, 24–5; evil and, 336, 338, 341; Progressive Christianity and, 210
Swainson, Donald, 105. *See also* Osborne, Brian
syncretism, 278. *See also* religious hybridity

tai chi, 32, 254–5, 327
Taoist Tai Chi Society, 32–3
Tarek, Abu Noman Mohammad, 228–30
tarot cards: 33, 210, 263; Kellye Crockett and, 275; 341; Elizabeth Greene and, 273–4, 370
Tataryn, Myroslaw, 162, 163, 168, 170
taxes, religious groups and property, 97, 183
Taylor, Charles, 26, 279, 288, 319
Teixeira, Carlos, 173
Thaqalayn Muslim Association, 292
Thekchen, Gen Kelsang, 280, 370
Theseus's Paradox, 313
Think, Inc., 291
Third Day Worship Centre: attendance at, 97; charismatic authority and, 98–100; governance of, 96, 99; and Jews, 97–8; location of, 216; as post-denominational, 95–6, 99, 101; preaching at, 97; same-sex marriage and, 98; schism and, 86, 94–100
Thurlby, Malcolm, 13–14
Tillich, Paul: and Ground of Being, 25; and Protestant Principle, 144; and ultimate concern, xxix, 181
Trothen, Tracy, 250
Trueheart, Charles, 113
Tulchinsky, Gerald, 10, 28–9
Turner, Isabel, 326–7

Unitarian Fellowship. *See* Kingston Unitarian Fellowship
United Church of Canada churches: Calvary United Church, 19, 205–6; Cataraqui, 216; Chalmers, 15, 34, 44–5, 64–5, 71, 85, 183–90, 204, 287; Cooke's-Portsmouth, 19, 23, 157–8, 185; Crossroads, 19, 34; Edith Rankin Memorial, 19, 46, 65; Faith, 19, 258–61; Kingscourt, 19, 35, 44, 112; Princess Street, 365; Queen Street, 19, 34, 44, 190; St Andrew's by-the-Lake, 23–4; St Margaret's, 19, 21–2, 34, 73, 185; St Matthew's, 19, 205–6; Sydenham Street, 12, 24, 47, 71, 105, 181–90, 203, 321, 365; Zion, 45–6
Unterschultz, Meghan, 274, 349
Urquhart, Jane, 299

Van den Hoonard, Will, 232–4
Vanderwerff, Andre, 94
Van Die, Marguerite, 331
Varley, Wayne, 50, 52, 54
violence, religious: 220–2, 230, 254, 355
visible minorities, 159, 213–14
Visser, Ed, 153–4, 176, 337
Vosper, Gretta, 44, 47, 210
Vyas, Rekha, 238–40

Wagner, Peter, 342, 343–4, 345–6, 348
Walker, Chris, 103–4, 178, 187–90, 369
Wallace, Bronwen, 371–2
Ward, David, 51, 362
Warfield, Benjamin B., 251–2
Weber, Max, 99–100, 118
Westfall, William, 13–14, 321
Wesley, John and/or Charles, 86, 106–7
Wesleyan Church, 83, 107–8, 178
White, Tom, 336–7, 348
Wicca (Paganism): 200, 313, 319, 341, 349, 354; Kellye Crockett and, 33, 274–6, 370; Bert Horwood and, 191; Justin Lewis and, 196–7, 209; 263–4
Wiesel, Elie, 28
Williams, Charles, 352
Wilson, Fergy, 369

Wilson, Hladini, 269
Wilson, Irene, 255–6, 369
women, religion and: 248–81; alternative spiritualities and, 261–78; in mainline Christianity, 252; and ordination, 249–51; Roman Catholicism and, 41–2, 251. *See also* Sisters of Providence

Yealland, Brian: as Queen's University chaplain, 284–7, 292, 298, 315; at Zion United Church, 45–6
Yoga and Relaxation Centre (Lila Centre): 276
Young, John, 47, 205

Zion, William P., 167